PUBLIC RELATIONS

Principles, Cases, and Problems

PUBLIC
RELATIONS

PRINCIPLES, CASES, and PROBLEMS

by BERTRAND R. CANFIELD, D.B.S.

DIRECTOR, DISTRIBUTION DIVISION
PUBLIC RELATIONS
BABSON INSTITUTE OF BUSINESS ADMINISTRATION

30525

1964

FOURTH EDITION

RICHARD D. IRWIN, INC.

HOMEWOOD, ILLINOIS

FOURTH EDITION

First Printing, April, 1964
Second Printing, August, 1965

Library of Congress Catalog Card No. 64–17242

PRINTED IN THE UNITED STATES OF AMERICA

PREFACE

THE FOURTH EDITION of this book (originally published in 1952 and last revised in 1960) has been completely rewritten and illustrated to include the latest developments in the rapidly expanding field of public relations. Thirty-three new cases describing the organizations, policies, practices, and public relations programs of large and small business, social service, and government organizations and associations are included in this edition. Thirteen new problems present the unsolved difficulties encountered by organizations in the administration of their public relations. New chapters on the Evolution of Public Relations and Public Relations Communications have been added to provide more comprehensive coverage of these important areas.

This edition has been prepared primarily as a basic text for undergraduate and graduate courses in public relations in colleges of business administration and journalism. It is not intended to teach public relations skills—how to write a press release or prepare an institutional advertisement. These skills can be learned better in journalism courses in news writing or advertising, or on the job. The purpose of this book is to prepare the student with a broad foundation in the area of public relations, communications, public opinion, international public relations, the place of public relations in the corporate organization, and opinion research. Study and discussion of these subjects provide broad training of maximum utility for future business executives, who should understand the role of public relations in management, as well as for practitioners who require a broader training than they can get from a "How to" handbook.

The public relations practitioner who is already established in the field and wants to increase his effectiveness will find in these pages much that will give him a broader perspective of public relations and a better understanding of its contributions to modern management. The public relations executive confronted with the increasingly complex task of developing public understanding for his organization will find in this edition descriptions of the public relations policies, practices, and programs of other business, as well as those of nonprofit

v

organizations, which may be adapted to the solution of the public relations problems of his own institution.

The twenty-four chapters in this edition are organized within five
sections. Each section is prefaced with an introduction to give the
reader a preview of the material to be found in the chapters of each
section. The subject is developed logically, beginning with the first
section on The Field of Public Relations, which defines public relations, describes its evolution, the role of communication, the nature
of public opinion and the organization for public relations. The second
section, The Corporate Publics, describes the nature of the eight principal business publics, and methods employed to develop sympa-
thetic understanding and good will. The third section, The Public
Relations of Associations, Social Welfare Agencies, the Armed
Forces, and Other Institutions, discusses the nature of these nonprofit organizations and their public relations objectives and programs. The fourth section, International Public Relations, describes
the rapid development of public relations throughout the world. Section five, Media of Public Relations Communication, is devoted to the
principal media of communication with the publics.

New in this edition is a chapter, Evolution of Public Relations,
which traces the historical development of the field from the early
press agents to its current stage of progress, its growth problems, the
search of practitioners for professional status, and ethical practices.
The prospects for future growth and influence as a management function of corporations are also described.

Another new chapter in this edition is Public Relations Communication, a major activity of every public relations program. The communication process is analyzed and principles of effective transmission of information are discussed. The importance of two-way communication between the publics and management is emphasized, and
various media of communication are described. The importance of
semantics and improvements in communicating skills are stressed so
that the effectiveness of public relations communication may be increased.

At the conclusion of each chapter are cases and problems that illustrate application of the principles that have been described. These
descriptions of the public relations organization, policies, objectives,
and activities of leading business and nonprofit organizations, supplied
by their public relations managers, give a realistic and practical approach to the study of the subject.

Teachers of public relations have found that study and discussion of cases and problems challenge the thinking and imagination of students by confronting them with realistic situations identical with those faced by public relations practitioners in planning and executing programs. In criticizing cases and proposing solutions to problems, students are required to do analytical thinking, know the fundamentals involved, consider alternatives, exercise judgment, make decisions, and defend their points of view in discussion—all of which makes for the best pragmatic education.

Cases and problems are included in this edition. The term *case,* as used here, refers to a description of the policies, objectives, organization, and procedures found in the public relations program of a particular organization and used in solving a specific public relations problem. The methods described in each case are assumed, by the management of the organization involved, to be the most desirable for the solution of the problem. The student is challenged to find more effective ways of solving the problem, and group discussion usually brings out alternatives which may seem more desirable than the "official" solution.

The term *problem,* as used here, is a description of the circumstances that surround a *recognized* deficiency in an organization in its relationships with a particular public. In contrast to a *case,* a problem does not present a solution. The student is expected to propose a solution to the problem by applying the principles and practices described in the chapter which precedes the problem.

All new illustrations used in this edition have been provided by leading business and nonprofit organizations to show their public relations organizations' activities and communication methods. An up-to-date public relations bibliography, recommended by educators and practitioners, is included to aid students, teachers, and practitioners in obtaining additional information on the subject.

The organizations that have contributed cases, problems, and illustrations to this edition, and for which assistance the author is indebted, are: Electric Companies Public Information Program; American Petroleum Institute; Wyandotte Chemicals Corp.; Ford Motor Co.; E. I. duPont deNemours & Co.; United States Army; United States Air Force; Galeries Orleanaises, Orleans, France; Westinghouse Electric Corp.; General Motors Corp.; New York Life Insurance Co.; Texas Eastern Transmission Co.; Consumers Power Company of Michigan; Michigan Consolidated Gas Co.; Monsanto Chemical Co.; Smith, Kline & French; Swedish Insurance Companies Information Service, Stockholm, Sweden; Association of American Railroads; Girl

Scouts of America; American Telephone & Telegraph Co.; Sun Oil Co.; American Motors Co.; Weirton Steel Co.; First Security Corporation; Salvation Army; Charleston Group Companies; Colonial Williamsburg; Western Electric Company; Caterpillar Tractor Co.; and International Business Machines Corp.

Valuable assistance in the preparation of this book has been received from Public Relations Journal, Public Relations News, Business Week and other business magazines, as well as from authors of authoritative books and articles on public relations.

I am particularly indebted to my wife, Elma S. Canfield, for the preparation of this manuscript.

BERTRAND R. CANFIELD

Babson Park, Mass.
February, 1964

TABLE OF CONTENTS

SECTION 1. THE FIELD OF PUBLIC RELATIONS

SECTION 4. INTERNATIONAL PUBLIC RELATIONS

SECTION 5. MEDIA OF PUBLIC RELATIONS COMMUNICATION

BIBLIOGRAPHY

INDEX

SECTION

1 •

THE FIELD OF
PUBLIC RELATIONS

THE ROLE of public relations has been obscured by much that has been written describing it as "the invisible sell," "the engineering of consent," and "projecting the corporate image." Its practitioners have been called "image merchants," and "hidden persuaders." These fanciful phrases have confused the public as to the real meaning of public relations which is described in the five chapters in this section.

Several definitions of public relations delineate its functions and explain the modern social philosophy of management which inspires effective public relations programs. The expression of this philosophy in policies and their interpretation to the public through various media of communication secures public understanding and good will.

The evolution of public relations from the first press agents to its current status of importance, the problems involved in its development, and its future significance are described.

The process of communication of information to the public through various media of communication to effect a two-way formal and informal exchange of ideas between an organization and its publics is explained as a major function of public relations.

As the molding of favorable public opinion is the primary objective of public relations, the student and practitioner of public relations should understand the nature of public opinion, its formation, the factors which affect it, and the role of opinion leaders.

The organization of public relations departments and outside counsel in various types of institutions is discussed to indicate the personnel needed to carry out public relations functions.

CHAPTER 1 · WHAT IS PUBLIC RELATIONS

MODERN ECONOMIC, social, and political life makes people increasingly dependent upon one another. Human beings look to others for recognition, respect, and understanding. They turn to employers, unions, churches, and social organizations for satisfaction of their basic economic, social, and spiritual needs. This dependence of people at work and in their social and spiritual lives has created serious problems of human relationships for business, social, religious, and political institutions.

Business organizations are dependent upon many people for the skills, materials, components, and markets for their products. Social welfare organizations, trade-unions, business and professional associations rely upon their members and the public in general for voluntary services and financial aid. Government depends upon people for financial support, manpower, and public approval. This reliance of people on public institutions is one of the significant social changes of the twentieth century.

It has become increasingly evident over the years that people and business, government, and social organizations have important elements of mutual interest that require specific management attention and action. Arising out of the mutual interest of individuals and institutions, a new philosophy and function of management has developed called *public relations*.

For many years business organizations, through labor relations, personnel, and industrial relations staffs have labored to gain the understanding, improve the working relationship, and increase the effectiveness of employees. However, as American business has expanded, broadened its base of public ownership, and the scope and public impact of its manufacturing and service operations, management has recognized that good relations are essential not only with employees but with others dependent upon the business. Shareholders, suppliers, distributors and dealers, community neighbors, consumers, and government are also mutually interested in the welfare of businesses upon which they depend

3

for products and services, dividends, taxes, sales, and profits. To satisfy the interests of people involved with business, public relations has become a major management responsibility.

Business organizations are seriously concerned with the way their policies and practices appear not only to their employees but also to their neighbors in plant communities, shareholders, customers, suppliers, distributors, dealers, and government. Management recognizes the need for establishing mutual understanding on the part of the corporation on one hand and the public on the other through public relations.

Today, effective management is giving as much attention to public relations as is devoted to financing, engineering, manufacturing, and marketing. The practice of public relations has become widespread in large as well as small business concerns, social service organizations, trade-unions, professional associations, political, and governmental bodies.

With the acceptance of public relations as an essential management function, the stature of public relations has grown. The ethics and competence of public relations practitioners have improved and new techniques have been perfected to increase substantially the effectiveness of public relations programs.

PUBLIC RELATIONS DEFINED

There are numerous definitions of public relations, many of which do not give a clear or comprehensive description of public relations. The definition of public relations appearing in *Webster's New Collegiate Dictionary,* 1958 edition, published by G. and C. Merriam Company is: "Public relations, (1) The activities of a corporation, union, government, or other organization in building and maintaining sound and productive relations with special publics such as customers, employees, or stockholders and with the public at large, so as to adapt itself to its environment and interpret itself to society. (2) The state of such activities or the art of organizing them."

Public Relations News, a periodical for public relations executives, favors a definition which is more specific and which emphasizes the important social responsibility of public relations: "Public relations is the management function which evaluates public attitudes, identifies the policies and procedures of an individual or an organization with the public interest, and executes a program of action to earn public understanding and acceptance."

The author prefers the following definition which also emphasizes the fact that public relations is a philosophy as well as a function of management which is communicated to the public: "Public relations is a philosophy and function of management expressed in policies and practices which serve the public interest, communicated to the public to secure its understanding and good will."

Public relations as discussed in the following pages has four basic characteristics: first, it is a philosophy of management; second, it is an expression of this philosophy in policies and actions; third, it is a function of management; and fourth, it is the expression of the philosophy, policies, and practices of an organization through communication to the public to secure its understanding and good will.

PUBLIC RELATIONS—A PHILOSOPHY OF MANAGEMENT

Public relations is basically a philosophy of management—an attitude of the management of an organization which places the interests of people first in all matters pertaining to the conduct of the organization. This philosophy assumes that an organization should function to serve the primary needs of people dependent upon it for employment, wages, income, goods and services, and social or spiritual satisfactions. This fundamental philosophy of public service is the foundation of the modern conception of public relations.

This philosophy of public relations is a revolutionary concept in management thinking—a premise that the primary objective of management is to serve the interests of the public. It is aptly expressed by Paul Garrett, a pioneer of modern public relations, as follows: "Public relations is a fundamental attitude of mind, a philosophy of management, which deliberately and with *enlightened selfishness* places the broad interests of the public first in every decision affecting the operation of a business."

This philosophy was applied to democratic government more than a century ago by Abraham Lincoln, Daniel Webster, and William Lloyd Garrison, each of whom referred to "government of the people, by the people, and for the people." The same philosophy has been accepted by the management of many business, professional, labor union, educational, and social welfare institutions today who recognize that the understanding and good will of people are essential to their welfare.

Business management in the nineteenth century was indifferent to public criticism of business policies and practices. The much quoted remark of the late William H. Vanderbilt, "Let the public be damned," typifies the philosophy of many business leaders before the turn of the century. Management felt that their only responsibility was to make a profit for the owners of the business, and managers in those days were usually the owners. As business ownership by the public became more widespread, management began to realize that it also had a responsibility to the stockholders. It was not until after the depression of the

FIG. 1–1. Public relations is a philosophy of management dedicated to serving people. The Caterpillar Tractor Co., Peoria, Illinois, serves education through its community relations program by providing a diesel engine to the Redwoods, Illinois, Community High School for its power shop course.

1930's that business managers began to recognize that they also had responsibilities to customers, employees, community neighbors, suppliers, distributor-dealers, government, and education. In recent years, the concept of a corporation as a social institution has been widely recognized.

The Corporation as a Social Institution

The managements of many progressive, modern corporations look upon them as institutions with social responsibilities. The chairman of a large farm equipment manufacturer expresses this point of view as follows: "After it has achieved a certain size, a corporation is a social institution which should be operated equally in the interests of stockholders, employees, and customers." In fulfilling its social responsibilities to employees, neighbors, customers, shareholders, suppliers, and dealers a corporation must serve the interests of individuals who comprise the corporation's publics. The interests of the individuals comprising these publics are different. However, they are similar in that they are basically selfish.

Employees are interested in steady employment, fair wages, good working conditions, recognition, opportunity for advancement, and retirement and disability benefits. If a business concern satisfies these interests of its employees, good employee relations result.

Customers have different interests. They are primarily interested in products and services of good quality at fair prices, and a continuous source of supply. If a company satisfies these interests, it enjoys good relations with customers.

Stockholders have still other interests. They are primarily concerned that their investment shall produce a reasonable return.

Suppliers of raw materials, parts, and equipment to manufacturers and merchandise to merchants are primarily interested in adequate profit, a long-term, friendly relationship, and honest dealing. A business which satisfies these interests of its suppliers gains good will and usually gets fair prices, prompt deliveries, and good service.

The community in which a company operates is interested in the business as a provider of jobs, a taxpayer, a contributor to local charities, a supporter of schools and churches, and an active participant in community affairs. If a business satisfies these interests, the community reciprocates with an adequate supply of labor, utilities, protection, and a good business climate.

Good Management Maintains a Balance of Benefits

In serving the interests of these various groups, management is faced with the fact that whatever it does to satisfy the interests of one group will affect the interests of each of the others. Accordingly, good management strives to maintain the fairest possible balance of benefits to each of the groups comprising the public. Management's effectiveness depends upon how well it satisfies the interests of these various publics without impairing the efficiency of the company. The company which best satisfies the interests of these diverse groups enjoys the understanding and good will of the public, which is the primary objective of public relations.

PUBLIC RELATIONS—A PHILOSOPHY EXPRESSED IN POLICIES AND ACTIONS

To achieve good public relations by placing the interests of people first in every business decision and action, management must establish policies which reflect this philosophy of serving the public interest.

General Public Relations Policy

The general public relations objectives of an organization should be described in a general public relations policy which reflects the philosophy of the organization toward the public. The general public relations policy of Standard Oil Company, Indiana, is:

We are in business to find oil, make good products, and sell them at fair prices and profits.

We try to operate in the best interests of shareowners, employees, customers, and the public.

We believe our company and all business and industry can do this best under American free enterprise and competitive, private management.

Our public relations is to treat people right, heed their opinions, and keep them informed.

Policies for Relations with Specific Publics

In addition to general public relations policy, it is essential to have public relations policies for specific publics. Policies are established for: employee relations, stockholder relations, community relations, supplier relations, distributor-dealer relations, educational relations, government relations, member relations, consumer relations, and press relations.

These policies that describe an organization's objectives in winning the understanding and support of various groups of people express the philosophy of management and are designed to inform those associated with an enterprise in carrying out the aims of the public relations program of the organization. A primary responsibility of management is to see that public relations policies are understood, accepted, and intelligently applied by management and all rank-and-file employees in developing good relations with people inside as well as outside the organization.

An example of a typical community relations, public relations policy is that of Tidewater Oil Company, which states:

Whenever possible convey to the community and its leaders the company's interest in good relations, the high quality of its products and services, and the company's desire to be a vital part of the community. Do everything within reason that is requested by or for the community and establish acquaintance with city leaders and officials. Make a positive effort to seek new and additional ways to identify the company as a good neighbor and asset to the community.

In each of the following chapters dealing with specific publics will be found statements of policies which have been adopted by well-known business and social institutions to describe their objectives in their relationships with a specific public.

Responsibility for Public Relations Policies

The management of an organization is responsible for formulating policies affecting all phases of its operations including public relations. The public relations manager should act in an advisory capacity to management in formulating statements of policy covering relations with employees, shareholders, communities, suppliers, dealers, consumers, and other publics.

The execution of public relations policies is the responsibility of everyone connected with an organization who, in the performance of his duties or through his personal relations, has contacts with the public. It is essential that all persons associated with an enterprise understand clearly its public relations policies and be able to interpret these policies to the public in the spirit in which they were written.

Policies Expressed in Actions

To be effective, a public relations philosophy must be expressed in action. Institutions are judged by the public by what they do, not by what they say. "Public relations is the philosophy of *doing* things people like and doing them the way they like. The *doing* is more important than the *saying*," says Paul W. Garrett, pioneer of public relations.

Good public relations involves acting in the public's interests. It means providing regular employment at fair wages and a good working environment for employees. It involves producing good products at reasonable prices with adequate service for consumers and contributing to the social, cultural, and economic welfare of the community in which the organization operates.

The Standard Oil Company, Indiana, considers the public relations effect of the things it does, and does many things deliberately for the public good. Its people participate in good works of many kinds, speak up for worthy causes, contribute to and work for local civic and welfare organizations. Directly, or through the Standard Oil Foundation, the company helps support colleges, grants scholarships and fellowships to worthy students, helps raise community welfare funds, contributes to Red Cross, and engages in youth activities such as those of the 4-H Clubs, the Future Farmers of America, and Junior Achievement.

PUBLIC RELATIONS—A FUNCTION OF MANAGEMENT

The attainment of good public relations is a major responsibility of every executive of an organization. Management cannot achieve good public relations by delegating responsibility to a public relations manager and a staff of public relations specialists. Public relations is primarily a line function of every operating department head as well as line and staff executives of the manufacturing, marketing, and finance departments.

Public relations is not a specialized activity like production, engineering, accounting, and sales. It is an activity of each of these departments that management must seek to apply in everything it does and says.

Each department of a company is concerned with maintaining good relations with one or more specific publics. The sales department seeks good relations with consumers, distributors, and dealers. The purchasing department needs the good will of suppliers. The personnel and labor relations departments want improved employee relations, and the finance department seeks the approval of shareholders.

To assist the management of each of these departments in developing good relations with their respective publics, is the function of a public relations department. The public relations manager and staff serve in an advisory capacity to the line operating executives and aid them in implementing public relations programs designed to improve relations with their publics. Public relations staff personnel have the communication skills and specialized experience not normally found in other staff and line departments.

In addition to aiding all levels of management in improving relations with their respective publics, a public relations department is responsible for planning and executing a program to interpret the organization as a whole to the public through institutional advertising, news publicity, periodicals, motion pictures, and other media.

PUBLIC RELATIONS—A RESPONSIBILITY OF ALL EMPLOYEES

The employees of an organization are the best spokesmen for its policies and acts. To the public, those who are employed by an organization *are* the organization. The public judges an organization by the people associated with the organization. The public will believe what employees of an organization say about it before they will believe its publicity or advertising.

Every telephone call received by switchboard operators, every sales presentation by salesmen, service call by servicemen, delivery by deliverymen, or letter written by a correspondent affects favorably or otherwise the public relations of an organization.

"In every successful program of public relations it is essential that all members of the organization take part. The philosophy of sound public relations and the recognition of its importance must permeate every phase of a company's operations. It is not a thing that you can delegate to a few people and then forget," says C. B. Reeves, vice-president in charge of public relations, Mutual Life Insurance Company of New York.

To inform and gain the active co-operation of all employees in building good public relations is a major responsibility of management at all levels.

PUBLIC RELATIONS—COMMUNICATION OF POLICIES AND PRACTICES TO THE PUBLIC

Public relations is not only a social philosophy which is expressed in policies and actions, it is also the communication of this philosophy to the public. Good public relations means not only doing good but also getting credit for it. Communication of good policies and acts is essential to make the public understand and appreciate what a corporation or organization is doing for the public welfare. This does not mean bragging nor pompous self-praise but rather the straightforward communication of policies and practices to the public.

It should not be assumed that the public fully understands and appreciates an organization's policies and deeds. Neither should it be taken for granted that the public is not interested in what an organization is doing. Unless management explains and justifies its actions, it is likely to be misunderstood and criticized by the public.

People want to know what a business, social, or political organization is doing to satisfy their interests. If an organization does not explain its actions, people supply their own explanations or through hearsay, gossip, and rumor, they acquire a false conception rather than the facts.

Employees want information about new policies, company progress, or operational changes which affect their jobs.

Stockholders are equally interested in the progress of the company in which they have invested their savings.

FIG. 1–2. Public relations is showing and telling neighbors in plant communities what goes on behind factory walls. To inform the public about its operations, the Corning Glass Works, Corning, New York, conducts a glass blowing demonstration for Girl Scouts and community neighbors. Photo courtesy Girl Scouts, U.S.A.

Neighbors in a plant community are interested in the expansion or curtailment of plant operations and their effect on employment, wages, and retail trade.

The principles of good public relations communications will be discussed in a later chapter.

UNWISE AND IMPROPER USES OF PUBLIC RELATIONS

Public relations is used sometimes as a temporary defensive measure to compensate for management's mistakes in dealing with customers, neighbors, employees, shareholders, and other publics. When faced with a strike of employees, a proxy fight by minority shareholders, or a government investigation, management sometimes resorts to a public relations campaign to solve the problem. This strategy of attempting to combat unfavorable public opinion is "fire alarm" public relations because it may be compared to calling the fire department after the fire breaks out. Effective public relations is not an emergency or transitory activity but a continuous effort to interpret an institution to the public, to secure its understanding and good will.

Good public relations cannot be attained quickly. To gain the confidence and respect of people requires time. A good reputation for a business or institution cannot be acquired in a few months and public relations programs must be carried on consistently over a long term.

Public relations is not a substitute for good management or a cure-all for poor policies, products, or services. Some poorly managed organizations make a fruitless attempt through a public relations program to gain a good reputation.

Public relations does not mean spending large sums for entertaining influential people, staging spectacular parties, nor posing models in bubble baths to attract attention. Sensational "stunts" are not good public relations.

EVOLUTION OF PUBLIC

RELATIONS

PUBLIC RELATIONS as practiced today is of comparatively recent origin. While many current public relations practices originated after World War II, public relations has a much longer history. The practice of public relations has evolved in three phases which merge into each other and are still evident in current practices.

The first public relations practitioner was the press agent employed by showmen to create situations designed to get the names and pictures of performers publicized in newspapers and magazines. The late P. T. Barnum, circus magnate, employed press agents whose philosophy was "Let the public be fooled."

In the early 1900's business first recognized the need for something more than press agentry to court favorable public opinion when the ruthless tactics of powerful monopolies in industry and transportation aroused a storm of public criticism. Big business was denounced as unscrupulous, greedy, and an enemy of the people. Popular writers, including Thomas W. Lawson, Ida Tarbell, Upton Sinclair, and others, viciously attacked the morals of business in exploiting labor and consumers.

In the face of mounting public criticism, press agents changed their philosophy to "Let the public be informed," and the second phase of public relations was born. A leading exponent of this era of publicity was Ivy Lee, a young New York newspaper man who scorned press agentry and believed that corporations should give the public accurate information about their policies and practices. He was employed by the Pennsylvania Railroad, the Rockefeller and Guggenheim interests, and I. G. Farben, the German dye trust, to inform the public about their activities. In 1903 he formed the public relations firm of Parker and Lee, which in 1916 became Lee, Harris and Lee. In 1919 he was joined by Thomas J. Ross to form Ivy Lee and T. J. Ross Associates. Ivy Lee has been called the father of modern public relations. Much public relations at that time was largely defensive.

In the 1920's publicity men recognized that their role was not only to

Reasons for the Rapid Growth of Public Relations

Public relations has become a major function not only in American business but also in politics, government, trade and professional associations, social welfare organizations, labor unions, schools, and the armed forces. The growing recognition of public relations has been brought about by widespread changes in our economic and social systems.

The rapid increase in population in this country and the expansion of business and social organizations has seriously disrupted communications between people identified with an enterprise. Formidable barriers exist to prevent a free flow of information from management to the rank and file of business and nonprofit organizations. People associated with large corporations often are unaware of what is transpiring within the organization that affects their interests. As a result, serious misunderstandings arise between management and employees. To explain its philosophy and intentions and bring about better understanding with workers, management employs public relations techniques.

In the past, corporations existed solely to make money for their owners. Today, corporations function as creators of employment, as social institutions, benefactors of their communities, philanthropists, supporters of education, patrons of the arts and sciences, defenders of the economic system, and advocators of good government. To fulfill these new roles in society, corporations have resorted to public relation programs in carrying out their responsibilities as good citizens.

Rising taxes, discriminatory legislation, increasing government controls, legislative investigations, and criticism of business by politicians have made it increasingly essential for business to become politically knowledgeable and active. To create a favorable political climate is an increasingly important function of corporate public relations.

Great progress in media of communication in the past decade has made possible rapid and widespread transmission of information by television, radio, motion pictures, newspapers, and magazines. This development has given national and international impetus to the communication function of public relations. Business can quickly communicate its views to millions of people by television, radio, and the press, thus exerting a tremendous impact on public opinion.

Higher moral standards and ethical conduct in business are products of sound public relations. To be effective public relations requires management to speak truthfully, act fairly, and deal honorably with the public. Public relations has contributed to giving business a corporate conscience.

Revolutionary developments in marketing, changing buying habits of consumers, the emergence of new channels of distribution, the introduction of new products and services have all made it essential for companies to seek the good will and support of consumers, distributors, and dealers through public relations.

Public Relations Experiencing Growth Problems

Public relations is undergoing many of the frustrations and handicaps that other management services have experienced before reaching maturity. There is considerable disagreement among practitioners and management as to the functions and objectives of public relations. In many corporations, public relations is largely product publicity. In others, it is confined to community work. In many companies public relations covers a multitude of miscellaneous activities such as editing employee publications, preparing the annual report and stockholder communications, institutional advertising, organizing open houses and plant tours, legislative activities, preparing educational materials, and a wide variety of special projects. Some corporate managements speak vaguely about creating a corporate image and building institutional good will, but few have a comprehensive public relations program reaching all of the major publics.

Public relations counselors and directors maintain that management fails to take them into its confidence or consult them on plans, policies, and decisions with important public aspects. Management, on the other hand, contends that public relations practitioners know little about corporate operations or problems. Furthermore, public relations people have an exaggerated opinion of the importance of public relations.

Many public relations practitioners recognize a need for improvment in the ethical standards and practices of public relations counselors and practitioners. The spectacular growth of public relations has attracted inexperienced, unethical practitioners who create a false image of public relations and detract from the honest efforts of the great majority of competent, ethical public relations people. Spurious publicity stunts, false organization fronts, the suppression of negative facts, influence peddling, deceptive publicity, and similar unethical practices have aroused public criticism of public relations.

Public relations practitioners have been charged by critics as being manipulators of public opinion or "hidden persuaders" who surreptitiously seek to influence public opinion in favor of products and institutions of questionable merit. One critic has called public relations "the business of the Invisible Sell."

That unethical practices exist in public relations cannot be denied, but there is no evidence that malpractice is more prevalent in public relations than in other management services in the early stages of their development. The ethics of public relations practitioners reflect the moral standards of corporations and public relations counselors. However, public relations counselors are becoming more discriminating in their choice of clients by rejecting accounts which do not measure up to their standards of morality.

A limitation of public relations, which it shares with other social sciences, is management's inability to appraise the effectiveness and measure the accomplishments of public relations programs. Measuring the good will and understanding developed by a public relations program, according to a leading public opinion researcher, is as difficult as measuring a gaseous body with a rubber band. The customary measurement of the effectiveness of public relations is the number of inches of publicity represented by press clippings. This is a very inconclusive measure as it does not prove that the publicity has been read or that better understanding or good will resulted. The impact of press publicity on special events or product popularity may be measured by the attendance at an event or sales of the product publicized. However, this evaluation may be inconclusive as attendance and sales may be influenced by other factors than press publicity.

Public opinion surveys are frequently used to measure the effectiveness of public relations. However, further perfection of opinion research techniques are necessary to insure a more conclusive appraisal of the impact of public relations on public opinion. Opinion research is costly and responses may be misleading. Public opinion may be influenced by corporate advertising, policies, and practices as well as by public relations activities which make it difficult to appraise the accomplishment of a public relations program.

Some practitioners seek recognition of public relations as a profession. State licensing of practitioners has been proposed as a step toward ethical improvement as well as professional status. However, when the performance of practitioners meets the standards of competence of other professions, recognition and professional status will inevitably follow.

To establish higher standards of public relations practice, the Public Relations Society of America approved in 1960 a Declaration of Principles and a Code of Professional Standards for the Practice of Public Relations as follows:

Members of the Public Relations Society of America acknowledge and publicly declare that the public relations profession in serving the legitimate interests of clients or employers is dedicated fundamentally to the goals of better mutual understanding and cooperation among the diverse individuals, groups, institutions, and elements of our modern society. In performance of this mission we pledge ourselves:

1. To conduct ourselves both privately and professionally in accord with the public welfare.
2. To be guided in all our activities by the generally accepted standards of truth, accuracy, fair dealing, and good taste.
3. To support efforts designed to increase the proficiency of the profession by encouraging the continuous development of sound training and resourceful education in the practice of public relations.
4. To adhere faithfully to provisions of the duly adopted Code of Professional Standards for the Practice of Public Relations, a copy of which is in the possession of every member.

CODE OF PROFESSIONAL STANDARDS FOR THE PRACTICE OF PUBLIC RELATIONS

This Code of Professional Standards for the Practice of Public Relations is adopted by the Public Relations Society of America to promote and maintain high standards of public service and conduct among its members in order that membership in the Society may be deemed a badge of ethical conduct; that Public Relations justly may be regarded as a profession; that the public may have increasing confidence in its integrity; and that the practice of Public Relations may best serve the public interest.

1. A member has a general duty of fair dealing towards his clients or employers, past and present, his fellow members and the general public.
2. A member shall conduct his professional life in accord with the public welfare.
3. A member has the affirmative duty of adhering to generally accepted standards of accuracy, truth, and good taste.
4. A member shall not represent conflicting or competing interest without the express consent of those concerned, given after a full disclosure of the facts.
5. A member shall safeguard the confidences of both present and former clients or employers and shall not accept retainers or employment which may involve the disclosure or use of these confidences to the disadvantage of or prejudice of such clients or employers.
6. A member shall not engage in any practice which tends to corrupt the integrity of channels of public communication.
7. A member shall not intentionally disseminate false or misleading information and is obligated to use ordinary care to avoid dissemination of false or misleading information.
8. A member shall not make use of any organization purporting to serve some announced cause but actually serving an undisclosed special or private interest of a member or his client or his employer.
9. A member shall not intentionally injure the professional reputation or practice of another member. However, if a member has evidence that another member has been guilty of unethical, illegal, or unfair practices

including practices in violation of this Code, he shall present the information to the proper authorities of the Society for action in accordance with the procedure set forth in Article XIII of the Bylaws.

10. A member shall not employ methods tending to be derogatory of another member's client or employer or of the products, business, or services of such client or employer.

11. In performing services for a client or employer a member shall not accept fees, commissions or any other valuable consideration in connection with those services from anyone other than his client or employer without the express consent of his client or employer, given after a full disclosure of the facts.

12. A member shall not propose to a prospective client or employer that his fee or other compensation be contingent on the achievement of certain results; nor shall he enter into any fee agreement to the same effect.

13. A member shall not encroach upon the professional employment of another member unless both are assured that there is no conflict between the two engagements and are kept advised of the negotiations.

14. A member shall, as soon as possible, sever his relations with any organization which he believes his continued employment would require him to conduct himself contrary to the principles of this Code.

15. A member called as a witness in a proceeding for the enforcement of this Code shall be bound to appear unless, for sufficient reason, he shall be excused by the panel hearing the same.

16. A member shall cooperate with fellow members in upholding and enforcing this Code.

Although the Public Relations Society cannot enforce compliance with this Code by nonmembers, this declaration of principles establishes standards of ethical conduct which are fundamental to achieving professional status for public relations counselors and practitioners.

The Future of Public Relations

Public relations has enjoyed a phenomenal growth in the past two decades. It has been widely recognized as an essential management function in the operation of large and small political, social service associations, labor unions, government, business, and professional organizations. It occupies a place of equal importance with manufacturing, research, finance, and marketing in the operation of a business. Business regards public relations with respect. Public relations practitioners sit on the boards of directors, are consulted on major policies with public aspects, and hold top management positions. This progress is not viewed with complacency by thoughtful public relations people. Improved person-to-person communication, more imagination, greater reliance on the social sciences, and greater competence of practitioners are essential if public relations is to progress at the same rate in the future as it has in the past.

More Person-to-Person Communication

In the future, public relations must employ more individualized person-to-person communication in contrast to the mass communication now generally used in public relations programs. Public relations categorizes people as "publics" such as "employees," "shareholders," "suppliers," and "dealers." As a result of this, most current public relations is impersonal. Messages are addressed to groups rather than individuals. Mass communications ignore the fact that the interests of the individuals in a group are different. In the employee group, for example, some workers are interested in security, others in working conditions, and others in fringe benefits or wages. Mass communications addressed to the group as a whole usually fail to appeal to the interests of individuals and the impact of the message is lessened.

The importance of individual person-to-person communications in community relations is emphasized by Paul Garrett, pioneer public relations executive, as follows: "What an organization grown large usually needs most is to put public relations on a personal plane that is natural in a small business. Most people like to do business with folks they know and trust. They pretty much make up their minds about a company by what they know of the folks in the company. The more we can atomize our contacts the better off we shall be."

The most effective person-to-person communications is achieved when every person associated with an organization—every employee, executive, or member—serves as a "communicator" to the public.

In community relations, employees of a company who speak about the company to their neighbors, tradesmen, and acquaintances are engaged in the most effective person-to-person communication. People in plant communities will believe what an employee says about his company before they will believe what the company says about itself in its publicity or advertising.

Wholesalers and retailers will accept what a salesman, whom they know and respect, says about the company he represents before they will believe the company's official communications.

A supplier will be more receptive to what a purchasing agent or expediter may say about his corporation than the supplier may read about the corporation in a trade magazine.

Every employee of a business, including all levels of management as well as rank-and-file workers, particularly telephone operators, receptionists, salesmen, deliverymen, servicemen, and messengers who are in constant contact with the public are key communicators in building public good will.

To obtain effective person-to-person communications through employees, sound personnel policies and good labor relations are essential. Employees should be informed and motivated to serve as communicators to the public. Too little is being done by corporations to teach rank-and-file employees how to communicate effectively with the public. The people associated with an enterprise should know that public communication is not something that is carried on by a small group of professionals in a public relations department. Public relations to be effective must be everybody's job.

FIG. 2–1. The importance of individual person-to-person relations in employee public relations is illustrated in the above presentation by a representative of top management, Benson Ford, vice-president, Ford Motor Co., of an award for good citizenship to an employee and his wife.

Mass Communication of Information Is Not Enough

Current public relations practice assumes that the best way to gain public understanding and influence public opinion is to deluge the public with information through mass communication media. Public relations staffs produce an unprecedented volume of news releases, articles, publications, and advertisements. Radio and television stations, and newspapers are working around the clock communicating information to millions.

However, public opinion studies provide convincing evidence that the great volume of mass communication exposing people to information has almost no effect on the amount of information they retain or their particular attitudes as a result of it. For six months the people of Cincinnati, Ohio, were subjected to an intensive information program to inform them about the United Nations. Mass communication media including newspapers, radio and television broadcasts, outdoor posters, car cards, blotters, matchbooks, and films carried the United Nations story. An opinion poll at the end of the campaign showed that there was no change in the number of people who knew what the United Nations was or how it operated.

People in Michigan were exposed to the greatest mass communication effort in the history of the state to convince them of the need for increased facilities by Michigan colleges and universities. Every newspaper, radio, and television station in the state bombarded the public for weeks with information about the need of the colleges for more housing. In addition, information about intercollegiate athletics was carried by all news media. Following this intensive information program, the Survey Research Center of the University of Michigan conducted a survey of "The Public's Picture of Higher Education in the State of Michigan." Not only did the great amount of information communicated by the mass media fail to impress the public with the plight of the colleges but 15 per cent questioned could not name one Michigan college. The public could not even name colleges much less know anything about them or their problems.

Other public opinion studies including the Katz and Lazarsfeld book, *Personal Influence,* confirm the fact that mass media do not necessarily influence opinion by explaining things to the public. Something more than mass communication of information is needed to influence public opinion.

The relative ineffectiveness of mass communication of information emphasizes the need for more person-to-person communication described previously. More individual communication with opinion leaders is more effective than communicating with everybody and ending up communicating with nobody. Mass communications has its place in a public relations program, but it is no alternative to person-to-person communications in winning the good will and understanding of the public.

Greater Competence of Practitioners

Management is finding it increasingly difficult to discover competent public relations practitioners to guide corporations in the higher levels of public relations policy and programing. Corporations are sponsoring educational programs for practitioners and fellowships for teaching public relations.

The Foundation for Public Relations Research and Education provides annual fellowships to college teachers of public relations to give them an opportunity of spending a five-week summer assignment with a public relations department of a corporation or a counseling firm.

The Public Relations Society of America is sponsoring annual summer Institutes of Public Relations to provide for an exchange of information and ideas between public relations executives and leaders in related fields of education, social science, and communications. Co-sponsored by leading universities, the Institutes provide public relations managers and counselors with forty hours of classroom work, lectures, panel discussions, and question and answer periods.

An increasing number of college graduates with degrees in liberal arts, business administration, and journalism are enrolling for graduate training in public relations in some twenty colleges, before engaging in public relations practice.

Imagination in Public Relations

Public relations offers a fertile field for creative imagination and new and original approaches to gain public understanding and good will. A high degree of originality is evident in many current public relations programs. Banks are forsaking traditional ultraconservative public relations programs for highly imaginative publicity. The First National Bank of New York boasts that the finger-painting earnings of Beauty, a three-year-old Cincinnati chimpanzee, are being deposited in a First National savings account. The Chase Manhattan Bank of New York City announces that "Queenie of the Plaza," an eight-month-old female cat, helps "guard" the bank at night. The Commercial Bank of Miami, Florida, sponsored a "Millionaire for a Week" contest to celebrate its tenth anniversary. The winner received the interest from a hypothetical $1 million fund for one week, or $575.40.

Corporation public relations is also becoming more imaginative. In a new approach to stockholder relations, Brunswick Corporation invited its stockholders to a Chicago golf course for its annual meeting to demonstrate its MacGregor sporting goods line "in action." Professional golfers staged a golf clinic and competed in a match with Brunswick directors who wore MacGregor tams for the occasion.

An imaginative technique in stockholder communications is American Telephone and Telegraph Company's special editions of its annual report for sightless shareholders. Two editions are produced, one in

Braille and one on a twelve-inch $33\frac{1}{3}$ rpm. record for the 3,600 sight-less owners of the company's shares. Copies are personally delivered to stockholders who request them by members of the Telephone Pioneers of America, an organization of retired telephone employees.

Scientists in Westinghouse Electric Corporation laboratories in Pitts-burgh, who are men of inventive genius ever in search of something new, turned their talents to community relations by sponsoring the Westinghouse Science Honors Institute to interest talented high school seniors in careers in science. Two hundred fifty scientists in the Westing-house laboratories devote their Saturday mornings to lectures and demonstrations of new scientific developments to more than 200 stu-dents. This imaginative and constructive community relations project has built good will for Westinghouse in several plant communities.

Imagination in employee communication thrives at the Caterpillar Tractor Company plant in Joliet, Illinois, where paper cups dispensed by plant vending machines keep employees aware of their "hidden pay checks" by carrying messages on the company's pension, retirement, and hospitalization programs and credit union.

Greater Dependence of Public Relations on the Social Sciences

The social sciences are playing an increasingly important role in pub-lic relations. The social sciences of psychology, sociology, anthropology, economics, political science, and semantics are contributing to the solu-tion of public relations problems.

Public relations has been slow to use the accumulated knowledge and research of social scientists. Practitioners of public relations have not appreciated what the social sciences can contribute to public relations. Social scientists, on the other hand have been reluctant to become in-volved in commercializing their scientific knowledge. They have studied the opinion forming process, the behavior of individuals in groups, the influence of emotion on opinion, and the role of opinion leaders. The effect of propaganda has been studied extensively. The communicating process of individuals and formal and informal organizations has been investigated. By utilizing the knowledge developed by the social sci-ences, public relations practitioners can improve the effectiveness of public relations.

CHAPTER

3

PUBLIC RELATIONS

· COMMUNICATION

A SOCIAL MANAGEMENT philosophy expressed in policies and actions is the basis of effective public relations. However, good deeds and policies alone are not enough to gain the understanding and good will of the public. The policies and acts of a business or nonprofit organization must be communicated to employees, customers, shareholders, community neighbors, and other publics if the organization is to receive public recognition for its good principles and performance.

Good public relations is impossible without good communication. Good relations can only take effect through the process of communication. If there is no communication there is no public relations because relations with people are established by communicating with them.

Public relations communication is a process involving an interchange of facts, viewpoints, and ideas between a business or nonprofit organization and the public to achieve mutual understanding. There are three significant points in this definition: first, communication must involve two or more persons; second, it is a two-way exchange of information; and third, understanding is implied. A bulletin board announcement is not communication. Only when the announcement has been read, understood, and acknowledged has there been true communication.

Although millions of dollars are spent annually on business communication it is the least understood, most ineffective, and inadequately measured management function. "We have been inept in communicating the ideas and information which create understanding among people," stated Austin S. Iglehart, former chairman of the board and president of General Foods Corp.

The rapid growth of business organizations has created a serious internal communication problem. A few years ago the owner of a small business knew intimately the people who worked for him. However, as the business grew and the number of employees increased, the former close and frequent communication between the head of the business and the workers disappeared.

29

As a result, employees were no longer aware of the problems of the business that affected their interests. Because the workers were not informed, they often misunderstood management's intentions. In one case, rumors and gossip spread that the owner was planning to close the plant and move the machinery elsewhere. Although these rumors had no foundation in fact, many employees were afraid they would lose their jobs. As a consequence, they sought work elsewhere. Unable to secure replacements the plant was forced to shut down; customers bought from competitors and the business failed. This complication of problems could have been largely avoided by good management communication with employees.

Communication by management with employees has become more difficult as the number of industrial workers and supervisors have increased. Communication from management in a large organization must be passed down through several levels of authority. In the transmission, the meaning of a message is often garbled and misunderstood. Supervisors and workers interpreted a communication not in the meaning intended by management but against the background of their personal attitudes and experience. Corporate decentralization, work specialization, resistance to technological changes and automation, and union propaganda have made it more difficult for management to communicate with workers.

Communication is poor in some companies because management is unwilling to explain its policies and actions. Supervisors and foremen are also reluctant to communicate to workers information they deem unimportant, that would adversely affect their interests or conflict with their own preconceptions.

Equally difficult is the problem of external communication with consumers, community neighbors, dealers and distributors, suppliers, shareholders, government agencies and legislators, educators, and other publics. The rapid growth of population has increased the numerical size of these publics and the magnitude of the communication problem. Competition for readers and viewers by mass communication media has drowned the public in a deluge of information. Newspapers, magazines, books, radio, television, all forms of advertising, and motion pictures are competing for a favorable audience for their messages. The capacity of the public to consume information is approaching the saturation point. The cost of mass communication has reached a level where only the well-financed organizations can afford to communicate with the public.

In spite of the numerous obstacles to the free flow of information from management to employees and outside publics, communication is being widely accepted by management as an essential function. Many companies have employed specialists with communication skills in staff public relations departments. Increasing sums are being invested in communicating with the public. Communication consultants are advising management, and numerous management books and periodicals discuss improved techniques of communication. Corporate executives and rank-and-file employees are being trained to communicate with each other and with the outside publics about the policies and accomplishments of their companies.

THE COMMUNICATION PROCESS

The process of communication may be compared to the procedure of production and consumption. It involves the production of meaning, using the raw materials of words, pictures, symbols, and actions by the communicator and the consumption of meaning by listening, seeing, touching, tasting, and smelling by the audience. Communication between an organization and its publics also may be compared to semaphore signaling in which a signalman standing on the bridge of a ship, with a flag in each hand, transmits messages to other ships by holding the flags in different positions to represent letters and numerals. A signalman acknowledges receipt of the messages with similar signals.

All communication involves three elements, the sender, the medium of communication, and the receiver. The effectiveness of communication depends upon all three elements. If the sender is incompetent, the message obscure, the receiver does not understand its meaning and the communication process has failed.

Communication may be either *verbal,* consisting of spoken and written words; or *nonverbal,* expressed by actions, gestures, facial expressions, and pictures. Communication is usually influenced by the feelings of the communicator as well as by his attitude toward the audience addressed and his purpose in communicating. The words used in a communication are often not as important as the meaning which may be inferred by the audience from the facts, actions, feelings, and intentions of the communicator.

Informal Communication

Communication may be either informal or formal. Much communication between people is informal. Conversation which occurs when two or more people meet in a social or business situation to discuss subjects of personal or business nature is informal. This face-to-face communication plays an important role in creating understanding as well as correcting misconceptions of an organization among employees at work and in informal conversation with community neighbors, shareholders, consumers, suppliers, and dealers.

Some informal communication, referred to as the "grapevine," consists of gossip, rumor, and misinformation and often creates misunderstanding and ill will. Because informal communicators are not held accountable for their utterances, they feel free to distort facts, exaggerate, misinterpret, and criticize. For these reasons informal communication is usually considered undesirable. However, informal communication can serve to carry good news as well as bad. By listening to the informal conversation of well-informed employees, their neighbors, shareholders, and consumers can learn how a business functions. In this way management can use informal communication to combat rumors, transmit the facts, and support the organization's objectives. What neighbors say about a company over the back fence carries more weight in a community than what the company may say in its formal communications.

Formal Communication

Formal communication is used by management to transmit information to other executives and employees within an organization. It is also used for outside communication with neighbors, consumers, shareholders, and other publics. Internal formal communication has two dimensions: vertical and horizontal.

Formal Vertical, Two-Way Communication. Internal, vertical, two-way communication follows the organizational chain of command *down* from the highest authority through the various levels of management to employees and *upward* from employees to management through the various levels of authority. Management's formal downward communication consists of formal directives, bulletins, employee periodicals, and verbal messages. Upward communication from employees is largely informal in the form of verbal suggestions, ideas, criticisms, and comments on policy and operations.

The long established flow of internal, management communication follows a one-way channel from the top level of authority down to the bottom of the organization. Employees are not expected to "talk back" to management which is not interested in the opinions of the rank and file. The same one-way communication has been used by management to communicate with community neighbors, consumers, shareholders, dealers, and others outside the organization. However, management is now adopting two-way communication with employees and the public by giving them an opportunity to express their views to management.

The opinions of employees are secured through suggestion systems, management-worker meetings, and in other ways. The views of the outside publics are secured by public opinion research.

Upward communication from employees and the external publics shows management whether or not its communications are being received and understood. It stimulates employee interest and participation and produces valuable ideas from workers. By listening to public opinion, management can improve policies and behavior to win public approval. The public has an opportunity through two-way communication to express its views and to enjoy a feeling of recognition which creates better understanding and good will.

Formal Horizontal, Two-Way Internal Communication. In addition to horizontal *informal* communication between staff executives, supervisors, and foremen, *formal* horizontal internal communication is encouraged in many organizations through conferences, closed-circuit television broadcasts, informative meetings, and discussions. Horizontal communication promotes co-operative effort and teamwork between staff groups and line executives and serves to better co-ordinate the various functions of an enterprise.

The Role of Listening in Communication

Since the process of communication involves not only sending but also receiving information, listening is an important part of the procedure. Management is listening more to workers, customers, neighbors, and the public. Talking to the public is not enough. Listening is a dual responsibility of the communicator and the auditor and is essential in good public relations. Listening enables management to determine how well its messages are being received, understood, and accepted by the public. Then adjustments may be made not only in the delivery of the messages but also in their content as well as in the policies and practices of the organization, to make them more acceptable to the public.

The process of listening to the public to determine if management communications are being understood and accepted is related to cybernetics. Derived from the Greek word "kybernetes," the term "cybernetics" means steersman and applies to control through the feedback of information. The electronic computing machine is a cybernetic device which is fed numerical information, computes it, and feeds back the answers. This is similar to the process by which management gives information to the public, listens to the feedback or response, and then adjusts its policies, practices, and communications to gain public acceptance and understanding.

Electronic computing equipment performs a memory function which holds information and combines it with other data when it is needed. This cybernetic process is comparable to what takes place in public relations when management listens to the feedback of public opinion, records and combines it with other opinion data to be used as needed to improve management policies and practices. Through opinion research management listens to the public, stores its views away in public opinion records, and uses this information in policy and decision making.

Listening by management is important in communication not only with employees but also with community neighbors, shareholders, suppliers, dealers, consumers, and other publics. Informal listening to employees occurs many times a day in the course of business. Listening to community neighbors takes place at civic and social gatherings, and informal meetings at which management has an opportunity to ascertain the public viewpoint, combat rumors, answer questions, and explain the corporation's objectives. Similar opportunities for informal listening arise at meetings with shareholders, dealers, suppliers, and educators. Formal listening is done by opinion research in which trained listeners interview consumers, employees, and other publics to determine public attitudes concerning the organization.

Listening skill may be acquired by employing good listening techniques. Listening is an active process in which the listener gives full attention to the speaker by looking him in the eye, acting interested, by alert posture and facial expression, and by asking questions and making comments to encourage the speaker to express his views. Stop talking and give the speaker an opportunity to communicate so that you can listen to his message. Exclude distracting noises and interruptions. Observe the nonverbal communications of the speaker—his tone, gestures, and facial expressions—which may amplify and clarify his verbal statements. Avoid prejudice and bias toward a speaker and his message by an unfavorable impression of his personality and vocabulary. Keep an open mind and ear to what the speaker says although it may differ from your point of view. Withhold evaluation of a communication until it is completely understood by avoiding interruptions, contradictions, and arguments. Listen primarily for ideas and underlying attitudes of the speaker.

Semantics in Verbal Communication

Communication is an exchange of meaning, and the science of meaning is called *semantics*. It deals with the meaning of words or symbols and with people's reaction to them. As communication is mainly carried on with words, the meaning of words is vital to clear, understanding communication. Communication with words is difficult because their meaning is affected by personal differences in the attitude, experience, and current situation of the communicator and his audience. The meaning that a listener gives to a word depends upon his personal feelings and experience. This meaning may not be at all what the communicator intended and misunderstanding results.

George Bernard Shaw once said that the American and British people are separated by the common barrier of a common language. This difficulty in communication is illustrated by an incident described by Winston Churchill in his book, *The Second World War*. The British and American Chiefs of Staff met to discuss an important subject. The British proposed to "table" it—which word meant to them to get it out on the conference table and discuss it immediately. The American officers protested that the subject must not be tabled—which to them meant deferred to a future meeting. The discussion waxed hotly until the participants realized that they all wanted to discuss the subject immediately.

The word "square," for example, has numerous meanings depending on the way it is used in communication. A square, used as a noun, may be a geometrical figure having four equal sides; an instrument used to lay out work; an area bounded by streets; a body of troops; and the product of a number multiplied by itself. Used as a verb, "square" means to bring to a right angle, as to square one's shoulders; to adjust, to settle accounts, to bribe, to cause the score of a match to become equal. As an adverb "square" may mean honest and fair, directly, firmly, and to be face to face. As an adjective, "square" means exactly adjusted, honest and just, even—leaving no balance, straightforward, and substantial—like a square meal. Nearly every word has many meanings which create semantic problems and misunderstanding.

Words describing tangible objects, persons, places, and materials such as "tree," "chair," "George Washington," "Boston," and "wood" present no semantic problem in communication as they convey the same meaning to almost everyone. Such words are called "extensional," which word is derived from the use of the term in physics, meaning a body which occupies a portion of space.

However, words describing abstract attributes, ideas, or conceptions such as "peaceful coexistence," "love," "justice," and "faith" which have different meanings to different listeners or readers depending on their personal attitudes and experience, create serious misunderstandings in communication. Such words are called "intensional" as contrasted with "extensional" words which convey the same meaning to all people.

To reduce the possibility of being misunderstood, use fewer abstractions and more extensional words which convey the same meaning to everyone; or explain the meaning of a word by demonstrating, using pictures or clear, simple examples.

The meaning of words is often determined by their context or the time, situation, or particular circumstances and environment in which the words are used. The same word expressed in one situation may have a completely different meaning in another situation. The statement, "He's aggressive," when referring to the performance of a salesman is complimentary. However, when "aggressive" is used in referring to a large boy who struck his smaller brother, it is derogatory. "He was driving 80 miles an hour" means excessive speed when referring to a motorist on a city street, but exceptionally slow when describing a racer on the Indianapolis speedway.

Make communication more understandable by choosing carefully the words used so that they will conform to the context within which the audience will interpret them.

In communicating, certain assumptions are made by the communicator which must be understood by the listener if the meaning of the message is to be understood. Sometimes these assumptions are clearly stated by the communicator but in many cases they are not apparent and the meaning of the message is obscure. A hidden assumption is illustrated in the following story recounted by Harry E. Maynard about a man who went for a walk one day and met a friend, whom he had not seen, heard from, nor heard of in ten years. After an exchange of greetings, the man said, "Is this your little girl?" and the friend replied, "Yes, I got married about six years ago." The man then asked the child, "What is your name?" and the little girl replied, "Same as my Mommy's." "Oh," said the man, "then it must be Margaret."

If the man did not know whom his friend had married, how could he know the child's name? Most people assume that the friend of the man in the story is also a man. On the contrary, the friend is the mother of the child. If the story had revealed that the man's friend was a woman, the answer to the question would have been obvious.

Another example of mistaken assumption is the following: Can you, with one line, turn IX into the number 6? The answer is simple when the assumption behind the question is understood. Most people assume that this is a problem in Roman numerals. On the contrary, this is a false assumption. When it is assumed that the question concerns Arabic and not Roman numerals, IX can be easily converted into the Arabic SIX.

Meaning in communication is often obscured by verbosity or wordiness. Every trade and profession has its own dialect and technical vocabulary often unintelligible to the uninitiated. Such dialect confuses the meaning of communication. An example of verbose bureaucratic communication from the Bureau of Standards of the U.S. Department of Commerce is the following exchange of communication between the Bureau and a New York plumber. The plumber wrote the Bureau that he had found hydrochloric acid fine for cleaning drains and asked if it was harmless. Washington replied: "The efficacy of hydrochloric acid is indisputable, but the chlorine residue is incompatible with metallic permanence."

The plumber wrote back that he was mighty glad that the Bureau agreed with him. The Bureau replied, with a note of alarm: "We cannot assume responsibility for the production of toxic and noxious residues with hydrochloric acid, and suggest that you use an alternate procedure." The plumber was happy that the Bureau still agreed with him. Whereupon the Bureau exploded: "Don't use hydrochloric acid; it eats Hell out of the pipes!"

For good communication choose words carefully, using simple, commonly understood words. Use extensional, concrete words rather than intensional, abstract words which mean different things to different people. Avoid wordiness. Use examples to give a clear picture of your meaning. Use words which conform to the context or situation in which they are used. State your premise or assumption so as to make your meaning clear; and listen attentively to determine if your words are being clearly understood.

Nonverbal Communication

Communication is also carried on not only through the use of words but simultaneously through actions, gestures, facial expressions, and pictures all of which are symbols of meaning. Nonverbal symbols or gestures when used to supplement a spoken communication clarify meaning which might otherwise be misunderstood. Meaning may be communicated with the use of nonverbal symbols alone. The growing use of visual and audio-visual materials in business, educational, and religious communication is recognition of the effectiveness of these methods of conveying meaning.

Actions often speak louder than words in communicating. A handshake and a pat on the back express friendliness and appreciation more than words. A scowling facial expression has the reverse meaning of a sincere smile. The clenched fist, the set mouth, and flashing eyes communicate anger more strongly than spoken or written words. Failure to act is also communication. Management communicates when it fails to promote an employee who has been promised advancement. Action may speak more clearly than verbal communication.

Visual communication is one of the oldest and most effective means of transmitting meaning. An ancient and much quoted Chinese proverb says, "One picture is worth a thousand words." Pictures are remembered longer than verbal messages. They convey meaning faster than words, making it possible to communicate information in a few seconds that would otherwise consume many minutes of verbal explanation. Pictures convey a meaning of reality and authenticity and are believed more readily than words. They gain and hold the attention of viewers and if the communication is interrupted the message may be readily picked up.

Tactual communication conveys meaning through the sense of touch. Scientists estimate that more than 5,000 sensory nerves terminate in one square inch of finger-tip surface to receive tactual messages and flash them to the brain. The meaning of the smooth finish of furniture, the rough texture of tweed, the softness of a peach can be communicated more readily by touch than in any other way.

Olfactory communication can make extensional the meaning of aroma that cannot be expressed by words. The fragrant aroma rising from a steaming cup of fine coffee tells a story that cannot be misunderstood. The scent of new-mown hay cannot be adequately described by verbal communication. This example also illustrates the effect of experience on the meaning of words. If you have experienced the scent of new-mown hay, you interpret the meaning of these words in the light of your sense experience.

Gustatory communication transmits meaning through the sense of taste. No abstract words can describe the deliciousness of a well-baked cake as well as a taste experience. A manufacturer of cake mixes, desiring to communicate the excellence of the product to shareholders at an annual meeting, baked and served cakes made from the cake mixes to communicate the delicious quality of the product which could not be adequately described by words or pictures.

Five avenues of communication may be used to communicate meaning to others. Communicate to the eyes, ears, hands, noses, and mouths of people in order to transmit meaning quickly and understandably. Use as many channels of communication as possible. Some persons understand more readily through one sense than another. The American Telephone and Telegraph Company communicates with blind shareholders by publishing its annual report in Braille, a system of printing with raised letters which can be read by the blind with their fingers.

MEDIA OF COMMUNICATION

Media of communication used by management in gaining the understanding and good will of employees, shareholders, customers, suppliers,
community neighbors, dealers and distributors, educators, and representatives of government may be classified as: written or printed, oral,
and audio-visual.

Written or Printed Media of Communication

Written or printed messages are the most widely used medium of
communication in public relations. They transmit information complete
and undistorted to persons at the place and time desired. Written
messages are used in communicating with the *internal* public composed
of managers, supervisors, and employees and the *external* publics including consumers, shareholders, neighbors, suppliers, government,
dealers, and others.

In Internal Communication. In internal communication, the following written or printed media are used: Management letters to all
employees, employee newspapers and magazines, bulletin board announcements, annual and interim financial reports, employee handbooks
or manuals, management bulletins for executives and supervisors, pay
envelope inserts, booklets explaining policies and procedures, daily news
digests, reading racks, indoctrination kits, and posters.

In External Communication. In external communication the following written media are used: annual and interim reports, publicity releases, newspaper and magazine advertising; consumer, dealer, and
shareholder magazines; correspondence; booklets reprinting policies
and executive speeches; program kits and study materials for women's
clubs; educational materials, library reference materials, letters, manuals,
and handbooks; outdoor advertising; and direct-mail advertising.

Oral Media of Communication

Oral communication is the most effective and persuasive method of
transmitting information to the internal as well as external publics. It
is growing in importance as the value of person-to-person communication is becoming more widely recognized and the limitations of mass
communication are evident. Oral communication provides opportunity
for discussion, clarification and two-way or feedback communication.
On the other hand, oral communication depends on the motivation and
skill of the individual communicator, it reaches a limited audience, is
costly and time consuming.

In Internal Communication. In internal communication, the follow-ing oral media are used: employee and executive meetings, a public address system, open houses, plant tours, family nights, visits by key executives to departments, new employee orientation, employee coun-seling, panel discussions, grievance discussion, performance appraisal, telecom system, open-door policy, employee-management committees, recordings, and participation in employee social affairs.

FIG. 3–1. Oral two-way communication occurs in a seminar in which management of Texas Eastern Transmission Corp. describes the operation of the company to security analysts who in turn ask questions.

In External Communication. In external communication, the follow-ing oral media are used: meetings of shareholders, consumers, dealers, suppliers, opinion leaders in plant communities, educators, and legisla-tors; open houses, plant tours, business-education days, speeches by employees and executives, visits to community institutions and suppliers, radio broadcasts, and in participation in community affairs.

Audio-visual Media of Communication

Audio-visual media of communication are enjoying growing recogni-tion in public communication. They make possible a dual impression on the sight and hearing of the audience, receive twenty-five times more attention than oral messages, are remembered five times more than what is read, and give a clearer understanding of the message. Audio-visuals transmit information more rapidly, accurately, and at lower cost. They secure and hold the attention of the audience for longer

THE NIMBUS SATELLITE, designed for long life and high reliability, will be permanently stabilized on all three axes so that its cameras will always face the earth.

PROGRESS POSTER FOR
SCHOOL AND COLLEGE
February 1, 1963

REPORTS WORLD'S WEATHER

Equipped with television cameras, NASA Nimbus satellite will cover the weather patterns of entire globe every 24 hours

Sometime in the near future, the first earth-oriented weather satellite will be launched into a near-polar orbit 500 miles above the earth . . . from California's Vandenberg Air Base. Nimbus, integrated and tested by General Electric scientists and engineers, will be placed in orbit at a precise 80.45° inclination by a Thor-Agena rocket. The satellite will orbit the earth 14 times every 24 hours and be timed to pass over the equator at high noon on each pass.

Mounted near the center of the sensory ring at the base of the satellite is a bank of TV cameras. They are placed side by side, with the first and third cameras angled slightly outward. Fixed in this position and always facing earthward, the cameras will produce composite pictures, each covering an area of the earth's surface 1500 nautical miles wide and 350 nautical miles deep. With each camera taking 33 pictures per orbit, the Nimbus will be able to send back more than 1300 photographs per day of weather patterns in every corner of the globe. The pictures are to be stored on four-channel magnetic tape recorders . . . then transmitted to a weather station in Fairbanks, Alaska. From here the data are relayed via the Goddard Flight Center in Maryland to a nearby Weather Bureau station for interpretation.

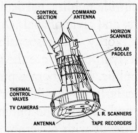

THE STRUCTURE OF THE NIMBUS consists of (1) a doughnut-shaped sensory ring about 5 feet in diameter which houses the TV cameras; (2) a "box" near the top of the satellite containing the control section which keeps the cameras constantly pointed toward the earth; and (3) two solar paddles which are supported by a shaft through the control section. Each paddle has 5740 solar cells that always face the sun.

Progress Is Our Most Important Product

GENERAL ⊕ ELECTRIC

PREPARED BY EDUCATIONAL RELATIONS, GENERAL ELECTRIC COMPANY, 570 LEXINGTON AVE., NEW YORK 22, N. Y.

FIG. 3–2. Posters are one feature of the educational relations program of the General Electric Company. They are distributed to science teachers of high schools and colleges for posting in science classrooms to inform students about scientific developments.

periods and the audience may be selected to suit the message. They are used most effectively in conjunction with oral and written media of communication.

In Internal Communication. In internal communication with employees the following audio-visual media are used: motion pictures, slides, film strips, closed-circuit television, sound slide film, flip charts, easel charts, posters, maps, flannel-boards, and product exhibits.

In External Communication. In external communication the following audio-visual media are used: displays and exhibits, motion pictures, slide films, sound slide films, charts, maps, posters, slides, television broadcasts on open and closed circuit, models and constructions, and demonstrating devices.

Responsibility for Communication

Communication is a responsibility of everyone employed by a business or nonprofit organization. It is not a function which can be delegated to a public relations department but is an activity in which all employees should participate, from the president through staff and line management to and including all rank-and-file workers. All levels of management are involved in the internal vertical flow of communications downward from higher to lower authority. All employees and line executives communicate upward from lower to higher authority, thus completing the circuit of two-way communication. At all levels of management there is, in addition, much horizontal cross-communication between executives. This cross-communication does not follow the vertical chain of command.

More important than internal communication is communication with the outside publics, particularly community neighbors, consumers, educators, and civic officials. All employees and management at all levels of authority are responsible for public communication and, when properly informed, are the most effective media of communication with the public. In corporate public relations, the marketing department is particularly responsible for communications with consumers, distributors, and dealers; the purchasing department with suppliers; the legal department with government; and the finance department with shareholders. All executives and employees of these departments are the major media of communication with their respective publics.

The ultimate responsibility for communication rests with top management and public relations staff specialists in communication, with operating responsibility for communication delegated to the entire management group. Administrative staff specialists are necessary to plan sound communication procedures and to stimulate, counsel, and assist line management in carrying out these procedures.

In some companies, administrative responsibility for internal communication between management and employees is delegated to the industrial relations or personnel staff. Outside communication is delegated to the public relations staff. As management and employees communicate not only among themselves but also to the outside publics, the public relations staff should assume responsibility for *both internal* and *external* communication procedures.

In carrying out this responsibility, the public relations staff should consult industrial relations or personnel in planning and programing internal communication procedures; and consult with the managers of marketing, purchasing, finance, and law in determining communication policies, objectives, and plans for effective communication with outside publics.

The increasing emphasis on communication has created a need for communication specialists and outside communication consultants to advise management on sound communication procedures. It is estimated that more than 100 communication specialists are now employed in industry, and optimistic advocates of improved communication predict that in the future a well-managed corporation will have a vice-president in charge of communication.

Improving Communication Skills of Management and All Employees

The ability of management and employees to communicate effectively not only with each other but also with the outside publics is essential in developing good employee and plant community relations. Communication training courses are being offered to management and hourly and salaried employees by several corporations to make company personnel more effective communicators both inside as well as with the outside public.

The New York Telephone Company trains management and employees in communication, using a 100-page manual entitled, *Help Yourself to Better Communication,* prepared by a professor of English and Education of a leading university after research of the oral communications of the company's employees. Topics covered include: talking with customers; making a speech; leading a meeting; listening, asking, and answering questions; meaning; and keeping supervisors informed.

The International Harvester Company, Chicago, trains foremen and supervisors in the techniques of communication by showing them how to transmit to employees management communications. The following principles of communication to workers are recommended:

Get all information to employees quickly, before the end of the shift. Give them all the news, both good and bad. Read letters or bulletins from management to the entire department or give them to the assistant foreman and have him group the people under his charge and read the news to them. Personal dissemination of news by the foreman is preferable to secure personal contact between the employees and management. Digest and discuss company news personally with every employee. Don't just put the news on the bulletin board which does away with all personal contact.

General Electric Company has a communication training course for plant supervisors to improve person-to-person communication and group conference leadership. The course consists of ten two-hour sessions and covers such topics as overcoming obstacles to oral communication, the communication process, developing skill as a communicator, and maintaining confidence in management decisions and actions.

The basis of communication skill is knowledge of the subject. If employees do not know they cannot communicate. The primary objective of a communication course should be to provide management and workers with information about the organization, its purpose, ideals, and mission; its philosophy and principles of management; its program; what it has accomplished and what it expects to do; and the people who manage and staff the organization. All employees and supervisors should have complete and current information on company policy, employment, and economic conditions affecting the corporation's operations, finances, research, plant expansion, sales, new product developments, taxes paid, and laws and regulations affecting operations. This information should be communicated to management and personnel through the written, oral, and audio-visual media described previously.

The role of management and workers as communicators to the outside publics should be emphasized in a communication training program. To the public each employee of an organization is the organization. The public will believe what an employee says about a company before they will accept what the organization says about itself in its advertising and publicity. If an organization cannot get its own people to speak well of it, all of its official communications will fail to gain the understanding and good will of the public.

Programs of Communication with the Public

In the following chapters are described programs of communication in which management and all employees communicate information about the organization to community neighbors, suppliers, consumers, shareholders, government officials, distributors, dealers, educators, and others upon whom the organization depends for understanding and good will. Everyone associated with an enterprise—telephone operators, receptionists, deliverymen, servicemen, installers, salesmen, and management executives—has an important role in these public communication programs. The task of all employees is to identify the organization with the interests of the public.

Case 3–1

INTERNAL COMMUNICATIONS

Westinghouse Electric Corporation

The Westinghouse Electric Corporation, Pittsburgh, Pennsylvania, manufactures and markets electric generating and transmitting equipment, home appliances, atomic and defense products in annual volume of more than $2 billion. The corporation employs about 110,000 workers in 60 plants in the United States. Westinghouse is owned by more than 170,000 stockholders, of which number 36,000 are employees.

A major activity of Westinghouse information is internal communication with employees. It is the policy of the company to communicate effectively at all times to employees within the organization by providing proper and adequate information and the means of transmitting it effectively. This policy is based on the premises that communications, both oral and written, constitute an essential management function in transmitting information about the company's policies, practices, plans, and actions; that employees should be informed to correct misunderstandings; and that employee reactions and attitudes toward Westinghouse policies and practices should be recognized.

The objectives of Westinghouse internal communications are sevenfold: to maintain confidence among employees in the company's integrity and actions; to develop in employees the belief that their own work is significant; to stimulate pride among employees in the achievements of the company; to give employees an understanding of management's objectives; to assure employees that their experience and thinking are valued by management; to convince employees who are members of unions that they have responsibilities to the company as well as to the union; and to keep the Westinghouse environment one of frankness, mutual respect, and confidence.

Responsibility for internal communications at Westinghouse rests primarily with the line organization through group general managers and division, department, and plant managers, as well as every regional and district manager and supervisor at every level of management.

To assist line management at all levels in developing employee communications is the function of the Employee Communications section of the Employee Communications and Community Relations Department of the Information Services staff at the company's headquarters in Pittsburgh. The Employee Communications section consults with line managers on problems of internal communications; plans and produces headquarters' sponsored company-wide employee communications programs; provides guidance and evaluation of Employee Communications to plant and headquarters' departments; assists divisions by producing employee periodicals, handbooks, and communicating media; and aids operating executives in the selection, guidance, and training of Communications Coordinators at local plants.

Communications Coordinators

At every local Westinghouse plant, communications with employees is the responsibility of a Communications Coordinator, who devotes 60 per cent of his time to internal communications and the balance to external community relations. In most cases a Coordinator gives his full time to these functions, but in a small plant he may also serve as a personnel or industrial relations man with internal communications and community relations responsibilities. In a large plant the Coordinator may have an assistant.

A Communications Coordinator is selected by each local plant manager, with the advice of the headquarters' Employee Communications section of the Employee Communications and Community Relations department. The assignment of the Communications Coordinator's responsibilities is a local management decision and his salary and expenses are charged against the local plant budget.

The employee communications function of a Communications Coordinator is to carry out the sevenfold objectives of Westinghouse internal communications described previously. Each Coordinator, with the approval of his local manager, is free to develop an internal communications program designed to fit local plant conditions within the framework of the company's communications policies and objectives. In this way local internal communications programs are active, timely, and flexible.

An Internal Communications Program

A typical internal communications program designed for the particular needs of the Buffalo division of Westinghouse by the division Communications Coordinator in co-operation with the headquarters Employee Communications staff illustrates the media and activities employed in local internal communications as follows:

A monthly employee newsletter in news brief format, to alternate with the local plant section of the company-wide employee publication, *Westinghouse News,* produced by the headquarters Employee Communications section.

A "Let's Take a Look" publication, to answer union claims and keep union periodicals honest and accurate.

Broader internal communications with supervisors through direct personal contact by the Communications Coordinator, who keeps a record of conversations with supervisors and foremen.

Bulletin boards painted in bright colors provide incentives to employees to read the boards in an "It Pays to Look" campaign. This campaign involves posting of employees' birth dates, the birth dates of employees' wives and children, employees' license numbers containing three 7's or a combination of numbers, with awards to the "lucky" employees who recognize these.

Supervisors' contacts with employees through formal safety and workplace meetings. Briefs on communication projects and related subjects sent supervisors for use in informal employee contacts.

Communications with department heads to keep them informed on monthly communications themes and to secure their counsel on local tie-ins.

Letters to employees' homes on special developments, Westinghouse in the community, vacations, and others.

Union communications through meetings with union leaders on United Fund, special events, and similar programs.

Company-wide Employee Communications

Company-wide employee communications programs are the responsibility of the Employee Communications section of the Employee Communications and Community Relations department at company headquarters in Pittsburgh. A national employee publication, *Westinghouse News,* is written, edited, and distributed once every two weeks to 110,000 Westinghouse employees. This publication is in newspaper tabloid size and format. For some twenty locations, one or two of the paper's normal four pages feature local news of that particular plant. This material, prepared by a local plant editor, is incorporated by headquarters into the issue distributed to employees of that particular plant.

A "Management Guide—Internal Communications," describing employee communications policy, objectives, and organization for the guidance of line managers and local internal Communications Coordinators, has been prepared by the headquarters Employee Communications and Community Relations department.

An annual program of employee communications projects, around which local plant Communications Coordinators can build their own plant communications programs, is prepared by the headquarters communications staff. This program is designed to accomplish the following internal communications objectives: to communicate to employees economic facts and concepts about the company; to develop loyalty among all employees; to build appreciation among the employees of the company as a good place to work; and to create greater recognition of the far-reaching contributions of Westinghouse.

To attain these objectives, a series of internal communications projects for each month of the year are proposed by the headquarters Employee Communications section. Typical projects are: "Help Build a Stronger Westinghouse," stressing the role of employees as "company salesmen"; "Report to Employees"; "Profits"; "Customer Is Boss"; "Education and Training in Westinghouse"; "Benefits"; "Automation and Productivity"; "Waste Prevention"; "Safety"; and "Good Housekeeping."

An annual two-day meeting of Communications Coordinators is held at company headquarters to give them a sense of direction in terms of corporate communications objectives and to criticize the proposed program. One day is devoted to employee communications covering such subjects as: improving plant sections of *Westinghouse News,* care and feeding of bulletin boards, communications gimmicks, making the management newsletter work, employee attitude surveys, workplace meetings, manager's letters, feedback, and employee opinions.

The headquarters Employee Communications staff works closely with Communications Coordinators at local plants by telephone, letter, and personal visit. Assistance may be given Coordinators in preparing important letters to employees or a special program involving a few minutes on the telephone, or several days spent at a plant by headquarters staffmen.

A continuous series of written communications goes out from the headquarters Employee Communications section to plant Communications Coordinators. An "Employee Communications Newsletter," reports internal communications techniques and new ideas gathered from Coordinators throughout the entire Westinghouse organization.

Monthly kits of employee communications ideas and materials for specific projects in the annual program are sent by headquarters to local Communications Coordinators. The kits state the objective of each project for the month, a plan, and suggested internal communications activities.

A typical monthly communications project was the "Westinghouse Employee Participation Identification Program," a part of the "Westinghouse in the Community" communications project. The objective of this program was to assure recognition of employee participation in community affairs and organizations during the month. Each employee participating in community activities was identified with a lapel button with a white circle "W" on a blue background. Buttons were provided by headquarters at cost. The program was announced to all employees in each plant, on bulletin boards, in the employee newsletter, letters to the home, and through informal personal contacts in the plant. Employees were encouraged to request a button by making known their community activities to their supervisors.

Idea letters are also used by headquarters to stimulate local internal communications programs. The letters suggest workplace meetings, mailings, and other communications techniques to Communications Coordinators in developing programs in line with local management objectives. Idea letters are "starters" designed to get each plant Coordinator into gear with his own variations and developments of suggested programs or other ideas which they may initiate.

The advantage of this combination of local activity and central co-ordination is effective localization of company-wide employee communications. The implementation of the company's internal communications program depends upon the effectiveness of local Communications Coordinators.

QUESTIONS

1. What is your opinion of the Westinghouse internal communications program? Give reasons for approving or disapproving of this program.

2. Should responsibility for employee communications in Westinghouse plants rest with the local management and Communications Coordinator? Give reasons for your decision.

3. Discuss the role played by the Communications Coordinator in Westinghouse internal communications. What are the advantages of the Coordinator? His limitations?

4. Are the methods employed by the headquarters Employee Communications section of the Employee Communications and Community Relations department to aid Communications Coordinators satisfactory? What additional service may be given by headquarters to local Coordinators?

5. Is the company-wide employee communications program of the headquarters Employee Communications and Community Relations department satisfactory? What additional company-wide communications are needed?

4 · PUBLIC OPINION

THE OBJECTIVE of public relations is the development of favorable public opinion. Public opinion is difficult to define. It is not an entity which has reality, form, and substance but an aggregation of different beliefs, ideas, illusions, and preconceptions of individuals who comprise a public.

What Is a Public?

A public is a group of people who exercise mutual opinion on *controversial* subjects. A group of workers confronted with the controversial question of deciding to strike or not to strike is a public involved in the process of forming public opinion. A group of workers waiting for a bus is not involved in public opinion formation as no controversial question confronts this group.

Every person is a member of numerous publics involved in opinion formation. A person may be identified with social, religious, political, economic, educational, recreational, and other groups faced with controversial questions and situations and engaged in formulating public opinion. Some of these publics consist of no more than two persons while others, such as religious and political groups, are composed of millions of persons. A group involved in opinion formation may not be assembled in one place but scattered throughout the world.

A public has a unifying interest which draws individual members of the group together. The common interest of employees in higher wages, fringe benefits, and improved working conditions draws them together in the process of opinion formation. A public is a cohesive body in which persons with like and unlike opinions are united in views held and advocated in common on controversial questions. The group is conscious of the similar interests which unite it.

The distinctive characteristics of a group involved in public opinion formation are enumerated by Carroll Clark, sociologist, as follows: Underlying common interests strong enough to override sharply op-

posed interests and sentiments; divergent interests and attitudes serving
to divide the group as to the course of action to be taken on an issue; a
common discourse in terms of which an exchange of views may be
affected; access through communication media to information on an
issue; tolerance of opposing views and willingness to discuss the issue;
and utilizing informal social mechanisms or formal political machinery
for reaching a collective decision and taking collective action.

A corporation has several important publics which are dependent
upon it for employment, dividends, goods, services, or taxes such as the
employee, shareholder, consumer, distributor, and government publics.

A college or university has several dependent publics, including its
graduates, faculty, community neighbors, suppliers, as well as its student
body.

A business, professional, or social service organization is concerned
with the opinions of its members, contributors, employees, neighbors,
and suppliers on controversial situations which arise in the conduct of its
affairs.

What Is Public Opinion?

Public opinion is an expression of the views held in common by
members of a group on a controversial subject. It is a process in which a
group rationally weighs and debates the facts or responds to nonlogical,
emotional appeals in reaching a collective decision on a controversial
question.

Public opinion is expressed as a consequence of controversy, dispute,
and debate over some situation or question which concerns the welfare,
beliefs, prosperity, doctrines, and value system of a group. There must
be an "issue" or a question or situation on which members of the group
take affirmative and negative positions in order to arouse public opinion.
An "issue" is a situation which threatens to disturb the prevailing
mores of a group, creating a crisis and arousing discussion and the formation of public opinion. Racial desegregation in the United States is one
such "issue" which confronts the American public. The testing of atomic
materials in the atmosphere is an international "issue" which causes
people throughout the world to take affirmative and negative positions
on the question.

Public opinion is not simply the opinion of the majority of a group.
It must be unanimous, otherwise it is simply a majority opinion or a
minority opinion. A majority is not enough, according to A. L. Lowell,
sociologist, and unanimity is not required. The opinion must be such
that, while the minority may not share it, they feel bound by convention

and not by fear to accept it and submit ungrudgingly to the views of the majority.

Attitudes in Opinion Formation

Public opinion originates in individual attitudes, although such attitudes are often influenced by the opinion of the group to which the individual belongs. Opinion is a verbal expression of an attitude which is a position assumed or studied to serve an individual's purpose. An attitude may also be defined as a predisposition to evaluate a situation in a favorable or unfavorable manner. More simply, an attitude is a way of seeing things, according to Edward J. Robinson, sociologist.

An attitude is a feeling or mood which is a product of numerous physical and mental influences. Body processes affect the attitude of an individual. Good health is conducive to positive attitudes, while illness creates feelings which may produce negative attitudes.

The cultural background of an individual may have a significant bearing on his attitude toward another person, an object or situation. The son of the president of a large corporation is likely to have a favorable attitude toward capitalism as a result of his heredity, family environment, and discipline.

Racial and religious beliefs affect attitudes. A person born and raised by devout Catholic parents will reflect in his attitudes on controversial questions the moral and theological principles of the Catholic religion.

Attitudes are aroused by the physical, social, or spiritual needs of an individual. A hungry man has a pronounced attitude toward food. A desire for safety, economic gain, social approval, or satisfaction of pride find expression in an individual's attitudes. A person's responses to these needs are expressed in his attitudes. A manager's failure to compliment an efficient worker may frustrate the worker's need for approval and create a critical attitude toward his employer.

Knowledge gained through education, reading, or experience influences an individual's attitudes on many questions. A graduate of a school of business administration has an educational background which influences his attitude toward capitalism. A mechanic who belongs to a union acquires from experience knowledge of unions which affects his attitudes toward organized labor.

Customs and habits affect the attitudes of individuals. A person who is in the habit of attending church regularly develops a favorable attitude towards religion. Racial customs affect the attitudes of members of racial groups toward food, clothing, and recreation.

Attitudes are latent within an individual until aroused by the needs of the person. The needs of an individual may be defensive or for self-protection; utilitarian for personal advancement; to express beliefs or to acquire knowledge. These are the motivating forces which arouse attitudes. External stimuli such as a speech, a newspaper article, radio or television broadcast, and other communication media arouse attitudes on controversial issues. A magazine article describing the disaster services of the Red Cross may be the motivating force appealing to the reader's desire for self-protection and arousing a favorable attitude to the Red Cross. This may induce the reader to contribute funds, give blood, or volunteer his services to the Red Cross.

The motivation which arouses attitudes is usually accompanied by feelings of emotion toward some person or object. A favorable attitude toward the country where a person was born is accompanied by emotional feelings for the ruler, the language, and the flag. Conversely, hostile attitudes toward an enemy are reflected in feelings of dislike, ridicule, or hate.

An attitude once aroused may be repressed by an individual as a result of external influences or will power. A critical attitude may be repressed by a person through fear of censure by other members of his group. The favorable attitude of a worker toward his employer may be repressed by fear of ostracism by his fellow-workers.

Types of Attitudes. Individuals manifest three types of attitudes; positive, passive, and negative. A positive attitude induces a person to react favorably toward another person, an issue, policy, or organization. Many industrial workers have a positive attitude and favorable opinion of labor unions and participate in union activities.

An individual's attitude toward an issue or organization may be completely passive. As a result, he will have no opinion on issues affecting the group. A worker who has a passive attitude toward labor unions will have no opinions on controversial questions involving union policy or activities.

Attitudes also may be negative, giving an individual an unfavorable opinion of a person, issue, or organization. A negative attitude is usually accompanied by feelings of unpleasantness or dissatisfaction. A worker may have a negative attitude toward labor unions. This negative attitude may create prejudice which causes the worker to prejudge the aims and activities of labor unions without understanding their contributions to the welfare of workers.

The intensity of an attitude is the strength of the belief or feeling of a person toward a person, object, or situation. Attitudes are also referred to as dominant or latent in respect to the strength of the feeling or belief of the individual.

Changing Attitudes. The purpose of public relations is to produce a change in the attitudes of people on controversial issues from misconceptions to accurate impressions or from little or no information to knowledge. Changes in attitude are accomplished by establishing belief by communicating information or appealing to the feelings to arouse favorable or unfavorable opinion. Changes in attitude also are brought about by a problem, a frustration, or dissatisfaction of an individual with his self-image, cherished beliefs, economic status, value system, and other circumstances. A worker dissatisfied with his wages and working conditions may undergo a change in attitude toward his employer after listening to a labor leader describe the hardships suffered by employees.

Changes in attitude occur when a prevailing attitude no longer provides a person with satisfactions or when his aspirations are raised. These are the motivations which coupled with appeals to belief or the feelings bring about changes in attitudes. Information communicated to the individual suggests new ways of obtaining satisfaction. Appeals made to the physical, social, material, or spiritual needs of people are most effective in changing their attitudes.

Public relations seeks to mold public opinion by persuading persons with a passive attitude to adopt a positive or negative attitude which will best serve the interests of the group to which they belong. Opinion research has shown that only about 15 per cent of all of the persons in a group have a positive attitude and definite opinions on issues affecting the group. An equal number have a negative attitude or are opposed to an issue. By far the largest number in the group, 70 per cent, have a passive attitude or have no opinions on questions confronting the group. The opinions of these neutrals may be influenced either for or against the question.

The passive attitude of the public on political issues is indicated by voter apathy in national and local elections. Many voters are indifferent to political questions until their interest is aroused and they express their opinions at the polls, frequently deciding the election.

Attitude change is directly related to the immediacy of the issue to the individual. An issue directly influencing the satisfaction or personal welfare of a person is likely to change his passive attitude to either a positive or negative opinion. Residents of communities where there is no local industry have a passive attitude toward the location of industry in residential areas. However, when a manufacturing concern proposes to erect a factory in a community where there is no industry, those with a passive attitude toward manufacturing in the community become concerned as to the effect the factory will have on local property values, traffic congestion, noise or odor nuisance and show an active interest and adopt a negative attitude on the question.

Attitudes are influenced by value symbols which are certain criteria by which persons, institutions, or events are judged to be either good or bad. Such criteria are wealth, material possessions, prestige, physical appearance, and others. These value symbols are important factors in determining value judgments and influencing the attitudes of people. When attitudes are organized or structured in a value system, such as conservatism or liberalism, socialism, or capitalism, they become difficult to change.

Events Change Attitudes.   Events play an important part in changing attitudes and opinions. Particularly, happenings or occurrences of significance to members of a group are a major determinant of attitudes and opinion. The dynamic, realistic, and sometimes dramatic character of events exert a strong influence on attitudes. Events provide information which often induces a change of attitude. The first orbital space flight by a Russian gave the American public an impression of Russian scientific progress which changed the attitudes of many Americans toward the Soviet Union.

Events which change the social or economic status of individuals likewise affect their attitudes toward social and economic systems. The national bank holiday of 1933 and the ensuing depression changed public attitudes toward the social reforms of the Roosevelt administration and turned public opinion in favor of social security, minimum wage, and maximum hour legislation.

Events may transform passive attitudes into positive opinions. An explosion in an industrial plant in a community arouses the latent attitudes of people about the danger of hazardous manufacturing in a residential neighborhood. This event may arouse public opinion against the company owning the plant and may bring about safety legislation to protect the community against a similar disaster. A large department store may sponsor an elaborate Christmas parade to entertain youth and adults of the community. This event transforms the passive attitudes of many persons toward the store and develops favorable public opinion of the business.

Events make a stronger impact on changing attitudes and forming public opinion than other media of communication such as news stories, broadcasts, speeches, or advertisements. Because actions speak louder than words in influencing attitudes, public relations recognizes the importance of events in transforming passive attitudes into positive opinions on controversial issues.

Some events have a temporary impact on public opinion while others, which may be termed continuous events, persist over a considerable period of time, and make a more permanent impression on attitudes. A crippling ten-day strike of transit workers will have a strong impact on public opinion while a creeping inflation, the effect of which is not immediately apparent, is a continuous event which has little impact on public opinion. The continuous activities of the United Nations do not make as strong an impression on public attitudes as the explosion of a hydrogen bomb by the Soviet Union.

Attitudes Become Opinions. Opinions are the public expression of active attitudes. Public opinion is aroused in response to motivation arising from the needs, preferences, and interests of individuals composing the public. The principal motives which induce persons to express their opinions are their desire for comfort and convenience, safety and protection, gain, satisfaction of pride, or satisfaction of affection.

The opinions of a person are activated by his motives which are aroused by mental and physical forces which induce him to express his opinions. Pride is one of the basic motives or drives which cause individuals to express their opinions on controversial questions. This motive is acquired as a result of environment, heredity, education, race, and other factors. People usually are not aware of the motives which impel them to express their attitudes in the form of opinions. The intensity of a person's motives varies from time to time as the urgency of his need increases or diminishes with circumstances.

It is important that the public relations practitioner understand the motives which cause people to express their opinions. By understanding motives of individuals, public relations communications can be phrased to appeal to the needs and motives of the public.

The importance of understanding a person's motive if you wish to influence his opinion is described by Baltsar Gracian in his *Art of Worldly Wisdom* written in 1653 as follows: "First guess a man's ruling passion. Appeal to it by word. All men are idolators; some of fame, others of self-interest, most of pleasure. Skill consists in knowing these idols in order to bring them into plan. Knowing a man's mainspring of motive, you will have the key to his will."

Opinion Leaders. Public opinion is shaped not only by events but also by certain individuals identified as opinion leaders. Opinion leaders are found in every economic, social, and political group. They exert an important influence on the opinions of the group. In business, opinion leaders are found in the employee group, the community, among shareholders, consumers, distributors, and dealers. Leaders of these groups are important communicators conveying to other members of the group information which influences the attitudes of individuals and shapes the public opinion of the group.

To recognize and appeal to these opinion leaders is a primary task of public relations. Opinion leaders are not easily identified. The characteristics which distinguish leaders from nonleaders vary as widely as the qualifications of leadership. Many who influence the opinions of others do not consider themselves as opinion leaders. Nor do they consciously seek to mold the opinions of other persons.

About one out of every five persons in a group may be identified as an opinion leader, according to Paul Lazarsfeld, sociologist. Not every one of these leaders may be equally effective in influencing the opinion of the group to which they belong. Some leaders influence group opinion on economic and political issues, others on educational questions, and still others on religious matters.

Opinion leaders usually read more and expose themselves to information, according to Lazarsfeld. They not only absorb information readily but they have a well-defined value system by which they appraise the utility and importance of the information which they receive. They are usually gregarious, sociable persons who enjoy the society of others. They leave the impression that they are successful and well adjusted in their business and social lives. These are the characteristics which induce other members of their group to ask their opinion and follow their leadership on controversial questions.

Opinion leaders may not hold high positions in community, social, political, or business groups to which they belong. They may not hold political office, elective positions in fraternal or civic organizations or volunteer to head charity drives. They may not be members of a profession, highly educated, or wealthy. Opinion leaders are found among laborers, artisans, students, housewives, clerks, salesmen, taxi drivers, and the "man in the street."

"The opinion leader," says John W. Hill, public relations counselor, "is almost always, regardless of any other sign of status or function, an individual who is demonstrating his alert interest in improving the lives of others, whether by helping them in their personal affairs as the doctor, lawyer, and minister or by improving the social and cultural environment in which they live."

Professional opinion leaders are demagogues who seek to capitalize for their personal advantage on social, political, or economic discontent by arousing public opposition. The professional opinion leader is a specialist in manipulating public opinion. He capitalizes upon events by emphasizing their significance to sway public opinion through appeals to the emotions of the noncommitted with promises of future rewards.

Formation of Public Opinion

Attitudes and their expression in the form of opinions are a psychological phenomena of the individual. A group is incapable of forming an opinion. Since a group cannot form an opinion, how is public opinion formulated?

Public opinion is formed by individuals composing a group expressing their own opinions on a controversial issue. Public opinion is a composite opinion resulting from the interaction of individual opinions of members of a group. The transformation of individual opinion by group stimuli is a distinctive characteristic of the public opinion process. This metamorphosis is sometimes referred to as the "group mind," which combines the opinions of individuals in the group into public opinion.

The *Dictionary of Mass Communications* defines public opinion as the expression of all members of a group who are giving attention in any way to a given issue. The process starts with more than individual opinions since there is an interaction of attitudes, mind-sets, beliefs, and other subjective states on an issue. It is essentially the product of a collective mental life, which in a democracy includes the expression of the majority, if there be a majority, and the minority or all minorities at any given time.

The stimuli exerted by a group on the opinion of an individual is illustrated by the example of a quiet, dignified worker who has never openly criticized his employer but, when stimulated by union leaders, joins a crowd of strikers and parades before a factory throwing rocks through the windows. Similar examples of the influence of group thinking on the opinions of individuals in the group may be observed at a college rally or any closely contested athletic event where ordinarily mild-tempered persons jeer the players and shout "Kill the umpire."

Public opinion involves a transformation of individual opinions into group opinion, brought about by the influences exerted by members of a group on the individual's opinion. The opinions of people in a group are influenced by what they hear from other members of the group or from persons outside the group; what they read in newspapers, magazines, and books; what they see in life about them or on television. Apart from group pressures, individuals' opinions are influenced by their knowledge, experience, heredity, culture, economic status, and education. Out of the interaction of individual attitudes, opinions, and the opinions of the group emerges public opinion.

An individual who is a member of a group manifests certain characteristics in his thinking and behavior which contribute to the formation of public opinion. The thinking of an individual in a group is characterized by identification, conformity, anonymity, sympathy, emotionalism, nobility, oppression, symbolism, and rationalization.

Identification or ego involvement causes a person to accept the opinion of the group in preference in his own opinion in order to gain the satisfaction of being identified with the group. A worker who may have no interest in labor unions will join a union because he wants to be identified with an organization which is influential. He wants to be accepted by his fellow workers who are members of the union. Many persons are willing to sacrifice their own opinions to enjoy the prestige of membership in a well-regarded group. They have no reluctance in changing their previous opinions in order to conform to group opinion when they know that others in the group are doing likewise.

Conformity in opinion to the views of the majority is characteristic of the thinking of many people in groups. The individual sacrifices his own opinion to conform to group opinion in order to secure the approval of the group. Many people prefer to "get on the band wagon" and follow the leader because they are habitual followers. It takes courage to oppose public opinion and many individuals would rather conform than oppose the current of public opinion.

Anonymity or the quality of being unknown is afforded by a group to individuals who are unwilling to express their own opinions openly on controversial issues. Many persons prefer to hide their individual opinions behind the anonymity of group opinion. An employee who is unwilling to criticize his employer openly has no reluctance in castegating the boss through the medium of union opinion. One reason why some employees join unions is to express their criticism of management without fear of personal reprisals.

Sympathy for other members of a group influences the opinions of all members. Uniformity of opinion is common in groups because whatever affects one member in controversial matters similarly affects all others in the group. Sympathy for members of the group causes individuals to sacrifice their own opinions and conform to group opinion. When a worker is discharged all members of the employee group conform in censoring management. Public opinion may be aroused by sympathy for the discharged worker to such an extent that a strike may be declared.

Emotionalism characterizes the thinking of members of a group confronted with a controversial question. The opinion of a group is likely to be influenced more by sentimental and emotional appeals than by reason and logic. Group thinking is rarely rational. A group either likes or dislikes, admires or loathes. Anger, fear, and hate is aroused over controversial questions. The amount of emotion aroused over an issue depends upon the nature of the question confronting the group. Issues which directly affect the safety, health, and prosperity of a group will arouse greater emotional response than questions which have no immediate impact on the welfare of individuals comprising the group. The closing of an industrial plant which deprives workers of jobs and local merchants of patronage is an issue which will arouse emotional opinion.

The opinions of some groups are often dominated by their least intelligent members, those whose views are determined by their emotions rather than intelligence. Lack of information, limited intelligence and experience make members of some groups incapable of rational judgment on all but the simplest questions.

On the other hand, the intelligent members of a group are not always rational in their judgments. Intelligent persons often lack sufficient information on many issues and are accordingly swayed by the emotional impact of the group. Emotional excitement over an issue pervades group opinion, sweeps reason aside, and reduces the intelligence of the group to the level of its least intelligent members.

This emotional response of groups to issues induces politicians, businessmen, and labor leaders concerned with influencing public opinion to appeal to feelings and emotions, particularly on issues of intimate concern to the group. Hatred of the opposition, fear of economic loss, envy, and greed are emotional appeals employed by opinion leaders to influence public opinion.

Some groups, particularly those of a more elemental nature, which have not enjoyed the advantages of education and information, are largely motivated in their opinions by instinct and emotion. The opinions of such groups are formed on impulse and with limited knowledge of the issue confronting them. This is particularly true of groups lacking homogeneity, hastily formed, loosely organized, and with little consciousness of their entity.

The customary methods of influencing the opinions of elemental groups is through appeals to emotion, falsifications, rumors, and exaggerations. This is the strategy employed by propagandists, as discussed later in this chapter.

Nobility is a characteristic of the thinking of groups confronted with a controversial question. Groups are inclined to be idealistic and moralize on issues. They are influenced by the nobler emotions of courage, praise, gratitude, and sacrifice. This nobility may be accounted for by the fact that the opinion of the group is openly stated to the public. Groups, like individuals, hide their baser feelings from others and show their nobler nature to the world.

Oppression is a delusion suffered by groups which feel that they are victims of oppression. Labor groups feel that they are oppressed by capitalists; minority shareholders feel that they are denied a voice by management; and citizens chafe under the restraints of government. A group's attitude toward opposing groups is usually characterized by dislike and suspicion. A group usually stands for "right," "justice," and "truth." This moral justification is sometimes a screen behind which a group hides its greed, envy, or baser emotions. A group's sense of oppression may arise from its feelings of importance and superiority.

Symbolism is employed by a group to express its character and ideals. The Republican party in the United States uses the elephant as a symbol to characterize the strength and intelligence of the party. The Crusaders used the Cross to symbolize their dedication to Christ. A symbol also may be a person who personifies a cause or ideal. A corporation may symbolize its president by describing him as a wise and beneficent "father of the corporate family." George Washington is symbolized as the "father of his country." And conversely, a group may symbolize its opponents as traitors or oppressors.

Rationalization characterizes group thinking. Groups explain or justify their actions to rational or creditable motives without adequate analysis of their true motives. A group which fails to achieve its objective rationalizes its failure by explaining that its loss was not significant. A corporation which loses a strike by employees for higher wages rationalizes its defeat by announcing that the wage increase was insignificant and concessions to the strikers were not important.

Groups justify their failure to attain their goals by rationalizing to relieve their sense of futility and frustration. Individuals rationalize their failure to vote by explaining that their vote would have little effect on the outcome of the election. There are some groups who rationalize their racial prejudice by claiming that other groups are inferior, uncivilized, and immoral.

Rational Basis of Public Opinion

While elemental groups are usually influenced in their opinions by appeals to their emotions, better-educated and adjusted groups are not influenced by emotion as much as by logic.

In arriving at opinions by rational rather than emotional thought processes, advanced groups are usually composed of persons who weigh and consider various courses of action on a controversial question, suspend their judgment until they have time to learn the facts, and evaluate the information they receive from various sources. They are likely to ask: "Who says this?" "What are his basic interests?" "How is he trying to influence our thoughts and actions?" "What exactly does he mean?" They are on guard against pernicious propaganda by analyzing the facts and opinions expressed in the press, over the air, in books, and conversations.

The reasoning group is not necessarily composed of persons of the highest intelligence nor is it made up of individuals with the broadest education, but usually includes men or women who have the greatest understanding of the issues confronting them. They have the facts and can clearly recognize the advantages as well as disadvantages of a course of action and formulate their opinions accordingly. As a result, a rational process determines the opinions of advanced groups. Group opinion is usually sounder and more in the public interest when formulated in this manner. Such a rational group is composed of persons of average intelligence and ability and not individuals especially gifted.

The outstanding characteristic of a logical group is that its members possess the facts about an issue which affects the group. Sound opinion is basically dependent upon adequate information. The group which has the most complete information about a controversial issue is likely to exhibit the most enlightened opinion. Given the facts, favorable and otherwise, the average man is capable of sound judgment and constructive opinions. When a person does not have the facts or is kept in deliberate ignorance by distorted propaganda, he is easily swayed by instinct and emotion to accept the falsehoods of the propagandist.

A worker who is unfamiliar with the problems facing his employer and does not know the facts about company operations easily becomes a tool for a demagogue who seeks to capitalize on his ignorance and influence his opinion by appealing to his emotions. Likewise, a shareholder who has no knowledge of the financial condition of the business in which he has invested is easily influenced by dissident shareholders who seek to control his opinion to their selfish advantage.

A rational group is one whose members have information about the controversial issues confronting the group. Since individuals are members of several publics, such as employee, shareholder, consumer, they are often unable to acquire adequate information on issues before these groups and express sound opinions about them. A factory worker is not only a member of the employee group but simultaneously he may also belong to the stockholder, community, and consumer groups. As the average individual cannot know the facts about issues affecting these groups, his opinions on many questions are by necessity influenced by emotion or group pressures.

A group, which is immediately concerned with the issues affecting it, usually has more rational opinion. There is a greater interest in acquiring information about matters of immediate concern to the group.

Employees as a group are closely related to the issues involving their daily work and therefore have a better knowledge of the facts and exercise more rational opinions on work controversies. Employees when faced with controversial questions of wages, hours, working conditions, and fringe benefits usually express intelligent opinions on these questions.

Residents of a community are closer to local issues and express more rational opinion than on national issues which are not of immediate concern and about which they are not in position to obtain and evaluate the facts. As a member of a community group, an employee does not exercise as rational a judgment on questions confronting the community as he does on labor-management issues. Employees are not as directly affected by community issues as by controversies with management and their interest in and knowledge of civic questions is limited. Accordingly, many residents of a community have no active opinions on community questions and are easily influenced by pernicious propaganda. Many persons are not interested in local issues to the extent of voting in town elections.

However, community opinion is easily aroused on certain issues directly affecting the taxpayer such as a bond issue to erect more schools. When the pocketbooks of the voters are affected, citizens are aroused to the point of getting and weighing the facts and more rational public opinion results.

Small shareholders have few opinions on issues affecting the corporations in which they have an interest. Large shareholders, on the other hand, are usually interested in corporate affairs and have definite opinions on questions affecting the welfare of the corporation in which they hold a substantial interest. The large shareholder studies his corporation's financial statements, gets the facts, and exercises more rational judgment on corporation issues.

Propaganda

Public opinion is influenced by propaganda. Changes in public opinion are often brought about by individuals or pressure groups through an organized effort or movement to spread a particular doctrine or information. Such an effort is usually referred to as "propaganda." Propaganda, according to the *Dictionary of Mass Communications* is an activity designed to advance a cause through enlightenment, persuasion, or a dedicated sense of mission. Propaganda is not to be confused with publicity, advertising, or promotion although it is sometimes a valuable adjunct to these.

No word in the English language has changed in meaning as much as the word "propaganda." In its original sense, "propaganda" was an honorable word and a legitimate effort of an organized group to communicate the truth and favorably influence the opinions of others toward a group. However, this conception of propaganda has greatly changed and now propaganda is generally considered as an insidious, dishonest, underhanded, and misleading effort to influence the opinion of the public.

According to Walter Lippman, propaganda consists of lies and stunts calculated to work on the emotional rather than the intellectual side of man from a hidden source of pressure. Lippmann characterizes propaganda as half-truths, lies, ambiguities, evasions, calculated silence, red herrings, unresponsiveness, slogans, catchwords, showmanship, bathos, hokum, and buncombe.

The hidden source of propaganda is emphasized by G. S. Viereck, sociologist, who says, "Propaganda is a campaign camouflaging its origin, its motives, or both, conducted for the purpose of obtaining a specific objective by manipulating public opinion. It differs from both education and publicity in that the element of camouflage in one form or another is always present."

Furthermore, objectionable propaganda does not attempt to present all of the facts, only those on one side of an issue. While it is impossible for one source to give full and complete information on all sides of an issue, propagandists do not attempt to present more than those facts which conform most nearly to their own interests.

The late Calvin Coolidge said, "Propaganda seeks to present part of the facts, to distort their relations, and to force conclusions which could not be drawn from a complete and candid survey of all the facts. Of real education and information we cannot get too much; but of propaganda —we cannot have too little."

The difference between honest persuasion and subversive propaganda, according to Max Lerner, is that in honest persuasion you never omit anything relevant nor do you ever distort anything crucial. In propaganda, you always omit or distort something relevant or important.

Propaganda is regarded with disfavor by the American people because they prefer to do their own thinking rather than have a propagandist do their thinking for them. Propaganda is considered an antidemocratic activity which attempts to manipulate minds, interferes with freedom of choice, and exerts pressures which independent thinking Americans regard as autocratic. Americans pride themselves on their independence of opinion, they are critical of any form of persuasion which attempts to deprive them of the privilege of thinking issues through to their own satisfaction.

Propaganda as a subversive activity has been prevalent during the past fifty years in which it has been used as a major instrument of aggression to further the aims of dictators in many countries of the world. Nazi, Fascist, and Communist propaganda which has appealed to bigotry and intolerance, hate, and fear by suppressing facts and releasing false and misleading information has identified propaganda as a vicious and reprehensible manipulation of public opinion. Propaganda has become an instrument of international conflict along with the atom bomb because it has been developed to a high state of effectiveness.

Never before in the history of the world has propaganda, either good or bad, attained such significance to humanity. The perfection of communication media through world-wide television and radio broadcasting facilities and international news gathering systems have enabled propagandists to influence the opinions and actions of individuals throughout the world.

The expansion of education in underdeveloped countries and growing literacy has made it possible for propagandists to reach through low-cost books, newspapers, and magazines millions of people who are now prime targets for organized propaganda campaigns by pressure groups to change public opinion.

Pernicious propaganda which is based on suppression of the truth and distortion has no place in the lexicon of public relations. Yet it cannot be denied that public relations seeks to influence the actions of individuals and groups. Every individual, corporation, social service organization, religion, political party, and nation seeks to impress others with its principles and ideals and gain their favorable opinion. Whether this is good propaganda depends upon the merit of the cause, the honesty and completeness of the facts presented, and whether the beliefs or ideals communicated contribute to the public welfare.

Techniques of Pernicious Propaganda

The evil propagandist relies upon various devices to persuade and win people to acceptance of his particular proposal or cause. Disregard of the truth is the most common characteristic of bad propaganda by suppression, distortion, diversion, and fabrication. Deliberate spreading of misinformation with intent to deceive the public of the true conditions; to communicate only that which will evoke the desired opinion and suppress the rest; to omit significant facts; to use words with double or obscure meanings; to divert the attention of the public from matters which the propagandist wishes ignored are all strategies employed by pressure groups to win public opinion.

Pernicious propagandists employ many devices to persuade the public to accept their particular point of view. Name calling is a favorite strategy of the propagandist who refers to capitalists as "robber barons" or organized workers as "communists." This strategy is employed to induce the public to condemn or reject a group or idea without considering the facts.

The use of cherished words is a common strategy of bad propagandists seeking to influence public opinion. Frequent reference to "motherhood," "America," "democracy," and "equality" is found in their propaganda. These words are employed to get the public to accept the propaganda without questioning its validity.

Imagery is a technique of propaganda by which the authority and prestige of an individual, who is respected and revered, is aligned with the appeal of the propagandist to make it more acceptable to the public. The image of George Washington as a symbol of patriotism is linked with an appeal to the patriotism of the American public. The humanitarianism of Abraham Lincoln is transferred to the motives of a social service organization in its efforts to persuade the public to support its activities.

The testimonial is a device used by propagandists to quote the words of a well-known and respected person in support of their appeal for public approval. "The President of the U.S. Steel Corporation stated today—" is a statement which may be used by a propagandist to support his economic theories and win public support for his views. When the well-known person is quoted accurately there is no objection to such a quotation but frequently a quotation is distorted, taken from context, or misrepresented by the propagandist to make his point.

Identification of the propagandist with his audience is a strategy designed to win the acceptance of the public. The propaganda of politicians describes their humble origins to identify them with the common people whose acceptance they seek. Mark Anthony, in his funeral oration over Caesar's body, used this propaganda strategy saying, in effect, "I am no orator, as Brutus is; as you know me all, a plain, blunt man."

"Loading" is a propaganda strategy in which only those arguments which give the best possible case for the propagandist's ideas are selected and conflicting arguments are ignored. Evidence is presented from only one viewpoint, that of the propagandist who maintains that he has exclusive possession of the facts. The propagandist "loads" his appeals by choosing only those facts or fallacies which support his case. Alternative proposals and evidence are not discussed so that the public hears only one side of the question.

Dramatization is a favorite technique of the evil propagandist who forms a parade, hires a band, fills a stadium, unfurls flags, sings songs, and illuminates with searchlights to make his propaganda more palatable to the public. These devices are used to stir up the emotions, the fears and enmities, prejudices and bias of members of a group and induce them to follow the leader.

Honest Public Relations versus Propaganda

A choice between honest public relations and evil propaganda faced the cigarette industry when called upon to defend its product against attacks of cancer specialists who charged that cigarette smoking contributes to lung cancer. The industry established the Tobacco Advisory Council and initiated a public relations program to answer the critics of cigarette smoking.

Should the public relations program present the views of only those scientists who are favorable to cigarette smoking or publicize the opinions of reputable scientists regardless of what they say?

"If you do it honestly by getting the best scientists you can," says Max Lerner, "regardless of what they are going to say, I think you have a right to do it. But if you pick your scientists in such a way that you know perfectly well what the results are going to be, then you are involved in dishonesty and immorality because there is a crucial distortion, a distortion of something crucial. And this really affects us. It may well be that somebody very valuable to this society will have his life shortened in the process."

Honest public relations openly reveals its origin but pernicious propaganda deliberately conceals its source and the identity of the propagandist. It hides its identity behind false front organizations. The late Ivy Lee, one of the first public relations counselors stated, "The essential evil of propaganda is the failure to disclose the source of information." Critics of public relations refer to its practitioners as "hidden persuaders" who surreptitiously mold public opinion in favor of certain products, ideas, and institutions. Public relations is condemned as "the business of the invisible sell" which makes the public the victim of veiled or camouflaged propaganda. These criticisms of public relations do not apply to honest communication but to the pernicious propaganda which seeks selfish advantage under the guise of serving the public interest.

Pernicious propaganda, according to Professor F. E. Lumley, sociologist, is a social danger because it "awakens passion by confusing the issues, it makes the insignificant seem weighty; it makes the important seem trifling; it keeps the channels of communication full of exciting stuff; it keeps people battling in a fog."

Honest public relations, on the other hand, is morally sound, concerned with facts and ideas which can be verified, originating from a recognized source, and intended to serve the public welfare. It is persuasion such as practiced by the minister in exhorting his congregation to a religious way of life; the teacher in informing his students of the facts and theories of science, and the ethical business or social organization in informing its employees, neighbors, and the general public of its principles, products, and practices.

Case 4–1

PUBLIC OPINION FORMATION

To illustrate the process of opinion formation and the way socio-economic status, personal interests, primary group affiliation, secondary group membership, sex, religion, occupation, and other factors enter into the formation of individual opinions on public issues, W. Phillips Davison has created a role-playing procedure or public opinion game.[1] The game shows the difference between public opinion and private opinion and illustrates how opinion leaders can influence the opinions of a group.

---

[1] Described in *Public Opinion Quarterly*, Summer, 1961.

In this game, the players are assigned roles and each player is asked to re-act to selected issues in a manner that he thinks is appropriate for his role. The group leader gives each player a printed statement of the issues and his personal characteristics—sex, marital status, socio-economic status, occupation, religious affiliation, organization membership, and primary group affiliation as shown on the following Instruction Sheet No. 1:

Instruction Sheet No. 1

You live in a medium-sized city in a Midwestern state with a large farming hinter-land. Recently a number of developments of some importance have taken place in your area, although these have not been publicly announced or generally discussed. First, geologists from the local university have discovered that one of the city parks has a large supply of oil beneath it. Second, the county clerk's office has noted that the percentage of unwed mothers has almost doubled during the past year. Third, several members of the city council are considering the introduction of a law to re-quire the installation of an exhaust-purification mechanism, costing about $25, on all vehicles.

Your personal characteristics are as follows (these characteristics differ with each player):

Sex: male.
Age: 45.
Marital status: married, two children.
Socio-economic status: upper middle.
Occupation: store proprietor.
Religious affiliation: Methodist—nominal.
Organization membership: trade association.
Primary group affiliation: "A"—active spokesman.

Players are next assigned by the play director to primary groups, each com-posed of four players (3 to 5 players may be used), all of whom are members of the same primary group. In Instruction Sheet No. 1 above, the player has been assigned to primary group "A." Typical primary groups are members of the same family, neighborhood groups, and work groups which tend to share a common outlook on most controversial issues. One of the four players in each primary group is designated as chairman, and records the opinions of his group on the issues.

After the participants have had time to study the three issues and their roles described in their Instruction Sheet No. 1 above, the players are "interviewed" for their individual opinions on the three issues by answering the following questionnaire, Instruction Sheet No. 2.

Questionnaire Instruction Sheet No. 2

You are approached by a public opinion interviewer, who asks you a number of questions. Please indicate your answers to these questions by placing a mark in the appropriate space below. (Remember that you are now playing the role of the person described in Instruction Sheet No. 1.)

1. Geologists have recently discovered that there is a large reservoir of oil under-neath Jones Park. If this oil can be brought to the surface and sold, without spoiling the park, do you think the money should be used to reduce taxes, to improve our school system, or for some other purposes?
   Reduce taxes _____. Improve schools _____. Other _____. No opinion _____.

2. Statistics in the county clerk's office show that the number of unwed mothers in this county has almost doubled during the past year. Some people think to counteract this trend it would be a good idea to introduce a compulsory course on sex and marriage in our high schools. Would you be in favor of such a course, or not in favor of it?

Favor _____. Oppose _____. Depends _____. No opinion _____.

3. Several members of the city council are considering the introduction of a law to compel all motorists to install an exhaust purification mechanism, costing about $25, on their vehicles. Would you be in favor of such a law or not in favor of it.

Favor _____. Oppose _____. Other _____. No opinion _____.

After each player has recorded his private opinion on Instruction Sheet No. 2, he is given Instruction Sheet No. 3, below. He first uses this sheet to record his weighted private opinions on the three issues and subsequently the position advocated by the spokesman for his religious group, spokesman for his organization, the consensus of opinion of his primary group, and the "final" opinion as the result of interplay of these factors.

Instruction Sheet No. 3

Issues	Weighted Opinion (A)	Religious Position (B)	Organization Position (C)	Primary Group Opinion (D)	Total (E)	Final Opinion (F)
1. Oil Revenue:						
Favor tax reduction						
Favor school improvement						
Other						
No opinion						
2. Unwed mothers:						
Favor course						
Oppose course						
Depends						
No opinion						
3. Exhaust fumes:						
Favor law						
Oppose law						
Other						
No opinion						

Instructions for Instruction Sheet No. 3.

Column A: If this is a personal opinion about which you don't feel very strongly, write down "1" opposite the alternative you would choose. If you would be prepared to defend the opinion vigorously in personal discussions, write down "2." If you would be prepared to act in favor of it (i.e., spend time or money), write down "3." If you have no opinion write "1" in the "no opinion" space.

Column B: If you are a *very devout* member of your religious group (or a spokesman), write "3" in the space opposite the position advocated by the spokesman of this group. If you are a devout member, write "2." If you are a nominal member, write "1."

Column C: If you are an official (or spokesman) of an organization, write "3" in the space after the position advocated by the organization spokesman. If you are an active participant, write "2." If you are a nominal member, write "1."

Column D: Write down "2" opposite the position on each question that has a majority of points in your primary group. If there is a tie, write "2" in the "no opinion" space. Your primary group chairman will tell you where to make the entry.

Column E: Total the points in each row and write the totals here.

Column F: Place an "X" in the three rows that have the largest number of points. If two rows are tied within one question, place an "X" in the "no opinion" space.

When all players have recorded their weighted private opinions on the three issues in Column A, following instructions on Instruction Sheet No. 3, the game director calls upon three religious spokesmen from among all of the players to present the position of various religious denominations on the three issues. Each spokesman, previously selected by the game director and so notified on Instruction Sheet No. 1, speaks briefly for his religious group. After hearing from the spokesman the religious position of his assigned religion on Instruction Sheet No. 1, each player records as directed in the instructions the position of his religious group in Column B, Instruction Sheet No. 3.

Next, three spokesmen for the secondary groups to which the players belong are called upon by the play director to discuss briefly the position taken by the leadership of three organizations on the three issues. There is one spokesman for business, one for labor, and one for a welfare organization as assigned on Instruction Sheet No. 1. After listening to the spokesmen of the secondary organization to which he belongs, each player records this position, as directed in the instructions in Column C, Instruction Sheet No. 3.

Next, the opinion of each primary group, as a whole, on the three issues is determined. Each primary group chairman, as previously assigned by the play director on Instruction Sheet No. 1, is supplied with a Work Sheet on which he records the scores entered thus far opposite each alternative by himself and for each of the other members of his primary group from their Instruction Sheets No. 3, Columns A, B, C. The chairman's Work Sheet, on which the individual players' scores are entered, appears on page 71.

The primary group chairman enters the scores of each player in his group opposite the appropriate positions in columns 1–2–3–4 of the chairman's Work Sheet. After the scores of all members of the group have been entered by the chairman, he adds up all the entries in each horizontal row and enters the result-score in the column marked "Total" on the chairman's Work Sheet.

The chairman next identifies the highest scores with certain alternatives shown on the Work Sheet, places an "X" after these alternatives in the column headed "Group Choice" on the chairman's Work Sheet.

Each member of the primary group then enters a "2" in Column D on his

WORK SHEET FOR PRIMARY GROUP CHAIRMAN:
SCORES OF GROUP MEMBERS

Issues	*1*	*2*	*3*	*4*	*Group Members*	*Total*	*Group Choice*
1. *Oil revenue:*							
Favor tax reduction							
Favor school improvement							
Other							
No opinion							
2. *Unwed mothers:*							
Favor course							
Oppose course							
Depends							
No opinion							
3. *Exhaust fumes:*							
Favor law							
Oppose law							
Other							
No opinion							

own Instruction Sheet No. 3, as the Primary Group Opinion opposite the three positions favored by the group as a whole. Instructions for Column D, at the bottom of Instruction Sheet No. 3, are followed at the direction of the primary group chairman by each player, who enters the group opinion on the three issues on his Instruction Sheet No. 3.

When all players in all primary groups have made appropriate entries in Column D, Instruction Sheet No. 3, they are in position to determine their own "final opinions." This is done by each player adding all the scores in each row opposite the alternatives on Instruction Sheet No. 3 and entering the total in Column E on the sheet. He then places an "X" in Column F, Instruction Sheet No. 3 after the three positions that have the largest number of points, which shows the player's "Final Opinion." If two alternatives under any one issue are tied, the player places an "X" opposite "no opinion" for this question.

Most players, by consulting the scores on their own Instruction Sheet No. 3, find that they have "changed" their opinions on at least one of the three issues as a result of the interplay of religious, secondary organization, and primary group opinion in the game. This may be verified by tabulating the "private" opinions of the players shown on the initial questionnaire, Instruction Sheet No. 2, and comparing these opinions with their "Final Opinions" shown on Instruction Sheet No. 3, Column F.

While the game is not a perfect device for simulating reality in forming public opinion, it is a valuable tool in pointing out some of the forces that mold public opinion, the difference between public and private opinion, and the interaction of various factors, particularly social forces in the opinion forming process.

CHAPTER
5 ·

ORGANIZING FOR PUBLIC RELATIONS

IN A SMALL ENTERPRISE, close relations with the public obviates the need for a formal organization for public relations. However, when a corporation or nonprofit organization attains such a size that it is no longer able to maintain close relations with the public, then responsibility for public relations should be organized and delegated to an individual, staff, outside public relations counsel, or a combination of the three.

More than 5,000 large industrial corporations, in addition to many small companies, in this country maintain separate public relations departments. This number is increasing yearly and indicates the growing recognition by industrial management of the importance of public relations as a function of modern business. Almost all of these departments are located at the headquarters of the company, although a growing number of large corporations are establishing public relations specialists in subsidiary companies and in local or regional offices of the parent corporation.

Many small companies do not have public relations departments but rely on other departments such as advertising, sales, industrial relations, and personnel to perform public relations functions in addition to their other responsibilities. This arrangement is often a prelude to the establishment of a separate public relations department. The obvious effect of depending upon other departments for public relations service is that public relations get second consideration and does not function effectively.

Some organizations which do not have a public relations department retain outside public relations counsel or advertising agencies on a continuing or special assignment basis to plan and program public relations. This practice may be effective for small enterprises with limited publics, but is no substitute for a well-organized internal public relations department.

A public relations department relieves operating executives of the responsibility for planning and carrying on public relations activities, assumes responsibility and authority for public relations, co-ordinates and unifies public relations functions, eliminates duplication of effort, insures a well-balanced program, and provides for specialized skills essential to the production of communication materials.

Types of Public Relations Organizations

In organizing for public relations, one or more of the following courses may be followed:

1. Assign public relations as a secondary responsibility to another department such as advertising, sales, industrial relations, or personnel.
2. Retain the services of an outside counsel or advertising agency to assume full responsibility for the public relations program.
3. Appoint a public relations manager to have sole responsibility for public relations.
4. Create a public relations department with staff specialists to handle the research, programing, and various functions of public relations and to be responsible to a public relations manager.
5. Appoint a policy group composed of the heads of the principal departments including manufacturing, sales, finance, personnel, industrial relations, and public relations to determine public relations policies and insure effective co-ordination of the program.
6. Decentralize public relations in subsidiary companies, regions, or plants.

Personnel of Public Relations Departments

Surveys of the personnel of public relations departments of corporations show that small companies, with annual sales under $50 million, employ an average of from one to six persons including those performing public relations functions in other departments. However, as the sales of a company increase, its public relations staff is expanded. In companies with sales in excess of a billion dollars, the number of persons engaged in public relations averages seventy-seven.

Public relations staffs are usually composed of young men and women with an average age of 35 years, although the age of public relations managers averages 46 years. Many of these people are college graduates, a majority of whom majored in journalism. Usually personnel in public relations departments were previously employed in the related fields of advertising, sales promotion, merchandising, or in newspaper and magazine reporting and editing.

Public Relations Policy Committee

To determine basic public relations policy and to co-ordinate all aspects of organization public relationships, the executive heads of various departments should constitute a public relations policy committee. This committee should be composed of the chairman of the board, president, general manager, and vice-presidents in charge of manufacturing, marketing, finance, personnel, law, purchasing, and the public relations manager. The policy committee meets with the public relations manager and counsel to discuss public relations policy, the attitude of the public toward the organization, and the effect of contemplated changes in policies or actions which may have an impact on the public relationships of the organization.

Public relations programs prepared by the public relations staff are usually presented to this committee for its approval. The effectiveness of current public relations activities is discussed with this committee. Through representation on this committee, top management is informed and its co-operation enlisted in accomplishing the public relations objectives of the organization.

Public relations programs involving several departments of an organization may be co-ordinated more effectively and the support of executives concerned may be secured more readily when they work together on a public relations policy committee.

Planning Committee of the Public Relations Department

To secure more effective co-ordination of the work of public relations staff members, a planning committee composed of the heads of the various sections of the public relations department is desirable. A public relations department is organized in sections representing particular publics, media of communication, or functions. A planning committee composed of the managers of each section should meet regularly with the public relations manager as chairman to plan the work of the department.

The planning committee determines program objectives, plans necessary research, prepares a time schedule, selects the media of communication, assigns certain persons to production, and arrives at a budget for each program.

If outside counsel is retained in an advisory capacity to conduct research or perform other services, a representative of the counseling organization should meet with the planning committee to insure effective co-ordination of the program.

Decentralized Public Relations Organization

Although most public relations departments are located at headquarters, there is a growing trend in large organizations toward decentralization of public relations by assigning public relations staff personnel to subsidiary companies, regional offices, or local plants. This decentralization provides closer contact with the public, better knowledge of public opinion, and improved communication. Many public relations problems of large corporations originate in local plants and communities and can be handled more effectively by local public relations personnel.

Large corporations are establishing regional public relations offices in charge of regional public relations managers to assist local plants and branches with employee, community, supplier, government, and dealer relations. Companies operating several plants assign a public relations manager to be responsible for plant and community relations in each plant. In small plants, personnel and industrial relations managers are responsible for public relations. Plant public relation managers work closely with the regional or headquarters staff but are responsible to the local plant manager.

Each subsidiary company of a large corporation usually maintains a public relations department with its own objectives and program, more or less independent of the parent organization. The parent company is usually responsible for comprehensive public relations programs involving the corporation as a whole. Subsidiary companies or divisions usually concentrate on plant and community relations. The public relations of the parent company usually counsels subsidiaries or divisions on their employee and community relations programs.

To insure effective co-ordination of the parent program with those of subsidiaries, periodic conferences are held by the public relations staff of the parent company and public relations managers of subsidiaries.

Basic Objectives of Public Relations Departments

The objectives, scope, and structure of a public relations department are determined by such factors as the number, size, and importance of the publics to be reached, the attitudes of these publics toward the organization; the size and financial resources of the enterprise; and the economic, social, and political climate in which the business operates.

One of the principal objectives of public relations departments is to interpret the public viewpoint to management. This includes:

1. Conveying and interpreting information about public attitudes and reactions to management.
2. Reflecting back to management trends in political, social, and economic thinking so that management may more effectively avoid the bad consequences of unforeseen changes in public attitudes.
3. Presenting for management's consideration any aspects of operating situations that may bear upon the relations of the enterprise with the public and make suggestions to management for handling such relations.

4. Studying public attitudes by opinion research to determine and reflect trends in public opinion to management for its consideration.

In addition to interpreting public viewpoints to management, an important objective of a public relations staff is to work with operating and administrative personnel to develop practices, create events, or present situations to secure public approval. An example of this is an "open house" planned and carried out by the public relations staff with the co-operation of management and operating personnel.

Communication is a basic objective of a public relations staff. The staff prepares communication materials such as publications, publicity, and advertising to inform the public. It establishes clear two-way channels of communication to enable the public to express its views to management.

To accomplish these objectives, a staff of public relations specialists competent to execute the work involved must be recruited, trained, and supervised.

Specific Activities of Public Relations Departments

The activities of public relations departments of corporations, governments, schools, churches, railroads, public utilities, banks, business and professional associations, and welfare organizations vary widely according to the size and nature of the organization.

Surveys of the responsibilities of public relations departments show the following major activities in order of frequency: publicity and press relations, employee publications, reports to stockholders, literature, advertising, community relations, speeches, photography, educational materials, radio programs.

Seven Public Relations Staff Functions

The seven principal functions of public relations departments are: research, planning, co-ordinating, administration, production, community participation, and advisory.

Research. Opinion surveys of employees, stockholders, consumers, dealers, distributors, suppliers, and the community; studies and interpretations of social, economic, and political trends; studies of public relations techniques.

Planning. Determining basic public relations policies, establishing objectives, determining methods of communication, timing, assigning personnel, and budgeting.

Co-ordinating. Contacting, informing, and advising general management, personnel, sales, finance, and manufacturing officials on public relations and co-ordinating their activities with the public relations staff and counsel.

Administration. Maintaining a public relations staff to provide service for all departments, supervision of services and personnel, control of budgets, and employment and direction of clerical and stenographic force.

Production. 1. Publicity. Planning, creating, and placing publicity material, holding press functions, answering press inquiries, distributing press releases, contacting editors, serving all departments with corporate and product publicity for newspapers, magazines, and trade papers.

2. Motion Pictures and Slide Films. Production and distribution of public relations films to further relations with employees, consumers, educators, stockholders, dealers, and distributors.

3. Publications. Production and distribution of company magazines (internal and external), handbooks, employee benefit publications, supervisory and training publications, speech reprints, company history and anniversary books, posters, inserts, annual and interim reports, policy manuals, and guide books.

4. Institutional Advertising. Planning and providing information for instituional advertisements in conjunction with an advertising agency, for radio, television, newspapers, magazines, financial advertising, plant community advertising, and special event advertising.

5. Special Events. Planning and conducting open houses; plant tours; exhibits; plant dedications; meetings for employees, stockholders, and community leaders; anniversaries; and parades.

6. Speech Services. Research for speech material for executives; preparation of speech manuscripts; clearance of manuscripts; publication of speeches; and providing speakers, through a speakers' bureau, for consumer groups, civic clubs, schools, and fraternal and social organizations.

7. Correspondence and Bulletins. Carrying on correspondence with stockholders, consumers, students, educators, and suppliers; keeping files of company data and historical materials, executive bibliographical files, and photographs of plants and executives.

Community Participation. Planning and taking part in community service projects for charity, health, cultural affairs, youth groups, and education.

Advisory. Advising management on public relations aspects of policies and practices and assisting line and staff executives in executing public relations programs.

PLACE OF PUBLIC RELATIONS IN A CORPORATE ORGANIZATION

Good public relationships cannot be achieved exclusively by a public relations department. Public relations is a function of the management and head of every department as well as all employees. "We like to think of public relations as anything and everything that all of us do and say which gives people an impression about our company," says the director of public relations of a large corporation. "Our department's job is but a part of the mass public relations job that all of our employees are doing every day."

Administration of Public Relations, a Staff Function

A public relations department should be an administrative staff functioning as a service department to all other departments. A public relations staff should have no operating authority but serve line operating executives in carrying out public relations programs and making decisions on public relations problems. It aids line, operating executives to communicate with workers and outside publics and through them increase the public acceptance of the company and its policies and products.

A public relations staff educates line executives and workers as to their public relations responsibilities and stimulates them to use good public relations techniques in winning favorable public opinion. An efficient public relations staff has the following advantages:

1. Public relations research and planning are in the hands of experienced specialists.
2. A staff organization results in the formation of sounder public relations policies.
3. It relieves line executives of excessive public relations details.
4. It subdivides, particularly in larger companies, the planning and production of public relations materials so that each phase of the program can be properly developed.
5. It develops experts in various areas of public relations, as stockholder relations, supplier relations, etc.
6. It facilitates co-ordination of activities directed to the various publics.

Public Relations Administration Functions Best at Top-Management Level

The public relations director and staff should be placed in the organization at top-management level and made responsible directly to the president and board of directors. As every action and policy of management affects corporate public relations, public relations should be in a position to advise management on the probable public response to policies and actions. A public relations director should be situated close to management to contribute the public viewpoint on operating problems and be able to inspire policies in the public interest.

At top-management level, a public relations manager and his staff can maintain closer contact with the heads of the various departments of the business and gain their support in carrying out public relations programs.

Relation of Public Relations to Other Departments

A public relations department cannot operate effectively without the close co-operation of other departments of an enterprise. The understanding and active support of managers of personnel or industrial relations, sales and advertising, legal, financial, and purchasing departments are essential for effective public relations.

To Personnel, Labor, and Industrial Relations Departments. There should be a close working relationship between the public relations director and staff and the personnel, labor, or industrial relations departments because all are mutually interested in developing good employee relations. The public relations department should explain management policies, actions, and benefits to employees so that they will understand and appreciate them and discuss the company's operations with their neighbors and friends in the plant community.

To the Marketing Department. A public relations staff assists the marketing department in creating good relations with two important publics—the consumer public and the distributor and dealer public. The marketing department is primarily interested in increasing product sales. The public relations department can be of valuable assistance to marketing in building corporate reputation and gaining its acceptance by consumers and dealers.

To Legal Department. In developing good relations with lawmakers and representatives of local, state, and national governments, the legal and public relations departments must work in close co-operation. In many companies, all government relations are handled by the corporation's legal department or counsel. However, legal departments are not staffed with personnel specialized in the techniques of communication and interpretation of legal matters to the public. A public relations department should be used in government relations.

To Purchasing Department. In improving relations with suppliers, close co-ordination of the functions of public relations and purchasing departments is essential. Purchasing is primarily concerned with day-to-day problems of buying and often gives little consideration to improving relations with resources. A public relations department should serve purchasing in improving resource relationships.

To the Corporate Secretary or Treasurer. In many corporations the secretary or treasurer is responsible for relations with stockholders. However, the secretary's or treasurer's staff does not have the specialized communications experience to enable it to carry on an effective stockholders' relations program. Accordingly, a public relations department should aid the secretary or treasurer in improving stockholder relations.

Division of Functions of a Public Relations Staff

The magnitude of public relations problems and the scope of public relations activities demand that public relations functions be divided among staff members according to: (1) functions to be performed, (2) publics to be served, (3) a combination of functions and publics, (4) geographically, and (5) by products. The organization charts shown in Figures 5–1 to 5–5 illustrate such distribution.

PUBLIC RELATIONS ORGANIZATIONS OF VARIOUS TYPES

The organization charts illustrated in Figures 5–1 to 5–5 show graphically the organization, functions, and division of responsibilities in typical public relations departments. Examination of these charts will show that the structure of public relations organizations is not standardized but their design is affected by the size and number of publics served, funds available, objectives of the public relations program, and other factors previously discussed.

Historical Nonprofit Organization

The public relations department of Colonial Williamsburg is representative of the public relations organization of an educational nonprofit organization. Colonial Williamsburg was founded by the late John D. Rockefeller, Jr., to recreate accurately the environment of the men and women of eighteenth-century Williamsburg, Virginia, and to bring about such an understanding of their lives and times that present and future generations may appreciate the contribution of these early Americans to the ideals and culture of our country.

To accomplish this objective the public relations department has a staff of nine, headed by a vice-president and director of public relations with an administrative assistant director of public relations who handles some secretarial work, monitors the departmental budget and performs other special duties.

Responsible to the assistant director of public relations is the director of the press bureau who prepares reviews and releases all current information and feature publicity material to local, national, and international media; serves as the point of contact for media representatives and assists various departments of the organization in carrying out plans for special events.

A radio and television manager is responsible for production of special television and radio programs relating to Colonial Williamsburg and distributes films to television stations.

A director of special events co-ordinates the various Colonial Williamsburg departments in plans and arrangements for visits by foreign dignitaries and other special events, and arranges speaking appearances by Colonial Williamsburg personnel, and co-operates with officials of the Commonwealth of Virginia, the College of William and Mary, Jamestown Festival Park, and the National Park Service to draw attention to the significance of the "historic triangle" of Williamsburg-Jamestown-Yorktown.

Electrical Equipment Manufacturer

The public relations organization of Westinghouse Electric Corporation, East Pittsburgh, Pennsylvania, is representative of the organization of a manufacturer of industrial equipment. The department is responsible for information services, employee communications, and community relations. The staff of six is headed by a vice-president of information services who is assisted by a director of employee communications and community relations. The director of employee communications and community relations has a staff assistant, a manager of employee communications, and a manager of community relations.

The manager of employee communications supervises planning and production of headquarters prepared employee communications, provides guidance and evaluation to plant locations and headquarters departments on employee communications, assists divisions to communicate to employees by producing periodicals, handbooks, and special mailings, assists in recruiting for employee communications positions in divisions, and provides emergency on-location services to divisions for concentrated communications programs.

The editor of *Westinghouse News* who reports to the manager of employee communications gathers, writes, and edits stories for *Westinghouse News;* supervises distribution of the *News* and plant inserts; guides local plant editors and does other special writing. The editor of *Westinghouse News* is assisted by the manager of plant sections who schedules, edits, and oversees printing of plant inserts for the *News;* guides division plant insert editors on content and handles special assignments in connection with specific *News* objectives.

The manager of community relations interprets and communicates company policy on community relations; serves as a clearing house for case histories and community relations techniques; advises divisions on community relations problems, programing, and budgeting; prepares special programs and guides; serves as liaison between divisions and headquarters staff organizations and helps recruit and train men assigned to community relations.

Industrial Association

The public relations department of the Association of American Railroads, Washington, D.C., is representative of the public relations organization of a large industrial association. The department of 35 is headed by a vice-president of the Association who is assisted by an assistant vice-president in charge of administration. Five division heads report to the assistant vice-president.

The manager of public and special services section is responsible for the publication of brochures, folders, charts, and wall maps about the railroads. More than six million pieces of literature are distributed annually in response to nearly 100,000 requests from educators, students, and the public.

The manager of school and college service is responsible for monthly mailings to 1,300 college professors; providing a Teachers' Kit on railroad transportation to more than one million teachers, distributing educational materials to teachers, and arranging for addresses by Association staff members to college students in courses in transportation.

The manager of news service is responsible for producing and distributing special and periodic news releases, special articles and information about the railroads to newspapers, magazines, television, and radio stations and wire services.

Telephone Service Organization

The public relations department of the American Telephone and Telegraph Company, New York, with a staff of 125, is representative of the extensive public relations organization of a large, public service

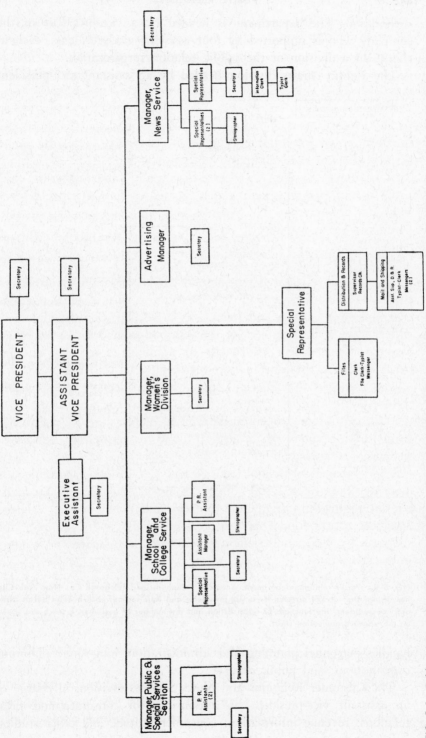

FIG. 5-1. Public relations department, Association of American Railroads, which includes public relations and advertising and sections specializing in news service, women's relations, school and college service, and special services.

corporation. The department is headed by a vice-president of the company who is supported by four assistant vice-presidents, each in charge of a division of the public relations organization.

The Public Affairs division headed by an assistant vice-president

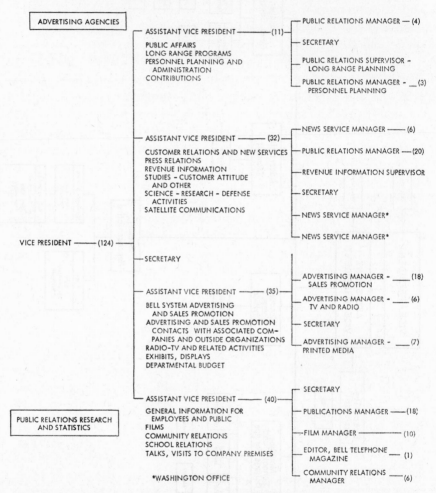

FIG. 5–2. Public relations department, American Telephone and Telegraph Co., New York City, has a total staff of 124 directed by a vice-president; and four sections each headed by an assistant vice-president. The functions of each section and the number of personnel in each are shown on the above organization chart.

handles personnel planning and administration, long-range planning, contributions, and public affairs.

The Customer Relations and News Services division, in charge of an assistant vice-president, is responsible for consumer and press relations; revenue information; consumer attitude and other studies;

science, research, and defense activities; and satellite communication.

The Advertising and Sales Promotion division, under an assistant vice-president, handles advertising and sales promotion; advertising and sales promotion contacts with associated companies and outside organizations; radio, television, and related activities; exhibits; displays; and departmental budget.

The General and Employee Information and Film division, in charge of an assistant vice-president, is responsible for publications, employee and general information, films, community relations, school relations, speeches, and visits to company properties.

Two advertising agencies provide the department with advertising services and a public relations research and statistics section serves all sections of the department.

Chemical Manufacturer

The public relations department of Monsanto Chemical Company, St. Louis, Missouri, with a staff of thirty is representative of the public relations organization of a large chemical manufacturer. The department is headed by a director of public relations, with an assistant

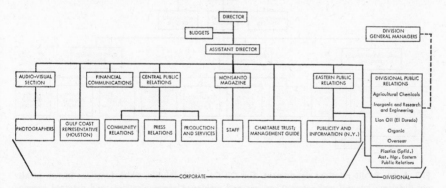

FIG. 5–3. Public relations organization, Monsanto Chemical Co., has geographical divisions for Central headquarters, Gulf Coast, and Eastern divisions, and public relations representatives for the principal product divisions. Separate sections handle financial communications, audio-visual materials, charitable gifts, and the corporation magazine.

director, who is in charge of six corporate divisions, each with a manager and staff, and a divisional public relations group representing the principal products of the company.

The six corporate public relations divisions are: Audio-Visual, responsible for photographs and audio-visual communication media; Financial, responsible for communications with stockholders and the financial community; Central Public Relations, responsible for community relations, press relations, and production and services; *Monsanto Magazine* editorial and production; Charitable Trust and Management Guide which handles contributions; Gulf Coast representative at Houston, Texas; and Eastern Public Relations headquarters in New York City to handle publicity and information in the Eastern section of the country.

The Divisional Public Relations group which works with product division general managers includes six staff members, one for each major line—agricultural chemicals, inorganic and research and engineering, petroleum, organic, overseas, and plastics. In addition, a staff member in charge of budgets reports to the director.

Petroleum Refiner

The public relations department of Sun Oil Company, Philadelphia, Pennsylvania, is representative of the public relations organization of an oil refiner. The department is headed by a director of public relations with two assistant directors and a staffman in charge of

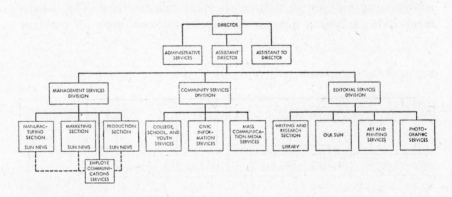

FIG. 5–4. Public relations department, Sun Oil Co., Philadelphia, which functions in two principal divisions: *internal* management services and employee communications; and *external* community relations with an editorial services division serving both external and internal relations.

administrative services. The department is organized with three major divisions: Management Services, Community Services, and Editorial Services, each headed by a division manager.

The Management Services division, responsible for *Sun News,* has a Manufacturing section, Marketing section, and Production section in addition to an Employee Communications Services section.

The Community Services division handles educational relations, civic information and mass communication through three sections:

College, School, and Youth Services; Civic Information Services; and Mass Communication Media Services.

The Editorial Services division handles editorial research, writing, graphic production, and a publication through four sections: Writing, Research, and Library section; "Our Sun" Publication section; Art and Printing Services section; and Photographic Services section.

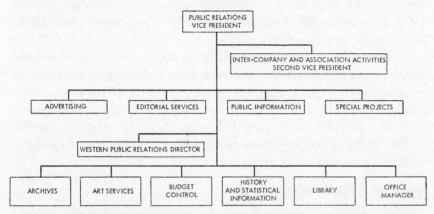

FIG. 5–5. Public relations department of New York Life Insurance Co., which has four principal divisions: advertising, editorial services, public information, and special projects. Secondary divisions are: Western public relations, archives, art services, budget control, historical and statistical information, library, and office manager.

Public Utility Organization

The public relations department of United Fuel Gas Co., Charlestown, West Virginia, with a staff of thirteen, is representative of the public relations organization of a regional public utility. The department is headed by an assistant vice-president and director of information, with an assistant director, who is in charge of seven staff members including three news bureau representatives, a public speaker, a darkroom technician and photographer, an advertising manager, and the editor of *Pipeline,* the employee magazine.

THE PUBLIC RELATIONS DIRECTOR

The director of a corporate or association public relations department should be able to deal effectively with top executives whose specialized knowledge of the enterprise often far exceeds his own. He must have the strength of his convictions and the character to defend his opinions of what constitutes good public relations, sometimes in opposition to management's conception of what it thinks public relations should be.

The director should be able to recognize the public relations problems of his organization and be aware of public opinion of the organization and reflect the public viewpoint to management. He must possess planning ability to take the facts disclosed by opinion research and build thereon a sound public relations program. He must have the executive ability to delegate, supervise, and carry out public relations plans. More important, he must be able to induce management to adopt policies which serve the public interest. He must be a persuasive counselor to management on public relationships.

Because public relations is involved in the activities of all departments, a public relations director must have a thorough knowledge of the affairs of the organization. He should possess the ability to deal with people successfully and be able to command their respect through his presence, personality, and good judgment. A public relations director should be apt at self-expression orally and in writing and understand media of communication.

Sources of Public Relations Directors

Public relations directors have a varied background before becoming identified with public relations. Some were advertising, sales promotion, media, and marketing executives experienced in dealing with the public and skilled in communication. Others were previously engaged in radio and television news broadcasting, newspaper reporting, and magazine writing. Paul Garrett, public relations counselor, was financial editor of the *New York Evening Post* before he organized General Motors' first public relations department.

Most public relations directors have served their apprenticeships in various capacities in public relations departments. Some were former staff members of public relations counseling organizations.

Title of Head of Public Relations Department

Directors of public relations departments have various titles, some of which reflect the principal function of the department and the responsibilities of its director. More than half of the heads of public relations departments are designated director of public relations. Others use the title of manager of public relations. From 15 to 20 per cent carry the title of vice-president. Other titles of persons responsible for public relations are: director of public relations and promotion, director of public relations and service, director of public relations and advertising, director of advertising and publicity, director of publicity, and assistant manager in charge of public relations.

Activities of Public Relations Directors

The activities of public relations managers vary widely according to the size of the organization and scope of the public relations program. Surveys of the responsibilities of public relations directors show that their activities include in order of frequency: public speaking; advising management on policy; writing and editing publicity, news letters, speeches, reports, booklets, articles, publications, institutional advertising, public statements; handling requests for contributions; community relations; employee relations; organizing open houses; government relations; press relations; supplying information to teachers and students; answering consumer complaints; trade association relations; administering scholarships; and making arrangements for special events.

PUBLIC RELATIONS COUNSELOR

The public relations counselor, the forefather of modern public relations, originated in the first years of the twentieth century as a publicity agent employed by large corporations to defend them against widespread public criticism. One of these publicity agents was the late Ivy Lee who, in the early years of the century, served the Pennsylvania Railroad and Rockefeller interests. Other early public relations counselors were Edward I. Bernays, Pendleton Dudley, Steve Hannagan, Albert Lasker, and John Price Jones who recognized that public relations includes many activities as well as publicity. Today, more than 500 consultant firms and individual counselors operating in all parts of the United States and internationally are members of the Counselors Section of the Public Relations Society of America.

Public relations consultants serve many large and small businesses, nonprofit organizations, and associations in one or more of the following ways, according to the Counselors Section of the Public Relations Society of America:

Establishment and definition of short- and long-range public relations goals.

Counsel and guidance to management on actions or policies which affect public relations goals.

Support of the marketing program including product or process publicity—news releases, feature articles, case studies, audio-visual aids, press, radio, and television coverage.

Stockholder and financial relations—annual, quarterly, or interim reports to shareholders, special releases to financial news media, assistance with the annual meeting, liaison with security analysts, investment dealers, and the professional investment community.

Employee and internal communications—company publications, information programs for employees on profits, the economics of industry, quality control, and over-all company operations.

Community relations—counsel on public relations policies at the local plant or branch office level, liaison with local news media, assistance in establishing policies of corporate giving, staging special events such as open houses and plant tours.

Government relations—international, federal, state and local—public relations counseling and liaison with agencies or government officials whose policies influence the operations of the client.

Evaluation and measurement—analysis of the effectiveness of public relations programs, application and use of budget, and attainment of objectives.

Industry-education co-operation—pioneered by the counsel firm of Hill and Knowlton, helps corporations and industries prepare teaching aids related to client interests in co-operation with teachers; creates programs for the recruitment of scientific personnel from colleges; conducts seminars in which industry executives meet and discuss with educators industry problems; arranges for educators to carry out research projects; develops plans for financial assistance to educational institutions; and provides programs of instructional assistance and in-service development for teachers.

Advantages of Retaining Public Relations Counsel

There are several advantages to retaining public relations counsel. An outside organization of specialists in public relations serving clients in various fields can provide objective advice uninfluenced by subjective problems which may exist within the client's organization. The opinion of an outside counsel is likely to carry more weight with management than the views of an inside public relations director. The services of an outside counsel may be more economical for a small organization than maintaining a staff of specialists on a permanent basis. A consulting firm brings to management a diversity of experience in dealing with the public relations problems of a variety of organizations. In retaining counsel, management has access to specialists with backgrounds in a wide range of business, government, journalism, and education and with experience in varied problems of public relations. A counsel serves several clients, the loss of any one of which does not seriously affect his income, giving him a more independent viewpoint. The outside point of view of counsel brings the public perspective to an organization's public relations. The services of a counsel are flexible and can be adapted to the variable needs of clients.

The Limitations of Public Relations Counsel

On the other hand, public relations counsel may have one or more possible limitations. An outside counsel cannot be as familiar with the internal operations and problems of an organization as an inside public relations staff. Some outside counseling firms are primarily concerned with press publicity and product promotion and have limited experience with the broader aspects of public relations such as relations with employees, suppliers, community neighbors, and other publics. An outside counsel may not be in position to influence internal policies and practices which are the foundation of an effective program. Some public relations counsel firms have a limited staff and experience with public relations problems. Internal public relations staff personnel may resent outside interference and consider employment of counsel as a reflection on their ability to deal with public relations problems.

How a Public Relations Consultant Functions

A public relations consultant starts work for a client by assimilating all the pertinent information that can be obtained about the client's business and existing public relations policies, objectives, and problems. Conferences are held with the management and public relations executives of the client organization. A study is made of the existing public relations activities, media of communication, and the economic and social forces affecting the client's public relations policy and program. In some cases, further research is recommended to obtain information about the attitudes and opinions of specific groups. This research may be conducted by counsel or outside specialists in opinion research may be employed.

Following such studies, a counsel uses this information as a basis for recommendations for short-term action and long-term projects, the techniques to be used, and the objectives to be attained. The program recommended may include communication of information to the press, stockholders, the community, government, and educators through the media of radio, television, visual aids, publications, public speaking, and participation in public affairs.

The decision to proceed on the recommendations of the counsel is the responsibility of management. A written contract may be employed although many counsel-client relationships exist without formal agreements.

The counsel may assume all public relations functions for clients who have no internal public relations staff and, in effect, become a public relations department for the client. The services of a counsel firm may be co-ordinated with an inside public relations staff so that both supplement each other and share public relations functions. A third course is for counsel to act as a consultant and only give advice without participating in the execution of the program. Most clients of counseling firms maintain internal public relations departments and use counsel on a continuing basis or for special projects. A combination of competent outside counsel and inside public relations staff is the most effective working arrangement for corporate, nonprofit, or association public relations.

Compensation of Public Relations Counsel

Compensation of public relations counsel depends on the extent of the work to be undertaken, the time involved, and the number of staff personnel required. If counsel is retained on a continuing basis, the fee may be established in one of three ways: a fixed monthly retainer; a retainer plus monthly billing for actual time on an hourly or per diem basis; or a base fee billed monthly to which is added charges for services performed beyond the retainer. Out-of-pocket expenses are generally billed at cost and are exclusive of the fee. On special, short-term projects, counsel may quote a single fee plus an allowance for expense.

Staff time charges at per diem rates cover the salary of the person assigned, plus overhead for account executives to co-ordinate the counsel's work for the client; the salaries of staff specialists working on assigned projects and research to assist the client in formulating a program.

Selecting Public Relations Counsel

The increasing number of public relations counsel firms, the scope of their services, their experience, and business and professional backgrounds pose a problem in selecting a public relations counsel.

To aid management in choosing a public relations counsel, the Counselors Section of the Public Relations Society of America suggests that the following questions be asked in selecting counsel: What is the professional competence and background of the principals of the counseling firm? How much of this experience has been in areas of particular importance to the organization seeking counsel? What is the general reputation of the counseling firm; does it adhere to the Public Relations Society Code of Ethics and are the counsel's integrity and professional standing above reproach? Who are the present clients of the counsel; how long have these organizations been served; and what is the rate of client turnover? Who among the principals and staff of the counseling firm will be working on the account; and what are their qualifications, special training, and background as related to the needs of the organization? Does the counselor make speculative presentations?

The practices of a counsel should conform with the ethical code of professional standards of the Public Relations Society which governs the practices of reliable counseling firms: Counsel should not represent conflicting or competing interests without the express consent of those concerned. The confidences of both present and former clients should not be disclosed to their disadvantage. Counsel should not engage in practices which tend to corrupt the integrity of channels of public communication. No use should be made of an organization purporting to serve some announced cause but actually serving an undisclosed private interest of a client. A counsel should not propose to a prospective client that the counsel's fee be contingent on the achievement of certain results.

THE PUBLIC RELATIONS BUDGET

There is no accepted standard amount to be appropriated for public relations. A public relations budget should be based on the specific needs of a business or nonprofit organization. A study should first be made of the public relationships of the organization. Next, the objectives determined, and then the public relations program needed to attain the objectives. The cost of the program should be estimated. If the cost of attaining the objectives is excessive, in relation to the anticipated benefit to be derived, then the objectives should be curtailed and the cost reduced.

To determine a public relations appropriation as a fixed percentage of either sales or profits is unwise, because the public relations needs of one organization will differ from those of another in the same industry. Furthermore, no two organizations classify the same expenditures as public relations costs. Some organizations consider advertising, customer entertainment, and contributions as public relations expense; whereas others allocate these costs to other accounts. For these reasons it is impracticable to compare the public relations expenditures of one organization with another of similar size or in the same industry.

Some organizations do not establish an annual budget for public relations but prepare a special budget for each project after careful study of the need and the cost of accomplishing the objective.

Case 5–1

E. I. DU PONT DE NEMOURS & COMPANY

Public Relations Advisors

E. I. du Pont de Nemours & Company was established in 1802 in Wilmington, Delaware. It manufactures and markets electrochemicals, industrial and biochemicals, organic chemicals, plastics, elastomer chemicals, coated fabrics, finishes, packaging and industrial films, pigments, photo films, textile fibers, and other chemical products in some 80 plants in 28 states in the United States.

Annual sales in excess of $2 billion are made to 75,000 customers in the textile, rubber, chemical, transportation, food, petroleum, machinery, paper, publishing, mining, agriculture, metals, construction, and other industries. Ninety-five per cent of all Du Pont sales are of products that go to industrial users rather than ultimate consumers.

Du Pont operates subsidiary companies in Mexico, United Kingdom, Belgium, France, Switzerland, The Netherlands, Venezuela, Brazil, Peru, Argentina, and Canada. Its total foreign business, including that of affiliates, amounted to $363 million in 1960.

More than 88,000 men and women, 48,000 of whom are shareholders, are employed by the company in its various facilities. There are 226,000 stockholders of the company. Some 30,000 suppliers provide Du Pont with raw materials, parts, supplies, and equipment.

Public relations at Du Pont is organized with a headquarters public relations department with four divisions: *Publications* is responsible for employee and other public relations periodicals; *Extension* provides public speakers to clubs and organizations; *Control* handles routine administration of the department; and *Information* maintains liaison with the press, informs the public and provides public relations counsel to managements of the twelve manufacturing and thirteen auxiliary departments of the company.

The managers of the four public relations staff divisions report to the assistant director of the department who is responsible to the director of public relations. Two executive assistants handle special projects. A policy committee composed of the above executives co-ordinates department operations and formulates public relations policy.

A unique feature of Du Pont's public relations staff organization is seven public relations advisors who are assigned to one or more of the twelve manufacturing departments of the company which are responsible for production and marketing of the twelve major product lines of the company. Each of these departments employs from 4,000 to 25,000 workers. The advisors who are on the staff of the public relations department are responsible to the assistant manager of the Information division of the department at Wilmington, Delaware.

A Du Pont public relations advisor has three basic tasks: (1) to provide the managements of the departments to which he is assigned with advice and assistance on all matters which have public relations aspects or consequences; (2) to serve as a source of information on the company's activities and problems which affect the company's over-all public relations objectives; and (3) to maintain contact with the press.

The most important function of an advisor is to provide public relations counsel to management of the manufacturing departments to which he has been assigned. The twelve manufacturing departments of the company are: Elastomer Chemicals, Electrochemicals, Explosives, Fabrics and Finishes, Film, Industrial and Biochemicals, International, Organic Chemicals, Photo Products, Pigments, Polychemicals, and Textile Fibers. Each of these manufacturing departments functions like an independent company in charge of a general manager who is responsible to the president and executive committee of the company. The department general manager is fully liable for the manufacturing and marketing operations of his department and its plants, laboratories, processes, and facilities and has authority over costs and selling prices.

The management of each of the twelve manufacturing departments is responsible for relations with the public, particularly employees and communities where facilities are located; including suppliers, customers, and media of communication with these publics. The general manager is fully responsible for his actions and for any public consequences.

The public relations advisor has no authority to require a departmental manager to follow any course of action. The advisor acts only in an advisory capacity and his task is one of persuasion. Departmental managements are regarded as the company's public relations practitioners and the advisors are the technicians.

Advisors deal with company executives of considerable stature, who will accept the counsel of no one for whom they do not hold respect. A major task of an advisor is to win the respect of the managements of the departments to which he has been assigned. Accordingly, advisors must have sound judgment based on intelligence, education, and experience. They must have the courage of their convictions and a willingness to fight for what they believe is good public relations even though the opponent be a general manager, vice-president, or president.

Although public relations advisors are assigned to manufacturing departments they are not located in plants. Even the largest Du Pont plants are too small to attract and hold highly qualified public relations men and most plants of the company are small. Each advisor keeps in touch with plant management by telephone and through periodic visits and assists the plant manager to be a director of public relations in his area.

An important function of an advisor is to correlate the actions of individual departments with the reputation of the company as a whole. The advisor through the public relations department has the freedom and responsibility to discuss with higher management a course of action decided upon by any department which may have potentially serious consequences for the company as a whole.

Each advisor is given a great deal of independence and given broad authority and responsibility by the Public Relations Department to deal with management. He makes his own recommendations to department management and only confers with the Public Relations Department when he is in doubt about the proper recommendations to make or needs help on a particular problem.

Advisors assume that departmental management is not only capable of dealing with the public but must do so. However advisors recognize that the heavy demands on management's time and pressure of responsibilities require specialized public relations experience and an independent viewpoint to deal with public relations problems. Management needs public relations advice just as it requires legal counsel.

An important aspect of an advisor's work is his relations with the press, the editorial departments of various media of public information: newspapers, magazines, radio and television, book publishers, and the public seeking information about the company. The advisors are a helping hand for the press which seeks information about the company rather than as buffers between management and the press. Advisors never go to editors unless they are convinced that they have genuine news of importance for readers. All Du Pont communication with the press is channeled through the Information division of the Public Relations Department which controls press relations for the entire company.

Public relations problems with which Du Pont advisors deal are similar to those of other large industrial companies. However, the size of the company and its leadership in the industry create more complex public relations problems than those found in smaller companies.

The principal public relations activity of Du Pont concerns its 88,000 employees in 80 plants in 28 states and more than 100 research, service, and plant laboratories.

One of the most difficult and challenging employee and community relations problems of Du Pont involves closing down obsolete manufacturing facilities. In communities where plants have been closed, the public relations advisor has been a key man over a period of months and years in assisting local management with its plans to close down operations, minimize the difficulties for employees, and to inform the community, suppliers, and customers.

A plant shutdown public relations program at Du Pont is not a public relations department responsibility. It is the primary responsibility of the local plant management to meet the various publics concerned and carry out the program with the advice of the advisor and the headquarters staff of the Public Relations Department in Wilmington.

The role of the advisor in the shutdown of the Du Pont, Arlington, New Jersey, works illustrates the character of Du Pont's public relations advisory service in respect to a critical community and employee relations problem.

The decision to shut down the Arlington plant which began operation in 1886 was made by the executive committee of the company several years in advance of the closing date. The decision to shut down the plant followed extensive engineering and marketing studies which indicated the obsolescence of the plant's products and processes and its unsuitability as a site for modern chemical manufacturing.

The company was faced with the problem of terminating, transferring, or retiring the plant's 732 employees, a majority of whom had more than 15 years' service. Involved in the problem were relations with the community, union, customers, and suppliers.

The public relations advisor was a party to discussions leading to the decision to close the plant. He became an active participant with the plant and departmental managements in planning procedures and timing the announcement of the shutdown to the public. He offered suggestions and was consulted on how to handle some of the difficult employee and community relations problems connected with the decision.

The advisor, with employee relations people and plant management, decided to notify employees of the company's plans about two years before the shutdown to enable them to make future plans, a decision which contributed in large measure to the success of the program from a public relations point of view. He assisted the plant staff in preparing announcement letters to employees, talks explaining termination benefits to employees, letters to community leaders and customers, and talks to civic clubs.

News releases were prepared by the advisor for nearby Newark and Kearney, New Jersey, newspapers. Employees were notified before the news was released to the papers. There was no unfavorable publicity in newspapers in the plant area. Relationships with employees, union officials, customers, and the community were cordial as a result of favorable public attitudes created over the years as well as by the orderly closedown procedures and good public relations.

Advisors counsel department managements on the public relations aspects of fires and explosions which are an ever-present risk in all chemical plants despite safety precautions. The company has an established disaster procedure which includes taking the press into the plant for a briefing by the plant manager, permitting photographs to be taken, and providing communication facilities for the press.

In Du Pont's overseas expansion program, advisors are playing an important role in establishing good relations between the local management, the press, and public.

QUESTIONS

1. Large companies with subsidiary plants and facilities in several locations are faced with the problem of securing effective public relations at the community level and at the same time co-ordinating the relations of individual units with the public relations of the company as a whole. Is Du Pont's use of advisors to department managements the most effective way to solve this problem? Give arguments for or against using advisors, and your conclusion.

2. Is there a better way to solve the problem of securing good community relations for multiunit industrial corporations? If so, describe how you would solve this problem.

3. Comment on the responsibilities of Du Pont public relations advisors? Are their functions too numerous? Should they have other duties?

4. Comment on the authority given Du Pont public relations advisors. Is this authority too broad or too restrictive?

5. Is the structure of Du Pont's headquarters public relations organization satisfactory? If you believe that this organization should be changed, describe what should be done.

Problem 5–1

PUBLIC RELATIONS ORGANIZATION

Leighton Corporation

The Leighton Corporation was established in 1902 in Philadelphia, Pennsylvania, by Henry R. Leighton who held patents on the first duplicating machine produced in the United States. He incorporated under the name Leighton Corporation to manufacture and market a machine for reproducing the typewriting of letters, reports, and bulletins and sold all the common stock to members of his family. Henry R. Leighton was president of the corporation and his son, Herbert, vice-president.

The company grew slowly in its early years but expanded after World War I by purchasing a competing duplicating machine manufacturer, enlarging its sales organization, and erecting new plants in Brooklyn, N.Y., Toronto, Canada, and Manchester, England. Twenty-five sales offices were established in the principal cities of the United States, Canada, and England. By 1962 the Leighton Corporation made and sold an annual volume of $10 million worth of duplicating machines, or about 10 per cent of all the duplicating machines made in this country. Sales of the corporation have been declining steadily since 1955 when an annual volume of $20 million was sold.

Henry Leighton died in 1962 at the age of 85 years having survived his son, Herbert, who passed away in 1953. Mr. Leighton was active as president of the corporation until his death. As there was no one in the family able to succeed Henry Leighton, the heirs decided to sell their interest to the Marcy Securities Corporation, New York.

The new owners of the business installed a new president to reorganize the corporation and revitalize its production, marketing, and finances. He found that the business had been under the autocratic control of its founder, Henry Leighton, who refused to delegate authority to his subordinates, assumed responsibility for all operations, and made most of the decisions. He also served as treasurer and refused to divulge information about the finances of the corporation to shareholders or executives. Officials of the corporation were no more than clerical assistants to the president. Department heads did not clearly understand their responsibilities and there was much duplication of effort and conflict of authority.

The new president reorganized the corporation by establishing a line and staff organization, headed by the president, supported by a staff consisting of a vice-president in charge of manufacturing, vice-president in charge of marketing, vice-president in charge of personnel, treasurer, advertising manager, and manager of foreign operations.

The new vice-president in charge of personnel found the corporation heavily overstaffed and, by eliminating nonessential workers and co-ordinating functions, reduced the number of employees from 1,100 to 800. He established new personnel policies to improve selection, training, and recruiting of personnel.

The manufacturing methods and facilities of the corporation were found to be antiquated and inefficient by the new vice-president in charge of manufacturing.

There were no production controls or cost accounting. The basic principal of the product had not been improved for fifty years. A multiplicity of models and obsolete production equipment contributed to high inventory and production costs. All new products had been designed by Henry Leighton, the founder, and were made by an individual worker who carried the blue prints in his mind.

The new vice-president in charge of manufacturing engaged a design engineer to develop a new model duplicator which is 30 per cent lighter than preceding models, has automatic controls, and is capable of producing 100,000 impressions an hour compared with 12,000 per hour of the old models. The new model has two attachments instead of 143 accessories used on the old machines. A foreman training program was initiated and steps taken to improve the skills of the workers.

The marketing of the corporation was reorganized by the new vice-president in charge of marketing, who established a new method of selection and training of salesmen, recruited new salesmen, opened new sales offices, and appointed regional sales managers for Chicago, Los Angeles, Dallas, and Atlanta. A new advertising program in business magazines and by direct mail was introduced to inform industrial and commercial companies, hotels, banks, transportation companies, and federal, state, and city governments about the new model.

The new treasurer installed a new budget system and is planning a large capital expansion program. The accounting of the corporation has been modernized.

Although the Leighton Corporation has a good and long-standing reputation for the quality of its products, its corporate image has suffered from the autocratic practices of its founder and its unprogressive policies so that it is identified in the public mind as an "old-fashioned" concern. The new president believed that if the corporation was to progress it would have to be known as a progressive, modern organization concerned with the needs of employees, customers, dealers, suppliers, stockholders, and the communities where it operates.

To secure better public relations, the president favored the employment of a public relations counseling organization to advise the management on a public relations program for the corporation.

Some of the executives opposed the employment of an outside counsel for the reasons that counsel would be primarily concerned with press publicity and not in a position to understand and influence internal policies and practices which are the foundation of a good public relations program. Some company executives resented the interference of an outside organization with the established procedures of the corporation.

On the other hand, other executives favored engaging public relations counsel, as the advice of counsel would carry more weight than the opinions of company personnel. Furthermore, counsel would have broad experience with a wide variety of companies and public relations problems. The services of counsel would be more economical than an internal staff for a small company. Counsel would not be involved in internal politics and would speak more freely. The services of counsel could be used as required and its outside viewpoint would be helpful in solving the corporation's public relations problems.

An experienced, well-qualified public relations manager and a secretary was all that the corporation needed at this stage, in the opinion of a vice-president of the corporation. Such a man should have executive ability and successful experience with the public relations of a business machine manufacturer. He must, in the opinion of the executive who favored a public relations manager, be able to command the confidence of top management and be aggressive and willing to fight for what he believes is good public relations with the president or board of directors. The manager must have sound business judgment based on intelligence, education, and experience, an unusual interest in human relationships and sensitivity to the attitudes of the public.

The responsibilities of the public relations manager, according to the executive who proposed him, would include: preparing news releases for the newspapers and trade magazines, speaking before various groups, writing a periodical for employees, participating in community affairs, answering inquiries from consumers about the company and its products, writing speeches for corporation executives, helping conduct labor-management negotiations, supplying information to students and teachers, and making arrangements for special dinners and parties.

Another vice-president of the company did not believe that the corporation needed a public relations manager, staff, or counsel. He maintained that every member of management and operating executive should have full responsibility for his actions and any public consequences of policies or actions by his department. Management people are the corporation's public relations practitioners who are fully capable of dealing with the attitudes of employees, customers, neighbors, and other publics. Department heads would be reluctant to accept the unsolicited advice of a public relations counsel, manager, or staff. If the public relations manager had no authority to force departmental management to follow his recommendations, he would be ineffectual. On the other hand, if the public relations manager had authority to require compliance, department heads would resent his interference with their responsibilities. Good public relations is not something that can be secured by simply employing a public relations manager or counsel, it must be the responsibility of every executive and employee.

The advertising manager of the corporation proposed that the advertising department be made responsible for public relations because the advertising staff had specialized skills in planning and executing communication programs. The cost of setting up and operating a separate public relations department would be unnecessary as the advertising department could handle both advertising and public relations. Furthermore, the advertising manager had previous experience as assistant advertising and public relations manager of a pharmaceutical corporation. Some large corporations successfully combine advertising and public relations in one department.

There was some opposition to the advertising manager assuming responsibility for public relations on the grounds that the major interest of the advertising manager and his staff was in advertising and that public relations would get secondary consideration. What was needed was a full-time public relations manager. Furthermore, advertising was mainly concerned with promoting product sales, whereas public relations was devoted to gaining the understanding of employees, community neighbors, suppliers, and stockholders of the corporation. The advertising manager would have a divided responsibility which would weaken his effectiveness in both advertising and public relations.

QUESTIONS

1. Should public relations be an organized function of the administration of the Leighton Corporation? Give reasons for your decision.

2. If you favor a public relations organization for the corporation, make a complete organization chart of the public relations function showing the functions and number of individuals involved in the research, planning, production, and co-ordination of the public relations of the company.

3. Should an outside public relations counsel be engaged by the Leighton Corporation? Give reasons for your decision. If you favor a counsel describe its services to the corporation.

4. If you believe that a public relations manager should be employed, describe the essential qualifications of such a person. What should be his functions?

5. Should the function of public relations of the Leighton Corporation be assumed by the advertising manager and his staff? Give reasons for your decision.

THE CORPORATE PUBLICS

IN PUBLIC RELATIONS terms a "public" is a group of people with a common interest whose understanding and good will is essential to the successful functioning of a business, union, social service, government, professional, or other organization. The principal publics of a corporation are: employees, stockholders, consumers, community neighbors, distributor-dealers, suppliers, educators, and government. Each of these publics has a common interest in a corporation as a source of benefits: employees in employment and wages; shareholders in dividends; consumers in products and services; the community in taxes; distributor-dealers in profits; suppliers in purchases; and education and government in financial support.

As the interests of each particular public of a business organization differs from the interests of other publics, a public relations program should be especially designed to appeal to the particular interests of each public. The development of good relations with each of the eight principal publics should consider the characteristics of each public, particular objectives, media of communication, and activities described in the following chapters in this section.

Corporate public relations programs often begin with the employee public, the most immediate group, whose understanding and good will are reflected in increased production, lower costs of operation, and improved products. Because most employees live in plant communities, community relations programs are used to supplement employee relations activities. Without good consumer relations, no business can succeed. As consumers provide the capital, pay the wages and profits, the importance of developing consumer relations is recognized. Special programs for stockholders, distributor-dealers, suppliers, educators, and government are included in corporate public relations.

6 · EMPLOYEE RELATIONS

MORE THAN seventy million men and women are employed in this country. Among the largest employers in the nation and the number of their employees are: General Motors Corporation, 605,-000; General Electric Company, 250,000; U.S. Steel Corporation, 225,000; Ford Motor Company, 160,000; Western Electric Company, Bethlehem Steel Company, and Standard Oil Company of New Jersey, 140,000 each; and International Telephone and Telegraph Company, 132,000.

The great expansion in the work force of American industry has been accompanied by serious problems in employee relations and communication. As corporations have grown and the number of employees increased, the communication between management and workers has deteriorated. Misunderstandings have arisen between employers and employees because management has failed to explain its intentions, and employees have had no opportunity to express their views to management.

Management Relations with Employees

Management gives attention to improving relations with employees through personnel, industrial relations, labor relations, and employee relations departments.

Personnel relations include recruiting manpower; employment; selection and placement; administration of employee benefit, retirement, and hospitalization plans; education and training; personnel planning; personnel research; and employee recreation.

Industrial or labor relations involve administration of wages, hours, employee benefits, relations with labor regulatory bodies, conformity with labor laws, handling grievances, relations with union representatives, and union contract negotiations.

Public relations is also involved in furthering the relationship between management and employees. It fills a need in improving employer-employee relations not satisfied by personnel, industrial, or labor relations. An important function of public relations is aiding personnel, industrial, and labor relations departments and management to communicate continuously and effectively with employees.

EMPLOYEE RELATIONS—COMMUNICATING WITH EMPLOYEES

To secure better understanding by employees of company policies and practices, the public relations department plans and produces communications to employees. It gives employees information about company affairs in which they have a personal interest such as: employment, working conditions, fringe benefits, sales, new products, finances, wage negotiations, plant expansion, payroll, personnel, promotions, and other matters. Furthermore, it provides two-way communication facilities whereby employees can express their views to management about company practices and policies.

The public relations function of employee communication is called "employee relations." In large organizations a separate section of the public relations department is responsible for employee relations.

Objectives of Employee Relations

The objectives of employee relations are typified by the objectives of the Borden Company employee section of the public relations department as follows:

To assist management in establishing a good employee relationship by: developing employee pride in the company by providing information about its varied activities; establishing the mutual interests of the company and its employees; improving employee understanding of the political and economic factors that affect the company and its employees; developing the employee market for the sale of Borden products; obtaining employee cooperation in general terms for greater safety, courtesy, efficiency, and waste prevention; establishing in general terms the fact that the company is a good place to work; and encouraging public relations work by employees with their friends and the public generally.

Responsibility for Employee Relations

The development of an employee communication and information program is the responsibility of the employee relations section of the public relations department. However, the execution of an employee communication program is a responsibility of top-management staff, executives in charge of personnel, employee or industrial relations, department heads, foremen, and supervisors.

In planning an employee communication program, the employee

relations section of the public relations department asks the management of each department of the organization what information should be communicated to its employees. Close co-ordination between the employee relations section and all staff and operating departments of the organization is essential in effective employee relations.

Good personnel policies and practices are the foundation of an employee communication program. What the employee relations section of the public relations department communicates to employees means nothing unless the words are supported by good personnel policies and management practices.

Importance of Employee Relations and Communications

Failure to inform employees leads to misunderstanding, false rumors, and confusion. If employees are not informed by management about matters which affect their work, they make their own assumptions or turn to outside sources for information.

Employees want to express to management their opinions about their jobs, working conditions, and other matters affecting their interests. Two-way channels of communication should be established to give workers an opportunity to ask questions about the business or to make suggestions to management.

Good relations with the community and general public begin with good communications with employees of the organization. No organization can have good community relations if its employees are uninformed or misinformed. The public will believe something bad that an employee may say about his employer before it will believe something good that the employer might say. "A company's public relations program, to get anywhere, must begin in the outer office and inside the plant," says Paul Garrett. "If the immediate family is not happy and informed, those whom it meets on the outside will not be. To outsiders, those who work for the company are the company—outsiders judge the company by the folks in the company they know."

COMMUNICATIONS FROM MANAGEMENT TO EMPLOYEES

The first step in initiating an employee communication program is to survey employee opinions of the organization, its management, policies, working conditions, operations, and other matters in which employees have a personal interest. The purpose of this research is to determine policies and practices about which workers are not informed or upon which they have misinformation. Employees are also asked what they want to know about the organization so that their questions can be answered by management. The method of conducting this investigation is described in Chapter 18, "Public Relations Research and Evaluation."

What Employees Want to Know

The National Association of Manufacturers, in co-operation with the National Industrial Council, held 150 employee communications clinics in all parts of the country to discover what information is wanted by employees and how management should communicate facts about the business. These clinics indicated that most employees ask for the following information:

1. Knowledge about the company—its background and present organization.
2. Product knowledge—how products are made and where they go.
3. Policy information—especially new policies as they affect themselves and their fellow workers.
4. Advance information about changes in methods and new products.
5. What is expected of the employees, and how they are measuring up to expectations.
6. How their jobs fit into the scheme of things and their chances for advancement.
7. The outlook for business and the prospects for steady work.
8. The company's income and its profits and losses.
9. The possibilities and reasons for layoffs, and how the employees as individuals are affected.

Fundamentals of Employee Communications

In an effective two-way communication system between management and employees, the following principles should be practiced:

Management must be genuinely willing to share information with employees. Communications cannot be successful if management assumes an air of secrecy about its acts and intentions.

Communication with employees must function as a two-way system, giving workers an opportunity to express their views to management.

The distortion of information which occurs in oral transmission from person to person should be avoided by written statements.

Communications should be expressed in terms with which employees are familiar, and consistent with their education and experience.

Communications media should be prepared by experienced, trained specialists. Communication of important information should not be entrusted to inexperienced personnel.

Communications should not be distorted or misleading, but based upon facts presented accurately and temperately.

· Information should be timely. Speed is important in getting facts to employees to avoid misunderstandings.

Repetition is an essential in good employee communication. Employees should be told the facts, and the same facts repeated again in different terms to make them understood.

Employees should be given information in small amounts for clear understanding.

Responsibility for employee communications should be assigned to the public relations department.

Employee Communication Employs Marketing Techniques

Good employee communication uses the same techniques employed in marketing products and services to consumers. An employee communications program sells the organization to employees to make them "organization customers."

The employee relations section of the public relations department, in planning an employee communications program, makes a "market research" of the attitudes of employees or "organization customers." This is similar to market studies made by the marketing departments before launching an advertising campaign.

On the basis of this research, an attractive "organization package" is designed to appeal to employee "customers." The organization package includes such features as regular work, good working conditions, good bosses, opportunity to get ahead, good pay, and desirable fringe benefits.

Communications to employees promote the "organization package" by describing the organization's sound financial condition, its progressive personnel and labor relations policies, experienced management, physical facilities, advanced research and development program, expanding sales volume, and social contributions.

In selling an "organization package" to employees, the same media are used as in selling a product or service to consumers. Personal selling and printed salesmanship properly co-ordinated are both used in selling the "organization package" to employees.

The sales force of the "organization package" is composed of all staff and operating executives of the organization. These management people are the "wholesale salesmen" of the company who deal with employees in offices, plants, warehouses, and branches. These "wholesale salesmen" direct the "retail salesmen" or supervisors and foremen who sell the "organization product" to the rank-and-file employees.

Employees are grouped into cells of from five to fifteen workers, each with its own supervisor or foreman. Because of his continuous contact with workers, a supervisor is in the best position to sell the "organization package" to the rank-and-file of employees. A supervisor or "retail salesman" is the most important person in the organization's communication program because most employee communications channel through him.

Product salesmen must be trained to sell effectively. Likewise, management must be fully informed about the company to make effective "organization package" salesmen.

In selling an organization to employees, the supervisor or "retail salesman" must prove that the "organization package" is worth the price which the employee pays for it in time, skill, and effort.

Organization marketing, like product selling, also employs newspaper advertising, posters, radio and television broadcasts, direct mail, periodicals, and other media to inform employees about the organization.

MEDIA OF COMMUNICATION WITH EMPLOYEES

The two general methods of communication with employees are oral and printed or graphic media, each of which has a place in the communications program. Frequently both methods are used simultaneously.

Oral Communication with Employees

Oral communication is the most common and effective method of transmitting information to employees. It provides two-way communication between employees and management so that workers can receive as well as give information.

The frequent personal contacts between line executives and workers makes oral communication a convenient, rapid, and economical means of informing employees about matters affecting their work interests. In small companies, conversations between management and employees keep workers informed about the business. In large corporations, the oral communications of line executives, supervisors, and foremen serve the same purpose.

Oral communication, however, should not be depended upon exclusively to transmit information to employees. Oral communications of top management are sometimes misunderstood and misinterpreted by line executives. The original meaning of a message may be lost in the process of oral transmission. Some executives are poor oral communicators and cannot express meaning clearly. Some supervisors do not realize the importance of giving employees information. Other supervisors may put their own interpretation on company information, color it with their own sentiments, or deliberately withhold information from employees.

FIG. 6–1. An oral report to employees on new and improved products is made by management of Caterpillar Tractor Co., Peoria, Illinois, in more than 100 meetings.

In spite of these limitations of oral communication with individual employees, the line executives, supervisors, or foremen are the key factors in the vital line of two-way communication of information from management to employees.

The employee relations section of a public relations department should be responsible for organizing and conducting an employee communications training program for staff and line operating executives, supervisors, and foremen.

To supplement individual face-to-face oral communications of line executives and supervisors with employees, several group methods of communication are used in employee communication, including public address systems, meetings of management and workers, radio and television broadcasts, open houses, and visits of key executives to departments.

Public Address System. Communication from management to employees by public address system gets information to workers quickly without calling people away from their tasks. It has an authoritative, personal appeal through the voice of the president or manager.

Meetings of Management and Employees. Well-planned and well-conducted management-employee meetings are an excellent medium of communication with workers. Management has an opportunity to speak directly to the workers about new policies, products, methods, and internal problems. Meetings of management and employees include mass meetings addressed by management, panel discussions by executives with questions by employees, and round-table conferences.

In some organizations, management meets regularly with small groups of employees. A group of eight different employees of the Tractor Works of International Harvester Company, Chicago, meets once a week with the works manager for an hour's discussion of company activities. A Midwest manufacturer conducts monthly employee information forums led by the president and personnel director who discuss sales problems, products, finances, manufacturing, relief and pension funds, economics, accounting, insurance and credit, advertising, and the company's position in the industry.

Television and Radio Programs. Local television and radio programs, describing the progress and operations of a company, are used in reaching employees as well as the local community in which a company's plant is located. The Lynn, Massachusetts, Works of the General Electric Company broadcasts information over local radio stations about company operations and weather reports to 20,000 employees living in 16 communities within a radius of 15 miles of the plant.

Open Houses for Workers and Their Families. The open house for employees and their families not only provides group communication with workers but is also a fine morale builder. Workers take pride in showing their families their part in the company's production. Supervisors and foremen have an opportunity to meet personally the families of employees. The open house combines telling and showing; it is particularly effective in informing workers about the nature and variety of products produced, the capital investment, new and improved machinery and facilities, and the significance of the individual's job in over-all company operation.

Many companies arrange "family nights" to inform workers and their families about their operations. Work schedules are rearranged so that a full shift can be in action during visiting hours, and all employees are off duty one night to have an opportunity to see the company's operations with their families.

Visits by Key Executives to Departments. Informal visits by the president and top-management executives to offices and plant departments for informal talks with small groups of workers maintain personal communication between management and workers in large as well as small business organizations.

Printed and Visual Methods of Communication with Employees

To supplement oral communications, a wide variety of printed or visual media are used to communicate with employees. Printed media of communication are inexpensive, reach many people in a short time, and tell a complete story. However, printed communication lacks the personalized appeal, immediacy, and flexibility of personal transmission of information. Many companies rely upon a combination of oral and printed communication methods.

Management Letters to Employees. A frequently used printed medium for informing employees is the management letter. Management letters are given general distribution to all employees by line supervisors or foremen, or are mailed to the homes of workers, where they are more likely to be given careful reading and consideration and the wife and family of the employee informed.

Employee Periodicals. The employee periodical, or house organ, is a basic medium of printed communication between management and workers. Some companies publish several employee magazines, one for each plant operation. The International Harvester Company publishes twenty plant magazines. The Ford Motor Company publishes twenty-one employee newspapers with a combined circulation of 143,000.

An employee periodical provides two-way communication between management and workers by informing employees about product developments and operations, as well as giving them an opportunity to express their views in the periodical. An employee magazine also combats unwarranted criticism, rumors, and misinformation.

Bulletin Boards. One of the least expensive, yet most neglected, media of group communication with employees is the plant and office bulletin board. Properly located and supervised, a bulletin board is an excellent supplement to the employee publication in transmitting spot news to workers. Robert Newcomb and Marg Sammons, specialists in the use of industrial bulletin boards, suggest the following: Locate the bulletin board in a spot where it can be seen and read conveniently. Cover it with glass, and keep it free from dust, excessive thumb tacks, and curling papers. Change material every ten days at least. Mix notices with company news, gossip, and a picture or two. Delegate one person to keep the board neat and up to date. Don't clutter it with too much material. Keep English simple and the message short.

Information posted on bulletin boards includes: building and production expansion plans, business notices, sales drives, cafeteria menus, community welfare drives, company club notices, company news, company policies, credit union notices, educational posters, group insurance and hospitalization plans, holiday and vacation notices, lost and found notices, plant tour notices, safety notices, shutdowns.

The total number of bulletin boards in plants and offices averages from seventeen to twenty in large organizations.

Product Exhibits. Employees should be shown the finished products which they produce and impressed with the part they play in creating them. Product exhibits may include samples of products, photographs of products in use, or cross-section or working models with charts and diagrams to point out important features and explain operation.

Annual and Interim Financial Reports. Surveys of employees show that many are interested in the financial progress of the employing company. Widespread misconceptions exist among employees about corporate profits and finances. To solve this problem, an increasing number of companies distribute annual and interim reports to employees.

A special employee edition of the annual report to stockholders, prepared in simple terms and illustrated so that it can be easily understood, is also distributed to employees. Financial reports also are published in the employees' magazine or run in plant city newspapers.

The annual report to employees of a large automobile manufacturer covers the following topics: employees' average hourly earnings, number of employees, total payroll, number of cars and trucks produced, receipts from sales, stockholders' earnings, income retained for use in the business, net profit per dollar, company's share of industry output, and highlights from each division.

Plant City Newspaper Advertising. Newspaper advertising is used to inform employees who live in plant communities about company operations. Newspaper advertisements are inexpensive and can quickly and regularly inform workers and their families about company activities. All employees read a daily newspaper and reader interest in local news is high.

Employee Handbooks and Manuals. Employee handbooks and manuals are widely used to inform employees about policies, procedures, hours, wages, benefits, and rules and regulations. Some companies publish a complete employee orientation packet for new employees containing booklets, periodicals, literature, manuals, and reports of interest to employees as follows: employee handbook, employee newspaper or magazine, history of the company, safety manual, annual report to employees, organization manual, policy book, product catalogue, employee benefit handbook, promotion chart, training manual, and suggestion system manual.

Payroll Envelope Insert. An inexpensive medium of employee communication is the payroll envelope insert. Inserts are used to inform employees of wage changes, pensions, hospitalization, group and accident insurance. They are also used to inform workers about the company's operations, growth, sales, and economic and political factors influencing the business.

Motion Pictures and Slide Films. Motion pictures and slide films are used extensively to inform and educate employees. Many companies use films to indoctrinate new workers in the history of the company, its organization, products, and employee benefits. Annual reports on corporate finances, sales, earnings, and plant expansion are filmed and shown to employees. Films are used in employee economic education programs to explain the advantages of the free enterprise system and the benefits of living in a democracy.

Reading Racks. A relatively new and inexpensive medium of communication with employees is the reading rack filled with reports and booklets about corporate affairs; national, political, economic, and social problems; health, thrift, safety, hobbies, cooking, sports, and other subjects of interest to employees. Reading racks are placed in offices and plants in locations readily accessible to employees. Estimates indicate that about 1,500 companies have installed reading racks for communication with workers.

A reading rack program may be handled entirely by the public relations department of the company sponsoring the program or by an outside reading rack supply company which provides the racks and the booklets, written by well-known writers, at a cost of six to eight cents each depending on the quantity ordered. Three reading rack supply companies: Good Reading Rack Service, Inc., Employee Relations, Inc., and National Research Bureau, Inc. periodically issue new titles, advise on programs, and keep racks filled.

An extensive user of reading racks for employee communication is Western Electric Company, with 140,000 workers in 45 plants and branches, in which are located 1,400 reading racks. About 60 million booklets and reports are taken from reading racks annually by Western Electric employees at a cost to the company of about $1.65 per employee. Typical subjects of booklets distributed by the company are: "Now Is the Time for All Good Men," a plea for political party support; "A Nation of Sheep," on foreign aid; and "Will Lower Tariffs Create Greater Prosperity?"

The public relations department of Western Electric produces about one fourth of the booklets placed in the reading racks and secures the balance from outside writers. A committee composed of representatives of management advises the public relations department in selecting titles. About one half of the titles deal with the company and industry, a third are on economics and public affairs subjects, and the balance are on miscellaneous subjects. The booklets are taken home by employees and read by families. Copies are also distributed to educators, opinion leaders, and plant visitors.

COMMUNICATIONS FROM EMPLOYEES TO MANAGEMENT

Good communications with employees is a two-way system in which workers have an opportunity to express their views on matters pertaining to their jobs, the organization, its policies, and management.

The principal methods by which employees communicate with management are: the employee audit or attitude survey; analysis of employee grievances; the open-door policy; employee participation; and conversations of workers with supervisors and foremen.

Employee Attitude Surveys

Employee attitude surveys give employees an opportunity to communicate with management. Through these surveys, management learns what employees want to know about the company and their understanding of company policies and practices. Surveys enable employees to express their views about the company. They enjoy a feeling of recognition and a sense of participation in company affairs.

Employee attitude surveys are conducted by five methods: (1) the individual, personal interview; (2) the employee essay; (3) the individual mail questionnaire; (4) the group questionnaire; and (5) a combination of mail questionnaire and personal interview.

Employee Grievance Analysis

Misunderstandings by employees of corporate policies and practices indicate the ineffectiveness of management communication with workers. Periodic reviews of employee grievances enable management to improve its communications and get the facts to people in the shops and offices and create a better understanding of the company.

The Open-Door Policy

The policy of many companies is to make management accessible to all employees by keeping open the doors of the offices of all executives to all employees who want to discuss the company and its operations. By this method of communication, an executive can maintain a close, personal relationship with workers, which is the essence of good communication and understanding.

Employee Participation

By inviting employees to meet with representatives of management to discuss company operations, clear, two-way channels of communication are established. Employee-management committees provide an opportunity to communicate and, at the same time, give workers a sense of participation in the affairs of the enterprise.

Employee Communication through Line Executives

Line executives, supervisors, and foremen play an important role in transmitting impressions from workers to management. Supervisors are in closest contact with employees and should be active transmitters of information from workers to management.

Employee Economic Education

An increasing number of corporations are educating employees for better understanding of business and the American economic system as well as the economics of individual companies and their industries. Employee economic education is devoted to increasing employee understanding of productivity, earnings and investment, capital, profits, taxes, monetary policy, competition, wages, prices, and inflation and their importance to employee and employer. The principal objective of economic education of employees is to motivate workers through a better understanding of applied economics to make their maximum contribution to the financial welfare of the business through reduced expenses, increased revenue, and greater individual and group productivity.

Economic education of employees is carried on through a variety of educational methods including formal courses, films, booklets, lectures, panel discussions, articles in employee magazines, notices on bulletin boards, letters, seminars, and literature in reading racks.

Formal courses in applied economics have been offered nonmanagement employees by Monsanto Chemical Company, American Telephone and Telegraph Company, Owens-Corning Fiberglas Corporation, and others.

The American Telephone and Telegraph Company and its subsidiaries has offered all nonmanagement employees a course entitled "It's Our Business." The course consists of three discussion sessions, two hours each, led by supervisors. The discussions are supplemented by three motion pictures: "The Changing Years," depicting the increased demand, "Stork Talk," about the population explosion, and "Tomorrow and Mr. Jones," portraying the competition of corporations for the investor's dollars.

Owens-Corning Fiberglas Corporation, Newark, Ohio, holds plant meetings once a month of employees with top management to discuss economic factors affecting the company. The meetings are voluntarily attended by 80 per cent to 95 per cent of all employees. Management of the Monsanto Chemical Company, Columbia, Tennessee, plant held a series of thirteen meetings with employees to discuss the annual report, in addition to weekly and monthly meetings to discuss competition, productivity, and other subjects.

E. I. du Pont de Nemours & Company published in each issue of its employee magazine, *Better Living,* an economic article. Subjects discussed include: "Competition," "Taxes," "The Free Market," and others. Du Pont has published a series of booklets on economic subjects for employee education on "The Profit Motive" and "The Story of Management."

Case 6–1

EMPLOYEE RELATIONS

Charleston Group Companies of The Columbia Gas System, Inc.

The Charleston Group Companies, all subsidiaries of The Columbia Gas System, Inc., include the following companies: Amere Gas Utilities Company, Atlantic Seaboard Corporation, Big Marsh Oil Company, Columbia Gas of Kentucky, Inc., Kentucky Gas Transmission Corporation, United Fuel Gas Company, and Virginia Gas Distribution Corporation, with headquarters in Charleston, West Virginia.

Three of the companies are wholesale suppliers of gas to local gas companies which serve industrial and domestic consumers in Cincinnati, Richmond, Washington, and Baltimore, as well as many smaller communities in the four-state area of Kentucky, West Virginia, Virginia, and Maryland. They also sell gas at wholesale to other Columbia subsidiaries in Ohio and Pennsylvania. In addition, four of the companies, including one of the above, serve directly about 240,000 retail gas customers in West Virginia, Kentucky, and Virginia. The seventh company is engaged solely in producing gas. Annual gas deliveries exceed one-half trillion cubic feet and total income is about $240 million. About 3,200 employees are engaged in production, distribution, transmission, and storage of gas in the four-state area.

Public relations of the Charleston Group Companies is the responsibility of the information department headed by an assistant vice-president and director of information. A staff of thirteen includes the director, an assistant director of information, a public speaker, three news bureau representatives, a photographer-darkroom technician, an advertising manager, an editor of the employee magazine, and four secretaries.

Well-informed employees are regarded as the most effective medium, of public relations of the company, particularly in view of its program of expanded service, stepped-up construction, and need for higher rates. To improve communications with employees, the president of the companies appointed a committee on communications composed of the assistant vice-president and director of information, chairman, the director of employee relations, and the manager of distribution operations. The committee reports to the vice-president and general manager.

To keep employees informed about company activities, management established three objectives of employee communications: (1) Better exchange of information through regular meetings of all levels of supervisors and employees. (2) Better and more tools of communications such as letters, pamphlets, and presentations. (3) Constant evaluation and exchange of communications procedures through definite research by assigned personnel.

Employee Communications through Meetings

To improve internal communications vertically as well as horizontally, regular meetings of all levels of supervisors and employees to exchange information are held throughout the organization.

At the top-management level, the president and his staff meet every Monday morning to discuss operations and policies of the companies. This important exchange of information starts the downward flow of communications to all employees and serves for evaluation of information which moves upward from employees through their supervisors.

Every 60 days the vice-president and general manager hold an all-day meeting with department heads representing middle management who report on their activities and have an opportunity to discuss, determine, interpret and adjust policies, and exchange information.

The department heads who attend the vice-president and general manager's conference hold monthly operating department meetings with their supervisors to acquaint them with company policy and discuss problems pertinent to their departments.

Supervisors within each department also hold monthly district and division meetings with their local managers to inform them and exchange information with them.

At the local level, supervisors in the production, transmission, and compressor departments meet regularly with their foremen and other key employees to disseminate information, interpret policies, and secure the reactions of foremen.

Individual employees of the Charleston Group Companies receive information direct from their immediate supervisor in workplace meetings. This is the lowest level of downward communication from management and the source of upward communication from employees.

An annual supervisor's forum gives officers of the parent company an opportunity to discuss the system's accomplishments, financial condition, customer growth, competition, and other phases of operations with supervisors. A question and answer period, following reports by system officers, gives supervisors an opportunity to get further information on subjects of interest to them. Supervisors pass along information from this forum to individual employees.

Special employee meetings and film presentations are held periodically by top-management officials to give employees more detailed information on new gas appliances, rate matters, economic subjects, and public relations. Employees attending these meetings are given an opportunity to question officers on subjects which the employees do not understand.

Veteran employees of twenty-five or more years of service meet once a year at five locations for luncheon with the president and other officials of the company. These meetings, at which awards for long service are presented, provide an opportunity for informal discussion between top management and employees.

Through an employee social club, the company sponsors picnics in the summer months for retired employees in their operating territory. On these occasions, top management renews acquaintance with former employees and discusses company progress.

Supervisors meet regularly with individual salaried employees for a personal appraisal of their progress and performance. These informal appraisal interviews give employees an opportunity to ask questions, make comments, and offer suggestions.

Printed Communications to Supervisors and Foremen

Supervisors and foremen are continuously informed about company developments through a series of letters, news bulletins, and manuals prepared by the public relations department.

"Supervisor's Newsletter" is published monthly by the public relations department for 475 supervisors to inform them of the latest happenings within the company and local and national developments that affect the company. This medium is used as reference material by supervisors in their conversations with employees and the public.

"Safety News Bulletin" written by the safety department and edited by the public relations department is published monthly for 600 supervisors and safety committeemen responsible for safety. This bulletin reports accidents, tells how they could have been prevented, and describes safety practices discussed at recent safety meetings.

"Rate Situation Manual" prepared by the public relations department gives local and district managers all available up-to-date information about rate schedules so that they can answer questions asked by employees and the public about the company's rates.

"Public Affairs Manual" gives employees information concerning important legislation affecting the company. It is a part of the company's Public Affairs Program designed to make known to employees the position of the company on legislation pending before Congress and the state legislatures.

"Supervisor's Manual" is designed to aid supervisors at all levels of supervision in interpreting company policies and procedures to employees. It is published by the employee relations department and distributed to selected supervisors.

The public relations responsibilities of each local office are described in the "Community Contact Plan" prepared by the public relations department to keep local managers aware of the importance of keeping the public informed about the company's operations.

Labor negotiations letters are sent to supervisors during labor contract negotiations, reporting meetings between company and union representatives. During the year, letters on grievance decisions are also sent to all supervisors.

Printed Communications to Nonsupervisory Employees

Printed communications with rank-and-file employees includes a wide variety of media such as booklets, reports, letters, a magazine, bulletin boards, contests, and pay envelope inserts.

An Employee Induction Program provides new employees with information concerning their new place of employment, its policies and people. It is designed to gain interest and good will of the new employee during the first crucial period of his employment. An Employee Induction Kit includes a booklet, "This Is Our Company," which describes company policy on hours of work, holidays, fringe benefits, vacations, company operations, sick leave, and other pertinent information.

"The Pipeline" employee magazine is published bimonthly by the public relations department to keep employees posted on important developments within the company and new construction, benefits, retirements, and promotions. It is mailed directly to the homes of 3,200 employees.

"Employee Letters" are used to keep workers informed about fast-breaking company developments such as rate filing, changes in personnel, and mergers. They are mailed at the same time as news releases to the press.

A handy "Data Card" giving basic information about the company is mailed annually to every employee. It is designed to be carried by the employee in his billfold or purse and is used for quick reference in answering questions from the public about the company.

The annual and quarterly financial reports made by the parent company to stockholders, carrying current financial statements and information regarding stockholders' meetings, election of officers and financings, are mailed to all employees.

A continuous series of contests designed to inform employees about gas appliances, fringe benefits, and company operations are conducted by the public relations department. Over 40 per cent of all employees compete in these contests for gas appliances, luggage, and other useful gifts.

Bulletin boards in offices, compressor stations, and other facilities are an important medium of communications with employees. The boards are kept current, uncluttered, and used exclusively for company information.

Employee relations booklets explaining the company's fringe benefits and the advantages that employees and their dependents enjoy through membership in various insurance, thrift, and retirement plans are distributed to all employees.

Booklets and folders on special subjects of interest to employees, such as the extent of gas reserves in the United States and an application for a rate increase, are published and distributed to all employees by the public relations department.

"Check-O-Gram," a pay envelope insert, carries brief news items about company operations so that employees are able to discuss the business more effectively with friends and neighbors.

Evaluation of Employee Communications

To improve employee communications through continuous evaluation and more effective procedures, the president of Charleston Group Companies appointed a staff committee on communications composed of the director of public relations, the director of employee relations, and manager of distribution operations. This committee meets twice a month to review employee communications, evaluate media, and improve the program.

This employee communications program, in the opinion of management, has improved employee morale and performance. The company has experienced less absenteeism, less overtime, a friendlier labor climate, and a better safety record. Employees are enthusiastic about the program. Better communications with the external public have also resulted from well-informed employees telling the company's story to their friends and neighbors.

QUESTIONS

1. What is your opinion of the Charleston Group Companies' employee communications program? Give your reasons for approving or disapproving of this program.
2. Discuss the company's Employee Communications through Meetings Program. What improvements can you suggest for this part of the employee communication program?
3. Discuss the company's Printed Communications to Supervisors and Foremen. What improvements can you suggest for this part of the program?
4. Discuss the company's Printed Communications to Nonsupervisory Employees. What improvements can you suggest for this part of the program?

Problem 6–1

EMPLOYEE RELATIONS

Employee Communication—Logan, Richards Corporation

The Logan, Richards Corporation was established in 1890 in Jackson, Michigan, to manufacture mattresses and box springs. The business grew rapidly and additional plants were established in Oklahoma City, Memphis, Los Angeles, and Atlanta. A line of living-room furniture, including upholstered chairs and couches, was added in 1935. After World War II a complete line of steel furniture—bureaus, desks, chairs, and side tables for hotels, motels, and hospitals was introduced. Annual sales are about $130 million. The corporation has foreign subsidiaries with manufacturing facilities located in Canada, Brazil, Mexico, Venezuela, France, and England.

The corporation employs 8,600 men and women in its various plants and offices in the United States and in foreign countries. Of this number, 6,000 own stock in the company. In other words, 20 per cent of the total number of shareholders are employees of the company.

Relations with employees are the responsibility of three staff departments at headquarters: personnel, industrial relations, and public relations. The public relations department is responsible for insuring continuous and effective communications between management and employees. It disseminates information about the company's activities for the purpose of improving employee understanding of the political and economic factors that affect the company and employees, establishing the mutual interests of the company and its employees and encouraging public relations work by employees with their friends and the public.

The public relations staff of ten specialists in communication is headed by a director of public relations who reports to the president. Four sections of the public relations department are devoted to: press relations, stockholder relations, consumer relations, and employee relations. The employee relations section is responsible for communications with employees. The principal medium of employee communication is a quarterly magazine, the *L.R. Times,* published for all employees of the corporation and its subsidiary companies. Most of the editorial material for this 64-page periodical is written by staff members, with photographic and art work provided by free-lance illustrators. In addition to *L.R. Times,* five monthly employee newspapers are published, one at each of the five plants of the corporation. The *L.R. Record* is published for employees of the Jackson plant; the *L.R. News* for Oklahoma City plant employees; the *L.R. Bulletin* for employees at the Memphis plant; the *L.R. Herald* for workers in the Los Angeles plant; and the *L.R. Review* for Atlanta plant employees.

Each of these plant employee publications is edited by an employee of each plant who reports to the plant manager. Each of these newspapers is 16 pages, tabloid size. It is primarily published to report company activities and developments but it also devotes considerable space to employee personals, promotions, retirements, births, marriages, and plant social and athletic events.

The employee relations section of the headquarters public relations department at Jackson distributes to each of the plant editors an editorial and photographic service, reporting company operations, new products, finances, and organizational changes. This service is mailed monthly to plant editors who may use, rewrite, or file the material for future use.

In spite of the fact that the corporation is spending in the neighborhood of a quarter million dollars annually on these six employee publications, the management is not satisfied with this as the most suitable method of employee communication. There is a recognized need for an employee communication program that not only informs employees but also has an impact on the opinions of their families. Management believes that employees can be a substantial help in securing public understanding and good will for the corporation if the workers were properly informed about the policies, practices, and plans of the business.

A committee of executives was formed to consider the existing relationships with employees and submit recommendations to management in respect to communications. Inquiries were made into what other companies were doing to improve communications with employees. However, nothing so far has been done and no decisions have been made in respect to improving the employee communication program. Recognizing that effective communications with employees is essential to the stability and progress of the business, the president decided to engage a well-known opinion research organization to find out what employees think about the communications of the corporation.

A personal interview survey was made by the research organization which questioned 800 employees at the Jackson, Oklahoma City, Memphis, Los Angeles, and Atlanta plants. Participants in the survey were selected at random at each plant and asked a series of questions on three areas of communication: (1) Communications in general, to determine how well the employee thought he was being informed. (2) Employee publications, to learn what employees thought of *L.R. Times* and their local plant newspaper. (3) Employee views about economic and financial conditions at Logan, Richards Corporation.

Employees were asked if they wanted more information from management about the company and its operations. More than 60 per cent of all workers questioned said that they wanted more information than they were getting about company developments and progress.

Since employees wanted more information, it was important to find out what the workers wanted to hear more about. More than 80 per cent of the employees questioned wanted to know more about the company's plans for the future. Subjects about which workers said that they wanted more information, in order of preference, were: job transfers and new job opportunities; prospects for steady work; practices and policies affecting workers; taxes and government practices affecting the company and employees; company union relations; work other company plants were doing; how the United States business system operates; economic information; company operations in foreign countries; company benefit plans; how the company is doing financially; and how each employee's work fits into the overall operations of the company.

Employees were asked from what sources they preferred to receive the above information. The information sources preferred by employees in order of their preference were: the employee's own supervisor, letters from management, employee meetings, the *L.R. Times*, employee plant newspaper, bulletin boards, and local community newspapers. Responses showed clearly that the supervisor was the main channel or preferred source of information. Employees said that they were not receiving as much information as they wanted from their supervisors, whereas supervisors said that they wanted more information from management.

The opinions of employees were secured about the quarterly employee magazine, *L.R. Times.* Eighty per cent of all workers questioned said that they read every issue or almost every issue. More than half of the respondents said that the magazine was interesting. Forty per cent said that the magazine was of little interest to them. Three out of four respondents said that the magazine was sometimes read by their families. About one half said that the magazine should be published more frequently. More than one fourth of employees responding questioned information they read in *L.R. Times.* Similar responses were received from employees about the monthly newspapers published in each of the five plants. As the employees expressed opinions on more than one question, the percentages on this and the other questions added up to more than 100 per cent.

The interest and understanding of employees on economic questions were investigated in the survey to determine the advisability of discussing economic principles in communications with employees. Thirty per cent of the employees questioned believed that the best way to raise the country's standard of living was by producing more per man hour. An equal number believed that lower prices was the answer. Ten per cent thought that increased wages and 18 per cent believed that lower profits were the surest ways to higher standards of living.

Employees were questioned about Logan, Richards Corporation as a place to work. Sixty per cent said the company was better than average, and 20 per cent felt that the company was one of the best. Seventy per cent thought that there was a good opportunity for people to advance in the organization.

The responses of employees in the survey indicate that the corporation's methods of communicating with employees through the *L.R. Times* and five plant newspapers are very satisfactory, in the opinion of the president of the company. He believes that the survey proved that the readership and employee interest in *L.R. Times* is high. He favors the magazine because it is issued regularly every ninety days and gains strength by repetition of accounts of the company's progress. It provides sufficient space to enable management to tell a complete story. The physical appearance of the magazine is impressive. The five plant newspapers also have many of these advantages, according to the president. He favors continuing use of these communicating media in the employee relations program.

A company magazine and plant newspapers alone do not insure an effective communication program, in the opinion of the personnel manager of the company. He stated that the survey of employee communication showed that 65 per cent of the employees questioned preferred to secure information about the company from their own supervisors as well as other sources. He questions the effectiveness of *L.R. Times* as 40 per cent of the employees surveyed said that the magazine was of little interest to them; and more than one fourth questioned information they read in the *L.R. Times*.

The plant employee magazines fail to make known the views of management on important questions affecting the employee welfare, in the opinion of the personnel manager. They lack originality and imagination and are little more than a collection of old jokes and trivial personals.

The survey indicated that more thorough economic education of employees was needed due to misunderstandings by employees of the finances, profits, and sales of the corporation, as well as how the business system operates. The personnel director believes that employee magazines should be used in this economic education but that other educational media should be employed also to secure the economic understanding of employees.

The president of Logan, Richards Corporation asked the public relations manager to analyze the responses to the employee communication survey and make recommendations for improving the employee communications of the corporation.

QUESTIONS

1. What specific advantages are to be gained by Logan, Richards Corporation from an effective program of communication with employees?

2. Is the employee communication program of the Logan, Richards Corporation satisfactory? Give reasons for approving or rejecting the existing program.

3. If you believe that the existing employee communication program can be improved, describe the media of communication and techniques which should be used to insure more effective communications.

4. Are the objectives of the employee communications of the corporation as described in the problem satisfactory? What other objectives should be selected?

7 . STOCKHOLDER RELATIONS

MORE THAN fifteen million men and women, more than double in the past decade, own shares in American corporations. This number includes 1,500,000 employees who are buying shares through stock purchase plans. In addition, thousands of banks, insurance, and investment companies are shareholders in corporations.

The increase in the number of shareholders is due to higher personal incomes, the growth of employee stock purchase plans, a rising stock market, better understandng of investment, and concern over inflation.

Not long ago the average publicly owned company could count by the thousands the number of people who were interested in its corporate affairs. Today, the same company has an audience numbering in the hundreds of thousands.

The Stockholder

Formerly, ownership of corporations was in the hands of a few large investors. Today, only about one fourth of all shareholders have incomes above $10,000 a year. About half of the total are in the rapidly growing middle class of incomes, ranging from $5,000 to $10,000.

The typical stockholder is a tradesman, farmer, teacher, mechanic, doctor, or salesman, who owns twenty-five shares or less in one or more companies. More than half of all stockholders are women. The ages of stockholders range from three to eighty-five years. Many have little or no knowledge of finance or accounting. They cannot understand or interpret a balance sheet or a profit and loss statement.

Not only are individuals shareholders of corporations, but numerous groups have large stockholdings and are an important segment of the stockholder public. Fraternal, social, and religious organizations, insurance companies, schools, hospitals, and charities invest millions of dollars of their funds in corporate stocks.

The stockholders of General Motors Corporation illustrate the size and diversity of the owner public. General Motors Corporation, at the end of 1962, had 1,059,000 stockholders: 770,000 were individuals of whom 54 per cent were women; 188,000 joint accounts representing two or more people; and 101,000 institutions. Over 75 per cent of these shareholders held 100 shares or less.

The Investment Community

Most stockholders acquire their shares as a result of information given them by stockbrokers, security analysts, trust officers, bankers, and financial advisors. These individuals comprise what is commonly referred to as "the financial community." They counsel not only individuals but also institutional investors such as banks, insurance companies, pension funds, mutual funds, charitable foundations, universities, hospitals, and other institutions in buying and selling securities.

The stock-in-trade of the investment community is knowledge of which corporate securities, among the many thousands available, represent the best investment opportunity at any given time. The primary function of corporation stockholder relations is to provide the investment community with current information not only about sales and earnings, dividends, and stock splits but the over-all environment of a company including the stability of product prices and profits, new products, new markets, research and development, capability of management, and available capital to take advantage of these opportunities.

Security Analysts

An important individual in the investment community is the security analyst employed by institutional investors, banks, brokerage houses, and insurance companies to keep informed about corporations and individuals so he can give an opinion on the future earnings of a corporation. The number of security analysts is increasing rapidly. Fifteen years ago, the New York Society of Security Analysts had thirty members; today it has 2,700. There are thirty societies with a total membership in excess of 7,000 analysts. The National Federation of Financial Analysts Societies is the national organization of independently operated societies which meet at frequent intervals. The New York Society meets several times a week and others, weekly or monthly.

The stockholder or financial relations section of the public relations department provides security analysts with facts about corporate operations and prospects through printed media, personal contacts, and features. Printed media include the annual report, quarterly reports, informative bulletins, news letters, booklets, speech reprints, financial advertising, and publicity. Personal contacts with analysts are made by corporate treasurers; research, product development, manufacturing executives; and members of the board of directors who address meetings of analysts; and by plant tours and seminars held for analysts. Features used to inform analysts include radio and television programs, motion picture films, exhibits, and distribution of samples of products.

Corporate information sought by analysts includes such basic information as sales, profits, costs, earnings, research and development costs, cash flow, reserves, mergers, inventory changes, foreign operations, labor relations, taxes, new products and markets, new distribution methods, changes in marketing policy, patents, dividend policy, and future plans. On the other hand, corporations should not reveal to analysts premature data on new products, unprotected products or processes, sales and earnings forecasts for stock price purposes, acquisitions or mergers under negotiation, or announcements in advance of employee notification.

The financial relations section of the public relations department should build a list of security analysts particularly interested in the corporation, using the *Directory of Memberships* published by the National Federation of Financial Analysts Societies as a basis.

Investment Clubs

A rapidly growing development in the investment community is the investment club. Tens of thousands of individuals throughout the country are members of investment clubs composed of small groups of friends, neighbors, business associates who regularly invest in corporate securities. Reliable estimates indicate that there are more than 20,000 investment clubs in the United States and their number is increasing rapidly. Investment clubs discuss investment objectives, the principles and techniques of investing, and make investments in corporations after gathering information, recognizing, and weighing the risks involved. Investor relations departments maintain lists of investment clubs and keep them informed through printed media and features about corporation finances and outlook.

What Is Stockholder Relations?

Millions of shareholders want to know how the corporations in which they have invested their funds are progressing. Additional millions who are planning to invest in securities are eager for corporate information. Thousands of banks, insurance and investment companies, and security analysts are seeking data to determine how and where to expand their portfolios.

To provide shareholders and the investment community with corporate information is an important function of public relations. Never before has so much been invested by corporations in keeping corporate audiences supplied with information about companies' current performance and future prospects. A stockholder who has a portfolio of ten or twelve stocks will be getting mail from one of the companies every three or four days, according to an official of a large corporation. Stockholder relations begins with a letter of welcome when an investor buys a stock and ends with a letter of regret when he sells out.

However, in spite of the rising tide of stockholder communications, many corporations do not recognize the importance of cultivating shareholders and keeping them informed and happy. This lack of interest in communicating with stockholders arises from several of the following assumptions. Shareholders have no other interest in corporate affairs as long as they get regular dividends. Stockholders are of all ages and both sexes with widely varying levels of business knowledge and education, many unable to understand a financial statement. The finances of a corporation should not be revealed to shareholders to prevent disclosure to competitors. Investors receive too much information, too many figures to digest, too many charts and photographs to look at. Most stockholder communications go into the wastebasket unnoticed. Stockholders are often critical of management, misunderstand its motives, and seek to organize opposition. Shareholders are not interested in corporate problems and few attend annual or regional stockholders' meetings.

The indifference, lack of understanding, and antagonism of some shareholders may be attributed to management's deficiency in stockholder communications. Management's efforts to communicate with the financial community are often ineffective because of fear of revealing secret information. Top executives are silent, reticent, or vague in speaking to stockholders. Printed media are not clear, concise, or interesting. However, as more corporations are appreciating the importance of good investor relations and giving more attention to communications, the interest of shareholders in corporate affairs is rising.

Objectives of Stockholder Relations

The objectives of a comprehensive stockholder relations program are: To build stockholder interest in the corporation. To create a better understanding between the company, its shareholders, and the financial community. To encourage stockholders to consume the products of the company or to recommend their purchase. To reduce the turnover among shareholders and promote holding of stock as a long-term investment. To reduce criticism, misunderstanding, and organized opposition to management by stockholders. To help stabilize the market for a company's securities. To raise the prestige of a corporation in the eyes of the community at large through enhancing its standing among its owners. To reflect and interpret to management the public attitude toward a company and serve as a barometer of public opinion. To win the allegiance and support of stockholders as a sound and durable basis for continued operating control by management. To secure the support of shareholders as a source of new capital—stockholders will either supply the money needed or approve fund-raising plans. To champion the cause of democracy by discussing the benefits of the free enterprise system with stockholders and, through them, reach the general public. To create new investor interest in the company and raise additional capital more readily and less expensively. To secure favorable recommendation of company securities by investment counselors and security analysts. To gain shareholder support for community relations projects.

The objectives of the stockholder relations program of the Borden Company, producers and distributors of dairy products, are to maintain a sound relationship with stockholders by: reporting to them fully and factually all pertinent information about the company; encouraging and expediting their support of company activities; providing special service in handling their inquiries and requests; and maintaining interest in the company's securities, and an active market for them, by informing the financial community and financial press of pertinent company developments.

The objectives of the stockholder relations of General Mills, Inc., are to stimulate interest on the part of its stockholders, to try to awaken them to the responsibilities of ownership, and to emphasize the stockholder's responsibility to management. An important though secondary benefit from stockholder co-operation is the word-of-mouth salesmanship which owners can give to company products.

Responsibility for Stockholder Relations

As the chairman of the board and president of a corporation are responsible to the stockholders, a stockholder relations program should have their general direction.

In corporations with a limited number of stockholders, the secretary or clerk of the corporation is usually responsible for carrying on correspondence with stockholders, arranging for the annual meeting, reporting the proceedings, and handling all stockholder relations.

However, corporations with a large and increasing number of share-holders assign responsibility for stockholder relations to the public relations department, which consults with the secretary and other corporation officers concerned with finance in planning stockholder communications. These officers and a representative of public relations may sit on a stockholder relations committee.

When the number of stockholders is limited, the director of public relations with secretarial assistance handles relations with stockholders.

In large corporations, a stockholder section is established in the public relations department directed by a stockholder relations manager on the staff of the public relations manager. For the past ten years, General Electric Company has centralized responsibility for stockholder relations in the Investor Relations Section of the Relations Services Department.

Stockholder Relations Policy

The objectives of a stockholder relations program are expressed in a policy of stockholder relations to serve as a guide to management and all who work in stockholder relations. An example of a good stockholder relations policy follows:

We believe that a successful business is one that is conducted in the interests of its stockholders, employees, consumers, and the general public.

We will encourage our stockholders to express opinions on matters of mutual concern and will give their opinions full consideration.

We believe that our stockholders have the right to know how management is conducting their business.

We will do our best to provide as complete information about the business as we believe stockholders want, consistent with the best interests of the company.

We believe that our stockholders should have a special interest in buying and promoting our products. We will encourage the use of our products by our stockholders and, through them, by their friends.

We believe widely held ownership of our stock will help promote confidence in the company and the economic system. We will seek continuously to broaden public interest in this company as an investment.

CONDUCTING A STOCKHOLDER RELATIONS PROGRAM

Surveying Stockholder Opinions

How stockholders regard the policies and progress of a corporation is of major importance to management in furthering relations with owners. An increasing number of corporations are trying to learn the views of their owners and improve communications with them by means of well-planned shareholder surveys. These surveys are conducted by mail and by personal interviews. The American Telephone and Telegraph Company and Western Union Telegraph Company carry on continuous surveys by personal interviews with shareholders in order to improve their communications with them. Western Union pioneered its visiting-the-stockholder program some thirty years ago.

The principal methods of conducting stockholder opinion surveys are mailed questionnaires and personal interviews by the stockholder relations section of the public relations department, by management officials, or by an outside opinion research organization. In the past six years some 250,000 stockholders of American Telephone and Telegraph Company have had good will visits from local Bell System management people. Opinions of shareholders are also expressed informally in annual meetings, regional meetings, open houses for shareholders, and in correspondence.

Typical questions asked shareholders in a mail survey by a large corporation were: How did you originally acquire your stock? How many shares of our stock do you own? Is the stock held by an individual, jointly, corporation, institution, estate, or trust fund? Why are you holding the stock? Would you buy more stock in this company? Do you own other stocks beside those of our company? Did you receive the company's annual report? If so, did you read it? What did you like about it? Dislike? Do you think the company is giving you enough information about its activities? How would you express your opinion of the management of your company? Do you use our products? Did you notice the ads enclosed with your last report? What did you think of them? Please give us the following information about yourself—sex, age, occupation, income, and income derived from investments.

Surveys of stockholder attitudes and interests indicate subjects about which stockholders want more information, misconceptions which should be corrected, shareholder opinion of management, and the effectiveness of a corporation's communications with owners. Responses suggest topics which should be discussed in annual reports, annual meetings, stockholders' magazine, shareholder advertisements, films, booklets, and other media of communication with owners.

Surveying Stockholder Characteristics

Effective communication with shareholders requires an understanding of the characteristics of the shareholder public. Analysis may be made of corporate stock records to determine number of shareholders by size of holdings; number of individuals; number of women; number of joint tenancy accounts; number of institutions and groups such as estates and trusts, insurance companies, foundations, employee benefit funds, and colleges; number of employee shareholders; geographical distribution, length of time shares are owned, and other information about shareholders.

In addition to securing information about stockholders from analysis of corporate stock records, mail surveys and personal interviews are used to secure facts about the age, occupation, earned income, income from investments, marital status, education, product ownership, readership of corporate communications, and other facts about individual shareholders which cannot be learned from stock records.

Nation-wide surveys of stockholders of American corporations by Opinion Research Corporation reveals that the stockholder public is a mass audience with 77 per cent having incomes of less than $10,000, 70 per cent have no college degree, and 53 per cent are women. The limited investment knowledge of shareholders is revealed by these surveys which show that while 78 per cent can give an accurate definition of "profits" and 59 per cent can define "dividends," only 26 per cent can define "bonds," 12 per cent can define "stock option," 5 per cent can explain "debentures," and 1 per cent can define "paid-in-surplus." Only a relatively small proportion of investors seek financial information with 5 per cent subscribing to a financial service of any kind, only 23 per cent consulting a broker for advice, and only 45 per cent reading a financial publication or the financial pages of a daily newspaper. Readership of annual reports runs as high as 65 per cent to 70 per cent but in many cases falls below the 50 per cent level.

By obtaining a better understanding of the shareholder public, communication problems may be solved more readily. Specific groups of shareholders may be singled out for special communications, the most suitable media of communication used, and the language of shareholder communications adapted to the educational and interest levels of the audience.

What Stockholders Want to Know

Surveys show that stockholders are interested in the following information about their corporations in which they have invested: characteristics of the stockholder group; labor relations, including wages, contract negotiations, benefit plans, and training; foreign operations, including export sales, plants, branches, foreign exchange situation, and executive personnel; advertising and public relations, including media used, radio and television programs, and trend of advertising expenditures; executive personnel changes, promotions, and deaths; legislation affecting the business, including tariffs, taxes, and labor;

litigations, such as antitrust suits, liabilities, patents, and rates; subsidiary companies' profits, dividends, and sales; raw material supplies, prices, and quality; history of the company, including executive personalities, growth, and subsidiaries; future corporate outlook, including wages, material and equipment costs, and demand and income trend; research, including new laboratories, process improvements, and product developments; profits and the financial outlook; current company problems; products and services; new products; research; company outlook; government relations; and pricing policy.

Fundamentals of Stockholder Communications

Communications with stockholders are most effective if the following principles are observed:

Information should be presented to stockholders in simple, clearly understood, nontechnical terms. Stockholder communications should be continuous. The investor relations consultant of a large corporation says, "We have a responsibility to the person who owns our stock today, who may buy today, or who may sell today."

Financial information is dull and uninteresting reading to most people. The techniques that are used effectively in popular magazines should be employed to gain attention and to arouse the interest of readers of stockholder communications.

Personal contact between management and stockholders is essential to the best stockholder relations. Printed media cannot take the place of personal contact.

Management should tell shareholders both sides of its business story—the bad news as well as the good.

Communications with stockholders should be based on knowledge of shareowners' characteristics, attitudes, and interests as revealed by continuous surveys.

MEDIA OF COMMUNICATION WITH STOCKHOLDERS

The media of communication with stockholders are: printed, audio, visual, oral, and a combination of these methods. Effective communications include media which provide for a two-way communication to obtain the views of shareholders as well as to give them information they desire.

Printed Methods of Communication with Stockholders

Communications with stockholders through printed media are: annual reports, interim reports, notices of annual and regional meetings, stockholder magazine, dividend and annual report advertising, stockholder correspondence, financial publicity, special offers to stockholders, booklets and folders, promotional literature, reports of stockholders' meetings, stockholder contests, employee-stockholder communications.

The Annual Report. The corporation annual report is the primary medium of communication in stockholder relations. It is also a medium of communication with employee, community, distributor, and supplier publics. In some corporations, the annual report merely serves to comply with legal requirements that the company publish an income statement and balance sheet.

However, an increasing number of companies are publishing comprehensive annual reports which discuss not only financial status but production, marketing, research, products, personnel affairs of the company.

The appearance of annual reports has been enhanced with dramatic photography, color printing, good writing, clear charts, and simplified financial statements that make annual reports compete in interest and attractiveness with modern magazines.

Annual reports of leading corporations show that they include the following features:

Financial Information. Summary of financial operations; statement of income; auditor's report; statement of financial position; long-term debt; cash flow in and out; amount spent for facilities; per cent income of sales versus per cent of operations; comparative operating and financial story for past years; earnings and dividends; investments, working capital, current assets, and current liabilities; taxes; funded debt; distribution of income and sources of capital expenditures and dividends; past years' summary of changes in working capital; cash dividends for past years; increase in sales and in property, plant, and equipment; growing number of stockholders; investment per employee; sales; earnings retained in the business; statement of earnings for past years; highlights of the last decade; division of the sales dollar.

Production Information. Inventories, plant equipment, manufacturing plants' operations, research, raw materials, plant facilities, new products, divisions and subsidiaries, transportation, production of raw material, production and shipments, rising wage costs, new and improved equipment, raw material prices, storage facilities, location of plants.

Marketing Information. Sales volume, foreign operations, warehousing, advertising, marketing, prices, price methods, supply and distribution, public relations, service, consumer relations, sales promotion, publicity.

Personnel Information. Directors and officers, employee benefit plans, employment data, organization changes, union relations, employees, employee relations, employment—hours and wages, pensions and insurance, employee safety, employee training, strikes, employee co-operative associations, fringe benefits, women's aid, fifty-year service buttons, labor, payroll, promotions.

Miscellaneous Information. Government relations—litigation, taxes, legislation; economics—business outlook, problems and opportunities, the future, inflation, circulation of cash; general—letter from the president, stockholder meetings, announcement of annual meeting, special problems.

Physical Features of Annual Reports. The customary page size of annual reports is 8½ × 11 inches, although a few are 7 × 9½ inches over all. The standard 8½ × 11 inch size is convenient for filing and affords more space for illustrations, charts, and maps. They have from 25 to 48 pages.

Illustrations include photographs of personnel, executives, plants, offices, production facilities, directors, products, and new construction. Graphs are used to show trends of earnings, dividends, production, sales, and stockholders. Bar charts show earnings, dividends, distribution of income, number of employees, and payroll costs. Pie charts indicate distribution of the sales dollar and disposal of assets. Figure charts show number of stockholders, employees, and units of production. Maps show location of plants and branches, distribution, and foreign subsidiaries or sales.

A survey of female stockholder preferences in an annual report by the Graphics Institute, New York, showed that 69 per cent favored text plus charts and photographs; 17 per cent, text plus charts; 9 per cent all text and no illustrations; and 5 per cent text plus photographs. Readership of annual reports by women questioned in this survey indicated that 47 per cent read parts of the report; 33 per cent read thoroughly; 26 per cent leaf through; and 6 per cent do not read.

Annual reports are sometimes published in unique form to secure attention and get an interested reading by shareholders. Annual reports may be made in the form of plastic phonograph records on which the president discusses progress of the company. An annual report may be the recording of a directors' meeting to give shareholders a review of accomplishments and information about the company. American Can Company packaged its annual report in a tin can. The American Telephone and Telegraph Company publishes a Braille edition of its annual report for reading by blind shareholders.

An annual report should have a central theme that serves to unify the various features of the report such as an anniversary or national advertising theme.

Annual reports present the principal features in the following order: Illustrated front cover featuring the theme of the report—exterior or interior of plant, products, consumers, or a dealer. Inside front cover— illustration of raw materials and products. Title page and table of contents. Highlights of the report—a summary of important facts about the company, finances, and operations. The president's or chairman's letter summarizing accomplishments. Financial review of the year. Nonfinancial review, including personnel, plants, equipment, research, products, stockholders, and advertising.

Distribution of Annual Report.   In addition to stockholders, an annual report should be distributed to television and radio commentators, editors and special financial writers for daily, weekly, and Sunday newspapers, financial publications, business magazines, and labor publications. Educational institutions, colleges, libraries, and people of influence in the community should also receive the annual report. Bankers, investment trust officers, brokers, and security analysts, who influence the sale of corporate securities, should be informed about the company through the annual report.

Local, state, and federal officials, senators, representatives, and heads of government bureaus, suppliers of materials or merchandise for resale, along with distributors and dealers, leading competitors, and trade associations should receive the annual report.

Employees of a corporation should get the annual report as published for stockholders or in a special simplified edition. It may also be reproduced in the employee magazine or published in plant city newspapers.

Interim Reports.   In the interval between annual reports, corporations communicate with stockholders through interim reports in the form of dividend enclosures, quarterly newsletters, folders, booklets, and bulletins. Most of these interim reports are devoted primarily to reporting earnings, statements, and recent dividend action. Many companies also cover in these reports important developments of interest to shareholders.

Notices of Annual and Regional Stockholders' Meetings.   Annual meetings of stockholders are usually required by law for the election of directors and to transact other business. Notices of such meetings are mailed to stockholders together with a proxy form on which absentee stockholders may vote for directors and on matters to be voted upon at the annual meeting. When regional stockholders' meetings are held, invitations are mailed to all stockholders.

Stockholder Magazine. An increasing number of corporations are publishing stockholder magazines and quarterly reports to interpret company policies and problems, and secure understanding and support of stockholders. In addition to financial news these periodicals discuss new products, plants and laboratories, research, and other subjects of interest to stockholders.

Stockholder periodicals are published by General Mills, Inc., "Horizons"; Union Carbide Corporation, "Stockholder News"; E. I. du Pont de Nemours & Co., "DuPont Stockholder"; Johns-Manville Corporation, "J. M. Stockholders' News"; Consolidated Edison Company of New York, "News and Views for Stockholders"; Westinghouse Electric Corporation, "Westinghouse Stockholders' Quarterly"; General Electric Company, "Shareowners Quarterly"; General Motors, "Shareholders Quarterly"; Sun Oil Company, "Shareholders Quarterly"; Pittsburgh Plate Glass Company, "Shareholder News Briefs."

Annual Report Advertisements. In addition to dividend advertisements, an increasing number of corporations are placing annual report advertising in national consumer magazines and newspapers in plant cities. Annual report advertisements, giving the highlights of financial operations, build prestige for a company in the community and interest small investors in corporate shares.

Share Ownership Advertising. A growing number of corporations are advertising in magazines to increase share ownership. These advertisements emphasize the investing public's role in our free and expanding economy. Public Service Company of Colorado, Iowa Power and Light Company, Union Oil Company, among others, are advertising share ownership.

Stockholder Correspondence. Individual correspondence with stockholders is an important factor in good stockholder relations. Correspondence with shareholders begins with a letter of welcome to the new stockholder from the president, and ends only when a stockholder sells his interest and receives a letter of regret, with an expression of hope that the former stockholder will soon again be numbered among the company's owners. Corporations that carry on extensive correspondence with shareholders are: The Borden Company, Standard Oil Company of California, International Petroleum Corporation, and others.

Financial Publicity. The stockholder relations section of the public relations department communicates much information about the company to stockholders and the general public through the medium of press releases to financial editors of magazines and newspapers, the press services, and radio and television commentators. Newsworthy financial releases include dividend declarations, annual and quarterly reports, new financing, mergers, annual and regional stockholders' meetings, organization changes, and employment figures.

Financial news releases are also distributed to financial services, investment counselors, brokerage concerns, and banks, which issue periodicals and reports to investors.

Gifts and Special Offers to Stockholders. Corporations making consumer goods gain stockholder good will, advertising, and patronage through various types of product offers, including gift packages of several products, Christmas Gift offers, special reduced prices to stockholders, and samples of new products. Minnesota Mining and Manufacturing Company gives new stockholders a kit of its tapes, ribbons, and sandpaper which would retail at $5.00.

Stockholder Booklets and Folders. Many companies keep stockholders informed about their operations through periodic mailings of booklets and folders. These publications cover a wide range of subjects including company management, personnel, products, production facilities, plants, the industrial outlook, and executive speeches. On anniversaries a commemorative history of the corporation is distributed to stockholders and other publics.

Promotional Literature. To inform stockholders about the company's advertising and products, promotional literature may be enclosed with stockholder correspondence or dividend mailings. Catalogues, booklets, folders, and proof sheets of advertisements are distributed to stockholders.

Reports of Stockholders' Meetings. The wide geographical distribution of shareholders of a corporation prevents all but a relatively small number from attending shareholder meetings. Stockholders who are unable to attend annual or regional meetings are mailed a postmeeting report of the proceedings. Some companies devote an issue of their stockholder magazine to a word and picture story of stockholder meeting proceedings, condensed speeches by executives, and illustrations of stockholders and executives taking part in the program.

General Motors Corp., General Electric Co., National Dairy Products Corp., Abbott Laboratories, Standard Oil Company, N.J. are among the many companies that publish postmeeting reports.

Stockholder Contests. Stockholders are encouraged to participate more actively in the affairs of their companies by means of contests offering suitable prizes for the best constructive criticism and suggestions on the operations of the company. A large radio manufacturer staged a "Stockholder of the Year" contest for the best letter suggesting improvements in company operations and policies. The winner was awarded a trip to headquarters as a guest of the company to meet executives, visit the factory, enjoy a week of entertainment, and receive a television and radio console at a banquet.

Employee Stockholder Communications. More than a million and a half employees of 233 companies whose stock is listed on the New York Stock Exchange participate in a variety of employee stock purchase plans. Communication with employee stockholders is getting more consideration by corporations whose employees are shareholders. The employee periodical is the principal medium, along with the annual report and booklets. The significance of stock acquisition programs has been described in employee magazines of Standard Oil Co., California; National Biscuit Company; Delta Air Lines, and others. Typical shareholder articles in employee magazines are titled: "You and Our Annual Report," "Where Did the Net Profits Go?" "Birth of An Annual Report," and "The Annual Meeting."

Audio-visual Methods of Communication with Stockholders

Stockholder Films. Motion pictures featuring company operations are included in many comprehensive stockholder relations programs. Films, based upon a corporation's annual report, make it possible for owners to visualize the progress of the business. A film can dramatize the teamwork of the producers of raw materials, employees who turn these materials into products, customers who buy these products, and stockholders whose investments make the business possible.

Television. A closed-circuit television broadcast of the annual stockholders' meeting to regional meetings of shareholders in other parts of the country makes it possible for more shareholders to participate in the annual meeting. American Machine and Foundry Company has televised its annual meetings.

Oral Methods of Communicating with Stockholders and the Financial Community

The principal oral methods of communicating with stockholders and the financial community are: annual stockholders' meetings, regional stockholders' meetings, open houses or plant tours, and meetings with members of the financial community. Printed communications with stockholders cannot substitute for personal relations in establishing effective two-way communications between management and shareholders.

Annual Stockholders' Meeting. By the laws of the state in which a corporation is incorporated, stockholders have the opportunity to exercise their rights at an annual meeting at which directors are elected, reports of executives are heard, and business is transacted. Annual meetings of corporations are often perfunctory affairs attended princi-

FIG. 7–1. Annual stockholders meeting of Standard Oil Company, New Jersey.

pally by the officers and a handful of larger shareholders. However, the increasing number of shareholders and interest in better stockholder relations is making the annual meeting an important corporate event. It provides an opportunity for the chief executives of a corporation to establish friendly, personal contacts with the people who are supplying the money to operate the business.

Annual meetings are usually held in the state in which the business is incorporated. However, more companies are holding the annual meeting in cities in areas where a large number of shareholders are located to encourage larger attendance. International Harvester Company broke a forty-nine-year tradition by moving its annual meeting from Hoboken,

New Jersey, to Chicago. Box lunches were formerly served, but this practice is being discontinued. Programs are well organized. Attendance of stockholders is encouraged. The meetings, instead of being dull, are informal, friendly, and enjoyable occasions.

The order of business at a typical annual stockholders' meeting includes: call to order by the chairman, presentation and examination of proxies, announcement of a quorum present, reading and approval of minutes of previous meeting, presentation of list of stockholders, reports of officers and committees, appointment of inspectors of election, opening of polls, election of directors, closing of polls, report of inspectors, declaration of election of directors, new business, and adjournment.

Novel programs are sometimes arranged for annual meetings. Brunswick Corporation invited stockholders to a Chicago golf course to see a demonstration of its MacGregor Sporting Goods line. American Machine and Foundry Company featured addresses on foreign trade by government representatives from Australia, Japan, Mexico, Pakistan, Turkey, and United Kingdom.

Regional Stockholders' Meetings. To make it possible for more stockholders to attend corporation meetings and participate in company affairs, many companies are holding regional stockholders' meetings at hotels in various parts of the country. Regional stockholders' meetings were pioneered by James F. Bell, founder of General Mills, Inc., in 1938.

Regional meetings are also held in plants located in various parts of the country and are attended by employee shareholders to hear executives discuss the annual report, answer questions, and announce plans for expansion.

Open Houses or Plant Tours for Stockholders. The open house or plant tour is becoming increasingly popular for improving stockholder relations, because it can be used to inform stockholders about the properties, operations, and products of the company and to give them an opportunity to see for themselves how their money is invested. These events feature speeches by executives, product exhibits, and motion pictures.

Open houses are described in detail in later chapters on special events and community relations.

Meetings with Members of the Financial Community. Many corporations arrange periodic meetings with members of the financial community to discuss corporate finances, corporation progress, and to answer questions. Security analysts, bankers, investment counselors, brokers, as well as the financial press are invited to hear the chairman, president, and other officers discuss corporate finances and the investment outlook for the corporation's securities. These meetings are supplemented with tours of the company's facilities, demonstrations of new products, and motion pictures.

The Texas Eastern Transmission Corporation, which moves a billion dollars worth of natural gas and oil by pipeline annually, holds annual meetings of financial analysts who specialize in natural gas stocks at the company's headquarters in Shreveport, Louisiana. Socony-Mobil Oil Company has run a series of seminars for security analysts in New York, Chicago, and Boston. Principal railroads regularly take analysts on trips over their lines.

Directors' Part in Stockholder Relations

Directors who are elected by the stockholders of a corporation to represent their interests are important factors in stockholder relations, as well as in the entire public relations program. Directors are usually important businessmen in position to influence public opinion favorably and serve as valuable public relations ambassadors.

Directors should be invited to attend annual and regional shareholder meetings, receive the annual report, interim reports, stockholder magazine, proofs of all financial publication advertising, special offers to stockholders, booklets, folders, promotional literature, and reports of stockholders' meetings. Directors should be kept continuously informed about the corporation's public relations program and its objectives.

Case 7–1

STOCKHOLDER RELATIONS

Texas Eastern Transmission Corporation

The Texas Eastern Transmission Corporation, Houston, Texas, owns and operates two natural gas and petroleum pipeline systems, one a 6,613 mile natural gas line extending from the Mexican border to New York City and the second, a 2,182 mile common carrier petroleum products pipeline system extending from the Houston-Beaumont, Texas, area to Chicago, Illinois, and Lebanon, Ohio, and through an interconnection with another system serves Detroit and Cleveland. The corporation is also engaged in exploring for and producing crude oil, natural gas, and in oil refining and natural gas processing. Texas Eastern also owns a substantial interest in Algonquin Gas Transmission Company which operates a 254 mile pipeline system from New York to Connecticut, Rhode Island, and Massachusetts.

The corporation supplies natural gas to 67 gas companies located in Louisiana,

Mississippi, Arkansas, Tennessee, Missouri, Illinois, Alabama, Kentucky, Indiana, Ohio, West Virginia, Pennsylvania, New York, and New Jersey through its own pipeline system.

The public relations of the corporation is the responsibility of a staff of sixteen located at headquarters and headed by a public relations director who reports to the financial vice-president. This staff organization is divided into two sections: community-stockholder relations and publications. Each section is headed by a manager who reports to the director of public relations. An advertising agency and public relations counsel provide outside counsel and services to the department.

A major function of the public relations department is communication with the some 70,000 shareholders of the corporation, security analysts, investment firms, banks, and financial publications. An annual report, interim reports, a quarterly magazine, *The Inch,* and a statistical yearbook covering the corporation's operations for the past ten years comprise the media of communication with shareholders and the financial community.

In 1959, the corporation decided to expand its stockholder relations program by initiating a series of seminars to inform security analysts, investment bankers, financial counsellors, stockbrokers, insurance companies, and the financial community about the natural gas industry and Texas Eastern's operations.

The investment analyst, in the opinion of the management, is playing an increasingly important role as an investment opinion leader and advisor of banks, brokerage houses, investment trusts, and insurance companies on the financial condition and potential of companies seeking funds. The views of analysts are given careful consideration by individual stockholders and institutions which are considering buying shares of common stock, preferred stock, or other securities of a particular company. The recommendations of security analysts frequently determine decisions to buy, hold, or sell a particular stock.

In order to determine the potential of a specific industry or company security analysts must be well informed about its financial history, organization, operations, and management. Texas Eastern Transmission Corporation recognizes that it is to its advantage to give analysts this information and to create a better understanding between the corporation and the financial community.

To improve communication with the financial community, the corporation began in 1959 to hold a series of educational seminars for security analysts. Small groups of analysts are invited to the company for a four-day meeting. The seminars are held in Shreveport, Louisiana, the center of the $23 billion natural gas industry. The second seminar was held at Shreveport from June 12 to 16, 1960, and applications for future seminars are booked through 1963.

Twenty-seven men and women financial analysts representing nationally known brokerage houses, life insurance companies, banks, and investment trusts from San Francisco to New York and Chicago to Houston attended the Spring, 1960, seminar as guests of Texas Eastern.

The faculty for the seminar comprised thirty members of the top management of the corporation including the president, financial vice-president, senior vice-president gas division, vice-president and chief engineer, vice-president of operations, controller, vice-president production, chief geologist, senior

FIG. 7-2. Field trip of security analysts attending Texas Eastern Transmission Corp. seminar on the gas industry, briefed by experts before going on to a drilling rig to observe at first hand the drilling of a new oil or gas well.

vice-president oil division, vice-president and general counsel, and their assistants.

The four-day session arranged by the public relations department with the advice of management is devoted to 22 hours of classwork in addition to field trips. Classes are held in the modern Shreveporter Motel, commencing at 8:00 in the morning and continuing until 4:30 in the afternoon with coffee breaks and an hour for lunch.

The first day's sessions covered the following topics presented by corporation officials: history of the natural gas industry, pipeline system design, pipeline operations, gas purchases, oil and gas sales, and rates.

The second morning lectures and discussions covered accounting, production operations, exploration, leaseholds, drilling, and production. In the afternoon, the group was flown to Opelousas and Lafayette, Louisiana, to visit a Texas Eastern drilling rig, a compressor station, and new cycling plant. All were briefed what to expect during the morning session and enroute while air-borne.

The third morning was devoted to lectures and discussions of the finances of the corporation, product diversification, transportation, production, processing, and refining. The afternoon was free for outdoor recreation including golf, fishing, tennis, trap shooting, and swimming with facilities provided by the corporation.

The morning session of the fourth day, which concluded the seminar, involved a discussion of legislation and regulation, conducted by the general counsel, followed by a seminar round-up in which top management participated.

The analysts who attended were provided with a complete kit of information about the gas industry and Texas Eastern. Visual aids were used extensively in each session in presenting a clear picture of the industry and corporation operations. Management and technical people were available at all times during recreation periods, social hours at the conclusion of each day's sessions, as well as in the classroom to answer questions and engage in informal discussion.

To appraise the effectiveness of the seminar, determine the interest in various features of the program, and secure suggestions for improvements in future seminars, each person attending the seminar was asked to complete a six-page, thirty-question questionnaire at the end of the four-day meeting.

Some of the questions appearing on the questionnaire are:

1. Considering the over-all nature of the seminar and comparing it with other conferences you have attended:
   a) How do you rate the worth of the seminar?
   High _____. Average _____. Average plus _____. Average minus _____. Low _____.
   b) What are your principal reasons for giving the seminar the above rating?
   c) What, in your opinion, are the strong points of the seminar?
   d) The weak points?
   e) Do you feel that any area of discussion should be expanded or reduced?
2. How do you rate the natural gas industry seminar on the following specific points?
   a) Information you can apply to securities evaluation?
   High _____. Average _____. Average plus _____. Average minus _____. Low _____.
   b) Having an opportunity to ask questions of a number of technicians in the natural gas industry?
   High _____. Average _____. Average plus _____. Average minus _____. Low _____.
   c) Getting to know the management of a natural gas company?
   High _____. Average _____. Average plus _____. Average minus _____. Low _____.
3. How do you rate each session? If any session was too technical or not sufficiently technical, please so state in your reasons for your rating.
   (Here followed questions on each topic discussed in each session of the four-

day seminar with a request for a rating of each as: high, average plus, average, average minus, and low, with reason for the rating.)

4. How do you rate the benefits derived from the field trips?
   High _____. Average _____. Average plus _____. Average minus _____. Low _____.

5. How do you rate the informal meetings with Texas Eastern Management?
   High _____. Average _____. Average plus _____. Average minus _____. Low _____.
   Reason for rating.

6. Do you feel the free time devoted to recreation was:
   Worthwhile _____. Free time could be better spent otherwise _____. Waste of time _____.

7. Do you have any suggestions for improving the participation in discussion periods?

8. Please give your comments on the way this seminar was run—general organization, physical set-up, facilities, etc.

9. Do you feel the length of the program should be:
   Shortened _____. Extended _____. Remain the same _____.

10. Should Texas Eastern undertake to continue the seminars?
    Yes _____. No _____.

11. What changes or improvements would you suggest that you haven't commented upon earlier in this questionnaire?

A comment by one analyst attending the seminar was: "Because of the many facets of the natural gas industry, it is exceedingly difficult to acquire the background necessary to evaluate the industry's securities. The seminar provided an exceptional educational opportunity."

The editor of the *Financial Analysts Journal* who participated in the seminar said, "To the financial analyst who, just a few years ago, had relative difficulty in getting corporate brass to talk, it is indeed something new to be invited into the corporate home, given a set of keys, and asked to sit on the ground floor. We think this is decidedly a good thing and express the hope that this will become the harbinger of many similar industry seminars. This is an excellent method of presenting the growth position of an industry."

The management of Texas Eastern considers the seminars one of the most valuable and worthwhile expenditures of time, effort, and money of all the financial relations activities of the corporation and they will be beneficial to the entire natural gas industry.

The seminar program was awarded first place for financial relations in the 1960 Public Relations Achievement Competition of the American Gas Association.

QUESTIONS

1. Should the financial analyst seminars of the Texas Eastern Transmission Corporation be continued as one feature of its stockholder relations program? Give reasons for your decision.

2. What changes, if any, should be made in the financial analyst seminars to improve their effectiveness? Be specific.

3. What improvements should be made in the stockholder relations program of Texas Eastern excluding the financial analyst seminars?

4. Should the corporation engage in other stockholder relations activities in addition to those described in the case? What? Be specific.

Case 7–2

STOCKHOLDER RELATIONS

Consumers Power Company

Consumers Power Company, Jackson, Michigan, is a combination gas and electric company serving approximately 539,000 gas and 874,000 electric customers in 64 counties and 331 cities and towns in an area constituting 70 per cent of the Lower Peninsula of Michigan. Gas sales total about 118 billion cubic feet annually with a revenue in excess of $100 million. Sales of electricity are about 9.6 billion kilowatt hours annually with a revenue of about $180 million.

The company operates nine steam-electric, 32 hydroelectric, and two diesel-electric generating plants and, with a subsidiary Michigan Gas Storage Company, has four gas storage fields where gas piped from the South in summer is held underground in Michigan for winter use. There are more than 10,000 employees in 12 operating divisions in the company's service area.

More than 67,000 stockholders own the common stock and about 16,500 the preferred stock of the company. Over half of these owners reside in Michigan and the balance in every state and several foreign countries. About one third of the shareholders are women, one fifth men, 38 per cent is in joint ownership; while insurance companies, banks, schools, estates, and investment trusts comprise the remainder of the stockholder group.

To create a better understanding by stockholders of the Consumers Power company's operations and problems, to encourage a continuing and expanding ownership of its common stock, and enhance the effectiveness of shareholders as a force for improved public relations, the company carries on a comprehensive stockholder relations program under the general supervision of the executive vice-president in charge of corporate affairs.

Responsibility for the conception of the stockholder program is assumed by the public relations department located at headquarters and headed by a public relations director who reports to the chairman of the board of the company. The public relations staff includes a general information supervisor; two photographers; an audio-visual specialist; editor, and managing editor of the Consumers Power News, employee newspaper; a man who devotes his time to public speaking; and a special public relations representative.

Managers of each of the company's 12 operating divisions are responsible for carrying out the company's general public and stockholder relations programs in their respective areas with the day-to-day assistance and counsel of the headquarters public relations staff.

The stockholder relations program of Consumers Power Company involves three major features: regional stockholders' meetings, open house programs, and printed and spoken communications.

Regional Stockholder Meetings

By legal requirement until 1960 the company's annual meeting had to be held in Portland, Maine. However, this location was inaccessible to most of the stockholders and, accordingly, few attended the annual meeting. In 1949, the company initiated regional meetings for stockholders in the principal cities of its service area during the month of April, immediately following the meeting in Portland, Maine. In 1960, Maine law was revised to allow the annual meeting to be held in Michigan. However, by that time the regional meeting program had become a part of the company's stockholder relations program to the extent that the program was continued in spite of the change in the Maine statute.

In 1949, four regional stockholder meetings were held; in 1950, this number was increased to six; and since that time at least 10 regional stockholder meetings have been held each year. Where facilities permit, the meetings are held in company quarters, otherwise in civic centers or hotel ballrooms.

In April, 1959, 11 regional meetings were held in the company's service area in which more than half of all shareholders reside. The location of these meetings and the attendance at each were as follows: Battle Creek, 185; Bay City, 350; Flint, 970; Grand Rapids, 600; Jackson, 360; Kalamazoo, 450; Lansing, 550: Muskegon, 400; Royal Oak, 170; Saginaw, 870; and Traverse City, 270. The total attendance at these meetings was 5,175 which was 8.2 per cent of the total of 62,600 shareholders. This was the largest attendance in the 11-year history of the company's regional meetings.

Attendance at regional meetings has increased regularly each year since 1955 as follows: 1955, 10 meetings with 3,797 shareholders; 1956, 10 meetings with 4,235 shareholders; 1957, 12 meetings with 4,598 attending; 1958, 11 meetings with 4,956 present; 1959, 11 meetings with 5,175 shareholders attending; 1960, 10 meetings with 5,100.

Program of Regional Meetings

The program of each regional stockholders meeting begins with a welcome by the division manager, in whose territory the meeting is held. He introduces the company officers and directors at the speaker's table. A report on the annual meeting is read by the secretary of the company. The chairman of the board, president, or a vice-president discuss the company's business progress and developments. Speakers are rotated on the programs of successive meetings to promote better acquaintance between shareholders and company officials. Recent company developments are shown in a brief color motion picture and with professional narration. Shareholders are given an opportunity to question officials in a question and answer period at the end of the formal program of each meeting. Refreshments and a social hour conclude each meeting at which time officers speak personally to many stockholders and answer questions that some stockholders are reluctant to ask in open meetings.

Graphic exhibits showing major aspects of the company's operations are installed in meeting rooms to inform stockholders about developments. These exhibits are changed each year. For example, recently a large illuminated display, "Here Comes Your Gas Supply," showed stockholders, most of whom are customers, how natural gas is piped from Southern gas fields to Michigan where it is held in underground storage fields and later delivered to homes and industries. Colored, translucent scenes from a motion picture, "Camera on Consumers," showing developments in the gas and electric industries were displayed on the walls of the meeting rooms. A scale model of the company's Big Rock Point Nuclear Plant under construction near Charlevoix, Michigan, was also exhibited.

Literature describing the company's operations, atomic power development, and gas industry progress is distributed to shareholders at each meeting. At a recent series of meetings, the following literature was given out: "Meet Your New Gas Industry," a 24-page booklet produced by the American Gas Association; "Consumers Power Facts," a four-page folder, and "Atomic Power for Peace and Prosperity," a 16-page illustrated booklet about nuclear progress in the electric industry.

Regional stockholder meetings are scheduled, wherever practical, in connection with open house programs at new company facilities in order to give shareholders a preview of new developments and increase their awareness of ownership. The regional meeting at Saginaw in 1959 was combined with a four-day open house program during which 12,000 persons visited the company's new $2,500,000 service center and saw a slide-film presentation produced by the company to tell the story of gas service in the area served by the company. Stockholders were also invited to visit the new service center in Lansing.

Related Publicity

Advance and follow-up publicity is planned by the public relations department in connection with regional stockholders meetings. Newspapers in each city where a meeting is to be held are given an advance news story about the meeting. Similar news releases are sent out to all daily and weekly newspapers in neighboring communities as well as to radio and television stations in the area.

A news release describing the proceedings of the annual meeting is distributed to all Michigan daily newspapers, and radio and television stations as well as to the financial press in New York City.

Advertisements inviting stockholders to attend regional meetings appear twice on the financial pages of Michigan newspapers in cities where regional meetings are held.

Following each regional meeting, a press release quoting the most significant statements made by officials at the meeting is sent to all newspapers in the meeting city and nearby communities.

Additional Stockholder Communications

In addition to annual and regional meeting publicity, Consumers Power Company publishes a modern annual report which is distributed to stockholders, the financial community, newspapers, schools, and libraries in the company's service area. The 1959 annual report of 32 pages profusely illustrated with photographs of company operations and personnel and graphic charts of financial data contained the following information: map of service area, operations summary, president's letter, breakdown of the company dollar, review of the year, annual meeting notice, St. Lawrence Seaway and its impact on the company's operations, balance sheets, statements of retained earnings, 10-year financial summary, 10-year electric and gas operating comparison, accountants certificate, names of directors, officers, division managers, and division operating data. This report won first award for utility companies with more than 400,000 customers in the 1959 Better Copy Contest of the Public Utilities Advertising Association. It was also awarded "Best of Industry" and "Best of Largest Operating Utilities" in the *Financial World* magazine, "Survey of Annual Reports."

Supplementing the annual report, a newsletter is mailed to all common and preferred stockholders with each quarterly dividend check to keep them informed about current developments and future progress of the company. Copies of this newsletter are also distributed to hundreds of financial analysts, bank officers, financial writers, and brokers with a monthly statement of income.

Twenty-six hundred employee stockholders are informed about company progress and industry developments through timely articles in the employees' publication, "Consumers Power News."

To tell about its Michigan service area and promote the industrial development of the state, the company has advertised in recent years in such national business magazines and newspapers as *Fortune, U.S. News and World Report, Newsweek, Barrons, New York Times,* and *Wall Street Journal.*

Company officials speak before financial groups such as the New York Society of Security Analysts and the Investments Analysts of Chicago to acquaint representatives of major stockholders with the company's progress. Copies of these addresses are distributed to the press and the financial community.

Effectiveness of Stockholder Relations Program

The effectiveness of Consumers Power Company stockholder relations program is indicated by the fact that the number of common stockholders has increased 122 per cent from 28,600 to 67,000 in 10 years. Average attendance per regional stockholder meeting has increased each year. The press has given much publicity to the regional stockholder meetings and numerous stockholders have complimented the company on its stockholder relations program.

QUESTIONS

1. Are the regional stockholder meetings of the Consumers Power Company a sound stockholder relations activity? Give reasons for your answer.
2. What changes, if any, should be made in the conduct and programing of the regional stockholders meetings to improve their effectiveness?
3. Is the publicity on the regional stockholders meetings fully effective? Should publicity be handled in another way? How?
4. Are the Consumers Power Company stockholder communications, aside from the regional stockholder meetings, desirable? If not, what changes should be made in these communications?

Problem 7–1

STOCKHOLDER RELATIONS

Electric Equipment Corporation

The Electric Equipment Corporation, New York, N.Y., is one of the ten largest electric equipment manufacturers in the United States, with forty plants making consumer, industrial, and defense products. The consumer products division makes household electric appliances, including mixers, toasters, irons, coffee makers, refrigerators, freezers, washers, ironers, air conditioners, radio and television receivers. The utility equipment division produces transformers, turbines, switchgear, and controls. Motors, generators, apparatus and components are made by the industrial products division. Electronic, atomic, and defense systems are produced by the special equipment division.

Foreign subsidiary companies are located in fifteen countries outside of the United States and Canada. Nineteen manufacturing or assembly facilities are operated in seven of these foreign countries to make consumer appliances and industrial equipment.

The annual sales volume of the corporation, including foreign subsidiaries, is in the neighborhood of $4 billion. The number of employees in United States operations is 230,000, with an additional 13,000 abroad.

The corporation is owned by about 500,000 common stockholders of which number 150,000 are employees who are participants in the corporation's employee stock ownership savings plan.

A public relations department was established in 1934 to create a favorable image of the corporation in the public mind by taking every opportunity to deserve and build good will, understanding, and confidence and to communicate to the public information about the practices and policies of the corporation.

A vice-president in charge of public relations is responsible to the president. A staff of sixty public relations specialists is divided into the following sections: employee and plant community relations, public information, government relations, educational relations, and stockholder relations.

The stockholder relations program was initiated in 1947 when a committee composed of the financial vice-president, treasurer, and public relations vice-president proposed that a stockholder relations section be established in the public relations department. The objectives of the section are to plan, produce, and distribute communications to stockholders to keep them informed about the corporation; to encourage stockholder participation in and support of corporation activities; and to inform influential bankers, investment analysts, and counselors about the corporation's financial status.

The stockholder relations section established a stockholder relations program based on a survey of the characteristics, attitudes, and interests of shareholders. This survey revealed the corporate policies, programs, and activities about which shareholders wanted more information; the misconceptions of stockholders; and their opinions of management.

The Electric Equipment Corporation's stockholder relations program includes: annual and interim reports; an annual meeting at corporation headquarters in New York City; a series of biennial regional shareholders' meetings held at corporation plants in Los Angeles, Detroit, Chicago, Atlanta, Boston, and Baltimore; a four-page shareholders' quarterly called "Elco Stockholder"; page advertisements in the financial sections of leading metropolitan newspapers and the principal financial journals featuring the annual report of the corporation; meetings with members of the financial community including security analysts, bankers, investment counselors, and financial editors to hear corporation executives discuss the company's financial affairs; and periodic stockholder open houses at the principal plants of the corporation.

The stockholder communication program was designed to keep owners of the corporation fully informed about its finances and operations; to secure favorable recommendations of company securities by banks and investment houses; and to create a better understanding between the company and its shareholders.

However, in the opinion of management, the program failed to secure the active support of its half-million shareholders in creating a better business climate in plant communities and in state and national government. The corporation needs more from its shareholders than just their capital. It wants them to actively work for its interests and for the American system of free and competitive enterprise. The owners of the company can aid themselves, their company, and the nation by striving to improve the climate in which the business operates.

To secure the active support of shareholders, the stockholder relations manager proposed a series of stockholder business climate symposiums. These would be a novel experiment in stockholder education to improve the economic understanding and secure the co-operation of the owners of the business in supporting the stand of the corporation on public issues, securing more favorable legislation, tax relief, and freedom from burdensome governmental controls.

Education of shareholders in improving the business climate is not entirely new at Electric Equipment Corporation. For several years stockholders have been receiving, along with executive and employee public affairs letters, bulletins and reports prepared by the employee and plant community relations section of the public relations department. These communications to executives and employees announce the corporation's stand on public issues, urge participation in local politics, support get-out-the-vote drives, and distribute legislators' voting records.

At several open houses for stockholders at corporation plants, executives have spoken about the business climate and its effect on corporate profits and have urged shareholders to participate in public affairs.

The proposed stockholder business climate symposiums would be another step in the corporation's program to interest executives, employees, and stockholders in the business climate. The symposiums would provide for face-to-face discussion with shareholders of some of the economic facts the corporation has been presenting employees in its economic education, political action, and business climate courses sponsored by the employee and plant community relations section of the public relations department.

The objectives of the proposed stockholder business climate symposiums would be to: focus the individual stockholder's attention on specific key elements affecting the national and local business climate and stimulate interest in and increase understanding of these elements; motivate stockholders to assume their responsibilities as individual citizens by taking steps to exploit the strengths and correct the weaknesses of the business climate, thereby enhancing the opportunity for economic progress by the corporation, stockholder, and nation; and foster in stockholders an awareness of and desire to participate in civic and political affairs.

The symposium method of attaining the above objectives offers an effective approach to stockholder education because it is a time-tested method of examining the facts and reaching a common understanding through individual participation and two-way communication. Symposium participation would motivate stockholders to support needed improvements in key elements affecting the business climate. The symposiums would create understanding of the need for a better business climate by a rational, objective, considered, and informed examination of the facts.

The curriculum for the symposiums would provide for discussion of the national economic climate in which business operates, the role of organized labor in the economy, conditions affecting the business climate in the state and area of the plant where the symposium is held, and what a stockholder can do to improve the business climate.

The business climate symposiums would be initiated on a trial basis at the Detroit plant of the corporation and extended to other plant cities if response of stockholders warranted. One four-hour session would be held each week for a period of four weeks in the reception building of the Detroit plant. A list of 500 men and women stockholders in the Detroit area, selected at random, would be invited by letter from the president of the company to participate in the symposium. An enrollment card to be returned by the stockholder would be enclosed with each invitation. An estimated 100 men and women shareholders would be expected to enroll for the sixteen-hour symposium program.

The faculty for the business climate symposiums would be headed by the vice-president in charge of public relations of the corporation, assisted by a headquarters staff composed of the stockholder relations manager, the employee and plant community relations manager, and the government relations manager. The general manager of the Detroit electric utility equipment plant, the local employee and plant community relations manager, and other local staff executives would speak.

These executives would lecture at the symposiums on various subjects affecting the economic climate nationally and locally. Subjects to be discussed would include government spending, inflation, government regulation, taxation, political participation, labor legislation, collective bargaining, unemployment, workmen's compensation, and welfare costs.

A typical symposium program would include: 2:00 P.M.—call to order; 2:05 to 2:15, statement of symposium's objectives; 2:15 to 2:30, speaker No. 1; 2:30 to 2:45, speaker No. 2; 2:45 to 3:00, speaker No. 3; 3:00 to 3:10 recess; 3:10 to 4:10, discussion period No. 1; 4:10 to 5:10, discussion period No. 2; 5:10 to 6:10 discussion period No. 3, and adjournment.

Each symposium participant would be given a resource kit containing a notebook, pen, reading matter, bibliography, and a booklet, "How Laws Are Made in the Congress of the United States."

Following the trial symposium at Detroit, questionnaires would be distributed to participants seeking their opinions, criticisms, and suggestions about the symposium to determine the desirability of extending the program to other cities.

Some executives of the corporation did not favor the proposed symposiums for several reasons. The symposiums would lead to a lot of talk and little effective action. Conflicts in political interests of participants would inject political bias into symposium discussions. Shareholders would be reluctant to give sixteen hours of their time to the symposiums. Only a limited number of shareholders would be reached by the symposiums. Stockholders are not interested in corporation problems as long as they get regular dividends. Corporation executives would have more important work to do.

On the other hand, advocates of the symposiums contend that nearly a half-million stockholders of the corporation can exert great influence for improving the business climate by speaking to their families, business associates, ministers, friends, and tradesmen about the importance of supporting free and competitive enterprise and creating a more favorable climate for business.

The vice-president in charge of public relations decided to give the proposal for stockholder business climate symposiums further consideration by referring it to the public relations policy committee composed of top-management executives.

QUESTIONS

1. Should the Electric Equipment Corporation adopt the proposed plan for symposiums on the business climate for shareholders? Give reasons for favoring or opposing this plan to secure the active support of shareholders in improving the business climate.

2. If you believe that there is a better way to solve the problem of securing stockholder support of the company's interests, describe in detail your proposition.

3. Is the stockholder relations program satisfactory? Give specific reasons.

4. What improvements can be made in the stockholder relations program of the Electric Equipment Corporation?

8 · CONSUMER RELATIONS

CONSUMERS WHO USE goods and services are the most important class of individuals in the American economy. The more than 185 million men, women, and children who comprise the consumer public in the United States determine the success and failure of every industrial and commercial enterprise. Accordingly, consumer relations which seeks the good will and understanding of consumers is a vital area of public relations.

"The paramount need of all businesses, big and small alike, is to plan their course mindful that their existence is of the consumer, by the consumer, and for the consumer," says Paul Garrett, public relations counsel. "With such a conception of public relations we will not go far wrong."

SPECIAL INTEREST CONSUMER GROUPS

To develop better relations with the massive consumer public is a tremendous task for even the largest corporations. Selective consumer cultivation of special interest groups with which an enterprise is most closely identified is essential. Special interest groups composed of consumers of similar age, sex, occupation, race, and economic status are: women, youth, farmers, businessmen, aged, military personnel, Negroes, and others.

Public relations programs are designed to appeal to the special interests of one or more of these groups of consumers. Producers of food, home appliances, cosmetics, and clothing focus their consumer relations activities on the woman public. Makers of farm equipment and supplies concentrate on the farm public. Farsighted corporations seeking the good will of the customers of tomorrow cultivate the youth public.

The Woman Public

The woman public is the most important consumer group for producers and distributors of consumer goods and services. Women control 65 per cent of the nation's savings accounts and an equal amount of the nation's privately held securities. They spend more than $4 billion a year on themselves and strongly influence the $290 billion annual personal expenditures by all Americans. The number of women is increasing more rapidly and women are living longer than men. By 1970, the number of women fourteen years of age and over in the United States, according to Bureau of Census estimates, will exceed 77 million. Of this number nearly 30 million will be employed consumers in their own right rather than dependents of their husbands or families.

Not only have women become more important economically but they are better educated, more independent, more sophisticated, and more receptive to new ideas than they were in 1950. With more money of their own and more confidence from exposure to the business world, the influence of women not only on consumption but also on public opinion is increasing. The understanding and good will of the woman public is essential to sound consumer relations.

The growing importance of the woman public has been responsible for the establishment by an increasing number of companies of special women's sections in public relations departments, staffed by women and devoted to developing good relations with women. Specialized women public relations counsel advise on the proper approach to the woman public and a growing number of women hold key positions in public relations departments. The National Association of Manufacturers has a women's department to further relations with women's clubs.

Joining for recreation, self-improvement, and social service more than 35 million American women are organized into over 200,000 women's clubs which are the most important channel of communication in most consumer relations programs. The women's clubs composed of opinion leaders in their communities present programs on a wide variety of cultural, economic, social, and political themes. They seek program materials on homemaking, community service, politics, fashion, cooking, and a host of subjects using information supplied by the consumer relations staffs of corporations, unions, and social service organizations.

The Youth Public

The spectacular growth in the population under twenty years of age in the United States is a national phenomenon. From 1950 to 1960 the population of the country increased by 18.5 per cent, but in the same period the number of youth under 20 years increased more than 34 per cent. By 1970 it is estimated that youth under 20 will number more than 92 million, or 42 per cent of the population at that time. The youth public is big and growing bigger and of increasing importance as an audience of American industry.

The youth public is actually three publics—the elementary, the high school, and the college publics. Each of these publics should be reached through its own media, be influenced by its own motivations, and convinced through its own interests. Teenagers are not adults with arrested development but individuals with drives all their own, quite apart from the motivations of adults. Effective communication with youth must take into consideration their behavior, attitudes, and interests in order to gain their understanding and good will.

Youth exercise a great influence on the attitudes of their families toward producers and distributors of many products and services consumed in the home from breakfast foods to television receivers and automobiles. Youth's influence on consumption is illustrated by the numerous television and radio programs appealing to boys and girls under twenty years of age.

The youth of today are the consumers of tomorrow. They are the future volunteer workers and contributors to nonprofit, social welfare organizations. The perpetuity of our economic system depends upon their support of free enterprise. To gain the understanding and support of youth for our democratic form of government, economic, and social institutions is a responsibility of business and nonprofit organizations through their youth public relations programs.

Youth organizations are a major channel of communication through which business and social organizations seek to inform and secure the good will of boys and girls. The principal youth organizations in the United States are the Boy Scouts, Girl Scouts, Future Farmers of America, Future Home Makers of America, 4-H Clubs, Hi-Y Clubs, Junior Achievement, YMCA, YWCA, and various religious youth groups.

Corporations encourage their employees to take part in the national, local, and regional activities of these educational and character building youth organizations. Companies sponsor programs and provide funds, awards, guidance, literature, visual aids, and other help to these groups.

The principal industry-sponsored youth organization is Junior Achievement, the objective of which is to teach youth about the American business system. Several hundred business concerns sponsor the approximately 1,800 Junior Achievement companies in operation throughout the country. A Junior Achievement company is formed and operated by from eight to fifteen boys and girls between the ages of 15 and 21 years, under the sponsorship of a business organization, whose executives act as advisers. The young people elect officers, apply for a charter, select a name, sell stock, buy raw materials, lease machinery, advertise, sell, keep accounts, and perform all of the functions of a business enterprise. At the end of the business year, each Achievement company goes out of business, liquidates its inventory, and decides whether dividends can be paid to shareholders and bonuses to workers.

Junior Achievement companies compete for national awards in various fields of business. These awards are provided by various national business associations. A "Future Unlimited" banquet is held for all of the Junior Achievers in a locality along with their sponsors, advisers, and civic leaders. Outstanding Achievers receive recognition through special awards and scholarships. All Junior Achievement companies in a city combine to hold an open house where all of their products can be seen and purchased by the public.

The youth activities of large corporations are typical of the interest taken by business in the youth of America. A large corporation sponsors youth activities through a youth committee headed by the director of public relations, with the manager of sales promotion and sales training and the advertising manager as members. A supervisor of youth and educational activities in the public relations department serves as co-ordinator of youth activities sponsored by the company. Regional management promotes the company's youth program and provides for the training of employees, especially salesmen and agents so they can co-operate effectively.

The Ford Motor Company sponsors an extensive youth consumer relations program, through its annual Industrial Arts Awards Competition, to encourage craftsmanship among junior and senior high school students. Cash prizes are given to young men for outstanding entries, among the 13,000 projects entered annually, in the following divisions: mechanical drawing, architectural drawing, woodworking, electrical, graphic arts, leather, ceramics, jewelry, models, wrought metal, machine shop, pattern making, molding, and plastics. In addition, Ford sponsors youth programs for Future Farmers of America, 4-H Club awards, and driver education.

Recognizing the importance of the youth public, the Fisher Body Division of General Motors Corporation sponsors the Fisher Body Craftsman's Guild to interest boys of high school and college age in fine craftsmanship and to drill them in its practice by means of an automobile model-building competition in which generous awards serve as incentives. Nearly two million boys have participated in this competition. The corporation provides university training for national winners and distrib-

FIG. 8–1. Judges selecting the winners in the annual Fisher Body Craftsman's Guild competition, youth public relations activity of Fisher Body Division, General Motors Corp. Half a million youth enter annually and more than a thousand divide $117,000 in cash and scholarships.

utes cash awards, in addition to providing educational trips for hundreds of boys.

The Chevrolet Division of General Motors Corporation has sponsored for many years the annual All-American Soap Box Derby for boys, in conjunction with local newspapers in the principal cities of the country.

The Farm Public

About a third of the nation's population, or around 54 million people, live on the three and a half million farms, or in rural areas. Agriculture directly or indirectly supports between 40 and 45 per cent of the population of the United States either through their working on farms, supplying farmers' needs, or processing or handling farm products. Significant changes in farming in recent years have made the farm public an important objective in the consumer relations programs of many large and small corporations. Farming, today, is a business and not merely a sentimental way of life. The farmer is a dual personality. He is a businessman who consumes a large amount of farm machinery and supplies. At the same time, he is an individual consumer like the city dweller in his tastes for television sets, electric refrigeration, and convertibles.

As business men, farmers own nearly five million tractors, three million motor trucks, and over a million grain combines. As an individual consumer, the farmer's standard of living has risen along with the improvement in farm production.

The modern farmer has a keen desire for information and a high capacity for becoming better informed. Many, especially younger farmers, are college graduates and actively interested in economic as well as social and agricultural affairs.

These are some of the reasons why the farm public is receiving increasing attention in the consumer relations programs of companies that supply farmers with farm equipment and also by producers of consumer goods as well.

Rural public relations programs are usually conducted with the co-operation of agricultural organizations and leaders, including the American Farm Bureau Federation with 1,600,000 members, the National Grange with 900,000 members, Agricultural Extension Service, leaders and teachers in Vocational Agriculture, the Land-Grant Colleges, and other groups concerned with the welfare of the farmer.

The most extensive farm public relations program in the United States is carried on by Sears, Roebuck and Company. This program is the joint responsibility of the educational programs, consumer education, rural programs, and medical programs sections of Sears national public relations department. These rural public relations activities are financed by the Sears, Roebuck Foundation to which the company contributes a portion of its profits for public service work.

The Sears farm program offers agricultural scholarships for farm boys and girls; rural swine, poultry, and dairy projects with awards to farm boys and girls for producing better livestock; national rural projects, including the national 4-H poultry program; rural films produced in co-operation with farm groups; and the National Grange community service contest with awards for community improvement by a local grange.

The Sears Medical Assistance Program is designed to attract physicians to rural localities, where there are inadequate medical services, by providing low-cost, long-term loans to keep the doctor in the community.

The Sears Consumer Education Service provides rural home demonstration agents, teachers, and 4-H club leaders with traveling exhibits and literature on a variety of products.

The Military Personnel Public

The U.S. military consumer public composed of Armed Forces personnel and dependents, totaling more than six million, is a group of growing size and importance to public relations. Reached by their own media, military personnel at home and abroad should receive more attention in public relations programs of American corporations.

The Negro Public

The Negro public in the United States has reached a population peak of nearly 19 million, with a $20 billion annual income and an all-time high urban population. The rising income, occupational level, and education of American Negroes make this group of increasing importance in public relations.

The Business Public

Businesses which consume raw materials, fabricating parts, installation equipment, and operating supplies are an important division of the consumer public. The business public in the United States, in 1961, according to the U.S. Department of Commerce was composed of nearly five million firms—manufacturers, construction concerns, wholesalers, retailers, and service establishments—in addition to transportation, utility, extractive, and commercial enterprises which serve the ultimate consumer.

Business organizations comprise the major public of thousands of large and small suppliers which employ public relations programs to secure the understanding and good will of the business public. Supplier relations programs conducted by the public relations departments of corporations seek the good will of business suppliers.

ORGANIZATION FOR CONSUMER RELATIONS

Responsibility for Consumer Relations

Consumer relations is a responsibility of every person employed by an enterprise which supplies goods or services to consumers. Every action or statement by an employee to consumers affects public opinion of the organization with which the employee is associated. Telephone operators, deliverymen, correspondents, service representatives, salesmen, and messengers, as well as executives, in the course of their business or personal activities have many contacts with consumers.

Because marketing effectiveness depends upon good consumer relationships, the marketing department of a company should be primarily responsible for carrying out a consumer relations program. Marketing executives and salesmen supported by advertising execute consumer relations planned by the public relations staff.

Salesmen are principally interested in selling products and services and they often neglect the important task of developing understanding and good will of consumers toward the company. Public relations with the assistance of salesmen sells the company as an institution.

Salesmen are qualified through continuous contacts and experience to win the understanding and confidence of consumers. Institutional advertising supplements the efforts of salesmen to win consumer good will. The combined forces of sales and advertising are employed to persuade present and prospective customers to think well of an enterprise through a well-planned program of consumer relations.

However, salesmen and advertising alone should not be expected to develop the good will of consumers for an organization. All of the rank-and-file employees should be actively enlisted in an organization-wide program for building consumer good will. Employees must be informed about the organization and encouraged by executives to speak well of it to their friends and the public in general.

Role of the Public Relations Staff in Consumer Relations

As pointed out above, responsibility for execution of a consumer relations program belongs to every person associated with an enterprise, particularly line operating management and personnel that have close and continuous relations with consumers through sales, credit, collections, service, adjustment, correspondence, and delivery. Personnel at all levels are the principal channel of oral communication with the large consumer public.

However, the research, planning, programing, and production of nonoral communication with consumers is the responsibility of the public relations staff. In large corporations marketing consumer goods, a special section of the public relations department is devoted to consumer relations. The consumer relations section, often staffed with women, has specialists assigned to product publicity, product testing, home economics, fashion, public speaking, women's club relations, consumer publications, and correspondence with consumers.

To co-ordinate the work of the consumer relations staff with the management of those departments of the business that have frequent contacts with consumers, a consumer relations committee composed of the heads of these departments is desirable. The head of the consumer relations staff serves as chairman of this committee. The function of this committee is to propose consumer activities and to critically examine the programs and communications prepared by the consumer relations section and evaluate the effectiveness of the program.

A large New York City department store has a consumer relations committee whose chairman is the general manager of the store, with the public relations manager acting as secretary. The committee is composed of representatives of the following departments: selling, service, adjustment, comparison, merchandising, warehousing, credit, supply, and methods and systems. The committee audits all points of consumer relations contact and recommends improved practices to gain consumer good will.

Owner Relations Activities

Owner relations is a specialized activity of the consumer relations programs of an increasing number of corporations. Chevrolet Motor Division, General Motors Corporation, established in 1959 an Owner Relations department to work with each department of the company on current and future dealer activities to retain owner satisfaction.

Owner Relations of Chevrolet functions through Forward Development Boards. Each board is composed of nine wholesale executives: regional manager, zone manager, city manager, regional department manager, zone department manager, four district managers, in addition to five dealers. Board members meet and make recommendations for improving owner relations for the company and dealers. A transcript of board discussions and recommendations is furnished to the central office department manager concerned, who reviews the proposals and submits them to general management for approval and activation.

Another activity of Chevrolet's Owner Relations involves Owner Panels representing a random selection of 1,200 Chevrolet owners, located in every state, who serve as owner counselors. There are two classes of Owner Panels—passenger car panels and truck panels. Panel members are contacted periodically by mail to secure their opinions on specific areas of Chevrolet products and services. Information from panel members is furnished to operating departments of the company for their guidance in improving owner relations.

A third activity of the Chevrolet Owner Relations department is conducting owner meetings at which groups of not more than fifteen

Chevrolet owners, selected at random, meet at luncheon with the Owner Relations staff in their home cities to express their views on Chevrolet products and services. Comments are tape recorded and forwarded to headquarters, where they are transcribed and distributed to operating departments to be utilized in improving products and services. Dealers also hold owner meetings to hear firsthand from customers their comments regarding dealer service to owners.

A fourth activity of Chevrolet's Owner Relations department is sending questionnaires to a representative number of new customers asking for their opinions on the product, delivery, and matters which concern owners at the time of making their purchases. These questionnaires are recapped and the results furnished to management so that they may be aware of owner interests. In addition, an outside independent research organization conducts depth interviews with Chevrolet owners, of up to three hours duration, to determine owners' buying motives and factors that influence rebuying decisions.

Consumer Relations Policy

The foundation of a consumer relations program is a consumer policy which defines the philosophy of management toward the consuming public. The customer policy of the International Harvester Company is a model for good consumer relations:

Customers rely upon us to supply them with machines that will do the job. They want quality—not just the frills that make a product look better in a showcase, but the kind of quality that will allow our machines to give maximum performance under all conditions. It is up to us to provide them with that quality and at the same time sell our machines to them at prices they can afford to pay.

Customers also expect, and get from us, service to back up the products we sell them. But we go further than providing them with service parts. Harvester service to its customers includes the publication of pamphlets showing how to get more out of their land, to increase their profits, or develop new uses for their equipment. We take an active interest in helping such organizations as the 4-H Clubs and Future Farmers of America, which develop farm youth and ultimately benefit the nation.

Customers want the promise that these goods and services will continue. We can keep this promise only if we run our business efficiently and maintain a sound financial policy.

A significant feature of this consumer policy is that good consumer relationships depend primarily upon the value of the products and services provided by producers to consumers. The consumer public judges a company largely by the quality of its goods and services. No public relations communications can change the attitudes of consumers toward a concern which produces inferior merchandise, sells it at an excessive price, or fails to give good service.

Objectives of Consumer Relations Programs

The objectives of a consumer relations program are determined by the consumer policy, goods or services supplied, the nature and size of the public served, as well as the resources of the enterprise.

The consumer relations objectives of large and small companies in various industries are:

To determine what consumers think and say about the policies, acts, products, or services of the organization.

To see that all statements made to consumers concerning price, value, service, and quality are truthful and unexaggerated.

To improve consumer service by more satisfactory handling of complaints and by analysis of complaints to discover what causes them, and to correct deficiencies in operation, procedure, or policy.

To gain acceptance of the products and services of a corporation by the consuming public.

To educate employees to give prompt, accurate, courteous, personal, and friendly service to consumers.

To disseminate information about the products, services, policies, and practices of an organization to the consuming public.

To answer the inquiries of consumers regarding the company, its products and services, their use or application.

To make a product or service more satisfactory to consumers through product research, study of consumer wants, or product testing.

To label products with specific data in understandable terms so as to aid consumers to understand the quality and characteristics of the products, and to establish grades or standards of product quality to guide consumers in their choice and use of products.

To establish lowest possible prices consistent with quality through the elimination of waste in production and distribution, and to pass along to consumers the savings from greater efficiency.

To co-operate with groups representing consumers in their efforts to inform and educate consumers in recognizing quality and satisfying their needs.

To maintain and develop relations with home economics teachers, home demonstration agents, home economists of other manufacturers and public utilities, and food editors and writers.

To prepare and edit printed material, package directions, recipes, and literature for consumers.

Determining Consumer Opinion

Knowledge of the attitudes of consumers toward an organization's operations, policies, products, and services is essential in establishing a consumer policy, objectives, and in planning a consumer relations program. To determine consumer opinion, research is carried on by the public relations department or by an outside opinion research organization. The methods of conducting consumer opinion research are described in Chapter 18, "Public Relations Research and Evaluation."

Complaint Analysis and Follow-up

Consumer opinion is reflected in complaints by customers of policies, products, or services. All customer complaints should be referred to the consumer relations department regardless of which department is responsible for settling claims. Every settled claim provides an opportunity to create good will which should not be left to a routine form letter from a clerk in the claims department. Top public relations management's attention should be given to claims. Complaints should be analyzed periodically to determine consumer opinion toward the company.

What Consumers Want to Know

Consumers have a natural interest in the activities of companies which supply them with important goods and services. The understanding and confidence of consumers in a business organization depend to a large extent on what they know about the company.

Consumers are interested in some of the following features of a company and its activities: history of the company and industry, executive personnel, personnel and labor relations, plants and branches, financial status and operations, management policies, marketing methods, organization, research and product development, competitive position, and contributions to the public welfare.

Planning a Consumer Relations Program

A public relations staff, in planning a consumer relations program, first gets a clear and complete understanding of the attitudes of the consuming public toward the organization, its products, policies, operations, and problems. Company executives in various staff and line departments which have relations with customers are consulted for their views on consumer opinion of the company.

Surveys may be made to gather further information on the nature of consumer prejudice and pressures that operate against a company. After a consumer relations program is functioning, surveys also should be made to determine whether the techniques employed are proving effective in creating more favorable consumer attitudes toward the company.

Correcting the Shortcomings Revealed by Consumer Surveys

When the attitudes, criticisms, and suggestions of consumers have been determined, action must be taken by management to correct those policies and practices which are disapproved by consumers. Only after action has been taken to correct objectionable policies and practices can consumer relations be improved.

When these corrections have been made, media of communication are chosen to inform consumers about improved corporate policies or practices, and to gain public acceptance. These media are discussed in the following pages.

MEDIA OF COMMUNICATION WITH CONSUMERS

Oral Communications

Oral communication between employees and the consumer public is the most effective means of presenting the facts and correcting misunderstanding of an organization's policies and practices. "The logical persons to interpret business to the public," says the head of a large corporation, "are those who are in the business—the employees. Primarily through them, the public gains confidence in the business as well as in its products."

Employee-Consumer Communication. Employee education in consumer relations is essential in an effective consumer communications program. Employees who are given information about the industry and company economics in simple, understandable terms can play an important part in correcting wrong impressions and informing consumers.

The public relations department, co-operating with line and staff departments, should develop a training program to give all employees a better understanding of company operations and achievements. The objectives of this training should be: to give employees a feeling of participation in developing good public relations; to give employees information about the company, its functions and business, financial, and personnel policies; to develop in employees a realization of the importance of good public relations; and to impress line executives with their responsibility to interest employees in speaking well of the company.

To train employees in consumer communication, organizations use planned group discussions with supervisory personnel, individual and group discussions with employees, pamphlets, motion pictures, visits to other departments, bulletin board posters, and employee publications.

Informal conversations of employees with their families, relatives, friends, and neighbors about the company and its activities are one of the most effective means of informing and gaining the good will of consumers.

Formal speeches by employees to community groups inform consumers about the company and industry. Employee speakers' bureaus, organized by public relations departments, are described in Chapter 24, "Oral Communication." Discussion groups composed of employees and representatives of community organizations are another medium of consumer communication.

Executive-Consumer Communication. Executives of a corporation or nonprofit organization are important communicators with individuals and groups of consumers. The chairman and members of the board, officers, department heads, and staff personnel can make a significant contribution to building good consumer relationships by speaking to consumer groups. Research, writing, and editing speeches for executives is a responsibility of the public relations department.

Public Relations Staff-Consumer Communication. The public relations executives of all types of organizations speak extensively to various consumer groups. Some corporations and associations maintain a speakers' bureau, as a section of the public relations department, staffed by professional speakers who address consumer groups.

Plant Visits by Consumers. Communication with consumers is obtained through plant visits by consumer groups, including church, civic, and fraternal organizations, women's clubs, clergy, students, teachers, and others to factories, warehouses, offices, and stores to see their operations and hear from executives. Plant visits give management an opportunity to explain a company's operations, to correct misconceptions, to create a favorable impression of good working conditions, and to discuss products with potential consumers.

There are two types of plant visitation programs: the special occasion open house, and regular visiting hours. Regular visiting hours on certain days during the week or month may be designated as "visiting days" for consumer groups. Effective plant visits require organization and administration, with oral communication through trained guides, lectures, or group discussions in which visitors have the opportunity to ask questions and hear about plant operations. Planning and administration of these visits is properly the function of the public relations department. The public relations department of E. I. du Pont de Nemours & Co. encourages managements of its 77 plants in 28 states to promote better consumer relations through plant visits. A manual, "Plant Visits," gives Du Pont local plant managements instruction in the organization and administration of plant visits.

Surveys of consumers who have visited a company's plant and have observed its operations indicate that consumer attitudes toward the company are much more favorable after a plant trip. The Bell Telephone System has found that the attitude of telephone users who visited a telephone exchange is 50 per cent more favorable to the company after the visit than before.

A further discussion of open houses and plant visits will be found in Chapter 9, "Community Relations."

Television and Radio Programs. Consumer television and radio broadcasts inform consumers about an organization, its accomplishments, policies, and operations.

Institutional broadcasts are increasing and are a basic medium of consumer communication of many large companies. Broadcasts provide communication with large numbers of consumers at relatively low cost and great flexibility. On an average day 73 per cent of the people in the country view television and 75 per cent of all women listen to radio, according to the Television Bureau of Advertising, and Radio Advertising Bureau. The principal types of consumer public relations broadcasts are: the service broadcast, the entertainment program, and the commentator program.

Consumer service television and radio broadcasts may be paid for by the sponsor at commercial rates or carried by the stations without charge as a sustaining, educational feature, providing the service to viewers and listeners outweighs the promotional aspects of the program.

Institutional entertainment television broadcasts on a national network are used by American Telephone and Telegraph Corporation, which broadcasts the "Bell Telephone Hour."

A third type of public relations broadcast to consumers features well-known news commentators who discuss current news, interpret recent events, and emphasize trends in social, political, or economic affairs. Institutional broadcasts carry brief announcements describing company operations, research, and products to create a better company image.

Printed Media of Communication with Consumers

Printed and audio-visual methods of communicating with consumers are used in conjunction with oral communication media. Printed communications reach large numbers of widely scattered consumers at relatively low cost. The principal printed and audio-visual methods of communication include press publicity, motion picture films, exhibits and demonstrations, program kits and study materials for women's clubs, library reference materials, publications, special events, correspondence, and publication advertising.

Publicity to Consumers. In the United States in 1962, there were 383 morning, 1,577 evening, and 582 Sunday newspapers, in addition to 9,774 weekly newspapers. There are more than 21,000 magazines of all kinds. All of these periodicals carry news stories and articles originated by the public relations departments of business and nonprofit organizations and read by millions of consumers in all parts of the country.

Public opinion is largely formed from information transmitted by the press, television, and radio. Public relations departments supply press publicity in the form of news releases, scripts for radio and television, special articles, photographs, clip sheets, and background information to newspapers, magazines, wire services, news syndicates, radio and television stations, and trade publications.

The two principal types of press publicity are institutional publicity to build good will for a corporation and product publicity to inform consumers about products and their various uses. The public relations department of a large food corporation has two sections specializing on publicity: an institutional publicity section to develop better understanding of company operations and policies, and a product publicity section to influence consumer buying habits by regular releases, recipes, and photographs to 700 editors of daily newspaper food pages, 300 television food commentators, and 800 radio food commentators.

Motion Pictures. Motion pictures are a major medium of consumer communication. They appeal to the eye as well as the ear, combine information and entertainment, speed up understanding, hold the attention, make a more lasting impression, and, by the combination of sound, action, and color, capture the interest and inform consumer audiences.

Public relations departments of large corporations have film sections responsible for producing or contracting for production, supervising, distributing, and evaluating institutional 16 mm sound motion picture films. The operations of these departments are described in Chapter 22, "Public Relations Films." Some companies maintain several film libraries in various parts of the country to expedite distribution of films to consumer groups, including civic, religious, fraternal, women's, and educational organizations. Films are available to the public for individual showings on a free loan basis. The sponsor pays the cost of shipping to the borrower who pays shipping charges on the return.

The public relations department, Ford Motor Company, has available for consumer showings 37 titles in five areas: the Automobile Industry, Americans at Home, Vacation Films, Educational Subjects, and Driver Education. Shell Oil Company distributes 24 subjects which have 225,000 showings to more than 14 million viewers annually. Many other corporations maintain film libraries for consumers.

Films are also produced and distributed to consumer groups by trade associations to create a better understanding of the operations and problems of an entire industry. The Association of American Railroads has produced "Mainline USA" which has been shown 47,000 times over a four-year period to more than 3½ million people.

Exhibits and Demonstrations. Exhibits and demonstrations are widely used to inform consumers about an organization's products, services, and activities. Exhibits portray the scope of a corporation's operations, the variety and quality of its products, its manufacturing processes, and its growth and progress.

Permanent industrial exhibits installed by large corporations in the Museum of Science and Industry, Chicago, and the Franklin Institute, Philadelphia, are viewed by hundreds of thousands of consumers annually. The model farm of the International Harvester Company at the Museum of Science and Industry, Chicago, shows the farm equipment produced by the company. A miniature oil refinery exhibited by the Sun Oil Company at the Franklin Institute, Philadelphia, informs users of oil and gasoline about the production of petroleum products.

Permanent exhibitions for consumers are maintained by some corporations in New York and Chicago. The Radio Corporation of America established, in 1947, the RCA Exhibition Hall in Radio City, New York City. General Motors Corporation has traveling exhibits, "Motorama" and "Parade of Progress" which have been seen by millions of consumers.

Program Kits and Study Materials for Women's Clubs. The 200,000 women's clubs in the United States, with some 35 million members, are an important means of communication with women consumers. Women's clubs participate in a wide variety of educational programs and seek information from business, social service, and political organizations for programs and discussions. The Women's Club program kits and study materials prepared by public relations departments are distributed to club program committees.

Library Reference Materials. Thousands of public school and special libraries in the United States are an important channel for the distribution of consumer relations publications. Public libraries are used extensively by women in preparing speeches and club programs, and by all members of the family for general reading. School libraries serve students seeking information about industry, home economics, social and political subjects. Business, professional, or technical libraries are consulted frequently for information about industrial organizations, processes, and operations. Libraries should be included on public relations lists to receive annual reports, executive speeches, institutional booklets, scientific reports, periodicals, and other public relations communications.

Consumer Periodicals. Large corporations publish magazines to entertain and inform consumers about the company, its products, policies, and accomplishments. The Ford Motor Company publishes a monthly, pocket-size magazine, the *Ford Times,* for owners and prospective customers. International Business Machines Corporation publishes *Think,* and Burroughs Corporation publishes *Burroughs Clearing House.*

Special Consumer Events. Special events to educate or entertain youth and the general consumer public are an important medium of consumer relations.

A well-known youth event is the annual R. H. Macy Thanksgiving parade in New York City, which attracts several hundred thousand children and adults, who see Macy employees parade with mammoth inflated rubber toys.

Neiman-Marcus, Dallas, Texas, department store, staged a "Far Eastern Fortnight," one of a series of international presentations featuring Oriental products, music, drama, and art. Exhibitions, fashion shows, luncheons, teas, and dinners at which distinguished guests participated, including the Ambassadors of India, Thailand, Malaya, and Ceylon, were arranged by the public relations department of the store.

Consumer Correspondence. Correspondence with consumers in response to inquiries, suggestions, and complaints is extensively employed in creating a better understanding of an organization. Some public relations departments have a separate section responsible for handling correspondence with consumers.

The volume of correspondence with consumers handled by a public relations department is indicated by the experience of the Association of American Railroads which, in a recent year, received and answered 161,000 requests from the public for railroad information and materials.

A leading food product manufacturer answers an average of 10,000 consumer requests a year and distributes 50,000 pieces of literature on food preparation.

Consumer Institutional Advertising. Institutional advertising to consumers is a public relations medium used by an increasing number of organizations to inform customers and the general public about a corporation's progress, operations, research, and contributions to the public welfare. Some corporations employ consumer advertising on public service themes, including safe driving, preventing forest fires, combating disease, and advancing education.

Westinghouse Electric Corporation carries on an institutional advertising campaign to inform consumers about its technical accomplishments, to establish public confidence in the company and its products, and to create a better understanding of the company by the consuming public.

John Hancock Mutual Life Insurance Company, for more than ten years, has paid tribute to great American leaders in page advertisements in color in consumer magazines.

Container Corporation's series of color advertisements in national magazines on the theme of "Great Ideas of Western Man" have been acclaimed as sound institutional advertising.

Consumer Literature. Consumer literature, including booklets, folders, bulletins, and pamphlets, is widely used in public relations programs to promote greater public understanding and appreciation of an organization and its activities. This direct-mail advertising medium is more selective than general advertising as it can be used to reach particular segments of the general public, such as youths, women, farmers, and other special-interest groups. It provides sufficient space to tell a complete story and to illustrate the message. In addition, it is a flexible medium as it may be produced in various sizes and forms. The preparation of consumer literature is a major function of public relations departments.

Case 8–1

YOUTH RELATIONS

General Motors Corporation

General Motors Corporation, Detroit, Michigan, is an operating company composed of 42 operating divisions and subsidiaries in the United States and Canada. Products manufactured include Chevrolet, Pontiac, Oldsmobile, Buick, and Cadillac automobiles, trucks, buses, Diesel locomotives and engines, heavy-duty off-the-highway earth-moving equipment, Frigidaire household appliances, automotive parts, and accessories. World-wide employment averaged 595,000 in 1960, and the corporation is owned by 830,000 stockholders.

Public relations in General Motors is the responsibility of the Public Relations Staff in Detroit headed by a vice-president. The staff is organized in the following sections: news relations with offices in Detroit and New York, plant city and field relations, institutional advertising, editorial planning, institutional writing and stockholder relations, divisional relations, and educational relations. This is a part of the staff organization, and each operating division of GM also carries on its own public relations activities, some on a comparatively large scale.

Both the central staff and the divisional public relations departments are active in youth relations. Some of the objectives are encouraging the development of creativity and craftsmanship among boys, providing teen-age boys and girls with information about careers, awakening young men to the importance of science and engineering, promoting safe driving by youth, and giving financial aid to highly qualified youth with limited funds to enable them to secure a college education. Following are some of the methods being used to pursue these objectives.

One of the principal mediums of communication with youth is the *American Youth* magazine edited especially for teenagers and mailed free bimonthly to the homes of more than a million recently licensed young automobile drivers throughout the United States and Canada. Each issue contains articles of interest to boys and girls of high-school age, including stories about hobbies, sports, school activities, vocational guidance, outstanding teen-agers, and at least one article designed to promote safe driving habits among the nation's young motorists.

Each issue of 24 pages, including covers, is 11 × 8¼ inches in size. It is printed in two colors and profusely illustrated. *American Youth* is published for General Motors by Ceco Publishing Company, Detroit, a division of Campbell-Ewald Company, national advertising agency. The only mention of General Motors in the magazine is in the masthead and in a full-page advertisement on the back cover featuring safe driving.

The editorial content is widely diversified in subject. The January–February, 1961, issue carried articles with these titles: "Young American of the Month," "President of the National Student Safety Association," "The Cleveland Youth Symphony Orchestra Is a Training Ground for Tomorrow's Talent," "This Is a Library," "Rate Your Date as a Driver," "Typing the Blind Can Read," "Airline Hostess," "Spectacular Showcase" (a story of General Motors Motorama), "Youth Employment Service in Phoenix, Arizona," "Hot Shots" (a story of youth skeet-shooting champions), "They Study Winter Survival" (a college course in survival in the woods), and "Young America Has Its Say" (comments of youth on controversial questions).

The names and addresses of young people to whom *American Youth* is mailed are secured from state automobile licensing departments. Each boy and girl selected to receive the magazine is sent a personally addressed letter by John F. Gordon, President, General Motors, congratulating him or her on receiving a driver's license and informing the recipient that *American Youth* is being sent. This letter emphasizes that a driver's license is not only a privilege but also represents a responsibility to drive safely and respect the rights of other drivers.

Readership studies of *American Youth* magazine indicate that safe driving articles rank among the highest in general interest. Thousands of letters have been received from youth, parents, safety authorities, and others expressing approval of the magazine's constructive stand on the problem of safe driving by teen-agers. Young people write that they appreciate a large company taking an interest in them and their driving. Parents are grateful for the company's interest in impressing their children with the importance of safe driving. More than 13,000 school authorities have requested that their school libraries be sent the magazine.

Relations with 4-H Clubs and Future Farmers of America

General Motors youth relations activities are planned to secure the good will of tomorrow's farm leaders through sponsorship of the national 4-H club program to reduce accidents in the home, on the farm, and on the highways. More than 600,000 farm boys and girls, members of the 4-H Clubs, which have a national membership of 2,250,000, participated in the General Motors safety training program in 1960. This program is conducted by 4-H Club leaders under the guidance of 11,000 county extension agents.

Safety awards on county, state, and national levels are provided by General Motors. National awards of eight $400 college scholarships are presented to the outstanding state competition winners. State winners also receive all-expense trips to the National 4-H Club Congress as representatives of the counties with the most outstanding county-wide 4-H safety programs in each state. In addition, certificates of merit are awarded to the ten outstanding 4-H Clubs in each state. County winners receive gold medals, and certificates are presented to the 4-H Clubs with the outstanding safety programs in each county. State winners are honored with a luncheon at the National Congress.

The corporation supplies 4-H Club leaders with highway safety and driver training materials including copies of the booklets: "We Drivers," and "How the Wheels Revolve"; the films "Your Permit to Drive," "We Drivers," and "Passing Fancy"; wall charts showing "Automotive Stopping Distances" and "Horsepower for Safety."

In addition to sponsorship of 4-H Club awards, General Motors also supports the Future Farmers of America Foundation which provides an opportunity for farm youth to receive training in leadership and citizenship.

General Motors dealers co-operate with 4-H and Future Farmers of America clubs, in their communities, by arranging for periodic inspections of leaders' and members' cars and trucks; by showing safety motion pictures, sponsoring dinners for presentation of safe-driving awards to local winners, and showroom displays in connection with 4-H and Future Farmers community events. Managers of General Motors plants arrange for plant tours by members of these organizations.

Fisher Body Craftsman's Guild

To develop creativity and craftsmanship among boys, the Fisher Body Craftsman's Guild was founded in 1930 by management of the Fisher Body

Division of General Motors in collaboration with leading educators. The Guild program is designed to give teen-age boys an opportunity to practice fine craftsmanship by means of model automobile building competitions in which liberal awards, including university scholarships, serve as incentives.

Annual awards of $38,000 in college scholarships, in addition to $79,000 in cash, and other prizes go to young men from 12 to 21 years of age who design and build model cars. Since 1930 the Guild has awarded 238 university scholarships valued at $650,500 to national winners. Approximately $1,100,000 in cash and other awards have been made to winners in state and regional competitions.

About 400,000 boys enter this competition each year and nearly five million young craftsmen have become members of the Guild since it was established. In addition to developing skill in craftsmanship, the Guild is one of industry's major talent sources and many former winners have achieved success in business and the professions through habits developed as Guild competitors.

All-American Soap Box Derby

To encourage youthful enterprise, competitive spirit, and good sportsmanship, Chevrolet Motor Division of General Motors has sponsored in conjunction with leading newspapers, radio and television stations, civic groups, fraternal organizations, and Chevrolet dealers the All-American Soap Box Derby.

The only competition of its kind, the Soap Box Derby which was initiated in 1934 is open to all boys 11 through 15 years of age who build and race

FIG. 8–2. Youth public relations activity of Chevrolet division, General Motors Corp., the annual All-American Soap Box Derby, held at Akron, Ohio, and dedicated to the youth of America.

gravity propelled cars of their own design. The National Championship is held annually at a specially constructed raceway at Akron, Ohio. Winners receive $15,000 in college scholarships, valuable merchandise, and trophies. About 50,000 boys build and race their cars annually in local races in the United States, Canada, Puerto Rico, South America, Europe, and the Philippines. From this number about 170 local champions are chosen to compete in the national championships in Akron.

Local winners who qualify for the All-American receive a trophy and an all-expense trip to Akron where they spend four days at Derbytown, a completely equipped lakeshore summer camp, enjoying swimming, baseball, horseback riding, and other sports under the direction of counselors. Prior to the race, contestants parade with bands through the city and appear in radio and television interviews. Popular actors, television stars, and singers entertain the champions. About 75,000 spectators from all parts of the country witness the event. After the race, all entrants are honored at a banquet of champions attended by nearly 1,700 parents, celebrities, Chevrolet executives, dealers, and local sponsors.

The Derby program is supervised by a national control and rules committee composed of sponsoring newspapers and Chevrolet executives. Each local race as well as the national competition is conducted under uniform rules which are enforced with rigid inspections. About three million persons witness and participate in the program, and for every boy who competes six adults are involved. Net proceeds are donated to Akron youth charities.

Education for Youth

Because General Motors is dependent upon a flow of trained young people into its organization, it provides financial assistance to well-qualified young men and women of limited financial means to enable them to attend college. The Scholarship Program is carried on by the Personnel Staff. The financial aid ranges from $200 to $2,000 annually and is given in the form of 304 four-year undergraduate scholarships to freshmen entering 111 private and 70 public schools in fifty states.

In addition, 100 four-year scholarships are awarded annually to secondary school seniors in a national competition based on the scholastic aptitude test of the College Entrance Examination Board, school records, and extra curricular activities. Private colleges which participate in either plan receive a grant-in-aid for each scholarship.

In its sixth year, this program is providing aid to 1,648 students in 216 colleges and universities. Graduates from this program have outstanding scholastic and extra curricular records. Forty-five per cent of the last graduating class were in the upper 5 per cent of their classes. Many were elected to Phi Beta Kappa, others were presidents of their student bodies, and others editors of their school publications.

The corporation also operates the General Motors Institute, Flint, Michigan, which offers four-year co-operative courses in engineering to outstanding high school gradates who alternate instruction with work experience in General Motors plants. Graduates receive degrees in mechanical, industrial, and electrical engineering and are employed in the corporation's plants.

QUESTIONS

1. What is your opinion of the youth activities program of General Motors Corporation? Comment favorably or otherwise on this program.

2. Is *American Youth* magazine a suitable medium of communication with the youth public? Why? Describe in detail the ways this magazine could be improved.

3. Is the program to gain the good will of farm youth satisfactory? Why? How would you improve this program?

4. Is the Fisher Body Craftsman's Guild a sound youth relations activity? Why? How would you improve this program?

5. What is your opinion of the All-American Soap Box Derby as a public relations event? In what ways would you improve the effectiveness of this event?

6. Is General Motors college scholarships program sound? Criticize this program.

Case 8–2

YOUTH RELATIONS

Electric Companies Public Information Program

The Electric Companies Public Information Program (P.I.P.) was established in 1949 as the national public relations arm of the investor-owned electric utility industry in the United States. Membership in the group is open to any investor-owned electric power and light company in the country.

The objective of the Public Information Program is to tell the positive story of the industry's achievements in terms of its betterment of the social, economic, and technical climate in the United States.

One of the principal features administered by P.I.P. is the National Youth Conference on the Atom. The purpose of this conference is to present to a group of the nation's most able high school students and teachers an authoritative and inspiring picture of the promise of the peaceful atom in its various applications and to help advance interest in the study of science in the United States.

The basic principles which govern the event are: it shall be primarily educational; specific public relations benefits to the sponsors shall not emanate primarily from publicity but mainly from a closer relationship of the utilities with educators, scientists, and high school students; the support of educators and scientists is essential; the role of the utilities shall be clearly shown as only one phase of the peaceful exploration of the uses of atomic energy; each participating company shall be given the responsibility for selection and sponsorship of the delegates; every company must obtain approval of local school authorities; and any investor-owned electric power company, even if not a member of the Electric Companies Public Information Program group, may participate in the conference.

The First National Youth Conference on the Atom was held in Atlantic

City, New Jersey, on April 30 through May 1, 1959. This event was so well received by students, teachers, scientists, and sponsoring companies that a second conference was held on October 20 through 22nd, 1960, at the Museum of Science and Industry, Chicago. A third conference was held on November 9 through 11, 1961, at the Palmer House, Chicago.

Second National Youth Conference

The Second National Youth Conference on the Atom held at the Museum of Science and Industry, Chicago, the largest of its kind in the world, was attended by 294 outstanding high school science students and 184 science teachers from 279 high schools in all parts of the country. This conference is

FIG. 8-3. Youth public relations—National Youth Conference on the Atom—a feature of the Electric Companies public information program sponsored by the investor-owned electric utility industry in the United States. Nearly 500 teachers and students from all parts of the nation hear atomic scientists discuss the future of the atom.

typical of the three meetings arranged by the Electric Companies Public Information Program.

The three-day event was co-sponsored by the National Science Teachers Association and Future Scientists of America Foundation with the co-operation of the American Association for the Advancement of Science, Argonne National Laboratory, Armour Research Foundation, Illinois Institute of Technology, Atomic Industrial Forum, Museum of Science and Industry, National Science Foundation, Science Clubs of America, and the University of Chicago.

The Second Youth Conference was addressed by national leaders in nuclear energy, science, business men, and educators including a U.S. Atomic Energy Commissioner, president of Commonwealth Edison Company, director of

Argonne National Laboratory, vice-president of The University of Chicago, and others.

The speakers discussed "Today's World of Science," "Things We Scientists Don't Know," "Mathematics as a Profession," and "Biology and Medicine in the Nuclear Age." Panel presentations were made on such subjects as "Five Different Approaches to Electric Power from Nuclear Fission," "Nuclear Propulsion," and "Atom Smashers and Strange Particles."

Following the speeches and panel presentations there were three hours and forty minutes of discussions of Science and Society: Atomic Frontiers, The Atom and Electricity, and Biology and Medicine. These discussions were led by sixty scientists and educators from Argonne National Laboratory, Armour Research Foundation, Illinois Institute of Technology, and The University of Chicago.

One entire day of the three-day conference was devoted to field trips to Argonne National Laboratory of the Atomic Energy Commission, operated by The University of Chicago, and to Dresden Nuclear Power Station, the nation's first privately financed atomic power plant, built and operated by Commonwealth Edison Company, Chicago.

The program was arranged by a program advisory committee of high school and college educators and the conference was endorsed by the United States Commissioner of Education.

The organization of the conference, building the program, arranging for speakers and tours, the mechanics of housing and feeding, procedure for selection of delegates, relations with participating companies and co-operating organizations, and publicity was the responsibility of Bozell & Jacobs, public relations counsel.

A 70-page Youth Conference Planning Guide was published for public and school relations executives of participating companies to provide basic facts about the conference, program details, advance program, names of participating companies and co-operating organizations, educators' reactions, lodging and feeding arrangements, selection of student and teacher delegates, public relations opportunities, and follow-up activities.

The cost of the conference was assumed by the participating companies, each of which paid for the travel, lodging, and food of its delegates sent to the conference. The average cost per delegate was about $100 plus travel expenses.

The high school student and teacher delegates were selected by the participating companies with the assistance of local educators. High scholastic aptitude, interest in science, achievements, character, and leadership were considered in selecting delegates. Examinations, essays, and science fairs were used in making selections. Both boys and girls from public and parochial schools were invited, along with one or more high school science teachers to accompany each delegation of students.

The conference was an exceptional vehicle for local public relations. Participating companies were mentioned in news stories in local newspapers; student delegates were featured on local radio and television programs and in full-page photo-feature articles. Company employee magazines carried illustrated articles picturing their delegates and describing the conference. An advance publicity kit containing announcements, news releases, and articles was sent each participating company by the Electric Companies Public Information Program to aid the electric companies in tailoring their local public relations efforts for the event.

Typical of local news releases prepared by participating companies was the following (by the Carolina Power & Light Co. Public Relations Department):

FROM: Jack Riley   *Immediate Release*
      Carolina Power & Light Co.
      Raleigh, N.C.

Cumberland Youth Wins
  C.P. & L. Award
w/illustration

Ken McAdams, Jr. of Route 6, Fayetteville, is North Carolina winner of Carolina Power & Light Company's expense paid trip to the Second National Youth Conference on the Atom October 20–22.

McAdams and his science teacher, Mrs. LaLuce Williams, will be guests of C.P. & L. at the three-day conference which will be held at the Museum of Science and Industry, Chicago.

Ken is a fifteen-year-old tenth grader at Fayetteville Senior High School chosen for the C.P. & L. award from among participants in the physical science division of the state's seven district science fairs. He was top winner in the district fair at Wilmington and won the Navy Cruise Award at the state fair at Raleigh.

His entry was a mock-up of a satellite cockpit with an apparatus for checking the reaction time of human beings in response to stimuli under long periods of isolation. He tested the machine on himself in the closed cockpit for a six-hour period.

The C.P. & L. winner is son of Mr. and Mrs. C. K. McAdams. His father is public relations director for the new Methodist College north of Fayetteville.

Following the conference, participating companies continued to capitalize on the public relations opportunities by suggesting that student and teacher delegates report on the conference to their classes. One company engaged its well-spoken student delegate to discuss the conference before civic clubs and other groups throughout its service area. Some electric companies have held nuclear conferences and seminars for students in their areas. Others have expanded their school and youth programs with plant visits, motion pictures, science fairs, and nuclear power meetings for the press.

Evaluations of the Second Youth Conference for the Atom by teacher and student delegates, educators, scientists, co-operating scientific organizations, and sponsoring companies have been highly complimentary.

Student reactions are expressed by a Cleveland delegate who said, "I will remember the experience throughout my lifetime. I hope to enter college and pursue a career in mathematics. My attendance has aided me in making a choice of a science career."

A teacher delegate expressed his approval as follows: "It can be stated unequivocally that the conference should be continued indefinitely and if possible expanded because it is an educational experience unequaled by any other extra-curricular activity of this type."

Forty-three out of 45 electric companies which responded to a postconference questionnaire believed that it was a worthwhile public relations activity for their companies, as well as the industry, from the standpoint of improved school relations, community and customer relations.

The conference enhanced the image of the electric industry among youth, educators, and scientists; demonstrated the industry's concern for education and its achievements in science and technology.

QUESTIONS

1. What is your general opinion of the National Youth Conference on the Atom sponsored by the Electric Companies Public Information Program? What are the advantages of this public relations activity to the electric industry? What are the limitations of this program?

2. Comment favorably or otherwise on the following features of the Second National Youth Conference on the Atom. (*a*) Location. (*b*) Duration. (*c*) Program. (*d*) Selection of delegates. (*e*) Planning. (*f*) Publicity. (*g*) Postconference activities.

3. In what way can the effectiveness of the National Youth Conference on the Atom be improved?

4. Should the Electric Companies Public Information Program undertake another type of public relations activity? If so, describe in detail a program which you believe would be more effective.

Problem 8-1

CONSUMER RELATIONS

The Optical Foundation

The Optical Foundation was established in 1959 by a group of prominent manufacturers of eyeglass lenses, frames, mountings, and ophthalmic products prescribed by ophthalmologists, optometrists, and opticians for the purpose of conserving eyesight. The foundation was incorporated in New York State with a capital of $100,000 subscribed by the incorporators to finance a public relations campaign to promote the welfare of the multimillion dollar optical industry.

The foundation is administered by a board of directors of twenty who are elected by members of the foundation. Each director, representing a member company, is elected for a term of three years. The board selects, from its twenty members, five who serve as an executive committee. In addition, the board elects a president who is the chief executive officer of the foundation. The directors, executive committee, and president serve without compensation.

In promoting the welfare of the optical industry, the foundation has several related objectives. It seeks to make the public aware of the growing prevalence of eye defects; to overcome the popular prejudice against wearing eyeglasses; to promote the custom of periodic eye examinations; and the correction of visual deficiencies by properly prescribed eyeglasses. The foundation desires to impress the public with the fact that glass technology and the ophthalmic sciences have progressed to the point at which it is possible for persons to obtain specialized eyewear for each specialized seeing need. The accomplishments of the ophthalmic profession in contributing to better seeing are publicized and educational programs employed to enhance the prestige of the profession.

Important factors in the foundation's campaign to conserve eyesight are the professional ophthalmologists, optometrists, and opticians who are specialists in the study and treatment of defects and diseases of the eye. Most of the eyewear of reliable optical manufacturers is available to the public only through optometrists, opticians, and oculists whose relations with the public are regulated by a professional code of ethics which prohibits advertising to the public. Accordingly manufacturers of eyeglasses have done no ophthalmic advertising direct to the public but restrict their advertising to the professional journals and direct-mail advertising to the profession. For this reason, identification by the public of the products of optical goods manufacturers has been indirect and complicated.

Because of the objection of the ophthalmic profession to the use of advertising in communicating with the public regarding the need for eye care, the Optical Foundation decided to use a public relations program which would not include paid advertising but would employ publicity to impress the public with the need for reducing eye strain and improving vision.

The board of directors of the foundation, after considering the qualifications of several public relations consulting organizations, selected the public relations firm of Macon, Howe, and Fuller, New York City, to research, plan, produce, and carry out a public relations program to accomplish the objectives of the foundation. The recommendations of the consultant are subject to approval by the executive committee of the foundation and the consulting firm is given full responsibility for executing the program.

The first recommendation of Macon, Howe, and Fuller was to make a survey of the prevalence of eye defects of the refractive type which are corrected or aided by wearing glasses. A representative sample of the population of various ages of adults and children was questioned and examined by qualified ophthalmologists to determine the prevalence of eye defects and ocular discomfort from headaches, eyestrain, blurred vision, tearing and burning of the eyes. It was anticipated that the survey would reveal a high percentage of persons with defective eyes and provide conclusive evidence of the need for sight conservation, the theme of the foundation's public relations program. The investigation would also determine the attitude of men, women, and children toward wearing eyeglasses.

The findings of the survey projected on a national basis showed that about one person in every five of the entire population of the United States wears eyeglasses, or some 36 million persons are dependent upon glasses for comfortable vision. A total of more than 72 million persons, or about 40 per cent of the people of the United States, have appreciable defects of vision of the refractive type.

Although nearly all infants are born with normal vision, by the time children graduate from high school about one out of four is suffering from nearsightedness. When they graduate from college one out of three has defective eyesight.

Forty per cent of the persons questioned in the investigation reported that they experienced ocular discomfort or inability to see clearly at all working distances. Approximately 70 per cent of the complaints involved headaches, eye ache, and blurred vision.

The survey revealed a widespread need for eyeglasses but also decided opposition to wearing glasses, particularly by women who felt that beauty and glasses were incompatible. The belief that glasses make a woman unattractive was held primarily by young, fashion-conscious girls. Other objections to glasses were that they are uncomfortable, particularly in warm weather, they are symbols of a physical handicap, expensive, inconvenient, and easily broken. For these reasons many persons with eye defects do not wear glasses.

The visual survey emphasized the need for a public relations program to correct the misconception that glasses were incompatible with good appearance; and convince people that they should wear glasses to reduce the burden on their eyes resulting from excessive viewing of television and motion pictures, close work in occupations where the tasks of seeing are severe; in studying and abnormal use of eyes under poor seeing conditions.

The first public relations project of the public relations counsel was a New York press conference to introduce the program to the press—newspaper and magazine editors, feature writers, radio and television news editors and commentators. A press luncheon at a large hotel was arranged for the press to meet the executive committee of the foundation and to hear the president discuss the prevalence of eye defects and the need for correcting the seeing difficulties of millions of people.

News stories were released through the wire services, articles were prepared for magazines, and editorials for small-circulation newspapers. One editorial, "Take Care of Your Eyes," appeared in more than 100 daily and weekly newspapers throughout the country.

In addition to news releases quoting well-known ophthalmologists on the need for sight conservation, the foundation launched a national competition to select the most beautiful women in the United States who wear glasses. The purpose of this contest was to prove that glasses do not make a person unattractive and to overcome the popular prejudice against glasses for this reason. The competition was designed to be more than a beauty contest. Professional opticians and optometrists were asked to nominate candidates for the winning award of an all-expense trip to Paris. From 300 entrants, a winner was selected by a committee of well-known artists and portrait photographers and crowned at a banquet at the Waldorf in New York. The winner was presented to the public on a popular television program by a well-known broadcaster. Motion pictures of the contest winner were taken by newsreel services and distributed to theaters and television stations. Stories in newspapers and in general magazines secured extensive publicity for the event.

A television film was produced in which the president of the foundation was interviewed along with reputable ophthalmologists to emphasize the prevalence of eye defects, the increasing burdens on the eyes, and the importance of periodic eye examinations and preventive measures for relieving eye strain.

A booklet, "Eyesight and Seeing," was distributed to 20,000 teachers in elementary schools and to the presidents of 300 women's clubs throughout the country.

Optical goods manufacturers who are members of the foundation supplemented the public relations program by producing attractive frames and mountings to appeal to the fashion-conscious woman and to overcome the impression that glasses make one unattractive. Tie-up publicity by individual manufacturers in their company publications and bulletins to salesmen and the profession was used extensively.

The executive committee of the foundation in appraising the program believes that it has not been as effective as it should have been because it was spread too thin. With an annual budget of $100,000 the foundation tried to blanket the nation with publicity to give the public an accurate understanding of the problem of seeing and the need for preventive measures to counter eyestrain. Poor targets were chosen. The program should have been concentrated on opinion leaders such as club women, educators, doctors, government officials, ophthalmologists, optometrists, and opticians rather than the general public, in the opinion of a spokesman for the committee.

Although members of the executive committee of the foundation did not deny that the campaign was beneficial, they would like to see future campaigns concentrated on opinion leaders and less publicity slanted. Although the effectiveness of the program cannot be accurately measured, a new approach is obviously needed.

The board of directors of the foundation is considering the desirability of affiliating with the Optical Manufacturers Association and operating from the association's national headquarters in New York City, with a full-time manager of the foundation to be responsible to the president of the association. Under this arrangement, the foundation would be the public relations arm of the Optical Manufacturers Association but continue to handle its own finances. If it affiliated with the association, the foundation would be closer to the public relations problems of the optical industry.

QUESTIONS

1. Why did the public relations program of the Optical Foundation fail to meet the expectations of its sponsors? What shortcomings in addition to those described in the problem account for the failure of this public relations program?

2. Prepare a new public relations program for the Optical Foundation describing the essential organization, financing, objectives, publics to be reached, and media of communication to insure a more effective campaign.

3. How should the public relations program of the Optical Foundation be financed? What amount should be appropriated for such a program? To what items of expense should the appropriation be budgeted? How much should be spent for each item?

9 · COMMUNITY RELATIONS

A COMMUNITY is a group of people living in the same place and having common interests in work, play, worship, learning, and social satisfactions. To satisfy their common needs for a good material, spiritual, and social life, people in communities have established in co-operation with their neighbors such institutions as churches, schools, factories, stores, government, and social service organizations.

The people and their institutions in a community have a responsibility to work together to solve their mutual problems and build a better community. Neither the institutions nor the people of a community can realize the opportunities and rewards of good community life without contributing to community welfare. They must be willing to give to the community as well as to take. The people living in a community and the stores, factories, and business firms serving them must balance the benefits they receive from the community with equal benefactions to the community.

Business derives numerous benefits from the community in which it operates. The schools provide educated workers with good attitudes, skills, and work habits. The churches develop employees of good morals and character. The local government furnishes fire, police, sanitary services, and highway facilities. The public utilities provide water, gas, electricity, and transportation; and the social service organizations contribute health, hospital, and medical facilities.

In return the community expects a business organization to provide regular employment, good working conditions, fair pay, and satisfying work; to purchase goods and services locally and put money in circulation in the community; to pay its share of taxes to support the local government; to contribute to worthwhile local charitable and cultural projects; and to be a good neighbor by keeping a clean and attractive place of business. A business should be operated for the benefit of the community in which it operates as well as in the interest of its stockholders, employees, and customers. A business organization, like any other community institution, can remain in existence only as long as the public permits it to survive.

A company's reputation in a community affects its success in recruiting good personnel, in securing reputable dealers, in selling its products, in maintaining the morale of its own employees, and in other important ways. It must create an image of good citizenship by each employee accepting his responsibility as a good citizen and by the company, as a corporate citizen, accepting its share of civic responsibility as well.

Business-Community Relationships

The role of business in community life has undergone radical changes since the first of the century. Fifty years ago, almost everything was made in the community and sold locally by hometown merchants. Business was largely local. However, as communities grew and industry expanded, many companies from outside the community built local plants or established stores in the area. These enterprises were regarded by residents of the community as outsiders with little interest in the welfare of the community. Companies regarded as outsiders experienced difficulty in building good community relations.

Poor community relations are caused by the failure of many companies to recognize their responsibilities to the communities in which they operate. Some companies assume that they have satisfied their community obligations when they have paid their taxes. They fail to recognize that they have a responsibility to contribute to the well-being of the community by matching the labor, skill, and services contributed by the community with an equal contribution to community development.

Benefits of Good Community Relations

Effective recruiting of desirable new employees depends upon the reputation which a company enjoys in its community as a "good company to work for." Good living conditions in a community also attract employees who prefer to work and live in attractive surroundings, send their children to good schools, enjoy facilities for recreation, attend good churches, live in modern housing, and have good transportation.

Good community reputation creates sales for producers of consumer products in plant communities.

Efficient business operation is dependent upon good public utilities, fire, police, sanitation, water services provided by the community.

Residents of a plant community are potential stockholders who can contribute to good plant community relations by creating good will for the company and defending it against discriminatory local regulations, taxes, or legislation.

Good community relations secure local identity for the local plant of a national corporation and allay public mistrust of absentee ownership.

Community Relations Policy

The foundation of a sound community relations program is the community relations policy. Typical of good community relations policies is the policy of Standard Oil Company, Indiana, which reads:

Standard Oil Company tries to be a good corporate citizen. Members of the management want the company to be known as just that in each of its many home towns.

A reputation for good citizenship must be earned. The company is continually striving to earn and maintain a reputation for good citizenship. It expresses good citizenship in its primary functions: to provide useful products and services, good employment, and profits to pay for continued growth and progress. It recognizes that good citizenship also calls for contributions of time and effort to civic, professional, and welfare activities.

Employee participation in community affairs is essential if the company is to be regarded as a good citizen. The company encourages employees to take part in such activities for the good of the community, the company, and the employees themselves.

Employees are encouraged to serve on boards of education, boards of trustees or regents of universities, library boards, planning commissions, and on similar bodies. It is understood that such responsibilities are not to interfere with good job performance. Employees who hold public office should avoid taking sides on questions appearing to involve company interests.

Employees are encouraged to do their reasonable share of the work in fund raising campaigns such as Community Chest and Red Cross drives.

COMMUNITY RELATIONS PROGRAM

Objectives of a Community Relations Program

The objectives of community relations programs vary widely according to the size and characteristics of the cities and towns in which they function and the needs of the organizations sponsoring the programs. Some of the principal objectives of community relations are as follows:

To inform the community about a company's policies, operations, and problems and to tell the story of what it makes, how many people it employs, the amount of its payroll, what it pays in taxes, what it spends locally, how it regards its community responsibilities, and what it contributes to the social and economic life of the locality.

To inform all people connected with a company about its operations and to stimulate them to tell the corporate story to their friends and neighbors in the community.

To correct misunderstandings, answer criticisms, and repel attacks on a company and its policies by local pressure groups who are misinformed about the company and industry.

To establish a company as an important factor in community life through contributions to local institutions and participation in neighborhood affairs.

To find out what the local public is thinking and saying about a company and its policies and operations.

To promote the welfare of a community by advertising its advantages and attractions to tourists, and by promoting its resources and industrial potential to attract new industry.

To win the support of a community during labor controversies through a candid discussion of the issues involved and the company's position.

To get acquainted with a community by inviting local groups and opinion leaders to meet corporate executives and see how a concern operates.

To aid community education through co-operation with schools and colleges in providing educational materials and furnishing facilities and equipment for training youths and adults.

To provide cultural leadership by encouraging a greater appreciation of art, music, and the drama, and an enrichment of community life.

To aid cattle raising or agriculture in areas where community welfare is dependent on the prosperity of the surrounding farms or ranches.

To promote community health by supporting local health programs and by aiding the local Red Cross and hospitals.

To support local sports and recreation activities by providing facilities and equipment and sponsoring events for neighborhood and community groups.

To support local youth programs to combat juvenile delinquency and gain the good will of future citizens of the town.

To promote a better understanding of national and local affairs through the organization of community forums and discussion groups for youth and adults of the locality.

To aid local government in the improvement of public services and facilities.

To co-operate with other companies in a community in promoting a better understanding of business and in advancing community welfare.

COMMUNITY RELATIONS OBJECTIVES OF A LARGE
INDUSTRIAL COMPANY

The community relations objectives of Westinghouse Electric Corporation, Pittsburgh, Pennsylvania, serve to illustrate the purposes of a company's community relations program.

The community relations manager at headquarters has as his main objective assisting local management in the execution of community relations policy and supervising and co-ordinating company-wide programs.

Maintaining good community relations is the primary responsibility of local management, division and plant managers. Divisions maintain a staff to establish and direct a program of community relations.

The objectives of Westinghouse community relations are:

To show the citizens of every plant community that Westinghouse is a good citizen and a good employer.

To demonstrate that the local plant is not just a branch of a large corporation, but is a local business which fully accepts and willingly acts upon its local obligations and interests.

To maintain harmonious relationships with community leaders, based on a spirit of mutual respect and interest.

To keep the local community fully informed of what the company is doing and trying to do and why, to the end that the best understanding and appreciation of the company's activities will be achieved.

To create an employee climate conducive to efficient and uninterrupted operations, and attraction of the most desirable people of the community as our employees.

To aid the community in maintaining itself as a desirable place in which to live and work, and as a partner in our growth, with full recognition of its obligations to its industrial citizens.

Co-operative Community Relations Program

In some communities, business organizations are co-operating in joint public relations programs to improve the social, cultural, economic, educational climates of the areas. In addition to conducting their individual corporate community relations activities, the public relations talent of many companies is being used to plan and carry out integrated community relations.

The objectives of co-operative community relations programs range from stocking the municipal zoo to slum clearance and neighborhood rehabilitation. The leader in a co-operative program may be a community-minded industrial corporation, a local Chamber of Commerce, a manufacturer's association, industrial development corporation, taxpayers' association, industrial foundation.

The Committee on Business Information of Worcester, Massachusetts, established in 1937 has a membership of 90 manufacturing, commercial, banking, and insurance firms which jointly sponsor a co-operative community relations program. The principal activity is an aid to education program consisting of business-industry education days for teachers, vocational conferences for students, an annual essay contest, economic education of teachers, plant tours for students, an educational film library. Other activities of the committee are church-industry discussion meetings; employer-employee communications library; industrial magazine editors council; speakers' bureau; radio, television, and newspaper publicity; library exhibits; and participation in fund raising for local charities.

Better Business Climate Programs

An increasing number of industrial corporations are co-operating in Business Climate Improvement Programs to better the social and political environment in which they operate and insure industrial and commercial growth and vitality, community progress and prosperity. The term "business climate" is defined as the net result of social, political, and economic factors which influence the cost and facility of doing business, and the ability of a company to contribute to the prosperity and well-being of the community.

The General Electric Company through its Community and Business Relations Service has adopted Business Climate Improvement as an important part of its community relations activities in the 123 plant towns and cities in which it operates. A handbook, "Improving Your Community's Business Climate," published by General Electric, describes the procedures and methods to be followed by corporations, civic groups, Chambers of Commerce, and industrial development boards in undertaking community business climate improvement programs.

The benefits of these programs are both tangible and intangible. Tangible results are: improved highways, better schools, more efficient local government, or more equitable taxation. Intangible results are: improved relations among community groups, increased community spirit, and the ability of a community to identify and solve its problems.

Community business climate improvement programs have been successfully conducted in Rome, New York; San Mateo County, California; Rhode Island; Syracuse, New York; and Ft. Wayne, Indiana. More than 200 community appraisals leading to community improvement have been made.

Some of the factors which handicap the profitable operation of business in communities throughout the country are: high unemployment costs, abuse in the administration of unemployment compensation, inadequate parking facilities, excessive workman compensation awards, failure of schools to prepare young people for business, discriminatory freight rates, inadequate planning for industrial growth, lack of urban redevelopment, bad employment practices, air pollution, poor transportation facilities, and others.

The work involved in community business climate improvement programs includes problem exploration, community development, political activity, and management practices. The first step is to make an appraisal to identify problem areas in need of improvement. Surveys are made, using a battery of three questionnaires prepared by General Electric Company, entitled, "Community Appraisal," "Businessman's Supplement to the Community Appraisal," and "Industrial Climate Audit." On the basis of information disclosed by the surveys, problem areas are designated for improvement. Further investigation is made of the problem areas, the feasibility of action is determined, and a plan for action developed and put into operation.

Role of Employees in Community Relations

Community relations should be an essential activity of every employee who lives in a community where a plant, branch, or store of the company employing him is located. Community opinion surveys show that every employee has regular contacts outside the plant or office where he works with approximately 50 people—members of his family, his neighbors, church people, tradesmen, and others. What an employee says about the company, its products, and policies influences the opinions of the company held by people in the community.

"Good community relations grow largely from the attitude of employees," says Paul W. Garrett, public relations counsel. "As citizens of the community in which the company has its being, they are the best spokesmen for its policies." The words and actions of employees have an important influence on corporate community relations. Community relations is not something that can be left to a headquarters or plant public relations office.

"The impressions we leave in our daily relations with neighbors, relatives, friends, and acquaintances are important in community relations," says Sydney Steele, director, public relations Atlas Chemical Industries, Wilmington, Delaware, speaking to Atlas employees. "A single employee grumbling over the back fence to a couple of neighbors about his job, or an inconsiderate Atlas driver, can tear down part of the reputation we've all worked so hard to earn. Every time you deal with someone outside the company, that someone forms an opinion of you and the company."

Community opinion surveys confirm that employees are either positive or negative in their comments about the company by which they are employed depending largely upon their own attitudes toward the company. A worker's satisfaction with his job and company affects not only what he says to his friends and neighbors about the company but how well they accept his comments about the company. For this reason good employee relations is the basis of good community relations.

Employee participation in civic affairs is an important factor in the effectiveness of a community relations program. Large corporations survey employees to determine their participation in community activities. The accompanying questionnaire form, used by International Business Machines Corporation, illustrates such a survey.

COMMUNITY RELATIONS SURVEY

The International Business Machines Corporation has always endeavored to be a good corporate citizen. In addition, many employees have been active in civic affairs on an individual basis. This has brought credit to them as well as to the company. In this survey, we are attempting to learn what types of community activities IBMers are active in—aiding by serving as officers, committeemen, or any other official capacity. This is merely a statistical survey, therefore, you need not identify yourself in any way.

Are you *active* in, or any officer of, any one or more of the following: (If an officer, board member or committeeman, please indicate title).

☐ School board

☐ Boy or Girl Scouts

☐ Other educational activities (PTA, teaching, lecturing, alumni(ae) association).

☐ Charitable organizations, (United Fund, Heart Fund, etc.)

☐ Public office (Write in name of office) Elected office (i.e. mayor)

☐ Junior Achievement (i.e., Advisor)

☐ Appointed office (i.e., Deputy Sheriff)

☐ Little League

☐ Civil Defense groups

☐ Service clubs (Rotary, Kiwanis, etc.)

☐ Hospital board

☐ Chamber of Commerce

☐ All others (please specify)*   ☐ Junior Chamber of Commerce
(YMCA, YWCA, professional   _____
organizations: Example: Nat'l   _____
Accountants' Assoc., NOMA,
etc.)

_____

_____

* Use this for categories not previously covered. We have only listed a few major areas of community service and realize there are many other important activities.

If employee attitudes toward a company are favorable, and if employees are informed about company policies, practices, and contributions to community welfare, good community relations are sure to result.

Organization for Community Relations

Administration and execution of a community relations program in plant communities is the responsibility of local plant management or a committee with the assistance of headquarters staff community relations specialists.

A basic community relations program is developed by the headquarters public relations department and made available to individual plants which adapt it to the needs of their particular plant communities. The headquarters public relations department prepares programs and media of communication and offers advice and assistance to local plants through field or regional public relations offices to insure effective operation of the programs by the local plant management.

The organization of a headquarters community relations department of a large industrial corporation illustrates the specialized functions and personnel found in such a department. The Caterpillar Tractor Company, Peoria, Illinois, community relations department is staffed with seventeen people reporting to the director of community relations. There are four sections, as follows: Administration—responsible for supervision of the department, expense records, and forecasts and contribution requests; Institutional Advertising in the area and company representation in community organizations; Literature, including mailings and racks, in additon to film and speaker scheduling, special events, and exhibits; Plant Escort Service—responsible for plant trip supervision, escort training of full-time guides, and visitor photographs. The heads of each section also make public speeches, write, and work in civic affairs.

The Ford Motor Company community relations program for all local

company installations is organized with 34 community relations committees in the principal cities of the country. Each committee is composed of
as many of the following executives as may be located in a particular
city: division general manager, controller, industrial relations manager;
regional sales manager; district sales manager; plant manager, controller, industrial relations manager, and depot manager.

The specific activities of these committees are: planning and coordinating company community relations projects such as special plant
tours and receptions, and premieres of company films; maintaining
contact with community leaders and meeting with them to discuss local
problems; promoting the use of company literature, motion pictures,
speakers, and other program material by school and community groups;
recommending company contributions and memberships, participation
in community programs and plant city advertising. The committees
meet at 30- to 60-day intervals.

The committees are given advice and assistance by one of the eleven
field public relations offices of the company and the community relations
department at company headquarters, which has published a *Community
Relations Handbook* for members of community relations committees.
This handbook covers in fourteen chapters: committee organization and
procedure, community projects, company mailings, company films,
speech activities, plant tours, press, radio and television relations,
company sponsored programs, contributions and memberships budget,
investigating contributions requests, making a company contribution,
company-type memberships, and donation of automotive equipment. In
addition, the headquarters community relations department also publishes a Community Relations Bulletin.

Sears, Roebuck and Company, with some 700 retail stores, 800
catalogue sales offices, and 11 mail-order plants throughout the country
gives responsibility for community relations to the individual store or
plant manager.

Sears' community relations programs, based on specific recommendations of local managers, are planned by Sears five territorial public
relations departments. These territorial public relations offices are in
close contact with the operational vice-president, zone management,
mail-order management, and local store management in their respective
territories to give advice and suggest methods of participating in
community affairs. The decisions, commitments, and activities in each
community are the responsibility of local management which is concerned with such problems as contributions, taxation, education, urban
renewal, and legislation.

General Electric Company maintains a national public and employee relations service department to aid the managements of the 123 General Electric plants throughout the country with their plant community relations programs. The headquarters department does not dictate methods nor attempt to carry out community relations programs for operating components.

The plant manager of each General Electric component is responsible for community relations in his plant area. In large plants, the plant manager is assisted by a manager of plant community relations and staff who plan and carry out local community relations programs. In small plants, the plant manager is assisted by a personnel supervisor who handles community relations.

What a Community Wants to Know about Its Business Neighbors

The people in plant communities have a natural curiosity about their business neighbors just as they have about the family next door. The community is interested in a company's operations including: the number of employees; their hourly earnings; total payroll in the community; number of local stockholders; investment in local property; products produced; output of local plant; expenditures for fuel, rent, supplies, and maintenance; contributions to community projects; taxes paid to the community; research and development, and other information.

What a Business Should Know about Its Community

An initial step in a community relations program involves securing an understanding of the attitudes of local citizens toward a company and, in addition, a knowledge of the social, political, and economic problems of the community.

Community opinion surveys made by opinion research organizations reveal the attitudes of opinion leaders and various community groups toward local industry and provide valuable information about the needs of the community. In addition to determining the attitudes of people in the plant community, the investigation should also provide information about the activities of various community organizations as well as the social, political, and economic problems of the area. The corporate community relations program should contribute to a solution of community problems revealed by a community survey.

Community Opinion Surveys

Manufacturers, public utilities, banks, and commercial organizations are making community surveys to discover the attitudes of their neighbors toward their policies, operations, and activities in the plant community. Such surveys provide an opportunity to discover the specific likes and dislikes of people in the neighborhood; to determine how much the community knows about the company, the source of this information, and the community's attitudes about the company and its employees.

A community opinion survey should be made before a company locates in a community to determine the public attitude toward the newcomer so that the community relations program can correct misconceptions and insure a more favorable reception.

Community opinion surveys should be conducted periodically in order to appraise community attitude toward the company and the effectiveness of its community relations program.

Community Climate Surveys

Business climate surveys should also be made to identify community problems in need of solution and to determine the influence of economic, social, and political conditions on business operations.

The three business climate questionnaires prepared by General Electric Company, discussed previously in this chapter, may be used in a community climate survey. Community surveys are the responsibility of a public relations department and community relations staff with outside assistance of opinion research organizations.

Planning a Community Relations Program

The first step in planning a community relations program is opinion research to determine attitudes toward the company and to give an understanding of the social, economic, and political conditions which determine the climate of the community in which the business operates.

Next, the policies and practices of the company should be critically examined for the purpose of correcting those which the survey shows the public dislikes, in order to deserve and secure favorable community understanding. Personnel policies and practices which affect employee attitudes and job satisfactions should be evaluated as these policies affect the morale of workers and their inclination to speak well of the company to their friends and neighbors.

Considering the information revealed by the survey of community opinion, the long- and short-range objectives of the community relations program are determined. This is necessary for the guidance of the public relations staff in planning a program to solve specific problems rather than merely communicating general information about the company.

The co-operation of local management and employees in carrying out the community relations program must be secured. Informal communication of employees with their friends in the plant community is essential to success of the community relations program.

The effectiveness of the program should be ascertained through opinion research of the community public.

The methods of communication to tell employees and community neighbors about company aims, objectives, and problems are selected. A program schedule of the dates for special events, local advertising, opinion leader meetings, broadcasts, and other activities should accompany the program plan.

Outstanding Community Relations Programs

Caterpillar Tractor Company. The community relations program of the Caterpillar Tractor Company, Peoria, Illinois, has the objective of developing and retaining the respect of the people in about 100 towns where the 21,000 employees of the main plant in Peoria make their homes. To accomplish this objective, the community relations department of the company carries on several major activities.

To inform the community about company affairs, local newspaper and radio publicity is regularly placed in three local daily papers, forty-two weekly papers, five radio stations, and in the company periodical, *News and Views.*

To keep community leaders informed, regular mailings are made to a list of 8,000 educators, business and professional men, clergymen, local government officials, tradesmen, and barbers and beauty shop operators.

More than 12,000 persons visit the company's Peoria plant annually to see and hear about plant operations from trained escorts of the community relations department. Regular plant tours are made daily and special trips arranged for specific groups such as students, rural organizations, Boy Scout troops, and civic, church, and luncheon clubs. Special tours are arranged for particular groups which see a company film, hear from executives, and have luncheon as guests of the company. Each group of visitors is photographed by the community relations department and presented with a folder containing a photograph of the group.

Participation by Caterpillar employees in community activities is encouraged by management. More than 150 memberships in the local association of commerce are paid for by the company and half of those who hold memberships serve actively on committees. Eighty-one employees hold positions in the governments of nearby communities.

Program chairmen of local parent-teacher associations and church, women's, and civic clubs are provided with program material, films, and speakers. As many as 886 requests for speakers have been filled by the community relations department in a year.

Community discussion groups, composed of representatives of local churches, business, education, and labor to discuss community social and economic problems, are organized by the community relations staff.

Contributions to community charitable, welfare, health, and educational organizations are an important factor in the Caterpillar program for building community good will.

Ford Motor Company. The Ford Motor Company's community relations committees in 34 cities across the country conduct in these communities company-wide community relations projects such as Industrial Education Days, Suppliers' Days, driver-training film premieres. In addition, there are individual committee projects such as plant tours, luncheons for opinion leaders or prominent visitors. They mail copies of executive speeches, booklets, and reprints of magazine articles to local opinion leaders; circulate company films to local groups; fill requests for speakers; provide for plant tours; keep channels to local news media open, and finally, arrange local tie-ins with company sponsored institutional programs for youth, handle company contributions in the community, and arrange donations of automobile equipment to schools.

General Electric Company. The General Electric Company's Public and Employee Relations Services department provides the managements of 123 General Electric components throughout the country with ideas, plans, and programs for local community relations. Community programs of various plants of the company are described monthly in the "General Electric Community Relations Review" circulated to the managements of all General Electric plants.

The General Electric Kit of community relations materials, prepared by the Public and Employee Services department, contains 25 manuals based on various problems and opportunities which the company's operating managements encounter in community relations. These manuals cover such subjects as: "Program for Clergy," "A Community Relations Program for Physicians," "Program for Women," "Plant Dedications, Plant Tours, and Open House," "Speakers' Bureau Source Kit," "The Use of Newspaper Advertising in Plant Community Relations," "Press, Radio, and TV Relations in Plant Communities," and "Mailings to Civic Thought Leaders."

The General Electric Check List of Plant Community Relations Activities, illustrates the nature of the community relations programs of various General Electric components.

GENERAL ELECTRIC

Check List of Plant Community Relations Activities

Does Your Plant Community Relations Program Include the Following?

Yes No

1. Periodic opinion surveys to determine community "likes" and "dislikes" and to serve as a basis for planning your plant community relations program.
2. Activities which will help you interpret your plant's aims and objectives to the following specific community groups: clergy, doctors, dentists, nurses, teachers, school children, lawyers, local businessmen, and other civic groups.
3. Community mailing lists for distribution of company booklets, employee papers, articles, letters, and other materials to area civic leaders.
4. A well-planned working arrangement with area press, radio, and television representatives to insure maximum coverage on local and national issues affecting your plant.
5. A series of newspaper ads prepared to keep community neighbors informed on the highlights of plant activities, aims, and objectives.
6. Radio and television sponsored programs to improve communications between the plant and the community.
7. Speakers' bureau and film library to provide information about the plant and its activities to civic, social, educational, and service clubs.
8. Special events such as open house and plant tours to show the community how the various products in the plant are made and to demonstrate the superior working conditions and other advantages in working for G.E.
9. Plant Community Relations Council enabling area department representatives to contribute their ideas and plans for participation in civic affairs.
10. A planned program to encourage company employees to participate in the activities of civic, educational, industrial, youth, hospital, health, and other similar organizations and agencies.
11. A card index system listing the names of all employees active in civic affairs so that foremen and supervisors can acknowledge employees' participation.
12. Participation in the exchange of plant community relations ideas and techniques by submitting material for G.E. Plant Community Relations Review.

COMMUNICATIONS WITH THE COMMUNITY

Several channels of communication are used by business organizations in informing community neighbors about their policies, operations, and objectives. The principal media of community communication are: (1) newspaper advertising; (2) television and radio advertising; (3) press, television, and radio publicity; (4) community publications; (5) open house and plant tours; (6) public speaking; (7) opinion leader meetings; (8) visits to community institutions; (9) employee contacts; (10) motion pictures; (11) exhibits and displays; (12) annual reports; and (13) direct mail.

Newspaper Advertising

Local institutional newspaper advertising is a basic medium for communication with the people in plant communities. Newspaper advertising reaches a large proportion of the population. It is selective, permitting an advertiser to concentrate a message in a particular community or to reach a specific segment of the community public. Quick action in communicating an important message to the community is possible with daily newspaper advertising. Newspaper advertising reaches a majority of the families in a community at comparatively low cost.

Newspaper advertising is employed in community relations to correct misconceptions of community neighbors; to win the good will of plant city people; to develop a favorable attitude by local government officials; to keep the community informed of good working conditions; to render a public service to local welfare organizations and associate a company with community activities.

Radio and Television Advertising

Advertising on local radio and television stations is widely used in communicating institutional messages to a plant community. It provides the impact of the human voice, has showmanship through sound effects and music, reaches all income levels, gains prestige, inspires pride of employees, affords instantaneous communication, and is easily understood and remembered.

Press, Television, and Radio Publicity

Good news publicity is basic in all community relations programs for securing public understanding of the aims and operations of an organization.

Good personal relations between a concern's community press representative and local newspaper, television, and radio news editors is essential to secure a maximum of local publicity. Headquarters public relations departments prepare press releases on corporate matters of

Justin Nowicki
helps make Milwaukee Quality
at Chain Belt Co.

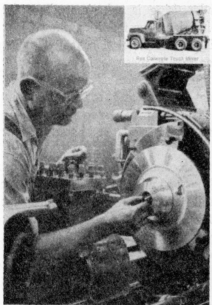

Justin W. Nowicki, 8450 W. Forest Home Ave., Greenfield
Member of Local 1527, United Steel Workers of America, AFL-CIO

Milwaukee Quality is made by people—people like Justin Nowicki—whose pride of workmanship shows in the work of his machine. Justin, a turret lathe operator for the Chain Belt Company, machines clutch plates with precision tolerances for the firm's Rex Concrete Truck Mixer (see inset photo above) ... and produces that something-extra quality that has made Milwaukee and Chain Belt famous.

Justin, an accomplished violinist and lover of classical music, demands true Milwaukee Quality in his beer, too. He enjoys practicing Chopin at home with a glass of beer. Naturally, he drinks Schlitz, famous the world over for extra quality. Schlitz—the only beer with just the kiss of the hops. Milwaukee brewed. Serve Schlitz proudly.

At Justin Nowicki's request, the Jos. Schlitz Brewing Co. is happy to send $100 to St. Mary's Catholic Church in Hales Corners for support of the choir.

Milwaukee Quality at its best

FIG. 9–1. Community relations newspaper advertisement, one of a series run in Milwaukee newspapers by Joseph Schlitz Brewing Co., Milwaukee, saluting the quality of Milwaukee products and the craftsmanship of the employees who make them.

special interest in local plant communities and send them direct to local newspapers. Local plant managers are encouraged to know members of their local press and to release news on plant construction, personnel, safety, employee relations, promotions, transfers, and other matters of local interest.

Public relations departments prepare publicity manuals for instruction of local managers in identifying news and in getting the co-operation of local editors and newspapers.

Company Publications

Some companies distribute their employee publications to selected lists of public officials, teachers, merchants, bankers, and other opinion leaders in plant communities. Others publish a bulletin for community leaders to bring them information about company employment, expansion, and operations.

A monthly "Community News Letter" is published and distributed to community leaders by the community relations departments of the General Electric Company in West Lynn, Massachusetts; Schenectady, New York; and Cincinnati, Ohio.

Open House and Plant Tours

One of the most effective ways to inform people of plant communities is to invite them to visit the plant and see and hear about its operations. The principal advantages of a plant tour are: People like to see how things are made and watch machines in operation. A plant tour establishes a company as a good place to work and shows that a company is interested in the welfare of its workers. It corrects misconceptions and gives the community an accurate impression of a business. An open house is a rapid means of building better community understanding. The hospitality and neighborliness of an open house give a company a "heart." Employee interest is stimulated by giving workers an opportunity to show their families and neighbors where and how they work. A plant tour attracts prospective employees and stimulates sales of consumer goods.

The number of companies using plant tours in their community relations programs has approximately doubled in recent years. Today, more than half of all companies with organized plant city programs use plant tours.

Visitors to plants of the Westinghouse Electric Corporation throughout the country create a favorable image for the company in plant communities. In a recent month, the following plant visits were made by various groups to Westinghouse plants: Eagle Scouts visited the Buffalo plant to learn more about electrical engineering; during National Electrical Week students from vocational schools visited the Chicago plant; Cornell alumni at the Friendship plant in Baltimore served on a panel when a group of high school seniors accepted for engineering and science at Cornell University visited the plant; foreign officers attending the Navy Supply Corps school in Athens, Georgia, visited the Athens plant; Brazilian mechanical engineering students toured the Atomic Power Division in Pittsburgh; a group of Soviet students visited the Columbus, Ohio, appliance plant; instructors and students in the Signal Material Maintenance Course at the Army Ft. Monmouth signal school toured the Metuchen, New Jersey, plant.

Procedure for Plant Tours and Open Houses. A procedure for a plant tour should be established by the headquarters public relations department after consultation with the local plant manager and his community relations staff assistant. Local plant managers are responsible for deciding when, where, and how plant tours and open houses should be scheduled and conducted. The community relations representative in the local plant confers with department managers in the plant to gain their co-operation and secure the support of employees. The plant community relations manager is responsible for preparing the materials required.

Public Speaking by Executives

Communication with citizens of a plant community is secured by public speeches made by company executives before local civic clubs, luncheon groups, professional societies, and school assemblies.

The community relations departments of numerous corporations have organized speakers' bureaus to provide information about the local plant and its activities to local groups. These bureaus are publicized by program planners' guides listing speakers and their subjects.

Speakers from Westinghouse Electric Corporation plants frequently address local organizations. In Lima, Ohio, plant executives are talking about submarines, "Return from Space" and the "Man on the Moon." Youngwood, Ohio, plant speakers are serving on the local high school speakers' bureau, discussing such subjects as "Does My High School Record Count?" and "What Industry Expects of High School Graduates." The Atomic Power Division in Pittsburgh is booking speakers on atomic power and other subjects. The Metuchen, N.J., plant has an active speakers' bureau, and the Baltimore plant is booking an average of sixteen speakers a month.

Opinion Leader Meetings

To promote better understanding of company policies and operations, many companies arrange meetings with community leaders in plant cities. Teachers, ministers, city officials, state and national legislators, civic club officials, bankers, and professional people who have opinions of their own and whose opinions influence the thinking of others in the community are invited to the local plant.

The Caterpillar Tractor Company, Peoria, Illinois, community relations department invites opinion makers in the community to be guests of the company for special days, including "Barbers' Day," "Clergy Day," "M.D. Day," "Business Education Day," "Visiting Fireman's Day," "Cops' Day," "Taxi Day," and others.

Visits to Community Institutions by Businessmen

At the invitation of heads of schools and social service organizations, business executives visit community institutions to learn about their operations and problems. Hundreds of business executives in many cities go back to school as the guests of city school authorities for luncheons in high school cafeterias and to hear about the operation of school systems, modern teaching methods, and future plans for school buildings.

Employee Contacts

The role of employees in community relations has been discussed earlier in this chapter. Employees are the principal medium of communication with community acquaintances, neighbors, relatives, and friends. A program to encourage employees to communicate information about company operations is essential in an effective community relations campaign.

Motion Pictures

Motion pictures and slide films depicting corporate activities are a valuable medium of community information and education. Films depicting corporate history, processes of manufacture, research, executive personnel, employee benefits, plant expansion are shown to schools, clubs, and civic organizations in plant communities. Films are frequently used to supplement speeches made by company executives to community groups.

Exhibits and Displays

Exhibits and displays of finished products, company history, raw materials, employee benefits, and production processes may be set up in display windows of local stores, railroad stations, banks, or in the office of the Chamber of Commerce to inform the community about company operations. They are also a feature of open-house programs and plant tours for community groups.

Union Carbide Corporation has a $175,000 educational exhibit of an atomic reactor at the Chicago Museum of Science and Industry. Other exhibits at the Museum of Science and Industry represent outlays of up to a million dollars by such companies as General Motors Corporation, International Harvester Company, Swift and Company, Commonwealth Edison Company, Radio Corporation, International Business Machines Corporation, and Santa Fe Railroad.

The Sun Oil Company, Philadelphia, has installed an educational exhibit of all operating phases of the oil industry in the Franklin Institute, Philadelphia, which is viewed by more than 200,000 visitors annually.

Annual Reports

Annual corporate reports mailed to community leaders, editors, schools and libraries, and distributed to employees and plant visitors are an effective medium for community communication. Local newspaper advertisements featuring the annual report should be included in a community relations program.

Booklets

Institutional booklets which commemorate a corporate anniversary and describe the history and operations of a corporation should be distributed to local opinion leaders, editors, radio commentators, educators, and plant visitors as well as to public libraries, hotels, schools, hospitals, and at meetings where company executives speak.

COMPANY CONTRIBUTIONS TO COMMUNITY WELFARE

A business organization has an obligation to contribute to the welfare of the community in which it operates. In addition to paying taxes, a business concern can contribute to developing a better community through: (1) cultural leadership; (2) educational assistance; (3) aid to health; (4) aid to agriculture; (5) service to youth; (6) civic improvement; (7) community promotion; (8) social and charitable assistance.

Cultural Leadership

By sponsoring cultural activities, a company makes it possible for people in plant communities to hear fine music, enjoy good art and drama, or listen to outstanding speakers. By making community life fuller and more satisfying to the people who live in plant cities and towns, a business gains the good will of its neighbors.

Educational Assistance

Educational assistance is an important feature of community relations programs. Sears, Roebuck and Company sponsors an agricultural scholarship program through which more than 17,000 scholarships have been awarded to boys and girls in farm communities. A city scholarship program has provided more than 2,200 scholarships to youth in 40 cities. The Sears Foundation Merit Scholarship program gives 100 four-year scholarships for outstanding high school seniors, at a cost of $250,000. In addition, Sears contributes $250,000 to colleges in the form of unrestricted cost of education grants.

Aid to Health

Community health is directly related to the welfare of employees and industrial production. Employees should be encouraged to participate in community blood donor campaigns, chest X-ray drives, crippled children and infantile paralysis activities, and school health projects. Financial aid to these worthy health campaigns should be given by corporations.

Corporations can contribute to improving the health of plant communities by making corporate gifts to hospital building fund drives. As an incentive to employee contributions, corporations are matching the gifts of employees dollar for dollar up to a specified amount. In-plant fund raising campaigns are organized by employees who are given time for these activities. Corporate aid to community health builds employee morale and good will for the company.

Aid to Agriculture

Manufacturers of agricultural equipment and supplies develop good will by assisting agriculture in farm communities by sponsoring improved livestock breeds; participating in annual county fairs, rodeos, or carnivals; awarding prizes for outstanding farm products; staging conservation demonstrations; operating a model farm; participating in surplus crop disposal campaigns; carrying on research on farm problems and products; aiding farm organizations; and establishing scholarships for outstanding farm youth.

Service to Local Youth

Industrial concerns contribute to community welfare by providing guidance and funds to Boy Scouts, Girl Scouts, Future Farmers of America, YMCA, YWCA, and Junior Achievement. Facilities are provided for youth groups for hobby clubs, teen-age canteens, and recreation. In addition, contributions are made by business concerns for

FIG. 9–2. An important community relations activity of many corporations is sponsorship of Junior Achievement Companies. Caterpillar Tractor Co., Peoria, Illinois, sponsors eight companies whose products are displayed here at a Trade Fair in Peoria.

scholarships, contests, educational trips, youth publications, and plant visits.

The employees of many companies serve as advisors for Junior Achievement companies in plant communities. Junior Achievement is a national youth movement that provides practical business training to high school boys and girls.

Caterpillar Tractor Company, Peoria, Illinois, sponsors eight Junior Achievement companies and provides 32 qualified sales, production, and business advisors.

Corporations serving agriculture sponsor 4-H Clubs which give "out-of-school" education to rural youth from 10 to 21 years of age. It is organized and conducted by the Cooperative Extension Service of the U.S. Department of Agriculture and state land grant colleges. Volunteer employees of sponsoring corporations serve as local club leaders.

Community Promotion and Improvement

To encourage new industry, attract tourists, and stimulate retail trade in plant communities, companies are running community advertising campaigns and sponsoring programs to aid local business and to develop the industrial, agricultural, and business resource of the area. Abatement of industrial smoke, noise, and odors and improvement of plant grounds wins community approval.

Social and Charitable Assistance

Business organizations contribute to the public welfare of plant communities by providing funds and manpower for social service organizations and groups engaged in rural social work, youth services, old-age assistance, recreational activities, maternal and child health, adult education, alien and foreign-born assistance.

Case 9–1

COMMUNITY SERVICE AWARDS

Ford Motor Company

The Ford Motor Company, Dearborn, Michigan, is the world's second largest automobile manufacturer. In addition to passenger cars, the company produces trucks, tractors and farm implements, industrial engines, and defense products. Sales of all products exceed $4¼ billion annually. The company has 36 foreign subsidiaries with manufacturing plants in England, Canada, Germany, and Brazil and assembly and sales branches in Belgium, Denmark, Finland, France, Holland, Italy, Portugal, Sweden, Norway, Egypt, Mexico, Uruguay, Venezuela, and Chile which sell nearly two billion dollars worth of vehicles annually.

The company employed in 1960, 160,000 persons in the United States and more than 100,000 men and women in the international operations. There are approximately 240,000 owners of the common stock of the company including 70 per cent of all salaried employees.

Ford passenger cars and trucks are marketed in the United States by about 8,100 dealers who employ some 162,000 persons. Ford tractors and farm implements are distributed by 26 independent distributors and about 2,500 dealers.

Public relations of the company is the responsibility of a vice-president in charge of public relations who reports to the chairman of the board. His staff includes a general public relations manager and a director of civic and governmental affairs. A manager of community relations reports to the director of civic and governmental affairs. The community relations department was established in 1947 for the purpose of improving the company's public relations in the cities where manufacturing and assembly plants, parts depots, and sales offices are located.

The Ford community relations policy is based on the principal of being a good neighbor and a good industrial citizen. This begins with company policies concerning relations with employees, customers, and vendors and the employees' compliance with these policies in their daily conduct of the company's business.

The company's primary service to the community depends upon providing a quality product and additional benefits in the form of job opportunities, taxes, and local purchases.

Hospitality, which is a normal part of being a good neighbor, means courtesy and friendliness to every company visitor, in every business interview, and telephone conversation. The interest of neighbors in company operations is welcomed and every provision is made to enable neighbors to visit plants to watch the manufacture and assembly of Ford products.

Corporate living habits at Ford plants conform to the standards of neighbors by well-kept grounds, clean plants, neat surroundings and no offensive smoke, noise, or odors.

The company and employees share their resources with the community to make it a better place in which to live by giving generously of their time and money to civic, health, and welfare groups and community projects.

To activate this policy, community relations committees have been established in 51 cities throughout the country where Ford plants and offices are located. These committees have the authority and responsibility for carrying out the company's community relations policy in their respective communities. Members of these committees are top-management executives of each local company installation. They are appointed to the local committee by the vice-president and general manager of the division with which each executive is associated. The committees elect their own chairman and the chairmanship rotates among the members on an annual basis.

The membership of each committee includes as many of the following as may be located in a particular plant community: division general manager, division controller, division industrial relations manager, regional and district sales managers, plant manager, plant controller, and plant industrial relations manager. Each of the company's nine field public relations managers and eight regional civic and governmental affairs managers serve as special consulting members of the committees in their respective territories.

Meetings of community relations committees are held at 60-day intervals and minutes are recorded and sent to the community relations department in Dearborn which directs and co-ordinates all committee activities.

Responsibilities of the community relations committees include:

Providing local direction to the company's public service programs, and planning and co-ordinating special community relations projects such as civic receptions, plant tours, and premieres of company films.

Assessing local and state legislative issues in which the company has an interest and assisting in the formulation and representation of company positions on such issues.

Representing the company through individual member participation in local and state civic improvement, trade, and commercial organizations.

Participating in community social, civic, and charitable programs; maintaining contact with community leaders and meeting with them periodically to discuss local problems; and representing the company at public events.

Promoting the use of company literature, motion pictures, speakers, and other program materials among educational, civic improvement, and other company groups.

Recommending company contributions and memberships and, when appropriate, special institutional advertising.

The committees give local direction to Ford's national public service programs which include educational round tables, traffic safety and highway improvement, driver education, Ford motion-picture films, 4-H achievement awards, information services, plant tour program, and speakers' bureau.

A major responsibility of community relations committees is to direct the local Ford Annual Community Service Award Program. To encourage employee participation in community affairs, this program is designed to give recognition and express company appreciation to Ford employees who have contributed to the social, civic, and political improvement of their communities.

In addition to the indirect benefits Ford obtains by fostering better communities and more representative local government, the Community Service Awards Program develops better community relations for the company by showing the public the company's interest in the welfare of its plant communities and develops better employee relations by providing mutual objectives for both the company and its employees.

The Community Service Award Program was initiated as a pilot project in 1955 by the Ford Ypsilanti, Michigan, community relations committee and subsequently tested in eight other company cities. In 1959 it was extended to all company cities across the country.

Each year the Ford community relations committees in 51 cities across the country, where major company plants and offices are located, invite Ford employees and their families, local civic organizations, or anyone acquainted with the community services of a Ford employee to nominate Ford employees who deserve recognition for voluntary personal services to the community.

About five Ford employees are selected annually in each plant community to receive an award in the form of a mounted silver scroll bearing an engraved commendation by Henry Ford II, chairman of the board of directors, for their outstanding service to the community. Employees submit nominations on special nomination forms which are deposited in distinctively marked nomination boxes located in Ford plants and offices.

When the community services of award winners are especially noteworthy, a committee composed of local management executives and/or prominent local citizens reviews the activities of the winners and selects one to be named "Ford Citizen of the Year." He receives a hand-cast bronze bell engraved with the employee's name and the figure of a town crier which the company adopted as a symbol of community service. In addition, the "Citizen of the Year" receives $100 to be presented to the local charity of his choice.

All Ford employees are eligible to be nominated for an award for active participation in the following, as well as similar, community activities: holding public office; political activity; citizens' groups including Chamber of Commerce, PTA, civil defense or volunteer fire department; youth programs such as Boy

Scouts, Junior Achievement, 4-H Clubs, Future Farmers of America, CYO, and others; community fund campaigns; and club community projects sponsored by Rotary, Lions, Kiwanis, or church groups.

Selection of candidates for a Community Service Award is made by a judging committee composed of representatives of local Ford management and sometimes community leaders. A 60-day nominating period is followed by a month of screening and selecting award winners. The criteria of the judging committee in selecting winners includes: the amount of personal effort contributed by the employee; results of the employee's service; the extent of his personal sacrifice; the degree of his selflessness and sincerity of motivation; the employee's position in the company or union; and the uniqueness or originality of his service to the community.

FIG. 9–3. Community service awards are made annually to Ford Motor Co. employees for voluntary personal services to their communities. Here, Philip A. Hart, U.S. Senator from Michigan, addresses and awards bronze bells for outstanding community service to Ford employees at Detroit area award dinner. Similar awards are made to Ford employees in 51 cities throughout the country.

The personnel of the judging committee for the Detroit area in a recent year included the editors of the three major newspapers, a Democratic Congresswoman, a Republican Congressman, and the executive vice-president of the United Foundation.

To aid community relations committees in announcing and promoting the Community Service Award Program, the community relations department of the company in Dearborn has prepared a chairman's kit which includes: a program planning guide; a judge's guide; a Community Service Awards descriptive brochure for mailing; a program poster, photographs of the silver scroll and bronze bell awards; set of sample announcement letters to employees, community leaders, and nominators; a letter of appreciation to nominees; forms for nominations; materials order form; preliminary report and budget estimate for the steering committee and summary report to the headquarters community relations department.

Community service awards are presented to the winners at a luncheon or dinner attended by the local Ford management and the leaders of the various community organizations or civic programs which the winners have served, the press, city officials, judges, and members of the local community relations committee.

The program for the award ceremony includes a reception, an invocation, welcome by the program chairman, address by an important community leader, presentation of awards and closing remarks by the chairman.

At a recent Detroit presentation dinner 400 guests were present including the award winners and their wives, company officials, media representatives, and 70 community leaders. The vice-president in charge of public relations presided, a U.S. Senator made the principal speech, and the awards were presented by Benson Ford, vice-president of the company.

Publicity for the program is handled by the local Ford public relations office and includes: advance news releases; announcement of the award winners and "Ford Citizen of the Year"; photo coverage; local press coverage; copies of prepared speeches; and follow-up publicity on the "Citizen of the Year" award which includes personal appearances before local organizations.

A summary report on each program is made by the local community relations committee to the headquarters' community relations department in Dearborn with photographs, press clippings, and program. The cost of local programs including awards, promotion materials, chairman's kit, and dinner are borne by the community relations department in Detroit.

About one half of one per cent of all Ford employees are nominated for awards, each receiving an average of 1.5 nominations. Approximately 22 per cent of the candidates are given awards and 2.1 per cent are named "Ford Citizen of the Year." In the Detroit area where more than one half of all Ford employees work, 535 workers have been nominated in a year.

QUESTIONS

1. What benefits accrue to the Ford Motor Co. from the Community Service Awards Program?

2. What are the limitations of this program from the company's standpoint?

3. How can the Community Awards Program be improved? Describe specifically what steps should be taken to make the program more effective from a community relations standpoint.

4. Is the organization of the program through the Community Relations Committees satisfactory? What changes, if any, should be made in this organization?

5. Is the method of selecting winners for the awards satisfactory? What improvements should be made in the selection process?

6. Is the publicity plan for publicizing the Community Awards satisfactory? What improvements should be made in the publicity plan?

Case 9–2

COMMUNITY RELATIONS

Westinghouse Electric Corporation

The Westinghouse Electric Corporation, Pittsburgh, Pennsylvania, was established in 1876 to manufacture electric generating and transmitting equipment and is now a leading producer of electric appliances, lamps, radio, television and radar equipment, electronic control devices, electric generation and distribution equipment, missiles, rockets, computers and nuclear power plants. Annual sales of about $2 billion are distributed as follows: apparatus and general products 55 per cent, consumer products 25 per cent, and atomic and defense products 20 per cent.

The corporation employs about 115,000 men and women in 60 plants in the United States. It is owned by more than 158,000 stockholders of which number 36,000 are employees.

An important feature of the Westinghouse public relations program is community relations which the company defines as the program which affects the sum total of what its neighbors in plant communities think and do about Westinghouse.

The corporation's community relations policy recognizes that effective performance in community relations is vital to the long-range success of any company and it is the policy of the corporation to conduct itself at all times as a good corporate citizen of every community in which it operates. To insure that the company acts upon its responsibilities for good corporate citizenship, it conducts continuing community relations programs in plant communities and other localities where the size of its operations warrants formal programs. The need for these programs arises from a desire to have the community think well of the company and its actions and also to have the community act well toward Westinghouse.

There are six major objectives of the corporation's community relations: to show the citizens of every plant community that Westinghouse is a good citizen and a good employer; to demonstrate that the local plant is not just a branch of a large corporation but a local business which accepts and acts upon its local obligations; to maintain harmonious relationships with community leaders; to keep the community fully informed of what the company is doing and trying to do and why; to create an employee climate conducive to efficient and uninterrupted operations; to attract the most desirable people of the community as employees; and to aid the community in maintaining itself as a desirable place in which to live and work and as a partner in the growth of the company.

Responsibility for Westinghouse Community relations belongs to local management, division and plant managers, and key local executives supported by all employees and a headquarters community relations department.

Each product division maintains a community relations staff function to establish and direct a community relations program. The responsibilities include: contacting local press, radio and television media; directing community relations advertising; holding opinion leader meetings; conducting opinion surveys; directing a speakers' bureau; co-ordinating company participation in community fund raising; supervising special events; directing programs with civic, government, educational, and youth groups; maintaining liaison with local and headquarters departments on community relations plans and programs; and carrying out recommended company-wide community relations projects.

A communications co-ordinator at each of the company's 60 plants is in charge of community communications at each plant. He is assisted by the headquarters community relations staff in carrying out community relations programs.

The community relations department under the direction of the community relations manager assists division and local management in the execution of community relations policy and supervises and co-ordinates company-wide programs. It consults with plant and division managers on community relations problems; maintains liaison with headquarters advertising and industrial relations departments in planning and executing community relations projects; prepares community relations programs; gives technical and editorial guidance on community relations material; serves as a clearinghouse for case histories on community relations; conducts community attitude studies; and arranges headquarters clearance for communications to the community.

The headquarters community relations staff informs local plant management, division public relations staffs, and communications co-ordinators about community relations activities of all Westinghouse divisions through the medium of a monthly "Community Relations Newsletter." Community relations activities reported in the "Newsletter" which have proven successful in plant communities are adapted by other Westinghouse plants for the solution of local community relations problems.

Recent typical Westinghouse community relations activities of various divisions include: "M.D. Day" with the Sharon, Pennsylvania, Transformer Division as host to 45 doctors for a plant tour, meeting, and luncheon. Informal luncheon at the Atomic Power Department for key community leaders to discuss radiation protection and other community problems. Formation of a speakers' bureau at the Metuchen, New Jersey, works with 21 volunteers speaking to community organizations. "Good Citizenship" awards conferred on 30 Westinghouse employees in 21 locations for outstanding service to their communities. Meetings with local civic clubs of Jersey City, New Jersey, by the Elevator Division to describe its growth, review its operations and the business outlook. A Science Honors Institute conducted by the Transformer Division, Sharon, Pennsylvania, in which eight transformer division scientists and engineers lectured to outstanding high school science students. A Christmas party for 175 cerebral palsy children, their families and guests conducted by the Lima, Ohio, Westinghouse plant. National Engineers Week celebrated in several plant communities with dinners and plant tours for the engineering faculties of nearby engineering schools, telecasts in honor of Westinghouse engineers, speeches by engineers to service clubs, and exhibits of engineering equipment. A series of dinner meetings with Maryland state senators and representatives held by the Baltimore division to discuss company operations. "Math Day" for outstanding mathematics students of local high schools held by the Newark, New Jersey, Meter division with lectures by division engineers.

An important community relations activity in many Westinghouse plants throughout the country is "Clergy Day." The objectives of this event are to gain the understanding of this important group of opinion leaders in the community. Major program emphasis is on the human values at Westinghouse, particularly safety, good housekeeping, medical facilities, working conditions, employee relations, and industrial programs.

Clergymen are often consulted by workers about problems at their place of employment, and well-informed ministers, priests, and rabbis are better able to counsel employees. Furthermore, "Clergy Day" gives management of the company the viewpoint of an important group of community leaders.

FIG. 9–4. Clergy Days are a feature of the community relations of many corporations. Here a group of clergymen visit the Friendship Plant, Westinghouse Electric Corp., to hear from management about plant operations and view products.

The program for "Clergy Day" at the Westinghouse Small Motor Division plant, Lima, Ohio, is representative of the procedure for this event in other divisions of the company.

"Clergy Day" at the Small Motor Division plant was opened by a personal welcome to the members of the Allen County Ministerial Association by the vice-president in charge of the division in the reception room of the plant at noon. Luncheon was held in the executive dining room. The visiting clergy were seated at tables of six with one or two Westinghouse executives at each table. Following lunch, the ministerial association held its regular monthly business meeting in the plant conference room.

Upon conclusion of the clergymen's meeting, the vice-president and division manager spoke for fifteen minutes on the corporation's organization, sales and profit, autonomy of operation, the small motor division, industrial motor department, its organization, products, and locations.

The manager of the aircraft equipment department discussed for ten minutes the history of the department, its organization, products and employment; aircraft and space vehicles using Westinghouse equipment; space development and the future of the department.

The industrial relations manager of the division described employee, union, and community relations in terms of wages, benefits, and charitable activities and the company's financial support of the community through its payroll, taxes, purchases, and contributions.

A question and answer period during which visiting clergymen had an opportunity to question executives about division policies and practices followed the presentations of three executives described previously. Typical questions asked by the clergy were: Is guidance given employees on personal problems? What is the extent of recreational facilities? What voice has labor in plant management? What effect has seniority on job security? What efforts are made to avoid strikes? How many employees belong to a union? What is the company's policy on contributing to churches?

Following the question period, each clergyman was given a plastic case, on which the recipient's name was lettered in gold, containing a fact sheet about the local plant, a folder describing educational scholarships sponsored by the company, a reprint of a speech by the president of the company, an article on plant safety, a copy of the company's creed, and a description of its insurance and pension plans.

After a one and one-half hour tour of the principal departments of the plant with management people acting as guides and answering questions the event was concluded at 3:00 o'clock.

Although "Clergy Day" programs in other Westinghouse plants are similar to the one described previously, arrangements vary according to the preferences of local managements, size of plant and community. In some plants the program begins in the late afternoon and concludes with dinner in the evening. In large communities attendance has exceeded 100 clergymen while in small places groups of three or four may attend.

The invitation list is compiled from several sources including local directories of clergymen, the membership of the local ministerial association or employees are asked to suggest the names of clergymen who should be invited. The works manager or division vice-president extends an invitation to each clergyman by letter which is usually followed by a telephone call. Clergymen who are unable to attend are followed up by letter in which is enclosed informational material.

"Clergy Day" is usually publicized in local newspapers which receive a press release and photograph of the group attending. This gives the company favorable publicity in the plant community.

QUESTIONS

1. Are the Westinghouse policy and objectives of community relations as described in this case sound? Comment favorably or otherwise and propose any changes in policy and objectives which you think should be made.

2. Is the delegation of primary responsibility for community relations to local management sound? Should the product divisions of the company maintain a community relations staff function? Why? What is the role of the head-

quarters community relations staff in community relations? Is this desirable? Why?

3. What is your opinion of the various community relations activities of Westinghouse divisions as described in the case? Should any additional community relations activities be undertaken? What?

4. Are "Clergy Days" an effective medium of community relations? Why? Is the program and conduct of this event satisfactory? How would you improve "Clergy Days?" Be specific.

Problem 9–1

COMMUNITY RELATIONS

Knight & Carney Corporation

The Knight & Carney Corporation was established in 1890 in Philadelphia, Pennsylvania, by Paul Knight, a retail druggist, and James Carney, a pharmacist with extensive experience in drug wholesaling. In its first year, the corporation had 60 retail customers, and sales volume during the first decade reached an annual total of $200,000. Then followed a period of rapid expansion in which the company brought new European therapeutic agents, botanicals, essential oils, antitoxins, and chemicals to the American market. At the turn of the century, the company was one of the ten largest drug manufacturers in the United States.

The company expanded into the manufacture of standard home toiletries and cosmetics including a lotion for chapped hands, face powder, lipstick, hair preparations, skin cleansers, astringents, deodorants, make-up products, and fragrances. Following World War II, the company entered the commercial market for bulk cleaning and germicidal agents, sanitary compounds, and disinfectants.

During this period, the company initiated long-range plans for development of foreign markets by acquiring a subsidiary company in Germany to manufacture disinfectants for hospitals and institutions. The company now has subsidiaries with plants in Berlin; Rome; Manchester, England; and Rio de Janeiro, Brazil.

The Knight & Carney Corporation now has annual sales in excess of $135 million and employs 8,000 workers in its United States plants and overseas subsidiaries. It is owned by 4,500 stockholders. The principal manufacturing facility and laboratory is located in Philadelphia, and a second plant in Clifton, Michigan, a community of 8,000 population near Detroit.

Shortly after the close of World War II, the company was faced with a rapid and extensive plant expansion in Clifton to provide for its growing domestic business. Imported foreign drugs and chemicals had been cut off during the war and the company was obliged to turn to domestic production of drugs, and plant expansion was imperative.

The management anticipated that the increased manufacturing facilities at Clifton would be welcomed by the community because it would provide more employment, increased purchasing power, and reduced taxes. The number of employees in the Clifton plant would be increased from 800 to 1,000 and payrolls would be 25 per cent greater.

However, as expansion progressed it became evident that the residents of Clifton were far from pleased with the new developments. The noise and dirt of new plant construction, the increased traffic congestion and inconvenience to neighbors aroused criticism of the company. Because of the specialized skills and training required for personnel employed by the company, it was necessary to go outside the community to employ people from all parts of the country. This aroused considerable local criticism of the company.

The growing national prominence of Knight & Carney caused some citizens to look with mistrust on the company as a stranger, a foreign corporation taking profits out of the community and putting nothing back. Townspeople considered employees of the company as separate and distinct from the rest of the community. Few citizens understood the scope and scientific character of the business.

During the period of rapid expansion, with many urgent problems to be solved, the Clifton plant's employee and community relations deteriorated. Internal communications in the plant became less effective and the company neglected to tell the community about its affairs. At that time there was a decided labor shortage in the area and considerable employee dissatisfaction and increase in labor turnover in the Clifton plant. Employees of long service as well as new personnel were discontented and their efficiency declined. Productivity decreased and costs mounted.

Dissatisfaction among employees within the plant was reflected among residents of the community. An editorial in the local weekly newspaper criticized the company for failing to employ more local people and to purchase more of its requirements from local suppliers. The former good will of the community was supplanted by increasing criticism of company practices.

These plant community problems were recognized by the management which called upon the public relations department to study the difficulty, make plans, and put into operation a program to create a better understanding between the company and the residents of Clifton. No organized plant community relations activities have been carried on at either Clifton or the home plant in Philadelphia.

The public relations department, headed by a public relations manager reporting to the president, was established at headquarters in 1945. The objectives of the department are to improve consumer relations by disseminating information about the company, gaining consumer acceptance of the corporation's products, answering consumer inquiries, handling complaints, and co-operating with women's clubs in promoting better grooming. A consumer relations staff of five beauty counselors speak to women's groups; a club service provides women's clubs with a series of planned programs on beauty care; and a news service prepares news stories and articles on skin care and personal appearance.

No effort has been made by the public relations department to improve plant community relations nor to gain the understanding of suppliers, dealers, and stockholders of the company.

Management believes that a plant community relations program should be introduced in Clifton to correct the prevailing impression that the plant is controlled by disinterested, absentee management unconcerned with community welfare. The program would emphasize that employees are an important factor in community life by identifying them as leaders and active participants in local civic, political, and social welfare activities.

This community relations program is essential to provide the local plant with a good labor supply; community support in event of labor conflict; a defense against discriminatory legislation; better civic services of water, sanitation, police and fire protection; increased product sales; and better community life for employees.

The public relations manager believes that good community relations begin on the inside with good employee relations. The company cannot have community understanding if its employees are misinformed about the problems and affairs of the business. The community will believe something unfavorable that an employee may say about Knight & Carney before it will believe something good that the company may say. The company's community relations must originate in the shops and offices of the company. If the immediate family is not informed about the company, the people on the outside will not understand either. In the opinion of residents of Clifton, those who work for the company *are* the company and outsiders judge the company by people in the company whom they know.

Failure to inform employees about company plans and developments leads to misunderstandings, false rumors, and criticism by townspeople about the company's affairs. Furthermore, Knight & Carney employees represent nearly one half of the families in the community and, accordingly, are in position to favorably influence community opinion about the company, in the opinion of the public relations manager.

However, the management of the company has been unwilling to share information with employees and neighbors about company affairs. This reluctance to communicate about company matters stemmed from an incident which occurred several years previously when a trusted employee informed a competing drug manufacturer about a secret formula used to compound a bulk cleaning product made by Knight & Carney. On the basis of the information furnished by the employee, the competing manufacturer produced a similar product at a lower price which soon outsold the Knight & Carney product. This incident made management secretive about company operations.

This reluctance by management to communicate with employees and the community is detrimental to public understanding and good will, in the opinion of the public relations manager. When employees and community neighbors are not told what the company is doing that affects their interests, they form their own conclusions which are often not compatible with the facts. Rumors and gossip spread misinformation throughout the community about the company's affairs. Practices and policies are exaggerated and distorted by the union and company critics to give the community a false conception of the company. Only by full and candid communication of the facts can the company combat this misinformation which is undermining the prestige of the company in Clifton, according to the public relations manager.

People in Clifton have a natural curiosity about Knight & Carney, just as they have about the family next door. It is the responsibility of the company to tell its employees and people in the community about its activities as well as its contributions to community life. Townspeople want to know what the company makes, the number of employees, payroll, investment in local property, taxes paid to the town, local expenditures for fuel, supplies, and utilities, and other information. The contributions which the company has made to the town in the form of an addition to the city hospital, public swimming pool, athletic field for the high school, and gifts to charities should be publicized.

Top management of Knight & Carney is not convinced that stepped-up communications would improve relations with employees and the town. Management does not believe that employees would be effective communicators of information about the company to the community. By the time information filters down from management through several layers of supervision to the rank-and-file employees it becomes so watered down and distorted that it does not reflect the facts. Much of the original message is lost in the transmission. Many employees are poor communicators and are not interested in discussing the company and its affairs with their friends and neighbors in the community.

To improve plant community relations in Clifton, management proposes that a committee composed of the plant manager, personnel director, and public relations manager from Philadelphia meet with a group of leading citizens of Clifton to consider various aspects of the problem.

QUESTIONS

1. What steps should be taken in planning a community relations program for Knight & Carney?
2. What method or methods of communication should be used in informing the plant community about the company?
3. Are employees of the Clifton plant of Knight & Carney an effective method of communication with the plant community? Give reasons for your opinion.
4. Who should be responsible for planning and executing a plant community relations program for Knight & Carney?
5. What should be the specific objectives of the company's plant community relations?

DISTRIBUTOR-DEALER

RELATIONS

NEARLY ONE HALF of the sales of all manufacturers in this country are made through wholesale and retail merchants who comprise the important distributor-dealer public. There are some 256,000 wholesalers and 1,200,000 retail merchants in the United States who distribute the products of manufacturers and influence public acceptance of these producers and their products.

Many manufacturers of industrial goods market operating supplies, parts, and accessory equipment through wholesale distributors, and most producers of consumer goods use wholesalers and retailers in distributing their products to the ultimate consumer. Many corporations producing consumer products have large dealer publics. The Shell Oil Company has about 20,000 outlets. Goodyear Tire and Rubber Company has 30,000 dealers, and Ford Motor Company has 40,000 dealers.

Importance of the Distributor-Dealer Public

The distributor-dealer public is one of the most important publics of manufacturers of consumer goods. Good relations with wholesalers and retailers are vital to a manufacturer whose sales and profits depend upon dealers buying, promoting, and reselling the manufacturer's merchandise. On the other hand, wholesalers and retailers are dependent upon good relations with manufacturers for their sales and profits.

The importance of good relationships between manufacturers, wholesalers, and retailers is expressed by the manager of dealer relations of a large electrical appliance manufacturer with thousands of dealers, as follows: "Dealers represent the very life blood of our existence and it would be foolhardy for us to march contrary to their best interests." A leading carpet manufacturer emphasizes the importance of dealer relations by saying, "There is nothing more important to us in marketing our products than the improvement of our relationships with our distributors and dealers."

Consumer relations for manufacturers depend on the good will of retailers. The only contact which many manufacturers have with ultimate consumers is through dealers. If retailers are loyal to a manufacturer and his products, consumers are favorably impressed and consumer relations of the manufacturer are improved.

Although the desirability of good distributor-dealer relations is generally recognized, good relationships do not always prevail. Dealers are critical of manufacturers' dealer franchise agreements, overproduction and overloading of dealers, direct-to-consumer selling, full-line stocking, pricing policy, too many outlets, phantom freight, arbitrary termination of franchises, high-pressure selling, and factory servicing. These dealer dissatisfactions are often the result of economic pressures, but they are also attributed to manufacturers' inequitable distribution policies which have aroused dealer resentment and resulted in deterioration of manufacturer-dealer relationships.

Many manufacturers are seeking improved relations with their wholesale and retail customers. To create a better understanding with dealers, responsibility for dealer relations has been given to top levels of management. Distribution policies and practices have been studied and revised to remove criticism of dealers. The opinions of dealers have been given more consideration. Impartial arbitrators have been appointed to adjudicate disputes with dealers. Joint manufacturer-dealer relations committees and boards have been appointed. New channels of communication have been established. As a result of these concessions to dealers, manufacturer-distributor-dealer relations have become more harmonious.

Partnership Philosophy of Distributor-Dealer Relations

"The relationship between the brand-name manufacturer and the wholesaler and retailer is a true partnership," says the president of a well-known textile manufacturer. "Their mutual interest is to make a fair profit in performing their respective functions in supplying the consumer with a product in which they both can be proud."

This philosophy may be described as a "partnership-in-risk" with the manufacturer risking millions in product improvement and promotion and dealers sharing in the risk by investing their capital in the manufacturer's products with the expectation of reselling them at a profit.

When manufacturers, wholesalers, and retailers work together sharing common problems and recognizing mutual obligations, a profitable relationship is assured.

Who Should Be Responsible for Distributor-Dealer Relations?

The public relations department should be responsible for research, planning, and preparation of media of communication for a distributor-dealer relations program. In large companies, a distributor-dealer relations section may be attached to the public relations department to give specialized attention to distributor-dealer relationships. The Ford Motor Company's public relations department has such a section for dealer information.

Execution of a distributor-dealer relations program, however, is a responsibility of the marketing department which has major relations with wholesalers and retailers at the headquarters, regional, or local levels. Marketing management, advertising and sales promotion executives, and salesmen, all of whom are in frequent contact with distributors and dealers, should be responsible for carrying on a distributor-dealer relations program.

In addition to marketing, representatives of other departments including accounting, credit, collection, traffic, and service are in frequent contact with wholesalers and retailers and should be included in executing a distributor-dealer relations program.

To co-ordinate all departments in a distributor-dealer relations program, a distributor-dealer relations committee, composed of the heads of all departments dealing with dealers, and the public relations manager, is established. The functions of this committee are to plan dealer relations policy and programs and to evaluate such programs.

To improve relations with dealers, a few large corporations have given a major executive or board responsibility for dealer relations. General Motors Corporation has appointed an executive vice-president in charge of dealer relations. The Chrysler Corporation has assigned a two-man team, composed of a vice-president and assistant to the president, to be responsible for dealer relations. The Ford Motor Company has a three-man dealer policy board.

Public Relations' Role in Distributor-Dealer Relations

In developing a distributor-dealer relations program, the public relations department should be advised by the distributor-dealer relations committee on the objectives of the program which should have the approval of the heads of all departments involved in relationships with distributors and dealers.

After consultation with the dealer relations committee, the public relations department conducts necessary research and determines procedures and methods of communication with distributors and dealers, prepares the media, and assists marketing management staff and operating executives in carrying out the program.

The public relations department should advise management and the distributor-dealer relations committee on policy and matters affecting company-dealer relationships; make suggestions to management regarding relations with dealers; and recommend specific courses of action for gaining dealer good will.

PLANNING A DISTRIBUTOR-DEALER RELATIONS PROGRAM

Objectives

The objectives of manufacturers' distributor-dealer relations programs vary widely according to the number and types of distributors and dealers involved, the nature of the product, and the marketing methods and policies of the company. The attitudes and interests of wholesalers and retailers in a manufacturer depend on the sales and profit derived from the producer's products. Distributors and dealers in staples such as drugs, foods, and hardware, who sell the products of hundreds of manufacturers, cannot be expected to be particularly interested in one manufacturer. However, those who distribute the products of a limited number of manufacturers are concerned with relationships with the manufacturer whose policies and practices directly affect their sales and profits.

The objectives of the distributor-dealer relations programs of manufacturers are as follows:

To determine the attitudes of distributors and dealers as a basis for dealer relations policies and practices.

To create a better understanding with distributors and dealers by explaining management policies and practices.

To retain present dealers by informing them of the advantages of distributing a product or line.

To give distributors and dealers and their personnel a better knowledge of the manufacturer's history, executive personnel, resources, organization, and services.

To provide distributors and dealers with a community relations program to improve consumer relations.

To aid distributors and dealers in increasing their sales by means of sales training programs, sales equipment, sales suggestions, improved selection and compensation of salespeople, and sales contests.

To aid distributors and dealers in advertising by providing them with advertising plans, store and window displays, outdoor displays, signs and car-

card advertising, store demonstrations, mail campaigns, sampling, and co-operative newspaper advertising.

To aid distributors and dealers in improving their management methods with better interior store arrangement and equipment, store lighting, stock control systems, improved accounting and credit control, store records and systems, delivery service, pricing, and better store organization and personnel.

To aid distributors and dealers in providing better mechanical service to users by providing dealers with improved service equipment, training dealers' service personnel, and offering a liberal service policy.

To adopt distribution policies designed to gain the good will and loyalty of distributors and dealers.

To provide consumer finance service to enable dealers to move a maximum volume of merchandise into the hands of consumers.

To seek out and place before management for its consideration company practices and policies which affect the position of the company with its distributors and dealers.

To stimulate distributor and dealer interest and loyalty in products, and establish a partnership relationship.

Distributor-Dealer Research

In launching a distributor-dealer relations program, a manufacturer should survey the attitudes of wholesalers and retailers toward the producer to determine the objectives of the program and needed improvements in the manufacturer's policies and practices. This research, carried on by the public relations department, determines not only what wholesalers and retailers think of the manufacturer but also how dealers expect the producer to serve them, and to secure suggestions from dealers for the improvement of a manufacturer's products, policies, and practices.

In addition to opinion research, a study should be made of dealers' operating methods to serve as a basis for aiding dealers in improving their management, merchandising, and advertising methods. Investigation should be made of the financial operations of representative dealers to determine their capital investment, net sales, cost of sales, gross margin, expenses of administration, occupancy, advertising, buying, selling, net profit, markdowns, markups, number of stock turns, and inventory.

The administrative practices of successful wholesalers and retailers should be studied to determine the most effective store arrangement, lighting, personnel policies, stock control system, buying methods, credit policy, location, warehousing, delivery, service, brand policy, and relations with employees and community. This information is essential in developing a dealer-help program for improving a manufacturer's dealer relations.

Sound Marketing Policy Basis of Good Relationships

Fair and equitable marketing and distribution policies are essential in an effective manufacturer's distributor-dealer relations program. A dealer policy should be based on an equitable franchise agreement, fair prices, product warranty, responsible mechanical service, territory protection, sales and advertising support, arbitration of disputes, and other features.

An example of a good dealer relations policy of a manufacturer is the following policy statement of Ethicon Suture Laboratories, Inc., a division of Johnson and Johnson:

What Ethicon Pledges Dealers

Continuation of the Ethicon policy of distribution through responsible dealers.

Quality products maintained by rigid manufacturing specifications and inspection.

Continued development of new products and improvement of present products through extensive research.

Nation-wide sales support by the Ethicon sales force in the interest of all dealers.

Outstanding advertising and convention support.

Substantial sales promotion help, displays, educational motion pictures, catalogues, dealer literature, and salesmen's training programs.

Fair and equitable treatment of all dealers.

Continued satisfactory yearly profits from the distribution of Ethicon products.

MANUFACTURERS' SERVICES TO DISTRIBUTORS AND DEALERS BUILD GOOD RELATIONSHIPS

Aside from a good product and a fair distributor and dealer policy, the service which a manufacturer gives wholesalers and retailers of its products is the most important factor in developing good distributor-dealer relations.

The services given wholesalers and retailers by manufacturers vary widely in nature, quality, and quantity according to the type of product, its importance from the standpoint of profit to the merchant and the resources of the producer. Manufacturers of staple consumer products, such as bread and sugar, which provide low profits, offer little service to dealers. Makers of luxuries and specialties, on the other hand, which provide more profit, carry on extensive dealer help and service programs to gain dealer good will and co-operation.

Distributors and dealers who are given an exclusive franchise for the sale of a product in their territories expect and receive considerable assistance from the manufacturer. Also, distributors and dealers such as automobile and gasoline retailers, who stock and sell the product or line of only one manufacturer, look to the producer for substantial merchandising aid.

Distributor-dealer relations service programs of manufacturers may include one or more of the five following services: advertising aid and counsel, sales assistance, mechanical service assistance, management services, and community relations assistance.

Advertising Aid and Counsel to Dealers

Many manufacturers provide distributors and dealers with advertising assistance to aid them in increasing sales and profits. This advertising includes: newspaper advertising—layouts, copy, mats, and complete advertisements; direct-mail advertising, including mailing cards, folders, calendars, and booklets; store and window displays, including exterior signs and window and point-of-purchase advertising; radio and television advertising—scripts, films, and tapes; and novelty advertising, including imprinted book matches and mechanical pencils.

Sales Assistance

Manufacturers' missionary salesmen aid distributors and dealers in increasing their sales and in selection, training, and supervision of wholesale and retail salesmen. Manufacturers' representatives also aid dealers in special sales and promotions.

Mechanical Service Assistance

Manufacturers of mechanical products give mechanical service aid to distributors and dealers by training retailers' servicemen at service schools and supplying service equipment.

Management Services

Management services provided by manufacturers to retailers include advice on pricing, stock control, store organization, and location; buying, credit, and collection methods; accounting and warehousing.

Community Relations Assistance

Manufacturers aid dealers in improving their community relations by providing them with press releases, motion pictures, public speech materials, open house plans, and programs for special community events.

A WHOLESALER-DEALER RELATIONS PROGRAM

McKesson & Robbins, wholesaler of drugs, liquors, and chemicals, the largest wholesale distributor in the United States, has earned good relations with nearly 40,000 retail drug merchants by providing them with a wide range of services.

The company provides aid to retail druggists in financing, and offers extensive store management counsel and training for store owners and salespeople. Store modernization assistance has been given to more than 11,000 retailers. If a merchant is considering opening a store, the company evaluates the proposed location and compiles a forecast of probable sales. Before the store is opened, the arrangement is planned in accordance with traffic flow analysis in other stores. A budget for store operation is prepared, estimating personnel and inventory requirements. The clerks are employed and trained by McKesson & Robbins. More than 100,000 drug retailers and salespeople have been trained by the company. The wholesaler handles the dealer's advertising, public relations, and merchandising program. It conducts co-operative advertising and promotion campaigns during the Christmas holiday season and runs national advertising to stimulate sales for its dealer customers.

A MANUFACTURER-DISTRIBUTOR-DEALER RELATIONS PROGRAM

Carrier Corporation, Syracuse, New York, the largest manufacturer of air-conditioning equipment in the world, has an extensive distributor-dealer relations program which is the joint responsibility of three departments—public relations, advertising and sales promotion, and divisional sales.

The program consists of four major services for building good relations with distributors and retailers: Publicity Service; Home Promotions; Advertising Workshop; and *Inside Carrier,* a monthly magazine for distributors and dealers.

Publicity is prepared to establish dealers as air-conditioning specialists in their communities and to publicize Carrier products by means of news releases, pictures, and press kits. *Home promotions* aid dealers in promoting the sale of air-conditioned residential subdivisions with Carrier specialists in publicity, sales promotion, and advertising giving personal guidance in the execution of these programs. *Advertising workshops* for the advertising, sales promotion, and sales managers of dealers are held at company headquarters to aid them in developing their local programs. To provide communications with distributors and dealers and guide them in their advertising, promotion, and merchandising programs, Carrier publishes a monthly magazine, *Inside Carrier.*

A MANUFACTURER-DEALER RELATIONS PROGRAM

The Bell & Howell Company, Chicago, manufacturers of photographic equipment distributed to camera, department, jewelry, and drugstores, has improved dealer relations by sending 25 executives into the field to discuss with dealers their problems and to discover their attitudes toward Bell & Howell and its products. These executives include managers of marketing, manufacturing, quality control, engineering, and finance.

Dealers choose, annually, a dealer representative to the Bell & Howell Retail Advisory Council from each of the company's sixteen sales regions. The Council meets with the management of the company at the company's headquarters in Chicago to discuss such subjects as improved dealer and manufacturer communications; the effectiveness of field representatives; motion-picture equipment trends; repair and guarantee policy; product packaging; photographic outlets; discount houses; improving accessory sales; industry marketing practices; price protection; trade discounts, guarantee, and franchise policy. Dealer representatives on the council are recognized with a plaque certifying membership on the council.

The company periodically surveys Bell & Howell dealers for their views on sales policy, delivery service, frequency of contact by salesmen, effectiveness of salesmen in training dealer salespeople, and other subjects.

MEDIA OF COMMUNICATION WITH DISTRIBUTORS, DEALERS

Manufacturers communicate with distributors and dealers in three ways: individual personal communication, group personal communication, and impersonal methods of communication.

Individual Personal Communication

The most effective method of communicating with distributors and dealers is through salesmen, sales supervisors, and company executives.

Good distributor and dealer relations must begin at home. If salesmen and executives who meet distributors and retailers are not informed about company's policies, operations, and plans, communication is ineffective. To insure good communications, salesmen should be fully informed about company history, financial status, research, management policies, practices, and development. This information should be included in sales training programs and sales manuals. Copies of the annual report, speeches of executives, and important publicity releases should be distributed to salesmen so they can sell the company as an institution as well as its products.

Group Personal Communication

Communication with groups of distributors and dealers may be accomplished by well-planned sales meetings. Good dealer relations may be developed at sales meetings when management explains its plans and policies. At the same time, management hears from dealers and good two-way communication results.

A Distributor-Dealer Advisory Group. Some manufacturers sponsor the establishment of distributor and dealer advisory groups composed of successful wholesalers and retailers. These groups meet periodically with management to discuss mutual problems and improvements in policies and practices for better distributor-dealer relations.

Manufacturers hold dealer relations meetings with small groups of dealers to hear their criticisms and receive advice and suggestions on mutual problems.

Impersonal Methods of Communication

Several kinds of printed media are used in informing distributors and dealers about company policies and operations, including dealer magazine; trade magazine advertising and publicity; films for distributors and dealers; dealer management manuals; radio and television broadcasts; booklets, folders, and literature; correspondence; annual report to dealers; exhibits and displays; and dealer awards.

Dealer Magazine. A major medium of communication used by manufacturers to inform distributors and dealers is a dealer magazine which develops dealer interest through regular publication, affords space to tell a complete story, is impressive in appearance, and recognizes dealer accomplishment.

Dealer magazines inform wholesalers and retailers about new products, policies, and promotions. These magazines also publish schedules and reprints of national magazine advertisements. Retail display material and dealer helps are illustrated. Editorial features include articles about successful distributors and dealers and their sales methods.

Trade Magazine Advertising. Advertising in trade magazines is widely used by manufacturers in communicating with distributors and dealers. Typical of the nearly 600 trade magazines published in the United States are: "Home Furnishings Daily," "Women's Wear Daily," "Hardware Age," "Electrical Merchandising," and "Chain Store Age."

Trade magazine advertising is used by manufacturers to inform dealers about company financial resources, assets, earnings, dividends, reserves, and profits; research facilities, laboratories, research personnel, and new product developments; mechanical service, advertising, discounts, and adjustments; management personnel, experience, and accomplishments; new distribution policies and expanding services to dealers.

Trade magazine publicity is also used by manufacturers to inform distributors and dealers about the previously mentioned features of a manufacturer's operations of interest to distributors and dealers.

Motion-Picture Films. Motion-picture films are used by manufacturers to assist distributors and dealers by showing them how to sell, display, service, and advertise the manufacturer's product. Institutional films are shown to dealers to visualize the resources of the producer, the plants, branches, warehouses, laboratories, research, plant expansion, and accomplishments of the manufacturer. The production of dealer films is a responsibility of the public relations and marketing departments.

Dealer Management Manuals. To assist distributors and dealers in improving their management methods, manufacturers produce management manuals, texts, booklets, charts, and outlines. The following dealer aids, an important feature of distributor-dealer relations programs, are produced by marketing and public relations departments and include:

Dealer management handbooks covering all phases of retail management including store location, organization, store management, advertising, delivery, lighting, displays, selling, credit and collections, and buying.

Retail sales management manuals discussing recruiting, selecting, training, supervising, compensating, and controlling the activities of salespeople.

Mechanical service manuals explaining methods and equipment used in servicing mechanical products.

Closed-Circuit Television Broadcasts to Dealers. An increasing number of manufacturers are using closed-circuit television to communicate with groups of wholesalers, retailers, and their personnel in manufacturer sponsored distributor-dealer meetings. These broadcasts make it possible for management to speak simultaneously to a nation-wide distributing organization.

Booklets, Folders, and Direct Advertising. Distributor-dealer communication employs various forms of direct advertising including booklets, folder, broadsides, and letters to inform dealers about new policies, products, and merchandising programs.

FIG. 10–1. Dealers of Caterpillar Tractor Co., Peoria, Illinois, inspect new 35-ton rear dump truck at the Peoria plant of the company. Exhibits of new products are an important medium of communication with dealers.

Correspondence. Correspondence with distributors and dealers is used by manufacturers to announce new policies, products, and advertising programs to wholesalers and retailers.

Annual Reports. Corporation annual reports, prepared by the public relations department, are also distributed to distributors and dealers to inform them about sales and profits, new facilities, new products or services, research developments, future prospects, and other matters of interest to wholesaler and retailer customers.

Exhibits and Displays. Exhibits of new products and processes at trade shows and conventions are widely used as a medium of communication with distributors. New products, research developments, new advertising and merchandising programs, are exhibited to present and prospective wholesalers and retailers.

Dealer Awards. In recognition of high sales volume, merchandising co-operation, and efficient operation, manufacturers award outstanding dealers with certificates, plaques, banners, and cups. These awards stimulate dealers to greater accomplishment and create a better relationship with the manufacturer. They are presented at dealer conventions and are publicized in the trade magazines. An honor club for outstanding dealers is a feature of the dealer relations programs of some manufacturers.

Case 10–1

DEALER RELATIONS

American Motors Corporation

American Motors Corporation, Detroit, Michigan, manufactures and markets automobiles and electrical appliances in annual volume exceeding $1 billion. The automotive division produces Rambler and Metropolitan automobiles. The appliance division makes Kelvinator refrigerators, clothes dryers, electric water heaters, dehumidifiers, room air conditioners, ice cream cabinets, frozen food merchandising cabinets, and beverage coolers. The appliance division also makes Leonard refrigerators and home freezers, automatic and wringer washers, clothes dryers, ranges, electric water heaters, dish washers, food waste disposers, room air conditioners, and ABC automatic and wringer washers and clothes dryers.

Subsidiary companies of American Motors are Redisco, Inc. (appliance sales financing); Kelvinator Limited, England; Kelvinator, Canada, Limited; American Motors, Canada, Limited; and American Motors Sales Corporation.

The corporation employs about 30,000 people in its plants and offices in the United States and in foreign countries. The corporation is owned by more than 90,000 stockholders.

The automotive division of American Motors markets passenger automobiles through a subsidiary, American Motors Sales Corporation, which distributes direct to approximately 3,000 retail automobile dealers located in all parts of the United States. There are 1,186 people in the American Motors field organization who give counsel, advice, and assistance to the corporation's dealers.

Twenty-three zone offices are located in the principal cities of the United States. Each zone office serves from 125 to 150 dealers. The 23 zone offices are grouped into five regions each with four or five zones under the direction of a regional manager.

Each zone sales office is headed by a zone manager, who has an assistant

and a staff to assist the 125 to 150 dealers in the zone to operate more efficiently and profitably. The zone staff includes a sales promotion manager who
aids dealers in hiring and training salesmen and organizing local advertising and
sales activities; a business management manager to assist dealers in training their
accountants and improving their financial operations; a car distributor to help
dealers get deliveries; and a parts and service manager who aids dealers in service management and training mechanics.

In addition to the above administrative staff, in each zone office are seven
to ten district sales managers. Each district manager is responsible for maintaining regular relations with about 18 dealers in his district. He calls on dealers
at monthly intervals to aid them in solving their merchandising problems and
advises them on every phase of their operations. There are also six to nine parts
and service representatives in each zone who call on about 22 dealers once a
month to assist them with their service problems.

The field sales organization is directed by five regional sales managers who
are responsible to the central management at Detroit composed of the executive
vice-president, director of automotive operations, sales manager automotive
division, and director of dealer development.

The basis of American Motors relationships with its 3,000 dealers is the
dealer franchise agreement. This bilateral contract consists of three basic parts:
(1) the franchise agreement; (2) the franchise provisions; (3) current price
list bulletins. All franchise agreements with dealers are signed by the zone
manager representing American Motors Sales Corporation and by the dealer involved. No franchise agreement is in effect until it is approved by an executive
in the central office.

The franchise agreement seeks the optimum relationship between American
Motors and its dealers by providing the advantages which each party hopes to
obtain from the association. The dealer wants a quality product which will insure customer satisfaction and repeat sales; an adequate market potential with
sufficient area to develop a reasonable return on capital investment, continuing
profit security, and confidence in factory personnel and policies. The manufacturer seeks dealers with adequate financial stability and sales, service, and used
car facilities of proper size and quality; dealers who practice sound business
management in the operation of their businesses, have good character and integrity and adequate sales and service personnel to fully develop the market
potential and provide good service for the product.

Dealer Advisory Board

Good relations between American Motors and its dealers depend not only
on an equitable franchise agreement, which provides the above advantages, but
also on good two-way communication between the factory and dealers. The principal medium of communication between American Motors and its dealers is the
Dealer Advisory Board, established in 1955, following the United States investigation of the relations of automobile manufacturers and dealers.

In addition to establishing a Dealer Advisory Board, American Motors also
announced an eight-point program designed to give dealers a greater voice in
the manufacturer's dealer policy including the shaping of franchise agreements
and to allay such dealer dissatisfactions as handling of franchise cancellation

grievances, unethical sales tactics, new-car bootlegging, overproduction, and franchise duration.

The American Motors eight-point dealer relations program includes: (1) Establishment of a company-dealer appeals board with final authority in dealer franchise cancellation cases. (2) Election of a dealer advisory board. (3) Periodic review with the dealer advisory board of all matters affecting factory-dealer relationships, including length and other aspects of the franchise agreement. (4) Solicitation of the dealer board's advice on all matters affecting dealers and customers. (5) Concerted action to prevent unethical advertising, selling, financing, or servicing. 6) Primary production reliance on dealer's sales projections and orders to avoid new-car bootlegging and unsound inventory accumulations. (7) Study of methods to avoid excessive fluctuations in car sales production volumes and to maintain these volumes at levels profitable to both dealers and the manufacturer. (8) Sharing with dealers the financial benefits for future company progress and growing sales volume.

The American Motors Dealer Advisory Board is composed of 23 members elected by secret ballot by the company's 3,000 dealers. One dealer representative is elected for each of the 23 sales zones in the country. The 125 to 150 dealers in each zone elect their representative to the Dealer Advisory Board. Ballots are mailed by the central office of American Motors to the dealers in each zone. A separate ballot for each zone lists every dealer in the zone who is eligible to serve.

The bylaws of the Dealer Advisory Board state that no dealer shall serve more than two consecutive terms and shall not serve for more than two years out of a five-year consecutive period. If a dealer serves on the Board for two years he is not eligible for re-election for the succeeding three-year period. This gives more dealers an opportunity to serve.

Dealers mark their ballots indicating their choice of the dealer to represent them on the Board and return their ballots by mail to a firm of public accountants in Detroit, which tabulates the votes and announces the names of dealers elected to the Board. No one connected with American Motors sees the ballots after they have been filled out by dealers, nor does an official of the manufacturer influence the election in any way.

When the Board convenes in Detroit it elects its chairman, vice-chairman, and secretary to serve for one year, with the chairman remaining in office until the next election is held.

The Board usually meets semiannually although, occasionally, there is only one meeting a year. Each delegate collects items for the meeting agenda from his fellow dealers in his zone, recaps them, eliminates the duplicates, and mails his agenda to the chairman of the National Board. The chairman, in turn, integrates the 23 agenda into one and mails his copy to the central office in Detroit about a week in advance of the scheduled meeting date.

In the central office the agenda is realigned by subject matter and categorized by department involved, such as engineering, manufacturing, quality control, sales, corporation policy, and others.

When the Board meeting convenes, the American Motors official in charge of each of the various categories on the agenda must be present to answer the questions directed to the department under him. For example: the chief engineer is present when questions involving engineering are discussed; the vice-president of manufacturing, along with his plant managers, is present when subjects pertaining to manufacturing and quality control are discussed and so on through other departments.

Items that deal strictly with factory policy are usually reserved for the afternoon of the second day of the two-day meeting. At that time the president of American Motors meets with the Board and discusses items which require top-management decision.

A complete tape recording is made of the two-day meeting and after the meeting the minutes are prepared by a central office employee who mails the minutes to the chairman and secretary of the Board for their review and approval. After approval has been received, a complete set of the minutes is sent to every American Motors dealer in the United States. Board members are not relied upon to pass back proceedings to dealers by way of regional or zone dealer meetings.

American Motors pays the travel expenses of all delegates from their home cities to Detroit and return, in addition to their lodging in Detroit.

The Dealer Advisory Board of American Motors differs from customary practice in the automobile industry in three respects: (1) Each of the zone dealer representatives is elected by secret ballot. Cliques are eliminated by the two-years-in-five rule. (2) The manufacturer pays the travel expenses of the delegates to the meetings. (3) A copy of the minutes of each meeting is sent to every dealer.

Management of American Motors believes that the Dealer Advisory Board makes several significant contributions to sound dealer relations. It permits top-level management to become acquainted with dealers and their problems at first hand. It gives dealers an opportunity to meet factory executives and hear dealer problems openly discussed and why some dealer requests cannot be granted. Both factory executives and dealers gain a much better understanding of each other's problems. By limiting service on the Board to a two-year period, and by permitting a dealer to serve only two years out of any five-year period, membership is rotated and more dealers have an opportunity to serve. By working together dealers and factory executives develop partnership with greater loyalty on the part of the dealer, lower turnover of dealers, and better sales and merchandising by dealers.

Reflecting the dealer's viewpoint toward the Advisory Board, a member of the Board wrote dealers in his zone, "I was surprised at top management's interest in our problems and feel as though I was personally on the factory board of directors."

QUESTIONS

1. Comment on American Motors automotive division program of merchandising and service counsel and assistance to dealers, pointing out its desirable features and also its weaknesses.

2. What specific changes or additions should be made in this manufacturer's counsel and assistance program to dealers?

3. Comment on American Motors automotive division Dealer Advisory Board as a means of improving dealer-factory relations. Point out the desirable as well as objectionable features of this program.

4. What specific changes should be made in the Dealer Advisory Board program?

5. Are the methods of communication employed by the American Motors relations with dealers satisfactory? If not, what other channels of communication should be used?

Problem 10–1

DISTRIBUTOR-DEALER RELATIONS

Briggs Tire and Rubber Co.

The Briggs Tire and Rubber Company was established in Chicago in 1906 to manufacture and market automobile, truck, and tractor tires; a wide variety of pneumatic tires of all types for wheeled vehicles; and in addition a broad line of industrial rubber specialties. The company operates six tire and rubber specialty plants—four in the United States and two in foreign countries. The number of employees has grown from 500 to more than 11,000. Annual sales exceed $700 million. The company is owned by 18,000 shareholders, 20 per cent of whom are employees.

All Briggs automobile and truck tires are distributed exclusively to 12,000 independent retail tire dealers throughout the United States and abroad. The average Briggs dealer has sold and serviced Briggs' tires for 15 years.

The company has for years followed a policy of aiding its dealers to expand or relocate, and of helping new dealers into the business. A retail management department at headquarters, staffed with specialists in tire retailing, provides, gratis, counsel to Briggs' dealers in designing new stores, improving store arrangement, establishing stock control systems, designing better store lighting and displays, training sales and service personnel, preparing advertising and promotion plans, and merchandising programs. Unlike other competing tire manufacturers, Briggs has confined its distribution to independent tire dealers.

Automobile tires present a special marketing problem. They are not an impulse item. Motorists are reluctant to buy tires and defer purchasing until necessity compels them to. When a consumer is forced to buy tires, the tire manufacturer who has his tires available gets the business, otherwise he loses the sale.

Availability of tires is no problem for consumers. Increased manufacturing capacity in the tire industry has created aggressive competition between large and small tire manufacturers who have distribution in thousands of retail tire outlets including filling stations, mail-order houses, supermarkets, auto accessory stores, department stores, discount houses as well as retailers specializing in tires exclusively.

On the other hand, for a manufacturer of a particular brand of tire such as Briggs, availability has become a serious problem. Shifts in population have altered the market for tires in many areas. Numerous tire-store locations that were formerly desirable are no longer profitable. Furthermore, new, aggressive tire dealers are hard to find. Progressive dealers have been pre-empted by competing tire manufacturers. In spite of Briggs' efforts to encourage its dealers to move to desirable locations or expand their operations, sales volume from existing dealers has declined. It is difficult to interest individuals with sufficient capital and experience to open a tire store as it requires a minimum capital of $50,000 to get started in tire retailing today.

To increase its share of the tire market, Briggs recognizes the necessity of stepping up its marketing efforts particularly in large metropolitan areas. However, in large cities rising costs tend to make independent tire retailing unprofitable. The large cities are a major source of tire volume essential to show a profit to the manufacturer in the highly competitive, narrow margin, price-conscious tire market.

Some large tire manufacturers have met this problem by establishing their own company-operated tire stores. The Firestone Tire & Rubber Company, in 1926, pioneered the establishment of company-owned tire stores to meet the competition of mail-order houses in metropolitan markets. Today it operates 785 company-owned stores. The Goodyear Tire & Rubber Company has established 620 retail tire stores in large cities throughout the country. The B. F. Goodrich Company, at one time, had 500 company-owned tire stores but has reduced this number to 458. The General Tire & Rubber Company has about 125 tire stores throughout the nation.

The company-owned retail stores of the big-four tire manufacturers are typically one-stop shopping outlets which sell a wide variety of products in addition to tires including large and small electric appliances, radios, television, hi-fi sets, refrigerators, washers, toys, hardware, lawn and garden supplies, outboard motors, and housewares. Firestone stores have 18 separate departments and sell more than 8,000 different items. In addition to marketing through their own stores, the major tire companies continue to sell their tires through independent tire dealers.

Briggs Tire & Rubber Company, despite changing market conditions and the retailing policy of its large competitors, has continued to market its tires exclusively through its 12,000 independent tire dealers. However, management of the Briggs company believes that in order to meet the competition of large tire company stores and take advantage of new market trends, it must assume more of the marketing function and integrate its distribution by opening its own retail tire stores.

The company plans to initiate its own specialty tire store operation in two metropolitan areas, New York City and Chicago, and from these two centers expand into other major metropolitan markets. Briggs tire stores will concentrate on tires and service rather than sell a wide variety of thousands of non-related items as in competing tire manufacturers' stores. In addition to a complete inventory of 30 different types of white wall, black wall, nylon, rayon, and various sizes of automobile and truck tires, the company will sell a limited line of its own brand batteries, auto accessories, antifreeze, cleaners, polishes, and ignition parts. No general merchandise will be sold in Briggs' stores to avoid competition with tires for the attention of consumers and the time of store personnel.

The new Briggs Company stores' program will create a serious dealer relations problem in the opinion of Briggs' management. Independent tire dealers throughout the country to whom the company is now distributing its tires will naturally view with suspicion the company's stores program. Independent dealers will resent the company going into competition with them. Although Briggs is planning to open its own stores in only two metropolitan areas in the beginning, independent dealers throughout the country will anticipate that Briggs' stores will be opened in their areas. Dealers may discontinue carrying the Briggs' line and take on competing tires and Briggs' sales and profits will suffer.

The Briggs Company is confronted with the task of securing acceptance by its independent dealers of its company stores' program. The company believes that its own stores will help independent dealers by serving as models of good store operation and show dealers how to run a dealership. Dealers would also benefit from the company's promotion and company stores would help stabilize prices as the price structure is chaotic.

The executive committee of the company believes that the threat to good dealer relations constitutes more than a marketing problem. It would have a far-reaching effect on the public relations of the company as the dissatisfaction of dealers would also create public misunderstanding and ill will. Accordingly, the committee proposes that the dealer relations problem should be a responsibility of the public relations department which should develop a program to secure acceptance of the new company stores' policy and gain the good will of the company's independent tire dealers and through them the general public.

The vice-president in charge of public relations proposes the following objectives for a dealer relations program: to determine the attitudes of dealers toward the company and its policies; to secure acceptance by dealers of the company's distribution program and policies; to retain present dealers by keeping them informed of the advantages of marketing the manufacturer's products; to aid dealers in selling more Briggs tires; to establish closer relations with dealers; to stimulate dealer interest and loyalty; and to interpret to management dealer viewpoints on Briggs' policies and practices.

If the public relations department assumes responsibility for dealer relations, it would be necessary to expand the public relations budget and staff.

The vice-president in charge of marketing of the company contends that relations with dealers should be the responsibility of the sales department whose representatives maintain frequent and continuous relations with Briggs' dealers and are in the best position to create understanding and win the good will of independent tire dealers.

QUESTIONS

1. Should responsibility for dealer relations be assigned to the public relations department of Briggs Tire & Rubber Company? Give reasons for or against this proposal.

2. Assuming the public relations department is given responsibility for dealer relations, who within the department should handle dealer relations and what specific steps should be taken to design a program to accomplish the objectives stated by the vice-president in charge of public relations?

3. What methods of communication should be used by the public relations department in a dealer relations program?

4. What part should the marketing department of the company play in such a dealer relations program?

11 · SUPPLIER RELATIONS

THE SOURCES from which manufacturers and merchants purchase raw materials, parts, accessories, equipment, operating supplies, or finished merchandise for installation, consumption, processing, or resale constitute the supplier or vendor public. Manufacturers are becoming more dependent upon suppliers for the specialized materials and components required in the complex products produced by American industry.

In modern mass production manufacturers depend upon thousands of independent resources for the hundreds of thousands of parts and materials which go into industrial and consumer products. Competition among manufacturers and merchants for the superior products and services of reliable suppliers is growing keener. A good resource is a primary source of profit for producers and marketers.

More than 76 per cent of the 30,000 suppliers of General Motors Corporation in the United States have fewer than 100 employees. More than 45 cents of every dollar received by General Motors goes to suppliers. Some 30,000 suppliers provide Du Pont with thousands of products, from test tubes to tons of sulphur. The Western Electric Company, manufacturing and supply unit of the Bell System, is supplied by 37,000 firms, with more than $1 billion worth of products annually. The Radio Corporation of America depends upon 7,500 suppliers, located in 43 states, for their inventiveness and resourcefulness that contribute to the quality and performance of RCA products. Other large manufacturers dependent upon small suppliers are International Harvester Company with more than 20,000 suppliers; United States Steel Corporation supplied by about 54,000 concerns, at least 50,000 of which are small businesses; and General Electric Company which has 42,000 suppliers.

Retail and wholesale merchants are equally dependent upon suppliers for finished consumer goods. R. H. Macy & Company, the world's largest department store, buys nearly 500,000 items from some 15,000 manufacturers. Sears, Roebuck and Company obtains its merchandise from more than 20,000 resources.

Causes of Poor Supplier-Purchaser Relations

Although the mutual dependence of suppliers, manufacturers, and merchants is becoming more widely recognized, much antagonism and mistrust still exists between buyers and sellers. In the past, some vendors were accused by buyers of misrepresenting the origin, quality, and quantity of merchandise offered for sale; misrepresenting the vendor's identity, character, and status; engaging in deceptive selling schemes, full-line forcing, exclusive dealing, imposition of arbitrary terms, and discriminatory pricing.

Purchasers, on the other hand, were accused by vendors of seeking special price concessions by oppressive methods; demanding special quality, prices, terms, or discounts; making unreasonable claims for the purpose of securing price reductions; misrepresenting prices and conditions offered by another vendor; and boycotting and blacklisting suppliers.

The New Partnership Philosophy of Supplier-Purchaser Relations

However, this is a new era of supplier-vendor relationships in which vendors and purchasers co-operate to their mutual advantage in producing and distributing products for the ultimate consumer.

Both parties to a supplier-purchaser partnership must have confidence in the integrity and capability of the other.

The buyer must be assured that the supplier is pricing his products fairly because of efficient, low-cost production facilities, sound engineering, and research. The purchaser, on the other hand, must recognize that the supplier must make a fair profit or he will eventually be lost as a resource; and the supplier must earn an adequate return on capital invested to provide for good research, engineering, and modern equipment.

Successful suppliers consult with buyers in planning the design, quality, and cost of merchandise to be produced. In committing a share of his engineering and production facilities to a buyer, a supplier must have definite assurance that a customer will buy regularly and in sufficient volume to sustain continuity of production for a reasonable length of time at a price which will return a fair profit.

Progressive manufacturers and merchants have found that aiding their suppliers to become vigorous and profitable producers benefits not only the suppliers but also the purchasers. Neither a buyer nor seller profits at the other's expense; both benefit by working together for their mutual profit.

A growing number of manufacturers and merchants are entering into partnership relationships with their suppliers. The buyer decides what goods shall be manufactured, the quantities required, the cost, and when the goods should be delivered. The supplier determines how to design, engineer, and manufacture the goods to satisfy the buyer's needs.

Sears, Roebuck and Company, Ford Motor Company, and other large manufacturers co-operate closely with suppliers in what amounts to a partnership. Manufacturers and merchants aid suppliers in improving production by counseling them on cost accounting, engineering, designing, and management. Suppliers are aided in obtaining equipment and plant facilities. In some instances, when suppliers need new machinery to lower production costs, or to expand manufacturing facilities in order to supply the quantities of goods required, buyers finance suppliers.

Purchasers Need Good Relations with Suppliers

Modern technology, which has evolved a wide variety of new products and materials, has contributed to a closer relationship between manufacturers, merchants, and suppliers. Customers are not the sole source of profits. Suppliers are often the primary source of profits for manufacturers and merchants.

When a manufacturer is faced with a shortage of raw materials, parts, or accessories, a reliable supplier is vital to continued operation. Without a source of supply, a manufacturer is forced to stop operations.

The technical laboratories of suppliers are producing new types of fibers, finishes, chemicals, and drugs which are creating new markets and increasing sales and profits for manufacturers and merchants. The suppliers of these new products are advertising and promoting them to create a demand for the products of manufacturers who are using these new materials.

Manufacturers who are dependent upon suppliers of raw materials, accessories, and parts are conducting aggressive campaigns to obtain reliable sources of supply. Competition among manufacturers and merchants for good suppliers is keen because the number of reliable suppliers of particular products is limited. An increasing number of suppliers pursue a policy of selective distribution and dispose of their output to a limited number of desirable buyers.

Suppliers are also an invaluable source of information for manufacturers and merchants on new materials, markets, prices, and consumption. Manufacturers and dealers who have good relations with suppliers are assured of a reliable source of supply in the face of unforeseen shortages created by abnormal demand or emergencies which curtail production. Suppliers are prospective customers for the products of manufacturers and wholesalers. Many purchasers follow a policy of reciprocity, giving buying preference to resources who are customers. Good relations with vendors assure prompt deliveries to purchasers. Delivery may be more important to a buyer than either price or quality.

Suppliers who enjoy good relations with purchasers give favorable publicity and word-of-mouth advertising to purchasers. Supplier salesmen, servicemen, and deliverymen who receive courteous consideration from buyers speak well of the buyers.

Most favorable terms and prices are usually quoted to purchasers who have good relations with suppliers. Purchasers who are on good terms with suppliers are often granted special privileges on returns and adjustments, allowances, special packaging, price guaranty, and other benefits which are not available to less-favored buyers.

The importance of suppliers to manufacturers and merchants is expressed in the following definition of a supplier by Edgar H. Savage in the United Business Service:

WHAT IS A SUPPLIER?

A supplier is one on whom our business depends.

A supplier is not dependent on us alone, but we are part of his business structure.

A supplier furnishes our raw materials, services, and information indispensable to us in the conduct of our business.

A supplier is a vital part of our organization.

A supplier is not to be treated coldly—he is too human and has much of value to offer.

A supplier does not try to be smart—he offers the best he has—we then make the decision.

A supplier keeps constantly in mind his customer's needs.

A supplier is entitled to a fair profit—but his costs must be right.

It is our job to select those who qualify as real suppliers and stick with them through thick and thin.

PLANNING A SUPPLIER RELATIONS PROGRAM

Organization for Supplier Relations

Responsibility for planning and preparation of media of communications for supplier relations should be assigned to the public relations department. Execution of a supplier's relations program, however, is in the hands of employees and supervisors engaged in purchasing, receiving, inspecting, accounting, merchandising, and engineering, all of whom have relations with suppliers.

Purchasing, in large corporations, is usually decentralized in regional buying offices or local plants. In these cases, local purchasing or plant management are responsible for execution of the supplier relations programs. When buying is centralized, headquarters' purchasing and other departments dealing with suppliers are responsible for carrying out the program.

As the purchasing department has more contacts with suppliers than any other department of a business, it should have principal responsibility for executing a supplier relations program. However, other departments are also involved in supplier relations and should have a part in the program.

Co-ordinating Supplier Relations

To co-ordinate the activities of all departments having dealings with suppliers, a supplier relations committee composed of the heads of the purchasing, receiving, inspection, accounting, merchandising, and engineering departments is desirable. The functions of this committee are to survey supplier relationships and establish policies and procedures for improving relations; approve a supplier relations program and communications as submitted by the public relations department after consultation with the committee; and appraise the effectiveness of the program. The public relations manager should chairman the supplier relations committee.

R. H. Macy & Company, New York City department store, has a vendor relations committee which has established a code covering relationships with vendors; instituted buyers' diaries for recording all important experiences with vendors; surveyed internal procedures and systems affecting relationships with suppliers; and supervised the training of executives and personnel involved in vendor relations.

The Personal Products Corporation, affiliate of Johnson & Johnson, has a Source Relationship Committee composed of heads of purchasing, research, finance, marketing, production, and the president. This committee periodically reviews resource relationships and reports to the board of directors of the corporation.

Functions of the Public Relations Department in a Supplier Relations Program

The public relations department is responsible for investigating the attitudes of suppliers toward the company; planning and preparing communications to suppliers; and proposing supplier relations policies and procedures of purchasing and other departments involved in relations with suppliers. The public relations department should consult with members of the supplier relations committee and with purchasing executives in regard to objectives of the program and communications with suppliers. The public relations staff serves all departments involved in developing good supplier relations.

Corporations supplied by a large number of resources have assigned responsibility for supplier relations to a supplier relations section of the public relations department. The Borden Company's public relations department has a farm section to develop supplier relations with more than 25,000 farmers in 20 states who supply the milk and cream used in Borden products. The farm section prepares a supplier relations program and local plant management adapts the program to local needs.

Objectives of a Supplier Relations Program

The objectives of a supplier relations program are as follows:

To attain a good working relationship with suppliers by:
1. Establishing the mutuality of interest between suppliers and purchaser.
2. Showing suppliers how they can improve their methods of production and thus increase their net returns.
3. Determining what suppliers think about the company's policies and practices.
4. Establishing the company as a friendly partner, genuinely co-operative in working out production and supply problems.
5. Maintaining a friendly relationship with supplier's representatives.
6. Providing materials and suggestions for improving supplier relations to the purchasing staff, receiving, inspection, accounting, and other departments which work with suppliers.

Supplier Relations Research

The first step in developing an effective supplier-purchaser program is opinion research to determine what suppliers think about the purchaser's policies and practices in dealing with resources. Continuous research determines and reflects supplier opinion trends to management and operating executives for their consideration in improving buying policies and practices. Methods of surveying supplier opinion are described in Chapter 18, "Public Relations Research and Evaluation."

In addition to external research, internal investigation should be undertaken by the purchasing department of purchasing procedures and systems leading to improved relations with suppliers. Analysis of complaints of purchasing, receiving, and inspection policies and practices received by the company will reveal deficiencies in dealing with suppliers that destroy good resource relations.

Supplier Relations Policy

Good relations with suppliers depend fundamentally upon sound purchasing policy and practices. Purchasing policy is determined by the executive responsible for purchasing and approved by management. It defines the buyer's responsibilities to suppliers as well as the obligations of suppliers to the purchaser. It considers the interests of good sources of supply by observing fair procurement practices which enable the purchaser to retain and develop good resources. Application of the company's purchasing policy by all personnel involved in buying is essential to good supplier relationships.

If a good supplier relations policy is not faithfully applied by all persons involved in purchasing, good relationships with resources cannot be developed. The public relations department should counsel the purchasing department on policy and its application, but responsibility for determining and executing buying policy is that of the purchasing department.

Internal Methods for Improving Supplier Relations

Congenial supplier relations begin "at home" in the buying offices and with the attitudes and actions of the people involved in purchasing, receiving, inspecting, accounting, and other departments that have direct relations with suppliers. It is the responsibility of the heads of purchasing and other departments that deal with suppliers, to develop in their people good attitudes and practices which are the basis of a mutually profitable and satisfactory relationship with resources.

To insure an effective supplier relations program, purchasing management should train the buying staff to deal more effectively with representatives of suppliers, appraise buyers' methods of interviewing salesmen, improve facilities for receiving salesmen, and keep records of experiences with suppliers. The public relations department should assist in improving purchasing practices by preparing training materials, and statements of buying policy, welcome booklets for salesmen, lists of products purchased, vendor policy, and in other ways aiding purchasing executives in improving relations with supplier's representatives.

Training Buying Staff. Internal education of personnel in supplier relations includes informing the buying staff about the corporate buying policy. The company's vendor relations policy should be studied by newly appointed buyers and personnel involved in vendor relations. Group meetings should be arranged between the buying staff and purchasing executives for a discussion of vendor relations policy and practices and how to improve them.

A supplier relations bulletin should be prepared by the purchasing department with the assistance of the public relations department and circulated at regular intervals to all who deal with resources. This medium should inform and transmit suggestions for improving supplier relations—covering correspondence with suppliers, treatment of salesmen, buying ethics, visits to suppliers, and other subjects.

Motion pictures produced by suppliers, showing their plants, facilities, personnel, and operations may be shown to purchasing officials and personnel to enable them to become more familiar with resources.

A purchasing handbook for the buying staff should be published describing buying policies and practices, the importance of good relations with resources, and methods of creating good will with resources.

Observing Buyers' Techniques in Interviewing Salesmen. In training buyers in improving supplier relations, buying interviews should be recorded and later discussed in meetings of the buying staff to show the best way to interview salesmen and improve relations with suppliers.

Improving Facilities for Receiving Suppliers' Representatives. Good relations with suppliers originate with good treatment of vendors' salesmen. A clean, well-lighted and ventilated reception room furnished with comfortable chairs, reading matter, toilet facilities, drinking water, and telephone service makes a favorable impression on visiting salesmen.

Recording Experience with Suppliers. Buyers' diaries describing their dealings with resources are useful in improving supplier relations. A knowledge of previous relationships with suppliers obtained from buyers' diaries makes for more intelligent purchasing and better relations with vendors. Such records should be maintained on suppliers from whom the purchaser does not buy as well as on those from whom purchases are made regularly.

COMMUNICATING WITH SUPPLIERS

The principal methods of communicating with suppliers are oral conversation of buyers, receivers, inspectors, engineers, and others connected with the purchasing organization; by printed and visual communications; or a combination of oral and visual methods.

Oral or Personal Communication

Personal communication by manufacturers and merchants with suppliers includes: personal interviews by purchasing executives and buyers with visiting representatives of suppliers; meetings arranged with suppliers; visits of buyers to suppliers' plants and offices; open house for suppliers; and expediters visiting with suppliers.

Personal Interviews with Visiting Representatives. The impressions salesmen representing suppliers receive in their conversations with buyers are an important factor in developing good supplier relations. Prompt and courteous reception of salesmen creates good relations with suppliers.

Group Meetings with Suppliers. Meetings arranged by manufacturers and merchants with suppliers are an effective means of promoting better supplier-purchaser relations. The program for supplier meetings includes a welcome by the purchasing director and a discussion of purchasing policy; films showing the buyer's products; a plant visit; a question and answer period, and luncheon.

Lockheed Missiles & Space Company, Sunnyvale, California, a division of Lockheed Aircraft Corporation, arranges one-day presentation conferences for potential suppliers with 40 Lockheed missile and space engineers and technicians in attendance. More than 150 technical presentations and demonstrations have been made by suppliers who are given a suggested procedure for product presentations. Samples and data on suppliers' products are sent to Lockheed by suppliers in advance of presentations. Lockheed's vendors' relations staff follows up the presentations by sending each supplier a list of engineers attending the meeting, their titles, projects, and addresses together with a critique of the presentation and a list of the companies in the area that might be interested in the suppliers' products.

Visits to Suppliers' Plants and Offices. Visits by purchasing executives and staff to the plants and offices of major suppliers establish closer relationships with resources and create a better understanding of suppliers' facilities, organizations, and policies.

Open House for Suppliers. Purchasers promote a better understanding with suppliers by inviting them to an open house to inspect the operations of the purchaser and hear from the director of purchasing and his staff.

A large automobile manufacturer holds supplier open houses in each of its principal assembly plant cities. Suppliers are served an informal luncheon followed by a tour of the assembly plant. Company executives address the suppliers and a motion picture is shown.

Traveling Expediters Contact Suppliers. Some companies employ traveling expediters to visit suppliers to expedite shipments, give counsel and assistance on production problems, and maintain friendly relations with vendors.

Printed and Visual Communication

Printed and visual media of communication are used by manufacturers and merchants in furthering relations with suppliers. The principal printed and visual media of communication with suppliers are: periodical publications; advertising; annual report; motion pictures; correspondence; publicity; and awards.

Periodical Publications. An effective medium for communicating with suppliers is a periodical edited and published by a manufacturer or merchant and distributed without charge to suppliers.

The farm section of the public relations department of the Borden Company publishes, for milk producers who supply Borden with milk and cream, a magazine called *The Dairy Digest.* This publication is also distributed to county agents, extension workers, agricultural college officials, farm editors, and agricultural writers to keep them informed of Borden's services to dairy farmers.

The First National Stores, New England regional food chain, publishes a bimonthly magazine for New England farmers who supply the stores with produce.

Advertising. Some corporations feature their suppliers in advertisements in leading newspapers and business magazines to create better supplier-purchaser relations.

General Motors Corporation sponsored a series of advertisements in national consumer magazines describing its dependence upon small suppliers.

Direct advertising folders and booklets describing the purchasing organization, products, policies, and services to suppliers are published by manufacturers and merchants and distributed to visiting salesmen. A large manufacturer gives each supplier's salesman on his first visit to the company's buying office a booklet entitled, "Welcome to purchasing," which discusses such subjects as: "Products Manufactured," "Purchasing Organization," Value Analysis and the Salesman," and "Purchasing Policy."

Annual Report. Many purchasers are furthering better supplier relations by mailing their annual report to their resources. The vendor relations committee of a large New York department store sends an annual report to vendors. This report discusses the importance of good supplier relations, the objectives of the store's vendor relations committee, the store's code of vendor relations, the store's buying procedures, and buyer training in improving resource relations.

Motion Pictures. Motion pictures are used by manufacturers to communicate with suppliers. The public relations department of a large automobile manufacturer produced a motion picture, portraying the vital role played by suppliers in the company's operations, for showing to suppliers and their personnel in a series of supplier meetings.

Correspondence with Suppliers. A large volume of correspondence continually flows between buyers and sellers. Good correspondence can make a substantial contribution to better understanding and improved relations between suppliers and purchasers.

Publicity. Manufacturers and merchants communicate with suppliers through news stories and articles describing purchasing policies and practices in the columns of business magazines read by management and salesmen representing suppliers.

Awards to Suppliers. In recognition of outstanding services rendered by suppliers, purchasers are making supplier honor awards. Recognition is given suppliers for their contributions to new or improved products, prompt deliveries, and technical competence. Neiman-Marcus Company, Dallas, Texas, department store makes annual awards to resources for "Distinguished Service in the Field of Fashion."

Case 11-1

SUPPLIER RELATIONS

Western Electric Co.

The Western Electric Company, with headquarters in New York City, is the manufacturing, purchasing, distribution, and installation subsidiary of American Telephone and Telegraph Company serving 23 regional telephone companies in the Bell System which operates more than 60 million telephones used to carry 80 billion conversations a year. At 16 plants in more than 20 cities Western Electric makes and distributes an annual volume of more than $1.5 billion worth of cable, amplifiers, automatic switching equipment, telephones, and supplies used by the Bell System.

In a recent year the company also made and installed over $600 million worth of defense products for the U.S. Army, Navy, and Air Force including guidance systems for missiles, underwater sound equipment, data transmission systems, and such projects as the Arctic DEW line.

Thirty-four Western Electric warehouses throughout the country distribute many thousands of supply items used by Bell Telephone companies. Western Electric employs over 140,000 men and women in its plants, laboratories, distributing houses, and offices throughout the country.

Western Electric Company spends annually more than $1.2 billion for 150,-000 different raw material items, finished products, and services purchased from 40,000 suppliers. Some 1,200 Western Electric employees are engaged in purchasing a wide variety of products including copper, steel, and other metals and plastic components, subassemblies and complete assemblies. The more than $300 million worth of supplies and special equipment purchased for Bell Telephone companies includes paper, printing, clay and concrete conduit, climbing irons, telephone poles, tents, and tarpaulins. In one year Western Electric buys over 100 million copies of telephone directories, 210,000 gallons of floor finishes, 276,000 cases of hand soap, 500 million paper towels, 35 tons of rubber bands, 100 million paper clips in addition to many other items of operating supplies. Nearly 50 cents of every Western Electric sales dollar is spent with suppliers.

The number of Western Electric suppliers has been increasing each year from 32,000 in 1954 to 37,000 in 1957 to 40,000 in 1961. They are located in 3,000 cities and towns in every state in the country. In the city of Yonkers, N.Y., for example, Western Electric spends over $3 million annually with over 60 suppliers. The company's suppliers vary in size from one-man operations to corporations employing tens of thousands of workers. The great majority— some 90 per cent—employ less than 500 people and are considered as "small" suppliers.

Many suppliers have been associated with Western Electric for more than 25 years. In a recent year some 7,000 firms became Western Electric suppliers for the first time. Some 135,000 suppliers' representatives call at Western Electric buying offices each year.

Relations with suppliers originate with buying personnel at over 50 locations including plants, distributing houses, and headquarters in New York. At each of Western Electric's 16 manufacturing plants there is a resident head of purchasing who also serves as the company's Small Business Liaison Representative for his area. He has the responsibility of carrying out the company's Small Business Policy which is to extend to small business concerns an equitable opportunity to compete within their capabilities for Western Electric's requirements. The buyer at each of the 34 Distributing Houses has the same responsibility. Responsibility for small business relations is therefore specifically assigned wherever buying authority is exercised.

Materials for manufacturing are generally purchased at the plant where the material is used. Commodities used at several locations or in large quantities are purchased on a centralized basis by Headquarters, the plant where engineering control of an item is assigned, or at the plant which is the largest user of the item. Distributing House buyers purchase against general or zone contracts negotiated at Headquarters and also purchase low-value items locally.

Western Electric's basic purchasing policies guide its relations with suppliers. The company aims to give fair and impartial consideration to any reliable concern, small as well as large, which is qualified to produce the material being purchased; to buy without favoritism on the basis of the best price for the material of the required quantity and quality for delivery at the right time; to make purchases competitively whenever possible; to develop multiple sources of supply for each important item of purchase; to avoid placing so much business with a single supplier that he becomes too dependent on Western; to give a courteous and prompt reception to salesmen; to keep quotations and other private information in strict confidence; and never accept gifts of any value whatsoever directly or indirectly from any supplier.

Co-operation with Western Electric suppliers goes beyond purchasing policy. Each new vendor who visits a Western Electric purchasing office is cordially welcomed and given an interview; his product and its possible use are evaluated; and he is briefed on the company's purchasing and contractual procedure.

Western Electric procurement representatives visit plants of suppliers to assess their capabilities. The company often gives its suppliers assistance in engineering, production control, and purchasing. This is a continuous program which helps suppliers cut their costs of production and assists them in introducing new efficiencies in their manufacturing operations. This service enables vendors to keep abreast of new developments and new designs of equipment, methods, and processes.

A Supplier Relations Program was initiated by the company at the Winston-Salem Works, North Carolina. A similar program is followed at all plant locations although at the North Carolina location the program is organized on a more formal basis because of the number of callers and complexity of the items purchased. Here, an experienced purchasing man with the title of Chief of Supplier Relations has been assigned the responsibility of encouraging and enhancing better vendor relations. When a receptionist greets a sales representative she has not seen before, she asks, "Is this your first visit?" If it is the visitor's first call, the Chief of Supplier Relations, who is always alert to new supplier capabilities, interviews the vendor and describes the various operations carried on at the North Carolina Works and the type of products purchased. The salesman is referred to the proper buyer or, if the salesman's product or service has no local application, he is advised to discuss his proposition with a buyer at the appropriate Western Electric buying office.

When several new noncompeting suppliers arrive at a Western Electric buying office at the same time, they may be interviewed in groups of three. As most of the information given salesmen on their first call is similar, the group interview saves time for the visiting salesmen and the buyer. A record is kept by each buying office of each visit of every salesman with the types of items or service offered, date of call, time spent with the buyer, size of the supplier's plant, and number of employees. Calls of suppliers are followed up promptly with letters of appreciation for the salesman's visit.

Western Electric maintains a staff of expediters who work with vendors and help build good supplier relations. These expediters have a complete understanding of material, labor, and equipment needed by suppliers to fill Western Electric orders. They have the initiative and imagination to suggest alternative ways of securing material which may be in short supply. They make the facilities of Western Electric available to suppliers when a shortage of parts or materials or a breakdown in equipment threatens to shut down a supplier's production line. In addition, expediters are located at strategic points throughout the country ready to go to the assistance of vendors as the need arises, and in some cases they are assigned to vendors' plants on a partial or full-time basis for a few days or weeks if necessary to help solve production problems.

All of these factors assure the timely delivery of material and equipment to Western Electric.

Suppliers welcome the assistance given them by Western Electric. One vendor describes the help given by a Western Electric expediter as follows: "Your expediter handled five supply problems on which the latest delivery was scheduled for September. As of July 14, every one of these items had been received by this laboratory. We not only appreciate the results which we have obtained but the attitude which has been shown throughout. Our problems were handled by your expediter as if he were one of our own staff."

Western Electric communications to suppliers, to encourage mutual under-

WESTERN ELECTRIC
AND ITS 40,000 SUPPLIERS

Last year, about 40,000 companies employing over 5,000,000 people in about 3,500 American cities and towns helped Western Electric with its job as manufacturing and supply unit of the Bell System and as a major government contractor. W. E. dollars paid to these firms – over $1 billion in 1961 – helped meet payrolls and pay taxes in communities throughout the nation. These companies ranged from major industrial concerns to three-man operations. Most were small businesses with fewer than 500 employees.

As our needs have grown, so has the number of our suppliers. Last year, for instance, there were close to 10,000 more than in 1955. In 1961 alone, about 7,000 new firms became Western Electric suppliers. To find the right companies for our special needs, we requested quotations from over 120,000 well-qualified concerns during 1961.

From some of our suppliers came raw materials, parts, components and assemblies for our factories where Bell telephones and communications equipment are made. Some helped with defense projects entrusted to us by the government. Others provided special services – like transportation. And still others supplied finished products – everything from linesmen's belts and pliers to telephone poles. The contributions of these suppliers enable us to focus our efforts on our main concern: manufacturing high-quality communications products for dependable service in the Bell Telephone network and furnishing production, engineering and management services for government projects.

FIG. 11–1. To develop good relations with its 40,000 suppliers Western Electric Co. published this two-page advertisement in business, telephone, and journalism

standing, are an important feature of the company's Supplier Relations Program. When a vendor's representative calls at a Western Electric buying office he is handed a booklet entitled, "Glad to See You," which welcomes the salesman and outlines the company's purchasing policy; its buying organization; what and where it buys; its manufacturing, distribution, installation, and defense activities; and its history.

The part played by small suppliers in Western Electric operations is described in a booklet entitled, "Western Electric and Its 40,000 Partners," which also is available to all visiting vendors. This booklet informs them of Western Electric's role as a consumer, its contributions to the nation's economy, its policies in dealing with small business, and its co-operation with suppliers.

A pocket-size booklet entitled, "Restatement of Policy of Western Electric Company," points out to all vendors the governing principles which guide the company's purchasing activities, particularly with respect to employees not accepting gifts from vendors.

An advertising campaign featuring Western Electric suppliers is appearing in business, press, broadcasting, and telephone periodicals. The primary objective of this campaign is to impress the public with the fact that many suppliers—small as well as large—are necessary to the successful operation of Western Electric and that these firms have a true partnership role with Western Electric in supplying the Bell System.

In effect, this advertising campaign stresses the benefits which suppliers, through their association with Western Electric, are able to pass on to their employees, their communities, and the nation. Brief case histories of small companies which are building profitable businesses from small beginnings are featured in the advertisements.

One of this series of supplier advertisements is reproduced on page 256.

The 140,000 Western Electric employees are informed of the important part played by suppliers in the company's progress through articles in the *WE* and *Western Electric News Features* publications. One article entitled, "Big Business–Little Business," in *WE,* for example, related how Western Electric depends upon thousands of small firms for goods and services used in the production of telephone equipment. Another article in a later issue of *WE* described suppliers in Elgin, Illinois; highlighting their history, operations, growth with the Bell System, and importance to the economy of the community.

Other publications such as the Western Electric and American Telephone and Telegraph *Annual Reports* also devote space to the importance of Western's suppliers. In addition, the significance of Western Electric's relations with its 40,000 suppliers is publicized in business magazine articles. *Purchasing* magazine described Western Electric's Supplier Relations Program in a 30-page feature article entitled, "Purchasing at Western Electric."

The effectiveness of Western Electric Company's Supplier Relations Program is shown by the letters of appreciation from vendors, the favorable comments by suppliers to the company's purchasing executives and the complimentary response by the public to the program.

QUESTIONS

1. Comment on the Supplier Relations Program of Western Electric Company. Describe its good features, also its shortcomings.

2. Describe how this supplier relations program can be improved.
3. What should be the objective of Western Electric Company's Supplier Relations Program?
4. Is the Western Electric Company's business magazine advertising campaign desirable? Give reasons for favoring or opposing this advertising.
5. How can the company's Supplier Relations Advertising Program be improved?

Problem 11–1

SUPPLIER RELATIONS

Monon Manufacturing Company

The Monon Manufacturing Company, Detroit, Michigan, manufactures and markets electric distribution and control equipment including safety switches, circuit breakers, panel boards, switchboards, switchgear, busways, and various types of motor controls in annual volume of $800 million. In addition, the company produces annually $80 million worth of components for guided missiles, rocket engines, and electronic systems for the U.S. Air Force and Navy. Production facilities are located in Detroit, Columbus, Los Angeles, and Pittsburgh.

The company employs 10,500 workers in its four plants and a sales engineering force of 200 men working out of 20 district sales offices located in the principal industrial centers of the country.

In the manufacture of its products, the company relies on 3,200 suppliers in 20 states to provide its requirements of raw materials, metals, plastics, parts, tools, machines, and operating supplies costing more than $400 million annually. The number of suppliers of Monon increased from 1,000 just before World War II to 4,000 during the war, but has declined in recent years to about 3,200. Each of these resources furnishes the company with $500 or more worth of products and services annually. Several hundred additional suppliers provide smaller amounts of materials and supplies. Most of the business concerns supplying Monon are small with less than 500 employees each. All purchases are centralized at the company's Detroit headquarters.

Relations between Monon and many of its suppliers have extended over a long period. More than 100 manufacturers have supplied Monon for more than 30 years; 20 per cent have done business with the company for more than 10 years; and 70 per cent have supplied Monon with goods and services for more than five years.

Suppliers range in size from multimillion dollar corporations to three-man operations. They are located in 500 cities and towns in 20 states across the nation. Purchases from these vendors range from an annual total of less than $600 from one concern in Montana to $85 million from 600 suppliers in the state of Michigan.

To serve its customers efficiently, the Monon Manufacturing Company believes that it is important to maintain an uninterrupted flow of materials and services into its manufacturing plants at the right time, in the right quantity, and in the right quality. Monon realizes that it cannot operate without the assistance of the hundreds of suppliers that furnish it with materials, parts, and services.

Monon is interested in maintaining a partnership relationship with its suppliers. Such a partnership requires that the company and its resources must have complete confidence in each other. Monon must be certain that it is buying competitively, that its suppliers believe in product development, have an adequate engineering staff, and efficient, low-cost production facilities.

To assure its suppliers continuity of production of Monon components and to make certain that Monon has reliable sources on which it can spend time and money in helping them produce improved products, Monon and its suppliers frequently sign long-term production contracts.

The research and development department of Monon provides technical services to some of its suppliers to aid them in determining quality standards, using alternative materials for a given component, investigating lower cost manufacturing processes, redesigning parts to provide greater utility and lower manufacturing cost, examining plant layout and determining how far to tool a new item, and solving similar technical problems. This assistance is patricularly effective with smaller suppliers, many of whose resources are too limited to enable them to support adequate engineering and development departments of their own and they turn to Monon's research and development department for advice.

In this manner an atmosphere of close co-operation has developed between the company and many of its resources. Monon recognizes that a supplier must make a profit or be lost as a source of supply. The company is seeking vendors able to earn a good return on their capital and to use a reasonable amount of this profit for research and new machinery so that they can continue to supply Monon with quality parts and materials at fair prices.

In some cases when a supplier is a satisfactory source and has need of financial assistance to purchase new machinery to lower production costs or expand output in order to provide the quality and quantity required by Monon, the company has given the supplier financial assistance and in return has obtained a small minority interest in the supplier's business.

To promote good relations with suppliers, Monon has modernized its reception room to provide greater comfort for visiting representatives of vendors. Each visiting salesman is supplied with reading matter while waiting to be interviewed. Reading materials include not only current business magazines but also company publications, the company's annual report, employee publications and newsletters describing new products, labor relations, and other topics. Receptionists and telephone operators are instructed in the proper public relations approach to callers.

The purchasing agent of Monon is concerned with the decline in the number of suppliers since World War II. He believes that it is necessary to increase the quantity and quality of suppliers and to become better acquainted with resources. To solve this problem, the public relations manager of the company proposes a one-day procurement symposium to be held at the Monon plant in Detroit.

The objective of the symposium would be to give suppliers a better understanding of the new and diversified electric distribution and control equipment made by Monon; to provide vendors with an opportunity to ask questions about Monon and its products; to find new competitive vendors to cut Monon's costs; to interest small business concerns in submitting estimates on parts and materials; and through publicity to inform the industry of the company's interest in its suppliers.

The public relations manager arranged several meetings with the purchasing agent and his staff to explore ramifications, obtain suggestions, and to anticipate problems that might arise in connection with the symposium.

The principal feature of the symposium would be a display of 500 identified parts which visiting suppliers could examine and select those they thought they could make, take notes, secure drawings and specifications of each part, and later submit quotations.

The symposium would be opened at 9:00 o'clock in the morning in the plant auditorium with a welcome by the Mayor of Detroit. He would be followed by the Detroit plant manager discussing plant activities and pointing out the mutual benefit to be derived by Monon and suppliers from the symposium. The purchasing agent would discuss the company's purchasing policy, co-operation with vendors, and interest in suppliers' offerings. He would urge visiting vendors to inspect the parts on display, request drawings and specifications, and submit quotations on the parts they were interested in supplying.

A company produced 20-minute color motion picture showing Monon's facilities, products, and their components would be shown to the visiting vendors to impress them with the desirability of Monon as a customer.

Following the showing of the film, visitors would be free to inspect the parts exhibit and to question members of Monon's purchasing staff. Air Force and Navy procurement officers would be on hand to instruct visiting suppliers on procedures for securing government subcontracts for parts for rockets, missiles, and electronic systems produced by Monon Manufacturing Company.

Luncheon would be served at noon in the company cafeteria where cafeteria employees would take trays to tables and seat guests with company representatives interspersed among the guests.

Following luncheon, suppliers would take part in a question-and-answer period moderated by the purchasing agent of the company. The plant manager, purchasing staff, mechanical and planning engineers would be present to answer vendors' questions. The remainder of the afternoon, the visiting vendors would be free to inspect the parts display and confer with company executives.

The co-operation of the Small Business Administration of the federal government would be enlisted in promoting attendance of small manufacturers at the symposium. In addition, representatives of the Small Business Administration would be present to aid small businessmen in understanding the procedure for securing subcontracts on parts for equipment for the Armed Forces. The names of small manufacturers interested in obtaining government subcontracts would be supplied by the Administration to serve as an invitation list.

Invitations would be sent to the operating heads of 800 small manufacturers throughout the Midwest. An attendance of about 500 was expected, representing some 350 companies. The symposium would be publicized in business magazines and local newspapers. The cost of the symposium was not expected to exceed $5,500.

The management of the Monon Manufacturing Company was not fully convinced that the procurement seminar was necessary, as the natural competitive interest of vendors would cause them to seek out Monon as a prospective customer. Furthermore, many of the potential suppliers who would attend the symposium would not have the manufacturing facilities to produce the type and quantity of components required for Monon electrical products. From the company's standpoint, a limited number of resources of proven ability to produce quality components would be preferable to hundreds of small suppliers.

The advertising manager of the company proposed an alternative plan for improving supplier relations. A series of advertisements would be placed in the business magazines featuring Monon suppliers and describing the advantages to vendors in supplying the company with parts and materials. The advertisements would explain how Monon co-operates with small suppliers in improving their production processes, reducing their costs, and solving manufacturing problems. These advertisements would reach a large number of suppliers at a relatively low cost per reader.

QUESTIONS

1. Do you approve of the proposed procurement symposium to improve supplier relations of the Monon Manufacturing Company? Give reasons for accepting or rejecting this proposal.

2. Do you favor the alternative advertising campaign proposed by the advertising manager of the company? Give reasons for accepting or rejecting this proposal.

3. Is there a better way for Monon Manufacturing Company to improve relations with suppliers? Describe in detail a better plan.

12 · EDUCATIONAL RELATIONS

THE FORTY MILLION pupils and one and one-half million teachers and administrators in American elementary and secondary schools, colleges, and universities comprise one of the largest and most important publics of business, social, and professional organizations. The educators and youth who compose this great public profoundly influence contemporary life and business in this country and the economic climate in which business must function in the future.

The educational public in the United States in 1960, according to the U.S. Office of Education, included 91,853 elementary and 25,784 secondary public schools, with a total enrollment of 36,146,591 pupils and 1,369,000 teachers. In addition, there are 4,061 private and parochial schools in the country. In the field of higher education, there are 701 public and 1,307 private universities and colleges of liberal arts, independent professional schools, teachers' and junior colleges, with a total enrollment of 3,891,000 students.

BUSINESS-EDUCATION RELATIONSHIPS

A better understanding between business and education is a real necessity today. The misunderstanding between the business and academic communities arises from inadequate communications by business of its philosophy, policies, and practices. "Due to the maintenance of a one-way street to the campuses of our schools by industry and its representatives," says Professor L. H. Ryerson, University of Minnesota, "the average faculty member has no firsthand knowledge of the industries to which he sends his graduates. It is now time for industry to make it a two-way street."

Business organizations, recognizing the importance of good communications with educators, are initiating programs of information and assistance to teachers. Corporations are providing teaching materials; furnishing speakers to schools; employing teachers and students; providing scholarships to needy students; inviting teachers and pupils to visit plants and offices; collaborating with school executives on community projects; serving on school boards and committees; advising on school problems; and contributing funds for buildings, equipment, and teacher compensation.

On the other hand, educators are improving their communication with business. Teachers are visiting business organizations to learn how industry functions; using more equipment, motion pictures, models, exhibits, and visual aids supplied by business; inviting businessmen to speak about business in the schools. Progressive teachers are incorporating business information in their instruction and are engaging in research on economic problems. Educators estimate that $50 million is spent annually by business for teaching materials.

Securing Acceptance of an Educational Program by Educators

An educational program of a corporation, association, or nonprofit organization intended to inform and aid teachers and pupils must be accepted and approved by school administrators and teachers. Educators are particularly sensitive to attempts by industrial or nonprofit groups or organizations to directly or indirectly commercialize instruction. Accordingly, all business-sponsored teaching aids are critically appraised by teachers for bias, propaganda, or sales promotion and those which have these characteristics are not used in the schools. Educators resist serving as a medium for business to reach the captive school audience. They oppose exploitation by an organization, and refuse to permit school children to become targets for propaganda or victims of thinly disguised sales promotion.

Much educational material distributed by business organizations for use in elementary and secondary schools is prepared by persons with limited knowledge of the current needs, aims, and methods of education. A teaching aid should be designed primarily to aid teachers in presenting an academic subject in a clearer, more interesting way or solving a particular instructional problem rather than to publicize a corporation. Teaching aids should be prepared by persons not only capable of interpreting the facts about a business or industry but also by those experienced in pedagogy.

The form and content of sponsored educational materials should recognize the preferences of educators and aim for quality rather than quantity. The advice and assistance of competent educators is indispensable in the development of educational materials for elementary, secondary schools, and colleges.

The educational materials acceptable to public schools is described in "Guiding Principles for School Selection and Use of Non-Listed Instructional Materials Not Purchasable Through School Allotments" published by the Board of Superintendents of the City of New York as follows:

Commercially sponsored materials should satisfy the following requirements:

The material should make a significant contribution toward educational goals.

The advertising content of the material should be minimal, unobjectionable, and unobtrusive.

The advertising matter should be in good taste. It should be fair, accurate, and free from excessive promotional or competitive presentation.

Wherever possible, the material used should be that provided by the industry as a whole rather than by individuals or companies.

In commercial and technical subjects in which identification of machines, apparatus, or other illustrative materials by reference to trade or firm name is necessary or unavoidable, materials containing such illustrative matter may be used.

Appropriate materials carrying advertising may be used in consumer education for the purpose of analysis and evaluation of advertising methods used. In this case, the purpose for which these materials are used should be made quite clear.

To secure acceptance of teaching aids in an educational relations program, an educational aids advisory committee composed of a representative group of classroom teachers, administrators, counselors, and guidance specialists should be formed by the sponsor of the program. This committee should collaborate in the preparation of educational aids by writing, reading, criticizing, and suggesting methods of presentation to assure the maximum suitability of teaching aids for use in the classroom. Educators experienced in the preparation and use of teaching aids should be consulted in the beginning and continuously during the execution of an educational relations program to assure that it will be favorably received and used by administrators and teachers. The National Association of Manufacturers has an educational aids advisory committee which advises on the preparation of publications and materials sponsored by the Association.

In addition to the collaboration of an advisory committee of educators, an educational program should be the responsibility of an educational section of the public relations department of the corporation or association. The educational section should be staffed by professional educators with the experience, interest, educational contacts, and understanding which comes from experience gained in teaching, educational administration, or service on a school committee.

In initiating an educational program on the local level in public and parochial elementary and secondary schools, the superintendent of schools should be consulted and through him the school principals, department heads, and teachers in the school system concerned with the use of the material to be developed. In introducing educational aids in colleges, the dean of the faculty, department heads, and professors who are expected to use the material should be consulted concerning the use of the teaching aids in their courses.

Objectives of Educational Relations

The objectives of educational relations programs vary widely, from broad economic education to providing information about the manufacturing processes of a particular company or industry. The choice of an objective is dictated largely by the product or service of the corporation or group sponsoring the educational program.

Some of the objectives of educational relations programs of business organizations and nonprofit groups are as follows:

Thrift Education. Thrift education programs to stimulate saving by pupils in primary and secondary schools are sponsored by banks and financial institutions.

Economic Education. Corporations and business associations sponsor economic education programs to inform students of the benefits of the American system of free enterprise, to expose the fallacies of socialism, and to explain the necessity for profits.

Teacher Education. To give teachers a better understanding of business operations, corporations invite college and university professors in marketing, social science, industrial relations, economics, and agriculture to attend forums and lectures by corporation officers. These programs run from two to five weeks at corporation headquarters, with the corporations paying expenses of teachers. The teachers have an opportunity to observe industrial operations, ask questions of company management, and, in some cases, make individual investigations of specialized phases of the business in the field of their individual interests.

School Problems. The objectives of the educational relations programs of some business organizations are to improve public knowledge of schools and educational problems including classroom and teacher shortage, growing enrollment, and inadequate teachers' salaries.

Highway Safety Education. Highway safety education of secondary school pupils is the objective of the educational relations programs of several automobile and petroleum corporations. Business organizations are co-operating with schools in driver-training programs.

Conservation Education. To interest teachers and pupils in the conservation of natural resources is an objective of educational relations programs. A large paper and woodpulp producing company conducts a forestry conservation program in the schools of the area where its forests are located.

Health Education. The educational relations programs of corporations producing food products are devoted to health education. The public relations and home economics departments of food manufacturers offer teachers booklets, films, and teaching materials on nutrition, food preparation, and diets.

Industrial Education. Industrial education is the major objective of the educational relations programs of some trade associations and large corporations which are seeking to give teachers and students a better understanding of the products and processes, as well as the history and contributions of industry to the public welfare.

Consumer Education. The principal objective of the educational relations activities of many manufacturers who produce consumer products is consumer education. Makers of textiles, foods, beverages, clothing, automobiles, and other consumer goods provide materials and services to teachers and pupils for use in courses in domestic science, nutrition, sewing, home economics, science, and social studies.

Vocational Guidance. Some educational relations programs are devoted to vocational guidance for secondary school boys and girls. Corporations are co-operating with teachers of vocational counseling and guidance to aid students in choosing a vocation. Industrial concerns publish career booklets describing job opportunities for high school and college graduates and make personnel available for speeches and school guidance forums.

Technical Training Assistance. Producers of technical products aid teachers in schools of engineering, science, and the trades by supplying technical information, exhibits, tools, charts, models, machines, and demonstrating materials for use in science, physics, electrical, chemical, and shop courses.

Social Studies Education. The emphasis in many secondary schools on social science and economic subjects has opened a new field of opportunity for educational service by business concerns that provide teachers and students with booklets, maps, charts, films, and exhibits.

A survey of 265 companies and 30 school administrators by the National Citizens Council for Better Schools, New York City, showed 30 different methods of business education co-operation including: making trained personnel available for school guidance forums; participating in teen-age career conferences; publishing pamphlets on careers in industry; co-operating with schools in the preparation of special exhibits; employing students under the co-operative education plan; employing students in summer; employing teachers during the summer months; taking part in Business-Industry-Education Days, in which students and teachers visit industrial plants; and taking part in Education-Business-Industry Days, in which businessmen visit schools.

Some corporations set special times for plant visits of students and teachers; prepare films for school use; put special research services at disposal of school teachers; and employ personnel from schools for special research projects.

Sponsorship of addresses and conferences is common in educational relations, with corporations maintaining speakers' bureaus and volunteer spakers giving lectures; sponsoring luncheon meetings where businessmen and educators informally exchange ideas; sponsoring workshops attended by both businessmen and educators; and encouraging company officers to speak on the value of education.

An increasing number of companies are encouraging employees to take part in school affairs; giving employees time off to participate in school activities; lending personnel to committees working for schools. Service to education is recognized by publicizing employee activity for schools in company house organs; running articles in company house organs on education in general.

Corporations support schools at bond elections; prepare and sponsor public service advertising on behalf of schools; participate in teacher recognition days; contribute equipment to schools; give special awards to students and teachers; give scholarships and fellowships to outstanding students and teachers; and make grants to colleges and universities.

Co-operative Business-Education Relations Programs

Co-operative business-educational programs are sponsored by community and regional groups of business concerns. The combined contributions of several companies in an area make possible a more comprehensive program and avoid the duplication which occurs when individual companies operate their own educational relations programs. Co-operative programs in educational relations are usually sponsored by a local Chamber of Commerce or industrial association which provides a co-ordinated educational program.

The Committee on Business Information, sponsored by 90 business organizations in Worcester County, Massachusetts, conducts a co-operative educational relations program of vocational guidance, student essay contests, student-teacher tours of industrial plants, speakers in the schools, and educational films.

The Tulsa, Oklahoma, Chamber of Commerce, through its Business Programs Liaison Sub-Committee, co-ordinates the educational relations activities of 45 local companies and professional organizations in an educational program which includes: providing business executives to speak and conduct conferences in the schools; inviting teachers and students to business meetings; providing business literature to schools; making industrial films and exhibits available to schools; conducting well-organized tours for students; donating or lending industrial equipment to schools; providing summer employment for teachers; giving financial aid to students on special projects; and providing scholarships for teachers and students.

The Industrial Information Institute, Inc., of Youngstown, Ohio, sponsored by industrial organizations in four counties in eastern Ohio and western Pennsylvania, serves more than 50 school systems in its area with teaching aids, films, recordings, speakers, supplementary readers, career literature, and an industrial exhibition. An educational advisory committee of 23 educators representing 70 school districts advises the Institute on teaching materials for the schools.

The Evansville Manufacturers and Employers Association, Evansville, Indiana, has carried on an educational relations program including essay contests, plant visits by students and teachers, and a textbook, *Career Opportunities in Evansville Industry,* for high school pupils.

DEVELOPING AN EDUCATIONAL RELATIONS PROGRAM

Organization for Educational Relations

The research, policy, planning, and production of media of communication for an educational relations program should be the responsibility of the public relations department. If the program is extensive, a special educational relations section should be established in the public relations department, staffed with experienced educators.

Execution of a corporation's educational relations program in plant communities belongs to the local plant management assisted by the public relations director who adapts the national program to local needs. The headquarters public relations staff aids the public relations managers of individual plants in carrying out the educational program in plant communities.

An effective educational relations program requires the participation of employees in their home communities who should be encouraged by management to join the local PTA, serve on the local school board, work for a school bond issue, and take part in school projects.

Educational relations sections of public relations departments have been established by the Ford Motor Company, General Motors Corporation, Sun Oil Company, Institute of Life Insurance, and other large corporations and associations. The School and College Services section of the public relations department of Sun Oil is responsible for counseling operating executives in school relationships, developing a better understanding of the company and the oil industry by educators and students, distributing educational material, and filling requests for motion pictures, plant tours, and speakers for the schools.

Research in Educational Relations

Research of the aims, methods, and needs of education for teaching aids and other assistance described in the preceding pages should be an initial consideration in the development of an educational relations program.

Teaching procedures should be investigated through a survey of curricula and instructional techniques to determine the objectives and type of materials to be included in an educational relations program. This research should be conducted by or with the counsel of educators who are experts in curricula and teaching methods and who can advise on the best techniques of conducting the survey. Educators familiar with courses of study and experienced in conducting research of teaching methods may be found in collegiate schools of education and teachers' colleges.

After an educational relations program has been under way, its effectiveness should be investigated periodically to determine if it is accepted by educators and attaining its objectives. Teachers involved in the program should be questioned to determine if the teaching aids meet their approval and whether they should be modified and improved. The methods of making such a survey are discussed in detail in Chapter 18, "Public Relations Research and Evaluation."

Educational Relations Policy

To define the objectives of an educational relations program and to serve as a guide to management, public relations staff, and operating executives in their relations with educators, a formal educational relations policy is desirable.

The following educational relations policy of a large industrial corporation reflects the growing interest of corporations in improving relations with educators:

We believe that good relations with the educational public, including elementary and secondary schools, junior colleges, and colleges, is important because our stability and growth are directly related to the welfare of our schools upon which we depend for the development of our future personnel, our technical progress, our community welfare, and our American way of life.

We believe that we have an obligation to American education to support its aims and contribute to its edvelopment by building better understanding between the schools and our business so that we may intelligently collaborate with the schools in their educational programs and attract and hold the good will of educators and students.

Therefore, it shall be our educational relations policy:

To establish friendly, personal relations with educators so that we can learn more about modern school methods and requirements and so that teachers can obtain more practical knowledge of business practices and policies to the end that boys and girls are better prepared for life and business upon graduation.

To give active assistance to teachers on educational projects and research; to provide educational materials of practical value to teachers; to furnish lecturers for schools; to aid in vocational counseling of students; to clarify our motives and objectives; and to describe our contributions to the social and economic life of the community.

Educational Relations Program

The following educational relations programs illustrate the various objectives and methods employed to gain the understanding of students and educators.

Economic Education of Secondary School Students. Washington Gas Light Company, Washington, D.C., conducts a program of economic education of high school students in its service area which includes the District of Columbia and five counties in Maryland and Virginia. Forty-one shares of stock of the company are awarded annually, one share to each of 41 outstanding high school juniors, by educators of eight school systems participating. The objective of the program is to teach teen-age boys and girls the principles of our American economy by involving them directly as owners in a business.

The Student Junior Stockholders are invited to participate in a "Junior Stockholder Meeting" at which the president of the company presents each student with a share of stock and reports on the history, current status, and future prospects of the company, just as reported at a regular stockholder meeting. Questions from the students are encouraged and answered honestly by management. A copy of the company's annual report is mailed to students before the meeting. After the meeting the Junior Stockholders are served lunch.

Before the program was announced to students, the management sought the acceptance of the educators concerned by inviting them to an informal luncheon at which the public relations director presented the plan and asked for their approval and recommendations. The teachers asked questions, made suggestions, and fully endorsed the plan.

Educational Program of National Association of Manufacturers. The National Association of Manufacturers, New York City, representing 20,000 large and small manufacturers, sponsors, through its educational department, an extensive program to make available to teachers information about industry; to bring about closer co-operation between industry and education, to assist schools in making available to youth a knowledge of the advantages of a free society, to encourage industrialists to support more adequate compensation for teachers, and better educational facilities and equipment.

The Association sponsors education-industry conferences, Business-Industry-Education Days, a teacher work experience program, a president's scholarship, student plant visits, an education and industry vocational guidance program, visual economic programs, and work-study for training young people for employment in plants, stores, and offices. The Association sponsors a college speaking program, employing leading industrialists to fill speaking engagements on college campuses and arranges for the appearance of industrialists before high school teachers and students.

Educational Program of the Board of Trade of the City of Chicago. The Board of Trade of the City of Chicago, the oldest and largest contract commodity exchange in the world, with 1,422 members who are buyers and sellers of grain and grain products, conducts an educational program to inform teachers and students about the functions of the commodity exchange and the part it plays in serving grain producers, processors, distributors, packers, and consumers.

The educational program of the Board ranges from explanations to elementary and secondary school children who visit the exchange to observe trading to information on complex projects for advanced college students and teachers about the operation of the exchange.

The principal educational project of the Board of Trade is an annual three-day symposium for teachers and administrators, held in Chicago, to which 60 educators from 35 schools of business, agriculture, and economics are invited at the Board's expense to tour the exchange, witness trading from the floor, and listen to lectures by specialists, followed by group discussions. The symposiums are planned by a college advisory committee, composed of six agricultural college professors, which selects the participants.

The Board of Trade publishes and distributes booklets describing the operations of the exchange to college students and professors of business, agriculture, and economics. A film, "After the Harvest," depicting the trading on the exchange, is distributed to schools and colleges.

Educational Program of Westinghouse Electric Corporation. The Westinghouse Science Honors Institute initiated at the Research Laboratories of the Westinghouse Electric Company, Pittsburgh, Pennsylvania, is a series of 12 Saturday morning lecture-demonstrations staged by Westinghouse scientists in company laboratories for outstanding high school seniors from the Pittsburgh area who are interested in science. One-hour lecture-demonstrations are followed by two and one-half hour discussions by small groups led by scientists. Discussions end in the company cafeteria with refreshments.

Science Honors Institute has been extended to other Westinghouse Laboratories of the Metallurgical Research and Development Plant at Blairsville, Pennsylvania, and the Transformer Division at Sharon, Pennsylvania. The science lectures have been published as a textbook and televised by the Westinghouse Broadcasting Company.

Educational Program Institute of Life Insurance. The Institute of Life Insurance, New York City, was established by 166 legal reserve life insurance companies in the United States and Canada to provide the public with a better understanding of life insurance and its contribution to the social and economic development of the nation.

The educational division of the Institute supplies secondary school teachers with teaching materials on life and family money management. Four study units, each comprising a text for pupils and a teacher's guide, have been prepared by the division, with the aid of an advisory committee of teachers, for use in secondary school courses in business education, home economics, social studies, and mathematics. A booklet has been prepared on the college level for classroom use in consumer economics, personal finance, and family economics courses. These booklets for secondary school and college use are supplemented with a series of film strips, showing how insurance works; wall charts; motion pictures; and a vocational guidance booklet for teachers, describing career opportunities in life insurance. Staff members of the educational division are in frequent contact with state and local school authorities, superintendents, and teachers.

The Institute works closely with the National Committee for Education in Family Finance in the establishment and operation of Family Finance Workshops for teachers, held at leading universities to discuss family financial problems, including life insurance. The Institute cooperates with the universities in arranging these summer workshops and granting scholarship funds to the hundreds of teachers who have attended. In addition to the summer workshops, the Institute co-operates with several city school systems offering in-service training programs for teachers of education in family finance.

BUSINESS SPONSORED AIDS TO EDUCATION

Industry sponsored aids to school administrators, teachers, and pupils include: films and slides; publications, including texts, booklets, and folders; teachers' kits, guides, and manuals; globes, charts, maps, and posters; exhibits, including models and samples; trips and plant tours; school and college speaking programs; vocational guidance; Industry-Education Day; association-education co-operation; employment of teachers; and participation in educational activities.

Films and Slides

Visual education through the medium of motion pictures and slide films has become an accepted technique of instruction in elementary and secondary school systems and in colleges. Visual education departments have been established in city public and parochial school systems to operate film libraries which stock films that are co-ordinated with the school curriculum. Industrial films sponsored by large corporations are exhibited to students in courses in engineering, mechanics, chemistry, physics, history, social sciences, economics, manufacturing, marketing, geography, agriculture, transportation, music, and other subjects in secondary schools and colleges.

Publications

Teachers in elementary and secondary schools and in colleges assign supplementary reading in addition to the textbook used in their courses. This supplementary reading consists of booklets, texts, and reports sponsored by industrial and nonprofit organizations prepared by or with the advice of educators. These publications are produced on a wide variety of subjects including family finances, home economics, transportation, food, fuel, housing, textiles, business, finance, and many others. From six to ten million booklets are distributed annually to schools by the public relations department of the Association of American Railroads.

Teachers' Kits, Guides, and Manuals

Many educational relations programs include a teacher's kit which gives teachers suggestions for using teaching materials provided by the sponsoring organization. A teacher's kit usually contains a bibliography, test questions, course outlines, and work procedures for primary, intermediate, or secondary school levels.

Charts, Maps, and Posters

Maps, posters, and charts for use in elementary and secondary schools, and in colleges are included in many educational relations programs of industrial and nonprofit organizations.

Demonstrating Devices, Exhibits, Models, and Samples

Miniature models of equipment; exhibits of industrial processes, mining, and farming operations; samples of raw materials or finished products; demonstrating devices to show scientific principles; displays illustrating the steps in an industrial process; and product samples are all produced by industrial organizations for use by teachers in laboratories and classrooms.

Plant Tours

Plant tours are a feature of many secondary school and college courses in business administration, manufacturing, economics, and social sciences. Visits to industrial plants provide students and teachers with an opportunity to observe at firsthand how industry functions and hear about business.

School and College Speaking Programs

Corporations and nonprofit associations have established speakers' bureaus with volunteer speakers addressing classes in secondary schools and colleges. Business executives lecture in high school and college courses in business administration, economics, social studies, marketing, finance, chemistry, physics, electricity, civil and mechanical engineering.

Vocational Guidance

Vocational guidance to students is an important feature of the educational program of secondary schools and colleges. Educators are inviting businessmen to visit schools to give students vocational guidance. In addition, students visit industry to observe and hear about vocational opportunities.

Secondary schools sponsor Career Days and invite business executives representing different occupations to speak to students about their careers; to give them information about specific occupations; to help them determine occupations which offer good opportunities; and aid them to obtain a practical viewpoint on employment conditions. The training requirements of specific occupations are described and how to plan for entrance into business upon graduation.

Career Clinics, a follow-up of Career Days, are held at industrial plants for selected groups of high school and college students who are interested in a specific occupation. Students visit places of business to discuss with business executives an occupation in the actual work environment.

Television and radio vocational guidance programs are presented by high schools and colleges in co-operation with broadcasting stations and businessmen. A moderator, usually a vocational guidance counselor, several businessmen, and students participate in the program.

Part-time work experience is given students by corporations during vacation, after school, and on Saturdays. This work experience enables students to choose a future vocation and puts the business in touch with prospective full-time employees.

Industry-Education Conferences

Industrial firms organize and conduct conferences for educators and businessmen to discuss mutual interests, the relationship of education and industry, and to make plans for co-operative action in plant communities.

Business-Industry-Education Day

Business-Industry-Education Day is a co-operative project of businessmen and the school authorities in plant communities to make it possible for teachers to observe and hear about the operation of local industries.

In reverse, Education-Industry-Business Day is arranged for businessmen to visit local schools and see and hear about their operations.

Association-Educational Co-operation

Some business and professional associations invite students and teachers to attend national and regional association meetings to hear speakers and to participate in the program.

Employment of Teachers

Business organizations employ secondary school and college teachers during the summer recess period to familiarize them with industrial organization and operations.

Participation in Educational Activities

Participation by businessmen in community education through membership on local school boards, college boards, and alumni councils is encouraged by employers to promote better education-industry understanding.

Financial Support by Industry to Higher Education

Financial support by corporations to universities and colleges is an important feature of the educational relations programs of many business organizations. Business management recognizes that it is dependent upon institutions of higher learning for trained personnel and has an obligation to support higher education.

Financial support to higher education by corporations includes: funds for research, capital funds for buildings, scholarships and fellowships, underwriting of specific instruction programs, funds for new equipment, and capital funds for endowments.

COMMUNICATING WITH EDUCATORS

Methods of communicating with educators are oral, printed, or a combination of these two media. Communication should be two-way to permit a free exchange of information and ideas between businessmen and educators.

Oral communication by industrial and nonprofit organizations with school administrators and teachers is carried on through industry-education conferences, business-industry-education days, representation at teachers' conventions, plant tours for teachers and students, participation by businessmen in Parent-Teacher Association work, membership on school boards, and personal visits with educators.

Printed methods of communicating with educators include advertising in periodicals published for teachers and students, a periodical published for teachers or students, direct-mail advertising to teachers, a listing in guides of free teaching materials, and publicity in periodicals read by teachers.

Advertising in Periodicals Published for Teachers and Students

Advertising in teachers' and youths' magazines is widely used by business to communicate with educators and students. Advertising in four types of educational periodicals is used to communicate with educators and students:

Weekly periodicals used by junior and senior high school teachers for supplementary study and class discussion in courses in current history, social studies, civics, literature, and vocational guidance.

Youth magazines such as *Boy's Life, Young America, Open Road for Boys* and *The Camp Fire Girl.*

School periodicals edited and published by the students in colleges and a few larger secondary schools in connection with courses in journalism, engineering, and English.

Professional educational periodicals edited for elementary and secondary school teachers and school administrators, such as *Scholastic Magazine, Grade Teacher, National Educational Association Journal.* Advertising in these periodicals informs teachers of the educational programs and teaching aids of business organizations.

A Corporate Periodical for Teachers and Students

A monthly or quarterly magazine for teachers is an effective medium published by a corporation to promote requests from teachers for teaching aids and to describe various features of an educational program. A periodical for students is published by some corporations as a feature of their educational program. The *Junior Fire Marshal* is published by the Hartford Fire Insurance Company for elementary school pupils to promote fire prevention.

Direct-Mail Advertising to Teachers

Direct-mail advertising is used to secure distribution of educational materials to teachers. Samples of teaching aids are mailed to teachers, with an offer to supply additional quantities upon request. Teaching materials should be supplied to teachers only upon request to avoid criticism of propagandizing the schools and to prevent wasteful distribution.

Guides to Business-Sponsored Teaching Materials

Teachers' guides listing sources of business-sponsored teaching materials are published by federal, state, and local school departments, teachers' associations, and universities. Corporations list their teaching aids in these guides to secure distribution to educators.

Publicity in Educational Periodicals

Publicity, in professional educational periodicals, about free business sponsored aids for teachers, is a valuable medium of communication with school administrators and teachers. Articles in teachers' magazines, prepared by educators, describe a corporation's teaching aids and publications, and how they have been used effectively in the schools. These articles increase the demand for educational materials.

Case 12-1

EDUCATIONAL RELATIONS

E. I. du Pont de Nemours & Company Educators' Conferences

E. I. du Pont de Nemours & Co., Wilmington, Delaware, manufactures and distributes an annual volume of more than $2 billion worth of electro-, industrial, bio-, organic, and elastomer chemicals, coated fabrics, finishes, textile fibers, films, explosives, pigments, plastics, and other chemical products in some 79 plants located in 27 states.

Public relations at Du Pont is organized in three major divisions: information, extension, and publications. Each of these divisions is headed by a manager who reports to the assistant public relations director who in turn is responsible to the director of public relations. Two executive assistants to the director handle special public relations projects.

One phase of Du Pont's public relations' program is directed toward the educational world. A major project is an annual educators' conference which was initiated in 1950 and has been continued each year. The conference is the outgrowth of Du Pont's concern over what it considers a major national problem— the lack of understanding between the intellectual and business communities. It was apparent to thoughtful company executives in the late 1940's that a wide gulf separated the thinking and attitudes of the academician and the businessman. It was equally obvious that the divisive influence was lack of knowledge rather than a reasoned reaction to fact.

Serious enough in itself, the divergence was considered a particularly alarming portent for the future. Du Pont's public relations officials were convinced from study and experience that in the long run the thinking of the intellectuals in any society eventually molds public thought and attitudes. All of the great revolutionary movements of history were, they found, based on ideologies that had been ripened long before by the thinkers of the time. Du Pont found it logical to conclude that contemporary opinions held by the nation's intellectuals could eventually become a fixed and governing set of public ideas.

If, they reasoned, the intellectuals of today believe that business is antisocial, that it is a selfish, predatory, inhuman machine that grinds down its employees and wrests exorbitant profits from the helpless millions that are its captive customers, the atmosphere in which business will have to operate a few decades hence will stifle the nation's economic and social strength. Yet these views were held, they believed, by a substantial number, if not a majority, of the nation's most influential educators.

Simultaneously, they found that many businessmen felt that college faculties consisted largely of flaming radicals. This, too, was viewed as a distressing omen, especially since, in the normal order of things, business and industry are the source of the wealth that supports institutions of learning.

Although Du Pont realized that the problem it had analyzed was far beyond its capacity, the company decided that prompt efforts toward solving it could produce some useful, if limited, results and might induce others to join the effort. A further motivation was a firm belief that the proper function of a public relations department lies not merely in responding to emergencies but also, and most important, in dealing with the major and long-range developments that inevitably have a profound effect on the course of events. The Educators' Conference grew out of these deliberations.

The conference covers nine working days plus a week end. There are six days of panel discussions in which about 40 college and university educators meet with the top management of the company at Wilmington headquarters for questioning, discussion, and debates. Three days are devoted to plant and laboratory visits, and, on the week end, trips are made to nearby places of interest. A get-acquainted session, chairman's dinner, president's dinner, cocktail party, and buffet luncheon provide social contacts between the educators and company executives.

Since the conferences were initiated, a total of 550 educators from 139 colleges and universities have attended, including 225 administrators, deans, or department heads; 162 professors; 147 associate or assistant professors; and 16 lecturers and instructors.

Forty-five educators representing 44 institutions attended the thirteenth conference held at company headquarters in June, 1962. Invitation letters, signed by the public relations director, were sent to the presidents of 48 colleges and universities in the United States asking them to select a representative from their faculty or administration capable of benefiting from as well as contributing to the conference. Educators from departments of economics, sociology, commerce and finance, business, political science, history, and government represented the following universities: Alaska, Bucknell, California, Colorado, Columbia, Cornell, Delaware, DePaul, Detroit, Duke, Florida, Fordham, George Washington, Harvard, Illinois, Lehigh, Miami, Minneosota, Missouri, New Mexico, Notre Dame, Ohio State, Oregon, Pennsylvania, Purdue, Rutgers, Texas, Vanderbilt, Virginia, Washington, Wesleyan, West Virginia, Wisconsin, and Yale; and these colleges and technical institutes: Athens, California Institute of Technology, Dartmouth, Gettysburg, Grinnell, Massachusetts Institute of Technology, Oberlin, Texas A & M, Whitman, and Williams.

Du Pont management is represented in the conference discussions by the following executives: the chairman of the board of directors; the president; the vice-presidents; general managers of the twelve industrial departments; directors of the legal, employee relations, central research, advertising, and public relations departments; plant managers of two Du Pont plants; and the treasurer of the company. Public relations department executives and staff members participated actively in the conference as discussion leaders, discussants, and tour chairmen as well as in planning, co-ordinating, and execution of the program.

Subjects discussed at the 1962 conference included the development and structure of Du Pont, its place in U.S. industry and methods of operation; management of a modern corporation with emphasis on the principles that guide and motivate Du Pont; employee relations, the company's philosophy and approach to employees with reference to wage roll, bargaining practices, and union relationships; research activities; community relations, and the impact of a major industrial unit on a typical American community; finance, involving the company's policies and practices in the field of financial controls and procedures; personnel, the Du Pont philosophy and personnel policies; production organization and development of technology, tools, and operating personnel; problems of bigness relating to the scale of a modern industrial enterprise; sales, including policies in distributing Du Pont products; and overseas operations. A special session, in which educators took the leading role, was devoted to economic problems of the '60's.

The sessions of the conference consist of a half-hour talk by a discussion leader, a Du Pont executive, followed by a panel discussion of three to five members of management, with a concluding question-and-answer period of about an hour and a half. Morning sessions begin at 10:00 A.M. and adjourn at noon. Afternoon sessions are from 2:00 P.M. to 4:00 P.M. Some sessions are held at company headquarters in Wilmington, Delaware; others at Du Pont laboratories; and one at the Martinsville, Virginia, nylon plant to discuss community relations; and one at Du Pont's largest plant, the Chambers Works, Deepwater Point, New Jersey, to observe employee relations firsthand.

The company defrays all travel and hotel expenses but pays no stipend for the reason that it seeks to avoid the implication that the educators, through receiving financial compensation, are beholden to Du Pont. The average cost for each conference guest is $500 or a total of about $22,500 for the 45 guests at the 1962 conference.

The social activity for the conferences is carefully planned. A get-acquainted session is held on opening night at the Du Pont Country Club to enable the educators to get to know one another and a few public relations staff members are the only company people present. The chairman of the board gives a dinner at his home for the educators and all top executives of the company. The president entertains in a similar fashion during the second week of the conference, and a buffet luncheon is given at the home of the director of public relations. A farewell cocktail party and reception at a local hotel closes the conference. These social occasions provide an excellent opportunity for the eudcators and company executives to exchange views and get to know each other, and they constitute an important feature of the conference.

The week end of the conference is planned to give the educators relaxation through visits to Winterthur, the Henry Francis du Pont museum of American antiques, near Wilmington; the Longwood Gardens created by the late Pierre S. du Pont at Kennett Square, Pennsylvania; and the Hagley industrial museum in the Brandywine River Valley on the outskirts of Wilmington which includes the ruins of the old powder mills that were for a century Du Pont's principal source of revenue.

The educators' conferences are planned to conform to certain basic principles. The number of educators included should number no fewer than 40 and not more than 45, representing schools of various sizes from all sections of the country. The size of the group is small enough not to inhibit free discussion and large enough to make it worthwhile for members of top management to give a good deal of their time to the project.

Invitations to the conference are not extended directly to college professors and administrators, but the presidents of the institutions are asked to select the participants because they are in a better position than Du Pont to determine who should be included.

Guest educators are brought in close contact not with a few but with all the top-management group of Du Pont who are available, including all members of the executive committee and 25 department heads. This principle is observed to give educators contact with the whole top-management group of the company.

Questions asked by educators are answered as fully and clearly as possible except in cases where answers would reveal competitive product or process secrets. No questions are barred in order to convince the educators that the conference is not intended to present only favorable features of the company's operations.

No attempt is made to "sell" Du Pont but rather to expose the teachers to the facts and permit them to probe where they wish and let them draw their own conclusions. Some of the guests arrive suspicious of company motives and practices, and these doubts can only be dissolved by clear and candid explanation by company executives.

No continuing effort is made by the company to measure how effective the conferences have been in creating an understanding of Du Pont in the minds of the educators. The management believes that this would give the project the color of a propaganda stunt which it is not. The educators are asked for their suggestions as to how the conferences can be improved from their point of view.

The objective of the conference is to give educators an opportunity to know Du Pont management, freedom to probe into the company, to determine what it does, how it does it, why it does it, and who gets what from the company. Conversely the top-management group comes to know educators through associating with them, arguing with them, exploring points of view with them, and reaches a better understanding of them.

In addition to the conference discussions, educators are informed about the company through the following printed material which is distributed during the conference: the company's annual report, the employee magazine, *Better Living,* the *Du Pont Magazine,* and *This Is Du Pont,* a series of booklets describing company operations and dealing with subjects of general business interest.

The effectiveness of the educators conferences is not easy to measure. However, several factors indicate that the seminars are achieving the objective of creating a better understanding between educators and the company. Company management and professors attending the conferences have established continuous contacts and even lasting friendships in spite of the fact that no conscious effort is made by the company to follow-up and maintain close relationships with those attending the conferences.

There is a perceptible difference in attitude on the part of the educators at the beginning and at the conclusion of a conference. Some educators before attending a conference have a knowledge of business almost wholly theoretical; others have surprising misinformation or lack of information as to how a company operates. Some of the participants have expressed their opinion that it has been helpful and enlightening to them to have this opportunity to observe an industrial corporation at work.

The executive committee of Du Pont asked the Opinion Research Corporation to interview some of the visiting educators a few years ago regarding their opinions of the value of the educators conferences and the response was highly complimentary.

The heads of colleges and universities invited to send representatives to the conferences have continued to send deans, department heads, and professors whom they rate as either their best or potentially best men. The company assumes that this would not be so if the conference did not have the reputation in academic circles as a rewarding experience.

Du Pont management believes that it is desirable to have to explain to highly intelligent people what management does and why it does it. The conferences clarify management thinking and expose company views to the critical scrutiny of outsiders.

The conferences have served to establish clearer communication between management and educators when the same words may have different meanings for each. Removal of semantic misunderstanding contributes to a greater comprehension by both Du Pont executives and educators.

QUESTIONS

1. Should the Du Pont educators conferences be continued? Give specific reasons for continuing or abandoning this type of educational relations activity.
2. What changes can you suggest to make the Du Pont educators conferences more effective?
3. What additional activities should be included in the educational relations program of the Du Pont company, which also provides substantial financial assistance to colleges and universities, arranges for speakers to colleges, and maintains close contact with many educators to build good relations with the educational community.
4. From the standpoint of the educators attending Du Pont conferences, what are the advantages to be derived from such seminars?

Case 12–2

EDUCATIONAL RELATIONS

General Motors Corporation

General Motors Corporation, Detroit, Michigan, is an operating company composed of 42 operating divisions and subsidiaries in the United States and Canada. Products manufactured include Chevrolet, Pontiac, Oldsmobile, Buick, and Cadillac automobiles, trucks, buses, Diesel locomotives and engines, heavy-duty-off-the-highway earth-moving equipment, Frigidaire household appliances, automobile parts and accessories. World-wide employment averaged 595,000 in 1960, and the corporation is owned by 830,000 stockholders.

In keeping with GM's policy of decentralization, much of the corporation's public relations activity is handled by the operating divisions. Most divisions have a director of public relations who reports directly to the general manager of the division. Public relations at the corporate level is the responsibility of the Public Relations Staff headed by a vice-president. While this Staff handles all matters of public relations which are of an institutional nature, it also works closely with the public relations directors in the various GM divisions to insure good planning and co-ordination of effort.

The Public Relations Staff is organized in two main groups, Field Operations and Communications. Communication consists of news relations, institutional advertising, editorial planning, and shareholder relations. Field operations comprises plant-city and regional activities, field relations activities, divisional relations and educational relations.

Educational Relations Section

The Educational Relations Section is responsible for informing educators and students about General Motors products and operating practices; providing information about career opportunities in the automobile industry; furnishing teachers with educational aids; promoting safe driving habits among the nation's youth; gathering information about current trends in education; and disseminating noteworthy information on education to executives throughout the GM organization. The program serves teachers and students in public, parochial, and private elementary and secondary schools, as well as public and private colleges and universities throughout the United States, Canada, and many foreign countries. An estimated two million students, and more than 20,000 educators benefit from the Educational Relations Section's programs annually.

Teaching and learning aids are generally furnished free in single copies, or at cost in large quantities to educators for instructional or reference use. Most of these materials are aimed at science, engineering, career guidance, social studies, economics, and driver education. They include booklets, charts, films, manuals, displays, and products or product components. While many of these materials are developed by the Educational Relations Section, others are developed by other sections of the Public Relations Staff, or by the various manufacturing divisions of General Motors.

The "General Motors Aids to Educators" catalogue, produced by the Educational Relations Section, lists over 400 booklets, charts, films, manuals, and other materials available from General Motors or its divisions. Typical titles are: "Transportation Progress," "American Battle for Abundance," and "The Automobile Story" for social study courses; "Short Stories of Science and Invention" and "Science at Work" for science instruction; "Troubleshooting Transistor Circuits" and "Ball-Bearing Screw and Spline Operation" for engineering education; "Doorways to Science and Engineering Careers" and "Can I Be A Craftsman?" for vocational guidance; and "We Drivers" for driver training in high schools.

Several series of wall charts are available to teachers for classroom instruction. One series of twenty 22 × 34 inch charts includes "Diesel Cycle Diagram" and others for study of power; "Body Construction," "Brake System," "Chassis" for automotive courses; "Automobile Progress" and "From Iron Ore to the Finished Automobile" for social studies and economics courses.

Demonstration kits and displays for use by teachers include a model aircraft engine kit, Chevrolet driver education kit, radio demonstration board, transistor demonstration, ignition coil and condenser demonstration kit, autronic-eye lab board and others.

For high school teachers of drafting, a basic drafting kit containing 14 selected mechanical drawings, illustrating current automotive drafting practice is available. Because General Motors has pioneered in drafting techniques and employs many apprentice draftsmen, this kit is especially useful to drafting teachers in high schools in GM plant cities.

To stimulate student interest in drafting and design in the engineering colleges, General Motors distributes to drawing and design professors, an engineering design problems kit containing four problems which illustrate the use of graphical techniques in the solution of engineering problems.

A series of resource leaflets entitled "Science at Work" has been prepared for high school teachers of physics and chemistry to aid them in teaching the fundamentals of such things as the pendulum, static electricity, electroplating, radiation, light waves, centrifugal force, sound waves, radioisotopes, elasticity, hydraulics, air pressure, and polarized light.

GM products and product components are supplied to high schools and colleges at special educational prices. This equipment includes engines, transmissions, rear-axle assemblies, and other automobile components, as well as heat exchangers, air-conditioning units, and household appliances.

To aid in driver training in high schools, General Motors and its dealers lend new cars to schools for instructional purposes. In 1960 the corporation contributed $480,000 toward the cost of lending 3,800 new cars to some 2,000 high schools.

Fifty sound motion picture films are loaned to teachers to supplement classroom instruction by General Motors film libraries in Detroit, New York, and San Francisco. These 16mm films listed in the corporation's 55-page film catalogue are on the subjects of driver education, operation of engines, industrial processes, economic progress, human relations, sports, and general subjects.

Typical film titles for safety and driver education are: "Passing Fancy," "We Drivers," "Safe as You Think," and others which were viewed by 3,250,000 in 1960. For instruction in engine operation, the films "ABC of Internal Combustion," "ABC of the Automobile Engine," and "ABC of Jet Propulsion" are available. Industrial processes are pictured in "Sand and Flame" about glassmaking, "A Thing of Beauty" about industrial designing, and others. Films for economic education are "American Harvest," "Our American Crossroads," and others. Human relations titles include: "Experiment" and "Doctor in Industry." Some films include "Fishin' for Fun" and "Derby Fever." Some general subjects are "ABC's of Hand Tools," "Farmer of Tomorrow," and "A Kitchen Is a Feminine Thing." Special purpose films are: "Selling America Today" on salesmanship, "Oil Films in Action" on the hydrodynamic theory of lubrication, and others.

Previews of Progress

A live, dramatic, noncommercial science stage show for junior and senior high school assembly programs, called "Previews of Progress" is designed to help motivate capable students into scientific and engineering careers by dramatizing opportunities in these fields.

This show is operated by the Field Operations Group of the General Motors Public Relations Staff. It went on the road in 1937 and, except for the war years, from one to twelve, two-man units have been staging the show in high schools throughout the country. "Previews of Progress" consists of eight major sequences which reveal interesting aspects of synthetic rubber, tailor-made molecules, microwaves, power from the sun, fuel cells, gyroscopes, and jet propulsion. Each unit is scheduled for ten shows weekly during the school year. Currently seven units are operating in the United States and 14 units overseas. During the past 14 years more than 26 million children and adults have seen this 45-minute science demonstration show.

FIG. 12–1. To interest high school students in scientific and engineering careers, "Previews of Progress," a traveling science show, operated by the Field Operations Group of General Motors Corp. public relations staff, has been shown to more than 26 million children and adults in the past 14 years.

Career Guidance Materials

General Motors, which employs over a half-million people, provides high school and college teachers and students with information about career opportunities in science, engineering, business administration, the skilled trades, technicians, office, and clerical work. A series of five guidance booklets has been prepared for various educational levels. "Can I Be a Scientist or Engineer?" is for ninth and tenth grade students. "Can I Be a Craftsman?" is for beginning high school students not planning to go to college. "Can I Be an Office Worker?" discusses opportunities for boy and girl high school and business college graduates in stenography, bookkeeping, and clerical work. "Can I Be a Technician?" describes the work of specialists who play a supporting role to the scientist and engineer. "Can I Get the Job?" gives high school seniors suggestions for getting a job upon graduation. A 36-page booklet for high school seniors, "Career Opportunities in the Retail Automobile Business," describes qualifications for positions as well as opportunities in automobile retailing.

FIG. 12–2. To satisfy the increasing demand of high school and college vocational guidance directors and students for information about careers, the public relations staff of General Motors Corp. produces and distributes the above booklets as one feature of its educational relations program.

Speakers to Student Groups

General Motors Public Relations Staff maintains a Speakers' Bureau in Detroit from which hundreds of requests from educators for speakers to high school and college groups are referred to corporation executives in all parts of the country who have volunteered to speak to students. For example, more than 100 school groups, each averaging 100 students have heard General Motors executives speak on "Traffic Safety." The Educational Relations Section of the Public Relations Staff prepared this talk and supplied speakers with a 38-page booklet giving answers to questions asked by students.

Financial Aid to Students and Colleges

The General Motors Scholarship Program provides financial aid to students of high ability to enable them to secure a college education. Financial grants are also made to colleges and universities to improve the quality of education. More than 400 scholarships are awarded annually to men and women seeking baccalaureate degrees. The corporation currently provides scholarship money to 1,648 students in 216 colleges and universities. In addition, General Motors makes annual gifts to educational foundations and associations of colleges. Coupled with the scholarship program, General Motors total direct financial support of higher education costs in the neighborhood of $5 million annually.

General Motors Engineering Journal

To inform educators in the fields of engineering and the allied sciences about General Motors research and engineering developments in products and manufacturing, the Educational Relations Section publishes quarterly the *General Motors Engineering Journal*. In its eleventh year (first published July, 1953) this 60-page technical periodical is read by some 7,000 scientists and engineers on the faculties of more than 800 colleges and universities throughout the world. In addition, some 18,000 General Motors technical and management people receive the *Journal*.

The *Journal* publishes papers prepared by scientists and engineers associated with General Motors Research Laboratories and manufacturing divisions. The papers are intended to show examples of how the fundamentals taught in the classroom are applied in practice. Educators praise the technical quality and appropriateness of the *Journal* as a classroom aid at the college level.

QUESTIONS

1. What advantages does General Motors derive, from a public relations standpoint, from the educational relations program described in the preceding case?
2. What improvements can you suggest to make the General Motors educational relations program more effective? Be specific.
3. Which features of the General Motors educational relations program contributes most to the public relations of the corporation? Give your reasons.

Case 12–3

EDUCATIONAL RELATIONS

Michigan Consolidated Gas Company

The Michigan Consolidated Gas Company, Detroit, Michigan, provides some 210 billion cubic feet of natural gas annually to 870,000 customers including 3,000 industrial users in the City of Detroit and more than 130 other communities in Michigan. The company was established in 1851 and employs 4,750 men and women.

The public relations department of the company conducts an educational relations program to communicate with more than 200,000 students in some 200 public and parochial junior and senior high schools in addition to 100,000 students in colleges and universities within its service area.

The objectives of this educational relations program are to communicate with students who are the gas industry's future customers, stockholders, and employees as well as tomorrow's business, civic, and political leaders; to secure their understanding of the free enterprise system, arouse their interest in science, correct misconceptions of the gas business, and develop favorable opinion of investor-owned gas utilities and their product.

The educational program of the company includes plant tours for teachers followed by dinner and a program including one of the 26 motion picture films from the company's film library. In addition, groups of high school students are given conducted tours of the company's operations, specialized according to the student's particular interests in the gas business. A booklet titled, "Bringing Gas to the City," prepared by the departments of language, education, social studies, guidance, and placement of the Detroit public schools with the assistance of the company and the Institute for Economic Education, is distributed to students in the schools and on tours of operations.

The home service department of the company, staffed with trained home economists, is in constant contact with schools to demonstrate the use of gas to home economics classes. Cooking classes are invited to the model kitchen, maintained by the home service department, to see demonstrations of gas cooking and the use of gas appliances.

The principal feature of the company's educational relations program is the "Gasarama," a show designed to develop student interest in science and to correct misconceptions that gas is dangerous, dirty, and in short supply.

"Gasarama" is a fast-moving, live, theatrical presentation featuring noise, mystery, and suspense which is staged in high school auditoriums. It was created by the public relations department with the assistance of the company's engineering department. A staff engineer from the laboratory and testing division was assigned to devise a series of dramatic demonstrations of the chemistry of gas.

Two basic scripts were written by the public relations department, one for high school and college students and a second for junior high school students. Slight variations were added for adult audiences.

The cast was recruited from company employees rather than professional entertainers to make the performance more believable, less expensive, and to provide personal contacts between company representatives, students, and educators. The narrator is a staff engineer who developed the demonstrations. He is assisted by an engineer who sets up and maintains the equipment, a young lady from the customer interview department who models clothes and displays articles from by-products made from natural gas. Two deliverymen and a special truck are employed for transporting the equipment. The cast was trained by a speech and dramatic teacher.

"Gasarama" opens on a darkened stage with the letters, *GASARAMA* illuminated in black light appearing on removable covers concealing equipment for a series of experiments atop a 25-foot table. Suspended above the table are maps of Michigan and the United States showing the routes of the company's and its suppliers' pipeline systems, a model of a gas holder that hides a tank of compressed gas, and a large cutout of a gas compressor engine.

The narrator introduces "Gasarama" by explaining that there have been many scientific advancements in the gas industry, that science can be fun, and "Gasarama" is presented to prove it. Following a brief description of the history of manufactured and natural gas, the narrator demonstrates how gas is discovered underground by seismograph. He fires a blank cartridge and uses a converted pinball machine to show how sound waves move through the earth's strata and reveal gas-filled dome formations.

FIG. 12–3. To stimulate the interest of high school students in science, Michigan Consolidated Gas Co., Detroit, has shown "Gasarama," a dramatic demonstration of the chemistry of gas, to nearly 200,000 students in its educational relations program.

Transportation of natural gas to Michigan is illustrated with the aid of the map of the United States which shows the location of pipeline systems. A one horsepower, natural gas-fired engine is operated and related to the cutout of a 2,000-horsepower compressor engine which is suspended above the demonstration table to show how gas is forced through pipelines to Michigan from the Southern gas fields.

Underground storage of gas by the company in Michigan is shown on the state map of the company's state-wide ground storage system and cutaway drawing of its underground storage fields. To show how gas passes through the porous sandstone of the storage fields, a piece of sandstone is affixed to the end of a pipe and gas pumped through the sandstone and ignited.

The chemistry of natural gas is explained by a series of experiments conducted by the narrator. The detection of gas odor is shown by an "odor camera." The mixture of gas with oxygen for combustion is demonstrated with a welding torch which is held in a glass tank filled with water and the gas-air mixture continues to burn. To show that gas is lighter than air, a balloon is filled with gas and as it rises to the ceiling of the auditorium the narrator explains that this characteristic of gas is a safety factor. To prove that gas is not toxic, a guinea pig plays in a glass tank in which a mixture of 20 per cent gas and 80 per cent air is flowing with a flame burning at the top to show the presence of gas. To demonstrate that gas must be mixed with air for combustion, a long glass tube is affixed to a gas burner and a sparking device within the tube ignites the gas-air mixture. When the ignition button is pressed there is a slight "Whoom" and the flame travels up the tube.

The part scientific research plays in the gas industry is portrayed with a "style show" in which a young lady models a rayon acetate dress, Dacron gloves, plastic jewelry, nylon stockings, simulated leather shoes and handbag, all made from natural gas.

The cleanliness and control of natural gas is shown by placing popcorn in a shining aluminum pan on a portable thermostatic burner. When the corn is popped to perfection, the bottom of the pan is displayed to prove that gas leaves no residue.

The operation of a gas refrigerator is shown by using a working model to demonstrate how cold can be created from heat produced by gas.

To show how a thermostat turns a gas furnace off and on, a bimetallic strip is held to a gas flame which warps the metal because of the difference in the expansion properties of the two metals.

The accuracy of a gas meter is demonstrated by attaching it to a clock. Gas flowing through the clock and ignited at a burner at the top keeps it operating in perfect time.

The final demonstration of "Gasarama" shows how compression moves gas through pipelines. A small cylinder of compressed gas is placed in a model of a rocket, hidden from view at the back of the stage. Following a count-down, the cylinder is punctured as a blank cartridge is fired and the rocket shoots across the stage on a wire trailing a banner which reads, "The End."

Before "Gasarama" was offered to all schools in the Detroit area, three trial showings were staged before educators and two high school assemblies. From audience reaction at these showings, several demonstrations were eliminated and replaced with others; more humor and less technical language was used; and to increase suspense the stage was darkened and a spotlight was used to focus attention on a single demonstration at a time.

"Gasarama" in the two years following its introduction was shown in 152 high schools and colleges, with an attendance of more than 176,000 students, in the territory served by the Michigan Consolidated Gas Company.

Following each showing, a letter of appreciation from the public relations director of the company is addressed to each school principal with a booklet entitled, "Experiments with Gas," and a suggestion that science teachers include gas experiments in their science courses.

Considerable press publicity has accompanied "Gasarama." Staff reporters and photographers of leading newspapers and television stations have covered many of the presentations. Advance news releases and matted pictures of the cast are distributed to each neighborhood weekly, prior to a showing at a school in the area. The editor is invited to attend the performance. Follow-up releases are sent to local weekly newspapers and the school publication. Special Sunday newspaper magazine feature articles about "Gasarama" have appeared in the metropolitan newspapers in Michigan in addition to radio and television coverage.

Letters and comments of teachers, school officials, and students about "Gasarama" indicate that the show has improved relations with educators and students; built company prestige; increased student interest in science; established personal contacts between teachers, students, and company personnel; corrected misconceptions about gas; and secured good publicity.

Statements of educators, in whose schools "Gasarama" has been presented, express their opinions of the show as follows: "The science implications from this program are challenging and the information presented is enlightening. A vital educational contribution is made through undertakings of this type." "The finest educational presentation of this type I have ever seen." "The show was entertaining enough to hold the interest of students and yet it included a great deal about the various sciences that relate to the production and distribution of gas."

The American Gas Association selected "Gasarama" as the gas industry's best public relations program of 1959.

QUESTIONS

1. What makes "Gasarama" an effective medium of educational relations for the Michigan Consolidated Gas Company? Give specific reasons why this educational program has been successful.

2. If you believe that "Gasarama" should be improved or perhaps eliminated in favor of another educational relations activity, describe in detail what should be done and why.

3. Should the company's entire educational relations program which includes conducted plant tours for students and teachers, motion pictures, educational literature, and demonstrations by home economists be expanded or curtailed? Describe what changes, if any, should be made in the present program.

4. Apart from this educational relations program, what community relations activities should be carried on by the company to increase its prestige and win the good will and understanding of the public in the area served by the company.

13 · GOVERNMENT RELATIONS

ONE OF THE MOST significant developments in American life is the increasing interest of citizens and corporations in government and politics. This growing awareness of the role of government in our national life may be attributed to the spreading influence of government in our affairs as well as an awakening public consciousness of the individual and corporation's responsibility for good government.

Since the turn of the century there has been an increasing amount of government control of business in the United States. A succession of federal laws beginning with the passage of the Interstate Commerce Act, in 1887, has given the national government control over wages, monopoly, restraint of trade, competition, prices, food and drugs, transportation, communication, and many other aspects of business.

While the federal government has been placing more restraints on business, state legislatures and municipal governments have likewise been curbing industry's and commerce's freedom of action with restrictive legislation.

In addition to exercising greater control over business, government is increasing the cost of doing business, with many forms of corporation and sales taxes levied by city, state, and federal governments. Regulations imposed on business by various government boards and commissions further increase operating costs and reduce profits.

The critical attitude of some government officials toward business has resulted in unfavorable publicity, investigations and antibusiness legislation. Industry has been subjected to increasing attacks by government officials. Congressional investigations have placed corporations, industries, and businessmen in a bad light. Censure of business by the White House has widened the gap of understanding between business and the nation's Chief Executive. Accusations of monopoly have given the public the impression that big corporations are evil. Inquisitions into earnings have aroused suspicion that corporations are making excessive profits.

Opponents of business, particularly labor unions, are politically active with well-organized programs to gain the support of legislators in Congress and the state legislatures and intensive political education of members to win votes for candidates pledged to support organized labor.

The growing unfavorable political climate in which business is operating is largely a consequence of its own conviction that "business and politics don't mix." As corporations have become more important economically, their interest and influence in public affairs and government has declined. Business management has long had the attitude that government is a minor activity not worthy of the consideration of reputable businessmen and organizations. Because it is controversial, many business leaders believe that politics is something to be avoided by business. This aversion to involvement in government and politics, which is typical of business management, is responsible for the poor relationship between business and government.

The "New Look" in Government Relations

However, a marked change is taking place in the viewpoint of business leaders toward government and politics. "We in business need to learn how to be politically effective," says Ralph J. Cordiner, chairman of the board of General Electric Co. "Government is becoming a more significant factor in business decisions with every passing year. There is a whole new field to be explored in this matter of discovering and organizing the political resources of business."

Business is seeking better government relations and taking a more active interest in legislation and politics in two ways: first, by taking a position on national, state, and city legislation affecting company operations; and second, by encouraging full and free participation by employees in government and politics as workers, voters, and office holders. To accomplish these two objectives, corporations have organized civic and government affairs offices with professional staffs to develop and carry out legislative and political education programs on the local, state, and national levels.

This new interest of business in government and politics promises to create a more favorable climate for business operation by reducing the cost of doing business through lower taxes; by relaxing controls that restrict business freedom of action; by meeting foreign competition through protective tariffs; by improving labor relations through more equitable labor laws and in many other ways.

On the other hand, some business leaders argue that business should not become involved in legislative affairs and politics. The business viewpoint is already adequately presented to politicians by industry lobbyists. The corporation is a legal and not a personal entity and has no right to political opinions. Corporation political action will antagonize more people than it will win. Businessmen have no experience in practical politics. These are some of the arguments against corporate action in civic and governmental affairs.

The desirability of educating employees in politics is questioned by some business leaders. The argument that corporations can conduct classes in politics without influencing the personal political views of employees is naïve, in the opinion of the chairman of a large corporation. Corporate political education of workers attracts the younger employee who then votes Democratic, is another objection from the standpoint of the Republican industrialist. In answer to this objection, others believe that if employees help elect pro-business Democratic candidates, business will benefit.

The negative position of business on public questions is criticized by James C. Worthy, vice-president, public relations, Sears, Roebuck & Co., "Unless business begins to be for things rather than everlastingly against; unless it takes more initiative in devising measures for dealing with urgent public problems, the public will react against corporation legislative activity."

Corporate Legislative Programs

A corporate legislative program to include national as well as state and city legislation is essential to effective government relations. A definite corporate policy on national issues such as foreign aid, taxation, defense, antitrust, social security, labor, tariffs, international trade, and other legislative questions that directly affect a corporation and industry is desirable. A long-range legislative program should be adopted by a corporation before legislation affecting the business is introduced in Congress.

Much of the legislative effort of corporations and associations is defensive, devoted to putting out legislative fires when they break out rather than in taking a position on legislation before it is enacted. This serious lack of corporate legislative policy and objectives handicap legislative representatives in securing the co-operation of members of the national and state legislatures in enacting legislation favorable to business.

Corporate management, after consultation with its legislative representatives, should take a definite position on national, state, and local legislation directly affecting the welfare of the business and its industry.

Then management should personally support competent candidates and elected Congressmen, irrespective of their party affiliations, who favor such legislation.

Gulf Oil Company. The Gulf Oil Company's legislative program has three major phases: local and regional political and legislative activity; national legislative activity; and political information and education of employees.

Local and regional legislative and political activity is handled by regional area political supervisors selected from the ranks of employees to train Gulf district managers of marketing, transportation, and production departments to work directly with local political leaders.

National legislative activity is directed from a Washington office staffed by an experienced legislative analyst registered as a lobbyist and, in addition, a political writer. A biweekly newsletter is prepared by the Washington office summarizing all legislative activities that affect the oil industry. It is distributed to all executives of the company down to the level of district manager.

Gulf employees are encouraged on a nonpartisan basis to be active in the political party of their choice. Leaves of absence are granted to employees elected to office.

American Can Company. The American Can Company has a comprehensive corporate legislative program. The company takes official positions on such public issues as a balanced national budget, government controls of business, and labor legislation. Official company policy on these issues is developed by four standing committees and when approved by the management committee is communicated to all company personnel as company policy.

Application of the company's legislative policy is assigned to 153 managers in plants and offices throughout the country who are the company's official spokesmen. Congressmen are invited to plants and offices to discuss legislation with the local managers.

Government relations letters discussing the company's legislative policy are sent to all company personnel, who are asked to study the company's views on legislation and the reasons for them. If company people approve of the company's official position they are urged to communicate their position to their legislators. However, no employee is required to support a corporate legislative position with which he disagrees. Endorsement by employees of company views on legislation is voluntary and no employee's status is affected by such disagreement.

Political Education of Employees. Many companies sponsor courses in practical politics for employees. "We feel that we are forwarding the business of democracy by offering our employees an education in the ways of government and by encouraging them to participate in local politics with the party of their choice," says Charles A. Thomas, board chairman, Monsanto Chemical Company.

The most popular method of encouraging employee political action is the practical politics seminar intended to motivate employees to become active members of the party of their choice at the precinct level. Political action seminars are conducted by industrial associations, Chambers of Commerce, universities, and individual corporations.

The United States Chamber of Commerce offers a course in practical politics consisting of nine, two-hour workshops. Classes are held once a week by business concerns, service clubs, or local Chambers of Commerce for groups of 12 to 20 persons. Course materials consist of eight pamphlets on the following subjects: the individual in politics, political party organization, the political precinct, the political campaign, political clubs, the political leader's problems, political meetings, and businessmen in politics. In addition, there are case problems for study and discussion, assignment guides and a discussion leader's manual. More than 100,000 people in 1,300 communities in 50 states have taken this course.

The National Association of Manufacturers has a similar political education course for employees called "Citizen at Work." The Effective Citizens Organization, a group sponsored by 50 major corporations conducts political workshops for executives and employees.

Industrial associations in several states including Texas, Kentucky, Pennsylvania, Illinois, Massachusetts, Florida, Missouri, California, and Ohio, have sponsored political seminars.

The University of Chicago conducted a course for employees of Republic Steel Company in Cleveland. Public Affairs Counsellors, a New York consulting firm, has developed employee political education programs for Allen Bradley Company, A. O. Smith Corporation, and Oxford Paper Company.

Monsanto Chemical Company has given employees a course in practical politics since 1959. A survey of the effectiveness of this course showed that the number of employees who have contributed money for political purposes has tripled; those who have affiliated themselves with political clubs or organizations has more than tripled; and those who have worked at the precinct level has quadrupled since this program started. Ninety-four per cent of those who took the course favored it. Almost 300 Monsanto workers hold elective or appointive political offices.

Caterpillar Tractor Company, Peoria, Illinois, pays half the tuition fee of employees taking the eight-week course in nonpartisan, practical politics offered by the Peoria Association of Commerce.

Continental Oil Company, Houston, Texas, has started workshops to teach employees and their wives how to participate in party politics, and grants time off with pay for work in either party.

American Cyanamid Corporation has employed a former mayor of Bloomfield, N.J., to run employee seminars on practical politics and requires all branch managers to meet their local legislators.

General Electric Company has sponsored courses in practical politics for employees: get-out-the-vote campaigns, surveyed political factors affecting the business climate, and taken an active part in political campaigns on issues concerning business since 1958.

Texas Instruments Inc., Whirlpool Corporation, Harvey Aluminum Company, and Aerojet-General Corporation have set up machinery to facilitate employee contributions to both political parties.

The Ford Motor Company's employee political participation program and government and civic affairs activities are described in a case at the end of this chapter.

Fundamentals of Corporate Political Action

Corporations which have established effective government affairs programs observe the following principles:

A corporate political program must be strictly nonpartisan and take no stand on candidates or parties. Good government can only be achieved by encouraging able people to become active in both political parties.

Legislative programs of corporations must embody genuine respect for the political liberties of all individuals affected by them. No attempt should be made to regiment the thinking or political behavior of employees. Employees should be encouraged to become active in public affairs for their own good rather than as agents of the company employing them.

Legislative programs must not be directed against other elements in society or just toward the achievement of specific or immediate objectives. The winning of an election or combating organized labor is not sufficient reason for a public affairs program.

A company must assume an obligation to give political issues mature study and weigh them in terms of the interest of the public. Business should apply itself imaginatively, constructively, and energetically to the problems of government.

Information on the political environment of plant communities, the local political structure, political issues, and developments affecting the profitable operation of business should be obtained.

The stand of elected representatives of national, state, and local government on controversial issues which affect business should be studied continuously.

All employees and levels of management should be educated in practical politics and encouraged to take an active interest in the party of their choice without prejudice to their status.

Friendly relationships should be sought with state legislators and elected town officials particularly in areas where the company maintains plants.

Corporations should co-operate with other business organizations in carrying on educational programs to inform all employees as well as the public on current political issues.

Communications of the views of the corporation on political issues affecting the business should be issued regularly to employees, the public, opinion leaders, and legislators.

Business men should actively participate as individuals in political campaigns, seek election to city and state legislatures and give voluntary service to government agencies.

Responsibility and authority for corporate political activity should be assigned to an individual and staff reporting to top management in order to insure a co-ordinated, comprehensive legislative program.

Organization for Government Relations and Political Action

The development and administration of a national, state, and local corporate program of government relations is logically the responsibility of the public relations department. Execution of the program on the state and local levels, however, must be a responsibility of division or local management and their staffs and employees. The encouragement and actual support of top management is essential to carrying out a legislative program.

Direct political activity by rank-and-file employees should not only be permitted but officially approved by management. Management and supervision in local plants must encourage employees to work for either party in their neighborhood precincts, ringing doorbells, stuffing envelopes, or serving on town councils, school boards, and commissions.

To secure political action at the local plant community level, the General Electric Company has appointed managers of public affairs attached to the employee and community relations departments of its principal plants. The public affairs manager is a political specialist in charge of employee political education and advancement of the corporation in public affairs in the plant community.

Civic affairs directors now occupy important positions in the public relations departments of large corporations. The Civic Affairs Office of the public relations and advertising department, Ford Motor Company, has an eight-section staff of associates responsible for relations with state governments, civic groups, municipal governments, the federal government, community relations, educational affairs, dealer information, traffic safety, and highway improvement. The Civic Affairs

Department of the public relations department of Sears, Roebuck & Company is responsible for a national program of civic activities executed by territorial public relations directors and individual store and plant managers in many communities throughout the country.

Many large corporations, trade and professional associations maintain government relations offices or representatives in Washington, D.C., for federal affairs. The typical Washington office for federal government relations is headed by a manager with the title of director of government relations, or legislative representative. He supervises a staff of specialists, varying in size from one to 40 employees, engaged in legislative research, analysis of proposed legislation, preparing briefs and testimony, publicity, and maintaining personal relations with legislators. The same type of organization, on a more limited scale, may be maintained in the principal state capitals or in large cities where the corporation's interests justify representation. In some companies, government relations is the responsibility of the legal department in co-operation with the public relations department.

FEDERAL GOVERNMENT RELATIONS

The increasing impact of the federal government on American business, labor, and the professions is causing many companies, industries, and professional and social organizations to take a more active interest in the legislative and executive branches of the national government.

The trend toward closer relations of business organizations with the federal government is acknowledged in a recent report of the Brookings Institution, Washington, by Cherington and Gillen on "The Business Representative in Washington." Says the Brookings report:

Defense expenditures, the use of fiscal and monetary policies to combat inflation and recession, social welfare, and extensive highway programs are but a few of the activities that have attracted the attention of business corporations to the significance of business government relations. The federal government has grown in importance as a purchaser of goods and services; as a source of scientific, technical, and economic information; a force for economic growth and social progress, and as a regulator of individual and commercial activities. These developments and indications that the trend will continue have made governmental affairs a consistently stronger influence on day-to-day operation.

Of the 200 largest manufacturers in the United States, approximately 130 maintain full-time Washington representatives according to the Brookings report. In addition, a number of relatively small companies are also represented in the nation's capital. While the objectives of this representation in some cases is strictly commercial, an increasing amount is in the area of legislative activity and in relations with the executive and administrative agencies of the federal government.

Not only are many individual corporations represented in Washington but an increasing number of industrial and professional associations and various types of government relations specialists are serving special interests at the seat of government. Some of these organizations are horizontal in character serving a cross section of business, such as the National Association of Manufacturers and the Chamber of Commerce of the United States. Others are vertical groups identified with a single industry, such as the Association of American Railroads, United States Brewers Association, or scientific and professional associations, such as the American Medical Association.

These groups sometimes sponsor luncheon and discussion meetings which provide a valuable exchange of information on Washington affairs for their members who are represented in Washington. Washington specialists in government relations, including lawyers and public relations counselors are also retained by corporations and associations for federal government relations. These counselors maintain close relations with the Washington representatives of their clients.

While many large manufacturers maintain their own government relations representatives in Washington, most small business concerns depend largely on trade associations, attorneys, or public relations counsel with Washington offices to carry on relations with the federal government.

Trade and professional associations, attorneys, lobbyists, and public relations counsel with Washington offices deal with government relations problems that company representatives cannot handle adequately. These specialists arrange "briefings" for corporation officials by government people on legislation, social security, pensions, and other matters affecting business; sponsor inspection trips to government laboratories and military installations; and provide legislators and government agencies with technical information and advice on framing legislation.

In some respects, associations are not as effective in government relations as Washington representatives of individual companies. The membership of most trade and professional associations is so large and the interests of their individual members so diverse that their legislative position on controversial questions is often weak and inflexible and they lack aggressiveness in obtaining favorable legislation and executive decisions.

Federal Government Relations Activities

The activities of Washington representatives of individual companies as well as associations and counselors vary widely but may be classified in the following categories: relations with the executive branch of the federal government; relations with the legislative branch, including members of Congress in the Senate and House of Representatives; relations with procurement agencies and the military services; and relations with the press.

Relations with the Executive Branch. Washington representatives of business, labor, social, and professional groups have a wide range of activities. They deal with federal government executives from the White House to minor officials in the many government bureaus, commissions, and agencies which execute the laws passed by the Congress. Washington representatives expedite executive action on legislation; furnish information and advice to executive agencies and aid them in formulating and enforcing regulations affecting a company or industry; familiarize government executives with the point of view of business; carry on research of executive rulings, regulations, and decisions affecting a company, industry, or profession; and keep agencies informed about the progress, policies, and problems of a company or industry.

Communication of a company's or industry's point of view to members of the executive branch is an important function of a legislative representative who may be assisted by staff specialists. Companies interested in additional tariff protection for their products present their case through their Washington representative to the U.S. Tariff Commission. Representatives, in the Capitol, of radio and television broadcasters deal with the Federal Communications Commission. The legislative agents of public utilities, subject to federal regulation, devote considerable time to the regulatory bureaus.

Federal government agencies which serve and regulate business include: the Departments of Commerce, Agriculture, Labor, Interior, State, and Treasury. In addition, numerous agencies regulate business including: the Civil Aeronautics Board, Federal Communications Commission, Interstate Commerce Commission, Securities and Exchange Commission, Federal Trade Commission, Federal Deposit Insurance Corporation, U.S. Maritime Commission, and others.

The amount of time given by Washington representatives to the executive branch depends on the size of the company, the extent of regulation exercised by government, and the company's interest in gathering information, assisting or projecting its point of view to executive agencies.

The Washington representatives of individual companies and trade and professional associations keep their corporation managements or members informed of the hearings, rulings, and activities of executive departments and agencies by telephone, news letters, and bulletins issued periodically.

Relations with the Legislative Branch. Legislative relations are carried on by Washington representatives of individual companies, business and professional associations with members of Congress, Senators and Representatives on Capitol Hill in the corridors of the House or Senate office buildings, in the offices of legislators and key committee staff members, at nearby country clubs, or Washington restaurants.

A Washington government relations representative may be compared to an ambassador for his company or industry, listening and reporting to the management of the company about legislative matters affecting the operation of the business. At the same time the representative serves as an advisor to his company or industry concerning its position on legislation and makes recommendations for support or opposition to significant legislation.

Activities of legislative representatives fall into two general classifications: legislative investigations and pending legislation. In respect to Congressional investigations, Washington representatives determine the likelihood of an investigation of the company or industry, the attitudes of members of the investigating committee, and its procedures. The Capitol representative may prepare testimony and assist witnesses at the inquiry and may assist a special company staff assigned to the investigation.

Most of the legislative representative's time is spent on pending legislation. A representative will be involved in from five to twelve measures a year, according to the Brookings inquiry; although in some cases he may be concerned with as many as 50 bills a year depending on the volume of legislation affecting his company or industry. Activities of Washington representatives on pending legislation include: answering Congressional inquiries; filing statements with Congressional committes, giving a company's or association's views on pending bills; communicating a corporation's position on proposed legislation to members of Congress; informing legislators about the economic importance and developments of a company or industry. A legislative representative becomes personally acquainted with members of Congress and discusses with them pending legislation. He keeps a record of the voting of legislators on important legislation and analyzes pending legislation. One of his most important functions is contacting by telephone or in person members of legislative committees and their staffs who are considering important legislation which will affect a company or industry.

A Washington representative keeps his company or association management informed of major developments affecting pending legislation, its scope, probable effects, and likelihood of passage; reports on the progress of legislation through Congress, and major developments in the executive departments of the federal government.

Specialists in government relations believe that local constituents of Congressmen can exercise more influence on legislation than Washington representatives. To supplement the efforts of their Washington representatives, many companies expect their local plant and branch managers to become acquainted with the Congressmen from their districts and gain their legislative support for measures which affect the welfare of the company.

Congressional Legislative Procedures

The legislative activities of government relations representatives of business, social, and professional organizations are determined by the procedures of Congress for introducing, considering, and acting upon legislation.

Congress has the power to regulate both interstate and foreign commerce. In the exercise of this power, it initiates bills or resolutions which, when approved by both Houses and signed by the President, become laws. It is in the interest of business that Congressmen be informed regarding the effects of proposed legislation and their cooperation secured in the passage of reasonable laws.

Consideration of federal legislation is the responsibility of committees of both the Senate and House of Representatives. There are 15 standing or permanent committees in the Senate and 19 in the House. There are, in addition, nearly 200 subcommittees in Congress and approximately 18 Congressional commissions and joint committees composed of members of both Houses.

All bills and resolutions introduced by members of the Senate and House are assigned to the committee having jurisdiction. A committee may report a bill out in its original form, vote against it in committee, make changes, or allow the bill to die in committee. When a bill is favorably reported out of committee of the House of Representatives, it is next submitted to discussion and vote in the House of Representatives, in which it originated. If passed by the House, it is sent to the Senate and referred to the committee of the Senate having jurisdiction. If the Senate committee approves of the measure, it is reported to the Senate and, if passed by that body, is returned to the House of Representatives. Differences between the Senate and the House over a measure necessitates its consideration by a joint conference committee to effect a compromise. Either body may also agree to the amendments of the other body. When a bill or joint resolution is finally approved by both the Senate and House of Representatives, it is signed by the Speaker and Vice-President and is sent to the President for his signature. Once the President signs the measure, it becomes a law. If he vetoes the bill, it cannot become a law unless repassed by a two-thirds vote of both Houses.

This process of enactment of federal laws gives legislative committees of Congress an important influence on laws affecting business. When considering proposed legislation, committees of both Houses obtain information and hear arguments of proponents, as well as opponents, of measures orally, by brief, and by letter. These committee hearings give representatives of business, professional, and other organizations an opportunity to express their views in regard to proposed legislation. Witnesses before legislative committees may also file briefs or submit to questioning by members of a committee considering controversial measures.

When representatives of business testify before legislative committees, government relations staffs prepare news releases featuring highlights of testimony of witnesses; arrange for press conferences with witnesses; publish reprints of statements made by witnesses; and in other ways publicize the viewpoint of a business or industry toward proposed legislation.

During the course of committee hearings on a measure, members of a legislative committee are interviewed by a legislative representative and provided with additional information in order to secure the approval, rejection, or amendment of a measure.

When a bill has been approved by a legislative committee and referred to the floor of the House or Senate for consideration, the government relations representative must next interest his local congressmen, other members of Congress, and possibly a federal agency in support or defeat of the measure.

Relations with Congressional Investigating Committees

Both the Senate and House of Representatives have authority to appoint special investigating committees to investigate a wide variety of matters ranging from crime syndicates, Communist activities, and economic problems, as well as the policies and practices of business concerns.

These investigations of business activities are usually preliminary to new legislation, but they are sometimes undertaken to bring the force of public opinion to bear on business and compel it to desist from some practice contrary to the public welfare.

Executives of corporations concerned are invited to testify before investigating committees considering business policies or practices. The appearance of a representative of a business or professional association before an investigating committee calls for sound public relations planning. To prepare testimony, the services of specialists in research, . statistics, law, and economics may be required. Charts, graphs, and illustrative materials must be drawn. Advice of legal counsel is usually necessary. A plan for press publicity is made to include news releases of statements of the principal witnesses, press conferences, individual interviews with witnesses, photographs of witnesses, publication of testimony in booklet form, television broadcasts, and newsreel coverage of important testimony.

Lobbying and Federal Government Relations

Relations of corporations, business and professional associations with members of Congress have long been identified as lobbying. Lobbying is generally considered a sinister activity involving influence peddlers, 5 per centers, or anonymous persons offering gifts for legislative favors. To regulate such lobbying, Congress passed in 1946 the Legislative Reorganization Act which controls lobbying. Section 307 of the act defines a lobbyist as any person who by himself or through an agent or employee or other persons in any manner whatsoever, directly or indirectly, solicits, collects or receives money or any other thing of value to be used to aid in the accomplishment of the following: the passage or defeat of any legislation by the Congress of the United States or to influence directly or indirectly the passage or defeat of any legislation by the Congress of the United States.

On June 7, 1954, the U.S. Supreme Court upheld the constitutionality of the Lobbying Act with Chief Justice Warren delivering the majority opinion, stating that a person to come under the act must have "solicited, collected, or received contributions intended to influence legislation and the intended method of accomplishing this purpose must have been through direct communications with members of Congress."

The Lobbying Act apparently does not apply to the following legitimate government relations activities, in the opinion of Bert C. Goss, president, Hill & Knowlton, public relations counsel: testimony before Congressional committees; distribution of information about legislation to newspapers and to opinion leaders generally; direct communication to Congressmen and their assistants about the state of business and matters of direct concern to a specific business, not involving the merits or demerits of a specific piece of legislation.

As far back as 1874, the United States Supreme Court recognized the existence of "lobby agents" and lobbyists existed for many years before that time. Today, lobbying has become a multimillion dollar activity. Since the enactment of the Federal Lobbying Act, more than 2,500 lobbyists have registered with the Clerk of the House and Secretary of the Senate. Of this number about 200 represent social, business, and professional organizations.

Constructive Lobbying

President John F. Kennedy, when a Senator from Massachusetts, recognized that lobbies play an important role in framing legislation, stating,

The "new lobby" emphasizes constructive activities designed to appeal to the judgment rather than to the personal advantage or gain of legislators. Included among these "new lobby" techniques is testifying before Congressional committees—lobbyists are in many cases expert technicians and capable of explaining complex and difficult subjects in a clear, understandable fashion. They engage in personal discussions with members of Congress in which they can explain in detail the positions they advocate.

Lobbyists prepare briefs, memoranda, legislative analyses, and draft legislation for use by committees and members of Congress; they frequently can provide useful statistics and information not otherwise available.

There is no more effective manner of learning all important arguments and facts on a controversial issue than to have the opposing lobbyists present their cases.

It is the responsibility of business, social, and professional groups to protect and advance their own interests through the "new lobby" techniques of communicating with members of Congress about matters of direct concern to a specific business or group.

Relations with Federal Procurement Agencies. Many federal government relations representatives of industrial companies devote a considerable portion of their time to aiding the marketing departments of their companies in supplying the government's requirements for raw materials, components, equipment, and specialized research and development requirements. Personal contacts are made by Washington representatives with the Departments of Defense, Agriculture, Health, Education and Welfare, Atomic Energy Commission, National Space Administration, and others. Representatives determine government buying policy, participate in the development of specifications for products required by the government, solicit sales, determine government requirements, submit bids, or assist their principals in securing government contracts.

Press Relations in Washington. The larger corporations, business, and professional associations represented in Washington, maintain press relations staffs in the Capitol. As much of the nation's news originates in Washington today, it is desirable to maintain relations with newspaper correspondents, radio and television writers, columnists and broadcasters at this important national news source. Local Washington news media, widely read by all members of Congress and those in the executive branch of the federal government, are also served by the press bureaus of manufacturers and associations.

Washington press relations involves personal contacts with newsmen; press conferences on important news; mailing of press releases, photographs, and clip sheets to all news media.

News from the Washington press bureaus of corporations and associations describes the effect of pending legislation or tariff agreements on employment, wages, and prices; the progress of federal mediation in labor disputes of companies or industries; the testimony of a corporation executive before a Congressional committee, or the visit of an important executive to Washington.

GOVERNMENT RELATIONS ON THE STATE AND LOCAL COMMUNITY LEVELS

Relations of business corporations and associations with state and local governments follow much the same pattern as those with the federal government, as described previously. Some large corporations and associations maintain permanent legislative representatives at the state capitals and in the cities where they are actively operating. The state and local government relations of many small concerns are handled by state or local trade associations.

State and Municipal Executive Relations

Numerous state, city, and county administrative agencies regulate and serve business both directly and indirectly through executive departments of public health, safety, labor, education, public works, and law enforcement. These agencies not only provide service to business in these areas but also have the power to regulate and control business, enforce regulations, and inspect business concerns whose operations fall within the scope of their authority.

State laws and city ordinances executed by a multiplicity of boards or commissions regulate the production and sale of food and dairy products, fish, and game; inspection of meat products; supervision of building construction; regulation of cold storage; suppression of animal and plant disease; the employment of labor; the accuracy of weights and measures; and many other activities.

State and local governments also regulate business licensing, franchising, and controlling entry into business; regulating prices, service, and quality; and preventing unfair methods of competition.

State and City Legislative Relations

Relations with legislators who are members of state legislatures and municipal councils follow much the same pattern as those with the federal congress. Proposed state and municipal legislation is referred to legislative committees which give a public hearing to advocates and opponents of proposed legislation. Representatives of business employ the methods of dealing with state and city legislative committees as described previously for Congressional committees. The lobbying process is followed in states and cities to bring to the attention of the proper legislative committees and regulatory agencies the views of business concerning proposed legislation. Investigating committees are appointed in most state legislatures to investigate various matters, including the practices of industrial corporations.

COMMUNICATIONS WITH FEDERAL, STATE, AND LOCAL GOVERNMENT OFFICIALS, LEGISLATORS, AND AGENCIES

The principal means of communication with legislators, the heads and personnel of government agencies on federal, state, and local levels is by personal interviews. Representatives of business can discuss the merits of particular measures with legislators, explain the problems of business to heads of government bureaus, and learn how government and business can work together.

Oral Communications

As the number of government executives and legislators is relatively limited, communication by personal interviews is simple, quick, and inexpensive. Representatives of business answer questions, meet objections, and fully discuss their views.

City, state, and federal hearings before legislative committees give representatives of business an opportunity to present their views on proposed legislation. In addition to giving oral testimony, businessmen may file briefs with the clerk of the committee or appear to answer questions. Committee hearings also provide opportunities for business to publicize its point of view to the general public.

Formal dinners or informal luncheons and breakfasts, arranged by legislative representatives for members of national, state, and city governments or for heads of executive departments, are excellent media for informing government officials about the problems, practices, and needs of business. Informal, round-table conferences between representatives of industry and government personnel present the case of business on controversial legislative measures or aid agencies in the enforcement of regulations and the application of controls.

Delegations representing a company or association visit the offices of city, state, and federal government officials to inform them about needed legislation. Top-management executives of local concerns may appear at public hearings to oppose or favor proposed legislation.

An increasing number of companies are informing city, state, and national legislators and officials about their problems, operations, and economic contributions by conducted plant tours and discussions. Observation by government officials of plants and operations make it possible for them to see at firsthand the importance of the industry and to better understand its problems in relation to needed legislation.

City, state, and national lawmakers and executives are also contacted by telephone calls, correspondence, and telegrams in respect to favoring or opposing pending legislation affecting business.

Printed Communications

Government officials should be continuously informed about business and its operations, objectives, and problems by means of printed media including advertising and publicity on radio, television, and in newspapers and magazines. Paid advertising, discussing legislation, taxation, or government controls may be run in newspapers and magazines which are read by legislators.

Booklets, folders, annual reports, and magazines describing the operations and problems of a corporation or group should be mailed to aldermen, senators, representatives, and executives of government agencies.

Communications with Legislators in Their Home Areas

Effective communication with legislators involves contacts with them in their home states and districts as well as at the seat of government in Washington or the state capitals. Legislators spend much time in their districts speaking and listening to their constituents. Meetings with legislators in the state or nation's capital should be supplemented by social and business contacts by local plant and branch managers. Corporations that maintain plants in several states have a potential audience of numerous Congressmen as well as state senators and representatives.

"Grass root" relations with legislators is increasing as business recognizes the value of local contacts with legislators. Meeting legislators in their own districts counteracts the political pressures of opposition groups such as labor unions and farmers which actively employ "grass roots" political action programs.

The local managers of plants, public relations, and sales are in the best position to make sure that their Congressmen understand the company's position on taxes, government spending and legislation and to get an expression from the legislators on issues of significance to the company.

Indirect Communication with Legislators through Voters

City, state, and federal legislators are responsive to the attitudes of their constituents on questions involving legislation. If the voters approve, legislators will do likewise. The most effective government relations of business organizations are not direct contacts with congressmen and legislators in state and local assemblies but in communicating the business point of view to the voters so forcefully that they will appeal to their elected representatives to vote for legislation beneficial to business.

It is essential that the voting public understand and accept the legislative position of business and vote for legislators who approve of legislation favored by business. The views of legislators on legislative matters are readily affected by public opinion, which must be courted by business through direct appeal to the voters.

Case 13–1

CIVIC AND GOVERNMENTAL AFFAIRS PROGRAM

Ford Motor Company

The Ford Motor Company, Dearborn, Michigan, is the world's second largest automobile manufacturer producing passenger cars, trucks, tractors, farm implements, industrial engines, and defense products. Sales of all products exceed 5.25 billion dollars annually. The company has 36 foreign subsidiaries with manufacturing plants in England, Canada, Germany, and Brazil and assembly plants and sales branches in Belgium, Denmark, Finland, France, Holland, Italy, Portugal, Sweden, Norway, Egypt, Mexico, Uruguay, and Chile which sell in excess of $1.8 billion annually of Ford products.

The company employs 160,000 persons in the United States and more than 100,000 men and women in its international operations. There are approximately 240,000 owners of the common stock of the company including 70 per cent of all salaried employees.

Ford passenger cars and trucks are marketed in the United States by about 8,100 dealers who employ about 162,000 persons. Tractors and farm implements are distributed by 26 independent distributors and about 2,500 dealers.

Public relations of the company is the responsibility of a vice-president in charge of public relations whose staff includes a general public relations manager and a director of civic and governmental affairs.

The Ford Motor Company established a civic affairs office at headquarters in 1950. A Washington, D.C., office previously established, watches federal, state, and local legislative proposals and administrative procedures affecting business in general and the automotive industry in particular. This office reports national legislative developments in Washington to top management of the company. It makes the company's viewpoint known to the government bodies concerned and, when issues are of sufficient importance, arranges for management to give direct testimony before legislative committees.

In 1959, the Ford civic affairs office was redesignated as the civic and governmental affairs office and its functions and staff broadened to include special departments for state and local government relations, community relations, traffic safety and highway improvement, research, dealer public affairs information. In addition, a field manager supervises the activities of eight regional civic and governmental affairs managers whose regions include all states of the country. The civic and governmental affairs office receives guidance on company policy from a committee on civic and governmental affairs composed of the president and chairman of the board and six vice-presidents. The director of civic and governmental affairs serves as chairman of this committee and the assistant director is also a member.

The civic and governmental affairs office in Dearborn is also responsible for community relations in cities where the company has plants and offices. Community relations at the local level are handled by 52 community relations committees composed of as many of the following Ford executives as may be located in a particular plant city: division general manager, controller, and industrial relations manager; regional and district sales managers; and local plant manager, controller, and industrial relations manager. Each of the company's nine field public relations managers and eight regional civic and governmental affairs managers serve as special consulting members of the committees in their respective territories.

The functions of the community relations committees, in addition to implementing the company's public relations program at the local level, are to further the development of Ford's civic and governmental affairs program. In this respect, the committees take inventory of the local business climate in plant communities using a Business Climate Inventory Form prepared by the Dearborn civic and governmental affairs office. This form of 41 pages lists 220 items affecting the community business climate including industrial and government factors, community services and facilities, highway improvement and safety, community organizations and participation by Ford employees in community affairs.

The community relations committees plan state legislative programs with state by state direction of the company's legislative effort in the hands of the eight regional civic and governmental affairs managers who have an intimate knowledge of government of the states in their regions.

Plant visits and luncheon meetings with local, state, and national public officials are arranged by community relations committees.

Ford Effective Citizenship Program

In co-operation with community relations committees and Ford plant and office management throughout the country, the civic and governmental affairs

FIG. 13–1. Training in practical politics is given Ford Motor Co. employees shown at a session of the Ford Effective Citizenship Course, a feature of its civic and governmental affairs program.

office at Dearborn sponsors the Ford Effective Citizenship Program to encourage individual participation by all Ford employees in political affairs.

The objective of this program is to interest Ford employees in becoming active in the party of their choice, not as agents of the company, but in their private capacities as a citizenship responsibility. The company believes that this program contributes to strengthening the organizations and improving the vitality of both political parties and thereby helps to strengthen and improve our free system of government.

Voluntary Political Contribution Plan

One of the features of the Ford Effective Citizenship Program is the provision of a convenient means for all salaried and hourly rated employees to give financial support to the political party of their choice. Contributions are entirely voluntary and no effort is made by company management to stimulate employee participation by personal contacts, contests, or other promotion. Employees are not counseled as to the amount of their contributions. No attempt is made by management to ascertain the identity of contributing employees, the amount contributed, party designated, or to assess participation by individual employees or departments.

Responsibility for installing the contribution plan rests with the top Ford official, at each company location, under the direction of the civic and governmental affairs office. The employee programs department, industrial relations staff at Dearborn is responsible for over-all co-ordination of the plan with plant industrial relations managers providing assistance as necessary.

A letter outlining the plan, a contribution form and two return envelopes are mailed to the home of each of the 156,000 nonsupervisory employees of the company. An employee who wishes to make a contribution to his political party places his check or cash and the completed contribution form in an envelope indicating thereon the political party to which it is to be delivered and places it in an outer envelope. This envelope is deposited by the employee in a container lettered "Political Contributions," several of which are placed at convenient locations in Ford plants and offices. At the end of a five-day collection period, all contribution envelopes are collected and the inner envelopes are sorted as to political parties and turned over to the state headquarters of the designated political party.

Political Party Activity Plan

To provide Ford employees with a convenient way to volunteer for political work, the Political Party Activity Plan was presented to all supervisory employees at the company's regular supervisory conferences held throughout the country. The plan gave employees an opportunity to decide whether they wished to engage during nonworking hours in political activities of the party of their choice and contribute financially to their party.

Every employee attending the supervisory conference was given a volunteer card, a contribution card, and two envelopes. An employee interested in political activity marked on his card the party of his choice, indicated his willingness to work for and contribute to that party, and signed his name and address. The volunteer card and contribution was addressed to a company collecting agent who forwarded the unopen envelope to the political party indicated thereon.

Providing Employees with Political Information

An Effective Citizenship Course in practical politics is offered to both supervisory and nonmanagement employees in Ford plants and offices throughout the country.

The objective of this voluntary course is to provide practical information on the political processes through which government officials are selected under the two-party system. It does not involve discussion of political issues nor serve as propaganda for the company's views about legislation.

The course is based on a manual prepared by the Ford civic and governmental affairs office. A two-hour course session is held weekly, after working hours, for eight weeks. The following eight topics are covered in this course:

Political leadership, its functions and problems, qualifications of leaders, how they get and hold their positions and what they do.

The political campaign, the structure of campaign organization, campaign planning and techniques, and media of communication with voters.

Political clubs and meetings, their influence on party policy, educational and social functions, planning and running political meetings.

The political party and determination of public policy, the role of party in developing public policy, influence of political factors on legislative processes and executive policies.

Organization of local government and parties in the community and state in which the course is offered.

Discussion with local political leaders of all parties who are invited to appear before the group taking the course.

The individual in politics, opportunities available to the individual, and how he can make his influence felt.

In addition to the Effective Citizenship Program, the Ford civic and governmental affairs office provides for recognition of employee service to the community through the Community Service Awards Program. All Ford employees are eligible to be nominated annually by other employees and community groups for service to the community including election or appointment to public office or activity for a political party. A mounted silver scroll or Town Crier's bell, in cases of extraordinary service, are presented to winning employees at an awards dinner attended by local civil leaders and company management.

If an employee is elected to full-time political office, he is granted a leave of absence by the company without pay but with continued participation in company benefit programs. A letter of congratulation from the president of the company is written to all employees elected to public office.

Ford dealers are informed about pending national legislation affecting dealers and the industry through a *Public Affairs Bulletin* published periodically by the civic and governmental affairs office of the company. Advertising to dealers in automotive magazines encourages dealers to participate in civic and governmental affairs in their communities. Dealer community relations committees have been established in various cities where the company has no installations. The purpose of these committees is to assist the co-ordinated efforts of Ford Motor Company dealers in maintaining a favorable reputation in their communities, elevating the status of the automobile retail business, and in keeping informed and taking effective action concerning governmental and legislative issues which affect their business.

Ford has produced a motion picture "Where Were You?" to interest employees, dealers, and the public in our political parties and to emphasize the importance of participating in the activities of political parties. This film is loaned without charge for showing by groups interested in representative government.

Employee newspapers published by 28 Ford plants carry editorials urging employees to participate in governmental affairs and to give recognition to Ford people who are active in politics.

QUESTIONS

1. What justification has the Ford Motor Company in sponsoring the governmental affairs program described in this case?
2. Should the Ford governmental program be altered in any way or further expanded? Describe in detail how this program can be improved.
3. Is the organization of the Ford Civic and Governmental Affairs program sound? Why? If not, what changes should be made in this organization?
4. Comment on the Ford Voluntary Contributions Plan describing the strengths and weaknesses of this plan.
5. Comment on the Ford Political Party Activity Plan, describing its strengths and weaknesses.
6. Comment on the Ford Effective Citizenship Course, describing its strength and weaknesses.

Problem 13–1

GOVERNMENT RELATIONS

The United Oil Corporation

The United Oil Corporation is a fully integrated oil company engaged in the production, refining, transportation, and marketing of petroleum and petroleum products. It produces crude oil in Texas, California, Canada, and foreign countries and transports it in its own tankers, pipe lines, and tank cars to refineries in Texas, California, and Pennsylvania. United products are marketed in New England, the Middle Atlantic, and Southern states, on the Pacific coast, and in 60 foreign countries. The corporation is owned by 30,000 shareholders, employs 18,000 workers, and sells more than $600 million worth of refined products annually.

In recent years the management of the corporation has observed the growing regulation by both national and local governments of business in general and the oil industry in particular. The corporation's ability to import oil which it produces in foreign countries has been arbitrarily curtailed by government decree. The corporation's ability to claim a tax adjustment to compensate for the exhaustion of its crude petroleum in the ground is under attack by members of Congress who are not familiar with the complex necessities of petroleum economics. The officers of the company on several occasions have devoted considerable time and expense to assembling facts and presenting testimony before government investigating committees which have disregarded the facts and issued reports placing the witnesses and the company in an unfavorable position.

In view of the increasingly unfavorable political climate, the management of the United Oil Corporation believes that it should take a more active interest in practical politics. The management has decided that shareholders, employees, dealers, and the public should be told what is happening to the corporation in national and state legislatures. The officials believe that if the public is properly informed about the company and its problems, it can be relied upon to vote for legislators who will act in the best interests of the corporation, the communities where it operates, and the nation.

The executive committee has approved of the appointment of a public affairs director to be attached to the public relations department and responsible to the public relations manager of the corporation. The functions of the public affairs director include the preparation of a political action program for the corporation, the co-ordination of company political activities, and development of a political education program for employees. In the development and administration of the political action program, the public affairs director will be advised by the legal counsel of the corporation. Execution of the program in the states and communities where the company operates will be delegated to division and local plant managers assisted by local public affairs officers in those areas where the company has principal plants.

The decision of the executive committee to involve the company actively in politics is inspired by the conviction that the efficiency of government, government regulations, the tax burden, and labor and welfare legislation are important factors in the profitable operation of the business; and that political training and participation by employees in government affairs equips them to cope more effectively with increasing corporation-government relations problems.

Furthermore, the executive committee believes that the corporation should seek grass-roots political support for company-endorsed positions and that by taking a public position on political matters the company will be favorably regarded by a large segment of the public.

National Political Action Program

The public affairs director has been asked to submit a political action program for the corporation to the executive committee. After studying the political programs of other corporations, the public affairs director has developed a program for national, local, and state political action. For national political action, the public affairs director proposes the establishment of a public affairs office in Washington, D.C. This office would be headed by a registered, legislative representative or lobbyist experienced in dealing with Congressmen and federal agencies. The staff of the Washington office would include a political analyst to gather facts of special interest to the corporation about the activities of the federal government, report on Congressional investigations, the progress of legislation, proposed legislation, and developments in executive departments and administrative agencies. He would also maintain records of the votes of legislators on legislation affecting the company.

The task of the Washington legislative representative would be to communicate with members of Congress and federal agencies concerned with the oil industry regarding the company's position on proposed legislation, inform legislators about the economic importance of the corporation and co-operate with legislators in the formulation of constructive legislation affecting the company.

Community Political Action

To build grass-roots support for corporation positions in the states and communities where the company operates, the public affairs director proposes that political action programs be developed at two levels—the community, city, or county level and the state level. The community political action program would focus on community government problems and legislation. This program would involve the personal participation and leadership of local plant managers with the assistance of a public affairs officer in the large plants and a local committee for political action composed of local management executives. The local committee would identify the community government problem areas in need of improvement, gather information on the problems, meet with lawmakers, secure the co-operation of community groups, and conduct publicity campaigns to improve the political climate.

State Political Action

The state political action program would be concerned with state legislation, government administration, and politics and would involve the personal participation of the division manager and a state committee of United Oil Corporation executives. In states where the corporation has extensive interests, a legislative agent or lobbyist would be employed to communicate with state officials and legislators. Advertising, seeking support of voters for the company's position on important state legislation and government administration, would be placed by the public relations department of the corporation in newspapers read throughout the state. A state-wide publicity campaign would supplement the newspaper advertising. An investigation of state political and governmental problem areas would be made by the state political action committee to identify the problems and determine the underlying causes.

Employee Political Education

To be conducted concurrently with the corporation's national, state, and local political action programs, an employee political education program is recommended by the public affairs director for the 10,000 employees of the corporation. The objective of this nonpartisan program is to interest United Oil employees in becoming active in the political party of their choice and better informed about government, political processes, and issues.

The employees of each plant would be asked to form an informal, nonpartisan, and voluntary Good Government Committee for political self-education. Each committee would be strictly nonpartisan; all political beliefs would be represented; the committee would not act as an instrument or spokesman of management; and its sole concern would be to arouse political interest among employees.

Each plant's Good Government Committee would develop an educational program to inform employees about the structure and functions of local and state government through discussing such subjects as city and state taxes and budgets, political party platforms and organization, campaign issues, and community problems such as parking, schools, and welfare.

Each committee would organize one or more discussion groups of 25 employees in each plant. For each discussion meeting one member of the Good Government Committee would serve as moderator of the discussion and make a short, formal presentation of the particular topic to be discussed. Following the presentation by the moderator, the balance of the one and one-half hour period would be devoted to round-table discussion of the topic, following which no attempt would be made to arrive at conclusions. The objective of the discussion would be impartial, informal talk without political bias.

As members of the Good Government Committees would have only a superficial knowledge of state and local governments, the corporation would retain the services of a political science teacher from a nearby university. He would conduct a series of lectures and discussions on local and state government with members of the local Good Government Committee and be responsible for technical guidance and development of discussion outlines and reference materials for the discussion groups.

To keep company employees informed about the Good Government Committee's activities and to present the topic to be discussed at the next meeting, a bulletin would be published by the committee and mailed to the homes of all participating employees who are notified of the date and hour of the meeting which is held on company time.

Following each discussion meeting, the committee would evaluate the discussion by sending questionnaires to employees attending and by informal comments made by participants.

When local government topics are discussed, the program would be explained to local government officials in advance of the meeting so there will be no misunderstanding of objectives. Municipal officials would be invited to attend and participate in the discussion to avoid possible misinterpretation by local officials that the company was critical of the local government.

When the political action program was submitted to the executive committee by the director of public affairs, several members of the committee questioned the propriety and desirability of the corporation becoming so embroiled in political issues. One member of top management expressed doubt that the corporation should adopt positions, as a corporation, on public issues without a vote of the stockholders. He maintained that businessmen would be more influential in politics if they spoke as citizens rather than representatives of corporations.

Another member of the committee argued that the corporation is a legal, not a personal, entity and has no right to political opinions. He maintained that corporate political action will antagonize the public and lose the corporation customers. The cost of such a program would be considerable and management does not have the time to devote to political work. The corporation would be faced with the problem of paying salaries of employees who are absent serving in city council or state legislature. The management of the corporation has no experience in politics and is likely to make mistakes that will give the company a bad image. A political education program will be regarded by employees as a way to avoid work or an opportunity to learn a few political facts on company time. Union leaders would accuse the corporation of influencing the votes of employees and dominating local government through political pressure.

In view of these objections to the proposed political action program submitted by the director of public affairs, the executive committee of United Oil Corporation decided to give further consideration to the proposal before committing the corporation to active participation in politics.

QUESTIONS

1. Should the executive committee of the United Oil Corporation accept the political action program proposed by the director of public affairs of the corporation? Give specific reasons for accepting or rejecting the proposal.

2. If you do not favor the program as submitted, propose a better corporate political action program for United Oil Corporation.

3. Is the organization established for government relations and political action satisfactory? If not, how should the corporation organize for political action?

4. Is the plan proposed for employee political education sound? Give reasons for favoring this plan or propose a better plan.

ted by the director of public affairs, the executive committee of United Oil Corporation decided to give further consideration to the proposal before committing the corporation to active participation in politics.

QUESTIONS

1. Should the executive committee of the United Oil Corporation accept the political action program proposed by the director of public affairs of the corporation? Give specific reasons for accepting or rejecting the proposal.

2. If you do not favor the program as submitted, propose a better corporate political action program for United Oil Corporation.

3. Is the organization established for government relations and political action satisfactory? If not, how should the corporation organize for political action?

4. Is the plan proposed for employee political education sound? Give reasons for favoring this plan or propose a better plan.

PUBLIC RELATIONS OF NONPROFIT AND SOCIAL WELFARE ORGANIZATIONS, BUSINESS AND PROFESSIONAL ASSOCIATIONS, THE ARMED FORCES, AND OTHER INSTITUTIONS

SECTION 3 •

NONPROFIT, social welfare organizations, business and professional associations are confronted with public relations problems which differ in many respects from those of profit-making enterprises. A substantial part of the work of nonprofit organizations is carried on by unpaid volunteers, often lacking in training and experience. As a result, public opinion is sometimes critical of these volunteer personnel and their performance, and the image of the organization suffers. To attract and retain the services of volunteers, a favorable public opinion of the organization must be developed.

The funds of nonprofit organizations are usually raised by voluntary contributions of many people and public confidence and support, acquired through public relations programs, is essential in meeting the financial needs of these organizations.

The principal objective of nonprofit organizations is public service and a continuous campaign of interpretation of their activities is essential to convince the public of the worth of their services. Furthermore, the services of many organizations are of an intangible nature and vary in quality with the caliber of their volunteer workers. For these reasons nonprofit organizations use public relations to secure new members, volunteer workers, contributors, and public support as described in the chapters in this section.

The Armed Forces of the United States recognize the importance of public relations and make extensive use of both internal and external programs to gain the support of the military and citizenry in the defense of the nation.

CHAPTER 14 · SOCIAL WELFARE ORGANIZATION PUBLIC RELATIONS

SOCIAL WELFARE organizations, which include social, charitable, religious, and educational groups, have particular public relations problems not common to industrial and commercial organizations. Because the primary objective of social welfare organizations is service to society, their activities are continuously subject to public attention. Accordingly, a clear and complete understanding by the public of the objectives, motives, and acts of social organizations is essential to their effective operation. Such public understanding can only be gained through sound public relations.

Social organizations differ from profit producing private enterprises in that they are dependent upon the public for contributions or membership fees from which supporters expect little or no tangible return.

A substantial portion of the work of nonprofit organizations is carried on by unpaid volunteers who give part-time service. To obtain the services of volunteer workers, a social organization must have good public relations. Because volunteer workers may be deficient in training, skill, and judgment, public opinion is sometimes critical of the personnel and accomplishments of some nonprofit organizations.

The services of nonprofit organizations are usually intangible in character, and a continuous campaign of interpretation and explanation is essential to keep the public convinced of the value of their activities. For these reasons, public relations is essential in securing new members, in maintaining the interest of present members, and gaining financial support to carry on their activities.

There are some 450 voluntary, national, social, welfare associations in the United States and Canada. Included in this group are such organizations as: the American National Red Cross, with more than 20,000,-000 senior and junior members, 3,730 chapters, and 4,184 branches;

the American Legion, with more than 2,700,000 members and 17,000 local posts; the Boy Scouts of America, with 2,900,000 members and 81,000 troops; the Girl Scouts, with nearly 1,500,000 members; the Young Men's Christian Association, with 1,715 locals and nearly 2,000,000 members; the Salvation Army, with a world-wide network of 17,000 corps; Community Funds and Councils of America, representing 2,100 fund organizations; and many other volunteer social welfare organizations.

More than 4,000 foundations, nongovernmental, nonprofit organizations have been established in this country by the wealthy to serve the public welfare. Five foundations—the Rockefeller Foundation, Ford Foundation, the Duke Endowment, the Carnegie Corporation of New York, and the Pew Memorial Foundation—each have assets in excess of $100 million. There are 350 foundations in the country with assets amounting to $10 million or more.

Religious welfare organizations have similar public relations responsibilities. The principal spiritual organizations in the United States are: the American Bible Society; National Council of the Churches of Christ in the U.S.A.; National Catholic Welfare Conference; in addition to 294,000 churches of all faiths with more than 95 million members. Hospitals and organizations for combating various forms of disease have important public relations responsibilities.

Growth of Social Welfare Public Relations

The growing interest of the public in social welfare, and the increasing membership of all types of welfare organizations have compelled the managements of these organizations to recognize the importance of public relations as an administrative function.

An increasing amount of public relations activity is being carried on by welfare organizations to inform and secure the support of present and potential contributors and members, and the general public. Numerous channels of communication are being used including newspapers, radio and television, publications, speeches, conferences, and exhibits to communicate with the public.

The National Publicity Council for Health and Welfare Services, composed of 2,000 social service organizations, is serving effectively as a clearinghouse for ideas and information on publicity and public relations for governmental and voluntary social and health agencies. The Council publishes a bulletin, a packet service of publicity examples, and a consultation and critical editorial service for member agencies.

Planning a Welfare Organization Public Relations Program

In planning a social welfare public relations program, the following steps should be taken: establish an organization, determine objectives and policy, conduct opinion research, choose media of communication, prepare communications, and appraise effectiveness of the program.

Organization for Public Relations in a Social Welfare Organization

The administrative staff for public relations in social welfare organizations varies in number and function with the size, scope, and objectives of the organization. In small organizations, public relations is a part-time responsibility of the executive secretary or his staff assistant. In large organizations, a public relations director with a staff of specialists handles public relations activities.

The public relations director of a social welfare organization should be placed at the policy-making level responsible directly to the head of the organization. The public relations director of the Boy Scouts of America functions as a member of management, attending all board meetings, participating in committee meetings, and serving as a member of the faculty of the national training school.

Public relations counselors and specialists who may be members of an organization frequently volunteer their services and advise the management on public relations. A public relations committee composed of members experienced in public relations volunteers to give supervision to the public relations program.

When fund raising is a major objective of a welfare organization, specialized personnel experienced in fund raising are attached to the headquarters staff to conduct a campaign for funds with the assistance of volunteer workers.

Community Organization

National public relations programs of social welfare organizations are usually supplemented by local public relations programs conducted in individual communities by local chapters, councils, or branches of the national organization. A volunteer public relations committee of the local unit is responsible for developing and executing a program to publicize the local activities of the organization. This committee consists of a general chairman, a member relations chairman, community relations chairman, and publicity chairman. The member relations chairman is responsible for communication with local volunteers of the organization; the community relations chairman seeks community support by working with community organizations and their leaders; and the publicity chairman communicates with the general public in the area through such publicity media as newspapers, radio and television, broadcasts, public speaking, exhibits, displays, and other media.

Policy for Social Welfare Public Relations

The governing board of a social welfare organization determines its public relations policy. The public relations director should be a member of this board, attend all of its meetings, and participate in formation of public relations policy.

The public relations policy of the Boy Scouts of America states:

The objectives of the Boy Scouts of America is to train boys to become good citizens while extending to these boys the fun, romance, and adventure they naturally seek. To attain this objective, boys must want to become scouts; institutions must want to sponsor units; men must want to give of their time as volunteer leaders; and communities must want to support the Boy Scout movement financially. For that to happen, the understanding and good will of all concerned must be obtained. This good will is obtained through having good public relations.

Public Relations Objectives of Social Welfare Organizations

The principal objectives of the public relations programs of social welfare organizations are: to increase membership in the organization; to interpret the objectives, practices, policies, and accomplishments of the organization to the public; to determine the attitudes of the public toward a welfare organization and its program; to aid in fund raising; to correct misconceptions and answer criticism directed at an organization and its policies and practices; to secure legislative support for the measures endorsed by an organization; to educate members of an organization to understand its services and participate in its activities; to aid individual members to carry on effective public relations programs in their communities; to recruit voluntary workers; to improve internal staff relations.

Opinion Research for a Social Welfare Organization

In developing a public relations program for a welfare organization, it is essential to know what the public thinks of the organization, its objectives, services, practices, policies, and personnel.

Professional opinion research specialists volunteer to conduct opinion polls for welfare organizations. Surveys of public attitudes may be made by mail, personal interviews, telephone calls, forum discussions, and informal conversations. Survey methods described in Chapter 18, "Public Relations Research and Evaluation," are used to determine public attitudes and evaluate the effectiveness of public relations programs.

Internal Relations of Social Welfare Organizations

Public relations of social welfare organizations begin with the inside staff, board of governors, administration, and membership. The people connected with an organization must understand its objectives and appreciate its accomplishments so that their knowledge may be communicated to their relatives, friends, and the general public.

Internal education of staff and membership about the activities of the organization is necessary to make everyone connected with the organization an enthusiastic and well-informed communicator of its accomplishments. This training should be planned and conducted by the public relations staff with the co-operation of the executive heads of the various departments.

One large social welfare organization keeps its local organizations informed of its activities through periodic conferences held by four area public information offices with the public information representatives of its community units.

MEDIA OF COMMUNICATION

Media of communication used in a social welfare public relations program to inform the organization's personnel and membership as well as the outside public about its objectives, policies, practices, and services may be classified as: internal, to inform members and obtain their co-operation in communicating with the public; and external, to inform the general public.

Internal Media of Communication

The principal media of internal communication used in informing the personnel and members of an organization are: public relations handbook, public relations report, organization publication, public relations kits, reprints of publicity, and radio and television scripts.

Public Relations Handbook. Welfare organizations' public relations departments prepare public relations handbooks for use by local units of the national organization in planning and carrying out effective community programs.

A public relations handbook for the guidance of local public relations committees in preparing a community relations program covers the following topics: understanding public relations; the local committee on public relations, its personnel and operations; general principles of public relations' national and local relationships; special events; newspapers, photographs; radio and television; motion pictures; and public relations policy.

Public Relations Reports to Members. To inform organization personnel and members about public relations activities, annual and special public relations reports are published.

Organization Publication. An employee publication is a desirable medium for explaining public relations programs and objectives to personnel and members.

Public Relations Kits. Public relations staffs of national organizations prepare kits to aid public relations committees of local units in conducting community public relations programs. Public relations kits contain press releases, radio scripts, copies of letters, radio spot announcements, manuscripts for public speeches, publicity pointers for working with the press and radio, newspaper fillers, and lists of literature available from headquarters' public relations.

Reprints of Publicity. Publicity reprints which have appeared in newspapers and magazines are distributed to local groups by national public relations offices to keep local publicity committees informed about the organization's national publicity.

Radio and Television Scripts. Radio and television broadcasts reach a larger audience simultaneously than any other channel of mass communication. The headquarters' public relations offices of social welfare organizations produce and distribute to local units scripts, tapes, and motion pictures for local radio and television broadcasts.

External Communication Media

The principal media used by welfare organizations in communicating with the general public are: press publicity; motion pictures; radio and television broadcasts; publications; public speaking; displays and exhibits; conferences; periodical advertising; outdoor advertising; booklets, folders, and printed matter; and open houses.

Press Publicity. Publicity in newspapers, magazines, radio and television is the major medium of welfare organization public relations programs. Publicity consists of spot news stories, feature articles, society stories, and editorials describing an organization's activities, personalties, accomplishments, and contributions to the public welfare on both the national and local level.

Headquarters public relations' offices release publicity direct to national magazines, news syndicates, wire and feature services, covering the nation-wide activities of an organization.

Motion Pictures. Motion pictures are playing an increasingly important role in the public relations programs of national social welfare organizations. Production of nontheatrical films is handled by organization national public relations offices which distribute them to local units. Showings are arranged by local public relations committees to luncheon clubs, school assemblies, women's clubs, and local commercial theaters. Short theatrical films of national organizations are also shown as trailers to newsreels in commercial theaters.

Radio and Television Broadcasts. Every national welfare organization's public relations program includes radio and television broadcasting. Headquarters' public relations staffs produce recorded programs which are distributed to radio and television stations. These programs are written by national public relations staff members and often feature top-flight professional talent who donate their services. Corporations also allocate time for social welfare presentations on their radio and television broadcasts.

Publications. Some social welfare organizations publish a magazine to inform the public about the current programs of the organization, fund-raising campaigns, and other activities.

Public Speaking. Speeches by executives and members of welfare organizations are a major channel of communication with the general public. Some organizations have established speakers' bureaus to recruit volunteer speakers to discuss the aims and accomplishments of the organization with professional groups, civic clubs, women's organizations, and social, religious, fraternal, and educational bodies.

Displays and Exhibits. Welfare organizations arrange displays, exhibits, and demonstrations in display windows, theater lobbies, office building lobbies, banks, railway and bus terminals. These exhibits use color, light, motion, and human interest to attract attention and tell an organization's story.

Conferences. Conferences and conventions on a national as well as a local level are a medium of internal and external communication. Meetings are used to inform members about the objectives of an organization so that they can carry the organization story to the general public.

Periodical Advertising. Social welfare organizations receive substantial contributions of space, time, talent, and services from advertisers, advertising agencies, and media. The Advertising Council, nonprofit organization of the advertising industry prepares and publishes complete advertising campaigns for social welfare projects with individual advertisers and media contributing time and space.

Outdoor Advertising. Outdoor advertising which is seen daily by millions of people traveling on the streets and highways is a powerful medium of communication for welfare organizations. The Outdoor Advertising Association, composed of some 1,200 poster-plant operators, has contributed outdoor poster space and service to the American

FIG. 14–1. Girl Scouts of the U.S.A. fiftieth anniversary Heritage Trail project took 72 Girl Scouts and Guides 16,000 miles through 40 states to acquaint them with the cultural, geographic, and human resources of the nation.

National Red Cross, Salvation Army, Community Chests, and other social service groups, in addition to campaigns for U.S. Savings Bonds, Crusade for Freedom, accident and forest fire prevention, and religion.

Booklets, Folders, and Printed Matter. An important medium of communication of welfare organizations is printed matter including booklets, folders, manuals, and reports distributed by national headquarters or local groups to the public.

Open Houses. One of the most effective methods of informing the public of the services of a welfare organization is the open house which provides the people in a community with an opportunity to inspect facilities and see at firsthand an organization's contributions to the public welfare. Special exhibits and demonstrations arranged by members increase the effectiveness of an open house.

TYPICAL SOCIAL WELFARE ORGANIZATION PUBLIC RELATIONS PROGRAMS

American Foundation for the Blind

The American Foundation for the Blind, a nonprofit, educational organization was established in 1923 to help the blind to use their capacities for a normal, social, cultural, and economic life. It surveys needs of the blind; sponsors institutes for teachers of the blind; produces talking books; conducts research on blindness; informs the public on the subject of blindness; and proposes legislation affecting the blind.

A public information department, currently with a staff of seven, was established at headquarters in New York City in 1952. The Foundation has initiated national radio and television program competitions on work for the blind with more than 60 universities preparing documentary and dramatic half-hour radio and television programs which have given the Foundation $5 million worth of free broadcast time a year. Seven series of radio programs in addition to 101 radio spots are distributed annually to 5,000 radio stations. Such network television programs as "Playhouse 90," "Wide, Wide World," and "Biography" have broadcast programs featuring the blind in co-operation with the Foundation.

One of the most important accomplishments of the Foundation has been to further relations with some 800 national, local, government, and voluntary agencies concerned with the blind. To aid these agencies with their public relations, the Foundation has held six annual public relations conventions which have brought together hundreds of leaders in public relations work for the blind. It created the first Public Relations Code of Ethics in Work for the Blind and publishes *Tip O' The Month,* a bulletin of public relations ideas for the agencies interested in the blind. Ten years ago only 2 per cent of the agencies had planned, public relations programs. Today more than 20 per cent have one or more full or part-time public relations executives.

All daily and weekly newspapers in the country are supplied with articles and fillers about the blind. The Foundation also provides information about the blind to writers for national magazines. Films and film strips dealing with blindness are distributed to clubs and civic organizations. Six portable exhibits are shown at important meetings concerned with blindness. Internal communication within the Foundation is furthered with a periodical *The Enlightener.*

The public relations program of the Foundation has been awarded three times the "Silver Anvil" of the Public Relations Society of America for excellence in public relations. In addition, the Foundation has received awards for its public relations work from the Boy Scouts of America, Westinghouse Electric Corporation, and a number of agencies for the blind. The public relations director was named Man of the Year in Work for the Blind.

United Community Campaigns of America

United Community Campaigns of America, representing United Fund and Chest campaigns in 2,200 communities, raising funds for 34,500 national, state, and local health and welfare agencies is engaged in the largest social welfare organization public relations program in the United States. This program raises more than $500 million annually from 30 million persons for numerous community public welfare services throughout the nation. A wide variety of public relations activities are involved in this annual fund raising campaign planned by a twelve-man volunteer plan board supported by a public relations advisory committee of 75 volunteer public relations practitioners backed by a paid public relations staff. Additional assistance is given by a Radio-TV-Films committee of 71 communications volunteers and Batten, Barton, Durstine, and Osborne Advertising Agency assisted by volunteers of other leading advertising agencies.

Numerous media of communication are used to carry the United Fund campaign messages to the public. In a recent year the public relations campaign was supported with a kit of over 150 promotion items ranging from window stickers to 24 sheet posters and from lapel buttons to award trophies. In addition, television and radio kits and a magazine editor's kit were produced and distributed to broadcasters and editors.

To secure the co-operation of media, a series of meetings were held in New York City and Hollywood to bring together representatives of the broadcasting and publishing industries and Advertising Council. Media representatives were asked to contribute space and time for the program, with the result that 212 full-page advertisements were given by national magazines, and broadcasters contributed 1.7 billion network television home impressions through sports and special shows. A total of more than $15 million of time and space was contributed by national media.

Internal communication with the 3.8 million volunteer leaders and workers was effected with a Campaign Leaders National Conference at which some 400 community leaders assembled for training and discussion of the campaign. The National Broadcasting Company produced a closed-circuit television show for each community's volunteers in 60 cities across the country. At the close of the campaign, Top Honor Roll Volunteers were honored at a special awards luncheon in New York City.

Motion pictures have an important role in the public relations program. The United Community Campaigns of America produced two films, "A Town Has Two Faces" combining a logical and emotional appeal; and a theater trailer, "Hands," featuring an emotional appeal to contribute. From the film "Hands" were taken color and black and white television film spots.

Newspaper advertising was used extensively with three of the four leading weekly Sunday supplements carrying full-page advertisements. The volunteer advertising agency working with the staff of United Community Campaigns created 37 newspaper advertisements ranging in size from two-line, one-column drop-ins to full pages which were used by newspapers in carrying the United Way message to more than 100 million newspaper readers.

Four hundred seventy-five industrial magazines and 600 labor publications ran advertisements, publicity, editorials, and cartoons prepared by the public relations department of United Community Campaigns of America.

The public relations program of United Community Campaigns has won the Silver Anvil of the Public Relations Society of America for excellence.

Metropolitan Hospital Council of Nashville, Tennessee

The Metropolitan Hospital Council, Nashville, Tennessee, composed of the five major hospitals in the community, sponsored a program of community public relations to control excessive visitations to patients which imposed a burden on hospital facilities, personnel, and patients. The Council consulted the local chapter of the Public Relations Society of America which recommended the employment of a public relations counsel. This counsel proposed a public relations campaign directed to hospital staffs, opinion leaders, clergy, patients, and friends to solve the problem.

Following the adoption of a uniform visitor-control policy by the hospitals involved, an internal public relations course for hospital personnel was initiated to inform them about the visitor-control program and secure their co-operation in enforcement of the visitor policy.

A "Guide to Visitors" was published and distributed in hospital and doctors' waiting rooms and to companies administering employee group insurance programs for distribution to employees. Letters were mailed to presidents of civic clubs and social organizations requesting the co-operation of these groups in restricting hospital visitations. A speakers' bureau was organized and volunteers addressed community groups on the hospital's program. News releases were distributed to the newspapers and broadcasting stations and radio and television stations gave time for spot announcements.

A survey of the effectiveness of the program showed that patients and public endorsed the visitation control policy of providing more rest and privacy for patients. One hospital reported that the use of tranquilizers among patients declined 50 per cent.

Park City Hospital, Bridgeport, Connecticut

The Park City Hospital, Bridgeport, Connecticut, conducted a community relations program to secure public support for a volunteer group to supplement the staff of the hospital in providing service to patients. A Volunteer Advisory Committee composed of representatives of the hospital administration, nursing, medical staff, hospital personnel, public relations, and the auxiliary was formed to plan the program.

A survey was undertaken by the committee to determine the hospital's need for volunteers, the nature of the jobs available for volunteers and a policy for selecting and training volunteers was established. A manual for volunteers was prepared and the staff was informed of the role of the volunteer and the responsibilities of the staff toward volunteers.

A community relations program to recruit volunteers was initiated. A booklet describing the program was prepared and distributed and a direct-mail campaign was directed to community leaders to obtain community support and obtain 40 women volunteers. Publicity was released to all newspapers within the hospital's service area.

As a direct result of the community relations program 86 volunteers were enrolled, who contributed 1,054 work hours a month to the hospital. Forty-eight per cent of the volunteers were recruited outside the hospital family. The program was so successful that the Volunteer Advisory Committee is undertaking a male volunteer program and expects to inauguarate a teen-age program in anticipation of the hospital's expanding needs. The program was awarded the Public Relations Society of America's Silver Anvil award for excellence in the hospital category.

Case 14–1

SOCIAL WELFARE ORGANIZATION PUBLIC RELATIONS

The Salvation Army

The Salvation Army was founded by William Booth, a Methodist revivalist, in London, England, in 1865, and established in the United States, in 1880. The Salvation Army is an international religious and charitable movement organized and operated on a military pattern, a branch of the Christian church.

The motivation of the organization is love for God and a practical concern for the needs of humanity. It preaches the Gospel, disseminates Christian truths, provides personal counseling, and undertakes the spiritual, moral, and physical rehabilitation of all persons of all ages regardless of race or creed.

The Salvation Army, in 1960, functioned in 86 countries through 19,725 work centers where 27,000 officers and cadets and 29,064 employees carry on religious and charitable activities to meet the physical, emotional, and spiritual needs of mankind.

For administrative purposes, the Salvation Army in the United States is divided into four territories with headquarters in New York City, Chicago, Atlanta, and San Francisco. Each territory is the responsibility of a territorial commander assisted by a chief secretary. National headquarters in New York City co-ordinates national policy through a commissioners' conference presided over by the national commander.

Membership in this country exceeds 270,000 including 5,300 officers and cadets in 8,487 religious and service centers. The corps is the basic unit of the organization. From 20 to 30 corps comprise a division under a divisional commander responsible to the territorial commander. The Army operated, in 1960: 125 men's social service centers, 19 settlements and day nurseries, 35 maternity homes and hospitals, 55 camps for children and adults, 173 mobile canteens, and 14 Red Shield clubs. The organization is sustained primarily through voluntary public support supplemented by fees and membership contributions.

Organization for Public Relations

National public relations activities of the Salvation Army were formally organized in 1957 with the establishment of the National Information Service at national headquarters in New York City. The Service provides the 1,113 local corps and other Army institutions and centers throughout the country with materials for their local public relations, distributes information of national interest to wire services and national media about Army activities and programs, and co-operates with United Funds or Community Chests in their public relations programs. The Information Service supplies information about the Army to book and magazine writers. Its aim is to interpret the basic purposes of the Army to gain broader community understanding and support for its religious and social activities.

The staff of the National Information Service consists of a director, a full-time assistant director, and three staff members who divide their time between the National Service and supplying information to communication media in New York City.

The efforts of the National Information Service and the material it prepares are designed to supplement publicity efforts on the local level. The basic public relations program of the Salvation Army is conducted on the community level, with the territories and divisional commands developing programs and materials to meet local needs.

Each of the four territories of the Salvation Army has a public relations secretary who reports to the territorial commander. Each public relations secretary is responsible for the public relations of his territory. To co-ordinate territorial and national public relations activities, to exchange ideas, to delineate needs and explore programs, the four territorial public relations secretaries and the director of the National Information Service meet semiannually in a public relations secretaries conference. This conference, after reviewing needs, plans programs and recommends action for approval of the Commissioners' Conference.

At the local level in the 1,000 or more communities where Salvation Army Corps are located are voluntary advisory boards composed of business and professional men and women who assist the Army in its religious and charitable activities. Each advisory board appoints a local public relations committee composed of public relations professionals from advertising agencies, newspapers, radio, and television who volunteer to assist in the Army's local public relations activities. These local public relations committees survey public opinion, recruit and train speakers, supply news releases to the press, and carry out the territorial and national public relations programs of the Army.

In rural areas and cities where there are no resident Salvation Army Corps, there are 6,356 service extension units operated by the Army in co-operation with a local citizens' committee. These service extension units assist the Army in the conduct of local public relations in addition to various religious and charitable activities.

In addition to the public relations activities of local corps, advisory boards and service units, there is, in some division headquarters, a full-time public relations person.

For the guidance of the Salvation Army officers and local public relations committees in conducting local public relations programs, a 70-page *Salvation Army Manual of Publicity* has been produced. This manual, issued by authority of the Commissioners' Conference, describes general public relations; the organization and formation of the local public relations committee; news publicity including kinds of news, the empire of the press, the press conference, press relations etiquette, and how to write a press release; advertising display promotion; radio, television, and motion pictures; printed materials; and special events.

Internal communications with officers and members of the Army is effected through a variety of media. *The War Cry,* the official gazette of the Army, is published weekly by each of the four territories. It carries articles of general interest and news of the Salvation Army. More than 20 million copies are distributed annually in the United States. Two foreign-language editions of *The War Cry* are published in this country, the *Stridsropet* for Scandinavian members and *El Cruzado* in Spanish for distribution in the Southwest and Mexico. There are, in addition, Salvation Army international publications including *Vanguard, All the World,* and *The Deliverer.*

The editorial and circulation departments of each of the four territories publish *The Young Soldier* weekly for youth, *The Musician* for Army bandsmen and songsters, and *Home League Quarterly* for 60,000 members of the women's organization of the Army.

The Salvation Army Christmas Appeal

A major public relations activity of the Salvation Army is its Christmas Appeal to the public for money to provide food, clothing, and gifts to more than 1½ million needy Americans. This appeal is made by the 1,113 local corps and some service units using letters, the traditional kettles on the streets, and various forms of publicity and promotion.

To aid about 1,500 Army officers in local communities and their public relations committees in securing publicity for the Christmas Appeal, the National Information Service produces annually a Christmas Publicity Kit. This kit contains publicity releases, feature stories, editorials, posters, letters, photographs, records, newspaper mats, electros, television slides, and film spots.

To supplement local Christmas Appeal publicity, the National Information Service secures publicity in national media. Eight hundred magazines, company publications, and newspapers are offered electros of advertisements featuring the Christmas Appeal which are published by the media gratis as their contribution to the Appeal.

Television film spots and slides, featuring the Christmas Appeal, are distributed from headquarters to all television stations throughout the country. "The Army of Stars," a half-hour Christmas radio program is produced annually under the direction of the Army's Western Territory's public relations department. In addition, two quarter-hour radio programs, "Reflections of Starlight," are broadcast by 1,000 radio stations in the United States and Canada during the Christmas season. These radio programs feature well-known radio personalities who contribute their talents to the Christmas Appeal.

Salvation Army Week

To arouse public interest in the Salvation Army and to publicize its manifold services to those in need, National Salvation Army Week is an annual special event publicized by Army public relations committees in thousands of communities throughout the country.

The National Information Service produces a National Salvation Army Week publicity kit for all local public relations committees containing news stories, editorials, fact sheets, newspaper advertising mats, photographs, television spot announcements and slides, records, posters, flags, and Salvation Army Lassie and Laddie dolls. These kits are widely used in securing publicity in local newspapers, radio and television stations by local public relations committees.

To support local publicity on National Salvation Army Week, the National Information Service obtains feature articles in national magazines, supplies them with editorial material and photographs, and distributes film to television stations and records to radio stations.

Exhibits

A series of exhibits telling the story of the Salvation Army services for use in store windows, hotel lobbies, fairs, conferences, and fund meetings have been produced by the National Information Service for use by local public relations committees in communicating the Army's message to local communities.

Literature

For general public information, a series of booklets and folders describing the history, organization, objectives, and operations of the Salvation Army have been produced by the National Information Service to Army officers throughout the country for local distribution. These publications include: "What Is The Salvation Army?" "Meet The Salvation Army," "The Salvation Army In Emergencies," "The Salvation Army Social Services," "The Salvation Army and the Alcoholic," "The Salvation Army and the Armed Forces," and others.

Radio, Television, and Motion Pictures

Much radio and television time is contributed to the Salvation Army by broadcasting networks, stations, and advertisers. Many religious programs allot a portion of their time to the Army. Interviews with Army officials, appearances of Army musicians, spot announcements and films, 15- and 30-minute programs are arranged by the National Information Service in co-operation with leading radio and television stations and networks.

Broadcasting media have co-operated generously with the Salvation Army in presenting information on specific areas of Army service. A Salvation Army sponsored television program, "The Living Word," consisting of four series of 13-minute films was produced by the Army's public relations department of Canada and shown on 82 television stations.

The Salvation Army's services to unwed mothers were presented in a series of interviews on the Columbia Broadcasting System's television network. A series of three radio programs entitled, "Faith In Action," were broadcast on the National Broadcasting Company's television network, describing the Army's services to the aging. A series of four radio programs on the theme, "Eighty Years of Service," were broadcast by the National Broadcasting Company describing the history, organization, work of local corps, and the rehabilitation program of the Salvation Army.

To dramatize the help given people by the Salvation Army, a half-hour recorded radio program, "Heartbeat Theater," was broadcast on 600 radio stations in the United States and 90 overseas stations in areas where American Armed Forces are serving.

A color motion picture story of the Salvation Army School for the Blind in Kenya, Africa, titled, "Conquest of Darkness," is distributed nationally by Association Films to more than 2,500 community and school groups throughout the country as well as to television stations for broadcast to the television audience. Each territorial public relations office maintains a film library from which films are loaned to service clubs, church, fraternal, and school groups.

Service to the Press

In response to numerous requests from the editors of magazines and newspapers as well as free-lance book and magazine writers, editors of encyclopedias and reference works, photographers, and advertising agencies for information about the Salvation Army, the National Information Service provides biographical sketches, background information, obituaries, photographs, reprints, and arranges for interviews and appearances of Army officials.

QUESTIONS

1. Comment on the Salvation Army's public relations program in the United States giving specific strengths and weaknesses of the program as described in the preceding case.

2. What specific steps should be taken by the Salvation Army in the United States to improve its public relations program?

3. Is the Salvation Army organization for public relations in the United States satisfactory? What, if any, changes should be made in the public relations organization?

4. Comment on the annual Christmas Appeal public relations program of the Salvation Army. What are its strengths, its weaknesses?

5. Are the media of communication used by the Salvation Army satisfactory? What additional media, if any, should be used?

Case 14–2

SOCIAL WELFARE ORGANIZATION PUBLIC RELATIONS
Colonial Williamsburg

Colonial Williamsburg was founded by the late John D. Rockefeller, Jr., in 1926, to restore and interpret the historical area of Williamsburg, Virginia, which for 81 years, from 1699 to 1780, was the capital of the Virginia colony and an important social, cultural, and political center identified with such leaders of American independence as George Washington, Thomas Jefferson, and Patrick Henry.

The objective of Colonial Williamsburg is to re-create accurately the environment of the men and women of eighteenth century Williamsburg and to bring about an understanding of their lives and times so that present and future generations may vividly appreciate the contribution of these early Americans to the ideals and culture of the nation.

The 130-acre restored area contains more than 500 colonial buildings and 84 acres of gardens and greens. More than one-half of the major buildings are original eighteenth century structures and others have been re-constructed on the exact sites of the original foundations following archeological and historical research. The buildings include taverns and ordinaries, craft and tradesmen's shops, public buildings, private homes, and outbuildings such as kitchens and smoke houses. An estimated 250,000 pieces of ceramics, glassware, metal, and other artifacts have been excavated on the sites giving added insight into the furnishings of the times. The work of physical restoration, which is continuing, has thus far cost more than $72 million. Nearly a million visitors come to Williamsburg annually.

The corporate structure known as Colonial Williamsburg includes two corporations. Colonial Williamsburg, Incorporated, a nonstock, nonprofit corporation carries out the historical and educational purposes of the restoration and holds title to the historical properties. A second corporation, wholly owned subsidiary of Colonial Williamsburg, Inc., is Williamsburg Restoration, Incorporated, a profit-making corporation which owns, operates, or leases commercial properties outside the historic area, including Williamsburg Inn, Williamsburg Lodge, the Motor House and Cafeteria, Craft House, King's Arms Tavern, Chowning's Tavern, Christiana Campbell's Tavern, and various business properties. All earnings of Williamsburg Restoration, Inc., are devoted to furthering the educational program of Colonial Williamsburg. About 1,900 persons are employed by Colonial Williamsburg which has an annual operating budget in excess of $10 million.

Public relations of Colonial Williamsburg is the responsibility of a public relations department of 14 persons. Its objective is to service the departments of development; curator of collections; corporate relations; architecture, construction, and maintenance; interpretation; presentation; visitor accommodations; and merchandising in creating a national as well as international awareness of the nation's heritage of self-government, public service, and personal freedom as exemplified at Williamsburg.

The public relations staff is headed by a vice-president and director of public relations who is assisted by an assistant director and a director of special events. The staff includes the director of the press bureau, radio and television manager, and staff writer for women's interests. The director of special events has two staff assistants. A special writer reports directly to the vice-president and director of public relations. An administrative assistant to the director supervises the work of four secretaries, monitors the departmental budget, and performs other special duties.

The eight major functions of the public relations department are as follows:

Providing advice and counsel to the president and other administrative officers on the development and modification of policies and programs which concern Colonial Williamsburg's relations with the public and internal communications.

Preparing reviews and releasing all current information and feature publicity material for use by local, national, and international news media.

Co-operating in the production of special radio and television programs relating to Colonial Williamsburg and distributing films to television stations.

Serving as the point of contact for representatives of the press, radio, magazines, motion pictures, and television media and assisting various departments of the restoration upon request in publicizing special activities.

Performing special assignments for the president and co-ordinating the plans and arrangements of various departments for visits of foreign dignitaries and other special events.

Arranging and co-ordinating speaking engagements for Colonial Willaimsburg personnel.

Developing, in co-operation with the president and with other departments, long-range plans to enhance the importance and significance of Colonial Williamsburg's program in future years.

Co-operating with officials of the Commonwealth of Virginia, the College of William and Mary, Jamestown Festival Park, and the National Park Service to draw attention to the significance of historic Williamsburg, Jamestown, and Yorktown.

Press Relations

Press relations of Colonial Williamsburg are handled by the press Bureau of the public relations department, which is headed by a director assisted by a radio and television manager and a staff writer. The Bureau provides a wide assortment of news and feature material for newspaper and magazine education editors; women's editors of food, gardening, and home furnishing magazines and newspapers; and news editors. Many specialized publications carry articles dealing with particular aspects of the restoration.

In its relations with news media, the Press Bureau emphasizes high-quality material based on authentic research presented in crisp, professional style in news releases and feature articles. In addition to routine production of news and feature materials, the Press Bureau co-operates with press, radio, and television representatives in covering special events or seeking their own material in Williamsburg.

One member of the Press Bureau staff maintains liaison with radio and television representatives. The radio and television manager books showings of Colonial Williamsburg films with stations throughout the United States and Canada and for overseas showings by the United States Information Service. Special radio and television scripts, providing still picture support or short pieces of motion-picture film, as appropriate, are also provided by the radio-television manager.

The Press Bureau staff maintains liaison with about 800 representatives of magazines, newspapers, radio, and television stations who visit Williamsburg each year. Press passes to visit exhibition buildings are provided to visiting press representatives. The Press Bureau staff also makes periodic visits to principal cities to call on media personnel. Twenty-five hundred copies of the president's annual report describing operations in Colonial Williamsburg are mailed to important editors, writers, and commentators to keep them informed about developments in Williamsburg.

Educational Relations

Colonial Williamsburg is engaged in extensive educational activities for students and teachers of public and private schools and colleges, as well as the general public. Daily presentations of eighteenth-century history and culture include a 45-minute orientation film in specially designed twin theaters, guided tours, and on-the-spot interpreters. Evening lectures, craft shop tours, candlelight concerts at the Governor's Palace, colonial games, eighteenth-century plays, bowling on the green, militia musters, and other activities interpret colonial life.

Other education projects include publication of books, pamphlets, and leaflets on colonial life and times; production of historical documentary motion pictures; slide sets with commentary, and film strips for school use; co-ordination of school tours with classroom study; sponsorship of events in the Williamsburg Forum Series such as the Antiques Forum, International Assembly, Student Burgesses, and Garden Symposium; and joint sponsorship with the College of William and Mary of workshops, courses and seminars on colonial life, culture, and architecture. Colonial Williamsburg library and files are open to students and research workers. The restoration also sponsors jointly with the College of William and Mary at Williamsburg, the Institute of Early American History and Culture devoted to research and publication in early American history.

The 1961, Williamsburg Student Burgesses, an annual event sponsored by Colonial Williamsburg, brought 88 high school seniors from 47 states and 22 countries to Williamsburg for a three-day forum on the problems of the democratic world. The 1961 meeting of the Williamsburg International Assembly,

FIG. 14–2. The public relations department, Colonial Williamsburg, is responsible for arrangements for visits of foreign dignitaries. King Baudouin of Belgium is presented with a silver brandy pipkin by William de Matteo, Williamsburg's master silversmith, while Winthrop Rockefeller looks on.

an annual event, attracted 58 outstanding graduate students from 42 countries for a three-day meeting to discuss, "The American Cultural Scene: Roots and Realities."

Special Events

An important part of Williamsburg's public relations program is concerned with publicity for a series of annual special events of historical significance.

A typical special event is the "Prelude to Independence" in the Williamsburg Forum Series, an annual commemoration of the 50-day period from May 15 to July 4, 1776, a time of great constitutional activity during which many of the principles of American democracy were established. The featured speaker of the 1961 "Prelude to Independence" was Dr. Charles Malik of Lebanon, former president of the United Nations General Assembly. Speakers at this event in other years were the late John Foster Dulles, the late Dag Hammarskjöld, Arnold J. Toynbee, and Dean Acheson.

Press coverage of this event was initiated 60 days in advance with a news release to 185 major newspapers, the wire services, and all dailies and weeklies in Virginia, Maryland, North Carolina, and the District of Columbia. Thirty days later a second news release giving more details of the event, a picture, and biographical sketch of the speaker, was distributed to the press. Ten days before the event, a "Memorandum to the Press" was sent out to all dailies, weeklies, wire services, Washington correspondents, newsreel companies, radio and television stations in Virginia, Maryland, North Carolina, and the District of Columbia. A final release was distributed to the press of Norfolk, Richmond, Newport News, and Washington for release the morning of the meeting and an advance copy of the address was delivered to the Washington offices of correspondents of leading dailies.

As a result this event was given extensive publicity in the *Readers Digest*, *U.S. News and World Report*, Scripps-Howard newspapers, *Christian Science Monitor*, *Richmond News-Leader*, *Roanoke World-News*, *Charlotte Observer*, and others.

Other special events of Colonial Williamsburg were publicized by the Press Bureau during 1961. The biennial commemorative sessions of the Virginia General Assembly were held in the Hall of the House of Burgesses at the eighteenth-century Capitol. The 353rd Anniversary of the establishment of the first permanent English colony in America at Jamestown was celebrated at Colonial Williamsburg. The Society of American Travel Writers met in Williamsburg for four days. The annual Associated Press Managing Editors meeting and the National Conference of Editorial Writers brought 500 press executives to restored Williamsburg.

QUESTIONS

1. Comment on the public relations program of Colonial Williamsburg, giving specific strengths and weaknesses of this program.
2. What specific suggestions can you make for improving Colonial Williamsburg's public relations program?
3. Is the public relations organization of Colonial Williamsburg satisfactory? What changes, if any, should be made in this organization?
4. Comment on the press relations of Colonial Williamsburg. In what specific ways can these press relations be improved?

CHAPTER

15 ·

BUSINESS AND
PROFESSIONAL
ASSOCIATION RELATIONS

PUBLIC RELATIONS is a major function of the more than 11,000 industrial and commercial and 500 professional associations in the United States. The original objective of most business associations was to defend their industries against attacks by labor, government, and competitors and to present a united front to opposition which threatened to undermine profits or disturb traditional practices. Associations, next, broadened their functions in order to help their members increase productivity, lower costs, improve quality, standardize operations, advance technical research, educate personnel, and exploit markets. Today, associations are involved in public relations for improving the public image of their industries, interpreting industry accomplishments to the public, and aiding members in improving their public relationships.

Association public relations programs are designed not only to inform the general consuming public but also federal, state, and local governments, as well as teachers and students in public and private elementary and secondary schools, colleges and universities. Association public relations programs are also used to inform the member companies and their personnel about the industry and its accomplishments.

Typical of the 11,000 voluntary, nonprofit business associations in the United States are: Association of American Railroads, American Trucking Association, National Association of Manufacturers, United States Brewers' Association, and National Safety Council in addition to 7,500 local, 600 regional, and 2,000 state associations.

All of the leading professions have national, state, and local organizations which, similar to industrial and commercial associations, carry on some form of public relations activity to inform the public and create a favorable image for the profession. Typical professional associations are: American Medical Association, National Educational Association,

344

American Bar Association, American Dental Association, and American Association for the Advancement of Science.

PUBLIC RELATIONS OBJECTIVES OF BUSINESS AND PROFESSIONAL ASSOCIATIONS

Business and professional associations have a variety of public relations objectives including:

To provide information about an industry's production, orders, shipments, sales, inventories, commodity prices, exports, imports, employment trends, taxes, plants, services, earnings, operations, expenses, developments, and problems.

To conduct opinion research to determine the public's attitudes toward an industry or profession, its products, or services.

To carry on government relations and legislative research, including reports for government agencies, reporting to members on proposed laws and the activities of government agencies, representing the industry or profession before legislative bodies, drafting model laws, co-operating with government statistical and technical bureaus, and making taxation studies.

To educate the public about an industry or profession and its contributions to the public welfare.

To provide information to industrial and commercial members on employer-employee relations by collecting and disseminating information on employee benefits, accident prevention, labor relations, collective bargaining, and employee communications.

To carry on a dealer and distributor relations program to improve an industry's relations with its trade through retail sales training courses, accounting service, store improvement service, stock control systems, and personnel recruiting and selection.

To provide educators and students with information about an industry or profession.

To furnish a public relations service to association members on employee and community relations activities.

To prepare publicity articles, press releases, and provide information to authors and editors about industry activities.

To stage exhibitions of industry products to dramatize the progress of an industry and its contributions to the public welfare.

Advantages of Association Public Relations

Association public relations programs have several advantages compared with the programs of individual companies. An association budget for public relations is usually larger and an association program can make a greater impact on general public opinion than the activities of a single company. The experience of the public relations directors of member companies are combined in planning and advising on the public relations activities of associations, thus insuring more effective programs. Association public relations programs are mainly concentrated on consumer, government, and educational relations; whereas individual companies are obliged to diversify their public relations activities and funds in developing the good will of several publics including employees, shareholders, plant communities, suppliers, distributors, and dealers. An association public relations program may enjoy more prestige with the public than the program of a small company. A more experienced and competent staff of specialists may be employed by an association than by a small company. A national association with a Washington office, staffed with specialists experienced in federal government relations and supported by the entire industry can exert greater influence on federal legislation and agencies than an individual company.

On the other hand, large corporations are in position to derive more benefit from association public relations activities than small companies. Association programs may not directly improve the public image of an individual company. An association program may duplicate the public relations activities of a company. A member of an association may exert little influence on the objectives and content of an association program.

CONDUCTING BUSINESS AND PROFESSIONAL ASSOCIATION PUBLIC RELATIONS PROGRAMS

Organization of Association Public Relations

National, regional, and local associations have public relations staffs headed by a public relations director reporting to the executive secretary or manager of the association. In small associations one person handles all public relations but an extensive staff is employed in the large organizations. The public relations managers of regional and local groups attached to a national organization work closely with the public relations staff of the national association.

Public relations executives of member companies are actively identified with the public relations programs of many associations. The program of an association is usually directed by a public relations committee composed of the public relations directors of member companies. This committee meets with the association manager, public relations director, and staff to plan the association public relations program. National associations with affiliated regional groups are assisted in planning public relations by an advisory committee composed of the managers or public relations executives of regional associations. Traveling field public relations representatives are employed by some national associations to aid member companies with their public relations programs.

A national association public relations staff is usually advised by a public relations counsel or advertising agency which may assume some of the functions of the public relations director and association staff.

Planning an Association Program

The public relations program of an association may be logically divided into two parts: the internal program, involving relations with members and employees of the association; and the external program, directed to the general public outside the industry or profession. The two programs, carried on simultaneously, are interdependent—good external relations depend on good internal relations, and vice versa.

The five principal steps in conducting a program of association internal and external relations are: organizing and financing public relations; conducting opinion research; establishing association policies and objectives; selecting methods of communication; and carrying out the program.

Organization and Financing. When a public relations director and staff has been employed, an adequate public relations appropriation or budget must be provided. Funds for public relations may be raised either by special assessment or from regular dues paid by the members. In some associations a special public relations fund is raised in addition to the customary membership dues. The public relations budgets of some industrial associations are raised by an assessment of members of a certain number of cents per unit of production or per dollar sales.

Conducting Opinion Research. The objectives of an association public relations program should be determined by opinion research of members and staff in addition to consumers, neighbors, and educators. Opinion surveys are usually undertaken by a national opinion research organization working with the public relations department of the association, using the methods described in Chapter 28.

The Association of American Railroads retains the Opinion Research Corporation to make an annual national survey of public opinion of the railroads. A representative group of 2,500 persons is asked basic questions concerning the operation of the railroads. In addition, the association makes a continuing analysis of editorial comment to provide a constant record of what is being said about the railroads in the press.

Establishing Sound Policies and Objectives. The policies and practices of an industry or profession must meet the approval of the public. Objectionable policies should be corrected if the industry's public relations program is to be effective. Policies should be established by agreement of the members of the industry along with fair-practice codes to eliminate unethical practices.

Selecting Methods of Communication.   To inform and educate the public and correct misconceptions about an industry or profession, the following media are used: newspaper and magazine advertising, press releases, radio, television, motion pictures, displays, posters, and exhibitions.

Carrying Out the Program.   The effectiveness of an association program depends on close co-operation and teamwork between the national association, regional and local groups, and individual members. It is essential to gain the support of the association membership in supplementing a national program with local tie-in campaigns to employees, neighbors, and consumers. Members of an association must be kept fully informed about the industry public relations program and their role in its effectiveness.

MEDIA OF COMMUNICATION IN ASSOCIATION PUBLIC RELATIONS

The media of association public relations communication are classified as: internal—to inform members and staff and to gain their co-operation in communicating the industry's or profession's accomplishments to the public; external—to inform the general public, government officials, and educators about contributions of the industry or profession to the public welfare. Both types of communication are used in a comprehensive association public relations campaign.

Communication with Association Members and Staff

The internal media for informing members of an association and staff about its public relations program are: association publications; business and professional magazine advertising and publicity; direct-mail messages; community public relations plans for member companies and their employees; personal contacts with members by public relations staff representatives.

Association Publications.   The most valuable and economical method of informing association members about an association's public relations program and gaining the co-operation of members and regional and local groups in carrying on public relations activities on the community level is an association magazine.

Business and Professional Magazines.   The business or professional magazines published for an industry or profession are an important medium to inform members about the accomplishments of the industry and to make them aware of the need for better public relations. Reproductions of association institutional advertisements, speeches by association executives, and articles about the industry should be placed in industry or professional magazines.

Direct Mail.   Mailing cards, broadsides, booklets, and letters describing the public relations program and mailed to members are valuable means of communication.

Community Relations for Member Companies and Their Employees. Employee and plant community public relations programs for use by association members in informing employees and communities about the industry are a feature of many association public relations campaigns. Association members are supplied with materials to inform the community public about the industry or profession.

Personal Contacts by Association Public Relations Staff.   Personal contacts by members of the national public relations staff with the public relations directors of member companies are the most effective way to gain their co-operation in carrying on public relations activities in plant communities.

Association Communications with the External Public

Media of communications used by associations in informing the external public, government officials, and educators include: association periodical advertising; press publicity; motion pictures; radio and television broadcasts; public speeches and forums; booklets and folders; educational materials; special events; displays and exhibits; and periodicals.

Association Periodical Advertising.   Periodical advertising should be used to tell the story of an industry or profession to the public to gain public confidence and cause the public to purchase the industry's products or services. Additional objectives of association periodical advertising are to dispel wrong impressions about the industry, to meet competition from other industries, and to render a public service.

Press Publicity.   National trade associations universally prepare press releases, hold press conferences, prepare background material on the industry, collect news photographs, and supply editors, radio commentators, writers, and reporters with information, copy, photos, mats, layouts, and ideas for articles featuring the industry or profession in newspapers and magazines.

Motion Pictures.   Motion pictures are used extensively in association public relations. They are produced for the following reasons: to show the contributions of an industry to the public welfare; to inform consumers about an industry's products; to correct misinformation and wrong impressions; to prevent the enactment of discriminatory legislation; to educate youth about a business; and to create a more favorable public attitude toward an industry or profession.

The Association of American Railroads' public relations films, "Mainline—U.S.A." and "Big Trains Rolling" are shown to more than two million persons annually.

Radio and Television Broadcasts. Network television and radio time is purchased by associations to communicate with the public. Stations also make free time available to associations on sustaining, public service, or educational programs. Associations have produced films which are shown by members on local television broadcasts.

Radio and television programs used by associations include speeches by industry leaders, spot announcements, sponsored entertainment programs, interviews with prominent industrial executives, round-table or panel discussions, and news broadcasts. Associations also release news publicity to radio and television news commentators.

Public Speeches and Forums. Speakers' bureaus are organized by associations to bring the story of an industry or profession and its accomplishments to the public. Association executives and officials of member companies speak to national organizations as well as to civic clubs, women's clubs, and school, college, and professional societies. Speeches, speech outlines, background materials, and visual aids for speakers are prepared by the public relations staffs of associations.

Booklets and Folders. Booklets and folders are published and distributed by associations to the public to interest young men and women in careers in the industry or profession; to describe the accomplishments of an industry and its contributions to the public welfare; to educate employees about the industry in which they are engaged; to correct public misunderstandings; and to combat adverse legislation.

Educational Materials. Educational materials are prepared by associations for use in schools. Similar materials are prepared for women's clubs for use by discussion groups.

The woman's department of the public relations division of the National Association of Manufacturers has produced a program kit for women's clubs entitled, "Are You the Victim?" which deals with labor union abuses. It was distributed by request to 8,000 clubs and followed up with a folder, "What's New in Labor Reform?"

Special Events. Special events are sponsored by associations to attract the attention of the public and create a favorable impression of an industry. Special event subjects range from the proclamation of a national day or week by an industry to the crowning of an industry queen, exhibits, and sports events.

National Library Week is sponsored annually by the National Book Committee in co-operation with the American Library Association to encourage a better read, better informed America. State, city, and community committees of the association conduct special programs during National Library Week.

Displays and Exhibits. Associations arrange displays of industry products to attract large numbers of people and produce valuable publicity in national and local publications. National fairs are sponsored by some industrial organizations as one feature of their public relations programs.

The Association of American Railroads exhibits at the annual conventions of the National Editorial Association, Associated Traffic Clubs of America, Union Industries Show, and at the Steel Pier, Atlantic City to show the public the progressiveness of the railroad industry and its contributions to better transportation.

Association Periodicals. Leading associations publish well-edited periodicals which compete in appearance and content with national magazines.

Steelways published bimonthly by the American Iron and Steel Institute, New York, fosters a better understanding of the steel industry. It is distributed to about 70,000 opinion leaders, schools, and libraries. Many of the articles appearing in "Steelways" are reprinted in other periodicals reaching between 30 to 40 million readers. This magazine is used in 50 different courses in 70 colleges and universities.

Association Public Relations Programs

The following public relations programs of national associations illustrate the various strategies and media of communications employed by associations in informing the public about industry accomplishments and developing good will.

Institute of Life Insurance. The Institute of Life Insurance, with a membership of 166 legal reserve life insurance companies in the United States and Canada, serves as a source of information and acts in a public relations capacity for the life insurance business. It gives the public a better conception of life insurance and translates public attitudes to insurance company members.

The public relations program of the Institute is the responsibility of a staff of specialists organized in seven divisions: statistics and research; information; press bureau; women's relations; family finance; education; promotion and advertising. The statistics and research division collects data from members and publishes the *Life Insurance Fact Book* which is distributed to the press, educators, publishers, and writers. The information division provides background material and technical information about life insurance to inquirers and assists authors. The press bureau prepares and releases information bulletins to the press and the Washington bureau handles news from the nation's capital. The women's division stimulates the interest of women in life insurance through work with women's clubs. The educational division supplies schools with information about life insurance and organizes family finance workshops as described in Chapter 12. The promotion and advertising division is responsible for a co-operative advertising program in national magazines and local newspapers.

The Institute also aids individual life insurance companies to improve their public relations through addresses to life insurance meetings, seminars, and conferences with insurance executives.

National Association of Manufacturers. The National Association of Manufacturers represents some 19,000 large and small manufacturers in many industries who employ about 75 per cent of all industrial workers in the United States.

The public relations objectives of the Association are to communicate to the public the views of industrial leaders on matters of national policy and to secure public understanding and support necessary to favorable government action; to enhance the confidence of the American people in privately owned, competitive industry; and to develop public awareness and understanding of specific legislative issues.

To further these objectives, the public relations division of the Association functions nationally through headquarters in New York City, and locally through the Association's five divisional and thirteen regional offices. Six departments of the public relations division are responsible for the Association's public relations program: public information, radio-television-motion-picture; clergy-industry relations; women's; education; and speakers' bureau.

The public information department prepares news releases, writes and publicizes speeches, produces booklets, arranges press conferences and luncheons, answers inquiries from writers, publishes the "Industrial Press Service," a biweekly clip sheet which goes to 3,000 editors of weekly newspapers, and "Service for Company Publications," which is distributed to 1,400 company periodical editors.

The radio-television-motion-picture department arranges for the appearance of association officers on national and local radio and television programs. A weekly newsreel-type television program on film, entitled "Industry on Parade" is shown regularly in public service time over 270 domestic stations, 36 stations abroad, and 26 stations of the Armed Forces network.

The clergy-industry relations department schedules joint meetings of the Association's clergy-industry relations committee and a clerical advisory council at which papers on important national issues are presented and discussed. These papers are published and distributed to clerical leaders throughout the country.

The women's department of the public relations division writes and distributes news releases on national issues to editors of the women's sections of leading newspapers, national women's magazines, and women's club periodicals. A bimonthly periodical *Program Notes* is published and distributed to 22,000 women's club officials.

The Association maintains a speakers' bureau staffed by three professional speakers who address civic, church, educational, and employee groups.

The education department is advised by an educational aids advisory committee composed of leading educators who approve the industrial program of the Association. A series of booklets on the American economy is published and distributed to schools and colleges. Outstanding college students and their teachers from all parts of the country are invited to attend the Annual Congress of American Industry held annually by the Association.

American Federation of Labor–Congress of Industrial Organizations. The American Federation of Labor–Congress of Industrial Organizations, a federation of 138 autonomous labor unions, has a public relations staff of nine located in Washington, D.C., headquarters. This staff is responsible for radio-television-films, speakers' bureau, press relations, publications, education, and direct mail.

Press relations of the AFL–CIO consists of preparing and distributing news releases covering statements and speeches by officials of the union and testimony before Congressional committees; providing press facilities for newsmen attending executive council, annual meetings of the board of directors and the biennial conventions; holding press conferences on important issues; and answering inquiries from the press.

A public service series of five television programs, "Americans at Work," has been shown by more than 150 stations throughout the country. In co-operation with the National Educational Radio and Tele-

John Luter (right) president of the Overseas Press Club, distinguished editor-correspondent, interviews Edward Swayduck, president, Local 1, Amalgamated Lithographers of America.

Featherbedding
is for the birds!

SAYS THIS UNION PRESIDENT

Q.
In the first of this series of advertisements, you indicated that a person who orders lithography in an ALA plant doesn't pay for featherbedding or obsolete processes. Since featherbedding has been in the news so much lately, I'd like to explore that situation with you.

A.
Good. This is a subject on which the Amalgamated Lithographers has very strong feelings.

Q.
And what are these feelings?

A.
We abhor it. We're absolutely opposed to such a practice. Featherbedding is for the birds.

Q.
Recently out of Cape Canaveral and Washington we learned of featherbedding as it affected our missile program. Would you care to comment on this?

A.
Absolutely! Let's go back in history, the history of labor unions. The philosophy of trade unions was to enhance our society for the benefit of all. Today, decent trade unions do not want to be looked on as a privileged class thinking only of themselves. Now it disturbs me when I see what's happening down at Cape Canaveral. According to the press, these people are not doing for the country what President Kennedy asked them to do. Members of a few unions down there allegedly are being paid for doing nothing. They watch components come in, already assembled, clock the time it takes to assemble them, and get paid for standing around for this time. It's outlandish.

Q.
What do you see as the solution for such a situation?

A.
The unions have to raise their voices against this kind of practice, just as I'm doing now. Nobody profits by featherbedding. A man might profit temporarily, but the industry and our country lose. The money goes down the drain. It's neither constructive nor profitable. Now if the public is aroused enough by these abuses there is certainly going to be some type of anti-labor legislation which is going to hurt

unions like my own which have consistently opposed featherbedding.

Q.
Then I take it you feel that leaders of every union should come out publicly against featherbedding?

A.
Yes! I don't like to see senators, or anyone in public life for that matter, having to do the job that labor officials themselves should have the courage to do. All union people should be saying that featherbedding is for the birds. Otherwise this could destroy in the public mind the proper mission of labor unions.

Q.
The Cape Canaveral problem got a lot of attention because of the importance of our missile program. But doesn't featherbedding exist in other areas?

A.
It certainly does. It's not detrimental to the country from the point of view of the missile program. But it's a practice that presents a form of immorality handed down into our society that negates the good unions have done and are doing in our country and the world. One example is "bogus type." There is a union which resets type that duplicates material already prepared on the outside, then throws away the type they've just set. Their idea is to use the same number of people to do a job which either has been automated or which the industry has found a better or less expensive way to do. Responsible trade unions have many ways to embrace industry innovations. In this way they benefit both the industry and themselves in the areas of training and rehabilitating their members, and in contract negotiations.

Q.
What has the Amalgamated Lithographers union done in this direction?

A.
Over the years, as we helped the lithographic industry to automate and create new processes, we were able to justify and attain for our members a 35-hour week, ten paid holidays a year, three weeks vacation, the finest welfare and pension programs and wage increases. This means our philosophy in fostering automation and being op-

posed to featherbedding made these gains possible. The volume of business has increased tremendously. Many more people are employed. This couldn't happen with featherbedding.

Q.
Can you cite any specific examples where you have actually cut down the number of men on a job to the benefit of the lithographic industry?

A.
Certainly. Only a few years ago there was a new press on the market. At the beginning, in negotiations, we thought it would require three persons to operate. However, it became evident that the press wasn't competitive with three men and it could be operated with two. We then volunteered to renegotiate and reduce the complement to two men so that the press could be run profitably.

Q.
Does your stand against featherbedding represent a new policy of your union or a shift in policy?

A.
No. It has always been a policy of our organization to oppose featherbedding. In our 80-year history we've stood for progress, not only in the graphic arts, but as an example for all industries. In the United States, through American ingenuity, we can manufacture at a decent high level and maintain the high standards of the American way of life—unequaled in world history.

Q.
Eddie, this has been an enlightening and unusual interview.

A.
Thank you. I hope that anyone concerned with graphic arts reproduction or who buys ink on paper is fully aware of this fact: the Amalgamated Lithographers of America is working in his best interests toward the highest craftsmanship and lowest cost. The ALA is unalterably opposed to featherbedding or any other immoral business practice. It knows and has proved that a good craftsman is good economy.

**AMALGAMATED LITHOGRAPHERS
OF AMERICA**
Craftsmanship and Fraternity Since 1882
LOCAL 1, EDWARD SWAYDUCK, PRESIDENT
113 UNIVERSITY PLACE, NEW YORK 3, N. Y.

FIG. 15–1. One of a series of advertisements in the public relations program of a trade-union, the Amalgamated Lithographers of America, which informs the public of the union's position on labor-management issues.

vision Center, the union produced "Briefing Session," a weekly public affairs broadcast. A documentary film, "Land of Promise," has been widely shown on television.

The publications department of AFL–CIO, with the co-operation of the public relations staff, produces a weekly newspaper, *AFL–CIO News,* and a monthly magazine, *The American Federalist,* in addition to numerous booklets on specific labor subjects.

A speakers' bureau, with a staff of volunteer speakers, serves as a clearinghouse to handle requests for speakers from colleges, social, fraternal, religious, and community groups to present the union movement's point of view. In a recent year the bureau provided speakers for more than 500 college and university meetings.

The education department supplies information about the union movement to students for secondary school and college debates. Films from the television series, "Americans at Work," are loaned to schools through the American Vocational Association. The AFL–CIO conducts regular seminars, schools, and classes on a variety of labor subjects with the co-operation of its international and national affiliates and state organizations. Publications are distributed on request to numerous educational institutions.

An annual exhibition of the products and processes of union-organized companies is sponsored by the AFL–CIO with the co-operation of the employers to develop good will for unions and to stimulate sales of union-made products.

Case 15–1

INDUSTRIAL ASSOCIATION PUBLIC RELATIONS

American Petroleum Institute

The American Petroleum Institute, incorporated in 1919 in New York as a national association of producers, refiners, and marketers of petroleum and its products, has some 11,000 members throughout the United States. The Institute serves as a forum, information bureau, technical clearing house, and national trade association for the oil industry.

The public relations of the Institute functions through its Committee on Public Affairs composed of representatives of 21 oil companies. The committee sponsors a comprehensive program of public relations and education for the oil industry. The objectives of the committee are threefold: first, to stimulate dissemination of information concerning the petroleum industry so that public opinion about it will be based on fact; second, to create a climate in which a privately managed and competitive oil industry can best serve the public and strengthen the national economy; and third, to secure the acceptance of all those engaged in the industry of their responsibility to assist government at all levels in matters of public interest affecting the oil industry and its customers.

In carrying out these objectives, the committee works with the Institute's staff of public relations specialists who are responsible for production of motion pictures, films for television, news releases, speeches, pamphlets, and magazine articles. A quarterly service titled "Oil Features for Editors" is distributed to editors of oil company magazines to give them timely articles, cartoons, and background material on the economy of the oil industry. A quarterly magazine, *Petroleum Today*, picturing and describing interesting developments in the oil industry all over the world is distributed to educators, opinion leaders, and libraries. A bimonthly economic bulletin, "Oil Facts," is circulated to newspapers, magazines, economists, and others interested in taxes, prices, production, and new products of the petroleum industry. A statistical handbook giving figures on oil production, reserves, and prices is also published by the Institute.

A major activity of the Committee on Public Affairs of the Institute is its school program intended to bring about a better understanding between teachers, students, and the petroleum industry by recognizing their interdependence in the perpetuation of the competitive enterprise system.

The school program has three objectives. The first objective is to provide useful teaching materials which will heighten students' interest in learning and enhance their understanding of the physical, economic, and social contributions of the oil industry to the public welfare. Specifically, the program is designed to develop a better understanding of the practical application of the physical sciences in petroleum exploration, production, refining, transportation, and distribution; the economics of the oil industry; the social and economic relationship of the industry to community life; and the role of the industry in the development of American industrial history and national progress.

The second objective of the school program is to encourage oil men to become better informed about the educational affairs of their communities and to participate actively in the work of their schools.

The third objective is to motivate and encourage young people to prepare themselves for careers in the petroleum industry, and to present the industry as an attractive and challenging place to work.

The Institute's school program was inaugurated on the basis of a survey in 1950 which revealed that teachers welcome business-sponsored teaching materials when they are specifically prepared for educational use and help to make classroom instruction more complete, realistic, and interesting.

In 1958, a group of 14 educators and oil industry representatives were invited to meet at Princeton, New Jersey, to review the Institute's educational program and to recommend changes to make the materials more useful to teachers and students.

From this meeting came the "Princeton Blueprint" which is a basic plan for developing materials for teacher and student use at all grade levels. The concensus was that the initial intent and general approach of the program provided a sound beginning but that major shifts in emphasis at various grade levels, changes in content and form of materials, and better adaption to curricula were necessary to insure that the program would continue to serve the needs of educators and the industry.

The following criteria for the development of teaching materials were adopted: The materials must offer authentic information designed as a resource material for easy incorporation into existing units of study and subject material areas. The materials must meet established standards for instructional materials as to format, authenticity, readability, timeliness, and availability, Planning and preparation should involve consultation at all stages with competent education specialists.

Since 1958, the Institute's educational program has concentrated on the production of materials for grades 7 through 12 and a substantial segment of this part of the program has been completed. The program will eventually include all grade levels from kindergarten through college.

Educators are consulted on each teaching aid prepared for the program. When the booklet "Physics and Petroleum" was prepared by Dr. Alexander Joseph, consultant to the Physical Science Study Committee of Massachusetts Institute of Technology, it was distributed with an evaluation questionnaire to more than 10,000 teachers whose names were supplied by the National Science Teachers' Association to determine their opinions on the value of the booklet as a study aid. Results were highly favorable.

A national survey of teacher reactions to the Institute school materials was conducted by Dr. Herman Remmers of Purdue University. Responses of teachers in this survey indicate that educators throughout the country give a high rating to Institute study aids in terms of their value for classroom use. Teachers were found to be using the materials extensively and appreciatively and they are eager to know about teaching aids which will make their classroom work more interesting and realistic.

A conference with educators was held recently to explore certain approaches to the content of study aids in the social sciences. Such materials are an important part of the "Princeton Blueprint." A similar conference is planned to discuss the need for teaching materials in the field of economic education.

The study materials prepared and distributed by the Institute for junior and senior high schools are of two types: teacher materials and student materials. Materials are furnished only on request of teachers. One copy of each teaching aid is available free of charge to a teacher. Student materials are free in classroom quantities.

For junior and senior high school teachers of general science, social studies, vocational guidance, physics, chemistry, and economics a reference handbook *Facts about Oil* describes the history of the oil industry, origin of petroleum, exploration, and drilling for oil, refining, marketing, and economics of the industry.

A 12-page booklet "Teacher's Resource Reference" lists the available teaching materials, a bibliography, and other resources on the industry. This is supplemented by a "Teaching Materials" folder listing Institute teaching aids.

A series of colored maps and charts showing oil and gas producing areas, oil production and consumption, formation and transportation of oil, and distillation and chemistry of petroleum refining are available to teachers for classroom use. These maps and charts are prepared especially for grade levels 7 through 12.

Student study materials include booklets featuring the chemistry and physics of petroleum and careers in the industry. For grades 7, 8, and 9, a 24-page booklet, "Science in the Petroleum Industry," describes petroleum geology, refining,

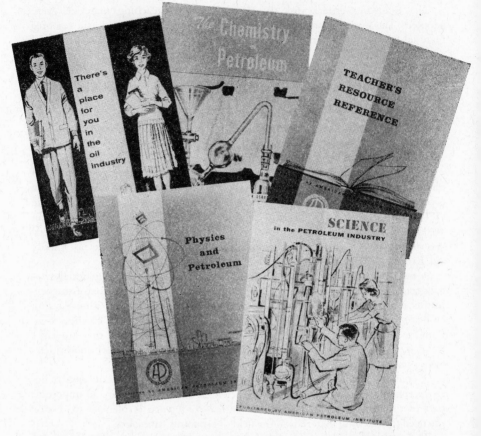

FIG. 15–2. Publications in the educational relations program of American Petroleum Institute. These useful teaching materials improve students' understanding of the physical, economic, and social contributions of the oil industry to the public welfare.

the story of gasoline, the chemistry of oil, petrochemicals, and the future of petroleum. To help teachers make the most effective use of this booklet in the general science curriculum a special folder is available suggesting several petroleum-related demonstrations and projects for the classroom.

For grades 10, 11, and 12, a 12-page booklet, "The Chemistry of Petroleum," describes the ways major chemical processes are used in the oil industry including fractional distillation, catalytic cracking, polymerization, isomerization, reforming, hydrogenation, and alkylation. For the same grades, a 20-page booklet, "Physics and Petroleum," describes applications of physics principles to the oil industry, such as seismic, magnetic, gravimetric exploration, well logging, the nature of petroleum, radioactive tracers, and jet propulsion.

Vocational opportunities in the oil industry are described in a 16-page booklet, "There's a Place for You in the Oil Industry," especially written for students in grades 7 through 12. This booklet describes the wide variety of jobs in the industry and offers suggestions as to personal qualifications and elementary skills required. This booklet is also supplied to vocational counselors, librarians as well as teachers. A student guide entitled "Projects Today—Careers Tomorrow" for grade levels 7 through 12 informs students about science fairs and suggests student fair projects relating to petroleum.

The Institute's teaching materials are introduced to educators and the program implemented throughout the country by local committees of oilmen. These committeemen call upon teachers, sponsor exhibits of teaching materials at teacher meetings, and conduct other programs to publicize the availability of study materials.

Local oilmen provide community resources by arranging trips for teachers and students through oil installations, oil fields, and refineries, by speaking before classes and school assemblies, and providing demonstrations and motion pictures for school use.

During the 1960–61 school year, teachers in 29,764 secondary schools out of a total of 42,000 such schools were reported to be using Institute school materials. The demand for these materials continues to increase because in many cases events are moving too fast for the textbooks and standard teaching aids used in the schools. Institute teaching aids augment materials now in use and update textbooks with current information. An increasing number of schools are being reached by the Institute's program and there is a growing use of the materials in individual school systems.

QUESTIONS

1. What are the specific advantages to the petroleum industry of the public relations program of the Committee on Public Affairs of the American Petroleum Institute?
2. Why should the American Petroleum Institute sponsor a school program when several of the large oil companies, particularly Standard Oil Company of California, Humble Oil and Refining Company, and Sun Oil Company have extensive school programs?
3. What are the specific advantages of the *school* program of the Committee on Public Affairs of the American Petroleum Institute? What are its limitations?
4. How can the American Petroleum Institute school program be improved? If so, describe in detail a school program which you believe would be more effective than that described in this case.

Case 15–2

SERVICE ASSOCIATION PUBLIC RELATIONS

Association of American Railroads

The Association of American Railroads, headquartered in Washington, D.C., was formed in 1934 as the organization of the principal railroads of the United States, Canada, and Mexico for dealing with matters of common interest in railroad operation, maintenance, engineering, research, traffic, purchases and stores, accounting and finance, valuation, taxation, law and legislation, and public relations. Members of the Association represent 96 per cent of the railroad mileage and 97 per cent of the business handled by railroads in North America.

The work of the Association is carried on by a number of standing committees and a headquarters staff organized in seven departments: operations and maintenance; law; research; finance, accounting, taxation and valuation; railroad economics; office of the vice-president and assistant to the president; and public relations.

The public relations department of the Association, created in 1935, is directed by a vice-president and an assistant vice-president. It has five sections: public and special services, school and college service, women's activities, advertising, and news service.

The public relations department works closely with the individual railroads and regional and state railroad organizations in bringing about greater public appreciation of the importance of railroads to the national economy, wider public knowledge of railroad progress, and better public understanding of the problems faced by the railroads and the need for sound transportation policies and regulations which will give the railroads a fair and equal opportunity to serve the public and the public interest.

Public Relations Theme

The railroad industry contends that it is faced with four major problems: discriminatory regulation, discriminatory taxation, subsidized competition, and lack of freedom to provide a diversified transportation service, all of which combine to create a major national crisis in transportation. To meet this crisis the Association has chosen the public relations theme "Magna Carta for Transportation" which features communications with the press, public, and the industry.

Booklets, news releases, slides, poster stamps, a news kit, background material, cartoons, and speeches on the theme "Magna Carta for Transportation" have been produced by the public relations department emphasizing the Four Freedoms for the railroad industry: Freedom from Discriminatory Regulation, Freedom from Discriminatory Taxation, Freedom from Subsidized Competition, and Freedom to Provide a Diversified Transportation Service.

Three publications with a combined distribution exceeding 650,000 copies are the principal media of communication in the "Magna Carta" program. A 76-page booklet, "Magna Carta for Transportation," tells what railroads mean to America and elaborates upon their problems, what they are doing to help themselves, regulation, diversification, taxation, and subsidies to competitors. "The Gathering Transportation Storm" illustrates with graphic charts the causes, impact, and cure of the nation's transportation problems. A booklet, "Magna Carta or Major Crisis," discusses the objectives of the program from the layman's viewpoint.

Public and Special Services

The public and special services section of the public relations department is concerned with cultivating public understanding of railroads and railroad problems and with the need for prompt attention to these problems in the public interest. The section produces a wide variety of material for public distribution. "Quiz on Railroads and Railroading," now in its 12th edition, has had a total distribution exceeding 5,000,000 copies. Other "best sellers" of the section include "American Railroads—Their Growth and Development"; "The Day of Two

Noons," which describes the railroads' role in bringing about standard time; "Last Rites for a Myth," which treats the railroad land grant myth; and a railroad map in color with the symbols of all Class One railroads reproduced around the borders.

A continuous, detailed analysis of newspaper editorials dealing with railroad topics is made by the public and special services section as one means of appraising the impact of the public relations program. In a recent year 5,360 newspaper editorials mentioning the railroads from papers in 50 states and the District of Columbia were analyzed. The fact that railroads are essential to the nation's economy was mentioned 1,374 times, the opinion that railroads must remain under private ownership was expressed editorially 224 times, and that railroads are overregulated 1,405 times.

School and College Service

To improve relations with 49,300,000 students and nearly 2,000,000 teachers in public, parochial, and private schools and colleges is the objective of the School and College Service of the public relations department. It prepares materials which enable the Association, its member companies, as well as regional and state railroad associations, to answer inquiries and requests from teachers and students, concerning railroads and rail transportation.

Relations with colleges are carried on through monthly mailings during the college year to some 1,300 professors who have requested information about railroad transportation; through addresses by Association staff members to college students in courses in transportation; by participating in panel discussions; by providing materials on national debate subjects; and by providing research materials for both professors and students for graduate theses or term papers. Pictures and reference data are also available to textbook authors and publishers.

Teachers in elementary and secondary schools are supplied from about 40 standard publications, teaching or learning aids on railroad transportation which are generally related to the curriculum taught in most public, parochial, and private schools.

Educational aids for teachers include unit materials such as a "Teacher's Kit for a Study of Railroad Transportation," "We Learn About Trains," wall charts, a wall map, and slide films. Nine cartoon-type booklets featuring railroads are distributed to elementary and high school students in addition to a variety of other publications, including "The Railroad Story," "Railroads at Work," and "Quiz Jr."

More than 90,000 requests for information are received from teachers, students, railroads, and the public annually. In response to these requests some six to ten million pieces of printed matter are distributed by the Association each year. Educational materials are provided on request only and without charge. In addition, an illustrated catalogue of publications is available to teachers, school administrators, and librarians who may also see publications on display at conventions of educators and librarians throughout the country.

Women's Division

In recognition of the increasing importance of women in economic and political affairs, a women's division was established in the public relations department to provide information about railroads to women through all means of communication. The division works closely with two major organizations of railroad women and with other women's groups.

The National Association of Railway Business Women with 55 chapters and 7,000 members, in co-operation with the Association, is conducting a two-phase program: (1) to inform members about the industry's problems and goals, and (2) to carry the railroad story to women's groups in their respective communities by public affairs dinners for presidents of local women's groups. The American Council of Railroad Women has organized a speakers' bureau to provide speakers for community organizations.

Public Relations Advertising

The Association has employed a selective public relations magazine advertising program to reach thought leaders. This group, which includes the higher-income, better-educated individuals, has proved most knowledgeable about railroads and most responsive to information about the industry's problems.

The principal objectives of this advertising in recent years has been to affirm that railroads are essential; that they are modern and progressive; that the need for railroads in the future will be as great as in the past; and that in the public interest transport policy should be corrected to permit the railroads to compete with other forms of transportation on a fair and equal basis.

Page advertisements have been run in such news and business magazines as *Time, Newsweek, Business Week, U.S. News and World Report,* and *Harvard Business Review,* all being recognized as having high readership among opinion leaders. To reach particular groups, with special interests in railroads, the press, radio, transportation and traffic, postal, and educational magazines have been used.

Association advertising has been keyed to the theme that railroads are modern and progressive. Examples are: the Minuteman Missile train, television in classification yards, piggyback truck service, microwave radio communications, and the potential use of atomic energy to power locomotives. Other advertising themes have included the essentiality and economy of rail transportation, the inequities in the transportation field, and changes in public policy needed to provide more equitable competition in transportation.

The effectiveness of the Association's public relations advertising has been proven by increasingly higher ratings by the established measurement services of Daniel F. Starch and Gallup and Robinson. Association advertisements have been named winners in the general competition as well as the special Public Relations category of the annual awards for Distinguished Advertising in the Public Interest sponsored by the *Saturday Review.*

The advertising section of the public relations department produces *Shop Talk,* a monthly publication for the Railroad Public Relations Association, to keep railroad public relations people informed about the public relations programs of individual railroads.

The advertising section circulates public relations films such as "Mainline—U.S.A.," which has been shown 47,000 times over a four-year period to audiences totaling three and one-half million persons in addition to frequent telecasts by stations throughout the country viewed by more millions. A new motion picture,

"Science Rides the High Iron," shows how the railroads modernized their operations. A film directory listing motion pictures produced by individual railroads and others is distributed to program chairmen of clubs and organizations. The advertising section co-operates with theatrical motion picture producers in the development of films on railroad subjects.

Press Relations

The news service section of the public relations department produces and distributes special and periodic news releases, special articles, and memoranda of basic information on a wide variety of events and subjects to newspapers, magazines, television and radio stations, and wire services.

In a recent year the news service section distributed to the press 362 special and periodic news releases, and nearly 450 special articles and memoranda of basic information. In addition, 2,000 photographic prints were furnished authors to illustrate books, newspapers, and magazine articles. Special memoranda were prepared and distributed on "Railroads: Major Arm of Defense," "Behind the Drive to Rig Transportation Prices," "The Iron Horse—Margin of Victory," "Freight Boom," "Facts on Railroad Piggyback Service," and others.

Spot news events such as federal government hearings are covered by some 600 news releases annually. A weekly "Information Letter" published only for railroad officials reports railroad news developments in Washington.

Survey of Public Opinion

The attitudes of the public toward the railroads and their problems are researched from time to time through nation-wide opinion surveys of a representative sample of the public. These surveys have been conducted for the Association by the Opinion Research Corporation. Findings are used in evaluating the public relations program, identifying the proper audience, determining the public's misconceptions about railroads, and indicating where emphasis should be placed in public communications. These surveys have indicated growing approval of the railroad industry, an understanding of its problems, and a belief that railroads are essential. They have also pointed up areas requiring greater concentration of public relations programing.

The public relations theme of "Magna Carta for Transportation" emphasizes railroad progress and indicates that the public could expect much more modernization if the railroads were given equal treatment with competing transportation methods.

QUESTIONS

1. What are the favorable features of the public relations program of the Association of American Railroads? What are its limitations?

2. What specific improvements can you propose to make the public relations program of the Association more effective?

3. Is the organization for public relations of the Association satisfactory? Give reasons for your answer. Suggest any modification of the present public relations organization which you believe desirable.

4. Discuss the activities of each section of the Association's public relations department. How would you improve the activities of each of the following divisions: public and special services, school and college service, women's activities, advertising and news service?

5. Discuss the use of public opinion research by the Association. Can the present research be improved? How?

CHAPTER   **ARMED FORCES PUBLIC**

16 • **RELATIONS**

THE UNITED STATES Department of Defense which includes the Army, Navy, and Air Force is America's biggest business. It may be compared to a giant corporation owned by 180 million shareholders who have invested billions of their tax dollars in equipping and operating this enterprise. Not only has the American public a tremendous financial investment in the business of national defense but, more important is the fact that millions of America's sons, daughters, brothers, fathers, and husbands have invested years of their lives in the Armed Forces. The Selective Service System reports that, from 1948 through 1960, 12,000,000 Americans with no previous military service served in the United States Armed Forces.

Not only is the Department of Defense America's biggest business in terms of money expended but it is also the most important, for upon its effectiveness depends the survival of every person in the country, the existence of the nation itself and of all nations allied with the United States in the preservation of freedom throughout the world.

Every American voter contributes to the control of this tremendous enterprise through the election of his national representatives and the administration. Millions of Americans are members of veteran and other groups which take a special interest in matters affecting the Armed Forces. Other millions are directly affected by the Armed Forces as members of communities with military installations or are involved as employees or the families of employees of the many thousands of research and industrial organizations which provide services and material to the Armed Forces. More directly involved are the many officers and enlisted men and women of various branches of the military services and the civilian employees of the Army, Navy, and Air Force throughout the world.

Millions of people in many countries throughout the world also realize that their national security depends to a large extent on the ability of the Armed Forces of the United States, in concert with their own, to

deter aggression or to win a war. United States Army troops help maintain freedom in West Berlin; U.S. Navy ships patrol the seas in many
parts of the world; and U.S. Air Force units are based on the territory
of allied nations in large numbers. Military forces of the North Atlantic
Treaty Organization are under the direction of a U.S. Air Force general
and U.S. Navy units with those of other allies in the Atlantic are under
command of a U.S. Navy admiral.

FIG. 16–1. Assistance to civilians in distress areas throughout the world is an important public
relations activity of the U.S. Air Force shown here air-lifting stranded flood victims by helicopter
from the Sidi Slimane area of Morocco. Aerial reconnaissance by the Tenth Wing and Military
Air Transport Service rescue crews brought to safety some 2,500 stranded Morocco flood victims.

Not only is it important that United States Armed Forces maintain
good relations with the American people, but it is equally essential that
they develop good relations with the military forces and civilian popu-
lations of allied nations with which we have defensive alliances throughout the world. Contacts with officers and enlisted personnel of our
Army, Navy, and Air Force stationed abroad provide the only direct
relations of the people of many countries with the United States. The
peoples of all nations of the free world comprise the international public of the Armed Forces of the United States.

Public understanding of the activities of the Armed Forces is essential
in overcoming the traditional apathy of the American public to a large

military establishment. The need for a strong military force and the funds to support it is not completely accepted by the American public. There is a natural desire on the part of taxpayers to reduce expenditures for defense. The desirability of military service as a career is not fully appreciated by many young men and women in this country. For these reasons, public relations of the Armed Forces is essential.

Significance of Armed Forces Public Relations

The importance of Armed Forces public relations is recognized by high officials of the United States Army, Navy, and Air Force.

Major General Arno H. Luehman, Air Force Director of Information from 1957 to 1961, emphasized the importance of public relations as follows:

Today, new movements and forces are forcing all of us in the military services to re-examine our relations with the public, with industry, the Congress, our schools, churches, and other public groups. The American people have a right to complete information, good or bad, about the Air Force, subject only to limitations of real security.

Admiral Arleigh B. Burke, U.S. Navy Chief of Naval Operations, said,

Military leaders are becoming more aware that they cannot do an effective job without the support of intelligent, clear-thinking and informed citizens. There is a vital need for all of us to have a determined public working with us—an alert citizenry that is conscious of the magnitude of the struggle our country is presently engaged in, and aware of the contributions the military services are making to our nation's cause.

Wilber M. Brucker, Secretary of the Army, stated,

Public understanding of the Army, not only in this country but in allied countries as well, is the foundation of public confidence which is a fundamental requirement if we are to carry out our mission effectively. It is imperative, therefore, that the public be kept as well informed as security will allow. They must know our plans and our day-to-day progress in meeting our grave responsibilities. Only then can we make them aware of the Army's ability to preserve the peace.

The Chief of Staff of the Air Force, General Curtis S. LeMay, emphasizes the importance of public understanding of the mission of the Air Force, as follows:

A highly motivated military force is essential to superior combat capability. Equally essential is a resolute and self-possessed citizenry. Constant esprit de corps and determination in a military force and calm resolution in the citizenry are founded on understanding. And understanding of the ever-changing situation is dependent upon information, truthful, current information. The Air Force information program is based on the belief in the right of all the people to know all the information about the Air Force that is consistent with national security.

Historical Background of Armed Forces Public Relations

Public information about the activities of the Armed Forces originated with President George Washington who submitted reports on the Continental Army to Congress. This practice has been followed by succeeding presidents who have informed the public about military affairs directly or indirectly through Congress. It was not until the Civil War that leading newspapers and illustrated magazines sent correspondents, illustrators, and photographers into the field to accompany the various armies and report on their progress. President Lincoln appointed an editor, Charles A. Dana, Assistant Secretary of War, to report to the public on the actions of field commanders. During the Indian Wars, newspaper correspondents accompanied military expeditions in the West.

Newspaper reporting of military operations was extensive during the Spanish-American War when correspondents Richard Harding Davis and Stephen Crane became famous for their reports from the front lines in Cuba. Army staff officers in the field issued daily bulletins to the press which is the first instance of commanders making war news available to the public.

The War Department issued its first formal press release by the Adjutant General of the Army in 1904. However, military public relations was a minor activity until World War I. The U.S. Marine Corps established the first armed services publicity bureau in Chicago, in 1907, and a second press bureau in New York City, in 1911, primarily to assist in recruiting. A public relations section was established at Marine Corps headquarters in Washington, in 1933, to handle relations with the press.

During the administration of President Woodrow Wilson, Newton D. Baker, Secretary of War, appointed as his press officer Major Douglas MacArthur, who publicized the famous Rainbow Division during World War I.

When General Pershing commanded the American Expeditionary Forces in France in World War I, he established a press section at his headquarters. This later became a subsection of the Army military intelligence staff where it remained until 1941.

After World War I, Army press relations lapsed, although it was revived when Air Force Major Henry H. Arnold was appointed Chief of the Information Division in the Office of the Chief of Air Service. His skillful public relations helped to bring about a separate Air Force in 1947.

In 1935, General Douglas MacArthur, then Army Chief of Staff, appointed Major, later Major General, Alexander D. Surles to head the public relations branch of the Army. He was in charge of an enlarged War Department Bureau of Public Relations from 1941 to 1945. In 1946, the public relations function was removed from the G2 and S2 sections of the Army and became a special staff section at the policy-making level. The name "public relations" was dropped and the term "public information" was adopted to describe the public information service of the Army. The Public Information, Legislative Liaison, and Troop Information and Education Divisions were co-ordinated under Chief of Information, General J. Lawton Collins.

The next reorganization of Army public relations occured in 1950 when the Legislative Liaison division was separated from Public Information, Troop Information, and Education. An expanded information program was established with external relations under the Public Information division and internal relations under the Troop Information and Education Division to develop educational programs for the civic, moral, and mental development of Army personnel.

As a result of the disloyalty of a few American prisoners of war during the Korean War and public criticism of the Army Troop Education and Information Program, Troop Information was separated from Education and staff responsibility for Troop Education was assigned as a G–1 function to the Deputy Chief of Staff for Personnel. Troop Information and Public Information, since 1956,, have been organized in separate equal divisions in the Office of the Chief of Information of the Army.

The public relations of the Navy was formally organized after World War II with the establishment of an Office of Public Relations and the Fleet Home Town News Center at the Great Lakes Naval Training Center, Great Lakes, Illinois. The entire Navy information program is under the direction of the Office of Information, Navy Department.

The public relations of the Air Force adopted the Army Troop Information and Public Information, since 1956, have been organized ated them throughout the Korean War. In 1954, the Air Force separated the Troop Information section from the Education section and established a new Office of Information Services. This department combined the internal troop and external public information programs, in addition to the historical services and protocol functions, in a special staff section. The Education and Library services remain in the Personnel Services Division in the Office of the Deputy for Personnel.

The public information activities of the Armed Forces were designated as "public relations" until 1946, but this terminology was discarded in favor of the term "public information" which was felt to have a less political and commercial flavor. However, Major General Arno H. Luehman, Air Force Director of Information, from 1957 to 1961, opposed the change in designation, saying, "I feel that it is unfortunate that the term 'public relations' was dropped, because to me it is much more meaningful than 'information.' Even the words 'public relations' do not reflect the full scope of the function or the responsibility of the job at hand."

Responsibility for Armed Forces Public Relations

Responsibility for public information of all the Armed Forces of the United States is centered in the Office of Public Affairs, Department of Defense, Washington, D.C. This office is the sole agency for dissemination of information about the Armed Forces to the six major publics: nonmilitary civilians; officers and enlisted men of the Armed Forces; men and women who have been in military service and are no longer on active duty; civilian employees and suppliers of the Armed Forces; citizens of foreign countries; and elected members of Congress and government agencies.

The military services have not been free agents in disseminating public information since 1949. The Army, Navy, and Air Force are all subordinate elements of the Department of Defense which is headed by a civilian secretary. Rules, regulations, and guidance pertaining to all of the public information activities of three services are prescribed in his name by a civilian Assistant Secretary for Public Affairs. These rules and directives are not inflexible but serve as broad guidelines governing what may be called precepts to be followed in communicating information to the public.

The Defense Public Affairs Council, composed of representatives of the Army, Navy, Air Force and the Director of the Office of Public Affairs of the Department of Defense, advises the Secretary of Defense on matters of public information which concern more than one branch of the service. The Council is concerned with national and international public information and internal information in the Armed Forces.

In addition to the Department of Defense, each branch of the Armed Forces has its own public information organization. The Army fixed responsibility for information in the Office of the Chief of Information, Washington. The Office of Information, Navy Department and the Division of Information, Headquarters Marine Corps, Washington, are charged with public information responsibilities for the Navy and Marine Corps respectively. The Air Force has its Office of Information, Office of the Secretary of the Air Force, Washington, D.C.

Department of Defense Organization for Public Information

Organization for public information of the Department of Defense, the sole agency for dissemination of information for all branches of the service, is the Office of Public Affairs. The Office of Public Affairs is organized in four sections: Office of News Services, Office of Public Services, Office of Security Review, and Office of Plans and Programs.

The Office of News Services is responsible for news releases and provides national news media with a central source of information. In addition to preparing and distributing releases which concern the three branches of the Armed Forces, the Office co-ordinates military information with other agencies and the executive branch of the government. The five specialized branches of the Office of News Services are: the Magazine and Book Branch, serving these media; the Audio-Visual Division serving the radio-television, still- and motion-picture media; the Production Branch co-operating with film producers; the Still Photo Branch, serving news media and releasing pictorial material; and the Radio-TV-Newsfilm Branch aiding the major networks and the newsfilm producers in producing military programs.

The Office of Public Services serves veteran and civilian organizations through five specialized branches: Liaison, Events, Speakers and Visitors, Special Projects, and Public Inquiries. The Liaison Branch arranges with veteran and civilian organizations conferences and visits to military installations. The Events Branch determines policy concerning Armed Forces participation in civic events, shows, fairs, and expositions. The Speakers and Visitors Branch provides speakers to address civilian and military groups. The Public Inquiries Branch answers inquiries from civilians about national defense. The Special Projects Branch is responsible for special events involving the military forces such as Armed Forces Day, Joint Civilian Orientation Conferences, the President's People-to-People program, High School News Service, and others.

The Office of Security Review of the Department of Defense clears for release to news media information about all of the Armed Forces

to insure that it does not endanger the national security. When classified information is subject to declassification and may properly be released it is cleared by the Office of Security Review.

The function of the Office of Plans and Programs is to review the
programs of the Office of Public Affairs and assure effective co-ordination of public affairs policies and plans of the Department of Defense.

Internal relations with members of all of the Armed Forces is co-
ordinated in the Department of Defense through the Office of Armed
Forces Information and Education which supports the internal relations
activities of the Navy, Army, and Air Force. This office operates a program to give the individual service person an understanding of our government, the mission of our Armed Forces, national and international
problems, international communism, and overseas orientation.

Through offices in Los Angeles and New York City, the Office of
Armed Forces Information and Education supports the world-wide
operations of the Armed Forces Radio and Television Service which
controls some 204 radio and 33 television outlets throughout the world,
including the Armed Forces Radio network. These offices also procure
and distribute films for use by service outlets; advise on programing;
and provide information and features for all service newspapers.

Army Organization for Public Information

Organization for Army public information at the seat of government
is headed by the Army Chief of Information who reports to the Chief
of Staff on all matters pertaining to public and troop information. The
Chief of Information prepares plans and policies for, and co-ordinates
and supervises Army public information in accordance with the policies
established by the Secretary of Defense and Secretary of the Army. The
Office of the Chief of Information is organized in four divisions: Policy
and Programs, Civil Liaison, Troop Information, and Public Information as shown in Figure 16–2.

The Policy and Program Division develops information plans,
policies, and programs and provides budgetary guidance on information
activities. The Troop Information Division prepares troop information
plans, policies, and programs through four branches whose titles explain
their functions: training and publications, troop radio and television,
Army newspaper, and special news service. The Public Information
Division informs the general public through three branches whose
functions are explained by their titles: news features, magazine-book,
and audio-visual. The Civil Liaison Division develops, co-ordinates, and
supervises public information plans and programs to maintain good re-

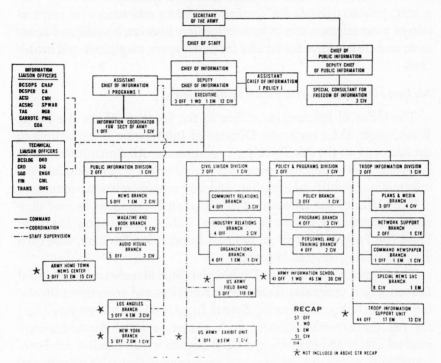

OFFICE, CHIEF OF INFORMATION
OFFICE, CHIEF OF PUBLIC INFORMATION
HEADQUARTERS, DEPARTMENT OF THE ARMY   DECEMBER 11, 1961

FIG. 16–2. Organization chart of the Office, Chief of Information, Headquarters, Department of the Army, showing external and internal functions.

lations between the Army, industry, and the general public through four branches whose titles explain their functions: organization, special projects, industrial relations, and community relations.

In the field each Army commander is responsible for the execution, review, and analysis of a sound information program concerning his command; the conduct of mutually good relations between subordinate elements of his command and neighboring civilian communities; and for the security of material submitted for publication which concerns his command. The field staff organization for information includes a public information officer, troop information officer, both of whom are responsible to the commanding general and his chief of staff.

The commanding officer of a post, division, regimental combat team and sometimes smaller unit, has a staff public information officer to advise and assist him in carrying out his public information responsibilities. A unit public information officer has two responsibilities: to keep the public informed about his unit and to keep his commander ad-

vised regarding public opinion. He arranges for the appearance of
speakers from his unit at civic affairs and on radio and television programs; writes addresses for speakers; prepares and supervises preparation of press releases; acts as an intermediary between his unit and newsmen; and creates ideas for articles for newspapers, magazines, and broadcasts.

Air Force Organization for Public Information

The Office of Information, Office of the Secretary of the Air Force,
Washington, D.C., under the Director of Information is responsible to
the Secretary of the Air Force for operating the Air Force Information
program. This responsibility includes planning and supervising internal
information, public information, and community relations programs.

The Office of the Director of Information is organized in four divisions: Community Relations Division, Public Information Division;
Plans and Programs Division, Internal Information Division, with each
division having several branches.

The Community Relations Division has four branches: the Industrial
Branch which maintains liaison with suppliers and contractors involving news releases; the Special Events Branch which has responsibility
for Air Force participation in such events as aerial demonstrations,
musical events and exhibits; the Civil Branch which handles Air Force
community relations programs and maintains liaison with veteran and
civilian organizations; the Speakers Branch which handles invitations
for speeches by the Secretary of the Air Force, and other Air Staff general
officers.

The Public Information Division has seven branches: Operations
Branch produces press releases, arranges travel to Air Force installations
for media representatives, monitors press tours, and arranges for interviews with Air Force officials; Pictorial Branch aids media in still- and
motion-picture coverage of Air Force activities; Magazine and Book
Branch provides information to publishers, editors, and writers; Radio
and Television Branch co-operates with the broadcast industry by supplying information, motion-picture film, personnel, and equipment for
use on programs; Press Branch is an integral part of the Department of
Defense, Office of Public Affairs, and is the official outlet for Air Force
news; Air Force Home Town News Center at Tinker Air Force Base,
near Oklahoma City, produces news stories on Air Force individuals for
use by their home town media; and Offices of Information in New York
City, Chicago, and Los Angeles provide service to news media in these
news centers.

The Plans and Program Division is responsible for planning and co-ordinating information activities in connection with the testing and development of new Air Force systems; training exercises and maneuvers; joint activities; and events of regional, national, and international interest. It works with the Office of the Assistant Secretary of National Defense for Public Affairs, and other government agencies.

The Internal Information Division has four branches: the Internal Projects Branch monitors the supervisory staff visit program to Information Offices at bases throughout the world; arranges an annual seminar for media representatives; supervises speaking engagements of officers of the Air Command and Staff College at selected bases; arranges an annual program for recognition of outstanding airmen; and exercises staff supervision over the Information Officers' course at Boston University.

The Editorial Production Branch of the Internal Information Division supervises about 400 Air Force newspapers in the Base Newspaper program and produces a weekly news service for base newspapers. It also supervises the operation of 85 radio and 14 television stations at overseas bases.

The Analysis Branch attempts to find more effective information programs by conducting and analyzing surveys of Air Force public information activities.

The *Airman Magazine,* the official journal of the Air Force, is produced monthly and distributed free throughout the Air Force by the Internal Information Division which also publishes the "Air Force Information Policy Letter" for commanders.

At the local level, the squadron or unit is the smallest operating organization within the Air Force. Each squadron has an Information Officer whose duties include: assisting in the advancement of the public information objectives of the Air Force; contributing news and feature articles to the base newspaper; assisting the Base Information Officer with news stories; making arrangements for special events, reporting on situations which may cause friction with the community, informing the Base Information Officer regarding any accident and aid in getting information about it, encouraging unit personnel to participate in community affairs, and assisting in publicity activities for community charitable drives.

Navy Organization for Public Information

The Chief of Information Department of the Navy maintains policy and operating liaison in matters of public information with the Director of the Office of Public Affairs, Department of Defense, Washington. He is responsible to the Secretary of the Navy and Chief of Naval Operations at the seat of government.

The Office of Information, Department of the Navy, is composed of the Chief of Information, Deputy Chief of Information and five divisions: Administration, Public Information, Civil Relations, Internal Relations, and Plans. The principal activities of the Office of Information are in the divisions of Public Information, Civil Relations, and Internal Relations.

The Public Information Division serves representatives of news media by answering requests for information, reviewing television and motion-picture scripts, and arranging Navy co-operation in filming pictures. It prepares news releases and provides pictures to the press and authors.

The Civil Relations Division administers the Navy Civil Relations and Navy Guest Cruise programs, handles visits of civilians to Naval installations and ships, conducts programs of co-operation with civic groups, answers inquiries from the public, and arranges for senior Navy department officials to speak before various groups.

The Internal Relations Division is responsible for relations with Navy men and women, both uniformed and civilian, as well as active duty, retired, and Naval Reserve personnel. This division disseminates information to ship and station newspapers and magazines; answers requests from commands for photographs and information; trains public information officers, and prepares current biographies of senior officers.

Marine Corps Organization for Public Information

Public information of the United States Marine Corps is the responsibility of the Division of Information, Headquarters Marine Corps, Washington, D.C. This division is organized with four branches: Administrative Branch, Plans and Policy Branch, Media Branch, and Community Relations Branch. In addition to this organization at the seat of government, the Marine Corps maintains information offices in New York City and Los Angeles and information sections at every major post, station, and fleet Marine Force unit.

The Media Branch initiates, stimulates, and evaluates information within the Corps for dissemination to the external and internal publics and co-ordinates the release of all Marine Corps public information of national interest. It answers inquiries from media, processes requests for accreditation and travel of media representatives, co-ordinates participation in national radio and television programs, and assists producers of films and broadcasts.

The Plans and Policy Branch develops information plans, policies, and programs and reviews and analyzes the current information programs of the Corps.

The Community Relations Branch initiates programs of information to inform the communities where Marine units are located by means of visits, open houses, speaking engagements, exhibits, and participation in community activities.

The Administrative Branch co-ordinates the activities of the Media, Plans and Policy, and Community Relations Branches of the Division of Information.

PUBLIC INFORMATION OBJECTIVES OF THE ARMED FORCES

The public information objectives of the Armed Forces are similar. These objectives in general seek to gain the understanding and support of the several publics, both internal and external, for a sound, national defense program by informing them of the mission of the military services.

Air Force Public Information Objectives

The public information objectives of the United States Air Force are typical of those of the Army and Navy and are in accordance with Department of Defense public information policy. The general objectives of Air Force public information are to help the American public, including members of the Air Force, to understand: *first,* the nature of the aggressive threats to the United States and the rest of the Free World, and national policy on the best military structure to deter a war, or win if one is forced on us; *second,* the day-to-day activities of the Air Force and its capabilities as an instrument through which national policy can be implemented to promote peace and deter war; *third,* the need for constant improvement in personnel and equipment of the Air Force and for keeping ahead of any potential aggressor in the most significant scientific and technological activities affecting aerospace forces.

Specific objectives of Air Force public information fall into four areas: internal information objectives, public information objectives, community relations objectives, and historical objectives.

The internal information objectives of the Air Force are to increase the effectiveness of Air Force personnel and their understanding of their responsibilities as citizens of the United States. This involves installing in each member a sense of personal dedication to country and duty; developing a devotion to career service in the Air Force; making each member an effective representative of the Air Force in the civilian community; developing an awareness of responsibility as a representative of the United States in the foreign community when assigned overseas; imparting an understanding of international communism; and understanding thoroughly the mission of the Air Force and its official position on key questions of doctrine and policy.

The public information objectives of the Air Force are to provide the American people, through established media, complete, timely, and accurate information about the Air Force; to explain the importance to national security of an adequate modernization program for all equipment and material used by the Air Force; to convey to the American public that aerospace power rests on men as well as machines; to make the full record of the Air Force available to the public, subject only to security restrictions; and to inform the public about the Air Force's utilization of men, money, and material.

The community information objectives of the Air Force are: to recognize the interrelationship between the Air Force and the communities where its units are located; to orient personnel as to their impressions on the public; to co-operate with the community, state, and organized civilian groups in furthering public understanding; to make the Air Force an important factor in community life; to determine community attitudes toward the Air Force; to establish and maintain mutual acceptance, respect, co-operation, and appreciation between the Air Force and communities affected by its operations.

The historical objectives supervised by the Air Force University are: to provide a permanent record of Air Force activities for planning, programing, and reference; to contribute to the military education of Air Force personnel; to assist in providing a sound, public understanding of aerospace power and the role of military aerospace forces in developing and exerting this power; and to increase the pride of the individual Air Force man in his unit and the Air Force.

THE ARMED FORCES PUBLICS

The Armed Forces have several distinct publics, each with its particular interests, but all similar in that they are composed of American citizens, both military and civilian, whose taxes and services support the Armed Forces in preserving national security. The six separate audiences of the Armed Forces are: the general public, which includes all nonmilitary civilians in the country; the Armed Forces public, including all Army, Navy, Marine, and Air Force enlisted men and women; the ex-Armed Forces public, which includes men and women who have been in the services, are no longer on active duty, but maintain an active interest in military activities; the civilian employee and supplier public which has direct contact with the Armed Forces as employee or supplier on posts, bases, airfields, and in ordnance plants; foreign nationals with whom members of the Armed Forces come in contact in the performance of their duties abroad; the Congressional public, composed of elected members of Congress and key government officials.

The general public comprising 180 million Americans is the primary Armed Forces audience because the existence and efficiency of the military services depend on the understanding and support of the civilian population accomplished through an effective information program. The general public includes civic organizations, trade and industrial associations, youth groups, women's organizations, clergy, educators, and communities.

The personnel of the Armed Forces and their families are an equally important public because an informed and motivated military force is essential to superior combat capability. Furthermore, members of the Armed Forces are a primary medium of communication of information about the military services to the civilian public.

Former members of the Armed Forces including retired officers and enlisted personnel, war veterans, reservists, and national guardsmen, not on active duty, and their families are an important audience and medium of communication with the civilian audience.

The civilian employees and suppliers of the Armed Forces at posts, bases, arsenals, post exchanges, and other installations are an audience that constitutes an important link between the military and civilian communities in this country and abroad. The Army alone has in the neighborhood of one-half million civilian employees and other branches of the service have a large number. The effectiveness of the members of this group and their awareness of their responsibility for national security is dependent on complete, timely, and accurate information about the Armed Forces.

The nationals of foreign countries in which our installations are located and where our personnel are stationed are an important audience of the Armed Forces. The Armed Forces inform this audience of our peaceful intentions and the strength of our military power.

The Congress is a very important Armed Forces public for its actions determine the size, type, and character of our military forces. Key members of Congress and members of committees involved in Armed forces' matters must be informed about the requirements, resources, and accomplishments of the military services in the interest of national security. Key government officials including members of the National Security Council Planning Board, representatives of the Office of Defense Mobilization, and Department of Defense officials make decisions which affect the military services and must be informed of the services' role in national defense.

Armed Forces Budget for Public Relations

The United States Department of Defense which co-ordinates and supervises public relations of the Army, Air Force, and Navy had an annual public information budget of $824,000 in 1960, according to the Associated Press. The Office of Public Affairs of the Department of Defense employed 73 civilians and 52 military personnel in four sections.

The United States Army had a budget of $387,850 for public information in 1960, and employed 50 civilian and 65 military personnel.

The United States Air Force had a budget of $295,700 for public relations, in 1960, and employed 39 civilians and 66 military personnel. The Navy operated its public information program on a budget of $111,000, and employed 39 civilians and 67 military personnel.

The combined budgets of the Department of Defense, Army, Navy, and Air Force for 1961 totaled $1,600,000, and employed 451 persons in their public information program. However, these cost figures, according to the Associated Press, do not include the compensation of the 250 military personnel employed in the public information activities of the three services and neither the budgets nor personnel totals included any military public relations activities outside of Washington. When the expenditures for public relations activities outside the seat of government are considered, the total investment in Armed Forces public information is considerably higher.

MEDIA OF ARMED FORCES COMMUNICATION

The Armed Forces employ all of the major media of mass communication in disseminating information to the various publics. Media used for internal communication with service personnel include: service newspapers, meetings, films, booklets, posters, fact sheets, radio and television broadcasts, news bulletins, bulletin boards, displays, information digests, press service, news service, and word-of-mouth publicity. External communication is carried on through commercial newspapers and magazines, house organs and trade journals, periodicals and books, still- and motion-pictures, radio and television broadcasts, news releases, public speakers, exhibits, service personnel and alumni, open houses, and tours.

Newspapers

Commercial and military service newspapers are the principal media for informing the external and internal publics of the Armed Forces.

Newspapers published for personnel of the Armed Forces are the basic medium of internal communications. There are more than 300 official Army unit and 400 Air Force newspapers published. They are published weekly by most commands and have a readership of almost 100 per cent of service personnel and dependents. Service newspaper editors are served with regular releases of news, editorials, and features by the Air Force News Service and Army News Service of their respective Offices of Information in Washington, and by the Armed Forces Press Service and the Office of Armed Forces Information, Department of Defense, Washington.

A typical news release of the Office of the Chief of Information of the Department of the Army follows:

Army News Service
News Release No. 100–57

DEPARTMENT OF THE ARMY
OFFICE OF THE CHIEF OF INFORMATION
WASHINGTON, D.C. 25

WASHINGTON (ANS). The Secretary of the Army has sent letters of commendation today to three commanders whose organizations have received awards in the thirteenth annual awards competition of the American Public Relations Association.

The Army recorded an unprecedented first in the competitions this year. According to an official spokesman, this is the first time in the thirteen-year awards that any service has won three awards in the same year.

The Southern European Task Force won a Silver Anvil in the field of international relations originating outside the United States for promoting good will between the U.S. Armed Forces and the Italian people. The Army was the only service to win a Silver Anvil in the competition this year.

The Seventh Army was awarded a Certificate of Outstanding Public Relations Achievement in the field of international relations originating outside the United States for fighting anti-American feeling in Germany after its restoration to sovereignty.

The U.S. Army Infantry Center received a Certificate of Outstanding Public

Relations Achievement in the government classification for its community relations program that won public approval from nearby civilian communities.

The awards were presented recently to representatives of the three winning commands at the annual awards dinner in conjunction with the national conference of the American Public Relations Association at Philadelphia, Pennsylvania.

This press release conforms to good mechanics and construction by showing the authority for the release at the top; using simple, concise, clear sentences; summarizing the principal facts in "lead" or first sentence; amplifying the details in the following paragraphs; avoiding overworked expressions; and making clear in the "lead" the time element in the story.

Commercial newspapers are the principal medium of communication of the Armed Forces with the external publics. The Offices of Information of the three services release to newspapers and wire services two types of news: spot news, a typical example of which is quoted above; and time copy including feature articles which are released to feature syndicates.

The sources of much Armed Forces newspaper publicity are the Home Town News Centers maintained by the Army, Navy, and Air Force. The Air Force Home Town News Center at Tinker Air Force Base near Oklahoma City, Oklahoma, produces news stories about Air Force personnel for their home town media. The Navy Fleet Home Town News Center at Great Lakes, Illinois, is under the Commandant Ninth Naval District and the management and technical control of the Navy Chief of Information, Washington. The Army Home Town News Center in Kansas City, Missouri, is controlled by the Army Chief of Information, Washington.

The functions of these Home Town News Centers include processing of home town news which originates at the individual's base, and standardizing the form and distribution of the releases to all home town daily and weekly newspapers and radio and television stations requesting them.

Several types of news stories are released by the Home Town News Center: "roster stories" which involve all of the personnel on a ship, post, or base; "form stories" based on a standardized form which personnel fill out on the occasion of an advancement or receipt of an award; "double-dub stories," a combination of "roster" and "form" stories which cover up to 200 persons; "flat stories" which feature better-than-usual news; and "feature stories" which present facts and background material on one or a small group of persons. The News Centers also release photographs, tape and disc recordings of service men and women to their home town newspapers, radio and television stations.

Radio and Television

Radio and television are widely used by all branches of the Armed Forces for both internal as well as external communications. Internal communications are facilitated by Armed Forces radio and television stations located in overseas areas and certain isolated sections of the United States. These stations provide Armed Forces personnel with information, education, and entertainment that would otherwise be unavailable to them. The Office of Armed Forces Information and Education of the Department of Defense supports the world-wide operations of the Armed Forces Radio and Television Service which controls some 204 radio and 33 television outlets throughout the world. Of this number, the Army has responsibility for 98 radio and 13 television stations. The Offices of Information of the Army, Navy, and Air Force have sections specializing in radio and television which support Armed Forces overseas radio and television stations and work closely with advertising agencies and commercial radio and television stations in the supervision and production of Armed Forces program material for the general public. Arrangements are made with stations and networks by the various offices of information of the military services for the appearance of service personnel and bands, for news broadcasts, special events, and clearance of scripts for radio and television broadcasts.

Pictorial Media

Audio-visual media, used extensively by the Armed Forces in communicating with both internal and external publics, includes still- and motion-picture films, official photographs, posters, drawings, charts, and aerial photographs. Information officers of all of the military services are responsible for disseminating audio-visual materials to newspapers, magazines, and broadcasting stations and networks.

The Public Information Division of the Office of the Director of Information, U.S. Air Force, has a Pictorial Branch which provides policy and guidance for still and motion picture coverage of Air Force activities for media as well as for historical and feature productions.

The Audio-Visual Branch of the Public Information Division of the Office of Chief of Information of the Army provides media with still pictures of Army activities; maintains a file of major officers; researches Army Signal Corps Library and other sources for still pictures to fill requests; and prepares spot news and still-feature coverage of

Army activities. It also initiates and supervises motion-picture coverage of Army activities, reviews films, approves scenarios submitted by commercial film studios, and appoints Army technical advisors to commercial film producers.

Printed Media

All of the information services of the Armed Forces produce and distribute booklets, folders, posters, and other forms of printed materials to inform both the internal and external publics. The Plans and Media Branch of the Army Troop Information Division is responsible for the production of posters and pamphlets to support the Army internal information program. The Office of Armed Forces Education and Information of the Department of Defense publishes literature for troop information on democracy, communism, citizenship, world affairs, orientation of overseas areas and code of conduct. A total of 53 publications and eight posters were distributed by the Department of Defense and the Army during 1961.

Magazines and Books

Publicity in magazines and books is an important medium of communication of the Armed Forces. The Magazine and Book Branch of the Public Information Division of the Air Force provides information and assistance to magazine and book publishers, editors, and free-lance writers about the activities of the Air Force. The Magazine and Book Branch of the Public Information Division of the Army and the Magazine and Book Branch of the Office of News Services of the Department of Defense provide similar aid to writers and book publishers. They arrange for authors' interviews with major officers, provide clearances for writers to visit military installations, review manuscripts of authors and editors, and answer requests from writers for information about military policy, procedures, and accomplishments.

Special Events

Special events including parades, band concerts, "fly-overs," ship commissionings and visits, open houses, tours, guest cruises, athletic contests, exhibits, displays, and demonstrations are important activities of Armed Forces public relations.

The Office of Public Services, Special Projects Branch, Department of Defense, is responsible for special events involving all of the Armed Forces such as Armed Forces Day, Joint Civilian Orientation Conferences, the President's People-to-People Program, the High School News Service, and others.

The Special Events Branch of the Community Relations Division of the Office of Information of the Air Force has responsibility for Air Force participation in public events and scheduled appearances of the "Thunderbirds," the famous aerial demonstration team; the U.S. Air Force Band and its subunits such as the Airmen of Note, Singing Sergeants, U.S. Air Force Dance Band, Strolling Strings, Drum and Bugle Corps, and the Air Force Orientation Group, which handles exhibits depicting Air Force missions, programs, achievements, and systems.

The Civil Relations Division of the Office of Information of the Navy administers Navy special events including guest cruises, visits of civilians to Naval installations, and Navy participation in civilian events.

Speakers

Speakers provided by the Armed Forces for meetings of civic clubs, lodges, churches, veteran, fraternal, and social orgainzations give the public authentic, firsthand information about the military services. The Speakers' Branch of the Community Relations Division of the Office of Information of the Air Force handles invitations to speak received by the Secretary of the Air Force, Chief of Staff, Vice-Chief of Staff, and other Air Staff general officers. Air Force Squadron Information Officers at the community level determine which officers and noncommissioned officers are available to speak to civilian groups and arrange for such speeches. Public speakers' guides for use by officers in preparing speeches on military topics have been prepared by the Offices of Information of the Navy and Army.

PUBLIC RELATIONS TRAINING IN ARMED FORCES

The United States Army and Air Force provide public relations training for selected staff officers, enlisted personnel, and civilian employees to prepare them for public and troop information assignments. The Army Information School was established at Carlisle Barracks, Pennsylvania, in 1946. In 1948, it was made a Department of Defense activity under the joint control of the Army, Navy, and Air Force and designated as the Armed Forces Information School. Here, were trained information personnel of all of the Armed Forces. In 1954, the school was returned to the jurisdiction of the Army and, today, is under the Chief of Information of the Army. The school has been located at Fort Slocum, New York, since 1951. It is administered by a Commandant with a staff and faculty. The faculty is divided into five academic departments: policy and plans; oral communications; applied journalism;

radio and television; and military, United States, and world affairs.

Three courses of instruction, two for training information officers and one for enlisted information specialists, are offered. Personnel of all services are eligible in addition to civilian personnel with certain qualifications. An eight-week course for information officers covers planning, supervision, and participation in the preparation and dissemination of information. A three-week course for radio broadcast officers trains in planning, co-ordination, supervision, and operation of an Armed Forces radio or television station. An eight-week course for information specialists trains enlisted personnel to participate in the administration of the Armed Forces information and public relations programs.

The Navy trains public information personnel at the U.S. Naval School for Journalism at the Naval Training Center, Great Lakes, Illinois. A four-week course covers the Navy and U.S. World Policy, foundations of public communication, Navy information programs, public information media, case studies, and problems.

The Air Force trains information officers at Boston University School of Public Relations and Communications, Boston, Massachusetts, in an eight-week Air Force information course which includes planning and evaluation of public relations activities, the United States Air Force and World Affairs, the publics and society, communications media and techniques, and U.S. Air Force information organization and policies.

The United States Armed Forces Institute, Madison, Wisconsin, makes available to personnel of the Armed Forces a course in public relations divided into five major areas and fourteen study units. The five major areas are: the field of public relations, the tools and techniques of public relations, the publics, public relations at work, and news releases. The fourteen study units of the course are: what is public relations?; what is public opinion?; organizing for public relations; public relations research; press relations; public relations periodicals; other media of public relations; internal public relations; consumer public relations; community public relations; trade public relations; public relations programs of special agencies; governmental public relations; and Armed Forces public relations.

PRESS RELATIONS OF THE ARMED FORCES

Good relations with the press, including newspaper, magazine, radio and television commentators, editors, publishers, and writers is essential to complete, accurate and impartial reporting of the activities of the Armed Forces.

Commanding officers through their public information assistants seek to maintain sound working relationships with the press in their areas by being immediately available to give the press prompt, truthful, and complete answers to queries; to initiate official releases of unclassified, newsworthy activities; to give equal access and privileges to bonafide media representatives; to invite newsmen to visit the command to observe and report unclassified activities and to seek the acquaintance, confidence, support, and understanding of media representatives.

The release of information concerning all of the Armed Forces at the seat of government is the responsibility of the Office of News Services of the Office of Public Affairs, Office of the Secretary of Defense, Washington, D.C. This office prepares news releases on all the Armed Forces and provides national news media with a central source of information. Information of national interest concerning the Army, Navy, and Air Force individually is relased by the Offices of Information of these services.

Accreditation of War Correspondents and Censorship

The Department of Defense, Office of Public Affairs, Accreditation and Travel Branch, Washington, D.C., accredits all news representatives assigned to areas outside of the United States for all of the Armed Forces. Certificates of Identity are issued to accredited correspondents. Accredited media representatives may ride on a nonreimbursable basis in military aircraft on assignments to cover Department of Defense activities and occupy a field press camp with facilities for administration, billeting, messing, transportation, briefing, and censorship.

Field press censorship is exercised over news material, entering, leaving, or circulating within an area to the extent deemed necessary by the commander for the maintenance of security. Commissioned officers of the respective services appointed by the theater commander act as field press censors. Information officers submit official releases to censorship and see that material submitted by correspondents is properly handled to insure good press relations. News material, still and motion pictures, radio and television scripts are submitted to field press censors who examine the material and stamp it as "Passed for Publication," "Not to be Released," or "Not to Be Released Before_____."

Press Conferences and Briefings

All of the Armed Forces employ press conferences arranged by local information officers. These conferences enable commanders to make important announcements; to enable news representatives to ask questions about involved subjects; and to provide background information for journalists. Conferences are also used to brief newsmen on tactical and operational plans and planned activities; to inform newsmen arriving within a command regarding procedure in clearing newsmatter; and to insure accurate news coverage of activities.

INTERNAL ARMED FORCES RELATIONS

Internal relations with members of the Armed Forces centers in the Office of Armed Forces Information and Education, Department of Defense, Washington, D.C., which has prepared programs to inform personnel of all military services. This office also controls the Armed Forces Radio and Television, the major medium of communication with military personnel throughout the world.

Each of the military services has its own internal communication program. In the Department of the Army, the Troop Information Division is under the Chief of Information and is divided into three branches: the Plans and Media Branch, the Network Support Branch, and the Command Newspapers Branch. The Plans and Media Branch develops Army-wide troop information plans, written and visual materials to supplement those produced by the Office of Armed Forces Information and Education, Department of Defense. The Network Support Branch is responsible for operating 98 radio and 13 television stations. The Command Newspapers Branch supervises the 300 official Army newspapers which are published.

The Internal Information Division of the Office of Information of the Air Force is divided into three branches: Internal Projects Branch, Editorial Production Branch, and Analysis Branch. The Internal Projects Branch monitors the supervisory staff visit program to information offices at bases throughout the world, arranges for an annual seminar for information personnel, monitors Air Force participation in the Foreign Service Institute's course on Communist Strategy. The Editorial Production Branch supervises 400 Air Force newspapers and the operation of 85 radio and 14 television stations overseas. The Analysis Branch attempts to find more effective informational programs by surveying Air Force personnel.

The Internal Relations Division of the Office of the Chief of Information, Department of the Navy, is responsible for internal communication with Navy personnel. It produces publications supplementing the program of the Office of Armed Forces Information and Education of the Department of Defense.

The objectives of internal communications of all of the Armed Forces are similar to those of the Army Troop Information Program which are: First, to develop in each soldier belief in the principles of American democracy and freedom; a sense of responsibility as a citizen; awareness of the threat of Communism to America and the Free World; determination to fight to preserve his American heritage; the will to continue resistance when facing military odds in combat and endurance under physical, mental, and emotional stress. Second, to convince each soldier of his personal importance to the Army; that the Army has an essential role in the defense of the Nation and Free World and that military service is a patriotic duty. Third, to explain to each soldier the mission of the Army and his unit; his military service obligations; his responsibilities in conduct and behavior; and the people, geography, climate, and importance of military-civilian relationships in the area in which he is serving.

INDUSTRIAL RELATIONS OF THE ARMY AND AIR FORCE

The Army and Air Force seek to develop good relations with contractors, subcontractors, and suppliers of materials and equipment. The Industrial Branch of the Community Relations Division of the Office of the Director of Information of the Air Force maintains liaison with contractors and resources on projects involving news releases and advertising.

The Industrial Relations Branch of the Civil Liaison Division of the Office of the Chief of Information of the Army assists industrial editors in assembling material for articles, reviews industrial magazine manuscripts for conformity to Army regulations, co-ordinates the placing of articles with appropriate technical publications, arranges for media representatives to visit industrial plants producing for the Army, plans visits of industrial workers to Army establishments, checks industrial advertisements to insure that they do not show the Army endorsing a commercial product, arranges for participation of soldiers in industrial ceremonies, and avoids involvement of the Army in industrial disputes.

COMMUNITY RELATIONS OF THE ARMED FORCES

Community relations of the Armed Forces is a command function which appraises the attitude of the command toward the civilian community as well as the attitudes of the civilian community toward the command, and initiates programs of action to earn community respect and confidence. Community relations of all Armed Forces is centered in the Office of Public Services of the Office of Public Affairs of the Department of Defense, Washington, D.C., which handles liaison with community organizations, provides speakers, and arranges for participation in special events.

Each of the military services has its own community relations program. The organization for community relations of each of the services at the seat of government has been described previously. The community relations objectives of the Air Force, which are typical of the objectives of the other services, have also been described previously.

Effective community relations of all branches of the services depend primarily upon the local commanders and their staff assistant information officers. A military post, air field, or installation is a part of the community in which it is located. Personnel stationed there mingle in many social, commercial, and other relationships, both official and unofficial, with the civilian population. Community opinion of the Armed Forces is composed of the personal impressions created by military personnel. Good or bad behavior of an individual soldier, sailor, or airman is regarded by the community as typical of all military personnel.

Understanding and good will of the community depends upon the awareness of the local commander and his staff of the problems involved and their ingenuity in winning the favor of the community. Civilian advisory committees, local officials, and businessmen, civic organizations, educators and professional men, opinion leaders, veteran organizations, and reserve components can help develop understanding and good relations between the military community and the civilian population.

Military installations are no longer isolated in remote communities throughout the country as in the past. They are found in hundreds of towns and cities not only in the United States but in many countries of the Free World. This makes the community relations of the Armed Forces more important than ever before.

Case 16–1

U.S. ARMY PUBLIC INFORMATION

Project MAN

The office of the Chief of Information Department of the Army, Washington D.C., is responsible for policy making, planning, co-ordinating, and supervising a continuing program of information and education about the U.S. Army for troops, civilian employees, Army National Guard, Army Reserve, industrial firms supplying the Army with equipment, and the American public.

The long-range objectives of the Army information program are: to secure public recognition of the scope and importance of the Army's mission; to gain the esteem and respect of the public for the Army and Army personnel; and to win public confidence in the Army's ability to execute its mission to be ready for combat now and in the future.

To achieve these objectives, the Office of the Chief of Information has selected the following five basic themes as major points of emphasis in presenting the Army story to the public: "The Army Is Essential," "The Army Is Modern," "The Soldier Is Tops," "The Army Insures Security, Any Time, Any Place, Any War," and "The U.S. Army Is One Army."

To implement the theme, "The Army Is Modern," the Office of the Chief of Information conceived "Project MAN" meaning Modern Army Needs. The objectives of this project were: to focus public attention on the Army's efforts to fulfill its mission to be ready for combat; to enable news media to get current, visual material on major weapon developments and their importance; to inform important government, military, and industrial leaders about the latest Army material and the Army's needs to enable it to fulfill its mission.

To attain these objectives the office of the Chief of Information of the Army planned a three-day, tactical exercise at Fort Benning, Georgia, the world's largest infantry training center, to demonstrate and exhibit 200 of the latest pieces of Army equipment, not classified for security, to leaders of the executive branch of the government, senior commanders, representatives of industry, and the press.

Invitations to "Project MAN" were issued by the Secretary and Chief of Staff of the Army to the President of the United States; high officers of the departments of Defense, Army, Navy, and the Air Force; civilian aides to the Secretary of the Army; important officers of the U.S. Army Reserves; U.S. Army National Guard; retired officers; North American Air Defense Command; overseas commands; and NATO Military Committee.

Two hundred invitations were extended to the press represented by reporters, editors, magazine writers, news broadcasters, wire services, and newsreel photographers.

Executives and scientists representing 35 industrial organizations producing tanks, aircraft, missiles, engines, automotive equipment, weapons, and electronic equipment were invited to the event.

Officials and opinion leaders of the Fort Benning community as well as newspaper, radio and television news broadcasters were also invited.

The three-day program began on May 2, 1960 with a welcome and remarks by the Chief of Staff of the Army, General Lyman L. Lemnitzer. He was followed by a night defense demonstration by a reinforced rifle company.

The program for the second day opened with an address by the Army Chief of Research and Development, Lieutenant General A. G. Trudeau. He was followed by a demonstration of river crossing techniques and equipment using new reconnaissance boats, assault boats, personnel carriers, a new-type infantry footbridge, rafts, and amphibians.

The arrival of Dwight D. Eisenhower, the President of the United States, and the Secretary of Defense was signaled with a 21-gun salute, inspection of the Guard of Honor, and Army equipment exhibit.

The President and guests witnessed a demonstration of modern Army equipment and a tactical display of weapons firing and airmobile assault.

Following the departure of the President, Secretary of the Army, Wilber M. Brucker, dedicated a bronze statue of the fighting American infantryman.

The second day closed with an official banquet in honor of the guests, with an address by Secretary of the Army Brucker, and entertainment by "The Bachelors," a quartet from the U.S. Army Field Band which tours the country under the sponsorship of the Army Chief of Information.

The program for the third day opened with remarks by the Deputy Chief of Staff for Logistics, Lieutenant General R. W. Colglazier, Jr., who discussed new Army equipment and its production. Displays of modern Army equipment and a demonstration of rangers in action preceded flights of new types of Army aircraft, paratrooper jumps, and supply drops. Farewell remarks were made by the Vice-Chief of Staff.

"Project MAN" was planned by two information officers and one clerical assistant in the office of the Chief of Information of the Army. The Deputy Chief of Staff for Logistics had primary staff responsibility for the execution of the program. Thirty-five industrial organizations supplying Army equipment participated in planning the event and provided material for press kits, arranging social functions, and transporting guests. The private, nonprofit Association of the United States Army co-operated by correlating many activities involved in the industrial participation. All subordinate Army commands supplied material and personnel for the event.

Execution of the project began two weeks in advance of the event with the establishment of an Advance Information Center at Fort Benning to co-ordinate rehearsals and promotional aspects.

The cost of the project was shared by the office of the Chief of Information investing $1,982; Fort Benning appropriating $663 for operation of Press Centers; and the Signal Corps spending $1,318 for media communication. Press kits, air-lift of newsmen, and mementos were provided by the Association of the U.S. Army and its industrial members. Troop participation, equipment, and its movement as in a training exercise was allocated to the training budget.

Six Press Centers were established throughout the Fort Benning reservation, five of which were adjacent to demonstration areas. Each center was equipped with typewriters and telephones. A total of 100 telephones were installed. The main Press Center was equipped with teletype machines. Twelve vehicles were provided to carry press dispatches from demonstration areas to the main Press Center.

To insure maximum photographic coverage, provision was made for three types of photographic operations: photographs produced by representatives of newspapers, magazines, and television; photographs by industrial personnel for their own advertising, house organs, and publicity; and official Army documentary coverage. Supervisory personnel from the office of the Chief of Information assisted photographers to obtain photographs of major interest.

An official photo display board in the Press Center illustrated and indicated by number photographs available to the press. Fifty-seven requests for 1,100 photographs were filled, in addition to 500 prints of major products on display or demonstrated.

Guests were transported by Army buses about the Fort Benning reservation to observe demonstrations of equipment. Special buses were provided for the press. Accommodations were provided for guests in the Student Officer Quarters on the post.

The 35 industrial organizations supplying Army equipment furnished 200 press kits each containing photographs, fact sheet, and news releases. Each guest was presented, by a leading supplier, with a bronze statuette of the statue of the American soldier dedicated by the Secretary of the Army. A special 16-page section on "Project MAN," published by the *Army Times,* was distributed to all guests.

"Project MAN" was publicized extensively to the Army throughout the world through a half-hour telecast by the 300 U.S. and overseas stations of the Armed Forces Television Network. The Army Hour, a radio program broadcast by 80 outlets in this country and 125 overseas, devoted a half-hour program to the event. The Army News Service supplied features to its 2,600 service media subscribers. The *Army Information Digest,* official magazine of the Army, read by 100,000 officers and enlisted men, devoted an entire issue to "Project MAN."

The project received extensive newspaper, magazine, television, and radio publicity through the 200 reporters, writers, and broadcasters who attended the event as representatives of 100 media. As a result of this publicity the confidence of the American public in the Army was increased. The public was impressed with the Army's extensive program of modernization and that today's soldier is proficient, versatile, and well trained. The President, Secretary of Defense, and other decision makers in government had an opportunity to see many new pieces of equipment. Key Army officers and producers of Army equipment were informed about current trends in equipment and how they are used on the battlefield.

QUESTIONS

1. What specific benefits were gained by the U.S. Army from "Project MAN"?
2. What are the limitations of an event of this kind?
3. In what specific ways could "Project MAN" be improved?
4. Were the program and arrangements for "Project MAN" satisfactory? What changes, if any, should have been made in the program for this event?
5. Was press relations for this event satisfactory? In what ways could press coverage have been improved?

Case 16–2

UNITED STATES ARMY COMMUNITY RELATIONS

U.S. Army Caribbean—"Operation Friendship"

Installations of the U.S. Army overseas are confronted with a growing spirit of criticism, instigated by communist agitators in the guise of nationalists, which creates a climate hostile to the United States and its armed forces. The mis-understanding of nationals of foreign countries in which Army units are located interferes with the mission of these military forces and poses a serious threat not only to the Army but also to the national security.

The same principles and practices underlying sound community relations of Army installations in the United States are being applied by the Army overseas. An outstanding example of Army community relations abroad is "Operation Friendship" which is being carried out by headquarters U.S. Army Caribbean, Fort Amador, Panama Canal Zone.

The problem confronting the Army in the Canal Zone was critical deteriora-tion of United States–Panamanian relationships created by incidents, some occur-ring as far back as the construction of the Panama Canal, and others of more recent origin stemming from the nationalistic activities of agitators. The Pan-amanian press slanted news to portray the United States and its citizens in Pan-ama in unfavorable terms. Automobile accidents involving U.S. soldiers and Panamanian citizens were reported in the press with sensational headlines. Antagonism between the United States of America and the people of Panama reached an all-time high.

It was apparent to the Army commander that immediate action must be taken to remedy an untenable situation and prevent further deterioration of relations and avoid an impending catastrophe in an exceedingly critical area of our na-tional defense. After analyzing the growing danger, the commanding general took immediate action in two ways: first, he announced that the community rela-tions of the Army would be given priority attention; and secondly, he invited representatives of the Panamanian press to a conference at the Fort Amador Officers' Mess.

At the press conference of newspaper, radio, and television newsmen, the commanding general complimented the Panamanians on the progress made by their country since World War II and expressed his concern over worsening United States–Panama relationships. He asked for the co-operation of the press in dispelling the existing antagonism and creating a spirit of understanding and friendship between U.S. military and civilian personnel and Panamanians.

The commanding general announced an Army community relations program called "Operation Friendship" designed to improve relations between the U.S. Army and civilian personnel and the people of Panama. The project was under the direction of the Information Officer, U.S. Army Caribbean and was directed to the following major audiences: (1) news media, (2) Panamanian civilians, (3) Panamanian military, (4) Panamanian youth, and (5) specialized groups.

The good will and understanding of these groups was cultivated by a variety of activities carried out by U.S. Army and civilian personnel as follows: personal contacts with the press; special events such as tours, open houses, exhibits, and social affairs; charitable activities; sports competitions; educational, religious, and cultural activities, and sports events.

The principal activity of "Operation Friendship" involved some 300 educa-tional, religious, and cultural events over a nine-month period. Thousands of hours of U.S. military and civilian labor were contributed to the construction of a school in the town of Arraijan. The building was dedicated by the President of Panama and U.S. Ambassador who paid tribute to the friendly co-operation of U.S. soldiers and civilians with Panamanians in the erection of the building.

Citizens of Panama City presented General Theodore F. Bogart, commanding general, U.S. Army Caribbean, with a diploma of merit as creator of "Operation Friendship" at the dedication of a new cultural center at the Republic of El Salvador school in Panama City.

Other cultural activities carried on by U.S. Army and civilian personnel for Panamanians included stage performances, motion pictures for children, spe-

FIG. 16–3.   An airfield for Chiman, an inaccessible jungle village in Panama was public relations "Operation Pista" (Runway) for U.S. Air Force First Commando Group stationed at Howard Air Force Base, Panama. Air Force aircraft is shown taking off after dedication of the new airfield which was constructed by townspeople with plans, equipment, and direction by the Commandos.

cial television and radio programs, and concerts by the Army band. Panamanians in turn staged musical and cultural programs for the U.S. military, their dependents, and United States citizens.

Charitable and Good Will Activities

Numerous charitable and good will activities characterized "Operation Friendship." Army personnel adopted several poor Panamanian families through Father Enrique Laburu, a Catholic priest who sponsors "Radio Hogar," a radio station which is the voice of his church in Panama and a potent force in combating subversive propaganda and communism. North Americans gave substantial sums to "Radio Hogar" to provide a stronger transmitter and increase its effectiveness.

A self-help project sponsored by an organization of U.S. Army wives was the furnishing of a school near Fort Kobbe. Lumber and material for chairs were provided with the understanding that Panamanians would make the chairs for the school. Active participation of Panamanians in the project won their good will and avoided the appearance of paternalism.

Other good will activities included: emergency blood bank donations by Army personnel; special assistance by the U.S. medical corps; visits by U.S. military and their dependents to Panamanian hospitals; benefit events staged by U.S. Army personnel and their families; charitable contributions by U.S. citizens and military to Panamanian individuals and groups, and the loan of U.S. Army equipment for the construction and repair of Panamanian schools and hospitals.

Press Relations

A minimum of "press agentry" and a predominance of meaningful projects of permanent value was responsible for the generous publicity given "Operation Friendship" by Panamanian newspapers, radio and television stations. More than 75 contacts were made over a nine-month period by the Information Officer and his staff of headquarters U.S. Army Caribbean with the Panamanian press in publicizing "Operation Friendship." Thirty-six formal press conferences were held with Panamanian news media in addition to numerous social meetings with members of the press. A leading Panamanian newspaper which was previously highly critical of the United States reversed its hostile attitude and gave a party for the entire Army headquarters information staff.

The day the Panamanian flag was raised over the Canal Zone, a United States citizen was stabbed by a Panama national extremist. The U.S. Army Information Officer released to the press his statement, "I know this act does not represent the feelings of the citizens of the Republic of Panama." Favorable editorials and news stories commented on the statement. Following his recovery, a television appearance was arranged by the principal television station, indicating the changed attitude of the Panamanian news media.

Panamanian Independence Day approached with widespread fear of anti–United States demonstrations and bloodshed but as a result of "Operation Friendship" the day passed without a single hostile incident.

The establishment of friendly relations with the Panamanian press is confirmed by an editorial in the Panama *Tribune,* a leading newspaper of the Republic, which stated in part: "We had our reservations about the real effectiveness of "Operation Friendship" but we shall not hesitate to admit that its aims have penetrated into the minds of all classes of Panamanians. Within the past year United States military and diplomatic representatives have made numerous gestures toward Panama and its citizens bearing sentiments of good will and friendship. The people of this country have not been insensible to these manifestations and it is encouraging to observe the many tributes of appreciation being extended."

Youth Activities

More than one hundred projects for Panamanian youth were carried out in "Operation Friendship" during a nine-month period. Parties were given for Panamanian children by U.S. military and civilian personnel who also organized sports competitions for Panamanian youth.

Activities for Panamanian Civilian and Military Personnel

A wide variety of projects provided individual and group contacts between the U.S. military and Panamanian civilians in "Operation Friendship." Special events including parades, open houses, social affairs, and exhibitions were staged by the U.S. Army for Panamanians. Joint meetings of U.S. and Panamanian professional groups were held. Numerous tours of U.S. military facilities were arranged for civilians. U.S. military and civilian officials visited Panamanian cities, towns, and installations.

Both United States and Panamanian military participated in "Operation Friendship" activities. Panamanian military forces took part in several U.S. Army sponsored events. The U.S. Army honored Panamanian military officials who visited our military installations in the Canal Zone. The Panamanian Army was host to U.S. Army officers at several special events and sponsored sight-seeing tours for U.S. military and their dependents.

Anniversary Celebration of "Operation Friendship"

One year after "Operation Friendship" was initiated, an anniversary party to commemorate the program was sponsored by the U.S. Army to which U.S. military and civilians and their Panamanian counterparts were invited. The objectives of this event were: to express appreciation to Panamanians who worked with U.S. military and civilians to make the program a success; to recognize those who made outstanding contributions in various ways; and to give assurance that the first year was only the beginning of an expanded, permanent community relations program which has become the basis for an entirely new concept of U.S.–Panama relations.

Effectiveness of "Operation Friendship"

"Operation Friendship" in the opinion of the commanding general U.S. Army Caribbean, was a successful program for improving relations between the U.S. Army and U.S. citizens and the people and military of the Republic of Panama. Carried out at no cost to the U.S. Army aside from the time of the personnel involved, "Operation Friendship" demonstrated that a well-conceived community relations program of sound activities and constructive projects based on the principle of self-help can dispel misunderstanding and win the good will of the civilian and military of Panama and other foreign countries where U.S. Army installations are located.

QUESTIONS

1. Comment on "Operation Friendship" as a medium of community relations for the U.S. Army overseas. What are the strengths and weaknesses of this type of program?
2. What change or improvement can you propose to make "Operation Friendship" more effective? Describe an improved program.
3. What were the basic conceptions underlying "Operation Friendship"? What other principles should have been followed to insure a more effective program.
4. How could relations with the press have been improved in the community relations of U.S. Army Caribbean?

SECTION 4 · INTERNATIONAL PUBLIC RELATIONS

PUBLIC RELATIONS is accepted today as an essential activity of business and professional organizations and government agencies in the principal industrial countries throughout the free world. Although the climate in which public relations functions in many countries is not as favorable as in the United States, imaginative practitioners from Scandinavia to South Africa and Australia to Japan are pioneering public relations programs to win the understanding and good will of the people of many nations.

Public relations societies composed of public relations directors and counselors have been organized in the principal countries to advance and enhance the status of the profession and raise the standards and ethics of practitioners. Educational courses have been initiated to train men and women in research, planning, production, and administration of public relations programs. Codes of ethics have been adopted and procedures for qualifying practitioners established.

Many government agencies in countries throughout the world use public relations not only in their internal relations with their own nationals but also in informing the people of other countries about their tourist attractions and products.

The most extensive public relations activity in the United States is the international public information program of the United States Information Agency which explains United States foreign policy, counters hostile propaganda, and presents a balanced, accurate picture of American life and culture to the world.

· INTERNATIONAL
PUBLIC RELATIONS

A GROWING INTEREST in public relations throughout the free world is a result of great technological, political, social, and economic changes which have given people of the emerging nations freedom of expression and recognition of the power of public opinion.

Great progress in telecommunications, making possible rapid and widespread transmission of information and ideas, has created unparalleled opportunities for people to communicate with each other and exert tremendous impact on world opinion.

The threat to the free world posed by communism and socialism is awakening the leaders of capitalistic countries to the need for exposing the fallacies of these doctrines and arousing public opinion in free nations in favor of capitalism.

United States' economic aid to foreign countries and private investments abroad make it necessary for business and government to employ public relations to protect our foreign investments and develop favorable public opinion abroad.

In undeveloped countries, expanded educational programs are making it possible for once illiterate people to read books, newspapers, and magazines and exert the power of enlightened public opinion on national and international issues.

In Europe, the Common Market of France, West Germany, Holland, Italy, Belgium, and Luxembourg has unified the European economy and created new opportunities to employ public relations to secure better understanding and good will throughout Europe. Higher living standards, rising employment, and a prosperous economy have combined to stimulate the practice of public relations.

Industrial, political, and social welfare organizations in many countries throughout the world are employing the public relations techniques, which have been originated and developed in the United States, to solve the problem of creating better understanding with employees, stockholders, neighbors, and consumers. Public relations associations have been established, and public relations departments created in government agencies, business, and social organizations in the most progressive nations.

Although the practice of public relations is making significant progress in countries throughout the world, particularly in Great Britain, Belgium, and France, public relations in the United States has attained a level of development unequaled in other countries.

Climate of Public Relations in Nations around the World

Public relations in many countries is developing in a much less favorable climate than in the United States. Established business practices and economic systems prevailing in many countries seriously handicap the development of the practice of public relations.

The traditional secrecy which surrounds the operations of many business concerns in many countries makes the management reluctant to reveal information about finances, policies, and operations. This reticence is detrimental to good public relations and restricts publicity opportunities.

European industry is monopolistic and does not recognize the desirability of cultivating the understanding and good will of the consuming public. Many large industrial enterprises are not concerned with informing and developing the good will of their employees. Industry in some countries is more interested in keeping the public in ignorance than in acquiring public understanding.

Many newspapers abroad refuse to use the name of industrial concerns in their news columns except for a consideration. News releases are only accepted from advertisers. Advertising contracts may provide that so many inches of advertising automatically entitles the advertiser to a certain number of "free news stories."

In many countries the term "public relations" has little or no meaning. It is usually used synonymously with advertising or product publicity.

In spite of these obstacles to the development of public relations, the practices of public relations in the United States are slowly being introduced abroad. The public relations associations in the principal countries, through discussions with the press and advertisers, are clarifying the meaning of public relations, adopting professional standards and codes of ethics, and securing acceptance of press publicity.

Public Relations of American Firms Abroad

Many American corporations engaged in foreign trade have adopted, in their overseas operations, the public relations practices and policies which have proven effective in the United States. The public relations departments of American corporations which operate abroad assist overseas subsidiary companies with their public relations programs.

General Motors Overseas Operations division of General Motors Corporation operates assembly plants in subsidiary companies in Pakistan, New Zealand, Mexico, Switzerland, France, Great Britain, Belgium, Germany, Denmark, Sweden, Australia, Venezuela, Peru, Argentina, Uruguay, Brazil, and South Africa. Each of these companies operates autonomously its public relations program.

The public relations department of General Motors Overseas Operations in New York City acts as a service group to foreign subsidiary companies and informs them about General Motors public relations programs in the United States. The companies abroad use American public relations programs in their entirety or adapt them to their local conditions.

Standard Oil Company of New Jersey operates abroad through 50 affiliate companies in Canada, Latin America, Europe, North Africa, and the Middle and Far East. Most of these companies maintain their own public relations departments, ranging in size from one or two-man operations to large staffs, which conduct programs designed to meet local needs.

The public relations programs of Standard Oil Company, New Jersey, foreign subsidiaries involve consumer magazines, pamphlets, booklets, press releases, the production and distribution of films, school programs, special events, speech preparation, and other public relations activities varied according to the need and scope of local operations.

The public relations departments of foreign affiliates of Standard Oil Company, New Jersey, are assisted by the Area Contacts Division of the public relations department of the parent company in New York City. This division keeps overseas companies informed of the parent company's public relations policies and activities, promotes exchange of public relations information between affiliates and the parent company, and supplies material and counsel. Contacts are maintained by the parent company public relations department with foreign companies by correspondence, frequent visits, periodic regional conferences attended by management and public relations representatives of affiliates, and an internal monthly public relations periodical, *PR Review.*

The *PR Review* reports on the public relations activities of Standard Oil Company of New Jersey affiliates throughout the world and serves as a medium for the communication of ideas between the parent company and foreign companies.

The scope of Standard Oil public relations abroad is illustrated by the

FIG. 17–1. Cartagena, Colombia fertilizer plant of International Petroleum, Ltd., affiliate of Standard Oil Co., New Jersey, officially opened, in 1963, with impressive public dedication ceremonies attended by opinion leaders, government officials, and parent-company executives.

following activities of subsidiary companies. The Creole Petroleum Corporation, Venezuelan affiliate, established the Creole Foundation for the advancement of cultural, educational, and scientific activities in Venezuela. Esso Standard Italiana, Italian affiliate, sponsored a Journalists Automobile Rally near Venice. A conference of leading British economists was arranged by Esso Petroleum, Ltd., Standard Affiliate in the United Kingdom. The International Petroleum Company, Ltd.,

Peru affiliate, arranged a series of window displays of the company's operations in the principal cities of Peru. A campaign of automobile silence on the streets of Tunis, capital of Tunisia was sponsored by Esso Standard Tunisie, S.A.

Public relations programs effective in the United States may not be equally successful abroad. The customs and point of view of people of other countries require a different public relations approach.

The foreign affiliate of an American corporation, following the practice of the parent company, offered scholarships to young people of the country. As is the policy in the United States, these scholarships did not require the recipients to work for the company after completion of their studies. The scholarship offer aroused no interest and there were no applicants for the educational benefits. Investigation revealed that the people of the country believed that since the company did not require winners of scholarships to work for it, the corporation must have some hidden motive of self-interest deliberately disguised in the scholarship offer which was probably dishonest and corrupt. When the scholarship offer was revised to require recipients of scholarships to work for the company, the scholarships were eagerly sought.

Another example of public relations techniques which are sound in the United States but which are not effective overseas occurred in South America. A foreign affiliate of a large American company desired to encourage employee participation in a suggestion plan by setting a goal of 101 new ideas from employees for a given period. To whet the curiosity of the workers, preceding announcement of the plan, the company posted the number "101," without explanation, throughout the works. A short time previously a reduction in the work force had been necessary. When the number "101" was posted, some workers believed that it was a subtle stratagem of management to suggest that 101 more workers would soon be discharged. So serious was the misunderstanding that a special meeting of workers was called and a special issue of the employee magazine was published to correct the misconception of employees.

These examples of the failure of American public relations practices in foreign countries confirm the desirability of giving foreign affiliates responsibility for conducting their own public relations programs to conform to the psychology and customs of the country.

International Public Relations Counsel

Some American companies engaged in foreign trade retain public relations counsel in the United States that specializes in public relations abroad. Other companies retain counsel in foreign countries to develop programs, communicate with employees, conduct research, prepare press releases, arrange press conferences, prepare public relations materials, act as a clearinghouse for public relations data from various countries, co-ordinate campaigns in several countries, and evaluate their effectiveness.

A well-known American public relations counseling firm has two foreign subsidiary companies; one located in The Hague, The Netherlands; and the second in Sydney, Australia. In addition, it is associated with independent public relations consultants in Paris, London, Toronto, Brussels, Stockholm, and Wellington, New Zealand.

Another public relations counsel located in New York City has established a network of foreign associates, independent public relations counseling firms, in 25 countries. These foreign public relations firms are familiar with the customs, prejudices, and communications media in their respective countries and are able to offer valuable assistance to American firms in planning public relations programs.

American public relations counselors also serve foreign governments, associations, and industries which are seeking to improve their public relations in the United States.

Public relations counsel in New York work closely with the public relations departments of their clients in the United States in planning foreign programs. An overseas program may be a short-term project involving a plant opening, anniversary, new product announcement, or visit by a headquarters executive; or have a long-term objective involving the building of a corporate reputation or a more favorable business climate for the client overseas.

Foreign Public Relations in the United States

An increasing number of foreign governments, associations, and corporations are carrying on public relations campaigns in the United States. These programs are usually handled by American public relations counseling firms. The principal objective of these programs is to develop favorable public opinion in this country for the foreign nation or industry, stimulate sales of foreign products in the American market, or correct unfavorable impressions of the foreign nation in this country.

The public relations program in the United States for the Commonwealth of Puerto Rico Development Administration, planned and executed by a New York public relations consulting firm, is a typical example of a foreign program in this country. The purpose of this program was to create a better understanding in the United States of the social and economic aims of Puerto Rico, to stimulate interest in capital investment in Puerto Rico, to develop a tourist industry, and to establish an atmosphtre of understanding between Puerto Rico and continental America.

A news bureau was established in San Juan, the capital of Puerto Rico. Journalists from leading newspapers and press services in the United States were invited to visit Puerto Rico to observe developments there. They reported in a series of feature articles on the social and economic progress in the Commonwealth.

The campaign produced 50 motion-picture news reels, motion-picture short subjects, documentary films by leading Hollywood producers for commercial theaters, and photographs for numerous newspapers and magazines illustrating significant developments in Puerto Rico.

This public relations program aided in bringing to Puerto Rico 350 new industrial enterprises which provided 30,000 new jobs and trebled the per capita income of the people of the country. Tourist income increased from $2 million to $20 million annually in the same period.

A public relations program in the United States for West Germany was credited with changing the attitude of the American public toward Germany, creating acceptance of German imports, particularly automobiles, and stimulating the flow of American capital to the West German industrial enterprises.

The government of Japan sponsored a public relations program in the United States to dispel war-born antagonism, create a favorable image of Japanese social life and economic progress, and secure acceptability of Japanese cotton imports.

PUBLIC RELATIONS AROUND THE WORLD

In many nations of the free world, public relations is in its infancy. The term "public relations" is unknown in many languages. Modern techniques of public relations are gradually being adopted abroad as an essential function of government and business. The value of public relations is slowly being recognized through the efforts of pioneering practitioners in progressive countries who are explaining the American conception of public relations and showing how it can be used to develop public understanding by business, the professions, and government.

Much of the impetus for the development of public relations throughout the world has come from the United States. Many of the techniques which have become accepted in this country as standard practice are being adopted as public relations practices in other countries.

Public Relations in Great Britain

The substantial progress of public relations in Great Britain reflects the enterprise of the British Institute of Public Relations, the only representative organization of practitioners of public relations in the United Kingdom. Established in 1948, the Institute has a membership of about 1,300 in Great Britain, in addition to overseas associate members. The membership includes public relations officers in local and central government, the armed forces, trade associations, industry, and counseling services. The Institute appointed its first full-time director in 1963.

The Institute has a 14-point development plan designed to protect and enhance the status of public relations in Great Britain and to raise the standard of practice of those engaged in public relations.

To place public relations on a par with the older professions, the Institute admits to membership only those persons who have a minimum of three years of practice, who are able to pass intermediate and final examinations of the Institute, and show evidence of professional competence. The Institute's written and oral examinations cover the principles and practice of public relations, printed material, advertising, press relations, opinion research, visual aids, and knowledge of a specialized field of public relations. The examinations are designed to evaluate a candidate's practical knowledge of the uses, techniques, and media of public relations.

To prepare candidates for admission to membership, the Institute has conducted an intermediate 60-period public relations course at the London Polytechnic consisting of lectures by practicing public relations executives supplemented with periods of field work and discussion. A final course of twelve seminars in public relations prepares for the final Institute examinations for candidates for membership. The textbook required in these courses is "A Guide to the Practice of Public Relations" published by the Institute in 1958. It was written by 24 leading practitioners who are members of the Institute and discusses the purpose and functions of public relations, the publics, consultancy, opinion research, and the media and organization for public relations in government, industry, and trade associations.

British Government Public Relations

British public relations is most highly developed in the areas of national and local government. In the central government ministries in England, the public relations officer and his staff keep the general public informed about the ministry's policies and functions. Close relations are maintained with the press through press notices, summaries, and conferences. Arrangements are made for radio and television features, photographs, news reels, and public visits. Educational campaigns and advertising are an important feature of the government public relations program.

Information service is an important function of the public relations staff in most British government ministries. Inquiry rooms are staffed to answer inquiries and provide information to the public calling in person, or by telephone, or to refer inquirers to government officials for further information. The public relations office of each ministry is also responsible for keeping the minister and officials aware of press and public opinion. Public relations offices are normally organized in three sections: press relations, publicity and inquiry, and intelligence.

In British municipal governments, the public relations officer is advised by a public relations committee and reports to the clerk of the municipal council. The public relations officer is politically impartial in his service to the corporate council and all departments of the local government. His functions include providing information and facilities to the press and other media; supervising public inquiries; arranging public meetings, lectures, and visits; producing and showing films; contacting local organizations; preparing and advising on publications; and providing the council with information on public opinion.

Some municipal governments operate central information centers to answer requests for information from the public. An important function of municipal government public relations is contact with local organizations—schools, clubs, and societies—to keep them informed about actions of the local government and use them as a sounding board of public opinion on major issues. Lectures and speeches by government officials to local organizations and schools are arranged by the public relations officer. A number of documentary films have been produced by the public relations departments of English cities for showing to local audiences, particularly, "A City Speaks," by the city of Manchester; "Capital County," by the London county council; and "Bristol, British City."

British Public Relations Counselors

Many British organizations employ no public relations officer nor staff but rely entirely upon public relations consultants and service organizations such as advertising agencies, individual counselors, publicity services, printers, and free-lance writers for advice and assistance in planning, research, budgeting, and production of public relations programs. About 250 counseling firms and service organizations are members of the British Institute of Public Relations.

Some British advertising agencies operate public relations departments to give public relations service to advertiser-clients although, in some cases, public relations counsel is provided without advertising service.

Some British government agencies and industrial concerns with public relations departments also retain private consultants to advise, plan, and prepare public relations materials. Some consultants specialize in government public relations, others serve industrial companies.

Consulting firms range in size from a proprietor with one or two assistants to staffs of 30 or more persons specializing in press releases, radio and television, photography, exhibitions, and press clippings.

British Public Relations Media

The principal medium of public relations communication in Great Britain is the daily newspaper. The 50 million people of Great Britain are the greatest newspaper readers in the world, buying more than 28 million newspapers daily. Accordingly, British public relations departments usually include a press office to answer press inquiries, prepare "handouts," and arrange press conferences, entertainment, and facility visits. Press officers maintain a press information desk and reference library to answer inquiries from newspaper writers and editors. A record of all press inquiries is maintained and periodic analysis indicates trends in public interest and opinion.

Radio and television are also important media of communication with the British public which is licensed to receive programs of information, education, and entertainment broadcast by the government-owned-and-operated British Broadcasting Company. Twelve types of radio broadcasts are provided by the BBC: news, religious talks and discussions, music, drama features, documentaries, variety and light entertainment, outside programs, children's, schools, and political. Many of these programs provide public relations opportunities for noncommercial material.

The British Broadcasting Company also televises news, talks, music, drama, films, and women's, children's, and school programs. A television network supported by advertising revenue is operated by the government television authority which contracts with program companies to provide programs. Advertisers purchase time on the programs from the program companies but have no control over the content of the programs. The program companies, in addition to providing programs, pay an annual rent to the government authority for use of the broadcast facilities.

Documentary films sponsored by government departments, armed services, and industry are produced by nontheatrical film producers for showing to schools, welfare organizations, societies, and clubs. Distribution of public relations films is secured through commercial film libraries such as Sound Services, Ltd., which distributes films sponsored by industry to 10,000 regular exhibitors. Large industrial concerns maintain their own film libraries for distribution of their films. The Petroleum Film Bureau distributes films of the major oil companies.

Public relations advertising is used in Great Britain by government departments to encourage national savings, to recruit for civil defense, advise immunization against disease, and to cope with emergencies. Industrial organizations employ institutional advertising to enhance prestige and create public good will.

Both internal and external public relations periodicals are widely used in Great Britain. The National Association of Industrial Editors has published a directory listing 800 British organization periodicals for employees, customers, and dealers. Most of these periodicals are produced by the public relations staffs of industrial organizations.

British Public Relations Programs

The following public relations of a British industrial corporation and a professional association illustrate the development of public relations in Great Britain and the similarity of British and United States public relations methods.

Ford Motor Company, Ltd. The Ford Motor Company, Ltd., a British company, located at Dagenham, near London, England, produces annually more than $300 million worth of Consul, Zephyr, Prefect, Anglia, and Popular automobiles, trucks, and tractors in 15 plants in England and Ireland. A public relations staff of 20 is organized in three departments: press and information, administration and publications, and visits and company entertainment.

Relations with the domestic and foreign press, radio, television, and newsreel organizations is the responsibility of the press and information department which works closely with the Labor Relations department of the company on labor news. As British newspapers and magazines devote considerable space to the performance of automobiles, the public relations department maintains a small fleet of vehicles which are loaned without charge to correspondents for test purposes. All written, spoken, or broadcast news issued by the company is handled by six press relations staff members.

Three periodicals are edited and published by the publications section: the monthly *Ford Times* for 80,000 motorists; the *Farm* for 35,000 agriculturalists; and weekly *Ford Bulletin* for 45,000 company employees. The publications department produces books, booklets, leaflets, and literature describing the company's operations which are distributed to the press, plant visitors, and opinion leaders.

Accommodations and entertainment for visiting overseas dealers, press representatives, and important guests are arranged by the visits and company entertainment department which also handles public tours of the Dagenham works. A staff of trained guides is kept continuously employed showing more than 50,000 visitors annually through the Dagenham plant.

Motion pictures on such subjects as public welfare, care of children, and the marketing of fruits and vegetables are produced by the public relations staff with the aid of the advertising department to enhance the prestige of the company and to contribute to public welfare.

Employee relations is furthered by employee service awards which are arranged by the research section of the public relations department and the labor relations staff, and presented at an annual dinner in London at which employees with long service are honored.

Racing publicity is obtained by the company in connection with stock car races or rallies held in various European countries. A half-dozen racing teams, two persons to each car, are sponsored by the company for the Monte Carlo Rally and similar events. The cars are prepared and entered by the public relations department.

British Medical Association. The British Medical Association was established in 1832, as a professional organization of medical practitioners to advance the welfare of the medical profession in Great Britain. In the past 50 years the British medical profession has been involved in political controversies over national health insurance and socialized medicine in which the profession has been denounced by the press and accused of sabotaging social security and selfishly opposing the public interest.

Faced with deteriorating public relations and a "bad press" the Association formed a public relations committee to consider matters involving the relations of the profession and the public. A public relations director and staff of seven was appointed to acquaint the public with the medical profession's position on controversial issues, to answer criticisms, and inform the public on all kinds of medical and medico-political subjects from medical education to geriatrics, spiritual healing, and local authority appointments.

The staff information officer provides a comprehensive information service to the public and press on social medicine and answers inquiries of business firms, government departments, embassies, and radio broadcasting and television organizations. Press publicity is prepared and distributed on scientific and political reports issued by the Association and major decisions of the body and council of the Association. Press conferences are held to announce scientific reports. All of the principal British periodicals are read and circulated to Association officers.

The national press and broadcasting authorities are invited to send representatives to the annual meeting of the Association. Accommodations for 40 journalists are made at the meeting place with a press room staffed by the public relations department with telephone facilities, typewriters, and synopses of scientific papers and news releases. Press conferences are held at which officials of the Association give background talks to the press and individual interviews are arranged between newspapermen and important doctors.

Correspondence with the general public is an important function of the public relations department. Misunderstandings in regard to medical practice or the regulations of the National Health Service are dissolved by correspondence and resentment toward the medical profession is dispelled.

Publications of the Association including "Care and Treatment of the Elderly and Infirm," the "British Medical Association Book of Medical Scholarships," "Guide to the British Medical Association and Its Activities," a list of forthcoming medical conferences, and other publications are prepared with the co-operation of the staff of the British Medical Journal and distributed to the profession and the public.

Meetings of the important committees of the Association are attended by the public relations officer and the department arranges for speakers to address professional meetings and aids them in the preparation of their speeches.

Each of the 200 local divisions of the Association has a voluntary public relations secretary, a doctor, who informs the local press, provides speakers for public meetings, and informs the headquarters public relations office in London of public attitudes toward the medical profession.

Public Relations in France

Public relations is becoming an important function in an increasing number of French commercial and industrial enterprises. French industrial public relations had its beginning in the period of economic progress following World War II, when a small group of public relations men led by Charles Louis Blondel, organized "La Maison de Verre" or "The House of Glass" which urged French managers to abandon traditional secrecy, live in "glass houses," and reveal their operations to the public. The Conseil National du Patronat Francais, the leading federation of French industries, co-operated by sponsoring a program of plant visits which increased the number of plant visitors fiftyfold. Individual companies held open houses, established relations with schools, and initiated public relations programs.

In 1955, the Association Francaise des Relations Publiques, the French public relations association, was established to facilitate the development of public relations in France and to guide practitioners in the objectives and professional ethics of public relations. Today, 280 public relations managers and counselors are members of the Association.

The development of public relations in France has been handicapped by lack of trained, experienced practitioners; the opposition of advertising agencies and the press which looks upon public relations as "free publicity"; public prejudice against big business; the indifference of business management; and the limited public ownership of shares in corporations.

The most significant public relations programs in France are found in large industrial organizations; a few medium-sized firms confine their public relations activities to product publicity. Government agencies are also practitioners of public relations. The French Ministry of Posts and Tele-Communications, under its director of external relations, has a staff of 130 public relations field men who are responsible for community and press relations on the local level. These field men meet annually at the Ministry in Paris to hear from the Minister, Secretary General, and Director of External Relations how to improve understanding of the postal service by the public. The External Relations Department of the Ministry also produced motion pictures, a monthly publication for the general public, booklets and exhibits.

Public Relations in Italy

The organization for the advancement of public relations in Italy, Associazione Italiana per le Relazioni Pubbliche was established in Rome, in 1954, and has a membership of about 500 public relations managers and counselors. The Association has held seminars and courses for its members and staged the International Congress in Stresa in 1956 and a public relations convention in Rome in 1957. Regional public relations groups are organized in Naples and Milan.

A growing number of Italian firms are becoming interested in public relations, but there is a limited number of trained practitioners in Italy. The practice of public relations is handicapped by fundamental philosophical and psychological misconceptions concerning what public relations can and should do. Many Italian public relations departments have the conception that their major function is to prevent publication of unfavorable information about their firm's activities. Many firms which urgently need public relations are not employing public relations although they are awakening to the need for both internal and external relations. The idea that a firm can provide legitimate news is not generally recognized by either the press or industry. Italian public relations firms are actually advertising agencies. Large American and international firms operating in Italy have experienced public relations managers heading their public relations departments, but most Italian firms do not have the same concept of public relations as corporations in the United States.

Public Relations in Belgium

The Public Relations Society of Belgium, which was established in Brussels, in 1953, as the Centre Belge des Publiques Relations, has a membership of about seventy including public relations officers of industrial firms, counseling agencies, government, education, and other groups. The objective of the Society is to promote a better understanding of public relations in Belgium. The organization held its first national public relations conference in Brussels, in 1956, attended by public relations representatives of government and industry. A similar event has held in 1957. In 1958, the Society was host to the first World Congress of Public Relations, attended by 237 delegates from 23 countries, which was held in connection with the International Exhibition in Brussels. As a result of the efforts of the Society, an increasing number of Belgian private enterprises, as well as government agencies, are establishing public relations departments. The Belgian postal and broadcasting departments have instituted public relations programs. The first public relations bibliography ever published in Europe has been issued by the Society. In 1961, a Belgian Public Relations Mission was sent to the United States to study public relations in this country.

Public Relations in Denmark

A number of international corporations, as well as progressive local industrial firms, are conducting public relations programs in Denmark. Press relations is the principal activity of most Danish companies, which stage "press demonstrations" and luncheons primarily for the introduction of new products. Other public relations activities include highway safety education for children, educational materials for schools, employee education, and plant visits. Public relations is usually a function of the advertising manager in Danish industrial firms.

Public Relations in Switzerland

The Schweizerische Public Relations Gesellschaft, or the Swiss Public Relations Society, was organized in 1957 and now has a membership of some 160 public relations practitioners interested in fostering public relations in Switzerland. Much public relations work is carried on in Switzerland under different designations and in different departments, principally by advertising staffs as an auxiliary function. Some companies publish employee periodicals; consumer product manufacturers conduct plant tours; others issue publicity releases; and a few have employee suggestion systems. Since Switzerland is a country with only 5 million people and only small industrial organizations, the scope of public relations programs is limited. To communicate with the Swiss population, it is necessary to use German, French, and Italian languages. Public relations is not carried on at the management level in Swiss concerns. A completely planned public relations program is uncommon. There are few public relations counseling firms.

Public Relations in Western Germany

The Deutsche Public Relations Gesellschaft has been established in the Provence of Westphalia to further the development of public relations in West Germany. The organization has about 80 members.

Public Relations in Norway

The Norwegian Public Relations Society with 38 members was established in Oslo, in 1949, to exchange ideas and experiences of practitioners in the field of public relations, to further the quality and ethics of the profession, and to inform the public about the public relations function. Membership in the Society is restricted to persons who are personally engaged in public relations and are responsible for the planning and execution of public relations programs. The limited membership of the Society is accounted for by the fact that few persons employed by Norwegian firms give a majority of their time to public relations work.

Business in Norway has accepted public relations to a very limited extent. Advancement of public relations is handicapped by the fact that the term, "public relations," is not found in the Norwegian language. Some of the most advanced public relations programs in Norway are those of industrial associations such as the Federation of Norwegian Industry, Norwegian Employers' Association, and Norwegian Merchant Fleet, which have public relations departments.

A series of lectures on public relations by prominent practitioners has been presented to students of the social sciences at the University of Oslo by members of the Norwegian Public Relations Society to create a better understanding of public relations. Meetings have been held with members of the Society, industrial leaders, and the press to bring about a better understanding of public relations and insure closer co-operation with the press. Norwegian government departments are beginning to employ public relations practices. The Foreign Department now has a Press Section and an Office for Cultural Affairs, and the Departments of Defense and Finance Ministry are served by public relations officers.

Public Relations in Holland

The principal organization of public relations practitioners is the Nederlands Genootschap Voor Public Relations, established in 1954. It has a membership of 59 and 35 associates. It sponsors a bimonthly public relations periodical.

Public Relations in Australia

Public relations in Australia is a growing activity with an increasing number of major industrial enterprises establishing public relations departments. The Australian Public Relations Society has two chapters: one in Sydney, New South Wales, with 70 members; and a second chapter in Melbourne, Victoria, with 85 members from government, industrial, and commercial organizations.

Public Relations in South Africa

The Public Relations Society of South Africa was organized, in 1957, in Port Elizabeth, Cape of Good Hope, with 22 members. An educational program was established in co-operation with the University of South Africa to train practitioners in public relations.

Public Relations in the Republic of China

Public relations in the Republic of China on Taiwan (Formosa) is largely a government activity which was initiated by the Ministry of Communications, in 1952, for the purpose of increasing efficiency of workers, improving public service, developing communications, and creating public good will.

Public relations departments are now operating in the following government bureaus: postal, tele-communication, railroad, harbor, shipping, weather, civil aeronautics, highway, and diving. In addition, three government ministries have public relations staffs. Three non-government organizations, an insurance company, newspaper, and sugar corporation have public relations programs.

Several media of communication are used including radio broadcasts, motion pictures, periodicals, advertising, press publicity, and exhibits. Radio stations regularly broadcast public relations programs. Documentary films have been produced by the railway and tele-communications administrations, and government power and steamship companies. Press releases and conferences are employed by the government information bureau and other government agencies. Periodicals are published by several government bureaus. Newspaper, magazine, and outdoor advertising carry public relations messages to the public.

Opinion research is carried on by personal interviews and mail questionnaires by a leading newspaper which has polled the public on such issues as lotteries, bus transportation, and political questions. The postal and power administrations regularly survey consumers on the quality of their services.

Courses in public relations have been offered by Taiwan University, National Cheng-chi University, Taiwan Normal University, and the College of Law and Commerce. Government bureaus also train employees in public relations. The Ministry of Communication and Transportation has published a guide for employees, "Manual on Customer Relations."

The Chinese National Association of Public Relations, with 381 members, has published three books on public relations and has sent members abroad to study the public relations programs of other countries.

The growing interest in public relations in Free China is indicated by the translation into Chinese of the first edition of this book by T. P.

Liang of the Department of Public Relations of the Ministry of Communications for use in training government and private public relations practitioners in public relations practice.

Public Relations in South America

In Brazil, the Associacio Brasileira de Relacoes Publicas, the professional public relations association of Brazil, was established in 1956 and has three chapters in Rio de Janeiro, São Paulo, and Niterol. The first Congress of the Association was held in 1958 with an attendance of government and private industry public relations practitioners. Graduates of the public relations course of the Brazilian Public Administration School, or other courses recognized by the Association, are eligible to membership. The Association has approved a code of ethics and professional qualifications for public relations practitioners in Brazil.

The Chilean Institute of Public Relations, Santiago, Chile, was host to the Third Inter-American Public Relations Conference in Santiago, in 1962. Delegates attended from the United States, Brazil, Venezuela, Mexico, Peru, Colombia, Uruguay, and Argentina.

Public Relations in Canada

The Canadian Public Relations Society, with 478 members throughout the Dominion, includes in its membership representatives of private, government, and consulting organizations. It is adopting professional standards for qualifying practitioners of public relations following the practice of the British Institute of Public Relations in testing and certifying applicants for membership in the Society.

The Society will be host to the Third Public Relations World Congress in Montreal, in 1964, with 4,000 delegates from 18 countries in attendance.

Public Relations in Japan

Many large industrial organizations in Japan have public relations departments which employ some of the media of communication used in public relations programs in the United States. Press conferences with important executives are arranged for editors and writers who are supplied with biographies and background material. Internal company periodicals are published by a few firms. Plant openings, open houses, and receptions are staged with guided tours, welcome by management, followed by refreshment and souvenirs. Press publicity is limited to major events such as plant openings as newspapers will not ordinarily mention a company or product in a news story. Television is rarely used for institutional messages.

It is estimated that there are more than a thousand public relations counselors in Japan although ten firms employing some 300 persons advise the major industrial organizations. Sales representatives, news-papermen, and interpreters identify themselves as public relations practitioners. There are many self-styled experts with little or no training or ability engaged in questionable practices under the guise of public relations.

The Pan Pacific Public Relations Group composed of public rela-tions practitioners from Hawaii, Canada, Taiwan, Thailand, India, the Philippines, Australia, New Zealand, Japan, and Hong Kong, or-ganized in 1958 held its biennial conference in Tokyo, Japan, in 1962, to promote public relations activities in the Pacific area and exchange information of mutual interest.

Public Relations in Malaya

The Federation of Malaya Institute of Public Relations, with a membership of 59 practitioners from government services, diplomatic missions, commercial, industrial, and labor organizations, was estab-lished at Singapore, in 1962, to further the development of public relations in Malaya. The first president of the Institute is the director of Information Services, Federation of Malaya and the secretary is head of the external affairs division of the Ministry of Information and Broadcasting.

Public Relations in Other Countries

In many other countries throughout the world, public relations is on the rise with the formation of organizations to explain the functions of public relations to the business community and establish standards of qualifications and better professional training for public relations practitioners. Public relations societies have been established in the following countries: Finland, the Public Relations Society of Finland, Helsinki; Eire, the Public Relations Institute of Ireland, Dublin; India, the Public Relations Society of India, Bombay; Mexico, the Associacion Mexicana de Professionales en Relaciones Publicas, Mexico City; New Zealand, the Public Relations Society of New Zealand, Auckland; Philippines, the Philippine Public Relations Society, Manila; and Sweden, Swedish Association of Public Relations, with 92 members, Stockholm.

International Public Relations Association

The international organization for public relations is the International Public Relations Association, Rome, Italy, which sponsors annual public relations conferences in various countries. Conferences of the Association have been held in Washington, D.C., and in Brussels, Belgium. The third international conference is scheduled for Montreal, Canada, in 1964, with the Canadian Public Relations Society and Public Relations Society of America as co-hosts. Conference discussion subjects include technical progress of public relations, education as a tool of public relations, the power of mass communications, and public relations and international relations.

INTERNATIONAL PUBLIC RELATIONS OF THE UNITED STATES

International public relations of the United States is the responsibility of the United States Information Agency, created by the President in 1953, and known abroad as the United States Information Service. The mission of the Agency is to submit evidence to the peoples of other nations that the objectives and policies of the United States are in harmony with and will advance their legitimate aspirations for freedom, progress, and peace; and to explain U.S. foreign policy, to counter hostile propaganda, and to present a balanced, accurate picture of American life and culture.

The director of the Agency reports to the President directly and through the National Security Council. He is a member of the Operations Coordinating Board which is concerned with the co-ordination of overseas programs. Foreign policy guidance is provided to the Agency by the Department of State.

The Agency is the largest public relations operation in the nation. It has an annual budget of more than $110 million and employs about 11,000 people including 1,200 Americans and 7,200 indigenous employees overseas and 2,500 in this country. The Agency maintains 223 overseas information posts in 102 countries of the free world. The informational and cultural program of the Agency in each foreign country is conducted by a Public Affairs Officer working directly under the U.S. Ambassador or Chief of Mission. The Public Affairs Officer is assisted by a small professional staff headed by Americans but largely composed of citizens of the country.

The activities of the Agency are carried on by six departments: press and publications; Voice of America; television; motion-picture service; information centers including exhibits and books; and private co-operation. The public information program varies in each country depending on the literacy and educational attainment of the area. In highly literate countries, libraries and printed material of many kinds are used, but in areas where literacy is low, motion pictures, slides, exhibits, and cartoon strips are most effective.

Newspapers and magazines throughout the free world are supplied with news releases, features, columns, magazine reprints, and picture stories prepared by the Agency's Press and Publication Service and distributed by overseas posts which adapt and translate news material and furnish it to the local press. The Agency publishes a Russian language monthly, "America Illustrated," sold in the Soviet Union; a similar publication in Polish is sold in Poland; and "Free World" is widely circulated in the Far East. The Agency originates cartoon features that are published by more than 8,000 periodicals in 88 countries. Overseas posts distribute about 98 million booklets, leaflets, posters, and other periodicals annually.

The Voice of America is the broadcasting element of the Agency with eighteen studios located in Washington, D.C., and program centers in New York City, Munich, and Cairo to give audiences on every continent the latest news about international developments, facts about the policies of the United States, and information on our way of life. Voice of America broadcasts seven days a week, 24 hours a day, in English and 38 languages. Million-watt transmitters are located in Germany, the Philippines, Hawaii, Greece, Morocco, England, Ceylon; and, in this country, in Ohio, New Jersey, New York, and California.

The television department of the Agency prepares "live" television programing on videotape, including programs on American achievements in science, education, and culture, and portrayals of American life, which are distributed by the Agency's overseas posts in 50 countries to foreign television stations which reach an estimated audience of 160 million persons.

The motion-picture service of the Agency produces, acquires, and distributes films in 40 languages supporting U.S. foreign policy and showing American life through 210 U.S. film libraries overseas. To show films in remote areas, the Agency has 350 mobile projection units which generate their own electric power and more than 6,000 sound projectors are maintained for use by U.S. Information Service personnel and loan to foreign organizations.

The Agency maintains 161 information centers in 65 countries, each of which includes a library of American books, magazines, and newspapers to acquaint people abroad with American life and culture and promote an understanding of United States policies and objectives. In addition, centers organize classes in English, provide lecture and concert programs, arrange film showings, and sponsor exhibits and cultural events. The centers co-operate with 110 autonomous cultural centers in 31 countries which conduct similar programs. The book translation program has put into circulation some 50 million U.S. books in 50 languages. An estimated 30 million people visit the centers annually.

The Agency's Office of Private Cooperation works with private industry, associations, and individuals in bringing about a better understanding of United States' objectives overseas. Advice and assistance is given to People-to-People program committees and hundreds of projects including sports, art, music, and educational exchanges in the interest of international friendship.

Public Relations of the United Nations

The United Nations Office of Public Information, headquarters New York City, under the direction of the Undersecretary for Public Information, carries on an extensive public relations program in three areas: external relations; press, publications, and public services; and radio and visual. The objectives of the Office of Public Information are to present facts regarding problems facing the United Nations, and to create a better understanding of the long-range purposes of the United Nations.

The external program of the United Nations functions through 35 Information Centers located in the capitals of the principal member countries. These centers are responsible for working with thousands of voluntary nongovernment organizations in member countries representing art, science, social welfare, education, health, labor, and agriculture endeavors whose members are interested in promoting the aims of the United Nations. United Nations Information Centers distribute United Nations films, documentary radio programs, publications, visual materials, and press releases to create a better understanding of activities of the United Nations.

The Press, Publications, and Public Services section of the Office of Public Information is responsible for publication of the official monthly magazine, *United Nations Review;* press coverage of meetings of the General Assembly, Security Council, Economic and Social Council, and the activities of intergovernmental agencies; publication of the *Year-book of the United Nations* and booklets about the activities of the United Nations.

Visitor services at New York headquarters include group visits, guided tours, lectures and film showings, and public inquiries and are the responsibility of the Press, Publications and Public Services section. Visual materials, including posters, charts, photographs, postcards, study kits, and flags are produced by the public inquiries unit of the Visitors' Service for sale to visitors.

The Radio and Visual section is responsible for UN radio news service consisting of news bulletins broadcast from UN headquarters in New York and Geneva, Switzerland, in 27 languages and rebroadcast by the national radio organizations of member states. Feature radio programs of 15-minute duration and 30-minute documentary programs are produced in 34 languages and broadcast over the national trans-mitters of 116 member and nonmember states. Recording and produc-tion facilities are provided at headquarters for delegates and news correspondents for recording reports on United Nations activities.

Thirty-six films and 33 film strips have been produced by the Radio and Visual section, covering the organization of the United Nations, its activities, recent world history, world communication and transporta-tion, economic aid, and health and welfare of the United Nations. These films may be rented or purchased through authorized distributing agencies.

Case 17–1

INTERNATIONAL PUBLIC RELATIONS

Galeries Orleanaises, Orleans, France

Galeries Orleanaises is a department store located in Orleans, France, a city of 80,000 population, with a trading area of 120,000 people, situated on the Loire River 73 miles south of Paris. It is affiliated with Galeries Modernes De-partment Stores Company, a chain of 27 stores situated in major cities of France. Annual sales of Galeries Orleanaises are in excess of $6,750,000 including $2,900,000 for the food department called Noveco Food Store, a separately incorporated company.

The store occupies a five-story and roof terrace, modern building with a total sales area of 36,000 square feet, embracing 4,000 feet for the self-service food store. There are 420 employees including management. The capital stock of Galeries Orleanaises and Noveco Food Store is $648,000 which is closely held by a family group active in the operation of the enterprise.

The public relations policy of Galeries Orleanaises defines public relations as a principle of action constituting a policy designed to inform the public about the role, organization, activities, and goals of the enterprise. The wishes of the public are considered in connection with all decisions pertaining to the operation of the business and its future activities. Public relations is not only a responsibility of management but also requires the participation and co-operation of all employees.

In conformity with this policy Galeries Orleanaises carries on a continuous program of internal public relations with store personnel and shareholders; an external program with consumers, the community, schools, suppliers, organizations, and with public relations practitioners in France and other countries.

The internal public relations of the store is designed to inform and secure the good will of the 420 employees. New employees are oriented in store operations with a guided tour of each department, a briefing on the organization of the firm, a personal welcome by top management, the presentation of a "cheque cadeau" or gift check, and an identification card bearing the employee's photograph and stating that the employee is a "member" of Galeries Orleanaises.

Communications with employees is mainly through the medium of *Echo des Galeries,* an internal employee magazine published bimonthly for all store employees and distributed to personnel of affiliated stores in the Galeries Modernes, Nouvelles Galeries, Galeries de France, and independent stores associated with the Societe Francaise des Nouvelles Galeries Reunies, Paris. The circulation of *Echo des Galeries* is 15,000 which includes 400 community leaders and 270 elementary school principals in the Orleans area.

Supplementing *Echo des Galeries* is a management bulletin "Galeries Vu et Lu pour Vous" (Seen and Read for You), which digests articles concerning the economy, retailing and department stores which appear in newspapers, general and business magazines. Two thousand copies of this bulletin are distributed eight times a year to supervisors and department managers of the store as well as heads of schools, banks, industries, and government agencies of 27 cities in which the associated stores of the Galeries Modernes chain are located.

A special bulletin describing store policy or special events, "Allo, Allo, la Direction vous Parle" (Hello, Hello, Management Speaking) is distributed to all employees as the need arises. A special edition of *Echo des Galeries* is also published from time to time to discuss such subjects as training, credit, the European Common Market, and others.

To promote good relations with employees, Galeries Orleanaises presents each employee with a birthday check on his or her birthday. A "Smile Award" competition among employees is held periodically in which customers vote for the salesperson who has rendered the most amiable service during the year. An employees' club organizes parties, trips, and social affairs.

Stockholders of the store receive an annual report on the finances and operations of the enterprise. This is supplemented with periodic mailings of store promotion materials.

Special Events

The external public relations program of Galeries Orleanaises is intended to inform and gain the good will of consumers, community organizations, suppliers, and the press. The principal medium of the store's community relations is the special event.

Upon the inauguration of dial telephone service to Paris and other French cities, Galeries Orleanaises invited all children in the city to telephone Santa Claus by calling the store's switchboard. The store Santa Claus answered all calls which were simultaneously tape recorded. A jury selected the 25 outstanding conversations and the winning children were presented with phonograph records of their calls. This event received extensive publicity in local and Paris newspapers.

To promote the welfare of the French Society for the Prevention of Cruelty to Animals, Galeries Orleanaises arranged for the distribution of 2,000 gold fish in small plastic bags filled with water to all children under 13 years of age who accompanied their parents to the store. Two hundred new memberships were obtained by the Society from this event.

To further good relations between 4,000 U.S. Army personnel and their families stationed in the Orleans area, the public relations department of the store, with the co-operation of community organizations, the U.S. Army Information Service, and U.S. Embassy in Paris, arranged a series of special events for U.S. military personnel and their families. A press conference was held to discuss ways and means of improving relations between French and American citizens. A monthly bulletin in English was published and distributed to all Americans living in the area to inform them about local events, concerts, theatricals, and recipes for the best-known French food specialties. Monthly luncheons of the U.S. Army "Officers' Wives' Club" were addressed by local authorities on French wines, cheeses, and the creation of French fashions. A meeting of the "Officers' Wives' Club" held at Chateau de la Mothe near Orleans was devoted to French Christmas customs; a French chef served Christmas specialties; and popular Christmas songs of different countries were sung by 40 boys and girls of the Holy Cross Choir. Tours of officers' wives were organized to visit the famous chateaus of the Loire Valley.

Each fall, Galeries Orleanaises organizes an automobile rally, a popular event throughout Europe, in co-operation with the Orleans Automobile Club for the purpose of promoting highway safety, touring, and the tourist attractions of the region.

The dedication of a newly constructed fifth floor and sixth floor terrace tea room was the occasion for a special public relations event. Immediate neighbors of the store were invited to a preview of new facilities, welcomed by the management, given a conducted tour of the property, and served a champagne buffet in the new terrace tea room. Following this preview, 21 officials of the Electric Energy Committee of the United Nations Organization European Commission watched the illumination of the monuments of the city from the roof-top terrace of the store.

The following day, the new facilities were officially dedicated by the leading citizens of the community and in the evening the Orleans Society of the Friends of Characteristic Music met on the terrace. The dedication ceremonies were followed by special events for the Boy Scouts of the community, the mayors of nearby cities, and the parish priests of the churches of Orleans.

Apart from special events, community organizations and school groups visit the store to observe its operations and hear from management about its procurement of merchandise, organization, sales, sales promotion, and public relations. Trained guides conduct tours of visitors through all departments and refreshments are served. "Information Days" are arranged to give students of local elementary, high schools, and colleges knowledge of the store and its operations through guided tours and lectures by executives.

Relations with customers are furthered by means of suggestions deposited by customers in suggestion boxes located at strategic places throughout the store. Cash awards are made to customers who make the best suggestions and the pictures of award winners are published in local newspapers.

Supplier Relations

Relations with 4,200 suppliers of Galeries Orleanaises are improved through visits by store personnel to the factories of suppliers and by store tours arranged for suppliers at which management discusses sales and special promotions of suppliers' products. A biannual report of sales and promotions is made by the store to all suppliers. When a new fleet of delivery trucks was put in service, a christening ceremony was held in front of the store attended by representatives of the supplier, gifts were distributed to guests, and the event was publicized in the press.

Press Relations

Press relations are an important feature of the external relations of Galeries Orleanaises. The press relations policy of the store is to release only such information as has genuine news value and reader interest. The press is not expected to give free space to commercial announcements and advertising which are paid for at space rates. Newspaper men have free access to company executives to obtain and verify information. News releases are not concerned exclusively with store affairs but feature local, national, and international news.

The public relations office maintains a complete list of editors, writers, and reporters to whom are mailed news releases, articles, reports, and pictures for publication.

The public relations program of Galeries Orleanaises includes several activities designed to create a better understanding of public relations by business men and the local community. The "First Public Relations Day in France" was sponsored by the store in 1956 and followed, in 1958, by the "Second Public Relations Day in France" which events were attended by French and foreign newspaper and public relations practitioners who discussed public relations practices.

To aid nonprofit organizations of the community in the improvement of their public relations, the public relations staff of the store offers its services and counsel free of charge to local organizations. The director of public relations of the store is a member of French and several international public relations organizations, speaks at their conventions, and actively participates in their programs.

The Galeries Orleanaises was awarded, in 1957, the International Silver Anvil Trophy of the American Public Relations Association for the most outstanding public relations program of foreign origin.

QUESTIONS

1. Does Galeries Orleanaises have a well-conceived and executed public relations program? Describe the good features of this program. What are its limitations?

2. Recommend essential improvements which should be made in the internal relations program of Galeries Orleanaises.

3. What improvements should be made in the community relations program of the store.
4. Describe in detail methods of improving the press relations.

Case 17–2

PUBLIC RELATIONS IN SWEDEN

Swedish Insurance Companies' Information Service

The Swedish Insurance Companies' Information Service, Stockholm, Sweden, was established in 1949 by the Swedish National Association of Insurance Companies composed of privately owned Swedish companies engaged in writing all types of insurance contracts including life, accident, health, casualty, and all forms of property insurance. Although Swedish insurance companies have been co-operating in a joint public information service since 1920, organization for public relations under sponsorship of the national association was not undertaken until 1949.

The objectives of the Swedish Insurance Companies' Information Service are threefold: first, to disseminate information to the public about all forms of insurance; second, to educate the public to prevent accidents at home, at work, and on the highways; and third, to inform member insurance companies about public attitudes toward insurance and provide them with public relations materials.

The staff of Information Service is headed by a public relations director who reports to the board of the Swedish National Association of Insurance Companies. The public relations director is assisted by a staff of seven including a press officer, the editor of *The Insurance Journal,* the assistant editor of the *Journal,* a school relations specialist, and three secretaries.

The principal function of the Information Service is to provide the public with facts about various forms of insurance and its importance to the country as a whole as well as to individuals. Communications are directed to important opinion-forming groups particularly teachers, doctors, politicians, journalists, and business executives. The principal medium used to inform 10,000 of these opinion leaders is *The Insurance Journal* which discusses not only insurance but also includes economic, social, and medical articles and news. It is published ten times a year.

In addition, communications are channeled to specialized groups such as homeowners, housewives, farmers, property owners, and industrialists. Handbooks, brochures, folders, and posters covering particular features of insurance of special interest to particular groups are published and distributed with the co-operation of the principal organizations representing these groups. Titles of these booklets are: "What Is Insurance?" "Facts About Swedish Life Insurance," "The Family and Finance," and the "Houseowner and Finance." The latter, published in collaboration with the Swedish Houseowners Association, deals with financial and insurance problems of houseowners, gives legal advice and suggestions for fire and theft prevention.

Paralleling communications with selected groups of adults, Information Service has published since 1953 a children's newspaper, *The Wink,* designed

Ju större hus — desto större tak

Ju högre standard — desto mer att skydda

ATP-året 1960 ökade livförsäkringstecknandet med 10 %

Att lindra den värsta nöden var förr livförsäkringens huvuduppgift. Nu behöver vi livförsäkringen för att trygga vår goda standard. Det är ingen tillfällighet att nytecknandet ökade med 10 % 1960 — ATPs första år.

Pensionsreformens förmåner — och kanske dessutom tjänstepension av något slag — ger nu grundtrygghet. Livförsäkringen förstärker tryggheten och skyddar därmed den goda standard, som varken vi eller våra anhöriga vill mista.

Vänd Er till Er försäkringsman eller annan sakkunnig och be honom utreda vilket skydd AFP, ATP och ITP ger just Er.

Ni betalar för en maska — och får ett helt skyddsnät

Redan från första premien har Ni full trygghet — hela kapitalet klart till skydd för Er familj.

Livförsäkringen, en av världens bästa sparmaskiner

Genom regelbundna, "automatiska" inbetalningar sparar Ni pengar, som Ni annars inte skulle spara.

Försäkringspengarna kan disponeras när de bäst behövs . . .

. . . utan att locka till mindre nödvändiga utgifter.

Er livförsäkring skall ha god passform

Den skall skydda utan att tynga. Låt därför försäkringsmannen — *fackmannen* — hjälpa Er.

HÖGRE STANDARD   HÖGRE SKYDD

FIG. 17–2. Newspaper advertisement of the Swedish Insurance Companies' Information Service, Stockholm, Sweden, explaining the importance of insurance to the public.

to make boys and girls safety conscious and reduce the number of accidents among children.

Motion pictures are an important medium used by Information Service in educating the general public on highway safety. The safety film, "To Kill a Child," was a prize winner at the Edinburgh, Scotland, Film Festival and has been shown extensively not only in Sweden but in Germany, England, and other countries throughout the world. Other film titles of Information Service are: "The Bus," "His Better Self," "Nothing Unusual," and a special medical film, "The Artificial Kidney," produced under supervision of Swedish medical authorities for showing to the medical profession. These and other films are loaned free of charge for projecting by clubs and organizations and to television stations for safety programs.

In addition to loaning films to organizations, Information Service stages film shows under the name, "Family Cinema." These shows are given in commercial theaters in 50 cities throughout Sweden in collaboration with local insurance societies. Both adults and children are invited to these showings which feature entertainment and instructional films combined with a short lecture on insurance followed by distribution of insurance literature to the audience. These free performances are attended by 100,000 persons annually. From two to four performances are given daily.

A newspaper advertising campaign of full pages, tabloid size, explaining the importance of insurance to the general public was sponsored by Information Service and appeared over a six-month period in leading Swedish newspapers during 1961–62.

Press Relations

Press publicity, articles, and news stories are released daily by the Information Service press officer to Swedish newspapers, radio and television stations, news services, and professional and scientific periodicals. Editors of member insurance company periodicals receive special articles and releases from Information Service. Close, personal contact is maintained with journalists to answer inquiries and provide insurance information. Newspapermen are often referred to spokesmen for the insurance business for authoritative statements on insurance subjects of current interest.

To give journalists background information on various aspects of insurance, regular biennial courses in insurance fundamentals are offered by the Information Service in co-operation with the Swedish Association of journalists.

Educational Relations

The Information Service staff specialist in educational relations collaborates with school teachers and administrators in developing textbooks, audio-visual aids, teacher guides, and brochures to give teachers and students a basic knowledge of insurance required in courses in social science, domestic science, commerce, and economics in secondary schools in Sweden.

To aid secondary and commercial school teachers in presenting insurance effectively to their students, teacher training programs have been established by Information Service with the co-operation of the Royal Board of Vocational Training, the Swedish Society for Commercial Education, and the Swedish

Association of Vocational Training Schools. With the assistance of the Royal Board of Agriculture, insurance courses are offered to teachers in colleges of agriculture and estate management. Teachers in primary schools are also invited to attend these courses. Lectures are also given by members of the Information Service staff before adult education groups and the state police school.

Accident Prevention

The second objective of the Information Service is education of the public for the prevention of accidents. Since it was established in 1949, Information Service has carried on extensive programs designed to reduce the number of accidents on the highway, in town and country, at home and at work. Annual accident prevention campaigns have been sponsored for the past several years in co-operation with government authorities and social welfare organizations. The themes of recent annual campaigns illustrate their objective of reducing various types of accidents as follows: "Accidents at Work," "No Drink for Drivers," "Accidents in the Home," "Protect Your Heart," "Road Safety's Model Towns," "School Safety Patrols," "Accidents to Children," "The Dangerous World of Children," and "Danger in the Fells."

In connection with these annual campaigns, Information Service publishes booklets such as "The Dangerous World of Children," describing how to protect children from accidents. This booklet was written by two well-known Swedish children's doctors and distributed free of charge by the Child Welfare Clinic. It was published in collaboration with principal social welfare organizations through their joint Committee for the Prevention of Accidents to Children. A booklet, "It Could Happen to You," advises housewives on preventing accidents in the home.

To reduce the number of accidents to school children, the Information Service initiated, with the co-operation of school and police authorities, School Safety Patrols which in recent years have been taken over by the Swedish National Society for Road Safety.

Internal Service to Member Insurance Companies

The third objective of Information Service is to serve member insurance companies by keeping them informed about public attitudes toward the insurance business and providing them with public relations materials, ideas, and programs. Several public opinion surveys have been sponsored by Information Service to appraise public attitudes toward saving and insurance. Information provided by these surveys is made available to member companies to aid them in planning their own public relations programs.

Educational booklets, folders, and posters produced by Information Service in connection with its public relations programs are made available to member companies for distribution to the public through their agents.

The Insurance Journal, published ten times a year by Information Service, is the principal medium of internal communication of the Swedish insurance business and expresses the opinions of insurance leaders on important insurance matters.

The Information Service exchanges experience and ideas with the Institute of

Life Insurance, New York, the public relations organization of the life insurance business in the United States.

QUESTIONS

1. What advantages are gained by the Swedish insurance business from the public relations program of Swedish Insurance Companies Information Service? What are its limitations?

2. Describe in detail how you would improve the Swedish Insurance Companies' Information Program.

3. Is the organization of Swedish Insurance Companies' Information Service satisfactory for effective public relations? If not, what changes should be made in this organization?

4. Are the media of communication employed by Information Service in its public relations program satisfactory? If not, what other media of communication should be used?

5. Is the educational relations program of Information Service satisfactory? What other steps should be taken to improve educational relations?

6. Is the press relations program of Information Services satisfactory? What other steps should be taken to improve press relations?

SECTION 5 · MEDIA OF PUBLIC RELATIONS COMMUNICATION

THE PRINCIPAL MEDIA used by business, social service, nonprofit organizations and government agencies in communicating with the public are: press publicity, advertising, periodicals, films, special events, and oral communications. The most widely used medium is press publicity prepared by public relations departments and distributed to newspapers, magazines, radio and television stations and networks, wire and news syndicates in the form of news releases, feature stories, magazine articles, photographs, videotapes, and films.

To promote the publication and broadcasting of this publicity, press relations programs are used to gain the co-operation of publishers, editors, writers, reporters, news broadcasters, and commentators. To communicate with the press, personal contacts, advertising in journalism periodicals, press previews, and press conferences are used to inform and secure the acceptance of newsmen.

To provide communication from the publics to business and nonprofit organizations, opinion research is used to learn what the public likes and dislikes about the policies and practices of an organization and what they want to know about its operations.

Opinion surveys determine the institutional image of an organization and discover why the public looks with favor or disfavor upon a company or an industry. Influence investigations are made to determine the effect of social, economic, and political changes on an organization's public image. Effectiveness surveys measure the impact on public opinion made by public relations programs.

The techniques of conducting public relations surveys including the use of personal investigators, telephone and mail surveys are discussed in this section in connection with employee, shareholder, community, supplier, distributor-dealer opinion research.

PUBLIC RELATIONS
RESEARCH AND
EVALUATION

MANY PUBLIC RELATIONS programs communicate what their sponsors think the public should hear without first establishing what the public really wants to know. This may be compared to listening to someone who ignores your views and monopolizes the conversation by saying what may be of interest to him but of no concern to you. The listener is so frustrated at not being able to express his opinions that he simply ignores the speaker's message and communication fails. A corporation that discusses its affairs and ignores the viewpoint of the public can be just as irritating as a person who does all the talking and no listening.

Effective public relations communication begins with a simple question that only the public can answer: "What do you want to know?" To learn the answer to this question, public opinion surveys and attitude research is undertaken. Opinion research enables an organization before communicating with the public to find out what the public really wants to know, like a person who pauses and listens to someone else talk.

The foundation of effective public relations communication is a "two-way" exchange of information from an organization to its publics and from the publics to the organization. Corporations like many individuals are not accustomed to listening and their "one-way" communication falls on deaf ears. However, the use of opinion surveys for public relations is developing rapidly with improvement in research techniques and recognition by management that communication is not only talking but also listening.

Business, social welfare, government organizations, trade and professional associations are using opinion research to ascertain the views of employees on company practices and policies, to find out what stockholders think of management, to determine how plant communities regard local industry, what distributors and dealers think about a manufacturer's marketing practices, and how members look upon the activities of a professional or social welfare organization to which they belong.

In planning its public relations programs and appraising their effectiveness, the Mutual Life Insurance Company of New York conducts as many as 20 opinion surveys a year, polling thousands of policyholders, field underwriters, the general public, and agency and home office employees. Policyholders are questioned about their satisfaction with various company services including response to inquiries, replies to correspondence, loan service, conversion from one type of insurance to another, and other subjects. Employees are questioned about internal communications, operating methods and procedures, and cafeteria food and service. Agents are questioned about sales meetings, promptness in paying commissions, underwriting service, and other subjects. The general public is surveyed to determine what people think of the company and what they want of it. Many improvements in communications, operating methods, and procedures result from these surveys with improved public relations for the company.

A chemical products manufacturer considered the construction of a new plant in a large Eastern city. Rumors of the building of the plant spread throughout the community, opposition developed, and the city council held hearings on a zoning ordinance prohibiting the erection of the plant. Faced with serious opposition, the company decided to conduct a community opinion survey to find out what the public really thought about the company and the contemplated construction.

The survey showed that the public opposed the new plant and that the company was poorly regarded in the community. The findings of the research convinced the management that a public relations program should be launched to explain the intentions of the company and gain the good will and approval of the community toward the construction of the new plant. Following a well-planned public relations program, the company was permitted to erect the plant, public misunderstanding was corrected, and the company enjoyed favorable public acceptance.

A Western railroad concerned about the public attitude toward the company retained an opinion research organization to determine the public opinion of the road. The survey showed the public so critical of the railroad that the company decided to employ institutional advertising in the 400 communities through which it operated. After the advertising appeared, a similar survey was made in the same area. This showed that the people in the cities in which the advertising appeared were better informed and regarded the railroad more highly than before the advertising appeared.

A national trade association employs a leading opinion research organization to make an annual survey of public opinion on various topics relating to the industry. Information from this research has proven helpful in formulating public relations programs of the association and its individual members.

The board of education of a large Eastern city was faced with the question of floating a new school bond issue for the construction of a new high school. Opinion research was used to determine the attitude of the community toward the new issue. The findings showed that the public was not aware of the need for the new school and would likely oppose the bond issue. A public relations campaign was launched to secure support of the community before the bond issue was submitted to the voters. The issue was approved by a large majority.

A large food-processing corporation conducts an aggressive campaign to interest shareholders in the affairs of the company. An elaborate annual report, regional stockholders' meetings, periodic mailings to shareholders, and newspaper and magazine advertising are used to gain owner understanding and good will. To appraise the attitudes of shareholders toward the company and the effectiveness of the stockholder relations program, the corporation makes annual surveys of shareholders.

A metal-products manufacturer sensed employee dissatisfaction with working conditions in one of his plants. A large university was asked to conduct an opinion poll of the workers. The findings of the survey indicated a need for improved personnel policies and working conditions. The policies and working conditions were improved with the result that employee morale was raised and production increased.

Opinion research should be conducted continuously, as public attitudes toward an organization and its policies and practices are never static but are constantly changing. A change in a corporate policy, some corporate act, a statement by management may affect public opinion favorably or otherwise. The public opinion of an organization may also be influenced by factors over which the management has no control, such as changing economic conditions, social changes, or the actions of pressure groups or government.

The scope of public relations research varies widely, from local studies of employee attitudes in a particular plant or the opinions of the residents of a plant city, to national surveys of dealers, suppliers, or the general public.

Every type of business, social service, and government organization should use public relations research in evaluating public attitudes. Social service organizations which are supported by the public and serve the public interest, all types of business organizations dependent upon public patronage, religious organizations, political parties, and professional groups—all should know clearly what the public thinks and wants from them.

ADVANTAGES OF PUBLIC RELATIONS RESEARCH

Public relations research reflects public opinion to management for its consideration in formulating basic policies so that better policies result. Opinion surveys give the public an opportunity to communicate its views and express its satisfaction and dissatisfaction. The effectiveness of public relations programs can be measured by determining what the public has learned about an organization and how well the program has been communicated to the public. Opinion studies satisfy the desire of people to express their views. They provide good communication between management and the employee public to improve teamwork and morale. Opinion research is a guide for determining the objectives, strategy, and effectiveness of a public relations program. Employee surveys produce suggestions from workers which lead to better working conditions, greater efficiency, and increased output. Opinion research defines, and makes management aware of, its public relations problems. It reduces the intangibles and nebulous impressions of public opinion to specific "likes" and "don't likes" and helps management avoid mistakes in dealing with the public. Research reveals reasons for public indifference and how to overcome it; it replaces guesswork with facts in dealing with the public; and it suggests ways to improve the quality of an organization's service to the public.

LIMITATIONS OF PUBLIC RELATIONS RESEARCH

Some professional opinion researchers question the effectiveness of opinion research in determining the effectiveness of a public relations program. "Measuring public relations effectiveness is only slightly easier than measuring a gaseous body with a rubber band," says Burns W. Roper, partner in Elmo Roper and Associates. "Unless a person is some way personally connected with a company, he is not very much concerned about the company. When a message is beamed at him about this company, he doesn't stop everything and pay strict attention. Thousands of messages are beamed at him from other companies, the government, his wife, his boss, his kids, his friends, and many of these messages come much closer to the mainstream of his life. How can you measure the effect of a particular flyspeck in this person's life?"

Because public relations deals with attitudes and opinions, it is one of the most difficult functions of management to measure. One method of measuring public relations effectiveness is to compute the inches of publicity given an organization or its products in newspapers and magazines. Although a sizable number of mentions may impress management seeking proof that its investment in publicity is paying off, it gives no positive assurance how many, if any, people noticed, read, and believed the publicity. Nor is there any evidence that their attitudes toward the institution or products publicized were more or less favorably influenced as a result of the publicity.

Critics of opinion research question its accuracy, citing errors in political polls such as occurred in the 1948 election when researchers predicted the election of Thomas E. Dewey over Harry S. Truman. Because the surveyors stopped sampling public opinion some time before the election, they were unprepared for the swing to Truman in the closing days of the campaign. In recent years, improvements have been made in political opinion survey techniques which are making forecasts much more accurate.

Some criticisms of opinion research are that it stifles creative thinking, encourages conformity to mass opinion, and is an invasion of privacy. To these objections, researchers reply that surveys are only informative and not designed to be slavishly followed.

Public opinion research is criticized for the reason that replies of respondents may be superficial and misleading. When a respondent is asked what he thinks about a company, he tries to make a favorable impression on the interviewer and his views may not reflect his real feelings.

Critics of opinion research contend that the number of persons questioned is too small to reflect public opinion in general. Interviewer bias or the nature of questions may influence the replies of respondents; questions are often asked upon which the public has no considered opinion; interviewers are incompetent; and the intensity of the feelings of respondents cannot be measured.

These criticisms of public opinion research may be attributed to faulty survey techniques which when improved provide reliable information. When opinion surveys are properly planned by experienced researchers, the questions carefully phrased and tested, and the interviewers adequately trained and supervised, conclusive results will be secured.

TYPES OF PUBLIC RELATIONS SURVEYS

There are five types of public relations surveys: image, motivation, effectiveness, individual public, and basic influences investigations. A corporation or association may employ one or more of these survey types concurrently in its public relations research.

Image Surveys

Image surveys determine the institutional profile or corporate image in the public mind. Such surveys determine the attitudes of the public toward an organization, what people think of it, how well they understand it, and what they like and do not like about it. Image surveys determine how well a company is known; its reputation; what the public thinks about its products, services, prices, advertising, personnel, and practices. The Opinion Research Corporation surveys the images of corporations using a 50-item "reputation profile" which determines public opinion of a company as a producer, distributor, manager, employer, and citizen. Image research provides information for evaluating policies, correcting misconceptions, determining the appeal of public relations messages, and improving the corporate image in the public mind.

Motivation Research

Motivation research involves a series of "depth interviews" to determine "why" the public looks with favor or disapproval upon a company or industry. It seeks to discover what motivates the public attitude toward an organization. It assumes that a person's opinions are largely a product of his emotional and mental state. To understand the reason for an individual's opinion it is necessary to explore the psychological influences which shape his attitudes toward a company. A company's public image may be affected not by its own actions but by the emotional attitude of the public toward the industry or business. Motivation studies are made to discover the underlying emotional factors which influence public opinion of a company or industry.

A motivation study was used by a metropolitan television station in determining public opinion of the station sponsoring the survey and four competitors in the same community. A representative sample of residents of the community was shown a list of paired adjectives such as: pleasant-unpleasant, loud-soft, active-passive, and others and asked to check off the adjectives which they thought best described each of the five stations. Respondents indicated on a scale which of the adjectives most nearly described each of the five stations.

A public opinion motivation survey made for a Southwestern state showed that most vacationers thought that the state was hot, uncomfortable, barren, and lacking in scenic interest. To correct this misconception, the state has changed its public relations program to emphasize its climatic and scenic advantages.

Effectiveness Surveys

Effectiveness surveys are used to measure the impact on public opinion made by public relations activities and programs. One method of appraising public relations activities is to question a panel of the public "before and after" the campaign. Prior to the start of the campaign members of the panel are interviewed to determine their attitudes and the extent of their knowledge of the company or industry. After the campaign, the same people are interviewed to see if there has been any change in their opinions as a result of the public relations messages.

The reliability of this type of survey is questioned by some public relations researchers because the initial interviews focus greater attention of respondents on the company or issues being investigated. As a consequence, respondents are more conscious of the messages, and their impressions of the campaign are not typical of the public as a whole.

Effectiveness surveys are used to measure the response to programs directed to employees, shareholders, community neighbors, and other publics. Effectiveness studies are also made to measure public response to particular activities such as open houses, anniversary celebrations, plant closings, strikes, or unemployment.

Individual Public Studies

In addition to researching the views of the general public, an increasing amount of study is being devoted to determining attitudes and interests of individual publics including stockholders, consumers, dealers and distributors, community neighbors, employees, suppliers, and opinion leaders.

Numerous corporations make annual surveys of their employees to determine their opinions of the company, its policies, practices, working conditions, management, and supervision. The attitudes of the families of employees are also investigated.

A food manufacturer, with 50,000 shareholders, makes periodic surveys of the opinions of the shareholder public to determine the interest of shareholders in stockholder publications, new products, special promotions, and policies; and the stockholder relations program of the corporation.

Basic Influences Investigations

Public opinion of corporations and institutions is affected by economic, social, and political conditions both in this country and abroad. It is essential that a company or industry understands trends in opinion which may affect public attitudes. Surveys of basic influences indicate factors affecting public opinion of companies and industries.

A large automobile manufacturer learned through basic influences research that the American public believed that large corporations are destroying small business enterprises. To correct this misconception, a public relations program was developed to show the mutual dependence of large and small business.

ORGANIZATIONS CONDUCTING PUBLIC RELATIONS RESEARCH

Public relations research is conducted by these types of organizations: business, government, and nonprofit organizations; public relations consultants; opinion research organizations; advertising agencies and media; and business and professional associations.

Corporations, government, and nonprofit organizations use their own staff research departments for public relations research in planning and evaluating their public relations programs. Some organizations rely entirely or in part upon outside opinion research organizations to make opinion surveys. Public relations department research sections conduct public relations investigations of the various types described previously.

The General Electric Company maintains a behavior research staff in its public relations department to undertake basic research in the behavior sciences.

Public relations consultants give research counsel and conduct public opinion surveys for clients. An objective viewpoint and experience in using opinion research enables them to give assistance to corporations and nonprofit organizations in the execution, interpretation, and application of opinion research. They sometimes provide a fact-finding service to clients on public relations activities, regularly reading and analyzing business publications for material and ideas pertinent to clients' interests.

Professional opinion research organizations conduct public relations investigations for leading business and nonprofit organizations. Leading opinion research organizations are: The American Institute of Public Opinion, Princeton, New Jersey; the Psychological Corporation, New York City; the Opinion Research Corporation, Princeton, New Jersey; Social Research, Inc., Chicago; Crossley S-D Surveys; Elmo Roper and Associates; Gallup & Robinson, Inc.; Alfred Politz Research, Inc.; and Institute for Motivational Research, all in New York City.

A few nonprofit organizations associated with universities conduct opinion studies for corporations and nonprofit groups.

The National Opinion Research Center, University of Chicago, measures public opinion in the United States using a national staff of trained investigators to question representative samples of the entire population on topics of current importance. It also analyzes and reviews the results of surveys made by other polling organizations.

The Office of Public Opinion Research, Princeton University, studies techniques of public opinion research to gain some insight into the psychological problems of public opinion motivation and to build up archives of public opinion data.

Advertising agencies and media also make studies of public opinion the results of which are made available to clients and advertisers. The *Chicago Tribune* Research Department has made many motivation studies which are helpful in determining public relations objectives and in planning public relations programs.

Public relations research is being employed by trade and professional associations in determining public attitudes toward an industry or profession. The Association of American Railroads sponsors an annual survey by Opinion Research Corporation to determine the attitudes of the public toward the railroads, rates, profits, progress, services, and personnel.

Public relations research is usually a product of the combined efforts of a public relations department and an outside consultant or opinion research service. The public relations department of a corporation or association is familiar with the business, but an outside research agency can contribute broad, specialized experience, and an invaluable objective viewpoint.

STEPS IN THE OPINION RESEARCH PROCESS

The successive steps in the opinion research process involve a statement of the problem, preliminary research, designing the questionnaire, testing the questionnaire, determining the sample, and interviewing, which is followed by tabulating the responses, analyzing the data, and conclusions.

Stating the Problem

The first step in opinion research is stating the public relations problem or problems that need attention. Too many public relations programs are planned without a clear conception of what they are expected to accomplish. The problem may first be stated in very general terms as: "Our stockholders are not interested in company affairs," or "We are not well regarded by our community." Discussion with people closest to the problem will bring out more specific definitions of the problem and what to look for in researching the problem.

Preliminary Research

After the problem has been discussed with persons within the organization who are most familiar with it, the next step is to discuss it informally with a few persons on the outside typical of the group which is creating the problem. Select a few representative people of the group involved and ask them some open-end questions bearing on the problem such as: "What are your ideas about that?" "Will you go into that a little more fully?" "Can you give us some examples?" A list of directive questions will help the questioner to explore the problem in informal interviews. Or a few tape recordings may be made of the ideas, reactions, questions, and likes and dislikes of respondents to uncover significant attitudes which may broaden the aspects of the problem or lead to new problems. This preliminary phase of the research is one of the most important steps of the project. From the preliminary interviewing will come a clearer definition of the problem, suggestions for questionnaire design, and the conduct of the research.

Designing the Questionnaire

Following the preliminary research, the questions to be asked in the survey are next prepared by the research staff taking into consideration the findings of the preliminary research, the objective of the survey, the complexity of the problem, and the variables involved. The questions should logically develop the area from the standpoint of the respondent and at the same time keep the respondent interested in the process.

The types of questions used may be simple "yes" or "no," multiple choice, ranking, or essay type. Whichever type is used, the questions should be stated so that they cannot be misunderstood. They should be sincere, arranged to facilitate flow of thought, and employ words in common usage. In dealing with technical features, questions should emphasize effects; questions should be worded to avoid bias in the minds of respondents; and questions on a series of items should be asked the same way.

Testing the Questionnaire

When the first draft of the questionnaire has been completed, it should first be tested on a small group of carefully selected respondents who are representative of the public to be questioned to determine if the questions are worded so that the issue involved is recognized and understood by the respondents. A test of questions is desirable to insure that they are clearly understood, are not leading respondents, and are not biased. Experienced researchers invariably favor testing the questionnaire and several tests may be necessary to insure reliable questions. When tests have been completed, revisions are made and the final questionnaire approved.

Determining the Sample

While the questionnaire is being tested, consideration is given to whom and how many persons should be questioned. When the public is small and readily accessible, as in the case of employees, everyone may be questioned. However, when the public is large, as is usually the case with consumers, stockholders, dealers, and plant communities, a small representative "sample" of these groups must be selected for questioning. Sampling is based on the theory that opinions of a small segment of the public resemble the responses that would be obtained if the entire public were questioned.

The three principal methods of sampling are random, quota, and area. The random method, also called "probability sampling," is the type of sampling in which the choice of who is to be interviewed is taken out of the hands of the interviewer. In this commonly used method, the areas to be sampled, rural counties or precincts in cities, are grouped into sampling units from which are selected segments or strata and then sampling points. In a city, each of these sampling points represents a certain number of blocks or in rural areas, townships. Interviewers sent into a city are instructed to go to specific intersections and interview the occupants of the first, third, and fifth houses, and so on. Call backs must be made upon those who are not at home in order to follow the sample pattern.

Interviewing

The individual personal interview in which the interviewer calls on respondents in person and records their responses to questions is the most commonly used method of opinion surveys. Other methods of questioning are by mail, telephone, or by group interviews in which individuals, such as employees, are brought together in groups for questioning. Each of these methods has its advantages and limitations and a choice of method depends on the size and accessibility of the group to be questioned, the objectives of the survey, the number of persons to be interrogated, and the funds available. A combination of methods is often used in a single survey.

In personal interview surveys, investigators must first be instructed and later supervised by one or more supervisors who assign the interviewers, check the interviews against the assignments, and determine the interviewers insight. The latter is particularly important on open questions calling for expression of opinion, such as: "Why do you feel that way about the company?"

Tabulating the Responses

When answers to the questions have been secured, the next step is to edit the questionnaires, to discard incorrect or incomplete answers, and to examine responses to open questions to determine if answers fit any one of the categories which are given code numbers for tabulation.

Next, the responses are punched on tabulating cards according to a tabulating plan which indicates the tabulations which will give the highest yield of useful information. The cards are fed to the tabulating machines and the raw information is forthcoming.

Analysis of Data and Conclusions

The next step in the process involves reading all of the data and making assumptions as to its meaning in respect to the objective of the survey. What the responses indicate in terms of decisions to be made and action taken is a most important phase of the research. Specific recommendations for action based on the findings of the survey are made by the researchers to guide management in formulating improved policies, correcting weaknesses, and planning a public relations program.

OTHER SOURCES OF INFORMATION ABOUT PUBLIC RELATIONS PROBLEMS

Public relations research is only one source of information about public relations problems. Much information is available on public relations problems which should be consulted before making a public relations survey. This information is not only found in public relations literature but in the related literature of the social sciences, psychology, sociology, communication, and business.

The major sources of information available to the public relations practitioners are: published materials, including company records, public relations textbooks and bibliographies, opinion research studies, current periodicals, reports of opinion research organizations, publications describing the public relations programs of individual companies. Individuals also have information on public relations, including teachers, librarians, editors, trade association executives, and government agencies.

Internal Records

One of the principal sources of information about employees, stockholders, suppliers, and dealers is company records and correspondence. Personnel records provide data about the employee public; salesmen's reports and sales records give data on distributors and dealers; the treasurer's records provide facts about stockholders; the purchasing agent's records give information about the supplier public; and sales and credit records tell much about the dealer and customer publics.

Reference Books and Bibliographies on Public Relations

In planning a public relations program, practitioners should read what has already been written on the problem under consideration. In the back of this book is a bibliography listing many of the books which have been published on public relations.

Opinion Research Organizations

Opinion research organizations publish reports on their findings, in addition to speeches and articles by their executives. These sources give valuable suggestions for conducting opinion researches.

Periodicals

Current periodicals on public relations and opinion research are a valuable aid in planning public relations programs. The principal periodicals for public relations are: *Public Relations News,* New York, and *Public Relations Journal,* published by the Public Relations Society of America, New York.

Magazines carrying articles devoted to opinion research are: *Public Opinion Quarterly, Journal of Applied Psychology, Journal of Consulting Psychology,* and *American Journal of Sociology.*

Advertising magazines, *Printers' Ink* and *Editor and Publisher,* carry articles on public relations, opinion research, and communications.

General business magazines which frequently publish articles on public relations are: *Fortune, Business Week,* and *Newsweek.*

Reports of Business, Social Welfare, and Professional Organizations

Leading business, social welfare, or professional organizations publish reports on their public relations programs. Business and professional associations maintain research departments which are actively engaged in collecting facts about the public. Some of these associations are carrying on industry-wide public relations campaigns.

Government Publications

Governmental sources publish information useful in planning public relations programs and in understanding the character of specific publics. The U.S. Department of Commerce, the U.S. Bureau of Internal Revenue, Interstate Commerce Commission, U.S. Department of Agriculture, Federal Trade Commission, U.S. Bureau of Labor Statistics, Federal Reserve System, and other agencies publish information about the business publics.

Colleges, Universities, and Foundations

The publications of the business, social, and economic research staffs of leading colleges, universities, and foundations furnish much data useful in public relations research. The National Opinion Research Center at the University of Chicago; The Office of Public Opinion Research, Princeton University; the Bureau of Applied Social Research, Columbia University; Institute of Communications Research, University of Illinois; Bureau of Audience Research, State University of

Iowa; and Public Opinion Laboratory, University of Washington, have contributed much to a better knowledge of public relations.

AREAS OF PUBLIC RELATIONS RESEARCH

In Employee Relations

Employee opinion research is used to measure employee attitudes toward the company, its policies, practices, and problems. The principal methods of conducting employee opinion surveys are: the listening-in or informal impression method; the individual personal interview; the use of mail questionnaires to employees' homes; the group opinion survey; and the essay contest.

Employee attitude studies are essential in determining the effectiveness of an employee relations program. They establish effective two-way communications; give workers an opportunity to express themselves, a better understanding of the business, and pride in the organization.

In Community Relations

Community opinion surveys are being made by leading corporations in plant cities. These surveys determine what people in a community think of a company and its policies, working conditions, participation in community activities, contributions in taxes, and other subjects.

The principal methods of conducting community research are: individual interviews with a representative sample of citizens; mail questionnaires to a sample of the community population; telephone survey of a typical cross section of the community public; and a combination of these methods.

In General Public Relations

Research organizations specializing in public opinion studies are retained by corporations and nonprofit organizations for surveys of the general public. These organizations employ investigators located in various parts of the country who can quickly question a nation-wide sample of the public in a personal interview opinion poll.

In Stockholder Relations

Research of the stockholder public is carried on regularly by corporations with a large number of shareholders. Personal interviews, mail questionnaires, and investor panels are used for stockholder relations research. The stockholder public is relatively small compared with the larger business publics and can be surveyed quickly and inexpensively.

In Supplier Relations

Questionnaires mailed to suppliers, supplemented by personal interviews with selected resources, are research methods employed in investigating the attitudes of suppliers. As the supplier public is relatively small, the research problems are comparatively simple. Little research has been attempted in the area of supplier relations, but growing interest in this field indicates that more studies will be made in the future of the viewpoints of suppliers to improve relations with resources.

In Dealer Relations

An increasing number of manufacturers are researching dealer and distributor attitudes and operations. Manufacturers' salesmen or trained investigators are questioning wholesalers and retailers. In some cases a combination of personal interviews and mail questionnaires is used.

A COMMUNITY RELATIONS RESEARCH PROGRAM

The General Electric Company appraises public attitudes toward the company in plant communities and measures the effectiveness of its community relations programs by mail questionnaires, personal door-to-door interviews, and by telephone surveys. In comparing the responses in door-to-door interviews with telephone surveys, the company has found that the two techniques yield comparable findings for the type of questions used in the telephone interviews.

In comparative tests the company found that when not more than 25 questions are asked, refusals by telephone respondents are fewer than normally found in door-to-door surveys. The ability to control interviews is an important advantage of telephone research over personal interviews and the cost of telephone interviews is lower. On the other hand, every household in a community does not have a telephone, but in most urban areas telephone coverage is high.

From its experiments with telephone surveys in three plant cities, the General Electric Company has found that the question wording which is effective in face-to-face interviews will not necessarily work on the telephone and questions which ask the respondent for a scale-type rating appear to yield results comparable to those obtained in face-to-face interviews.

The General Electric Company's telephone surveys have covered five attitudinal areas: public attitude toward the General Electric plant as a place to work; toward the plant as an asset or liability to the community; toward plant personnel as citizens and neighbors; toward business in general and channels of communication open to the plant community; and public receptivity to various aspects of the plant's communications.

Twenty-four questions General Electric asked in surveys in Roanoke, Virginia, were worded to elicit responses on a five-point scale of excellent, very good, good, fair, and poor. Two hundred interviews were conducted by five telephone interviewers supervised by a survey consulting organization. The interviews, averaging eight to ten minutes each, were completed in three evenings from 5:30 to 9:00 o'clock. The sample consisted of a cross section of 200 male and female household heads in the county in which the plant was located.

An example of the type of question asked in the survey was: "From what you know, or have heard, how would you rate the General Electric plant here as a place to work?" Responses on a five-point scale were recorded on tally sheets during the interview for each question by the interviewer, thereby eliminating the data processing cost of tabulation encountered in conventional surveys.

Case 18–1

PLANT COMMUNITY RESEARCH

Wyandotte Chemicals Corporation

The Wyandotte Chemicals Corporation, Wyandotte, Michigan, was established in 1943 from a consolidation of the Michigan Alkali Company, founded in 1894 by John B. Ford, pioneer plate glass manufacturer, and the J. B. Ford Company, producer of washing compounds, organized in 1890. After World War II, the corporation expanded into new chemical fields by purchasing several producers of synthetic detergents, mineral absorbents, organic chemicals, and oxide products. Manufacturing plants are located in California, Michigan, Mississippi, Georgia, Louisiana, New Jersey, Canada, Venezuela, and Mexico. District sales offices are in 22 cities of the United States and Canada.

Annual sales of all products are about $100 million and net earnings approximately $5 million. There are some 4,000 employees in all plants and offices. The corporation is owned by 1,500 shareholders. For 65 years shares of the corporation were largely held by the Ford family but in 1955 stock was offered to the public.

When the company was controlled by the Ford family, little or no information about its finances or operations was made available to the general public. However, when shares were offered to the public in 1955, management recognized the necessity for communicating with the public about its affairs, and a public relations program was inaugurated.

The public relations department is a section of the Employee and Public Relations division under the direction of the vice-president of Employee and Public Relations who is also responsible for the departments of industrial relations and medical service. These departments provide for personnel administration, training, wage and salary administration, safety programs, recruiting, and employment.

The public relations director is assisted by a staff consisting of a publications editor, two photographers, two staff assistants, and secretaries. The functions of the public relations staff include servicing all divisions and departments of the company for communications and public relations. A communications advisory committee established by the department co-ordinates news and information for all departments.

The objectives of the public relations department are to stimulate a free flow of news throughout the company, to achieve believability in employee publications, and to assume an aggressive posture in all aspects of public relations.

Like many companies which are the mainstay of their plant communities, Wyandotte Chemicals employs 3,200 persons or about 76 per cent of its total workforce in its main plants in Wyandotte, Michigan. These employees represent about one fourth of the total number of families in the community of 43,000 population located 12 miles southwest of Detroit on the Detroit River.

The corporation provides about 40 per cent of community revenues in taxes. As the largest taxpayer and biggest employer, Wyandotte Chemicals has been the target of criticism and unfounded rumors about its policies and practices. It is misunderstood for appealing a portion of its personal property taxes and is accused, along with other "downriver" industries, of polluting the air and streams with noxious odors and waste.

The corporate tax policies and practices of the state of Michigan have involved many Michigan corporations in state and community tax battles which have generated public confusion and criticism. Wyandotte Chemicals has appealed its local personal property tax assessments as excessive every year for the past six years. In 1960 for the first and only time, the state tax commission ruled in favor of the company. As the result of this ruling the city of Wyandotte was forced to cut its budget $40,000 and reduce its services to the community.

Industrial odors and smoke from numerous factories in the area have aroused many complaints from residents of the community. The company shares in the responsibility for this situation but has invested more than $1 million in special equipment to combat objectionable smoke and odors and spends $200,000 annually on an antipollution program, administered by two full-time antipollution experts. The company has organized an engineering pool of engineers from companies in the vicinity to cope with the problem, but many people in the community see only smoke stacks of the company's two major plants dominating the skyline.

The attitude of some residents is that the corporation makes nothing but money and contributes only smoke and noxious odors to the area. On the contrary, the company has for years given liberally to local charities and the development of the city by financing a public library, hospital, and marina, and making its employee recreational facilities available to community organizations.

The management believes that many people in the community did not know about these contributions, the company's large tax payments, its efforts to abate pollution, and the influence of its employment and payroll on the economic life of the city.

To evaluate the company's image in the community, management appointed a committee of middle-management executives to examine community relations and make recommendations to improve the local business climate and community understanding. The committee considered the encouragement of more employee participation in civic affairs, a corporation stand on political issues, and such community problems as parking, shopping facilities, education, and the future of the city.

After much discussion, the committee decided that it needed more information about the attitudes of employees and citizens on these matters in order to make constructive recommendations. A comprehensive employee and community survey was proposed to determine the attitudes of people in the community toward the city and Wyandotte Chemicals to provide a blueprint for community and company action. Such a survey would have a dual purpose in aiding community government and organizations to understand local opinion and plan for city development and at the same time help the company plan its community relations program.

A well-known public opinion research organization, the Opinion Research Corporation, Princeton, New Jersey, was engaged to conduct personal interviews with residents, employees, members of their families, and community leaders. A total of 725 persons were interviewed in the city and surrounding communities over a two-week period. The survey included 500 interviews with citizens of various ages, sex, economic, and educational status; 200 interviews with Wyandotte Chemicals employees; and additional interviews with 25 community leaders.

Sampling segments were selected by probability procedures. With each segment, interviewers were given a specified starting place and a prescribed route. Interviewers were instructed to obtain half of their interviews with men and half with women. Only adult residents of a household were questioned. Names of employees were selected at random from name and address cards furnished by the company. The names of community leaders were supplied by the company. Reliability of the sample was plus or minus 4 per cent of responses which would have been obtained if every person in the survey area was interviewed.

In advance of the survey, personal letters, news releases, and advertisements informed employees and residents that the survey would be made and why, in order to obtain their co-operation. The public was told that survey results would be published as soon as available.

The questions asked in the survey were thoroughly pretested with actual interviews in the Wyandotte area and found to be generally understood, as free from bias as possible, and most likely to provide useful information about the attitudes of people in the community toward the city and company. Most of the 56 questions in the survey were of the multiple choice and "yes" or "no" type supplemented by opinion type. Names of respondents were not asked.

The questionnaire was divided into five main categories: (1) Resident's opinions of the city of Wyandotte. (2) The company's relations with the community. (3) How the community gets its information about the company

(4) How residents and employees appraise the company as a place to work.

(5) Attitudes of community leaders toward the city.

THE QUESTIONNAIRE

1. How do you feel about the city of Wyandotte as a place to live, would you say it is a good place to live, average, or a poor place to live? Good, average, poor, no opinion.

2. What things do you like most about the city of Wyandotte?

3. What things can you think of that might be done to make Wyandotte a better place to live?

4. Ten years from now do you expect the city of Wyandotte to be more prosperous or less prosperous than it is now? More prosperous, less prosperous, about the same, other, no opinion.

5. What makes you say that?

6. Have you heard of a proposed two-year junior college? Yes, have heard; no, have not; don't recall.

7. Do you think the downriver area needs a tax-supported junior college or not? Yes, needs it; no; no opinion.

8. How do you feel about Wyandotte as a place to shop, would you say that it is a good place to shop, average, or a poor place to shop? Good, average, poor, no opinion.

9. (If "average" or "poor" response to 8.) What do you think needs to be done to make downtown Wyandotte a better place to shop?

10. How do you feel about the local taxes you pay; are the taxes too high or are they reasonable? Too high, reasonable, other, no opinion.

11. What makes local taxes (high) (reasonable)?

12. In your opinion does waste material in the river create much of a problem? Yes, creates a problem; no, it doesn't; no opinion.

13. (If "yes, creates a problem") Do you think the problem of waste materials in the river is getting better, getting worse, or is about the same as it was a few years ago? Getting better, getting worse, about the same, no opinion.

14. Why do you say that?

15. Who or what do you think is responsible for its getting (better) (worse)?

16. Are you ever bothered by smoke, unpleasant odors, or dirt in the air? Yes, no, no opinion.

17. (If "yes" on 16) Would you say that this happens frequently or just occasionally? Frequently, just occasionally, no opinion.

18. Do you think the problem of smoke, odors, and dirt is getting better, getting worse, about the same, no opinion.

19. Why do you say that?

20. Who or what do you think is responsible for its getting (better) (worse)?

21. (Interviewer hands respondent a list of 19 statements that have been made about companies.) Please read through the list and see which statements fit Wyandotte Chemicals. Every time you come to a statement that fits your ideas or impressions of Wyandotte Chemicals, state the number of it. You may pick as many or as few as you like.

22. What would you say are the advantages of having a company like Wyandotte Chemicals in the city of Wyandotte?

23. Well, there are two sides to most everything. What are the things that aren't so good about having a company like Wyandotte Chemicals in the city?

24. Is there anything else about Wyandotte Chemicals, or anything that Wyandotte Chemicals does, that people in the city don't like so well?

25. Aside from providing jobs, can you name any other things that Wyandotte Chemicals does for the city of Wyandotte? What?

26. Do you approve or disapprove of the management of a company like Wyandotte Chemicals publicly stating its opinion about public matters or community problems? Approve, disapprove, no opinion.

27. Why do you say that?

28. Have you heard or read anything about city taxes paid by Wyandotte Chemicals? Yes, no, don't recall.

29. (If "yes" on 28) What have you heard or read?

30. What is the company's position on this tax question, as you understand it?

31. Just as a guess, what share of all taxes collected by the city of Wyandotte are paid by Wyandotte Chemicals? Less than 10%, 10%, 20%, 30%, 40%, 50%, 60%, 70%, 80%, 90%, 100%, and no opinion.

32. Do you have as much information about Wyandotte Chemicals as you want, or would you like to know more about the company? Have enough, would like more, no opinion.

33. (If "would like more" on 32) What things about the company would you like to know more about?

34. (Interviewer hands respondent card listing some of the ways people learn or hear about companies.) From this list would you pick out the chief ways you have learned or heard about Wyandotte Chemicals in the last year or so?
    Have read news about them in the papers. Read letters or booklets from the company. Read their magazine, *The Chief*. Know company employees. Know company top-management people. Work for the company now. Have talked with foremen or supervisors. Used to work for them. Have business dealings with the company. Read company's "Management Newsletter." Their advertisements in national magazines. From Union sources. Hear talks and speeches by company employees. Visited their plants. Other. None or don't know.

35. What have you heard or read about Wyandotte Chemicals most recently?

36. Where did you hear or read this?

37. Have you seen Wyandotte Chemicals' 1959 annual report? Yes, no, don't recall.

38. (If "yes") What are some of the main ideas or facts that you remember from the annual report?

39. What do you think is a fair per cent of profit on total sales for a company like Wyandotte Chemicals to make?

40. Do you ever see the company's magazine called *The Chief?* Yes, no, don't recall.

41. (If "yes" on 40) Would you say that you get to see most issues of this magazine, just some of them, or do you hardly ever get to see this magazine? Most of them, some of them, hardly ever or never, no opinion.

42. Where do you usually get to see *The Chief?*

43. Do you remember any particular articles in recent issues that were interesting to you? What were they about?

44. On the whole, how would you rate Wyandotte Chemicals as a place to work; would you say it's good, average, or a poor place to work? Good, average, poor, other, no opinion.

45. What would you say are some of the good points of Wyandotte Chemicals as a place to work?

46. Most companies have both good and bad points. What are some of the things about Wyandotte Chemicals as a place to work that aren't so good?

47. (Interviewer hands respondent list of statements about companies as em-

ployers.) Please read through this list, and every time you come to a statement that fits your ideas or impressions of Wyandotte Chemicals as an employer state the number of it.

48. Now, taking everything into consideration, would you say that Wyandotte Chemicals is a better place to work, about the same, or not as good a place to work as it was ten years ago? Better place to work, about the same, not as good, no opinion.

49. Why do you say that?

50. What kind of work does the chief wage earner in this household do?

51. What kind of business is that—what do they make or do? Owns business, hires others; self-employed, hires nobody; works for someone else, other. Respondent is housewife, student, retired, unemployed, working person.

52. How many people in your household are employed?

53. Do you (does the chief wage earner) happen to be a member of a labor union? Yes, no, don't know.

54. What was the last grade you completed in school? No schooling; 1st to 7th grade; 8th grade; 9th to 11th grade; 12th grade; college incomplete; college complete; graduate work; other; don't know.

55. Do you (does the chief wage earner) happen to work for Wyandotte Chemicals? Yes, no.

56. (If "no") Do any members of your family happen to work for Wyandotte Chemicals? Yes, no.

The survey findings ran to 150 pages of statements, verbatim replies and evaluations. They were reported in local newspapers and were generally favorable to both community and company. Eighty per cent of the respondents want management to speak up on public and community problems. Seventy per cent believe that air and water pollution are the greatest problems of the company, and 40 per cent think no improvement is being made. Seven out of ten residents think the company a good place to work and 75 per cent of employees rate the company "good."

In respect to the community, eight out of ten residents think the city is a good place to live. Sixty per cent criticize local shopping facilities. An equal number think that local taxes are "reasonable" and a high percentage favor a junior college.

The company is acting on the survey findings by increasing its communications with employees with an employee magazine, newspaper, newsletter, new bulletin board program, and letters from the president. A slide-film was prepared, narrated by the president, covering the survey, company growth, position, and prospects. Communications from the company to the community include an extensive advertising campaign in local newspapers discussing findings of the survey, meetings with the press, and a speakers' bureau. Management believes that the survey which cost about $20,000 to conduct and $5,000 to report provides a blueprint for constructive action for both the community and the company. Future meetings with community leaders are scheduled, at which time the slide-film will be shown.

QUESTIONS

1. Is the community survey of Wyandotte Chemicals Corporation a desirable step toward improved community relations for the company? What are specific advantages of this survey? What are its limitations?

2. Should an outside opinion research organization have been engaged to make this survey? State reasons for your decision.

3. Was the research properly designed from the standpoint of the size and nature of sample, method of securing the information, advance publicity, and reporting the findings?

4. What is your opinion of the questionnaire used in the Wyandotte Chemicals' survey? What are its good features? Its weaknesses?

5. Should another research method or technique have been used in determining the attitudes of residents of the community and employees? What?

6. What steps should the corporation take, in addition to those described in the problem, to use the findings from the survey?

Case 18–2

OPINION RESEARCH ON SPEECH

Smith Kline and French Laboratories

Smith Kline & French Laboratories, Philadelphia, Pennsylvania, is a manufacturer and distributor of ethical pharmaceutical products prescribed by the medical profession and dispensed by retail pharmacists. Typical products of the company are "Thorazine," one of the earliest tranquilizers, used in moderate and severe mental disorders; "Dexedrine," a central nervous system stimulant used in treatment of depression and overweight; and "Ornade," an oral nasal decongestant for relief of upper respiratory distress.

The company has four subsidiaries in the United States. The Wholesale Division operates three wholesale drug houses in the Delaware Valley. The Avoset Company, located in California, produces milk products. Norden Laboratories, Lincoln, Nebraska, produces veterinary medical products for treatment of diseases of animals; and Julian Laboratories, Chicago, is engaged in development and production of steroid drugs. The International Division of the company includes subsidiaries in England, Canada, Puerto Rico, South Africa, Australia, Mexico, Brazil, and Venezuela.

Sales volume of the company and subsidiaries exceeds $145 million annually. There are about 4,600 employees in the United States and foreign plants, laboratories, and offices. About 10 per cent of sales are invested annually in research and development of new products.

Smith Kline & French Laboratories, in common with other ethical pharmaceutical manufacturers, is faced with mounting criticism and Congressional investigation on the grounds of monopoly, high prices, excessive profits, high-pressure selling and advertising, and unethical dealings. To overcome this criticism, the company recognizes the need for interpreting the drug industry to the public, medical profession, and legislators.

The public relations department of Smith Kline & French has published a series of statements describing the company's position on various issues raised in hearings of the pharmaceutical drug industry policies and practices before the U.S. Senate Sub-Committee on antitrust and monopoly. These statements have been circulated to stockholders, the press, legislators, and leaders in health and medicine.

In addition, a speaking program on the contributions and economics of the pharmaceutical drug industry was initiated by the public relations department. Medical representatives of the company spoke on the subject "Prescription for Tomorrow" before civic clubs throughout the country. More than 1,700 speeches were delivered over a period of a year before audiences numbering approximately 75,000 persons.

To appraise the effectiveness of this speech in enhancing the public image of the industry and building more favorable attitudes toward the pharmaceutical drug industry, Smith Kline & French retained the Opinion Research Corporation, Princeton, New Jersey, to make an audience reaction evaluation of the speech.

The Opinion Research Corporation conducts public opinion studies on a wide variety of issues of general interest to business executives and publishes its findings monthly in its Public Opinion Index for Industry reports. In addition, the corporation conducts opinion research on specific public relations problems of individual companies such as the audience reaction study of the speech by representatives of Smith Kline & French Laboratories.

The method used by Opinion Research Corporation in evaluating audience reaction to "Prescription for Tomorrow" illustrates current techniques for appraising a public speech, a medium of communication which has been subjected to little critical evaluation.

The speech was evaluated at eight evening meetings of four men's civic clubs located in eight towns and cities in the Southern and Middle Atlantic states over a period of 60 days. The clubs which participated in the study were: Lions Club, West Oak Lane, Pennsylvania; Rotary Club, New Castle, Delaware; Lions Club, Perkiomen Valley, Pennsylvania; Kiwanis Club, Hatboro, Pennsylvania; Rotary Club, Washington Crossing, Pennsylvania; Y's Men, Millville, New Jersey; Lions Club, Piedmont, Alabama; Lions Club, Island Park, L.I., New York.

Arrangements were made in advance with each organization for a representative of Opinion Research Corporation to have a part in the program for the purpose of administering the questionnaires used in evaluating the speech.

The basis of the research design was the before and after matched sample. Before each speech was delivered by a Smith Kline & French medical representative, the audience was divided into two groups. About one half of the audience identified as Group "A" was asked to complete a questionnaire on the prescription drug industry, the results from which constituted the "before" speech data. The other half of the audience identified as Group "B" served as a control group and completed prior to the speech a questionnaire on a totally different subject, fallout shelters.

The "after" speech data was based on responses to the prescription drug industry questionnaire completed by the control Group "B" after the speech. This is the same questionnaire filled out by Group "A" before the speech. After the speech Group "A" filled out the same drug industry questionnaire which it completed before the speech but the after-speech responses of this group were not included in the findings since, in the opinion of the investigators, there is likely to be some resistance to changing a previously recorded opinion.

A total of 93 respondents in Group "A" completed the prescription drug industry questionnaire before as well as after the eight speeches. Eighty-five respondents in Group "B" completed the control questionnaire on fallout before the speeches and the drug industry questionnaire after the speeches. The findings of the survey are based on a comparison of the responses of the before Group "A" which completed the drug questionnaire prior to the speeches with the responses of Group "B" which completed the drug industry questionnaire after the speeches.

The research was not designed to cover a highly representative sample of all audiences that heard the speech "Prescription for Tomorrow." The principal objective was to measure the changes in attitude toward the prescription drug industry immediately after hearing the speech. It is assumed that the extent of attitude change observed in the eight audiences studied is a good general indication of the extent of change that occurred among most of the audiences that heard the talk.

The research was designed to measure change in attitudes of the audience in three broad areas: image of the industry; attitudes on prices, profits, government price regulation and research, and competition; and industry favorability and familiarity.

The basic device of image measurement used in the study was a list of statements describing various facets of the prescription industry's reputation. Respondents selected from the list of statements those that most nearly fitted their mental picture of the industry. The purpose of this technique is to help respondents verbalize their impressions of the industry which may be vague and difficult to express without the aid of descriptive statements that the respondents can recognize as corresponding to their ideas about the industry.

The statements used in this image study of the pharmaceutical drug industry were grouped in three broad categories: social concern and contributions, competition and communications, and product attributes and product development. This list of statements from which respondents selected those reflecting their image of the industry with the percentage before and after the speech and the change in attitudes follows:

Image of Prescription Drug Industry

Area I—Social Concern and Contributions of Industry

Favorable Statements	Before (%)	After (%)	Change (%)
1. Their drugs have almost eliminated certain diseases......	67%	79%	+12%
2. They help family doctors learn about new drugs....	62	78	+16
3. They deserve respect for their contributions to health......	61	75	+14
4. They are devoted to better medical care for all Americans......	57	71	+14
5. They donate money to universities for medical education and research......	47	51	+ 4
6. They have high ethical standards......	31	53	+22
7. They are interested in serving the public, not just in making money......	27	44	+17
8. Favorable average for this image area......	50	64	+14

Unfavorable Statements			
9. They try to make too big a profit......	49	16	−33
10. They put fancy names on ordinary drugs and charge a higher price......	47	15	−32

	Before (%)	After (%)	Change (%)
11. They sometimes try to profit unfairly from sickness	33%	9%	−24%
12. They use high-pressure sales tactics to get doctors to use their products	18	14	− 4
13. They are sometimes unethical in their dealings	13	8	− 5
14. Unfavorable average for this image area	32	12	− 20

Area II—Competition and Communications of the Industry

1. A highly competitive industry	38	55	+17
2. They do a good job of letting the public know about their field	27	38	+11
3. Favorable average for this image area	33	47	+14

Area III—Product Attributes and Product Development

Favorable Statements

1. Their products help most of us live longer	66	78	+12
2. You can depend on most of their products	63	67	+ 4
3. You can get most of their products everywhere when you need them	49	64	+15
4. Most of their products are of the highest quality	48	62	+14
5. They are outstanding for scientific achievement	34	58	+24
6. Considering everything, drugs are a bargain	15	42	+27
7. Favorable average for this image area	46	62	+16

Unfavorable Statements

8. Some of their products had bad side effects	53	52	− 1
9. Some of their products are overrated	52	32	−20
10. They tend to imitate each other's products	43	47	+ 4
11. They sometimes put new drugs on the market before they have been thoroughly tested	18	16	− 2
12. They are slow in developing new drugs to cure sickness	9	7	− 2
13. They don't do enough research	2	4	+ 2
14. Unfavorable average for this image area	30	26	− 4
Over-all favorable average for areas I, II, III	43	58	+15
Over-all unfavorable average for areas I, III	31	19	−12

Attitudes on Prices, Profits, Government Price Regulation, Research, and Competition

Following the image measurement of the reputation of the prescription drug industry, specific questions were asked about prices, profits, government price regulation, research, and competition as follows:

Drug Prices

Rate the prescription drug industry as "very good" or "good" on:	Before (%)	After (%)	Change (%)
1. Providing value for the money in its products	31%	62%	+31%
2. Effectiveness in keeping the prices of its products down	9	40	+31
Costs of prescription drugs and medicine are "about right" "or low"			
3. Compared with other medical costs	55	75	+20
4. In relation to their effectiveness in treating disease	42	54	+12
5. Compared with prescription drug costs of twenty years ago	22	53	+31
6. Compared with costs of other things	17	62	+45

	Before (%)	After (%)	Change (%)
7. Since 1939, prices of prescription drugs have gone up about the same as, or less than, other prices...	45%	75%	+30%'
8. State correctly the cost of the average prescription in the United States ($3.14).....................	0	39	+39

Profits

1. Average (Median) estimate of prescription drug companies' net profits per dollar of sales..........	37¢	12¢	−25¢
2. Think this profit is reasonable..................	30%	61%	+31%

Government Price Regulation

1. The government should *not* fix the prices of prescription drugs.............................	59	84	+25

Research

1. Rate the prescription drug industry as "very good" or "good" on progressiveness in developing new products.....................................	81	94	+13
2. State correctly the industry's annual research expense ($200,000,000)........................	2	24	+22

Competition

1. Say there is a great deal of competition among companies in the prescription drug industry.......	41	56	+15

Industry Favorability and Familiarity

As a broad measure of how the respondents regarded the prescription drug industry, the following questions were asked:

Favorability	Before (%)	After (%)	Change (%)
1. Favorable......................................	45%	72%	+27%
2. Half and half.................................	36	23	−13
3. Unfavorable..................................	10	4	− 6
4. No opinion...................................	− 9	1	− 8

Familiarity			
Which of the following statements best describes how well you feel you know the prescription drug industry?			
1. I know the industry very well..................	3	7	+ 4
2. I know a fair amount about it..................	23	28	+ 5
3. I know a little about it........................	42	45	+ 3
4. I know practically nothing about it............	32	20	−12

The survey showed that the speech "Prescription for Tomorrow" produced substantial gains in the social concern and contributions area of the industry's image and a sharp reduction in the association of unfavorable concepts with the industry. It increased understanding of the competitiveness of the industry and reinforced respect for the industry on product attributes, research, and development. On six out of the eight questions on "price" the "after" responses are 30 percentage points more favorable to the industry than before the speech. Twice as many respondents after the speech say they had a "very favorable" impression of the industry than they had before the speech.

QUESTIONS

1. What are the advantages to be derived by Smith Kline & French from the audience reaction research of the speech "Prescription for Tomorrow"?

2. Comment on the research technique used by Opinion Research Corporation in the study of audience reaction to the speech? What are its desirable features? Its weaknesses?

3. What is your opinion of the list of statements of the drug industry's reputation to obtain audience reaction to the industry?

4. Was the sample used in this survey satisfactory? Give reasons for approving or propose improvements in the sample.

5. What other method of opinion research may be used in determining audience attitudes to a speech?

PRESS RELATIONS AND
PUBLICITY

THE PRESS INCLUDES the personnel of newspapers, magazines, radio and television stations and networks who are responsible for the collection, preparation, and publication or broadcasting of news and information. Members of the press are editors, publishers, feature and editorial writers, reporters, news editors, announcers, and commentators. Good relations with the press is essential to secure publication of news and publicity about a corporation, industry, association, or non-profit organization.

Relations between the press and management of corporations and nonprofit organizations are not always amicable. Some managers are hostile to the press, refuse to grant interviews, or to be quoted; others antagonize the press by demanding publicity in return for the purchase of advertising space, by seeking to suppress unfavorable news, by criticizing the press for failing to publish news releases, and by playing favorites among newsmen.

On the other hand, management is critical of the press for over-emphasizing unfavorable news about business, inaccurate reporting, misquoting, misleading headlines, and giving advertisers publicity space while refusing space to nonadvertisers.

However, the press and industry are reaching a better understanding as business management becomes better informed about the operational problems and ethics of journalism and appreciates the value of good press relations. The press, on the other hand, recognizes that business has general news to report and that corporations can give the press valuable aid in the developing of news stories and articles.

PUBLICITY MEDIA

The principal publicity media employed in public relations programs are daily and weekly newspapers; general, women's, farm, business, and professional magazines; and radio and television broadcasts.

Newspapers

Newspapers are a basic medium of communication for public relations because they are read by many millions, enjoy the confidence of readers, exert influence on public opinion, appear frequently, and provide concentrated coverage of the areas in which they circulate. Special sections and features appealing to women, businessmen, sportsmen, motorists, gardeners, and others provide opportunities for product publicity on these subjects.

The number of daily and Sunday newspapers in the United States and Canada exceeds 2,500 according to N. W. Ayer & Son's *1963 Directory of Newspapers and Magazines.* There are more than 60 million readers of daily newspapers and more than 47 million readers of the Sunday editions. Nearly 10,000 weekly newspapers are published in the United States and Canada. In addition, about 500 papers are published triweekly, semiweekly, fortnightly, and monthly. These newspapers provide a valuable channel of communication from corporation and nonprofit organizations to the public.

Magazines

There are nearly 20,000 magazines published in the United States appealing to the general public and special groups. In addition to general magazines such as *Life, Look,* and the *Saturday Evening Post,* there are women's magazines such as *Ladies' Home Journal, Good Housekeeping,* and *Seventeen;* business magazines such as *Fortune* and *Business Week;* agricultural magazines, as *Capper's Farmer, Farm Journal,* and *Progressive Farmer;* professional magazines, as *Oral Hygiene* and *Journal of the American Medical Association;* special interest magazines, as *Holiday* and *National Geographic;* religious magazines, such as *Presbyterian Life* and *Christian Herald;* and many other periodicals for special-interest groups. The readership of these and other magazines exceeds the total population of the country.

Magazines are an important medium for product, corporation, and nonprofit organization publicity as they are read leisurely and thoroughly by several persons; have a long reading life; and are often filed for future reference. Magazines which afford sufficient space to tell a complete story are particularly suited to service or educational publicity articles; the attractive appearance, good paper, and color reproduction of magazines make them ideal for photo publicity. For these reasons magazine publicity is a medium of communication eagerly sought by business, social service, and associations for public relations programs.

Radio and Television Broadcasting

Radio and television publicity has developed rapidly with the expansion of radio and television facilities in the United States. The total number of radio and television stations in the nation is 5,501, according to the 1963 edition of *Broadcasting Yearbook*. Of this number, there were 3,749 AM and 1,062 FM radio stations and 645 television stations. Each of these stations allocates a portion of its broadcasting time to public service programs, documentary films, news, and product publicity provided by the publicity staffs of industrial, commercial, and nonprofit organizations and associations.

Ninety-four per cent of all households in the country, or 51,690,000, have radio receivers and 91 per cent, or 49,800,000 homes, have television sets according to the 1963 *Broadcasting Yearbook*. Nearly every household in the country receives radio and television news and information released by public relations staffs.

Newspaper Feature, Picture, and News Syndicates

There are about 175 newspaper feature, picture, and news syndicates operating in the United States. News syndicates are associations of newspapers or private concerns which provide newspapers with special articles, photographs, and cartoon strips. Syndicates are a major channel of distribution for publicity of sectional or national interest. There are four principal types of news syndicates: wire news syndicates distribute news by wire nationally and internationally to member newspapers and broadcasting stations and networks; feature syndicates specialize in the distribution of columns, articles, background information, cartoons, and comic strip serials to newspapers and magazines; illustration syndicates distribute photographs and drawings by mail and wire to hundreds of newspapers; and distribution syndicates operate a nation-wide system of distribution for news publicity, features, articles, and illustrations.

PRESS RELATIONS POLICY

A comprehensive press relations policy is the basis for establishing good relations between a business or nonprofit organization and reporters, editors, feature writers, and radio and television commentators. The following press relations policy of the public relations department of the Standard Oil Company, Indiana, is a good example of a comprehensive press policy:

It is company policy to help and stimulate the press—newspapers, magazines, and other publications, as well as radio and television, to report and interpret the Standard Oil business story to the public.

To extend public understanding of the Standard Oil Company, it is also company policy to:

Issue news releases or statements on matters of genuine news value and public interest.

Provide the press with news releases and abstracts or copies of talks by company people.

Supply factual information willingly and promptly in answer to inquiries from bona fide representatives of the press.

Report newsworthy examples of employee and corporate good citizenship.

Willingly and immediately state the known facts of an emergency situation in answer to inquiries from responsible representatives of the press, even though the facts may not always be favorable to the company.

Willingly and immediately permit access to plants for bona fide reporters and photographers in times of emergency such as fires and floods, to the limits of national security and human safety.

Provide factual information to correct misstatements.

At all times maintain good working relations with the press.

In the interest of company public relations it is also policy to:

Limit statements to subjects related to company business and the petroleum industry.

Refrain from expecting or requesting any preference in treatment of news about the company because it is an advertiser.

Refrain from giving construction costs of monetary damage resulting from fire, flood, accidents unless authorized by the manager.

Fundamentals of Good Press Relations

Good relations between the management of a corporation or non-profit organization and the press are furthered by the observance of a few simple principles. The International Labor Press Association, AFL–CIO advises publicity officers of local unions to observe the following "Dos" and "Don'ts" in dealing with the press:

"Dos"

Be Friendly, polite, and even tempered.

Be Helpful. Only by meeting the needs of the news outlets can you get their help in meeting yours.

Be Accurate. Every name, fact, and figure must be right.

Be Prompt. Nothing is deader than old news.

Be Truthful.

Be Frank. You may not be able to tell everything you know; if that's the case, say so.

Be Thorough. Make sure to include every significant fact.

Be Fair.

Be Patient. Good relationships take time and perseverance.

"DONT'S"

Don't Lie, not ever under any conditions.

Don't Bluster, threaten, or demand.

Don't Lose your temper.

Don't Exaggerate the importance of your news.

Don't Write a news release as though it were an editorial; your job is facts, not opinion.

Don't See a plot against your organization every time a story gets less space than you think it is worth.

Don't Blame a reporter for his paper's policies.

Don't Be self-important.

Don't Expect miracles.

Don't Give up.

Organizing for Press Relations

Many people associated with an organization are directly involved in press relations, from the receptionist who greets reporters, the telephone operator who handles their calls, the branch office or local plant manager, the public relations staff, and top management. The principal responsibility for press relations is with those who determine policy which creates news, all who execute policy, and those who meet the press.

The headquarters public relations department or the press section thereof is responsible for the over-all guidance of the company's relations with the press and the dissemination of news. Headquarters makes available to local plant management publicity programs and offers advice on executing such programs.

Large corporations with regional public relations offices assign press relations to the regional public relations manager. He is usually responsible to the company's regional or district manager who is spokesman for the company in his territory.

A company with several plants holds each plant manager responsible for press relations in the plant community. A local community relations manager in large plants deals with the press. News of major changes in company policy, shutdowns, expansions, and layoffs at a local plant usually originate with the headquarters public relations department which sends news releases direct to local newspapers and radio and television news editors. Routine news of less importance is disseminated by the local plant community relations manager.

General Electric Company—Press Organization. General Electric

Company press relations organization is decentralized in approximately 100 product departments located in various parts of the country. Press relations for corporate plans, programs, policies, activities, and achievements are the responsibility of the Press, Radio, and TV News Relations department, New York City, which has sections for the business press, radio-TV news, daily press, and general magazines. Similar responsibilities are performed by four regional public relations offices in Atlanta, Chicago, San Francisco, and Washington, D.C. About half of the product departments maintain their own press relations personnel, while in the remainder publicity is supervised by the company's News Bureau in Schenectady, N.Y.

FUNCTIONS OF PRESS, RADIO, AND TELEVISION MEDIA

Knowledge of the news functions of newspapers, news services, magazines, radio and television stations and networks is desirable in the preparation of publicity and relations with the press.

Newspaper Organization and Publicity

The editorial departments of daily, Sunday, and weekly newspapers receive publicity prepared by the public relations staffs of companies and nonprofit organizations.

In charge of the editorial staff of a daily and Sunday newspaper is the publisher, who is responsible for the general policies of the paper and plays a more or less active part in determining its editorial content. Subordinate to the publisher is the managing editor who is responsible for the news content of the paper. He supervises the city editor and, in some cases, the editorial and feature writers.

The city editor is in charge of all local news. The staff of the city editor includes local news reporters, rewrite men, and special editors including the business editor, sports editor, women's editor, Sunday editor, picture editor, and feature writers. The city editor and these special editors are the principal outlets for local publicity and news photographs distributed by public relations departments.

State, national, and international news is the responsibility of state, national, and international editors, on large papers, who usually report to the managing editor. They handle news from the Washington bureau of the paper, from staff correspondents in the principal cities of this country and abroad, and from the press wire associations.

The chief editorial writer and his staff, who are usually responsible to the managing editor, interpret editorially current national and local events and significant developments. Annual reports, news releases, and company publications are sent regularly to the editorial writers of newspapers in the area served by a company to keep them informed of its activities.

The editorial organization of a daily newspaper is illustrated in Figure 19–1. The editor of a weekly newspaper is the person to whom

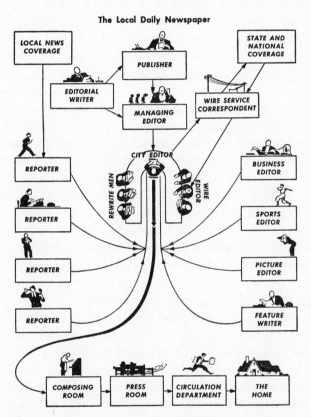

The Local Daily Newspaper

FIG. 19–1. Editorial staff of a metropolitan daily newspaper, showing the various departments which handle publicity releases from public relations departments. This chart was produced for American Iron and Steel Institute by Hill and Knowlton, Inc., public relations counsel.

press releases, pictures, and news material are distributed.

Types of Newspaper Publicity. Four types of press publicity appear in daily, Sunday, and weekly newspapers—news, opinion, service, and entertainment publicity. News publicity, including pictures, may be one of four types: *local* publicity, involving company news of new construction, increases in personnel, promotions and transfers, employee relations, safety awards, disasters, speeches of executives, and news about a particular plant or office; *state* publicity, involving news about a company of state-wide interest; *national* publicity, concerning the national activities of a company; *international* publicity, concerning the operations of a company outside the United States.

Sources of News Publicity. News publicity for daily, Sunday, and weekly newspapers and radio and television stations originates from three sources: a local plant manager or public relations manager; a regional public relations office; or a national public relations office. Much company news concerns the operations of a plant in the community where the newspaper or broadcasting station is located. This news is prepared by a local public relations manager subject to the approval of the plant manager or someone authorized to speak for him. State and national news releases which concern basic policy, major shutdowns, expansions, and layoffs of a company, as a whole, are prepared by the regional or headquarters public relations department and transmitted to the local plant manager or public relations manager to be released to local papers. The preparation and distribution of news publicity will be discussed later in this chapter.

Opinion Publicity. Opinion publicity, which is distinct from news publicity, expresses publication policy and the views of newspaper editors and editorial writers. It is published in the form of editorials and cartoons on the editorial page. Opinion publicity is obtained through personal contacts and correspondence with editorial writers who are sent annual reports, executive speeches, and company publications from which editorials may be prepared.

Service Publicity. Newspapers and radio and television stations publish and broadcast to readers and the listening public service material, such as recipes and menus for homemakers, financial advice for investors, horticultural hints for gardeners, and beauty aids for women. Much service publicity is produced by public relations departments of manufacturers of consumer products. This publicity is used in special broadcasts and printed in the financial, women's, garden, book, and business pages of daily, weekly, and Sunday newspapers. Syndicated editorial services also prepare and distribute to newspapers reader service material supplied by the public relations departments of corporations.

Entertainment Publicity. The public relations staffs of entertainment, recreation, and sporting enterprises prepare publicity on sport and theatrical personalities and events which is used by sport, theatrical, and boating editors of daily and Sunday newspapers and by radio and television commentators.

News Syndicate and Wire Service Publicity. Publicity is also distributed by corporations and nonprofit organizations to news syndicates and wire services which distribute it to newspapers and radio and television stations throughout the country. The Associated Press, United Press International, feature and picture syndicates write and distribute spot news, features, and pictures to newspaper and radio and television subscribers.

Magazine Organization and Publicity

The editorial departments of general, business, women's, professional, farm, religious, technical, and class magazines are interested in newsworthy publicity prepared by the public relations departments of business and nonprofit organizations.

The editorial staff of a magazine is headed by an editor-in-chief with an executive editor and a managing editor as assistants. The editorial staffs of news magazines include a chief editorial writer, art director, copy editor, picture editor, and chief of research supported by senior editors, staff writers, photographic staff, associates, researchers, and reporters. News magazines also maintain national and foreign news service departments with correspondents located in the principal cities of the United States and foreign countries. General magazines have special editors for sports, education, science, travel, books, and other interests. Women's magazines have editors for fiction, general features, food and homemaking, architecture and gardening, and fashion and beauty.

Publicity and articles are accepted by magazines for publication according to their news value, reader interest, and conformity to editorial policy of the publication. Magazine publicity is placed through personal contact with the editors of the specialized departments of the magazines interested in the news or articles prepared by the public relations staff. To supplement personal relations with editors, public relations departments maintain lists of magazine editors classified according to the types of editorial material which they use.

The publicity writers of food manufacturers are personally acquainted with the editors and writers of women's magazines and submit to them articles on foods or offer to assist them in the preparation of editorial material.

Radio and Television Organization and Publicity

Publicity for radio and television broadcasts is distributed to the program director or to the news editor. The station program director is assisted by a producer who directs public service programs. Radio and television organization is illustrated in Figure 19–2.

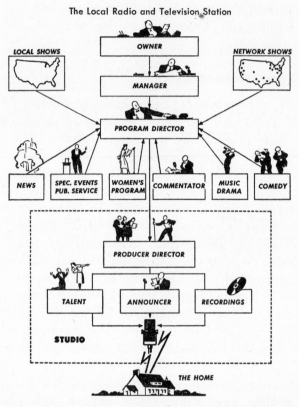

FIG. 19–2. Organization of a radio and television station showing the various departments which are outlets for news publicity and features from public relations departments. This chart was produced for American Iron and Steel Institute by Hill and Knowlton, Inc., public relations counsel.

Radio and television stations broadcast two types of publicity programs: the commercial program, sponsored and paid for by a company, association, or nonprofit institution; and the sustaining or public service broadcast sponsored by a station or network at its own expense.

Commercial Publicity Programs.   Institutional commercial radio and television broadcasts of "live," taped, or recorded material are used by large corporations and associations to inform the listening and viewing public about an organization and its products, provide a public service, or entertain. These broadcasts are 30 or 60 minutes in length with musical or dramatic entertainment accompanied by 60-second publicity, institutional announcements preceding, during, and following the program. Public relations programs are not intended to directly promote sales of the products or services of the sponsors. A typical corporation commercial institutional television broadcast is the "Telephone Hour," sponsored by the American Telephone and Telegraph Company.

Sustaining Publicity Programs. A portion of all radio and television broadcasting time is devoted to sustaining programs which are planned and produced at the expense of stations and networks as a public service. Publicity may be obtained on the following types of radio and television sustaining programs: speeches, round-table discussions, interviews, special events, news, sports, fashion, homemaking, farm, educational, and other types of programs.

Publicity departments co-operate with broadcasting stations in producing sustaining programs by providing background information, facts, and stories to script writers or program directors, as well as properties and settings. Institutional motion pictures for television broadcasts are also loaned by public relations departments to television stations and networks. Radio and television stations broadcast corporate special events such as plant openings, anniversaries, and open houses.

Newsreel Publicity

Newsreel publicity reaches millions of viewers in commercial theaters and on television. Newsreel producers photograph events of national interest such as ship launchings, unique scientific and technical developments, important labor agreements, and interviews with well-known industrialists.

COMMUNICATIONS WITH THE PRESS

Effective relations with the press require clear channels of communication with editors, reporters, publishers, writers, and commentators through personal contacts, press conferences, mailing of news releases, press previews, press-management luncheons, clip sheets, press books or portfolios, and publicity distribution agencies.

Personal Contacts

The principal method of communicating with the press is by personal calls on editors, publishers, writers and newscasters on newspapers, magazines, wire services, syndicates, and radio and television stations. Personal contact is the most effective way to place news stories and publicity articles; to determine what editors want; to learn their editorial policies; and to secure their co-operation.

Press Conferences

Press conferences are called by public relations directors to obtain publicity in connection with the introduction of a new product by a manufacturer, labor negotiations, change in management, plant expansion, corporate reorganization, and accidents of disaster proportions. A press conference should be timed so that the news will secure the widest coverage in newspapers and on television and radio. A chief executive of the organization or a representative of management should be present to make the announcement and answer reporters' questions.

Photographs may be taken by the press depending upon the purpose of the conference. Prepared press releases, official statements, background information, and photographs or a press kit should be distributed to reporters attending.

Mailing of Press Releases

Routine press releases are distributed by mail to editors of newspapers, magazines, and radio and television broadcasters for publication or broadcast. An up-to-date mailing list of editors and writers is essential. To this list is sent news releases and other publicity material. As the editorial requirements of publications and broadcasting stations differ, it is important to send publicity and pictures only to those editors who may give it space or broadcast time. The list of news outlets should be classified according to the type of material which they will publish; or the press list may be divided into preferred and secondary lists. The preferred list to include those publications which use the publicity more or less regularly; the secondary list to include publications which use publicity releases occasionally.

The press list should be compiled on cards showing the name and address of the publication, frequency of issue, names of editor and assistants, telephone number, circulation, special information on editorial requirements, and a code classification number.

Press Previews

Press previews are essential for informing and securing press and radio co-operation in introducing new models and opening new plants and facilities. The day before the official public showing of a new product or opening of a new facility, the press is given a preview; company officials are on hand to meet the press and answer their questions. Press news releases, photographs, and press packets, giving complete information about the new product or facility, are distributed to the press at the preview.

Press-Management Luncheons

Press luncheons for local newspaper editors, magazine writers, and television and radio broadcasters to meet management and discuss organization developments or inspect facilities create better press relations.

A large food manufacturer holds a press-management luncheon preceding each of its biannual, regional stockholders' meetings. Invited to these meetings are business and financial writers, food editors, women's page editors, managing editors, city editors, publishers, and correspondents of business magazines. Company officials speak informally during the luncheon. Questions from members of the press are answered, and a motion picture featuring the company's operations is shown.

Clip Sheets

Clip sheets are distributed by publicity departments to editors of daily and weekly newspapers. Clip sheets reproduce in newspaper format news stories and illustrations to show news editors how stories and pictures will appear in print. Editors clip out news material and send it to the composing room for setting in type.

The Industrial Press Service is a clip sheet published by the public relations department of the National Association of Manufacturers, and distributed to 6,000 weekly newspapers.

Press Kits

Press kits containing mimeographed news releases, photographs, biographies, and background material are produced by public relations departments and distributed to the press at special events such as anniversaries, plant openings, and new product announcements.

Publicity Distribution Agencies

Newspaper feature syndicates and publicity distribution agencies serve publicity departments in providing low cost distribution of news and publicity material to editors and news writers.

Determining Volume of Press Publicity

The volume of press publicity about an organization may be determined by using commercial clippings services which clip all news items, pictures, and articles appearing in daily and weekly newspapers

and magazines. The publicity staff also examines newspapers, magazines, and business publications for publicity appearing therein.

PLANNING AND PRODUCING PRESS PUBLICITY

Planning a publicity program for a business or a nonprofit organization involves: research of the publicity needs of the organization;
determination of publicity policies; assignment of responsibility for
press publicity; selection of media to be used; timing the program;
preparing the publicity; and determining the budget.

Publicity Research

Before launching a publicity campaign, research is necessary to
determine the audience to be reached, the best media to reach the
audience; the type of editorial material desired by editors and
writers; and newsworthy and interesting information about the organization to be featured in the publicity.

Publicity Policy

A publicity policy statement should be prepared to define the objectives of the organization's publicity which may be to give the public
accurate and interesting information to create a better understanding
of the organization in the eyes of the public; to build prestige and good
will for the organization and its products or services; to establish the
organization as a reliable source of information; to increase sales and
counteract unfavorable publicity that sometimes occurs. Publicity
should be newsworthy and limited to statements related to the business
of the organization and its industry.

Selecting Publicity Media

The publicity media should be carefully selected to reach the
particular public which should be informed. News of interest to the
community or employees should be sent only to local media. Whereas,
news of state-wide or national importance should be released to press
associations, newspapers, magazines, or radio and television networks.
Financial publications should be sent news for stockholders and investors; trade publications, news of interest to distributors and dealers;
and supplier news should go to periodicals read by manufacturers.

Timing Publicity Releases

Timing is important in releasing news to the press. Editors and
reporters work toward deadlines and should have ample time to
process a story or article. In distributing publicity, broadcast times and

publication hours and dates should be taken into consideration. All routine news stories should be in the hands of city editors of afternoon papers or radio or television editors by 9:00 A.M. and spot news, by 11:00 A.M. for publication in afternoon editions and broadcasts. News for morning papers or broadcasts should be on editors' desks by 6:00 P.M. and spot news by 11:00 P.M. the day preceding publication. Sunday news should reach Sunday editors before noon on Friday, or earlier for special departments. Spot news for Sunday may be submitted as late as 4:00 P.M. Saturday. State editions close earlier.

Publication dates of magazines must be taken into consideration in submitting articles for publication. Many monthly magazines "close" their columns to editorial material six weeks or more in advance of publication.

It is easier to secure publication of news releases on certain days of the week. Monday is normally a lighter news day than the latter part of the week, and the chances of getting a publicity story into a daily paper are often better on Monday. The heavy volume of newspaper advertising carried on some days of the week limits the space available for publicity. When important local, national, or international news is breaking, it is more difficult to get publicity in newspapers.

Announcements, speeches, or programs for future events should be realeased to newspapers and radio and television news editors in advance and the release date plainly indicated on the copy.

Production of News Publicity

News releases should be prepared to conform to standard journalistic practice. The first paragraph of a news release should summarize the principal facts and answer the five questions of "who, what, when, why, where," so that if the balance of the story is eliminated, the opening paragraph, or "lead," constitutes a complete story. There are two reasons for writing all the principal facts of a news release in the opening paragraph. Most readers scan newspapers, reading the headlines and first few sentences and not taking time to read the full details. Also, when space is limited, news editors eliminate the last paragraphs of stories that are in type if they are too long to fit the available space. Following the lead paragraph in a release comes news of secondary importance, and from then on elaboration of the subject follows to the end of the story.

News releases should be brief and factual. However, when there is additional detailed information which should be incorporated in the story, attach a supplementary fact sheet giving important details which can be included by the rewrite man or news editor if he desires.

The standard form for a news release is on 8½ by 11 inch paper with the heading of the company's public relations department, address, and telephone number, so that editors can contact the organization for further information if desired. Double spacing and wide margins should be used. Copy should be written on only one side of the paper. Preferably, the length should be limited to one page.

The release date should appear in the upper left margin of the page. When news releases are distributed in advance, as in the case of special announcements, speeches, or programs scheduled for the future, they should carry the release line, "Hold for Release Monday Morning, April 10, or Anytime Thereafter." A headline should not be written on the release.

The pages should be numbered in the center at the top of each sheet if the release is more than one page long, and each page closed with a complete sentence so that there will not be any carryover, as copy is often distributed to typesetters in "takes" of several pages at a time to expedite composition. These principles are illustrated in the following:

News from USO

USO Public Relations Department
237 East 52nd St., New York City 22, Plaza 1–3020
Date of Release

New York—General A. C. McAuliffe, National Campaign Director for USO—the private nonprofit agency for welfare and recreation for men and women in the armed forces—today stated that Vermont is the first state in the union to report through its United Fund–Community Chest organizations a one hundred per cent inclusion of USO in their community plans.

Six communities in the Green Mountain State—Barre, Brattleboro, Burlington, Putney, Rutland, and Springfield—comprise the entire state's roster of organized community giving. The budget committee of each individual community organization studies the needs of national, as well as local, charities and social agencies, deciding to include or refuse the separate agencies' fund requests in their particular collection of public subscription.

"This is the first time in several years," the former battle commander at Bastogne said, "that all of Vermont's Chest and Fund committees have included USO, and we are grateful." He expressed hope that the remaining forty-nine states will see fit to follow Vermont's lead.

He stated that USO faces the need to serve military personnel stationed in remote areas of the world, providing some degree of civilian support through clean and comfortable hospitality centers, and by sending troupes of live entertainers in long jumps from the United States to put on shows, even at gun sites.

Spontaneous News. Spontaneous news is often of such widespread local, sectional, or national interest that editors, on their own initiative, will send reporters to the place where the news originates to get facts and pictures. Supplementing personal coverage by the press, the public relations staff should prepare news releases for distribution to newspapers and broadcasting stations.

Planned News Publicity. News publicity is also created by an imaginative publicity staff from novel, human interest, controversial, or humorous incidents which occur in an organization. Through contacts with executives, a publicity staff learns of newsworthy events or information which would serve as the basis of press releases. Regular organized coverage of all news sources in an organization is essential to the development of news releases.

Material for news publicity will be found in an annual report, in significant or newsworthy statements made by executives, statements by important visitors to plants or offices, unique discoveries in company laboratories, human-interest stories, new product developments, and numerous other subjects.

FEATURE STORIES AND ARTICLES FOR NEWSPAPERS AND MAGAZINES

Feature stories and articles are prepared by public relations departments or developed in co-operation with the staff writers of daily and Sunday newspapers, Sunday supplements, business magazines, and general and special publications. They appeal to the specialized interests of readers in business, science, fashion, food, home decoration, and other subjects.

Examination of articles published in newspapers and magazines will indicate to a publicity staff the preferences of editors, editorial policies, the amount of space allotted to articles, and the possibility of getting articles accepted. Some magazine editors only publish articles written by their editorial staffs. In this case, a public relations department may provide the information and illustrations which can be used by the staff writer of a magazine in preparing an article or feature.

RADIO AND TELEVISION PUBLICITY

Several types of institutional radio and television publicity programs are sponsored by corporations and nonprofit organizations, including drama, musical, audience participation, commentators, interviews, and round-table forums. The type of program chosen depends upon the type of audience, the hour of the broadcast, the time available, current popularity of a program type, available talent, cost, and other factors.

A radio or television speech by an executive of the sponsoring organization is a common type of publicity program. A speech on a timely, interesting subject delivered by a forceful speaker can create a favorable public image for a corporation or nonprofit organization. A radio or televised interview between the head of an organization and a skillful interviewer on a subject of public interest may be effective institutional publicity.

A variation of the interview program is the round-table discussion, in which several persons participate in a discussion of controversial issues. The material to be discussed is outlined in advance, and each participant is assigned one or more topics in the outline.

The symposium broadcast is similar to the round-table discussion in that several persons participate. In this type of broadcast there is no discussion of viewpoints and no attempt to stimulate conversation. Prepared scripts are usually used and each speaker is allotted a specific time to speak.

Another type of publicity program is the dramatic broadcast. This type of program is the most expensive and requires specialized skill in writing, acting, and production.

Radio and television publicity may be obtained from special event broadcasts such as the opening of a new plant, an anniversary celebration, or an open house. Speeches of executives and well-known guests may be broadcast. Interviews with visitors give an informal and human interest appeal to the broadcast.

Publicity may also be obtained by social service and nonprofit organizations from participation in the commercial radio and television programs of national advertisers. Arrangements may be made with the sponsors to include in their broadcasts a reference to the nonprofit group.

To insure a large radio or television audience, a publicity program should be planned to publicize important institutional broadcasts by: press releases; advertisements in local papers; announcements in company publications and on bulletin boards; and aid from radio and television stations in building an audience with their press releases, station program résumés, published schedules, special announcements, and newspaper advertising.

HANDLING EMERGENCY AND DISASTER PUBLICITY

"A serious emergency, if not handled correctly, can destroy a good company reputation. Handling of press relations during critical moments can determine what the general public will think of a company for years to come," says A. L. Roberts, public relations director, Texas Gas Transmission Corporation. Serious industrial accidents and disasters present the most difficult press relations and publicity problems. Proper handling of emergency publicity by a public relations staff of a corporation is remembered by the press long after the emergency is forgotten.

Plant personnel and supervisors are the key to effective emergency publicity. At times of emergency, supervisors are excited and preoccupied in caring for the injured, keeping the public out of danger, stopping spread of the damage, or restoring service. Under these conditions, supervisors regard the presence of reporters as an intrusion. They may try to "cover up" the emergency by barring reporters from the scene, obstructing their efforts to get the facts, or refusing to give out information. This is the worst possible way to handle emergency publicity.

To insure effective handling of press relations during an emergency, the public relations department of every corporation, likely to have an emergency involving the public, should prepare a carefully considered emergency publicity program. This plan should include the following features:

Designation of one person in each plant or facility to serve as the company spokesman to give out information to the press and answer questions of reporters. This person may be the ranking supervisor, manager, or foreman at the emergency site. Later, when the division manager, superintendent, department head, or representative of management arrives on the scene, he is the logical person to deal with the press. No other employee should be permitted to speak to the press for the company. The public relations director acts as liaison between the spokesman for the company and the press. Information issued by the company spokesman should be channeled through the public relations representative for the benefit of newsmen who will be calling the public relations department for information.

Supervisors, foremen, and company executives should be instructed in dealing with the press in emergencies. A number of companies have prepared press relations guides for supervisors giving specific instructions for informing reporters. "Meet the Press," a manual prepared by the Texas Gas Transmission Corporation, advises supervisors to have answers for newsmen to five basic questions about an emergency: What? Who? When? Where? and Why?

What—Nature of accident; physical damage to pipeline, compressor station, and other company property and equipment; physical damage to the property of others and owners' names and addresses; how service will be affected by the emergency; what repairs will be made; and how long they will take to complete.

Who—Nature and extent of injuries; names, ages, addresses, occupations of any injured; what injured were doing at accident scene; disposition of injured; if removed to hospital, what hospital and where; name of doctor who treated injured.

When—Time of accident.

Where—Location of area where emergency occurred; approximate distances to nearest landmarks or towns; type of terrain.

Why—Cause of accident, if known.

Company spokesmen should give the press only established facts—not guess at the cause. It is better to say "The cause has not been determined" or "the extent of the damage is unknown." Estimates of damage should be made only by responsible company authority.

Bad news should not be hidden, but favorable facts should also be given to the press, such as prompt and brave action which minimized a more serious situation, steps being taken by the company to relieve the distress of the injured and their families, and the company's favorable safety record.

Blame for the emergency should not be plaecd upon an employee, as later developments may show that he was not at fault and the company should not be placed in a position of accusing an employee of neglect of duty.

Terminology used in describing an emergency to the press should not be inflammatory, as "I thought for sure it was the end," or "She really blew." An accident should be described as a "failure," not an "explosion" and an "emergency," never a "disaster."

The press should be notified immediately of an emergency. Newsmen arriving at the scene should not be ignored. Guards and receptionists should be instructed to honor press cards and conduct reporters to the public relations representative or person in authority. Reporters should not be greeted with such statements as: "No comment," "I don't have time to talk now." Refused information, a reporter can write only what he sees and hears and his account will be more sensational than factual.

In major disasters, a press room should be set up near the scene of the disaster with telephones, typewriters, darkroom for developing pictures, and refreshments for newsmen. A press conference with top management should be arranged by the public relations department. Frequent statements should be released to the press in the name of management when the facts become known. The public relations staff should be at the scene to "cover" the disaster, prepare news releases, and secure pictures which should be made available to the press. The name, telephone number, and address of the company's press representative should be given in advance to all local newspapers, radio and television stations so that he can be reached in time of emergency. After the emergency has passed, the press should be thanked for its coverage and co-operation.

To secure effective publicity in emergencies, a carefully considered emergency press relations program should be planned in advance by the public relations department. A press relations handbook should be published for supervisors telling how to deal with the press in emergencies and build a good reputation for the company with the press and public. Press relations should be included in supervisory training programs. The public relations staff should be briefed on its role in an emergency; specific tasks should be assigned individuals; procedures should be planned; and additional facilities provided. There is no question whether a company will have press relations in an emergency; the question is whether they will be good or bad. A sound emergency publicity plan will avoid misunderstandings with the press likely to arise in an emergency.

Case 19–1

DISASTER PUBLIC RELATIONS

Monsanto Chemical Co.

Monsanto Chemical Company, established in 1901 in St. Louis, Missouri, is the third largest chemical company in the United States and the fourth largest in the world, producing thousands of chemicals, plastics, petroleum products, and chemical fibers. The company has total assets of more than a billion dollars and is owned by about 86,000 shareholders. It employs some 35,000 persons approximately 28,000 of whom work in 22 plants, 11 laboratories, and 27 sales offices of the parent company and six subsidiary and associate companies in the United States. Monsanto has manufacturing facilities in 11 foreign countries, employing 7,000, with sales offices in the principal cities of the free world.

Public relations was initiated by Monsanto in 1938 with the employment of a full-time public relations executive with the title "assistant to the president." In 1939 he established the Department of Industrial and Public Relations which embraced personnel, advertising, and public relations. Later, the personnel and advertising functions were dropped and since 1954 public relations has been the sole function of the present Public Relations Department.

Monsanto's public relations department is staffed with 47 persons, 17 of whom are clerical. The department is organized in eight sections as follows: Audio-visual, with six staff photographers; Financial Communications; Central Public Relations, which embraces community and press relations, production, and services; *Monsanto Magazine;* Eastern Public Relations office, New York, which handles publicity and information; Gulf Coast Public Relations office, Houston; Charitable Trust, which handles contributions; and Divisional Public Relations, with a staff manager for each of five manufacturing divisions. The heads of each of the eight sections are answerable to an assistant director of public relations. He is responsible to the director of public relations, who reports direct to the president of the company.

As a victim of the greatest industrial disaster ever to occur in the United States, Monsanto Chemical Company has experienced disaster publicity problems on a scale never before encountered by an American industrial company. From this experience, the company has established public relations policies and practices which may serve as a pattern for any industrial organization in communicating with the public in time of disaster. Although the disaster to the Monsanto Chemical plant in Texas City, Texas, occurred in 1947, the public relations problems would be similar today in an industrial catastrophe of equal magnitude.

To understand the disaster public relations problems of the company it is necessary to describe the tragedy which occurred the morning of April 16, 1947, when the burning French freighter, *Grandcamp,* loaded with 2,500 tons of ammonium nitrate, exploded at a quay 700 feet from the Monsanto plant in Texas City. The explosive force of ammonium nitrate, which is about half as great as TNT, subjected the plant to an impact equivalent to 250 five-ton blockbuster bombs exploding simultaneously. To this force was added the destructive power of tanks and pipelines filled with propane, ethylene, and benzol in the Monsanto plant which were pierced by red-hot fragments of steel from the disintegrated ship. The whole constituted a disruptive force comparable to an atomic bomb.

The $20 million Monsanto plant was a shambles. The main power plant of steel, brick, and concrete was flattened along with the walls of manufacturing buildings; windows of offices and laboratories were shattered; roofs were ripped off; pipelines carrying inflammable liquids and explosive gases were torn apart starting fires which, added to those of nearby oil refineries, formed a pillar of smoke 3,000 feet high, visible nearly 500 miles away. A large wave, rushing in from the basin where the ship exploded, inundated the adjacent area and drowned many fleeing for safety.

Approximately 450 out of 658 employees were at work in the plant at the time of the disaster. Of this number 154 were killed or missing, another 200 were hospitalized, and only a few escaped completely. In addition to Monsanto's casualties, nearly one half of 123 employees of an outside contractor working in the plant were killed and the remainder injured. Of the combined forces in the plant 215 persons were dead or missing.

At the same time, the community of Texas City suffered serious losses. Out of a total population of 25,000, over 500 persons were killed and 1,000 seriously injured. Hundreds of homes were damaged beyond repair, scores burned, 1,000 automobiles were flattened, banks and stores were destroyed and all electricity, water, gas, telephone and transportation services, as well as police and fire protection were wiped out by the blast. State police ordered the city evacuated completely before a second ship also loaded with ammonium nitrate exploded.

When news of the disaster reached Monsanto headquarters, the president ordered the entire resources of the company mobilized to bring relief to the survivors. Public relations staff executives along with the president, chairman of the board, medical director, nurses, and executives from other Monsanto plants throughout the country flew in company planes to Texas City.

Press facilities were immediately established by the public relations staff in a completely equipped pressroom in the Galvez Hotel, Galveston, 16 miles from the scene of the disaster. Typewriters, direct telephone lines, copy paper, mimeograph machines, messengers, and hotel accommodations were provided for the press. Automobiles were rented to provide transportation for reporters to Texas City and return. All information about the disaster in the company's possession was immediately made available to the press.

The principal public relations problem confronting the company was to correct the inaccuracy of early reports that the Monsanto plant had exploded. Engineers and explosion experts were called in to explain to the press that the plant was not engaged in hazardous operations, handled no explosive materials; that the ship was not at the company's pier; that the explosive did not originate in any company plant; and the company did not use ammonium nitrate. First reports in newspapers and magazines stated incorrectly that the plant manufactured ammonium nitrate and was located near rich ammonium nitrate deposits. Ammonium nitrate is a combination of air, natural gas, and water, and is not found in natural deposits.

Erroneous statements that the plant was improperly designed were made by an employee of a contractor engaged in its construction. These statements were refuted by an announcement by the president of the company which built the plant that no construction fault was accountable for any part of the disaster.

Reports in financial circles that insurance coverage on the $20 million plant was inadequate were corrected by Monsanto's president who announced that plant and contents were insured for $14,750,000 plus $7,500,000 use and occupancy insurance, and $2,500,000 public liability insurance.

Simultaneously with the establishment of press headquarters, the company set up its public relations staff headquarters in the Galvez Hotel, Galveston, and arranged for two 24-hour-a-day teletype circuits to the field headquarters of the company in Texas City and to Monsanto headquarters in St. Louis. All communications were channeled through public relations headquarters and all statements from the company were released there. At the company's St. Louis office, the public relations staff was put on 24-hour duty and information was transmitted from Galveston to St. Louis for simultaneous release there.

The president and chairman met with reporters in a press conference to announce the company's policy to rebuild the plant in the same location and to appropriate an emergency fund of $500,000 from which immediate payment of $1,000 over and above insurance and legal liability would be made to the family or dependents of each deceased employee. The company agreed to pay full hospital costs of each injured employee not covered by Blue Cross, full salary or wages through the next pay period, and further consideration for those who were able to work and for whom no work could be provided. The company stated that it would pay for the removal of bodies to other cities for burial where the families wished it; repairs to damaged homes of employees; and return to the home cities of widows and dependents of employees who had been transferred to Texas City.

Monsanto bought time on Galveston radio stations and ran full-page advertisements in local papers announcing the names of the dead, missing, and injured and seeking to determine the whereabouts of employees who had not reported to the company since fleeing the disaster site. After the emergency, local newspaper advertisements published by the company thanked volunteer workers and organizations for their assistance.

Within a week, the company published a four-page report to stockholders, employees, and friends written by the chairman of the board discussing the tragedy and the steps taken by the company to aid the injured employees and dependents of the deceased.

Personal relationships with employees and the community were handled by a disaster group of Monsanto employees from other cities organized in three service departments: Personal Service, Community Service, and Property Service. Personal Service was responsible for identification of unknown dead, payments to the next of kin and the hospitalized, reimbursement for damaged property, and medical care for the injured. Community Service maintained liaison with the Red Cross, directed two trained welfare workers in aiding survivors, and issued daily bulletins on casualties to the press. Property Service aided employees in repairing their property, finding new homes, moving household goods, and reimbursing them for loss of wrecked automobiles.

From its public relations experience in the Texas City disaster, Monsanto developed the following Check List for Disaster Community Relations covering the facilities and services needed in time of emergency.

CHECK LIST FOR DISASTER COMMUNITY RELATIONS

I. *Disaster Staff*
   1. *Operation*
      a) Organization
      b) Operations base
      c) Medical supervision
      d) Food
      e) Lodging
   2. *Communication*
      a) Phone and teletype
      b) Transportation
      c) Liaison with Red Cross, police, etc.
      d) Special public announcements

II. *Information*
   1. *Press Relations*
      a) Press room
      b) News releases
      c) Accommodations
      d) Press conferences
      e) Background information
      f) Special services

III. *Help for Employees*
   1. *Personal Service*
      a) Physical condition and whereabouts
      b) Identification of dead
      c) Hospital check-up
      d) Put able to work
      e) Keep all on payroll
      f) Home canvass by welfare workers

2. *Property Service*
    a) Financial aid
    b) Emergency home repairs
    c) Transportation

IV. *Help for Community*
  1. *Community Service*
    a) Community public relations
    b) Aid to other affected industries
    c) Co-operation with local officials
    d) Financial aid to local hospitals and welfare groups

V. *Follow-up of Disaster*
  1. *Public Relations*
    a) Rehabilitation of injured employees
    b) Re-employment
    c) Community co-operation
    d) Media
    e) Periodic check-up

In addition to these steps to be taken to improve employee and community relations at time of disaster, Monsanto believes that first concern of management should be for the relief of company personnel and their families. Outside relief workers should be relied upon in case of serious disasters. Up-to-date expanded personnel records should be maintained with duplicates kept at another location. The damaged area should not be disturbed until it has been examined by experts for bodies and clues to the disaster. Rumors should be rejected in the absence of facts. An advance emergency plan should be prepared describing what should be done and who should do it.

QUESTIONS

1. What good principles of disaster relations were observed by Monsanto Chemical Company in the Texas City disaster?
2. What should be the specific objectives of public relations at time of an industrial disaster?
3. What publics were reached by the company in the Texas City disaster? Should other publics have been informed? What? How?
4. What media of communication were used by the company in the disaster? Were these media used effectively? What other media should have been used?
5. Should the public relations staff have taken other action in the Texas City disaster? What?
6. Comment on the Monsanto Check List for Disaster Public Relations. What changes or additions should be made to this list?

Case 19–2

SOCIAL WELFARE ORGANIZATION PUBLICITY

Girl Scouts of the United States of America

Girl Scouts of the United States of America, national headquarters in New York City, was founded by Juliette Low in Savannah, Georgia, in 1912 to help girls aged 7 through 17 to develop as happy, resourceful individuals willing to share their abilities as citizens in their homes, communities, country, and the world.

Total membership of the Girl Scouts is approximately three and one-half million including 2,685,000 girls and 769,000 adult leaders organized in almost

FIG. 19–3. Publicity photograph released by National Girl Scouts News Bureau showing Girl Guide Rangers from Denmark, France, England, and Scotland participating in the Girl Scout Heritage Trail tour of the United States sponsored by Girl Scouts of the U.S.A.

950 councils and 166,000 troops in the United States and at U.S. military and civilian locations in 49 countries around the world. Since 1912, there have been some 18½ million members, 14½ million girls and 4 million adults. The organization is affiliated with the World Association of Girl Guides and Girl Scouts which includes representatives from 51 nations of the free world.

Girl Scouts from 7 through 9 years of age are Brownie Scouts; from 10 through 13 years they are Intermediate Scouts and from 14 through 17 years they are Senior Scouts. The three age groups participate in a single Scouting program adapted to the girls' interest levels. The program includes activities in 11 fields of interest: agriculture, arts and crafts, community life, health and safety, homemaking, international friendship, literature and dramatics, music and dancing, nature, out-of-doors, sports and games.

The public relations program of Girl Scouts of U.S.A. is designed to promote public knowledge and understanding of the objectives and activities of the Girl Scouts through publicity in newspapers and magazines, on radio and television, in the house organs of industry and in local media, as well as through relationships with community, national and international groups and organizations.

To accomplish these objectives, the organization maintains a public relations department at headquarters which is advised by a standing public relations committee of adult members and subcommittees on community relations, relations with religious organizations, school relations and international relations. Public relations chairmen in the councils are responsible for public relations at the local level, but depend to a large extent on the advice and materials supplied by the national public relations staff.

The annual budget of Girl Scouts of the U.S.A. for public relations, publications, and periodicals exceeds $800,000 and employs such communications media as council public relations kits including public relations plans, publicity suggesions and sample copy, television spots, motion pictures, film strips, cook books, the Girl Scout *Leader* magazine which goes without charge to 775,000 adult volunteers and professional workers, and the *American Girl,* a subscription magazine for teenagers, with a circulation of 800,000.

Heritage Trail Public Relations Program

An outstanding example of national and local public relations of Girl Scouts of the U.S.A. is the Heritage Trail public relations program planned and activated by the national headquarters public relations department with the co-operation of the public relations chairmen of the 52 hostess councils participating in the Heritage Trail project.

The Heritage Trail project, representative of major national Girl Scout activities, was an eight-week exploration across the country in the summer of 1961 by 72 Girl Scouts-Guides between 15 and 19 years of age. The participants included 48 American Senior Girl Scouts, 24 Girl Guide Rangers from 12 foreign countries, and eight adult leaders. The Girl Scouts involved came from all parts of the United States and Girl Guide Rangers (equivalent to U.S. Senior Scouts) were from Brazil, Canada, Denmark, France, Germany, Great Britain, Ireland, Italy, Mexico, The Netherlands, Norway, and the Philippines.

The purpose of Heritage Trail was to acquaint young women of this and other countries with the land, peoples, cultures, and history which created the United States of today. It was one feature of the celebration of the fiftieth birthday of Girl Scouts of the U.S.A. in 1962, and carried out the anniversary theme of "Honor the Past—Serve the Future."

The participants were grouped into four teams, each having 12 American Scouts, six Rangers from three different countries and two adult leaders. The country was divided into four sections: Northeast, Southeast, Northwest, and Southwest, and a team was assigned to travel by chartered bus over a carefully planned route in each section. The teams visited and studied local industries, agriculture, and historical sites and met people of different national origins whose ancestors developed the area.

In eight weeks the four teams traveled a total of 16,000 miles through 40 states, stopping in 33 states and the District of Columbia as guests of some 1,000 Girl Scout families in 52 communities across the country.

Each team confined its travels to the particular section of the country to which it was assigned. For example, the itinerary of the Southeast team included 13 communities from the District of Columbia to Louisiana with visits to the White House, Supreme Court, and Senate in Washington; Jamestown and Williamsburg, Virginia; New Orleans; a cruise on the Tennessee River; and a visit to the American Museum of Atomic Energy at Oak Ridge, Tennessee. The other three groups visited places of interest in the Northeast, Northwest, and Southwest.

A five-day orientation period for the two Western teams was held at Stanford University and for the Eastern groups at International House, New York City. At the conclusion of the tour the four teams met at the University of Kansas for a ten-day evaluation and discussion of their experiences.

Heritage Trail Local Publicity

The Heritage Trail project provided the Girl Scouts' headquarters' public relations staff and 52 hostess councils with an unusual publicity opportunity on both the national and local levels. The national public relations department placed publicity with national media and provided press, house organ, radio, and television publicity material to the participating councils for local usage.

To assist the 52 hostess councils on the Heritage Trail in securing maximum publicity for the project in their local media, the national public relations department provided each council with three press kits: one for the council public relations chairman; one for the council executive director; and the third to the person in charge of local Heritage Trail arrangements.

The council press kit was arranged in three sections: "How to Do It" suggestions for securing press coverage for Heritage Trail; recommended publicity and background material for the project; and an order form for additional publicity materials.

The "How to Do It" section of the council press kit gave specialized advice to the hostess council public relations chairman for listing all community news media, interviewing editors, suggestions for features and news photos, local magazine coverage, co-operating with participating local organizations in publicizing Heritage Trail, and radio and television coverage.

The second part of the kit included a fact sheet describing Heritage Trail, a sample news release for local papers, a sample editorial, a program schedule of local events, Heritage Trail itineraries, a glossy print map showing the Trail across the country, and background information on Girl Scouts of the U.S.A.

An order form to be used by council public relations chairmen in procuring additional fact sheets, tour itineraries, maps, and background data from the national public relations department completed the press kit.

Advance National Publicity on Heritage Trail

The national Girl Scouts public relations department opened the national publicity campaign on Heritage Trail 60 days in advance of the event with an illustrated feature story distributed by a commercial news service to editors of national newspapers, magazines, and house organs. Approximately 100 leading magazines and newspapers used it.

This initial story was followed 30 days later by a media kit mailed to almost

300 outlets, including the New York metropolitan and out-of-town press; wire services; national syndicates; women's youth, education, and travel editors; the foreign language press; and foreign correspondents of other countries represented on the tour. This media kit contained a letter to the editor describing the project, a Heritage Trail fact sheet, news release, trail itineraries, a national map showing the route of the Trailers, the names and addresses of the American and foreign girls participating, and background information on the National Girl Scouts organization.

A luncheon to launch Heritage Trail was held at United Nations headquarters, New York City, for the 40 members of the Northeast and Southeast teams. Invited to the luncheon were representatives of United Nations delegations of the United States and the six foreign countries represented on the teams. The deputy representative of the United States Mission to the United Nations was the great speaker. A news release on the luncheon was sent to 100 editors, including all metropolitan press, wire services, foreign language press in the United States, and correspondents of foreign press of countries represented.

A special kit was distributed to all media representatives attending the luncheon. This kit contained a news release, a luncheon fact sheet naming the speaker, prominent guests, a list of names and addresses of all U.S. and foreign participants, a Heritage Trail fact sheet, a national map showing the cross-country routes of the Trailers, and background information on the national organization.

Photographs of the luncheon were serviced to national media, including the foreign language press.

Internal Public Relations on Heritage Trail

During the orientation sessions held in New York and California in advance of departure, the participants were briefed on the public relations aspects of the project. The leaders and girls were told why public relations coverage was important and what to expect in press, radio, and television interviews throughout the trip. The American girls were asked to serve as photographers and reporters during the tour to provide picture and story material for their home town newspapers. The leaders of each group reported to national headquarters on all publicity received by the group.

Publicity Coverage of Heritage Trail

About 500 newspaper stories and feature articles on Heritage Trail appeared in newspapers in all parts of the country. Much of this publicity was secured by hostess council publicity chairmen using the council public relations kit supplied by the national public relations department. United Press International carried a feature story and photograph of the United Nations luncheon for the Trailers.

Magazine coverage included illustrated articles in two *Junior Scholastic* issues (one, a cover story) and one in *Newstime*. *Seventeen* covered parts of the Southeast Trail and prepared a photo feature in another issue.

A total of 112 radio and television programs were secured by hostess councils as well as by the national public relations department. These included

55 radio news items and interviews and 57 television news spots and interviews. At the United Nations luncheon, radio station WRUL taped an 18-minute interview in Danish, English, Norwegian, and Spanish which was broadcast over its European network. The Voice of America also carried a radio news report in French of the event. The National Broadcasting System program "Today" carried a 12-minute broadcast about Heritage Trail from New York at the conclusion of the tour.

The United States Information Agency produced a ten-minute film covering three of the stops on the Trail for showing in the native countries of the international participants.

QUESTIONS

1. Comment on the Heritage Trail public relations program, giving specific reasons for approving or disapproving the program.
2. What specific suggestions can you make for improving the Heritage Trail public relations?
3. What additional media of communication should have been employed in the Heritage Trail public relations program?
4. Comment on the local and national publicity and press relations of Heritage Trail suggesting specific ways to improve these features of the program.

CHAPTER

20 ·

PUBLIC RELATIONS
ADVERTISING

ADVERTISING is included in many public relations programs of business, social welfare organizations, and trade and professional associations to communicate with employees, plant communities, consumers, stockholders, distributors, and dealers and to supplement other media of communication.

Some public relations advertising is called "institutional advertising" used to create a favorable image of a company or institution. Much public relations advertising, however, is not institutional but serves a wide variety of purposes such as explaining the issues in a strike, announcing the establishment of a new plant, explaining interruptions in service, inviting the public to an open house, and other uses described later in this chapter.

Other public relations advertising is called "public service advertising" and is used by corporations to serve the public welfare by combating inflation, promoting good health, advocating good government and participation in politics, aiding education, restraining racial and religious prejudice, and many other service objectives.

Advertising is an effective medium of public relations communication for several reasons. It is economical, making it possible to transmit a public relations message to a large number of readers at relatively low cost per reader. It can be highly selective and concentrated on a particular segment of the public such as stockholders, suppliers, or opinion leaders. It is flexible and may be used either for a national campaign or a local program in a plant community. Quick communication is possible through advertising in daily newspapers or over the air. Intensive community coverage may be secured through the use of local newspaper, radio or television advertising. Advertising in newspapers, magazines, and by mail provide sufficient space to tell a complete story and inform and educate readers. The advertiser can control the timing and space given a public relations message by buying a certain size space in a particular position in a specific edition of a publication.

PRINCIPAL OBJECTIVES OF PUBLIC RELATIONS ADVERTISING

To Create a Favorable Image of an Organization

Advertising is used to create a favorable image of an organization so that the public will have more confidence in the organization and be more favorably disposed toward its products or services. A company that uses advertising to develop the good will of the public is able to sell more of its products, to attract desirable employees, to reduce labor turnover, to secure the support of the plant community, to attract and hold stockholders, to win the favor of government officials, and to build a loyal dealer organization.

The Weyerhaeuser Company has used national magazine advertising for ten years to create a favorable company image.

To Correct Misconceptions

Public misconceptions about a company may seriously affect its sales, progress, and profits. To correct misunderstandings, many companies use advertising to inform the public about their policies and practices.

The Bankers Trust Company, New York City, uses magazine advertising in European publications to dispel the misconception of many Europeans that Americans live only for money and bigness. The advertisements feature the cultural aspects of American life.

Industries or professions are sometimes criticized by the public because of misunderstanding, prejudice, or adverse conditions over which the industry or profession may have no control. Advertising can be used to give the public information about the economic importance of an industry, its policies, practices, and contributions to the public welfare so that the public image of the industry or profession can be improved.

To create public acceptance of the professions of medicine and pharmacy, Parke, Davis & Company, pharmaceutical manufacturer, has used national advertising since 1951, which pictures in color great moments in medicine and the history of pharmacy.

To Interest Suppliers

To secure reliable sources of supply, an increasing number of manufacturers and merchants are using advertising in trade papers and magazines to interest suppliers in selling their products to the manufacturers and merchants.

To Arouse the Interest and Secure the Support of Stockholders

Corporations are advertising in newspapers and magazines to develop closer relations with shareholders. Formerly, stockholder advertising consisted of small, dividend announcement advertisements on the financial pages of daily newspapers. Today, corporations are running full-page, color advertisements in general magazines and pages in the Sunday editions of metropolitan newspapers to inform shareholders and the financial community about their financial condition.

To Win the Good Will of Community Neighbors

Advertising in plant city newspapers is a feature of many corporate community public relations programs. Community newspaper advertising informs local citizens about the operations of an industrial concern and impresses employees with the contributions of the company to the welfare of the plant community. This advertising points out that the company creates jobs and employment, helps pay the cost of government, and promotes civic affairs and community projects.

In addition, advertising is used to create a favorable awareness of a community. Lafayette National Bank of Brooklyn, New York, advertises in New York City and Brooklyn on the theme, "Helping America Wake Up to Brooklyn."

To Develop a Favorable Attitude by Legislators and Government Officials

Advertising is also used to inform voters about the issues involved in pending legislation and win their support and the support of city, state, and national legislators.

To Inform Dealers of Company Policies and Programs

Trade magazine and mail advertising is used by manufacturers to inform wholesale and retail dealers about the manufacturer's policies, programs, and developments. Advertising in trade publications is used not only to inform but also to instruct merchants in better merchandising and management methods, more effective displays, store arrangement, lighting, advertising, stock control, and credit policy.

To Inform and Win the Good Will of Employees

Advertising in plant community newspapers and on radio and television is used in many employee relations programs to inform workers about company policies, plans, and accomplishments. In addition, advertising in employee magazines gives employees facts about company operations, dispels rumors, and creates a better understanding between workers and management.

Baxter Laboratories uses advertisements in its employee magazine "Baxter World" to translate company finance into personal terms for employees.

To Serve Consumers with Helpful Information

Public relations advertising is used to give consumers helpful information and thereby win their good will and patronage. The Metropolitan Life Insurance Company builds good will with full pages in national magazines to educate the public on the proper care of health and how to live longer.

To Improve Labor Relations

Public relations advertising placed by employers in local newspapers improves their labor relations by keeping employees and the community informed and by counteracting the propaganda of labor agitators. Advertising is also used to present the employer's position in a labor dispute and to dispel misunderstanding of an employer's motives.

To Win the Support of the Press

To cultivate editors, publishers, and radio and television broadcasters, corporations advertise in the journalism and broadcasting magazines. Advertisements inform the press about business operations and accomplishments. Advertising is a logical medium to gain the understanding and support of the press essential to effective public relations.

To Render a Public Service

Much public relations advertising is used by corporations to promote the public welfare. Advertising sponsored by business organizations through the Advertising Council advocates going to church, forest fire prevention, better schools, accident prevention, and the American economic system. Advertising paid for by business concerns also furthers the objectives of the American Red Cross, CARE, United Nations, and Community Chest.

To promote the cultural life of northern New Jersey, Bamberger's, Newark department store, has carried on a campaign of public service advertising for better theater, concerts, and entertainment in the area served by the store.

MEDIA OF PUBLIC RELATIONS ADVERTISING

The principal media of public relations advertising are: newspapers, magazines, radio and television broadcasts, direct mail, outdoor bulletins and posters, motion pictures, and miscellaneous forms of advertising.

In selecting media for public relations advertising, consideration should first be given to the audience to be reached—employees, shareholders, neighbors, the press, suppliers, educators, opinion leaders, or others. Next, the fitness of the media to reach the desired audience from the standpoint of circulation, flexibility, prestige, and cost must be considered.

Certain media are more suitable for communicating with specific publics. Newspapers are the primary medium for community relations advertising. General magazines are most suitable for reaching the general public. Direct advertising is desirable for informing shareholders. Combinations of media are often most effective in public relations communication.

Public relations newspaper advertising is used in local community programs as well as in national campaigns. Local advertising is prepared by headquarters public relations departments for individual plant cities. Newspaper advertising in daily newspapers throughout the country provides broad coverage of the general public. Large corporations with plants throughout the country use both local and national newspaper advertising in their public relations programs.

Advertising space may be purchased in certain sections of newspapers to reach particular publics. Advertising to reach women is placed on the women's or society pages; to reach men, the sports pages are used. In Sunday papers, a variety of special sections appeal to the interests of music lovers, gardeners, motorists, travelers, or book lovers.

Institutional public relations advertising appears in newspaper supplements such as *Parade* and *This Week,* which are distributed in Sunday newspapers published in the principal cities.

To communicate with particular racial and foreign language publics, racial and foreign language newspapers are used in public relations programs. The Negro press is used to reach the Negro public. The foreign language press, which includes newspapers printed in German,

Danish, French, Greek, Norwegian, Arabic, Polish, Portuguese, Spanish, and other languages, is used for communicating with employees and consumers of foreign extraction in their native tongues.

Magazines

Magazines, including trade, technical, and business magazines and specialized religious, agricultural, fraternal, and recreational publications are a major medium of communication with the general and special publics.

General magazines are used for institutional advertising to the general public. Many institutional messages, however, are directed to specific publics, including influential persons, youths, farmers, teachers, women, business executives, parents, ministers, doctors, and other groups. Class magazines, which are published for special interest groups, enable a public relations advertiser to appeal to readers in terms of their particular interests.

Trade, professional, and industrial magazines are used for public relations advertising to suppliers, dealers, distributors, and professional people.

Radio and Television Broadcasts

Radio and television broadcasts are used to communicate with local, sectional, and national publics. The two types of radio and television advertising broadcasts are: *network,* involving the use of several stations simultaneously in a region, or nationally; and *spot* or *local* broadcasts by individual stations. Most public relations broadcasts are local spot announcements, although a few large corporations broadcast national network institutional programs.

Public relations radio and television advertising programs are of several types: talks and information programs, interviews, entertainment, and round-table or panel discussions by executives. One type of public relations program is a news broadcast, sponsored by a corporation as a public service and interspersed with institutional announcements describing a company's activities. Special events programs feature corporation open houses or anniversary celebrations. Audience participation programs include customers, employees, suppliers, neighbors, and representatives of various publics. Music, comedy, and dramatic programs are accompanied by institutional announcements. Public service programs inform listeners of the best ways to prevent accidents, to sew, cook, play golf, make a garden, or engage in many leisure activities.

Many radio and television public relations broadcasts are station-break announcements of one minute or less; talks and information programs running 15 or 30 minutes. Fifteen-minute consumer, day-time, public relations service programs feature homemaking, cooking, and child care.

Direct Advertising

Direct public relations advertising includes folders, envelope en-closures, leaflets, letters, broadsides, booklets, handbills, blotters, and company magazines. These forms of advertising are used in com-municating with specific publics such as employees, stockholders, cus-tomers, dealers and distributors, opinion leaders, government officials, and suppliers.

Direct advertising has the advantages of selectivity of audience, highly personalized appeal, minimum waste circulation, great flexibility in timing and coverage, directly traceable response, and ample space to tell a complete story.

Outdoor and Transportation Advertising

The principal types of outdoor and transportation advertising used in public relations are posters, painted bulletins, electric bulletin spec-taculars, car and bus cards, and station posters. This medium is used for institutional and public service advertising to the general public. It has the advantages of reaching a large audience at comparatively low cost and can be concentrated in a section of a city, state, or region. Outdoor advertising makes a strong impact on the public through large-sized space, color, and illumination. It has cumulative impact through repeated impression and may have local appeal in copy and illustration.

Motion Pictures and Miscellaneous

Motion-picture advertising is seen by an estimated 80 million per-sons weekly. Three types of public relations pictures are shown in com-mercial theaters: films running 40 to 80 seconds; three-minute films, and single-reel pictures.

Motion pictures are also an important medium of communication with employees, the community, stockholders, suppliers, and con-sumers. Many companies and associations sponsor and distribute films to schools, clubs, churches, and other groups.

Miscellaneous advertising media including calendars, ash trays, pencils, book matches, and similar novelties, are used principally as gifts in connection with public relations events.

ORGANIZATION FOR PUBLIC RELATIONS ADVERTISING

Responsibility for public relations advertising should be given to the public relations department. In some cases, both public relations and product advertising are handled in one department. In a majority of companies, however, public relations and product advertising are handled in separate departments. Product advertising is properly a function of the marketing department where advertising is used primarily to promote product sales.

In corporations that use a large volume of institutional advertising in their public relations programs, a separate section to handle institutional advertising is established in the public relations department. An institutional advertising section is responsible for the public relation advertising in the public relations department of General Motors Corporation.

Subsidiary companies of large corporations usually have public relations advertising programs which are developed by the public relations department of the parent company and adapted by the subsidiary to meet its own needs.

Advertising agencies plan, produce, and place public relations advertising under the supervision of the public relations department.

Many public service advertising programs to further the objectives of social welfare organizations are prepared and financed by the Advertising Council, a nonprofit organization supported by advertisers, advertising agencies, and media. The Council approves requests for advertising assistance from social welfare organizations and leading advertisers, media, and agencies who are members of the Council prepare and run the advertising at their expense. Some of the public service advertising programs which have been sponsored by the Council are: Better Schools, CARE, Civil Defense, Forest Fire Prevention, Red Cross, National Blood Program, Religion in American Life, U.S. Savings Bonds, Stop Accidents, Community Chests and Highway Safety.

A PUBLIC RELATIONS ADVERTISING PROGRAM

Public relations departments of business and nonprofit organizations depend on advertising agencies to plan, produce, and place public relations advertising because they have broad experience, outside viewpoint, and creative talent to execute an effective advertising program.

The first step in developing a public relations advertising program is to make an opinion survey of public attitudes toward the company or organization. This survey determines the public misconceptions about the organization which should be corrected and indicates the information which should be communicated to the public by the advertising.

Themes of Public Relations Advertising

When the opinion survey has been completed, the findings will suggest a theme for the advertising program. The principal themes used in public relations advertising are: the institutional theme, the public service theme, the economic theme, the labor relations theme, and the special event theme. The choice of these themes depends upon the particular objectives of the public relations program.

The Institutional Theme. Much public relations advertising is based on an institutional theme which depicts a corporation or nonprofit organization as a public service institution. Institutional advertisements describe how the advertiser has served the public through research, good products, progressive policies, and modern facilities.

Public relations institutional advertising informs the public about the size, number, and location of plants and branches; financial resources; management policies, distributing methods, research and development; and social contributions.

The Public Service Theme. Public relations advertising on a public service theme presents solutions to social problems. Public service advertising advocates curbing highway accidents, preventing forest fires, helping public schools raise funds for teachers' salaries, soliciting contributions for nonprofit organizations, combating infantile paralysis, increasing the prestige of the armed forces, selling government bonds, and solving other social problems.

The Economic Theme. Public relations advertising on an economic theme promotes better understanding of how our American business system operates and gives the public a greater appreciation of the advantages of the free enterprise system.

The Labor Relations Theme. To improve labor relations, advertising in plant magazines and community newspapers informs employees about company policies, problems and practices, employee services and benefits, employment stabilization, equitable wage rates to secure the understanding of workers.

The Special Event Theme. Public relations advertising in plant

Rockwell Report

by W. F. ROCKWELL, JR.
President
Rockwell Manufacturing Company

EVERY MANAGER of a business must wish at one time or another for a crystal ball from which he might divine the future of his enterprise. In the absence of such a godsend, however, it is his essential job to *define* the *present* enterprise as a key to the future.

We ask our managers to define the business in terms of *customer needs*, rather than the products we make. They must ask themselves, "Do we make valves and meters, or do we really make the means to control and measure gases, liquids, time and distance? Do we make Drivotrainers, or the means to educate many youngsters to good driving habits? Do we produce voting machines, or answer the need for faster, incorruptible voting? Power tools, or a method to shape and build useful products? Do we maintain regional parts warehouses, or assurance to the customer of uninterrupted performance of his equipment?"

We then ask these managers, "What do we want the company to be? What should we be doing about meeting the changing needs of our customers? What can the company do about planning, rather than merely accepting, its future?"

If we accept that our business *is* control and measurement, the means to shape and build products, better voting procedures, teaching good driving habits, etc., then we must accept the responsibility that goes with it. This responsibility is to the customer, and involves the improvement of existing products or the development of new ones that better satisfy these needs as they change or develop.

The original emergence of any successful company is linked to the satisfaction of a customer need. The decline of such a company is equally linked to some point in time when it either forgets or chooses to ignore that needs change or become altered.

The job of defining our business today is relatively easy. Defining—and shaping—its future is much more difficult. The key, we feel certain, lies in properly evaluating the future needs of the customer.

* * *

We have discussed many phases of communications in this column from time to time. Having just completed our annual management meeting, we are reminded of what a valuable internal communications tool this is. It includes all domestic, Canadian and International Division managers, along with division sales managers and headquarters staff. Its success is due largely to open discussion of intimate operating and financial data which we believe is paramount to our management people in planning and executing their responsibilities.

* * *

Interested in the increasingly complex subject of driver education? We have just published a comprehensive booklet on the substantial contribution to driver education programs that can be made through the Aetna Drivotrainer System.

* * *

A new automatic valve lubricator is now available to provide lubricated plug valves with a continuous and regulated supply of lubricant. It is particularly suited for use in connection with remote valve installations where controlled and automatic lubrication is a necessity. The unit can also be equipped with a switch which triggers a warning system on a panelboard at remote control stations.

This is one of a series of informal reports on

ROCKWELL MANUFACTURING COMPANY
PITTSBURGH 8, PA.

*Makers of Measurement and Control Devices, Instruments.
and Power Tools for twenty-two basic markets*

R-6103

FIG. 20–1. The Rockwell Report advertisement reproduced here is one of a 12-year-old corporate advertising campaign in business magazines to tell the business and financial community that the company is well managed, progressive, and growing.

city newspapers, radio and television broadcasts, and outdoor posters is used to invite the public to a special event, such as an open house for the community or families of employees, an anniversary celebration, a stockholders' meeting, the dedication of a new plant or office building, the introduction of a new product, or a display, exhibit, or parade.

Planning and Producing Public Relations Advertising

Following the selection of a theme for a public relations advertising program, a plan is prepared by the advertising agency and approved by the advertiser, stating the media to be used; the number of advertisements, their size, frequency of appearance, and position in the medium; and the cost of the proposed advertising.

When the plan for advertising has been approved, the agency writes, designs, illustrates, and prepares the advertisements or radio or television broadcast scripts, purchases space or time, and places the advertising with the media. When the advertising has appeared, the agency verifies the insertions or broadcasts, audits the accounts, bills the advertiser, and pays the media for the space and time.

PUBLIC RELATIONS ADVERTISING TO SPECIFIC PUBLICS

Advertising is used in transmitting public relations messages to employees, stockholders, consumers, dealers and distributors, suppliers, government, and neighbors in plant communities to secure their understanding and good will.

In Employee Relations

Advertising to employees in plant communities appears in the following media: daily, Sunday, and weekly newspapers, company magazines, radio and television, direct mail, outdoor, and motion pictures. Media are selected that reach the greatest number of employees with maximum reader or listener interest at the lowest cost per employee.

A corporation with one or more plants in a single community concentrates its employee advertising in media with maximum coverage in the plant community. Companies operating plants in several cities may use the same advertising program for employees in all plant cities. Employee advertising is usually on the institutional, labor relations, or economic themes.

In Stockholder Relations

Advertising to stockholders and the financial community appears in the following media: direct mail, business and financial magazines, and the financial pages of daily newspapers. Direct mail is the principal medium for stockholder advertising and includes letters, annual and interim financial reports, dividend enclosures, invitations to open houses for stockholders, reports of annual meetings, special product offers to shareholders, and stockholder periodicals. Periodicals which carry stockholder advertising are: *Financial World, Wall Street Journal*, the financial pages of the *New York Times* and *Chicago Tribune*.

In Community Relations

Advertising in plant communities reaches consumers, suppliers, stockholders, municipal government officials, and employees. It is used to present facts about corporate affairs which would not be acceptable as news. In paid advertising, a corporation can control the content and assure the appearance of its messages, which is not possible with newspaper publicity.

The major medium of community advertising is the local newspaper, supplemented by local radio and television broadcasts and outdoor and transportation advertising. Direct-mail advertising is also used to reach community leaders, including ministers, city officials, civic and women's club officers, and teachers.

Co-operative community relations advertising, sponsored by a local Chamber of Commerce or industrial association, featuring the contributions of local industry to community welfare, creates favorable community opinion of local industry.

In General Public Relations

The principal media used in public relations advertising to the general public are magazines, newspapers, and radio and television broadcasts. The theme of this advertising is institutional, emphasizing corporate development, executive personnel, plants and branches, good labor relations, sound financial status, and social contributions.

In Dealer and Distributor Relations

Dealer relations advertising in trade magazines and by direct mail informs merchants about a manufacturer's sales promotion program and describes new company policy, new products, finance plans, and merchandising aids.

Other objectives of dealer advertising are: to educate dealers and their personnel in improving their efficiency and increasing sales of the manufacturer's products; persuading dealers to maintain a complete stock; to advertise, display, and promote aggressively; to maintain an adequate sales force; and to give good service.

NEW BUILDING...

The new Ocean Cable building at Western Electric's Baltimore Works, now nearing completion, will provide almost four acres of floor space for the manufacture of underseas telephone cable for the Bell System.

NEW PRODUCT...

A brand new type of submarine cable will be manufactured on the machines shown here and is scheduled to go into production in Western Electric's new Ocean Cable building early this year.

NEW YEAR

B. J. Ramsey, Baltimore Works Manager

1962 promises to be an exciting year for Western Electric's Baltimore Works. In addition to making a new armorless underseas cable, developed by Bell Laboratories, we'll continue to produce here a wide range of other essential products necessary to help meet many of the diverse communications needs of the Bell System.

Meeting these needs takes teamwork. Lots of it. Western Electric people at the Baltimore Works and 12 other major plants across the nation work in close harmony with Bell Telephone Laboratories engineers. Together, we create the equipment needed by the Bell Telephone companies to provide Baltimore and the nation with

the world's most versatile and reliable communications services.

Helping to perform this essential manufacturing job made 1961 a busy year for your neighbors employed at Western Electric's Baltimore Works. To help us do our part of the Bell System job, we purchased more than 27 million dollars' worth of supplies and equipment from over 800 Maryland suppliers.

In 1962 — we look forward to a busy and productive year.

BALTIMORE WORKS: MAKER OF COMMUNICATIONS EQUIPMENT FOR THE BELL SYSTEM

FIG. 20-2. This advertisement in Baltimore newspapers, featuring a new addition and a new product of the Baltimore Works, Western Electric Co., is one of a series of newspaper advertisements run in plant communities throughout the country by Western Electric to inform community neighbors of the company's local developments.

In Supplier Relations

Advertising is used by manufacturers and merchants to interest resources in supplying their products to the advertiser. The institutional theme is used to emphasize the reliability of the purchaser and describe his financial resources and requirements.

Manufacturers and merchants who wish to establish and maintain profitable relations with reliable sources of supply advertise in business magazines and by direct mail to a selected list of resources.

A NATIONAL PUBLIC RELATIONS ADVERTISING PROGRAM

The Sinclair Oil Corporation, New York, has conducted a national public relations advertising program since 1955 on the theme of conservation to interest Americans in visiting and conserving their national parks and historic shrines. A series of full-page advertisements in national magazines feature national parks, forests, and historical places. Each advertisement carries a "salute" to a national organization such as the Boys' Clubs of America, National Geographic Society, General Federation of Women's Clubs, Daughters of the American Revolution, Girl Scouts of the U.S.A., 4-H Clubs, and others.

The objectives of this Sinclair public relations advertising program are to obtain the good will of motorists, influential people on all levels of government and commerce, and prominent groups working in the cause of conservation; to promote automobile travel which influences sales of Sinclair products; and to serve the public interest by making the public aware of America's heritage.

A well-planned publicity program, in conjunction with the public relations advertising campaign, is directed to organizations mentioned in the advertisements, Senators and Congressmen, local newspapers, motorists, and Sinclair executives, employees, and dealers, to enhance the value of each advertisement in the series.

A reprint of each advertisement accompanied by a letter signed by the president of Sinclair is mailed to the officials of the organization mentioned in the advertisement. Reprints are mailed by the organizations to their members. Officials and legislators of the state, in which the park or shrine featured in the advertisement is located, receive a reprint of the advertisement. Sinclair executives, employees, and dealers are informed about the advertisement in the company's dealer and employee magazines. Articles about the national parks and shrines mentioned in the series appear in the Sinclair monthly consumer magazine, *Picture News*.

Special public relations events are arranged by the Sinclair public relations department in connection with the appearance of each advertisement featuring a national park or shrine. Luncheons attended by officials and prominent members of the organization featured in the advertisement are held at the park or shrine, with publicity for Sinclair.

The effectiveness of the advertising is indicated by the citations and resolutions of commendation of the organizations honored; by commendatory letters from U.S. Senators, Congressmen, state governors; and thousands of inquiries from motorists planning visits to the national parks and historic places mentioned in the advertisements.

Case 20–1

PUBLIC RELATIONS ADVERTISING

New York Life Insurance Company

The New York Life Insurance Company founded in New York City in 1845 provides financial protection for individuals, families, and business organizations of the United States and Canada against the hazards of death, accident, sickness, and decreased earning capacity in old age. The company has more than $24 billion of individual and group life insurance in force covering nearly seven million persons. An additional 800,000 persons are protected with health insurance. Annual benefits and dividends in the neighborhood of $510 million are paid to policy holders and beneficiaries.

The company has more than 6,000 field underwriters who operate out of 239 offices in 50 states and 12 provinces of Canada. In addition, the company employs about 9,300 men and women in the Home Office, General Offices, and Central Service Offices.

The Public Relations Department of New York Life was established in 1948 with four principal divisions: advertising; editorial services, which includes speech writing and communications improvement; public information, which embraces publicity and press relations; and special projects. Each division is headed by a director who reports to the vice-president for public relations. Other subordinate sections handle Western public relations; intercompany and association activities; archives; art; budget control; statistical and historical information; and library and office administration. Thirty men and women comprise the public relations staff, and there are another 30 clerical personnel.

Public relations advertising is one of the principal features of the New York Life public relations program. The objectives of this advertising are fourfold: to provide a genuine service to the public and meet a worthwhile need; to make a strong family appeal because life insurance provides for family financial needs; to create a favorable image of the company, a receptive attitude toward life insurance; and to support the efforts of the New York Life agents.

To achieve these objectives the public relations department initiated in 1953 an advertising program based on a relatively new idea, which had little competition and presented an unusual opportunity for public service. A series of advertisements was planned by Compton Advertising, Inc., the company's advertising agency, based on the theme of helping young people choose a vocation by informing them of the opportunities, requirements, rewards, and limitations of the principal occupational fields open to youth.

Each advertisement in the series is presented in the form of an illustrated magazine article written by a skilled magazine writer collaborating with a well-known authority in a particular vocational field. This joint authorship secures maximum readership for each advertisement. Each article gives a general idea of a particular occupational field and objectively appraises the advantages and disadvantages of a career in this field.

The first advertisement, captioned "Should Your Child Be a Doctor," appeared in 1953. This advertisement and the 44 others which have followed it have appeared in two-page, black and white spreads in *Life, Look, Saturday Evening Post,* and *Scholastic* magazines. Five advertisements, featuring five different occupations, appear in these magazines each year. Each advertisement is seen by an estimated total audience of more than 80 million readers.

The great number of requests for reprints induced the company to reprint each advertisement in a handy, pocket-size booklet. Since the advertising campaign was initiated in 1953, more than 40 million booklet reprints have been distributed to inquirers all over the world. For greater convenience to those interested in reading the entire series, New York Life has reprinted the first 39 articles which appeared in advertisements in a paper-bound book titled *Career Opportunities.*

The advertisements in the career series carry one of two uniform titles: "Should Your Child Be . . ." or "Should Your Child Go into . . ." followed by the name of the particular occupation featured in each advertisement. Titles for the booklet reprints are changed to "Should you . . ." because these are usually read by the young people themselves. The following vocations and professions have been featured in 45 article-advertisements: accounting, advertising, aeronautical engineering, architecture, armed forces, atomic scientists, banker, biologist, self-employment, chemist, city and regional planner, clergy, dentist, doctor, electronic engineer, engineer, farmer, food retailing, foreign service, forester, counselor, home economist, hospital administrator, lawyer, librarian, life insurance, mathematician, medical technologist, mineral industry, newspaperman, nurse, personnel work, pharmacist, physicist, printing industry, public servant, public relations, rehabilitation, retailing, salesman, scientist, secretary, social worker, teacher, and traffic manager.

More than one million requests for reprints have been received for each of the following advertisement-articles: accountant, architect, armed forces, banker, chemist, dentist, doctor, electronic engineer, farmer, food retailer, home economist, lawyer, newspaperman, nurse, pharmacist, printer, public servant, and teacher.

Among the well-known authorities in various occupational fields who have collaborated in the preparation of the articles featured in the advertisements are: Igor Sikorsky, aeronautical engineer; Admiral Arthur W. Radford, armed forces; Dr. Irving Langmuir, chemist; Roscoe Pound, lawyer; Arthur H. Compton, physicist; and Robert Moses, public servant.

FIG. 20-3. One of a series of vocational counseling advertisements run by New York Life Insurance Company in national consumer, business, and professional magazines to help young people choose a vocation by informing them of the opportunities, requirements, and rewards of the principal occupational fields open to youth.

To handle the great number of requests for booklet reprints of the career advertisements, New York Life maintains a special career information service staff. Inquiries average 3,000 a week—the record week was 12,000 requests. A career mailing list of more than 50,000 names has been established in response to requests from vocational guidance counselors and others for each new career booklet as issued.

Vocations featured in the advertisements are selected after thorough consideration. To qualify, a career must be of wide, general interest, have a clearly defined national need for additional people, and be neither too broad nor too limited in scope. More than 200 different career areas ranging from agricultural scientist to zoologist have been suggested for featuring in the advertisements.

To supplement the magazine advertisements and career booklets, New York Life has published a booklet titled "The Cost of Four Years of College" which gives information about the location, type, enrollment, and costs of more than 2,000 colleges in the United States and Canada.

An annotated bibliography of current occupational literature titled *Guide to Career Information* was prepared by the public relations department of the company and published by Harper & Brothers in 1957. Fifty thousand copies of this book were distributed by New York Life to libraries, schools, colleges, and youth organizations. It is available through local book stores and the publisher.

To aid schools, libraries, and youth organizations in displaying and distributing the career booklets, the company has prepared do-it-yourself plans for constructing a self-service display rack which can be easily and inexpensively built in any school industrial arts or home workshop.

The public relations department of New York Life has also produced a career motion picture called "The Big Question" which is loaned without charge to show young people and their parents the importance of early career planning.

New York Life's career advertising program has been honored by special citations for excellence by such organizations as American Personnel and Guidance Association, University of Oregon School of Journalism, Social Work Committee of Greater New York, Public Relations Society of America, and First District Dental Society of New York. The program has received seven consecutive distinguished advertising awards from the *Saturday Review*. The George Washington Honor Medal has been awarded to the company for the campaign by the Freedoms Foundation of Valley Forge, Pennsylvania.

Thousands of complimentary letters are received annually from students and teachers in high schools and colleges. A New England teacher writes, "Congratulations on the great strides you are making to assist America's youth by placing at their disposal the valuable material contained in your career articles. I have reread my copies several times and require my students to write an essay on choosing a career."

A student writes: "I am no longer confused as to what I should be. Your information helped me to evaluate the careers which I was interested in entering. One by one I decided which ones I did not like and after all I ended up with teaching and am glad to have had your help. I feel much better now that my confusion is cleared up."

An agent writes: "As I have written you in the past, these booklets have really been well accepted and have served me very well as a prestige builder.

Again, let me thank you for your splendid cooperation that enables me to make such a favorable presentation."

QUESTIONS

1. Is the public relations advertising program of New York Life Insurance Company good public relations? What benefits does the company receive from this program? If you do not approve of this program, state your objections.
2. What changes or additions, if any, should be made in this program to make it more effective?
3. Prepare a publicity plan to supplement this advertising program describing the publicity media and communications with the press.
4. What public relations research and evaluation should be undertaken in connection with this advertising program? Describe the objectives of such research and tell how it should be carried out.
5. How can this career advertising program be used to improve relations with educators and guidance counselors in secondary schools and colleges? Describe the media and methods which should be employed in furthering educational relations in connection with this program.

Problem 20–1

PUBLIC RELATIONS ADVERTISING

Northwestern Lumber Company

The Northwestern Lumber Company was established in Eugene, Oregon, in 1910, for logging and milling in the Douglas fir timberlands of Washington and Oregon. The company built its first sawmill in Springfield, Oregon, in 1910, and expanded its operations by acquiring stands of timber and logging rights and absorbing small lumber mills in the Northwest. By the close of World War II, it was engaged in diversified manufacturing of forest products including milling, plywood, bark, wood pulp, and fabrication of plywood panels.

The company established wholesale distributing yards at West and East coast ports, acquired intercoastal ships for shipping lumber to the East coast, and organized a national sales force to sell to retail lumber and building material dealers throughout the country. All of the products produced by the company were branded and a brand advertising campaign appeared in the principal building magazines.

In 1964, the company had developed into one of the leading forest product producers in the country with annual sales exceeding $500 million and more than 8,000 workers employed in its forests, saw, pulp, bark, plywood mills; yards; offices; and marketing organization.

To attain complete utilization and conversion of the forest crop, the company established a research and development center in Seattle, Washington, adjoining its headquarters offices. The center is staffed by wood scientists and engineers who carry on extensive research in timber cultivation, disease prevention, wood fabrication, and new uses for forest products to meet the competition of other types of building materials.

Shortly after it was established, the company pioneered in the establishment of a scientifically operated tree farm of 100,000 acres and proceeded to grow a continuous crop of trees with intensive protection from fire and disease, planned harvesting, and orderly removal of mature timber crops. Today, the company has 30 large tree farms under intensive cultivation.

The Northwestern Lumber Company shares with other companies in the forest product industries serious public relations problems. The public image of the industry is unfavorable. The forest industries consume trees, a natural resource, which the public regards with strong sentimental attachment. An emotional public attitude toward the industry criticizes lumber companies for destroying the natural beauty and wildlife of the nation and creating soil erosion which washes away the rich soil and creates floods. Other natural resources such as oil, iron, and coal are buried underground and their depletion goes unnoticed by the public. However, cutover woodlands are readily noticed by the public which assumes that lumber companies are robbing the country's natural wealth and depriving future generations of timber resources.

The forest industries are also condemned by the public for logging operations which create temporary employment and unstable communities filled with smoke and odor of refuse burners and unsightly buildings. Timber trucks congest the highways in logging areas and create hazardous driving conditions.

These public relations problems brought about the establishment of a public relations department at the company's headquarters in Seattle. Community relations programs were organized by the company in ten mill communities under the directions of plant community relations managers who are assistants to the mill superintendents of each of the company's principal mills. These mill-community relations managers work closely with the headquarters public relations staff in developing the mill-community relations programs.

The mill-community relations programs followed a similar pattern including: school relations with visits by junior and senior high school pupils and teachers to the local mill for a conducted tour and refreshments; speeches by mill management before school assemblies; and an annual high school essay contest with cash prizes for the best compositions on the subject of "Conserving America's Woodlands" and related topics. An educational film library is maintained at headquarters from which teachers may borrow free of charge sound films for showing in classrooms.

To keep mill communities informed about company operations, the headquarters publicity staff prepares publicity releases for local newspapers and radio and television stations. Editorial material about the forest industries is furnished local editors and reporters who are invited to visit the mills and attend luncheons with mill management for discussion of company operations.

Special events such as open house and mill tours to show people of mill communities how the various wood products are made are arranged by local mill-community relations managers. These tours also demonstrate the good working conditions and other advantages in working for Northwestern.

A program to encourage company employees to participate in the activities of civic, educational, industrial, youth, hospital, health, and political organizations in mill communities is conducted by the company which makes annual awards for good citizenship to employees most active in community affairs.

The annual report of the company is mailed to community leaders, local editors, school teachers, and presented to mill visitors to give them timely information on the company's financial status, production and marketing operations, research, new products, and industry progress.

Although the company's community relations activities are considered effective in creating a more favorable image of the company and industry in mill communities, the public relations manager believes that the scope of the public relations program should be broadened to inform the general public throughout the country. As a leader in the forest products industry, the company should, in his opinion, sponsor a national public relations advertising program to improve the public image of the industry in general and Northwestern Lumber Company in particular.

Before initiating the public relations advertising program, the public relations manager favored a national public opinion poll to be conducted by an opinion research organization to determine what the general public, the company's employees and dealers are thinking about the forest products industry and the Northwestern Lumber Company. Some of the questions to be answered were: What does the public know about the industry's plan for permanent operation to provide steady jobs, stable communities, and fair tax structure to support government and schools? What does the public know about the industry's tree farming program? Does the public favor government ownership of timberlands and, if so, why? These and other questions would be asked by the researchers.

The findings of this survey would be analyzed and the specific public relations problems confronting the industry would be identified, the misconceptions to be corrected, and information to be communicated would be determined. Objectives of the advertising would be established, the theme selected, the media chosen, the number and size of advertisements and budget necessary to accomplish the aims of the program decided upon.

Responsibility for this national public relations advertising campaign would be assigned to the public relations department of the Northwestern Lumber Company which would be assisted by a national advertising agency responsible for planning, illustrating, writing, and placing the advertisements in suitable media.

The objectives of the public relations advertising would include: informing the public about the company's policies and practices of land and plant management; its product research and development to provide needed products and conserve timber resources; its efforts to grow a permanent timber supply to assure conservation of water, wild life, and recreational facilities; and to create a consumer demand for the company's products.

The cost of a national public relations advertising campaign should not be less than $1 million a year for a ten-year period, according to the public relations manager of the company. Such a long-term institutional campaign is essential to create a favorable image of the company and industry, in the opinion of the public relations manager.

The public relations manager believes that the proposed advertising would be a potent force in improving the public image of the forest products industry and informing the public about the company's progressive policies and practices, ethics, and leadership. The advertising will reflect the company's awareness of its responsibility for conserving the nation's timber resources. It will help build a good image of the company at a relatively low cost. The advertising will build confidence of stockholders and the financial community; win the respect of men in all areas of government; hold present employees and attract new talent; maintain acceptance of current products; improve trade relationships; and pave the way for the company's sales force.

The executive vice-president and general manager of the company opposed the proposed advertising campaign as wasteful and expensive. In many areas in the country, where Northwestern has no distribution, its products are not available to the public. The general public is less than interested in conservation of natural resources; criticism of logging operations is confined to a few forested areas; and the benefits to be derived by the company from the advertising are intangible. Competitors would benefit from the advertising as much as Northwestern. Stockholders would oppose the advertising as a needless expense. The current public relations program of the company is a more potent force for building good will in mill communities than national advertising. For these and additional reasons, the general manager prefers to expand the current community relations program rather than engage in a national public relations advertising campaign.

The question of running a national public relations advertising campaign was discussed by the executive committee and referred back to the public relations department which was asked to present a national advertising plan.

QUESTIONS

1. Should Northwestern Lumber Company engage in a national corporate public relations advertising campaign as proposed by the public relations manager? Give reasons for or against this proposal.
2. Assuming that a national public relations advertising program were used by Northwestern Lumber Company, what should be the specific objectives of such a program.
3. What particular publics should be reached by the proposed advertising?
4. What class or classes of media should be used in a national program for this company?
   a) Name the specific media which should be used in each class.
   b) Name the particular publics to be reached by each medium.
   c) State the sum which should be budgeted for each medium on an annual basis.
5. What theme or themes should be used for the national advertising?
6. Describe the publicity which should accompany the national advertising program.

CHAPTER
21 •

PUBLIC RELATIONS
PERIODICALS

THE PUBLIC RELATIONS periodical, sometimes called a "company magazine," "house organ," or "industrial publication," is used by corporations, associations, and nonprofit organizations in communicating with employees, shareholders, suppliers, dealers, and the general public.

A survey by the House Magazine Institute shows that the total circulation of all house magazines published in this country exceeds 300 million copies per issue for an annual investment of more than $500 million.

Business enterprises have published periodicals for more than a hundred years. The earliest company periodical in this country was the *Lowell Offering,* published around 1840 by the Lowell Cotton Mills, Lowell, Massachusetts. Among the best-known early company periodicals was the *Travelers Record,* published by the Travelers Insurance Company, Hartford, Connecticut; the *Houghton Line,* published by E. F. Houghton & Company, Philadelphia; *Through the Meshes,* by W. S. Tyler Company, Cleveland; and *Ford Times,* first published by the Ford Motor Company, Dearborn, Michigan, in 1908. *Ford Times* now has a circulation of more than one and one-half million readers.

Value of Public Relations Periodicals

Public relations periodicals have numerous advantages as media of communication. They have high reader interest. Only one medium, the country weekly, can compete with the public relations periodical in reader interest. A periodical can be edited to appeal to the particular interests of the people who read it. Published at regular intervals, it gains strength of impression through frequent appearance. It affords sufficient space to tell a complete story. Waste circulation is at a minimum when the list of readers is carefully selected and maintained. It is flexible as the size and format can be readily altered to suit the volume of editorial matter available and budget of the publisher. The cost of distributing a periodical by mail is low.

515

Limitations of Public Relations Periodicals

The mortality of public relations periodicals is high. In periods of economic recession, public relations periodicals are curtailed or eliminated for reasons of economy. There are various other reasons for the short life of many public relations periodicals. In many organizations a periodical is not recognized by management as an essential channel of public relations communication. Less than a third of the editors report to the public relations managers. Editors are burdened with other duties. In some companies, the editor must obtain approval of material by ten people. Many editors have inadequate budgets and insufficient help.

From an editorial standpoint many periodicals do not have specific objectives endorsed by management and subjected to its continuous scrutiny. Many company publications avoid controversial issues and do not make known the views of management on important questions. The entertainment value of employee publications is limited to sport and social news. Company publications often lack originality and imagination. They fail to discuss problems that concern the company and its future and do not arouse a feeling of mutual interest within the corporate family.

TYPES OF PUBLIC RELATIONS PERIODICALS

There are three principal types of public relations periodicals: internal, published for employees of a business or association or members who belong to a nonprofit organization; external, published for the general public, suppliers, dealers, stockholders; and combination periodicals, published for both internal and external publics.

Internal Public Relations Periodicals

Internal periodicals are published by manufacturers, merchants, banks, social welfare, transportation, and public service companies for their employees. There are an estimated 8,000 internal publications with a combined circulation of 20 million.

Employee Periodicals. Magazines, newspapers, and newsletters for employees are the principal type of internal periodicals and the most important medium of communication from management to workers.

Large corporations publish several employee newspapers, one for each of their principal plants. The International Harvester Company, Chicago, publishes 23 employee newspapers. The American Telephone and Telegraph Company, New York, publishes 24. The Borden Com-

FIG. 21–1. Employee newspapers are published to inform employees in individual plants and product divisions of many corporations. Typical editions of the employee newspapers of International Business Machines Corp., Sun Oil Co., E. I. du Pont de Nemours & Co., and Ford Motor Co. are illustrated above.

pany, New York, publishes 30 employee newspapers in its plants in the United States and Canada. E. I. du Pont de Nemours & Company issues more than 40 employee newspapers.

Outstanding examples of employee magazines are: *GM Folks,* published monthly by the public relations department of General Motors Corporation for the employees of all divisions of the corporation; *Better Living,* bimonthly, published by the public relations department of E. I. du Pont de Nemours & Company, Wilmington, Delaware, for its 90,000 employees: *Torch,* edited and published by the Standard Oil Company, Indiana, public relations department for 50,000 employees; and *News and Views,* published bimonthly by Caterpillar Tractor Company, Peoria, Illinois, for 30,000 employees.

Weekly employee plant newspapers are published by large employers in combination with monthly or bimonthly employee magazines. The newspapers serve employees of individual plants and the magazine goes to employees of all plants.

Management Periodicals. Corporations with large executive staffs publish management periodicals to keep management personnel informed about company policies and developments and educated in the most efficient management methods.

The public relations department, Sun Oil Company, publishes five management periodicals: *Daily News Digest,* a summation of what the daily press in seven cities says about the company and industry; *Periodical Highlights,* a weekly, carrying abstracts of interest to management from 30 weekly and monthly business publications; *Public Relations Memo,* a biweekly, four-page memorandum on company and industry public relations policies, problems, activities, and results; *Company Encyclopedia,* an annual digest of facts about company operations; and *Petroleum Reference Sheet,* a weekly compilation of data on oil industry operations.

The Relations Services of the General Electric Company publishes a monthly periodical, *Community Relations Review,* which is circulated to the plant and community relations managers of the company's 131 plants for the exchange of community relations ideas and programs. *Community Relations Newsletter,* published by Westinghouse Electric Corporation serves the same purpose.

Salesmen's Periodicals. Many companies publish magazines for their salesmen. Most salesmen's magazines are published monthly, although a few are issued bimonthly or weekly. Typical of salesmen's periodicals are *Sales Kraft,* published monthly by Kraft Foods Company, Chicago; the *Royal Standard,* published by the Royal Typewriter Company, Hartford, Connecticut; and *The Kodak Salesman,* published by the Eastman Kodak Company, Rochester, New York.

External Public Relations Periodicals

External public relations periodicals are published for persons not employed by a corporation including stockholders, suppliers, distributors and dealers, and their personnel.

FIG. 21–2. More than a million teenagers in the United States and Canada receive the *American Youth* magazine published bimonthly by the public relations staff of General Motors Corp. A typical cover and article from *American Youth* are illustrated here.

Consumer Periodicals.   Consumer periodicals are published for the consuming public by large corporations. *Ford Times* has been published by the Ford Motor Company since 1908 to gain the good will of motorists and promote travel by automobile. *Dodge News* is the consumer publication of the Dodge Division of Chrysler Corporation.

A few large corporations publish business magazines which carry paid advertising such as *Burroughs Clearing House,* published by Burroughs Corporation and *Dun's Review,* published by Dun and Bradstreet, Inc.

Professional, fraternal, and business associations publish periodicals for their members, such as *The American Legion* and the *Journal of the American Medical Association.*

Distributor-Dealer Periodicals.   Periodicals are published by manufacturers of consumer goods for their distributors and dealers. *The Ford Dealer* is published by Ford Division, Ford Motor Company; *Mohawk Rug Retailer,* by Mohawk Carpet Mills; and *Exide Topics,* published for battery dealers by Exide Battery Company.

Stockholder Periodicals.   Corporations with a large number of stockholders publish quarterly stockholder periodicals to give stockholders information about company finances, new products, research, expansion of facilities, and developments of interest to investors. *Horizons* is published by General Mills, Inc., three times a year. Union Carbide Corporation publishes *Stockholder News,* and General Foods Corporation issues *Item* quarterly to shareholders.

Supplier Periodicals.   Manufacturers and merchants with many suppliers publish supplier periodicals. The Borden Company publishes *The Dairy Digest* for milk suppliers; and First National Stores, New England food chain, publishes a monthly magazine for its New England resources.

Combination Periodicals

A few public relations periodicals are edited for distribution to the outside publics as well as internal personnel. These combination periodicals carry information of interest to employees as well as customers, stockholders, dealers, suppliers, and opinion leaders of plant communities.

Frequency of Publication

Public relations periodicals are published at various frequencies. A survey by the House Magazine Institute of company periodicals in the New York metropolitan area showed that 40 per cent are published monthly; 29 per cent come out every other month; 5 per cent, twice a month; and 11 per cent, quarterly.

External publications for customers, suppliers, dealers, and salesmen are usually published monthly; while internal periodicals are published at weekly or biweekly intervals.

Objectives of Public Relations Periodicals

A written statement of objectives should be prepared for a public relations periodical to give direction to the editorial content of the medium and to establish a definite standard with which its effectiveness can be measured.

Employee Publications. The major objectives of employee periodicals are to inform employees about company policies and practices; to increase production by publicizing good individual performance and the need for increased output by workers; to stimulate improved morale and promote loyalty; to inform employees about a company's products and operations and show them their part in the manufacture of the final product; to increase company prestige among employees; to counteract union propaganda and improve labor relations; to explain the financial structure and operation of the company and the role of profits; to expose rumors that breed misunderstanding and dissatisfaction; to build a favorable attitude toward the company by families of workers; to promote safety practices; to educate workers on economics, Americanization, and safety; and to promote employee activities, including sports, entertainments, and social affairs.

The Atlantic Log, employee magazine of the Atlantic Companies, insurance organization, has the following written objectives:

> To inform and educate the staff about the company, its history, its products, and its goals. To keep alive the traditions and image of a company founded many years ago and to take pride in them. To emphasize the importance of people in our enterprise. To recognize and understand their needs as human beings. To persuade and educate employees that what is good for the company is good for them, to the end that they understand and appreciate the position of insurance in our economy today and how it affects them.

Distributor-Dealer Publications. Major objectives of distributor-dealer magazines are to develop dealers and their employees; to cultivate a partnership relationship with distributors and dealers; to provide information about company policies, products, service, merchandising, programs, personnel, and developments; to show dealers how to increase their sales and profits; to aid dealers in solving their management problems; to stimulate dealers and their salespeople to recommend to their customers the manufacturer's products; to increase the number of efficient dealers; to reduce dealer turnover; to give recognition to outstanding dealers; and to gain the maximum co-operation and good will of distributors and dealers.

Consumer Periodicals. Periodicals published by manufacturers and merchants for consumers have the following aims: to inform and educate consumers about a company, its policies, and program to gain their understanding and good will; to cultivate the respect of the public by showing how a company is operating in the public welfare; to counteract adverse pressures of special groups which threaten a company's reputation; and to promote customer loyalty.

Stockholder Periodicals. Periodicals for stockholders are published to increase the stockholder's knowledge of his company; to keep the financial community, including bankers, brokers, investors, and consultants, informed about a company and its financial status; to secure the confidence of investors; to stimulate the use of company products by stockholders; to enlist the aid of stockholders in promoting company welfare; to stabilize the market for company securities; to attract new capital; to increase stockholder participation in corporation affairs; and to educate stockholders on current corporate problems, including labor relations, taxation, government controls, prices, and other threats to profitable operations.

Supplier Periodicals. Periodicals published for suppliers have the following objectives: to obtain reliable sources of supply; to inform suppliers about a company, its policies, operations, resources, and ability to consume or distribute the supplier's products; to gain the co-operation of resources in adjusting supply to demand; to stimulate reciprocal purchases by suppliers; to secure prompt deliveries; to promote good trade practices and fair dealing; to win the good will of suppliers' salesmen; and to secure the co-operation of resources in special promotions.

Association Periodicals. Periodicals published by trade and professional organizations have the following objectives: to inform the membership about the activities of the organization; to secure participation by members in organization affairs; to increase the number of members; to recognize members who have given unusual service to the organization; to inform the general public regarding the contributions of the organization to the public welfare; to advance the objectives of the organization; to correct misinformation about an organization; to educate members to give more effective public service and secure public approval; to inform and secure the understanding of government officials and legislators; to describe the activities of the association to community leaders; to provide a channel of communication from the membership to management; and to raise funds for operation.

Multiple-Audience Publications. Public relations periodicals which are distributed to several publics serve various objectives. Employee publications distributed to stockholders, opinion leaders in the plant community, customers, and dealers give them a better understanding of the company's operations. Stockholder periodicals are mailed to editors and commentators, financial institutions, important customers, trade association executives, and government officials. Consumer periodicals are circulated to libraries, reading rooms, schools, barber shops, and doctors' offices where they will be read by the general public.

Organization for Public Relations Periodicals

Public relations periodicals are planned, designed, and written by the public relations department or a special section thereof staffed with specialists experienced in editing publications.

The Sun Oil Company's public relations department's editorial services section is responsible for the company magazine, *Our Sun,* and a staff representative is assigned to each of the major operating departments—refining, marketing, and production—to supervise the employee monthly tabloid for each department, *Sun Refinery News, Sun Marketing News,* and *Sun Production News.*

A special section of the public relations department of Standard Oil Company, New Jersey, is responsible for publication of *The Lamp,* a quarterly stockholder and employee magazine written by a staff of four, supplemented by free-lance authors and illustrators. *The Lamp* has a circulation of 575,000.

The publications division of the public relations department of E. I. du Pont de Nemours & Company is responsible for *Better Living,* the employee magazine; the supervisory news letter; plant paper liaison service; and special publications. The staff of *Better Living* includes an editor, three assistant editors, two photographers, and 25 associate editors, each representing a product and administrative department of the company.

A publication advisory committee composed of representatives of management should meet with the editors and staffs of company periodicals to counsel them on editorial policy and practices and evaluate the effectiveness of periodicals.

The Publication Editor and Staff

Second only to the interested support of management, the success of a public relations periodical depends upon the caliber of the editor and staff. Many company periodicals fail because responsibility for editing them is delegated to a person who has neither the time, interest, nor ability to produce an effective periodical. Many periodicals are edited by an employee who is overburdened with other work. A survey by the House Magazine Institute showed that 90 per cent of company periodical editors have other duties; an average of 40 per cent of their time is devoted to preparing speeches, press releases, letters, bulletin boards, and booklets.

Qualifications of the Editor. A public relations periodical editor should be primarily a creative idea man who can dramatize the company message in terms which will arouse reader interest. "Talent is a shamefully neglected area in publications designed to sell ideas," says T. W. Stephenson, manager, publications of E. I. du Pont de Nemours & Company. "Management would not think of assigning an accountant to laboratory research, nor a chemist to keep the accounts. Yet, too often those assigned to industrial publications have no qualifications for the job. Many times, a man after repeated failures elsewhere has been assigned to a plant paper as a kind of last resting place."

A good reporter, feature writer, or editor of a newspaper or trade magazine who knows news and has an objective viewpoint and an understanding of publication layout, make-up, and production has a good background for editing a public relations publication.

Plant Reporters and Correspondents. Much of the editorial material of employee periodicals is assembled by volunteer plant reporters and correspondents. One of the important responsibilities of an employee periodical editor is to secure, train, stimulate, and maintain close contact with plant reporters and correspondents who should be given specific descriptions of their duties, the type of news and pictures desired, mechanics of reporting, and editorial policy.

Plant Editors. Plant editors are employed in large corporations to supervise volunteer reporters, edit local news, procure illustrations, and send editorial material to headquarters when production is controlled by the headquarters public relations department.

In some corporations, publication of employee periodicals is decentralized, with each plant editing and printing its own employee publication subject to general supervision by the headquarters public relations department.

In some companies plant publications are a joint production of the plant editor and headquarters public relations department. The headquarters staff prepares the body of the publication with the exception of the cover and a few pages of local news and pictures which are assembled by the plant editor and forwarded to the home office for incorporating as a section of the employee publication.

Contents of Public Relations Periodicals

The contents of public relations periodicals vary widely depending upon the public relations objectives of the corporation and interests of the reading audience.

Employee Publications. Analysis of the editorial content of employee periodicals shows that the following subjects are included, arranged in order of the amount of space devoted to each subject: social news of employees; management activities, company progress, management development program, employee benefits, company suggestion plans and awards; health and safety; national economy including profits, unemployment, taxes, prices, growth, and foreign affairs.

Stockholder Publications. Stockholder periodicals feature the following subjects: corporation earnings, government controls, report on annual meeting, public relations, advertising, president's annual message, production report, expansion of plant facilities, new products, regional stockholder meetings, answers to questions asked by stockholders, controller's report, recipes for using products, executive personnel changes, research and development, and executive speeches.

Distributor-Dealer Publications. Distributor-dealer publications which are edited to inform and stimulate the sales of wholesalers and retailers contain articles on sales training, advertising, descriptions of the methods of successful dealers; articles showing how dealers increase sales, reduce expenses, and raise profits; the sales methods of outstanding dealer salesmen; and the service methods of successful dealers.

Consumer Periodicals. Consumer periodicals published by corporations feature subjects of public interest related to the business of the publisher. Leading consumer publications are *Ford Times,* published monthly by Ford Motor Company; and *Think,* published monthly by the International Business Machines Corporation for customers and the general public.

Physical Features of Public Relations Periodicals

The format of public relations publications varies widely according to the preferences of the publisher, purpose of the periodical, size of the audience, funds available, and editorial content.

About seven out of ten public relations periodicals are magazines.

The size of public relations magazines ranges from pocket size, 5 by 7 inches, to large size, 10½ by 14 inches. About two out of three are 8½ by 11 inches in size, although a considerable number are 6 by 9 inches in size. The larger size is most suitable for pictorial presentations, effective typography, and art layouts. It is more impressive, carries more prestige, and has greater eye appeal.

Notable among pocket size public relations publications is the *Ford Times*. The 5 by 7 inch size was suggested by the late Henry Ford who visited the editorial office, picked up a copy and tried to put it into his pocket. After several unsuccessful attempts, he turned to the editor and said, "Make it so it will go in my pocket," and it has remained pocket size ever since.

About one out of four public relations periodicals are newspapers. The newspaper format is favored for employee news periodicals. There are two basic newspaper formats—the standard page size, 16½ by 21½ inches, with eight columns to the page; and the tabloid page size, 10¼ by 14¼ inches, with five columns to the page. The tabloid is the most popular size for employee news periodicals as it provides ample space for pictorial display and, at the same time, is suitable for short stories and features.

The mimeographed bulletin, 8½ by 11 inches in size, is an economical medium for organizations with a limited number of employees. Many employee periodicals originate as one-page bulletins produced on the office duplicator and are enlarged to magazine or newspaper formats as reader interest and circulation grow.

The number of pages of public relations publications ranges from 4 to 64 pages, with the majority in the 16- and 32-page sizes.

About two out of three periodicals are printed by letter press process and the balance by offset or a duplicating process. Most are printed in one color with the addition of a second color for headings or to brighten the cover.

Cost of Public Relations Periodicals

The investment in public relations periodicals published in this country has been estimated to exceed $40 million per month. The cost of individual periodicals varies widely. A mimeographed four-page employee bulletin, for a company with less than 100 employees, can be produced for less than $50; while a modest 16-page, 8½ by 11 inch magazine, two-color cover, 5,000 circulation, will cost in the neighborhood of $1,000 per issue to print in addition to the costs of preparation and distribution.

Evaluation of Reader Interest and Effectiveness of a Public Relations Periodical

To maintain reader interest in a public relations periodical, a periodic study should be made by the editorial staff to determine what interests readers. A questionnaire may be inserted in one issue of the publication or mailed separately to readers to secure reader opinion of various editorial features; questions about the publication may be included in a general survey of opinions of employees, stockholders, and consumers; or an outside research organization may be employed to conduct personal interviews with the readers of the periodical.

In addition to researching reader interest, surveys should also be made to determine if the periodical is fulfilling its objectives in terms of better understanding, good will, higher morale, and others.

Appraising Periodical Effectiveness. To determine the effectiveness of its consumer magazine, *Home and Highway,* Allstate Insurance Company, a subsidiary of Sears, Roebuck & Company, employed a research firm to conduct 1,000 personal interviews of recipients of the magazine. The company learned that 81 per cent of the persons questioned were familiar with most of the articles in the magazine; while 19 per cent were nonreaders. Confidence in the company's promptness in settling claims was 18 per cent higher among readers than nonreaders. The willingness of readers to recommend the company was increased 16 per cent by regular reading of the magazine.

To determine reader opinion of its employee magazine, *Better Living,* the public relations department of E. I. du Pont de Nemours & Company polled a representative sample of employees. The survey showed that 70 per cent of the employees questioned said that three or more persons read their copies of *Better Living,* and 25 per cent reported that six or more persons read each issue. Respondents were given a list of 26 magazines, including *Better Living,* and asked to name those they read regularly. Some 88 per cent selected *Better Living* as their favorite magazine. Employees were asked if they read *Better Living* more thoroughly than other magazines and one third said that *Better Living* received more attention than other magazines.

Distribution of Public Relations Periodicals

Most external publications for customers, stockholders, distributors and dealers, suppliers, salesmen, and opinion leaders in plant communities are distributed by mail.

About half of all employee periodicals are mailed to their homes;

one quarter are picked up at the plant; and the balance use both methods of distribution.

Distribution of publications by mail requires continuous revision of the periodical mailing list. To avoid waste circulation, some companies mail periodicals only to those who request them. Others make a small subscription charge; while the majority send public relations periodicals free.

To insure an up-to-date mailing list, changes in names and addresses of customers, stockholders, suppliers, employees, and dealers should be reported to the public relations department by the various departments of the company who have contact with these publics.

Editorial Service to Publication Editors

In addition to editorial material written by the public relations staff, the talents of outside writers and illustrators should be employed to give variety and enrichment to the periodical.

The public relations departments of business and professional associations serve editors of members' periodicals with news and pictures of the industry or profession. The public relations department of the National Association of Manufacturers publishes "Service for Company Publications," a monthly bulletin which provides industrial editors with ideas for use in company publications.

The headquarters public relations departments of some large corporations that operate several plants provide editorial and picture service to the editors of the employee periodicals published by the individual plants. This service includes news and articles about company operations, new products, policies, the industry, personnel, mergers, and plant acquisitions. Local plant magazine editors use, rewrite, or file the material for future use.

A PUBLIC RELATIONS PERIODICAL PROGRAM

Nationwide Insurance Company, Columbus, Ohio, with affiliated companies, is engaged in fire, life, and automobile insurance, mutual funds, radio and television broadcasting, home and commercial development, and mortgages. The public relations department of Nationwide Insurance is organized in five sections: administration, advertising and press relations, graphic arts services, policyholder relations, and publications and editorial services.

The publications and editorial services section is responsible for editing and illustrating three public relations periodicals: a weekly newspaper for home office employees, a bimonthly magazine for all employees, and a bimonthly publication for policyholders.

The policyholder publication, *Minutes,* is published to interpret the operations and interests of the companies to some 85,000 holders of Nationwide automobile, fire, and life insurance policies. The objectives of *Minutes* are: to establish a friendly bond between the companies and their policyholders, to tell the companies' story in human interest terms, and to promote causes that are of benefit both to the companies and the public.

Minutes is published by the policyholder publications division of the publications and editorial services section of the company's public relations department. The staff includes an editor, a photographer, an editorial assistant, and a business manager, with art work, layout, and production handled by the graphic arts service department. Some editorial material is purchased from writers and photographers outside the company.

The initial issue appeared in 1949 as an eight-page quarterly. The size of the magazine was increased to 24 pages in 1952 and to 36 pages, its present size, in 1954. Since 1955, it has been published six times a year. Four colors are used on the cover and two colors on heavy coated paper stock are used throughout the 5½ by 8 inch magazine. The periodical, with the exception of the cover, is printed and mailed by the Farm Bureau Printing Corporation, Spencer, Indiana.

Minutes will circulate eventually to about 20 per cent of the company's total number of policyholders. It goes only to those policyholders who request the magazine and others selected by the company's agents. Distribution is restricted to a select audience of influential teachers, politicians, editors, ministers, doctors, lawyers, farm leaders, bankers, and merchants who are leaders in community life.

The effectiveness of *Minutes* is evidenced by numerous complimentary letters received from policyholders and company agents and requests from editors of other company publications asking permission to reprint material from *Minutes.*

Case 21–1

EMPLOYEE PERIODICALS

E. I. du Pont de Nemours and Company

E. I. du Pont de Nemours and Company, established in 1802 in Wilmington, Delaware, manufactures and markets electrochemicals, industrial and biochemicals, organic chemicals, plastics, elastomer chemicals, explosives, coated fabrics, finishes, packaging, and industrial films, pigments, photo films, textile fibers, and other chemical products in some 80 plants in the United States.

Annual sales in excess of $2 billion are made to the textile, rubber, chemical, transportation, food, petroleum, machinery, paper, publishing, mining, agriculture, metals, construction and other industries.

In addition, Du Pont operates through subsidiary companies in Mexico, United Kingdom, Belgium, France, Switzerland, the Netherlands, Venezuela, Brazil, Peru, Argentina, Chile, and Canada.

More than 88,000 men and women, 48,000 of whom are shareholders, are employed by the company in its various facilities. There are more than 226,000 owners of Du Pont.

Public relations at Du Pont is organized with a headquarters public relations department with four divisions: Information, Extension, Control, and Publications. Information maintains liaison with the press, informs the public, and provides public relations counsel to the managements of the 12 manufacturing departments of the company. Extension provides public speakers to clubs and organizations throughout the country. Control handles routine administration of the department. Publications publishes employee and other public relations periodicals.

The managers of these divisions report to the assistant director of the department who is responsible to the director of public relations. Two executive assistants handle special projects. A policy committee composed of the above executives co-ordinates department operations and formulates public relations policy of the company.

The Publications division was established as a staff section of the department in 1945 to plan and produce periodicals for all employees, supervisors of the level of foremen and above, and stockholders of the company.

This division has responsibility for the following employee and supervisor periodicals: *Better Living* a bimonthly picture magazine for all employees; *This Is Du Pont* a semiannual publication about the company for employees and others; *Supervisory News Letter* a monthly bulletin of information and interpretation for all supervisory employees of the level of foremen and above, including salesmen and technical people, so that they can speak for the company with knowledge and authority; and *Du Pont Facts Book*, a loose-leaf encyclopedia revised periodically to give supervisors of the level of foremen and above basic, timely data on Du Pont. The Publications division is also responsible for *Du Pont Stockholder*, sent three times a year to the company's 226,000 owners.

The Publications division provides a plant publication service which acts in an advisory capacity to improve the usefulness and quality of 40 employee periodicals published by Du Pont plants throughout the country. Other objectives of the plant publication service are to recruit and train personnel for plant employee periodicals, to impress upon local management the benefits which can be derived from well-edited employee periodicals and to help the plant editors to plan and produce good publications. Employee plant periodicals are the responsibility of the managers in the plants in which they are published. They vary in form from mimeographed bulletins, to tabloid newspapers, to slick paper magazines and are published at intervals that vary from bimonthly to monthly.

The all-employee periodical of Du Pont is *Better Living,* a 32-page and

FIG. 21–3. Magazines are a major medium of communication with employees in the employee relations programs of many corporations. One of the outstanding employee magazines is *Better Living* published bimonthly by E. I. du Pont de Nemours & Co. A typical cover and article from this magazine are illustrated here.

The Creative Process In Du Pont Research

A Leader in Industrial Research, Du Pont's Efforts are Based on Belief that Current and Future Projects Will Top its Past Gains

cover picture magazine published six times a year and distributed to 88,000 employees as well as 30,000 persons outside the company including the press, schools and colleges, libraries, community leaders, and opinion molders. It is aimed directly at Du Pont employees, their families and neighbors, and more specifically plant production and maintenance workers.

This magazine is typical of the company-wide "all employee" periodical which is published by large corporations to supplement the employee periodicals of individual plants. While the objectives of the individual plant employee publication are to report and interpret important local developments and deal with local plant problems, the goals of the "all employee" magazine are much broader as described below.

The objectives of *Better Living* are: to help employees to acquire a feeling of identification and association with a worthwhile enterprise; to increase employees' understanding of and support for the kind of economic, social, and political climate in which Du Pont and large business can maximize their usefulness; to interpret to employees the essential role and function of business and inform them on economic, political, and social subjects which bear on their jobs and opportunities.

Better Living is a joint production of its editor, two assistant editors, two photographers, the manager of publications and the executive assistant to the director.

There are 25 associate editors, each representing one of the following units of the Du Pont organization: elastomer chemicals, electrochemicals, explosives, fabrics and finishes, film, industrial and biochemicals, international, organic chemicals, photo products, pigments, polychemicals, textile fibers, advertising, central research, development, economist's office, employee relations, engineering, general services, legal, purchasing, secretary, traffic, treasurer, and Remington Arms, a subsidiary company.

Associate editors co-operate with the headquarters staff of the magazine in preparing editorial materials and serve as liaison between the editorial staff and principal departments of the business.

The magazine is produced on a five-month cycle (or five months elapses from the day an issue is planned until it is off the press). Planning begins with a conference of the editor, executive assistant to the department director, and manager of publications who determine the contents of each issue to conform to the basic objectives described previously. This is in contrast to the policy of some large all-employee company publications which rely upon local plant employee publications editors to suggest and develop stories. The editorial plan for each issue of *Better Living* specifies the purpose of each story, the general approach to the subject, and the pictures and art treatment.

Better Living is primarily a picture magazine because its ideas must be communicated quickly and dramatically in order to attract attention and compete with popular commercial magazines as well as the many diversions of modern living. In a representative issue there will be as many as 120 separate illustrations in the forms of photographs, graphs, cartoons, and drawings executed by the editorial staff. As *Better Living* is a company-wide employee publication it does not depend on the personal news and pictures which are characteristic of local plant employee publications.

The editorial content of *Better Living* covers a wide variety of subjects. Typical articles from representative issues are: "Labor Shortage Ahead," a story designed to increase employees' understanding of the role of technology and to gain their support for the process changes and new products of Du Pont. "How You Can Be a Conscientious Constituent" urges employees to assume their obligations, responsibilities, and privileges as citizens. "My Job," a series of articles, in which production workers describe in their own words their roles in making various Du Pont products. "How Du Pont Is Doing" describes how the company is keeping pace with competition in the rapidly growing chemical industry. "How Du Pont Families Live," a series of articles about the problems and way of life of employees and their families in this country and abroad. "Mama's Getting Younger Every Day," a human interest story in words and pictures of young mothers, employed by Du Pont, and their daughters. "The Profit Pinch" describes the effect of declining earnings of industrial companies in the U.S. economy.

On the back cover of each issue appears a full-page advertisement in color featuring a Du Pont product. Aside from the covers, no advertising appears in the magazine.

Better Living is distributed to employees at 280 plant, office, and laboratory locations throughout this country and abroad. Since distribution costs are borne by the individual departments, each location selects the methods most consistent with its budget, personnel, and desires. Some plants mail the magazine to the homes of employees, which practice is recommended by the Publications division. Other plants distribute it to employees on the job or at exits when the employee leaves the plant.

Readership surveys of *Better Living* have shown a consistently highly favorable reception by employees. Ninety per cent of the company's employees regularly look at the magazine and from three to four people on the average see each copy.

In a recent readership survey, employees were asked to indicate on a list of 24 mass-circulation magazines those that ranked highest in terms of reader interest and those which were read regularly. Eighty per cent of the respondents selected *Better Living* as their favorite. Its nearest rivals were *Life* with 56 per cent and *Reader's Digest* with 53 per cent.

There is no way to measure precisely the impact or influence of *Better Living* on the viewpoints of employees, in the opinion of the editors, because it presents ideas and intangibles the impact of which cannot be determined exactly. Readers' attitudes are the result of conscious or subconscious assimilation of impressions from conversations, television, radio, newspaper and magazine stories, pictures, and headlines. Which of these impressions is most influential in determining the attitudes of employees cannot be identified.

QUESTIONS

1. What are the specific values of *Better Living* as a medium of communication with Du Pont employees or what can it do for the Du Pont organization?

2. Comment on the objectives of *Better Living* as described in this case. Should there be other objectives of this magazine?

3. What are the limitations of *Better Living* or what specifically *cannot* this magazine do for the Du Pont organization?

4. Is the organization for editing and publishing *Better Living* suitable? What changes, if any, can you propose to improve this organization?
5. Is the magazine format of this publication suitable? Why? What are the limitations of this format?
6. Is the distribution of *Better Living* satisfactory? If not, what method of distribution should be used?
7. What specific steps should be taken to improve the effectiveness of this magazine?

Problem 21–1

PUBLIC RELATIONS PERIODICALS

Rutherford Corporation

The Rutherford Corporation was established in Detroit, Michigan, in 1920, to manufacture and sell farm tractors. Later, the company expanded into the production of earth-moving and road machinery and diesel engines. Six manufacturing plants are operated, four in the United States and two in Canada. The total number of employees has increased from 500 to more than 20,000. Annual sales of all products exceed $300 million. The corporation is owned by 22,000 shareholders, 20 per cent of whom are employees. Annual expenditures for research and development exceed $20 million.

Rutherford products are distributed through 1,000 tractor, farm equipment, and road machinery dealers who operate 1,500 places of business throughout the United States and Canada. The average dealer has sold and serviced Rutherford products for 15 years and employs 23 sales and servicemen.

The Rutherford marketing organization of 40 sales representatives operates out of ten district sales and service centers located in the principal cities of the country. These centers include service and parts depots so located that dealers in the United States and Canada can receive overnight service.

A public relations department was established by the company, in 1950, with the following objectives: communicating information about the corporation to residents of plant communities to secure their understanding and good will, researching public opinion of the company, and conveying and interpreting public attitudes to management for its consideration in improving policies and practices of the corporation.

The public relations department retains an outside opinion research organization to make an annual survey by personal interviews of a random sample of customers, employees, dealers, suppliers, and plant community residents to determine their attitudes toward the corporation, its policies, practices, working conditions, participation in community activities, and other subjects. The purpose of this research is to determine the public relations problems confronting the organization so that recommendations for action may be made to management based on the findings of the survey.

The findings of this opinion research for the current year revealed some critical attitudes of dealers and employees which, in the opinion of the management, constituted serious public relations problems.

Rutherford dealers, in response to survey questions, criticized the company for overproduction of tractors and engines and expressed dissatisfaction with Rutherford distribution policies and practices. When asked what they disliked about Rutherford a substantial number of dealers questioned mentioned: the dealer franchise agreement, the company's pricing policy, direct sales to contractors, overloading of dealers, and arbitrary termination of franchise agreements.

Rutherford dealers believed that the company should give them more individual consideration and recognize their importance. Over the years Rutherford dealers have attained substantial incomes and economic, civic, and political influence in their communities. Their standing with the company does not, in their opinion, reflect their increased stature and status. Dealers are considered by the factory as the business equivalent of the village idiot, according to one prominent dealer.

The findings of the dealer survey were further confirmed by an incident which occurred in the Pacific coast district. Thirty of the leading dealers met with Rutherford's regional and district managers and warned them that unless immediate action was taken by the factory to cease objectionable practices, the dealers would give up their Rutherford franchises and distribute a competing line.

Not only were Rutherford dealers critical of the company's policies and practices but employees, when questioned anonymously by the researchers, were equally critical of the company. The principal criticisms of employees concerned low wage rates, limited opportunities for promotion, unfavorable working conditions, inadequate employee fringe benefits, arbitrary attitudes of supervisors, and no recognition for good performance.

When asked, "What do you think of working conditions at Rutherford Corporation as compared with other companies?" only 10 per cent of the respondents said "above average," 20 per cent said "average," and 60 per cent said "below average," with the balance expressing no opinion. In response to the question: "Do you think the Rutherford Corporation is a good company to work for?" only 30 per cent said "yes" and 70 per cent replied "no." Employee attitudes toward supervisors were critical. In answer to the question, "Are the supervisors or bosses at the Rutherford plant extremely fair, very fair, fair, moderate, or unfair?" 5 per cent were considered "extremely fair," 8 per cent "very fair," 30 per cent "fair," 40 per cent "moderate," 10 per cent "unfair," and the balance expressed no opinion.

These criticisms by employees were inspired by action taken during a recession to curtail employment, cut wages, and reduce overtime of employees, according to management. At the same time, the company tried to maintain production by forcing dealers to take a larger number of tractors and engines and to cut their prices. This policy was resisted by many dealers. In view of these criticisms by employees and dealers, the executive committee of the corporation asked the public relations director to make specific recommendations to improve relations with employees and dealers.

The current public relations program is devoted to developing a favorable public image for the corporation in the six plant communities. A plant public relations manager responsible to the local plant manager is located at each plant. His duties include interpreting the company to community groups of doctors, attorneys, businessmen, and teachers; supplying the local press, radio, and television with news of plant activities; providing volunteer speakers to local civic, social, and service clubs; arranging for special events such as open houses and plant tours to show community neighbors how the various products in the plant are made and to demonstrate good working conditions; and participating in community social service and charitable fund raising campaigns and projects.

The six plant public relations managers meet with the headquarters public relations staff every three months to exchange ideas and plan community relations activities. One project planned at a recent meeting was a newspaper advertising campaign to keep plant communities informed about the policies, practices, and development of the corporation and to improve the image of the industry and company. A series of 24 half-page advertisements prepared by the company's advertising agent, are appearing in the principal daily newspapers of plant communities at biweekly intervals. There was little evidence of the effectiveness of this advertising aside from occasional comments by local residents and employees who said that they had read the advertisements and found them interesting.

Although many company employees live in the plant communities where this newspaper advertising and other public relations activities were carried on, the program, according to the responses to the employee opinion poll, did not cause employees to regard the corporation more favorably. Something more than the current community relations program was needed to develop employee understanding and loyalty.

Up to this time, the public relations department had made no attempt to improve the company's relations with dealers because the management considered that this was the principal function of the marketing department. Marketing executives, salesmen, advertising and sales promotion people were in frequent contact with dealers and were the most logical persons to secure the understanding and support of the company's dealers. However, the findings of the dealer opinion poll which showed that dealers were highly critical of the policies and practices of the corporation convinced the management that the marketing department was not developing sound relations with dealers and that the public relations staff should take an active part in creating a more favorable image of the corporation in the minds of dealers.

The public relations staff concluded after discussion of the problem that the critical attitudes of the dealers were caused by inadequate communications between the company and its outlets. Dealers were not aware of what the company was doing to help them increase their sales and profits. Because dealers were uninformed they criticized the company's policies and practices. The dealer organization had grown from 300 to 1,000 dealers since World War II and the former close relationship, good communications, and understanding between the company and its dealers no longer existed. Improved communications with dealers were urgently needed to improve dealer relations, according to the public relations staff.

Similar conclusions were reached by the public relations staff in respect to improving relations with employees. Employees were not informed about the company's progress, expansion, and the outlook for jobs and advancement. As a result, they were critical of the management. Furthermore, the number of employees had increased from 1,000 to 20,000 which had created internal communications problems. Messages from management were often distorted or lost in transmission through several levels of authority to rank-and-file employees.

To improve communication to employees and dealers, the public relations staff proposed a communications program based on public relations periodicals as the most effective medium for telling management's story to the 20,000 employees and 1,000 dealers. Periodicals were favored because of their low cost of distribution, high reader interest; regular appearance; attractive appearance; flexibility in size; complete coverage of all employees and dealers; and adequate space to tell a complete story. The fact that most large corporations publish several periodicals is proof that this is an effective medium of communication.

To carry out the proposal to publish one or more periodicals, the public relations staff would have to be increased with specialists experienced in publication layout, make-up, production, and editorial preparation. A publication advisory committee, composed of members of management, would be established to advise the editors and staffs of the periodicals on editorial policy and content and evaluate the effectiveness of the periodicals.

The public relations manager recommended to the executive committee of the company the use of public relations periodicals in the public relations program. Upon approval by the executive committee of this proposal, the public relations staff would determine the number, size, type, objectives, personnel required, cost, contents, and method of distribution of periodicals for the company.

QUESTIONS

1. Should the Rutherford Corporation use periodicals in communicating with its 20,000 employees and 1,000 dealers? Give specific reasons for using this medium. What are the objections to using this medium?
2. Assume that one or more employee periodicals will be used:
   a) State the objectives of the periodical or periodicals.
   b) State the type or types of employee periodicals which should be used.
   c) Describe the physical features of each periodical.
   d) Describe the contents of a typical employee periodical.
   e) How should the employee periodical or periodicals be distributed?
3. Assume that one or more periodicals will be used in communicating with the 1,000 dealers and:
   a) State the objectives of the periodical or periodicals.
   b) State the type or types of periodicals which should be used.
   c) Describe the physical features of each periodical.
   d) Describe the contents of a typical dealer periodical.
   e) How should the dealer periodical or periodicals be distributed?
4. Should periodicals be used to communicate with other segments of the company's publics? Name objectives of each periodical.
5. What personnel would be required for the publication of these periodicals?
6. How should the effectiveness of these periodicals be evaluated?

PUBLIC RELATIONS films are used in communicating with various publics by corporations, associations, government, trade-unions, social organizations, and the armed forces.

Public relations films are sometimes called "educational films," "documentary films," and "nontheatrical films," and include both sound motion pictures and filmstrips. Other related audio-visual materials used in communication with the public are slides and transparencies.

The annual expenditure of business and industry in public relations and nontheatrical films in the United States, in 1960, was $389 million, according to John Flory and Tom Hope of Eastman Kodak Company. Federal, state, and local governments invested $59 million; educational institutions, $103 million; religious organizations and churches, $18 million; civic, social welfare, and recreational groups $16 million; and medical and health organizations, $8 million, and business and industry, $184 million, for a total of $389 million.

The expenditure in public relations films, in 1960, was divided according to production, prints, distribution, equipment, and other audio-visual materials as follows: production, $115 million; prints, $64 million; distribution, $93 million; equipment, $36 million; and other audio-visual materials, $81 million.

Production of public relations films has shown consistent growth in recent years. The total number of public relations nontheatrical motion pictures produced in 1960, as estimated by Flory and Hope, was 8,900. Of this number, business and industry produced 5,000 motion pictures; federal, state, and local governments, 1,500; educational institutions, 1,600; medical and health organizations, 300; churches and religious groups, 190; civic, social welfare, and recreational organizations, 210; and experimental films, 100.

The number of 16 mm. sound motion-picture projectors in use for public relations film projection in the United States, in 1961, was 727,-

000, according to Flory and Hope. Schools have the largest number with 220,000 projectors; business, 179,000; religious organizations, 127,000; government, 75,000; homes, 65,000; civic and social welfare organizations, 50,000; and medical groups, 11,000.

ADVANTAGES OF PUBLIC RELATIONS FILMS

Visual communication is not only the oldest but also one of the most effective methods of conveying ideas. Scientists believe that visual impressions receive 25 times more attention than those received by ear. The sense of sight is by far the fastest to register images in the mind. Vision is believed to account for 83 per cent of all acquired knowledge, outdistancing all other senses combined by four to one.

When visual impressions are combined with appeals to the ear in sound films, the combination is one of the most powerful methods of communication for public relations. The auditory appeal of films commands attention and carries the force, emphasis, and persuasiveness of the human voice.

Sound films command attention of the viewing audience through dual appeal to sight and sound, and motion and color secure and hold attention to the message presented.

Viewers receive a clearer understanding of public relations messages presented visually and orally by sound films. The lapse of time in a situation or series of events can be clearly shown on film. Past events or those remote can be brought into the immediate presence of the audience. The size of objects can be enlarged or reduced on film so that viewers can see them more clearly.

Films combine drama, sound, color, music, action, and emotion to exert strong impact on an audience sitting in a darkened room and giving its full attention to the picture.

The viewer's attention to the message is not interrupted and is held for a longer period of time than is the case when reading a newspaper, magazine, or poster. The average public relations film offers sustained observation for 30 minutes.

Information received from films is retained longer than information obtained from other sources. The United States Air Force has found that a good film can convey twice as much information on a subject as other methods of communication.

Films are particularly effective in communicating information to groups by giving all of the group information simultaneously. Furthermore, public relations messages may be communicated to groups with substantial savings in time and cost over individual methods of communication.

Films are a selective medium as the film audience may be chosen by sex, occupation, age, or special interest in the subject of the film. An accurate count of the size of the audience may be obtained and the response of the viewers can also be determined.

Films provide a record of past events such as anniversaries, dedications, open houses, outings, award ceremonies, and other special events which can be revived at any place or time and before any audience.

Films are used in a wide variety of ways in employee, economic, and educational programs, general consumer education, institutional publicity, dealer and distributor relations, and stockholder meetings. They supplement other methods of communication such as public speeches, exhibits, and displays, television broadcasts, plant tours, and open houses.

TYPES OF VISUAL COMMUNICATION MEDIA

Visual communication media used in public relations includes not only motion pictures but a wide variety of audio-visual techniques including silent filmstrip, sound slide film, 2 by 2 inch slides, 3¼ by 4 inch slides, overhead transparencies, opaque projections, tape recordings, and records and closed circuit television.

A survey of the visual communication media used by 341 manufacturers, made by the National Industrial Advertising Association, showed that 79 per cent use motion pictures, 74 per cent use flip charts, and 86 per cent use slides and filmstrips.

Sound Slide Films

Slide films or filmstrips are produced on strips of 35 mm. motion-picture film, each strip with 30 to 150 "frames" or individual pictures which are projected by a special filmstrip projector. The operator advances each picture manually. The sound which is synchronized with each picture, produced on records revolving on a turntable, is amplified by an electrodynamic speaker incorporated in the projection unit.

Sound slide films with illustrations and text, in either black and white or color, are projected to 8 by 12 feet in size. They are convenient to use and economical to produce. There is no possibility of the illustrations getting out of the proper order. A spoken message, synchronized with the illustrations may be accompanied by sound or music.

Sound slide films are particularly effective for showing subjects in which motion is not an essential feature of the presentation. In employee relations, slide films are used to orient new employees in company history, operations, plants and facilities, policies, organization, and employee benefits.

Western Electric Company produced a filmstrip, "Supply Computer," to inform employees about the uses and advantages of a computer system installed in several company locations.

In furthering relations with distributors and dealers, sound slide films are used by manufacturers to inform dealers about management methods and merchandising programs. Other uses for sound slide films include showing at open houses, suppliers' days, plant tours, and opinion leaders' meetings, as well as meetings of church, civic club, and community groups.

Filmstrips are also used without recorded sound of voice or music, leaving the spoken message to the commentator who times his remarks and the speed of film projection to the comprehension of the group viewing the film.

The principal disadvantage of slide films is the absence of motion which viewers have become accustomed to in motion pictures. The illustrations are less impressive, the sound is inferior, and the mechanics of projection distract the audience.

Motion Pictures

Motion-picture film is produced, in two sizes: 35 mm. wide, used in commercial motion pictures; and 16 mm. wide, in which size pictures for public relations are produced. In the near future 8 mm. sound film will be widely used for public relations motion pictures.

The most important technical development in the past quarter century is the introduction of sound to 8 mm. film which promises to revolutionize the nontheatrical motion-picture industry, according to Tom Hope of Eastman Kodak Company. The advantages of 8 mm. sound films are: more portable equipment; economy of release prints; less bulky prints; lower cost, smaller-size projectors; lower postage charges; and less storage space. However, it may be several years before public relations can take advantage of this new development. The number of 8 mm. sound projectors is limited and technical difficulties of freezing the sound on a magnetic track must be solved. Professional film producers are reluctant to enter the 8 mm. field. Nevertheless, 8 mm. sound promises to be another milestone in the communications revolution.

Seventy-eight per cent of all business films are produced in color and 22 per cent in black and white, according to *The Dollars and Cents of*

Business Films, published by the Association of National Advertisers. Color motion pictures are more realistic and effective in creating moods of heat, cold, calmness, and dignity than black and white films. The attention value of a film is enhanced by color which emphasizes features of the presentation and adds brightness to what might be a dull picture.

LENGTH OF MOTION-PICTURE FILMS

The running time of an average-length public relations motion-picture film is 26 minutes, according to the Association of National Advertisers' survey of 157 films produced by 67 companies. Some films are released in two lengths: a condensed version which may run from 10 to 20 minutes, and a complete version running from 35 to 50 minutes.

The running time of a motion picture is determined by the nature of the subject, the purpose of the film, and the type of audience, as well as funds available. Public relations films produced for use on television should be either 14½ or 29½ minutes in length. Films for showing in schools should not run longer than 30 minutes.

LIFE OF PUBLIC RELATIONS MOTION PICTURES

The life span of public relations motion pictures depends upon the quality of the production and viewer interest in the subject. Skillfully staged, directed, and acted, films are circulated for many years. Five years is the life of an average public relations film, according to a survey of film longevity by the Association of National Advertisers.

Examples of public relations films in active circulation are: American Telephone and Telegraph Company's "Adventure in Telezonia" which has circulated more than 14 years to an audience in excess of 15 million; and "Mr. Bell" which has been viewed for more than 14 years by 35 million. National Livestock and Meat Board's film "Meat and Romance" has been viewed for 19 years by more than 50 million persons.

NUMBER OF PRINTS REQUIRED

To satisfy the demand for showings of public relations films, an average of 100 duplicate or release prints are made from the original production by sponsors seeking national distribution.

An adequate supply of release prints is needed to replace damaged and worn-out prints, delays in returning prints, as well as prints lost in transit. When film libraries and commercial distributors are used to get national distribution of films, several release prints of each film are required for each distributor and library.

EXPENDITURE FOR PUBLIC RELATIONS FILMS

Expenditures of large sponsors for public relations films vary from $100,000 annually to several million dollars, according to Flory and Hope, with the ratio of visual communication expenditures to gross sales of less than 1 per cent. Representative annual expenditures by large selected film sponsors are: an airline, $1,050,000; an automobile manufacturer, $6,000,000; an oil company, $5,000,000; a public utility, $4,000,000; a food processor, $175,000; an electronics company, $375,000; metal products company, $1,000,000; and oil and mining equipment company, $200,000.

The latest survey of the cost of production of public relations motion pictures was made in 1954 by the Films Steering Committee, Association of National Advertisers. Although the costs of film production are higher today, the following figures indicate expenditures for public relations films.

The major cost of a public relations film is production, which includes research, preparation of script, photography, editing, and recording. The production cost of 116 films included in the ANA survey ranged from $1,732, the lowest, to $426,600, the most expensive, with a median of $25,800. The median cost per screen minute per film was $1,168.

The number of duplicate or release prints required for distribution to exhibitors averages 100 prints and the average cost per print including costs of reel, can, case, and inspection is $122.74.

The cost of distribution by sponsors, commercial distributors, noncommercial film libraries, and combinations of these methods on 51 films showed a median cost of distribution per print of $91.40.

The costs of producing a professional sound slide film using professional talent, high-fidelity recording, art, and titling will range from $2,000 to $5,000 depending upon the number of frames, use of color, and settings.

PUBLIC RELATIONS FILM AUDIENCES

The major audience for public relations films, as determined by the number of 16 mm. sound projectors in use in 1961, was in the schools and colleges, according to Flory and Hope. Educational institutions in the United States own and operate more than 220,000 projectors. The second largest audience for public relations film is found in business and industry. Churches, synagogues, and religious groups comprise the third largest audience. Government agencies, homes, and civic groups represent the fourth, fifth, and sixth audiences respectively.

The size of the audience of well-produced public relations films compares favorably with that of successful, entertainment-type commercial pictures. As a public relations film may be produced for specific audiences with little waste circulation, some sponsors choose to make a film for limited, highly specialized groups, with the quality of audience more important than quantity. Many public relations films are shown to total audiences ranging from several hundred thousand to several million a year.

The total number of viewers per film, excluding television showings, of 116 films studied by the Association of National Advertisers, ranged from 40,000 to a high of 21,852,465; and the median number of viewers of a film was 1,268,851. The size of individual audiences varies widely from a few to several hundred persons, with the average for school and club groups ranging from 25 to 50.

Educational Audiences

Elementary, secondary schools, and colleges provide the principal audiences for public relations films. The major school audience is in the elementary schools which have 118,000 projectors; second are the public high schools with 68,000 projectors; third are the colleges and universities with 17,000 projectors; and fourth, private and parochial schools with 16,400 projectors.

Films for educational audiences should be planned with the advice of educators for use in courses in the social sciences, economics, homemaking, mechanics, business, geography, science, and history at specific educational levels—elementary, secondary, or college. The films should be free of advertising and promotion and of biased and misleading information.

Procter & Gamble's film on personal cleanliness, "Scrub Game," has had over 200,000 showings in elementary schools over a period of 13 years to audiences of more than 13 million children.

Club Audiences and the General Public

Civic, women's, social welfare, and fraternal organizations own and operate 50,000 projectors for showing public relations films to their members.

About 10,000 women's clubs with nearly 30 million members are a primary audience for public relations films featuring women's interests.

Service clubs, including Rotary, Kiwanis, Lions, Optimists, and other civic organizations, composed of business and professional men, are logical audiences for public relations films on business and professional subjects.

The National Live Stock and Meat Board's film, "Meat and Romance," has been shown to civic groups comprising more than 50 million persons, not counting television audiences. The Weyerhaeuser Forest Products Company's forestry film, "Green Harvest," has been viewed by over 13 million persons in 11 years, plus an estimated 54 million in television showings. The Ford Motor Company's public relations film, "American Cowboy," has been seen by 12 million persons. "How to Catch a Cold," produced for Kimberly-Clark, manufacturers of Kleenex tissues, has been viewed by an estimated 170 million persons in groups and on television in the past seven years.

Business Audience

Business and industry uses 179,000 projectors in showing public relations films to employees, stockholders, dealers, and suppliers. Films are used to inform these publics about the history of the company, its organization, products, policies, earnings, taxes, reserves, production, and marketing operations.

Westinghouse Electric Corporation has produced a series of films, "Westinghouse in the News," for showing to management and employees at 23 Westinghouse plants.

Religious Audience

Churches, synagogues, and other religious groups own 127,000 projectors for showing religious and public relations films. These religious groups represent persons of all ages, sex, and economic status.

Industrial Management Audience

To inform management about company operations, finances, organization changes, and new products, slide and motion-picture films are used extensively.

Stockholder Audience

Annual report films are produced by corporations for showing at the annual and regional meetings of stockholders. Corporations with a limited number of shareholders are not justified in the expense of a motion-picture film so a slide film is produced at low cost. Films primarily produced for stockholders are also shown to executives, employees, and community neighbors. When a stockholder film is shown to several groups, the additional circulation justifies the expense of a motion-picture film.

General Mills, Inc., produces biannually for showing to stockholders entertaining and informative annual report films describing new products and facilities, subsidiary company operations, and future corporate outlook.

Television Audience

Approximately 50 million homes had television sets in the United States, in 1963, according to the Broadcasting Yearbook. These sets are served by about 645 television stations. Ninety out of every 100 stations use public relations films an average of 3.7 hours a week, according to a survey sponsored by Modern Talking Picture Service, in 1958. A typical local television station in a city of one-half million population reaches an estimated 400,000 sets, each operated for five hours a day, and viewed by an average of four persons per set.

An increasing number of public relation films are being shown on television because television stations have a substantial amount of public service time to fill as the Federal Communications Commission requires that a reasonable amount of station time be devoted to the public interest.

Eighty-five per cent of the television stations, surveyed for Modern Talking Picture Service, telecast public relations films supplied by industry or associations at least once a week. More than 71 per cent of these films are shown in the afternoon.

Some public relations films are programed in a series of related subjects, as travel or sports. Seventy-eight per cent of the stations questioned preferred the series format.

Typical public relations films shown on television are: "Quest for Red Trout," sponsored by Alcoa; "The Case of Officer Hallibrand," Ohio Oil Company; "The Miracle Kitchen," Whirlpool Corporation; "The New Paul Bunyan," Weyerhaeuser Sales Company, and others.

DISTRIBUTION OF PUBLIC RELATIONS FILMS

Public relations films reach exhibitors through an estimated 5,000 film libraries which distribute from one to several thousand titles. The nontheatrical film libraries in the United States, in 1958, according to

Flory and Hope, were: educational, 1,400; business, 1,150; government, 560; civic and social welfare organizations, 500; medical, 440; and religious, 400.

Public relations films are distributed on one or more of three bases: free, rental, or sale. The free films outnumber those which are sold or rented in ratio of six to one. The majority of business- and government-sponsored films are free; while films for education and religion are usually rented or sold.

Noncommercial film libraries are of two types: those with restricted circulation, and those which offer general circulation. The restricted circulation libraries are usually found in city and county school systems, co-operative organizations, state departments of education, and universities. General circulation libraries include public libraries, government agencies, trade associations, social service, and commercial distributors. These libraries distribute films to any reputable organization willing to defray transportation charges.

Four methods of distributing public relations films are: sponsor distribution, commercial distributor, noncommercial library, and combinations of these three methods.

Sponsors distribute 43 per cent of all public relations films, according to the Association of National Advertisers' survey of film distribution. Sponsor distribution is usually employed by large corporations with many titles and film libraries stocked with release prints at strategic locations throughout the country.

Commercial film distributors handle entirely or in part the distribution of 37 per cent of all public relations films. Film distributors charge sponsors a fee for distribution service. The largest distributor represents 400 sponsors and distributes to schools, industry, social groups, television, and 17,000 commercial motion-picture theaters.

Noncommercial film libraries distribute about 20 per cent of all public relations films. Sponsors sell or provide free release prints to the libraries which agree to maintain, inspect, and distribute prints and provide the sponsor with reports on the number of showings, size of audience, and reaction to the film.

The public relations department, Standard Oil Company, Indiana, distributes its own films and also uses a commercial distributor who charges on the basis of each booking secured. The company spends about $100,000 annually on film distribution.

Films distributed to commercial motion picture theaters reach exhibitors through 458 commercial film exchanges in 39 distribution areas throughout the United States.

While the distribution of public relations films is primarily restricted to the United States, an increasing number of American films circulate abroad. American public relations films have been remade in many different languages. U.S. government films are widely distributed abroad by the U.S. Information Agency.

Promotion of Film Distribution

Public relations film circulation depends on the method of distribution, the quality of the film, and the promotion. Direct-mail advertising is the principal method of promoting circulation to program chairmen of service clubs, church groups, the visual education directors of school systems.

The film catalogue is the basic medium of promotion for sponsors and commercial distributors circulating numerous titles. The American Telephone and Telegraph Company's film catalogue lists some 300 titles classified according to subject and type of film.

Display advertisements, featuring new film releases, are published in periodicals devoted to visual education and in business and professional magazines to stimulate circulation of public relations films. Reviews of new film releases in business and professional magazines and listings in standard film catalogues build acceptance for films and increase distribution. The Library of Congress publishes catalogue cards on every film which is produced in this country. Any sponsor, exhibitor, distributor, or library can order the catalogue cards of public relations films from the Library of Congress.

PRODUCTION OF PUBLIC RELATIONS FILMS

Public relations films are produced in the United States by some 6,800 production units of two basic types, commercial and in-plant. The majority of films are made by commercial producers, but a few large corporations operate their own film production units.

The successive steps in the production of public relations film are as follows:

Planning, involves the collection of suggestions; determination of the subject and the audience; the basic philosophy of the film; preliminary research; preparation of an outline of the picture including its scope, coverage, and objectives; organization and film treatment.

Preparation of the script by an experienced writer following the plan previously described.

Approval of the script for content and technical accuracy, with revisions as necessary, by an advisory committee representing the sponsor.

Production of the film, involving arrangements for a location, operators, cameras, sets, actors, and direction.

Sound recording of the actors' voices which explains the things that are seen in the film and smoothes the transition between scenes.

Delivery of the finished picture for distribution to exhibitors.

The final decision to produce a film depends on approval of the script by the sponsor at which time a definite decision is made to undertake or abandon the production. If the sponsor is dissatisfied with the script, the producer is compensated for the preliminary work and production of the film is shelved. Otherwise, the producer estimates the cost of the film and, if the amount is acceptable, production proceeds.

Film production is a co-operative enterprise, with the sponsor providing information and assistance when needed and the producer assuming full responsibility for the technical excellence of the production. Producers are selected on the basis of their demonstrated ability to produce the type of picture desired by the sponsor, and their location, facilities, skilled personnel, and cost.

DETERMINING THE EFFECTIVENESS OF PUBLIC RELATIONS FILMS

The effectiveness of public relations films is measured by audience-opinion questionnaires distributed to viewers following showings; comments by exhibitors; records of showings which indicate the type and number in the audience and their geographical distribution.

Opinion surveys are also used to determine the audience reaction to a film. These opinion surveys employ personal interviews, mail investigations, or telephone surveys.

The most comprehensive tests of the effectiveness of public relations films have been sponsored by the American Telephone and Telegraph Company to determine the size of audience, audience interest, communication, attitude effect and behavior. The majority of tests have been conducted by Schwerin Research Corporation in its theater in New York City, with the audiences recruited by mail. Two audiences, each consisting of 300 to 350 people are used on two consecutive nights.

As the picture being tested is projected, small numbers appear in the corner of the screen at intervals of 20 to 30 seconds. The audience checks on a form whether they consider what they have just seen is "very interesting," "mildly interesting," or "not very interesting." From this information an interest profile for the film and an over-all interest rating is obtained.

To measure communication or understanding of the audience, members of each audience are asked to check, on forms provided, their answers to a set of questions relating to the subject matter of the film.

To determine the attitude effect of the film, certain members of the audience are asked to answer three standard sets of attitude questions designed to determine their opinions of the quality of telephone service, what they think it costs, and how they feel about the telephone company in general.

One of the two audiences, called the "test" or exposed audience, answers the questions *after* they have seen the film and it is assumed that their responses may have been affected by the film. Members of the second or "control" audience give their responses *before* seeing the film and it is assumed that their responses could not have been affected by the film. Differences in the responses for the two audiences indicate what the film has accomplished in communicating information and understanding and influencing attitudes.

The results of the testing have had practical usefulness, have led directly to more effective films, and some useful generalizations, in the opinion of telephone company executives responsible for the tests.

Public Relations Film Programs

Ford Motor Company. The Ford Motor Company was one of the first sponsors of public relations films. The "Ford Newsreel," a weekly newsfilm, was produced in the period from 1911 to 1920 in the company's own studios, distributed to 3,000 commercial theaters, and viewed weekly by an audience estimated at five million persons. The current Ford film program was initiated after World War II and is the responsibility of the motion-picture staff of 18 persons in the public relations department. The department has a motion picture production unit which makes motion pictures and slide films for public relations, training, and sales promotion.

The Ford film catalogue lists 36 film titles in five classes: Americans at Home, The Automobile Industry, Travel, Education, and Highway Safety. Distribution of films is made from libraries located in Dearborn, Michigan, New York City, and Oakland, California. The libraries have about 11,000 prints in circulation. The Ford International Division distributes films in 15 languages in 29 countries.

The annual number of showings of Ford films exceeds 560,000, before audiences of 34 million viewers in addition to an estimated 30 million persons who see the films on television. The cost of producing and distributing Ford films ranges from about $800 a screen minute to $5,000 a minute depending upon whether black and white or color is used, the size of the film, indoor or outdoor location, original or stock music, or professional actors, all of which factors affect the cost of film production. This cost averages about one cent for each person who views a Ford film. The company estimates that its cost of distribution is less than one-half the cost of commercial distribution.

Prudential Insurance Company. Prudential Insurance Company, Newark, New Jersey, has built a public relations film library with subjects originally shown on its successful public relations half-hour Sunday television program, "The Twentieth Century," a Columbia Broadcasting System network documentary featuring important personalities and events of this century. To capitalize on the national network program, the 35 mm. film used on television was converted to 16 mm. release prints, representing 25 titles, and offered to schools, churches, and adult groups on a free loan basis. Additional titles are added as new subjects are televised.

A commercial film distributor handles distribution of the films, stocks the prints, ships to exhibitors, makes necessary repairs, and follows up film borrowers who fail to return film. Requests for showings are channeled through the public relations department of the company and forwarded to the distributor.

To promote showings, a Teacher's Guide, giving a synopsis of the "Twentieth Century" shows for the coming month as well as collateral information useful to teachers in integrating "Twentieth Century" with social studies classroom work, is mailed to 70,000 teachers in 10,000 junior and senior high schools each month. In addition, the company's sales organization is supplied with a list of available titles, a synopsis of each film, and an order form so agents can request films on behalf of organizations in their communities.

The first year of operation of the program more than 25,000 requests for films were received, representing an audience of over one million persons. The second year the total audience for all films in circulation totaled almost seven million people. Schools and colleges account for approximately 75 per cent of all film requests. Requests for the films now run about 4,000 a month and the size of the average audience is about 44 per cent higher than many other public relations films.

Case 22–1

PUBLIC RELATIONS FILMS
The Bell Telephone System

The Bell Telephone System comprises the American Telephone and Telegraph Company, New York City, N.Y., 21 associated telephone companies in which it owns all or the greater part of the stock, two associated but noncontrolled companies, and the Western Electric Company and the Bell Telephone Laboratories.

The Bell System provides a nation-wide communications service, operating about 63 million telephones or more than 83 per cent of all the telephones in the United States.

Each of the associated companies is a separate corporation with its own board of directors, officers, and employees. Each has available the resources of the entire Bell System which include the centralized manufacturing, purchasing, distributing, and central office installation services of the Western Electric Company; the research and development activities of the Bell Telephone Laboratories; and the advice and assistance of the American Telephone and Telegraph Company's general staff on important operating, engineering, marketing, financial, personnel, public relations, accounting, legal, and other related services.

The companies in the system are: Bell Telephone Company of Nevada, The Bell Telephone Company of Pennsylvania, The Chesapeake and Potomac Telephone Companies (four), The Cincinnati and Suburban Telephone Company, The Diamond State Telephone Company, Illinois Bell Telephone Company, Indiana Bell Telephone Company, Inc., Michigan Bell Telephone Company, The Mountain States Telephone and Telegraph Company, New England Telephone and Telegraph Company, New Jersey Bell Telephone Company, New York Telephone Company, Northwestern Bell Telephone Company, The Ohio Bell Telephone Company, The Pacific Telephone and Telegraph Company, Pacific Northwest Bell Telephone Company, Southern Bell Telephone and Telegraph Company, The Southern New England Telephone Company, Southwestern Bell Telephone Company, and Wisconsin Telephone Company. The territories of the companies are interconnected by the long-distance telephone lines provided, maintained, and operated by the Long Lines Department of the American Telephone and Telegraph Company. The Long Lines network carries radio, TV programs, and other services from city to city across the nation. It also handles calls to and from overseas locations.

The Bell Telephone Companies recognize as a primary responsibility telling the public about their service aims, policies, and how the business operates so that their customers may derive maximum satisfaction from the telephone service. This is a function of the public relations departments in the associated companies and at the American Telephone and Telegraph Company.

An important activity of the public relations department of the American Telephone and Telegraph Company is the production of films of nation-wide interest for the use of the telephone companies. The companies consider the sponsored industrial motion picture a powerful medium for informing the public and employees.

The Film Section, headed by a film manager, has two departments: the Film Project and Planning Department, responsible for the direction and co-ordination of film research, script work, evaluation, and release promotion; and the Film Production and Distribution Department, which takes over once a script is approved and supervises casting, photography, editing, and laboratory processing. Both departments work in close co-ordination from the start of a film idea until the finished prints are ready for distribution by the associated companies.

Films play an important part in the public relations program of the Bell System. They are used to show the public new services and facilities; how to use the telephone; how research and engineering of the Bell Telephone Laboratories and the manufacturing, installation and supply services of the Western Electric Company make possible better telephone service at lower cost; what the Bell System is doing in areas of defense and space communications; and how the companies try to make their people competent and friendly. Almost 200 million persons see telephone films annually.

"Seconds for Survival"

"Seconds for Survival," a Bell System film released in 1960, is described below to illustrate the method used by the Film Section in the development of story treatment, production, evaluation, and distribution of a public relations film.

"Seconds for Survival" was produced for the Bell Telephone Companies by Audio Productions, Inc., New York City. It was made in Eastman Color, 35mm. and 16mm. sizes and runs 27½ minutes. Its purpose is to describe our continent's over-all defense system and to show the Bell System's part in providing instant, reliable, and flexible communications for that system. The film has had wide distribution. In the first nine months following its release, it was seen by 10 million viewers on television; and 2.5 million persons in theaters as a public service; by 710,000 school children; and by 867,000 persons in clubs, civic and service groups, religious and fraternal organizations. Because of the importance of the subject, various branches of the U.S. government and the armed forces purchased over 550 prints for their own distribution.

"Seconds for Survival" combines in one film all the elements of our integrated defense structure—NORAD, BMEWS, the DEW Line, picket ships, patrolling aircraft, blimps, White Alice, SAGE, SAC, guided missiles and missile systems.

Raymond Massey, who narrates the film, tells how this continent's vast existing telephone network, designed for peacetime use, is also ready to serve the cause of defense. It shows how telephone men have built great networks of communications that bypass critical military targets and avoid large cities by means of express routes which connect with the main routes around and between our cities to insure continuous communications in event of disaster or enemy attack.

A simulated enemy air attack provides a highly dramatic sequence and shows how modern communications sprint into action to alert the nation and all elements of our defense system. We see interceptors roaring up toward the "invaders," missiles being launched, and nuclear-armed bombers heading for the "enemy's" bases.

How Ideas for Films Originate

Ideas for films may originate in one or more of the Bell Telephone Companies, at Western Electric or the Bell Telephone Laboratories, or at the American Telephone and Telegraph Company. The idea usually comes from a realization that there is a need for a public audio-visual in the areas of sales promotion, customer instruction, and information or institutional advertising. Films for employee information and training are also considered under the heading of public relations, for the telephone companies recognize their employees as one of the most important factors in creating and maintaining desirable public opinion.

The need and desire for a film are studied by the Film Section which gives particular attention to whether or not a film seems to be the most reasonable, economical, and effective medium in terms of its purpose, content, and intended audience. The Film Section canvasses the Bell Companies for their comments and approval.

"Seconds for Survival" illustrates how an initial idea is modified by this process. Originally, it was thought that there was need for a film covering civil defense. The Bell System had produced a film in 1954 on this subject. It was soon out of date due to development of the hydrogen bomb and changes in civil defense techniques.

However, as the problem was discussed it became evident that before the subject of civil defense could be made meaningful, it might be desirable to present the story of continental defense so that the public would be better able to place its own individual defense activities in proper perspective. Furthermore, the Bell System had a big story to tell in connection with its contribution to continental defense.

A film on a subject of national importance such as this required, of course, the co-operation and approval of the Defense Department. The idea was discussed with them and their approval and co-operation received for the project.

Story Treatment

A professional film producer was now recommended by the Film Production Department of the Film Section on the basis of its knowledge of producer capabilities. The suggestion was accepted by the Film Project and Planning Department whereupon the Film Production Department contracted with the producer.

A project supervisor is assigned to each film and he stays with the project until its completion. Preparatory to the production of "Seconds for Survival" he worked closely with the producer's script writer and co-ordinated a number of subsequent script meetings with the Defense Department. As the project supervisor worked with the script writer, the objectives and scope of the film were crystallized. Meanwhile, the Production Department arranged for the producer to photograph at certain military locations. It also busied itself with the acquisition of innumerable scenes that existed as stock footage in the company or outside film libraries.

The outline, preliminary script, and then final script were presented at various group meetings and gradually the project developed to a point where it could be turned over to the Production Department.

The proper presentation of a script at a script conference is vital to the success of the project. The operating people, technicians, and other laymen, who normally attend such conferences to approve the content and treatment, are not familiar with film production. They find it difficult to visualize the finished production in this early form. Yet they must be given a fairly accurate appreciation or costly changes and modifications may be required as the film moves through the production stages.

A script may be presented in a number of ways. In the case of "Seconds for

Survival" the writer read the script, being careful to explain the accompanying visuals, and dramatizing certain sequences in order to give the group a better idea of treatment and balance. If the visuals are complex, a story board is often used. A story board may consist of a sequence of an artist's rough drawings on a display board; or the drawings may be photographed as a filmstrip and narrated by the script writer or by a synchronized recording.

A recording is particularly useful if the narration involves a number of speaking parts; or certain scenes may be acted out to clarify complex sequences. There is no attempt to make such presentations professional.

Production of Film

When the script was approved, the producer with the help of the Production Department prepared a shooting schedule to show which scenes were to be shot on location, which to be taken in studio, and which to be provided by stock footage. Casting was the next step. In this case, since the film was to portray actual defense facilities, the actors would consist of the people who would normally operate these facilities. However, it would be necessary to select a narrator.

Raymond Massey was chosen because he was well known and respected by the public. It was felt that his stage presence and manner of delivery would be in keeping with the seriousness of the theme and that what he said would be accepted as coming from one who knew what he was talking about.

Each day's shooting was thoroughly planned by the producer, project supervisor, and technical advisers. During studio shoooting, company representatives were present to be sure that technical details were properly covered where company operations and facilities were involved.

Evaluation of Bell System Films

"Seconds for Survival" was tested with public audiences before its release. The basic purpose of a public relations film is to inform or to influence favorable public opinion toward the business. An audience test aims to discover whether the audience understands what the film is designed to convey, the amount of audience interest, and the influence the film may have on attitudes of the audience toward the telephone company, its service, and the cost of service.

Some 40 or more Bell System films were tested from 1946 to 1956. A vast amount of information has been gained on how a film should be constructed in order to achieve desired results. It is no longer felt necessary to test all Bell System films. Now tests are limited to films that present unusual problems of content or treatment.

Originally tests were made by inviting groups of people in the New York metropolitan area to the testing theater for a series of evening sessions. One half of the sessions were "control" audiences, the other half were "test" audiences. Both types of audiences were carefully matched according to their responses to a series of questions on age, sex, economic status, occupation, and certain opinions and attitudes toward the telephone company. Sessions for both control and test groups were conducted identically with the exception that control audiences answered questions before they saw the film. The test groups answered attitude questions after seeing the film. Presuming that the groups are matched properly any changes in audience impressions, opinions, and attitudes should be expected to result from the influence of the film alone.

Tests are now made using the "before and after" questionnaire technique. The accuracy of this system was validated by running both types of tests on the same film. It was found that the "before and after" questionnaire technique gave the same results as the "control and test" audience technique. The "before and after" technique has certain advantages. It is less costly because the same audience acts both as control and test. Matching samples is eliminated. It is possible to observe changes in the group and various members of the audience can be interviewed after the show to determine just why there was a change in opinion or belief.

Interest in the film is obtained by having the audience register its reaction to the program on a televote machine.

"Seconds for Survival" was tested at Mirror of America, Gallup and Robinson's theater and test center in Hopewell, New Jersey. Respondents were drawn from localities within a radius of 25 miles of Hopewell, served by Bell System Companies.

Sixty of the theater seats are equipped with dials with which the occupant of the seat can show his degree of interest as he views the program. The machine produces a continuous graph showing the average responses of the audience as it changes throughout the program. At each showing approximately 30 men and 30 women registered their reactions to the program, using this Hopkins Televote Machine. A total of 191 persons were included in the test.

The film rated an average interest level of 80 with highs of 93 and a low of 47 which occurred at the start.

Movement in the Service, Cost, and Company attitude batteries plus specific questions to test information gain and understanding were obtained from respondents' answers to the "before and after" questionnaires.

"Seconds for Survival" showed significant positive movement in the Cost (+3.6) and Company (+3.2) battery indices. Analysis of the change showed that women and people with less education were responsible for most of the movement.

The audience was asked to rate their agreement or disagreement on a five-point scale with specific statements dealing with the telephone company. A significant favorable change was noted for the following statements:

1. The company has a strong sense of civic responsibility to the community and nation. Men, +5; Women, +6.2.
2. Most people saw the company's role in defense as that of a good citizen who also wanted to protect himself as well as others.
3. The company plays an important part in the defense of the U.S. Men, *; Women, *.
4. The company never does anything without an eye to its own profit. Men, −5; Women, −5.2.
5. The Telephone Company has too much influence and power in this country. Men, *; Women, −5.2.

---

* Indicates no significant change. Changes on questions #4 and #5 are *minus* which are favorable changes for these particular questions.

Releasing and Distributing Bell System Films

Prints of completed films are sent to the associated companies where they are previewed to determine whether the company desires to show the film in its territory.

Because of the universal application of the "Seconds for Survival" message all Bell System Companies accepted the film and proceeded to order prints for local distribution.

Distribution is accomplished in a number of ways. The many Bell System business offices serve as distribution points for local club and school showings. They promote bookings through direct mail, distribution of catalogues, posters, bill inserts, personal contacts, and through employees.

However, the prints are usually stored, maintained, and shipped from a centralized library in each state to reduce print shelf time and yet keep shipping time within reason.

Some theater and television bookings are also made from the business offices. Usually, however, theaters are handled through booking agents who charge a small fee for booking a film with a theater. Booking agents also provide similar services for bookings to television stations, clubs, and other groups.

In the case of "Seconds for Survival" a contract was made by the Film Section with Sterling Motion Pictures, Inc., to handle television bookings on a national basis. Arrangements were made, however, so that some of the Associated Companies could exclude themselves or certain of their areas from the national distribution where it was felt that contacts could be handled more effectively on a personal basis.

Experience of sponsors of industrial motion pictures has been that theater managers and TV program managers accept industrial films when they involve subjects that are of public interest, educational, timely, and free from overt commercialism.

QUESTIONS

1. Describe the successive steps in originating, story treatment, production, evaluation, and distribution of public relations films of the American Telephone and Telegraph Co.

2. Is the American Telephone and Telegraph Company organization for producing, evaluating, and distributing public relations films for the Bell Telephone System satisfactory? How could this organization be improved?

3. Comment on each of the following features of the film "Seconds for Survival":
   a) Title of film.
   b) Purpose of film.
   c) Distribution of film.
   d) Narrator.
   e) Audience.

4. Discuss the American Telephone and Telegraph Company methods of evaluating audience reaction to public relations films. What are the strengths

and weaknesses of this method of testing a public relations film? What other methods of evaluation of films, if any, should be used?

5. Is the Bell System method of distributing public relations films satisfactory? What other methods, if any, should be used?

6. What methods should be used to promote showings of Bell System films?

Case 22–2

PUBLIC RELATIONS FILMS

First Security Corporation

The First Security Corporation, Salt Lake City, Utah, is the largest intermountain banking organization, operating a system of 80 banks in the states of Utah, Idaho, and Wyoming. The corporation operates through three banking subsidiaries: First Security Bank of Idaho, First Security Bank of Utah, and First Security Bank of Rock Springs, Wyoming; all serving 350,000 depositors with deposits of over $559 million and total resources in excess of $619 million.

The corporation employs 1,600 men and women and is owned by 3,900 shareholders, 82 per cent of whom are residents of the three states in which the banks operate. An affiliate, First Security Company provides economic, investment counsel, purchasing, credit, business development, and public relations services to the three banking subsidiaries.

The public relations department of First Security Corporation was established in 1953 with the appointment of a public relations officer who is responsible to the senior vice-president in charge of public relations, business development, and new business. Three secretaries serving the vice-president, public relations officer, and statistical clerk complete the public relations staff. An advertising agency provides advertising, publicity, and public relations counsel to the corporation's public relations executives.

The objective of First Security's public relations program is to impel people to want to do business with the corporation so that a profit may be made for the company and its owners, the stockholders.

The public relations program of First Security Corporation includes employee, stockholder, and general public relations. An employee magazine, *Branch Clearings,* goes monthly to the 1,600 employees of the corporation. The 3,900 stockholders and the investment community receive a profusely illustrated 24-page annual report describing not only the financial status of the corporation but also the economy of the region which it serves.

The general public relations program of First Security Corporation is largely carried on through the medium of motion pictures. Through arrangement with a commercial distributor of films, the corporation sponsors films on banking and historical subjects for showing to students in the high schools of the area. Five American Bankers Association films and four historical pictures are exhibited to more than 50,000 high school students annually at a cost of one cent per viewer. An American Red Cross film, "Rescue Breathing," is also sponsored by the corporation.

After distributing films produced by other organizations for several years, First Security decided in 1958 to sponsor its own motion picture titled, "Frontiers," a dramatic and informative color film of the life, economic, and recreational resources of the intermountain states of Utah and Idaho. This film is one of the outstanding documentary motion pictures produced in this country and has been accorded numerous national and international honors.

"Frontiers" was selected by the National Association of Manufacturers as one of the 15 outstanding films produced in 1960 for American industry. In the 1961 American Film Festival, New York City, sponsored by the Educational Film Library Association, "Frontiers" received honorable mention in the business and industry category. At the Columbus, Ohio, Film Festival, in 1961, the film was awarded the top honor, the Chris Statuette, as the best film in the travel section of the festival. "Frontiers" won first place in the public service category in the National Visual Presentation Association awards competition sponsored jointly by the National Visual Presentation Association and the Sales Executives Club of New York City.

International honors accorded "Frontiers" are even more impressive than the recognition given the film in this country. It was selected as the best film in the Western regional screenings of the Committee on International Non-Theatrical Events (Cine) to be entered in the Edinburgh and Venice Film Festivals. Although the Edinburgh Film Festival is noncompetitive, a film to be selected for showing is considered as having won a top honor. At the Venice Festival, "Frontiers" was awarded a first prize gold medal. At the Brussels Film Festival, the picture won first prize as best tourist film with cultural interest.

At the International Industrial Film Festival, Turin, Italy, "Frontiers" was awarded a special prize of a silver cup which was presented to First Security Corporation by the president of the National Association of Manufacturers which selected the picture for European showings.

The United States State Department is circulating "Frontiers" for exhibition in foreign countries and the United States Information Agency is showing the picture on Belgian television and in Belgian schools.

"Frontiers" is dedicated to the people of Utah and Idaho to dramatize their lives, history, and desire for adventure, risk, and achievement which sets them apart as frontiersmen in what is still the Great West. It enables them to show others their way of life, the wide variety and unusual beauty of their land, and their accomplishments. It is a film to inspire new generations and attract new industry with which to build a greater community in the intermountain region.

The film makes several contributions to the public relations program of First Security Corporation. It builds prestige for the corporation with the people of the region who regard it as a generous public-spirited contribution to the welfare of the area. It engenders appreciation of the sponsor for providing a valuable promotional medium for business and industry in Utah and Idaho. It is an effective medium of internal communication with employees of the corporation. The film provides teachers in high schools with a valuable educational tool for teaching the history, geography, and resources of the region served by the bank.

"Frontiers" recounts the history and pictures the activities of the young, energetic, expanding intermountain region of Utah and Idaho through narration of the personal experiences of typical pioneers, ranchers, farmers, miners, sheepherders, and industrial workers of the area. An old settler recalls the principal historical events, significant places and adventures of the early days of the pioneers. A young steel worker at the Columbia Geneva plant of the United

States Steel Corporation tells of his satisfaction in living and working in a big industry set in the scenic grandeur of the Wasatch mountains. The wife of a fruit rancher in Idaho describes the beauty and solitude of the frontier and the enjoyable life she lives.

A Utah mining engineer recounts his adventures in discovering uranium and the importance of the modern prospector's role in the development of a new industry in what is still the Great West. A Utah sheepherder brings to life the wool industry and emphasizes its importance to the intermountain region. A potato farmer praises the superiority of the Idaho potato and tells of the improvements in agricultural methods and the better way of life of the farmer. A salt miner illustrates how dredging salt from the Great Salt Lake is a unique contribution to the economy of the region.

Through these and other sequences, the audience is impressed with the economic wealth, scenic grandeur, and satisfying life in the intermountain West —the significance of copper mining in Bingham Canyon, Utah; the development of the oil and gas industry; the awesome scenery of Hell's Canyon, the deepest gorge in North America; the colorful beauty of Bryce Canyon and Zion National Park; and the enjoyment of informal living in the high mountain country. The picture portrays the recreational resources of the region, the opportunities for skiing in Sun Valley, big game hunting in the Idaho wilderness, fishing in the Salmon River, and river running in the colorful canyons of the Colorado River.

Production of "Frontiers"

"Frontiers" was produced by Dick Durrance Films, specialists in the production of 16mm. sound color films. Dick Durrance, famous skier, formed his own motion-picture company in 1948, in Aspen, Colorado. He has directed and photographed "Sun Valley Ski Chase" which won first prize at the Cortina, Italy, Film Festival as the best sports film of the year; "Ski Champs" which received the highest award at the Cortina Festival; and "Wings to Austria" top award winner in 1957 of the National Scholastic Visual Aids Committee.

The production personnel included a leading screen writer who wrote the treatment and final narration; a composer of the musical score; a film editor to cut the film; a camera crew to do the photography; only a few professional actors; professional voices for the narration; and sound technicians.

The successive steps in the production procedure were: preparation of the shooting script, planning of shooting schedule, completion of color photography, editing of picture and sound, preparation of final narration, preparation of separate music track, recording of voice, mixing and recording of the composite sound track, printing of first answer print with sound, approval of answer print, and ordering of release prints.

Eighteen months were consumed in preparation, planning, and shooting the footage on locations throughout the intermountain region, and consummation of the various steps enumerated above to the submission of the final picture by the producer in the summer of 1960.

The cost of "Frontiers" at the all-inclusive rate of $1,250 per running minute for the first answer print with sound was $39,000. A total of 32 release prints were ordered at an additional cost of $216 per print.

Distribution of "Frontiers"

The estimated potential audience of "Frontiers" is some 105 million viewers. In addition, families in more than 32 million homes served by over 500 television stations see sponsored films as part of their regular television viewing. There are some 500,000 16mm. sound projectors owned by organizations that meet regularly and view films.

Distribution of "Frontiers" is to the national film audience through repetitive showings by the nation's television stations; luncheon groups throughout the three intermountain states of Utah, Idaho, and Wyoming served by First Security Corporation; schools and colleges for showing to students in courses in history, geography, and economics; business organizations for showing to employees; local Chambers of Commerce, civic clubs, women's clubs; banking organizations and affiliates throughout the country; employee groups and their local community organizations; and social, religious, and fraternal organizations throughout the intermountain West.

The picture was premiered by First Security Corporation before a distinguished group of business and government leaders in Salt Lake City in the fall of 1960. Following this initial showing the corporation distributed the film through the managers of its 80 branch banks in Utah, Idaho, and Wyoming. Audiences totaling more than 200,000 persons saw the film in the intermountain area in its first year and continuous exhibition is contemplated for an estimated period of five to seven years. Numerous requests for showing of the film have come from leading corporations, colleges, banks, insurance companies, and government agencies in all parts of the country and abroad.

Promotion of "Frontiers" has been carried on by branch managers of the corporation, calling the film to the attention of program chairmen of clubs and organizations and by viewers telling others about the film. Extensive favorable publicity on the picture has appeared in newspapers throughout the intermountain region and has stimulated requests for the film. Free prints of "Frontiers" were distributed to the Utah Tourist and Publicity Council, the Idaho Tourist Bureau, the Latter Day Saints Church, and several large school districts for their continuous use.

QUESTIONS

1. Was First Security Corporation warranted in sponsoring the documentary motion picture "Frontiers" illustrating the history, resources, and way of life of the intermountain region? Give reasons for your answer.
2. Was the production of "Frontiers" by a professional film production organization the most desirable way to handle the production of this film? Give your reasons.
3. Discuss the distribution of "Frontiers." Is the method of distribution sound? Should other methods be used? What?
4. Discuss the promotion of "Frontiers." Describe the methods of promotion which should be used.

23 · SPECIAL EVENTS IN PUBLIC RELATIONS

SPECIAL EVENTS or functions including open houses, fairs, parades, anniversary celebrations, dedications, exhibitions, conferences, and special days or weeks are sponsored by business, social service organizations, trade-unions, or government agencies as features of their public relations programs. The objectives of a special event are to inform the public of the aims, policies, and activities of an organization and gain the good will of employees, community neighbors, the press, shareholders, suppliers, dealers, government officials, and the general public.

Special events are an effective public relations activity because they appeal to the universal desire of people to witness and participate with others in public affairs. They satisfy the desires of young and old to acquire knowledge and experience and enjoying the pleasures of seeing, hearing, and participating in an exhibition. People are attracted by crowds and the action, light, color, and motion of a special event. The presence of management at a special event humanizes a corporation in the public mind and dispels the impression that big business is impersonal and cold. The job interest of employees is stimulated by an open house which gives them an opportunity to show their work to families and friends.

Some types of special events have been discredited by press agents who have created sensational affairs to secure publicity for personalities or causes of questionable merit. While such spurious events may attract public attention, they do not create a favorable public image of a company or organization.

PRINCIPAL TYPES OF SPECIAL EVENTS

One or more of the following types of special events are in the public relations programs of corporations, associations, or nonprofit organizations.

Special Days and Weeks

A day or week devoted to a particular objective—industry, organization, group, product, or social problem—serves to inform and educate the public regarding the objective of the week.

National Fire Prevention Week is an example of an annual event in the public relations program of the National Board of Fire Underwriters. This event is officially proclaimed each year by the President of the United States as Fire Prevention Week. Fire insurance companies and fire prevention organizations throughout the United States and Canada feature this week in their public relations programs.

The National Board of Fire Underwriters promotes the organization of community fire prevention committees and provides the press with publicity on fire prevention.

Special days for community groups are a feature of the community public relations program of the Caterpillar Tractor Company, Peoria, Illinois. Barbers, clergymen, taxi drivers, policemen, firemen, and other groups are invited for a plant inspection tour, a luncheon, and an open discussion period on special days designated as: Barbers' Day, Clergy Day, M.D. Day, Farm Youth Day, Cops' Day, Visiting-Firemen's Day, and Taxi Day.

Family Days and Family Nights are special public relations events in many industrial concerns. The families of employees and their friends are invited to see a plant in operation. Westinghouse Electric Corporation plants hold Family Days which are attended by employee families and friends in plant communities.

The Bowling Proprietors Association, with 6,000 members sponsored "Bowl Down Cancer Week" in its 1962 public relations program.

Displays and Exhibits

Special displays and exhibits are special events included in public relations programs. They range in magnitude from a World's Fair exhibit to a product display.

Fifty corporations have invested more than $25 million in exhibits at Chicago's Museum of Science and Industry including Union Carbide Corporation, General Motors, International Harvester, Radio Corporation, Swift and Company, and others.

An educational exhibit, "Oil Serves America," showing the principal operating phases of the oil industry, is maintained by the public relations department of Sun Oil Company in Franklin Institute, Philadelphia. It is seen annually by more than 200,000 persons.

FIG. 23–1. Display of Texas Eastern Transmission Corp., gas division, of a modern electrically powered compression station, used to inform the public about the company's operations, is shown here at a special event for security analysts.

Meetings and Conferences

Conferences, conventions, and discussions of representatives of a corporation with groups of consumers, employees, stockholders, suppliers, distributors and dealers, educators, the press, and opinion leaders are special events in corporate public relations programs.

Meetings give the management of a company, nonprofit organization, or association an opportunity to meet the public in person, to correct misconceptions, and to discuss the policies and program of the organization. At the same time, the public has an opportunity to express its views to management. Many corporations make an annual personal report on finances, sales, expansion, problems, and future developments at meetings of employees, shareholders, dealers, and suppliers.

Anniversaries

Anniversaries of business and social service organizations offer opportunities to publicize their progress, accomplishments, and resources and to build public confidence and prestige.

The Camp Fire Girls celebrated their fiftieth birthday, in 1960, with a Golden Jubilee celebration publicized with an extensive public relations program.

Special Awards

Special awards made to employees, customers, stockholders, dealers, or consumers or received by organizations provide public relations opportunities. Awards ranging from cash to loving cups, certificates, medals, trips, and promotions are made to employees for suggestions, attendance, length of service, safety record, sales, and other accomplishments.

General Electric Company gained favorable publicity in connection with receipt of President Kennedy's "E" award for excellence, in developing export trade, at a special ceremony at the Department of Commerce, Washington, D.C.

Annual cash awards for exceptional voluntary service in the United States have been made by Lane Bryant, New York specialty store, since 1948.

Open Houses

The open house, which includes a plant tour, exhibits, and other activities, is the most widely employed special event in public relations. To open houses are invited school groups, including pupils, teachers, and administrators; customers, including purchasing agents, housewives, and buyers; opinion leaders, including ministers, doctors, and women's and civic club officials; suppliers who provide raw materials, parts, and equipment; and social and fraternal groups, civic clubs, and veterans' organizations.

The objectives of an open house are to create a better understanding of the operations of a company, dispel misconceptions, gain prospective customers, and to demonstrate good working conditions. The conduct of an open house is discussed later in this chapter.

Contests

Contests and competitions are special events in the public relations programs of many business and nonprofit organizations. Contests stimulate public interest in an organization, its activities, and accomplishments. They are used in combination with other activities in special events for employees, stockholders, and dealers.

A large Southern public utility sponsored a competition for community improvement, with awards to communities in the area served by the company which showed the greatest improvement.

Parades and Pageants

Parades and pageants are special events in public relations programs of commercial, religious, political, fraternal, military, social, and industrial organizations.

The annual Thanksgiving Day parade sponsored by R. H. Macy & Company in New York City, witnessed by more than two million adults and children, is the principal public relations activity of the world's largest department store.

Sponsored Community Events

Industrial and commercial organizations sponsor community events to promote civic beautification, education, cultural life, health, recreation, and youth activities. Bamberger's, Newark, New Jersey department store sponsored a series of dramatic, art, and musical events in the area served by the store.

Sponsored Organizations

Corporations sponsor community and youth organizations to build good will for the sponsoring organization. The Ford Motor Company

FIG. 23–2. Annual special public relations event of Chevrolet division, General Motors Corp. is a banquet honoring the winners of the All-American Soap Box Derby held at Akron, Ohio, and attended by leaders of business, education, and parents of the winners.

sponsors the 4-H Clubs and Future Farmers of America to provide encouragement to boys and girls active in these organizations.

Public Relations Personalities

Some corporations and industries choose attractive young women of charm, beauty, and talent to serve as their public relations personalities.

The National Cotton Council, representing growers, processors, and distributors of cotton and its products, annually selects a Maid of Cotton to dramatize cotton fashions.

ORGANIZATION FOR SPECIAL EVENTS

Special public relations events of national scope are planned and executed by headquarters public relations departments. Responsibility for local events belongs to the manager of the local plant or facility where the event will be held, with the assistance of the plant community relations manager in large corporations. For some cases a regional public relations manager and headquarters public relations special events staff assist local management in planning and publicizing an event.

To insure the success of a special event, the active co-operation of district, regional, and local executives, supervisors, department heads, and employees of the plant or plants involved must be secured. A *special event committee,* headed by the local plant manager and composed of plant department heads, with the plant community relations manager as secretary, should be formed. To secure the co-operation of local civic leaders in a community event, they should be included on a special event committee.

To assist in planning and carrying out the program for a special event, subcommittees should be appointed by the special event committee. For the dedication of a new plant of an electrical manufacturer, the following subcommittees functioned: advertising, parking field, greeting, guidance, good-by, telephone, safety, first aid, and hospitality.

SPECIAL EVENT POLICY AND OBJECTIVES

A policy and specific objectives for special events should be established for the guidance of the management and public relations staff. An example of a special event policy is the following, of the Standard Oil Company, Indiana:

It is company policy to hold open houses, conduct tours, and participate in special events that give us an opportunity to show our good will toward the community, as well as gain new friends and customers. Such public relations activities give our neighbors a chance to meet us and see how we live. When properly conducted, they offer visible proof that we keep our house in order, that we spend funds wisely, and that we are a desirable neighbor, a good citizen, and a steady, considerate employer.

Objectives of the Special Event

While a special event is generally intended to create good will for an organization, there should be more specific reasons for the affair which are consistent with the public relations objectives of the organization. A comprehensive statement of objectives is necessary in determining the theme, emphasis, scope, and program of the affair.

As a special event attracts a particular segment of the public such as stockholders, employees, and community neighbors, the objective should consider the particular interests, background, and knowledge of the group invited to the event. General Electric Company plants hold a special event known as "M.D. Day" for physicians of plant communities. The objective of this event, taking into consideration the interests of physicians, is to gain the understanding and co-operation of community physicians in the General Electric health, safety, and welfare program. The objective of General Electric's "Clergy Day" is to show clergy in plant communities the good employee relations, working conditions, and benefits prevailing at General Electric.

Some of the objectives of special events in community public relations programs are: to secure the good will of a plant community; to dispel misconceptions about a company; to show that a company is a good employer, provides good jobs and good pay; to inform the community of the volume and value of the company's local purchases; to give people in the community personal contact with plant management; to show neighbors that employees enjoy good working conditions and other benefits; to celebrate a company anniversary; and to obtain the understanding of particular community groups, such as physicians, clergy, and educators.

The objectives of stockholder events are to give investors an opportunity to observe their company's operations, to meet the officers and directors, to express their opinions and ask questions, and to learn the views of management.

Distributor-dealer special events are held to introduce new products; to explain distribution policies; to impress dealers with the company and its resources; to recognize dealers for outstanding performance; to

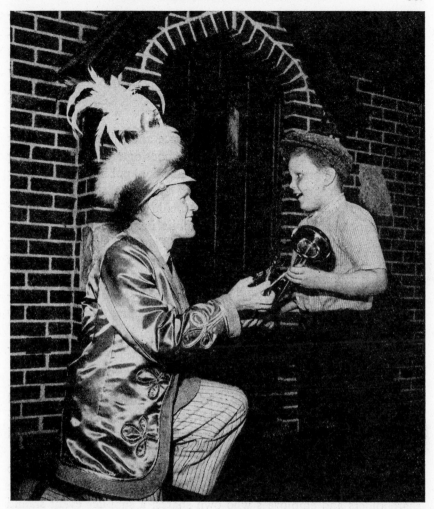

FIG. 23–3. Scene from the "Music Man," a community special event staged by a mixed chorus of employees of Caterpillar Tractor Co. in the Shrine Mosque, Peoria, Illinois, for the entertainment of the people of Peoria and vicinity.

educate distributors and dealers in management; and to show dealers how a product is manufactured.

Supplier events are held to impress resources with the facilities of a manufacturer or merchant as a consumer or distributor; to create a better understanding between buyer and sellers; to provide vendors with an opportunity to "speak their minds"; to give suppliers an opportunity to see their material or parts incorporated in the purchaser's product; and to explain the reasons for reductions in purchases.

Employee special events for workers and their families are held to build employee morale; to give supervisors and foremen an opportunity to meet personally the families of workers; to show employees the nature and variety of products produced by a company; to impress workers with the significance of their individual contributions to the total product; and to present the outlook for the business.

Preparations for a Special Event

Preparations by a special event committee and subcommittees for a special event involve: naming the event, choosing a date; determining the guests, transportation and parking, reception, publicity, community co-operation, program, and follow-up of the event.

Naming the Event. A special event should have a name descriptive of its purpose and to appeal to the public imagination. Community events are called: "Community Days"; "Family Days" or "Family Nights," for employees and their families; "Business-Industry-Education Days," for educators, and similar designations for other groups.

A "Cavalcade of Cartwheels" is the name of a special event to dramatize the contribution of a business to the economy of a community by paying employees with silver dollars.

Anniversary events are often named "Silver Anniversary," "Diamond Jubilee," or "Centennial."

Choosing the Date. The date for a special event should be selected, after thorough consideration, far in advance of the affair, so that it will not conflict with other events in the community, legal holidays, the completion of facilities which figure prominently in the celebration, and to allow ample time for preparation.

The Guests. The objective of a special event will determine who should be invited. For a stockholder event, the guest list should include shareholders and employees who own shares; a supplier event should be primarily restricted to suppliers and the same applies to dealer events. However, for events involving the general public and plant community, any or all of the following should be included: employees, present and retired; their families and friends; stockholders; opinion leaders; bankers; merchants; city officials; educators and students; club officials; the clergy, doctors, and lawyers; fraternal and cultural organizations; and the general public.

Invitations should be personalized for selected, limited groups using a printed card or personal letter from management, with a return reply card, mailed a month in advance of the event. Invitations to employees and their families should be by form letter from management, supplemented by bulletin board notices and the employee periodical. The general public should be invited by newspaper advertising, radio and television announcements, and press publicity, with personalized invitations to opinion leaders.

Transportation and Parking. Arrangements should be made for transportation of guests to the event. When guests are invited from out of the area where the event is held, air or rail transportation should be provided. Local transportation by bus, taxi, or rapid transit should be arranged for employees and the general public. Directional signs should be posted on highways approaching the site of the event. Sufficient parking space located near the event should be provided with parking attendants and traffic police on duty to guide visitors. Directional information should be included in invitations if the site is difficult to locate.

Reception. Provision should be made to greet personally all guests and register important guests. For this purpose a welcoming committee of company officials, identified by name tags, should greet the guests. Coat racks should be provided and ushers selected to seat guests. Provision may be made for the care of small children, and rest rooms made available for all guests. A staffed information desk and telephone facilities should be located at the reception center with a public address system for reaching individual guests in case of emergency. Identification badges may be provided for guests. A welcome sign may be erected outside the reception center. Grounds, plant, offices, and meeting place should be clean and "No Smoking" signs posted.

Tour Preparation. When a special event includes a plant tour, thorough preparations are necessary. The best tour route from the standpoint of visitor understanding and interest, safety, minimum interference with work, process flow, and even flow of visitors, should be laid out in advance and marked with direction signs. Safety precautions should be planned, including the erection of safety signs and barriers, stationing safety men along the tour route, and providing for accidents. Tour guides should be selected, trained, and rehearsed, identified with name tags, and provided with a planned talk for each step in the process. Machine operators should be identified with badges showing name and job. Foremen should serve as hosts in their areas to explain processes. Arrangements should be made for displays and exhibits of products, processes, materials, parts, safety program, employee relations, literature, and motion pictures.

Refreshments and Souvenirs. Provision should be made to serve refreshments to the guests during intermission in the program, or at the conclusion of a plant tour, in the company cafeteria or meeting place.

For all-day events, luncheon or dinner should be planned at the site or at a nearby club or hotel for special guests. At the close of the event each guest should receive a souvenir booklet, featuring a welcome by the plant manager, illustrations of the plant, story and steps in manufacture, history of the company, pictures of plant personnel, description of good working conditions, the contributions of plant to community, safety record, diagram of tour route, and distribution of sales dollar. A souvenir for adults related to company production or a novelty such as a mechanical pen or pencil should be distributed to adult guests. A special souvenir for children should be provided if they are invited to the event.

Pre-Event Publicity. Press publicity should be planned by the publicity section of the public relations department and the special event committee to precede the event by 30 to 60 days.

A press conference with editors, business magazine writers, and local reporters should precede an important special event. At this conference memo releases should be distributed by the public relations department announcing the event and giving the time, the place, the features of the program, the purpose of the occasion, and names of featured speakers.

News releases should be distributed by mail or in person to all local and nearby daily, Sunday, and weekly newspapers, and radio and television stations in advance of an event.

Photographs of the local facilities, participating officials, and important guests, details of new construction, and other features should be sent with captions to all local newspapers and business magazines.

Feature stories describing an event, the history of the organization, features of the program, personalities involved, unique demonstrations, and exhibits should be prepared in advance of the event and released to Sunday, weekly, and daily newspapers, and trade publications with accompanying pictures.

Special supplements to Sunday newspapers are used to publicize plant openings, anniversaries, open houses, and similar events.

A day or two in advance of the event, news releases describing parking arrangements for visitors, a statement by the president or board chairman, pictures and statements of guest speakers should be distributed to local and nearby papers.

Important events are preceded by a press preview the day before the event to give newspaper editors, feature writers, reporters, and radio and television commentators advance information about the event.

Advertising in local newspapers and announcements on radio and television should precede a community event to invite people of the community and describe features of the program. Direct-mail invitations or announcements should be sent in advance of the event to local community leaders, stockholders, important customers, dealers, and suppliers.

Publicity on events of regional or national importance should be distributed to the editors of regional or national business magazines, as well as to the news editors of local newspapers and radio and television stations in areas served by the organization.

The employees' newspaper or magazine should carry advance articles and pictures on the event and give recognition to employees for their contribution to the event.

Co-operation of the Community. A subcommittee of the special event committee, composed of local opinion leaders, town officials, presidents of civic clubs, the local Chamber of Commerce, and educators, should be appointed to assist in planning important community events.

Program for a Special Event

The program for a special event includes some of the following features: speeches by executives or guests, inspection of facilities, exhibits, demonstrations of equipment, guided tours, entertainment, refreshment, motion pictures, and round-table discussions.

A Plant Dedication Program. The program for the dedication of a new electronics plant followed by open house included: dedication ceremonies opened with music by a local civic band; invocation by a local clergyman; welcome by the governor of the state; addresses by the company president and plant manager.

Following the dedication ceremonies, an informal luncheon was held at a local country club for the principal guests and speakers. In the afternoon, an open house and guided tour were held at the new plant for employees, their families and friends, stockholders, community leaders, and the general public. The open house program included inspection of the plant in operation, explanation of processes by escorts, exhibits of parts and finished products, refreshments served in the company cafeteria, and souvenir of visit.

A "Clergy Day" Program. The "Clergy Day" program of a large corporation includes a welcome by the works manager and brief discussions by heads of the engineering, manufacturing, marketing, and finance departments. The employee and community relations manager discusses the company's job security program and activities in employee and community relations. The wage rate manager speaks about the establishment of wage rates. The personnel manager describes safety and employee benefits and training. Finally, the labor relations manager tells about the company's attitude toward unions and the status of company-union relations.

Following these presentations, the visiting clergymen, accompanied by representatives of management, are taken on a plant tour and shown manufacturing operations, with emphasis on good working conditions and safety. Following the plant tour, the guests meet in the company cafeteria for luncheon with representatives of management.

After luncheon, a group discussion is conducted by the plant manager assisted by department heads who answer questions of the clergy. The question period is followed by a motion picture describing employee security. Visitors are given packages containing company literature, the employee newspaper, and the annual report.

National Anniversary Program. Camp Fire Girls, national social service organization, commemorated its fiftieth anniversary, in 1960, with a five-month celebration initiated by a Golden Jubilee Convention, in New York City, attended by some 3,000 girls and adult leaders from all parts of the country. The national public relations division, assisted by the national public relations advisory committee of the organization, prepared a program for this special event designed to increase public understanding of the organization, enrich its program, serve the nation, and recognize the efforts of volunteers.

The public relations activities planned for the Golden Jubilee Celebration included the issuance by the United States post office department of a commemorative postage stamp bearing the organization's insignia in color. Three hundred twenty-five thousand Camp Fire Girl stamps were canceled the day they were issued. At a private ceremony held in the White House, President Eisenhower was presented with a specially bound edition of the *Conservation Book,* prepared and published by the Camp Fire Girls, describing its reforestation program in which more than two million trees were planted by girl members from Maine to California. A tribute by a Congressman to the Camp Fire Girls for its conservation work appeared in the Congressional Record.

"Thank Your Community Day" celebrations were staged by every local council at which recognition was given to adult volunteers by the presentation of awards to citizens who gave the Camp Fire Girls special service. "Founders Day" and "Birthday Week" celebrations with dramatic demonstrations, pageantry, and exhibits were held by local councils throughout the country. The governors of 37 states issued proclamations honoring Camp Fire Girls during the "Birthday Week" celebration.

Extensive national and local publicity was given to the Golden Jubilee Celebration by newspapers, magazines, radio and television. Five hundred radio and 200 television stations used publicity kits prepared by the national public relations office. The estimated value of the broadcast coverage given the Golden Jubilee amounted to $2 million for local and $3 million for national public service time.

Publicity at an Event

Plans should be made in advance of an event to secure publicity at the time of the event by issuing invitations to national and local press and radio and television representatives. Facilities should be provided for the press at a special event. A press room should be set aside for the use of newsmen and equipped with telephones and typewriters for those who want to prepare their stories there. Provisions should also be made for photographers and radio and television broadcasting.

Advance mimeographed copies of speeches, program, and background material should be available for distribution to the press. Press kits containing information about the company, new facility, biographical material on top executives, and pictures should be provided the press before the start of the ceremonies. Important guests should be made available for interviews with the press.

Radio and television broadcasts of an event should be arranged with local stations and network special event departments to feature well-known speakers, interviews with important guests, and other activities.

Publicity on a special event should also appear in the company's periodicals and on plant bulletin boards. To supplement coverage by the press, the public relations staff should take photographs, interview guests, and prepare features for distribution to the newspapers, magazines, and industry periodicals.

Following up a Special Event

After a special event, the souvenir booklet and other material should be mailed to important guests who were unable to attend. "Thank you" letters should go out to press and civic leaders for their contributions to the event; and a "thank you" advertisement may be published in local newspapers.

Persons who attended should be questioned to secure their reactions to the event, to evaluate the good will created by the occasion, and to obtain suggestions for conducting similar affairs in the future.

Co-operative Special Events

Special events are sometimes sponsored by a group of industrial concerns in an area. By pooling skill, effort, and expense, the sponsors of a special event can make a greater impact on community opinion than can an individual concern through its own efforts.

Co-operative special events include open houses, plant tours, luncheons, and community forums. These special events are usually arranged by a committee composed of the public relations directors of the sponsoring organizations.

Case 23–1

ANNIVERSARY CELEBRATION

Sun Oil Company

Sun Oil Company, Philadelphia, Pennsylvania, is an integrated producer, transporter, manufacturer, and marketer of petroleum, petroleum products, and petrochemicals. Through subsidiaries it is also engaged in ship building, ship repair, mercury mining, and the manufacture and marketing of oil well surveying instruments and services. The company is the nation's fifth largest producer of lubricating oils and ranks between tenth and fifteenth among American oil companies with annual revenues in excess of $755 million.

The company produces crude oil and natural gas in 20 states, Western Canada, and Venezuela. It owns and operates oil refineries at Marcus Hook, Pennsylvania; Toledo, Ohio; and Sarnia, Ontario, Canada; a fleet of 20 tankers and over 3,100 miles of pipelines. It markets 550 separate products in most of the principal countries of the free world and through 9,500 service stations in 23 Eastern and Midwestern states and Canada.

More than 17,000 persons are employed in the oil division and over 3,000 in the shipyard. Almost half of the company's 28,000 shareholders are employees.

Sun Oil Company was established in 1886. In 1961, the 75th anniversary of the founding of the company afforded a public relations opportunity to commemorate the event with a world-wide anniversary celebration.

Plans for the anniversary program were made by an anniversary management committee headed by a senior vice-president and including the director of production; the assistant to the vice-president in charge of manufacturing, transportation, research and engineering; general sales manager; comptroller; director of industrial relations; manager of general accounting; and director of public relations.

Execution of the anniversary program was the responsibility of local managers, assisted by a staff member of the public relations department in handling the press and by a "Guidebook for 75th Anniversary Observance" prepared by the public relations department.

The anniversary management committee considered various ways of celebrating the anniversary and rejected the customary complimentary advertising, banquet, and product promotion in favor of seeking the co-operation of employees in the attainment of management's goals.

Sun Oil Company, in common with other petroleum refiners, had been through a period of declining profit. To reduce costs Sun sought to effect economies by consolidating offices and introducing laborsaving measures and equipment but unlike most competitors it avoided general layoffs of employees. Despite the company's efforts to communicate its intentions to employees there was considerable employee unrest, concern over the future prospects of the company and job opportunities, in addition to union resistance to management's efforts to effect operating economies.

In view of these factors which affected employee morale, the anniversary management committee decided that the bulk of the time and money devoted to the observance of Company's 75th Anniversary should be spent internally in a well-conceived and executed program to increase employee understanding, strengthen loyalty to the company, improve morale and performance on the job.

Seventy-Fifth Anniversary Party Program

To attain these objectives, the president of the company proposed a series of anniversary parties for present and retired employees of the oil division and their spouses and escorts. Sixty anniversary parties were scheduled over a nine-month period in the principal cities of the United States, Canada, England, the Netherlands, and Venezuela where the company is operating.

A typical anniversary party program opened with a personal greeting of employees and guests by the president of the company and his wife. Dinner was preceded by singing of the Star-Spangled Banner after which an appropriate employee or a local clergyman gave the invocation. At the close of the meal the president's wife cut an anniversary cake. The master of ceremonies, who was the ranking local company executive, made brief introductory remarks describing the purpose of the party, introduced the guests at the speaker's table, and, at some locations, presented special employee awards for safety and long-term service. In some instances an employee glee club or choral group entertained during or following dinner. In a few cases a small professional orchestra was engaged to play during dinner.

The master of ceremonies then introduced the departmental vice-president accompanying the president, who in turn introduced the president of the company. In a 30-minute address, the president expressed confidence in the future of the company and emphasized that opportunities for employees depended upon how well the company fulfilled its responsibility of serving the interests of customers and stockholders. Employees were urged to strive with renewed determination and unity to be of increasing service to the company and the nation.

When large attendance (1,200 to 1,400 persons attended a number of the dinners) precluded personal greetings to employees and guests upon their arrival, the president and other members of his party remained after the program to greet as many persons as possible.

An anniversary souvenir gift of a vacuum bottle made of plastic produced by a Sun Oil Company affiliate, AviSun Corporation, was presented to each employee attending each party.

Other Anniversary Activities

In addition to the anniversary parties for employees, special commemoration of the event was arranged for dealers, shareholders, and customers.

To bring the anniversary celebration to Sunoco dealers, a special program was prepared for dealer meetings. Featuring this dealer program was a 24-minute color motion picture "Power for Progress" which opened with a personal message from the president and reviewed the history of the company and described its facilities. The dealers' magazine, *Sunoco Diamond*, gave special coverage of the anniversary celebration.

The officers and crews of Sun tankers at sea were shown a special version of the film, "Power for Progress," with an introductory leader which depicted the president and manager of the marine department on the bridge of a Sun tanker.

Shareholders of the company were made aware of the anniversary celebration through special exhibits and decorations at the annual shareholders meeting and through articles in the *Shareholder Quarterly*.

Customers were informed about the anniversary and the company's history through articles in *Sunoco-Grams*, a publication circulated to all charge customers.

Sun employees were given further particulars about the anniversary celebration in three editions of *Sun News*, employees' newspaper, and in a special anniversary edition of *Our Sun*, a quarterly magazine which goes to all employees, shareholders, and community leaders.

The general public was told about the anniversary through Sun's radio news broadcasts "Three Star Extra," with postage meter cancellation stamps bearing the slogan "Pioneering Petroleum Progress for 75 Years," and the use of this slogan and anniversary emblem on Sun stationery.

Management of Anniversary Program

The anniversary management committee decided that wide latitude should be given to local managers to organize and conduct the birthday parties in their areas. To provide local managers with information about the committee's plans for the celebration and their execution, a manual "Guidebook for 75th Anniversary Observance," was prepared by the public relations department.

This 45-page handbook contained suggestions for handling invitations, arranging the menu, distributing the anniversary souvenir, decorations, seating and entertainment, the program, hotel accommodations for the president's party, and press arrangements. The manual also described accounting procedure to be followed and gave local managers suggestions for handling anniversary activities for dealers, shareholders, and the public. A list of all anniversary parties and arrangements managers was included.

Press, Radio, and Television Publicity

Although the anniversary parties were primarily internal celebrations, they created many publicity opportunities. The headquarters public relations department assigned a staff man to each party to assist representatives of the press, radio, and television in obtaining information and pictures. The public relations representative also called on local media and invited editors and writers to attend anniversary parties in their area.

News releases prepared by the public relations department were distributed to newspapers, radio and television stations in adjacent communities in advance of each party. Press conferences with the president were held in New York

City and Philadelphia followed by 20 local press interviews preceding the parties in various cities throughout the country.

Numerous news stories appeared in newspapers in areas where anniversary parties were held. The president's speech was released after all of the parties had been held, and again attracted newspaper and trade publication attention.

Evaluation of Anniversary Celebrations

The anniversary parties which were attended by 90 per cent of the employees fostered a stronger feeling of interest in the company and aroused employees' desire to advance the welfare of the business in the opinion of management. The large number of employees attending the anniversary parties was evidence of employee interest. Employees not only attended but participated actively in the parties by providing music and helping with decorations and arrangements. Recognition was given employees of long service and those with safety records. The good will of the wives of employees was gained by the celebrations. The parties also provided an opportunity for employees to renew old friendships and gained the good will of retired workers. Personal greetings by the president established a more personal relationship between management and employees.

The local celebrations also brought the company numerous expressions of good will and recognition from local business and community leaders in cities where birthday parties were held. In several cities business firms called attention to Sun's 75th anniversary and celebrations in their newspaper advertising. The president of the Toledo, Ohio, Chamber of Commerce presented the head of the company with a scroll honoring Sun Oil Company's contribution to the economic welfare of the community. In other cities, the president of the company was named an honorary citizen.

QUESTIONS

1. Should Sun Oil Company have celebrated its 75th anniversary with a series of birthday parties for employees? Give reasons.

2. If you believe that there is a better way to celebrate the 75th anniversary of Sun Oil Co. describe what should have been done.

3. Was the company's organization for handling the anniversary celebration satisfactory? If not, what change should have been made?

4. Were the program and the arrangements for the anniversary parties satisfactory? What changes, if any, should have been made in the program and arrangements?

5. Comment on the press coverage of the anniversary celebration. What improvements might have been made in this coverage?

Problem 23–1

STOCKHOLDER OPEN HOUSE

Hall Milling Company

The Hall Milling Company, Kansas City, Missouri, was established, in 1921, by a merger of three flour milling companies: Tozier Mills, Kansas Milling

Company, and Kent Flour Mill Company. In 1940, the company purchased the Sunshine Cereal Company, manufacturer of packaged corn and wheat cereals; in 1961, the Pet Pal Company, producer of dog and cat food, was acquired; and in 1954, the company entered the frozen food field with the purchase of the Frost Fair Industries, packers of frozen vegetables and fruits. The company employs 6,000 workers in six plants located in Kansas City, Sioux City, Los Angeles, Camden, Houston, and Buffalo, and sells nearly $310 million worth of food products annually. The company is owned by 12,000 shareholders, one half of whom are women. Employees participate in a common stock ownership plan and comprise one third of the total number of shareholders.

The growth of the company is attributed to sound, imaginative management committed to policies of quality products at fair prices, product research and improvement, fair profits, extensive advertising, aggressive merchandising, realistic accounting, maximum output at lower costs, and sound public relations.

The public relations policy of Hall Milling Company is to give the public essential facts abouts its operations and to establish it in the public mind by good deeds as an organization of good character which serves the public interest faithfully and well. The company recognizes its business responsibility to manufacture and market quality products at fair prices and to work for continual improvement of its products and services. It recognizes its social responsibility to employees, stockholders, dealers, suppliers, customers, the general public, the communities in which it operates, and the nation. It is the policy of the company to strive for better human relations in its contacts with employees, stockholders, and customers and to conduct itself in the public interest at all times.

A public relations department was established, in 1946, to make the company more widely and favorably known to the public. The director of public relations is responsible to the president. A staff of 20 is organized in four sections: customer relations, employee relations, educational relations, and press relations. The department is engaged in five major functions: research of public opinion and the effectiveness of public relations activities; planning public relations programs, establishing objectives, choosing methods of communication, budgeting; co-ordinating public relations within the company and with an outside public relations counsel; administration of personnel, control of budget and employment; and production of publicity, publications, motion pictures, public relations advertising, correspondence, and special events.

Communications with the 12,000 shareholders of the company are handled by the treasurer and secretary, advised by an outside management counsel. The president of the company has asked the public relations department to assume responsibility for a stockholder relations program, and plan, produce, and distribute stockholder communications.

A stockholder relations committee was established, composed of the financial vice-president, treasurer, secretary, and public relations director to survey past stockholder relations procedures of the company and other companies in the food industry and set up a new stockholder communication program.

The company holds annual meetings for stockholders at its headquarters in Kansas City for the purpose of electing directors, appointing public accountants, hearing reports by the president and treasurer, and the transaction of other business proposed by stockholders. Notices of this annual meeting are mailed by the secretary of the corporation to all stockholders, with a proxy to enable those stockholders who cannot attend the annual meeting to indicate the manner in which they wish their shares voted. Only about one half of one per cent of all shareholders attend the annual meeting although about 40 per cent are represented by proxy.

The company mails to each stockholder an annual report which includes a consolidated balance sheet, statement of consolidated income, statement of consolidated surplus for the year, auditor's report, and a signed statement by the president describing the year's operations and outlook for the future.

The stockholder relations committee agreed that the corporation's communications with stockholders was inadequate and proposed the following objectives for a stockholder relations program: (1) To keep stockholders informed about the company and to encourage their participation and support of company activities. (2) To sell the company as an institution to the stockholders. (3) To inform the financial community and influential investors' groups about the company and its operations. (4) To emphasize the importance of human relations in company operations by bringing the president and principal officers of the company to the owners and showing that the corporation is an institution of human beings, not a cold, impersonal corporate entity.

Although the corporation is in excellent financial condition, owes nothing to banks or bondholders, the stockholder relations committee maintained that the long-range financial needs of the company would be best served by interesting new sources of equity capital and that future financial stability would be assured only by securing a substantial number of new stockholders. A more intensive stockholder relations program was needed to secure wider ownership of company stock by new stockholders, by present stockholders, employees, and the general public. To retain the confidence of the present owners and attract new investors in a competitive market for investment funds, it would be necessary to provide more information to stockholders and investors than in the past.

To accomplish the objectives of the stockholder relations committee, the public relations director established a stockholder relations section in the public relations department. The first step in improving stockholder communications was a stockholder survey in which the 12,000 stockholders were questioned by mail to determine their attitudes toward the company and their interest in stockholder communications. Stockholders were asked: How did you originally acquire your stock? How many shares do you own? Why are you holding the stock? Would you buy more stock in this company? Did you receive the company's annual report? If so, did you read it? What did you like about it? Dislike? Do you think the company is giving you enough information about its activities? Do you attend the annual meeting? If not, why?

More than 5,000 stockholders responded to the questionnaire and indicated that they were interested in the company's stock as a long-term investment. Most said that they received the annual report but found it dull and uninteresting. Few had attended an annual meeting. Many wanted more information about the corporation's operations and how management is conducting the business. A majority were not interested in buying more of the company's stock. The responses of stockholders confirmed the opinion of the stockholder relations committee that a better stockholder relations program was needed.

A more attractive annual report was prepared with dramatic photography, color printing, good writing, amplified financial statements, clear charts, non-financial information on personnel, labor relations, research, new products, and public relations.

Interim reports, in the form of dividend enclosures, were mailed to stockholders every quarter giving information on sales and profits. A series of four mailings to stockholders was used to secure proxies and to stimulate interest in the annual meeting. Correspondence from shareholders was invited and a letter of welcome was mailed to every new stockholder over the signature of the president. When a stockholder sold his shares, he was mailed a letter of regret over the signature of the president who expressed the hope that the former shareholder would again be numbered among the company's owners. A quarterly eight-page stockholder periodical was published to promote owner interest, interpret company developments, and report on new products, research, and subjects of interest to shareholders.

A page advertisement in color, featuring company stockholders, was published in the *Saturday Evening Post* and copies were mailed to stockholders. The advertisement discussed the advantages of investing in American business and the highlights of the company's operations.

After the new stockholder program had been in operation a year, another stockholder survey was made to appraise the effectiveness of the program. A marked increase in shareholder interest was revealed by the survey. More attention was given by shareholders to communications from the company. The number of shareholders who increased their holdings mounted. The number of new stockholders increased and the number selling their shares declined.

However, the program failed to bring the management of the company into personal contact with many shareholders to emphasize the personal assets of the corporation and create an image of the company as a human institution. Personal contact between management and stockholders is essential to the best stockholder relations. The annual report, dividend inserts, and the shareholder quarterly cannot take the place of personal contact, in the opinion of the president. Although attendance at the annual meeting increased as a result of the four mailings to stockholders, less than one per cent of the total number of shareholders attended.

To provide personal contact with shareholders by the management, the public relations director proposed that special events be held for stockholders at each of the six plants of the corporation in Kansas City, Sioux City, Los Angeles, Camden, Houston, and Buffalo. Shareholders residing in the vicinity of the six plants would be invited to a one-day open house at the plants to give them an opportunity to meet in person the president, vice-presidents, treasurer, and other company officials, inspect the facilities, observe products made, watch machines in operation, and see how their investment was used.

The advantages of these special events for shareholders were several: They would be a rapid means of building better owner understanding. The friendliness and neighborliness of an open house would give the corporation a "heart." The events would arouse owner interest in company affairs. They would show shareholders that the company is interested in its employees. Misconceptions of shareholders would be corrected, and they would have a more accurate impression of the company. Stockholders would be encouraged to consume the products of the company. There would be more favorable recommendations of the corporation's shares by stockholders. And the events would create a more personal relationship between management and the owners.

The president of the company was favorably impressed with the suggestion of the public relations manager, but the secretary of the company maintained that shareholders were only interested in dividends and not concerned about company operations; the company's manufacturing operations would be of little interest to shareholders, many of whom were women; only a small percentage of the total number of shareholders would attend the special events and management time and expense involved would be considerable.

The president asked the public relations manager to develop a program for special events for stockholders at the company's six plants and submit it for consideration by the executive committee.

QUESTIONS

1. Should open houses for stockholders of Hall Milling Company, as proposed by the public relations manager be held at the six company plants? Give specific reasons.

2. Assuming that the executive committee approves of these special events, what should be the objectives of these events?

3. Plan an open house for shareholders of the Hall Milling Company giving your views on each of the following: (a) Name of the event. (b) Date for the event. (c) Pre-event publicity. (d) Guests to be invited. (e) Transportation and parking. (f) Reception arrangements. (g) Preparation for plant inspection. (h) Refreshments and souvenirs. (i) Program for the event. (j) Publicity at the event. (k) Follow-up of the event.

4. What internal organization is required for these special events?

5. What other public relations special events should be sponsored by the Hall Milling Company?

ORAL COMMUNICATION
IN PUBLIC RELATIONS

SPEECH is the most effective and least expensive medium of public relations communication. Informal speech in the casual conversations of supervisors and workers, employees and their neighbors, management and shareholders, is the most effective means of transmitting information and securing understanding.

Formal speeches, addresses, or lectures by skillful public speakers before employees, neighbors, and other groups are second only to personal conversations in efficient communication of corporate messages.

As there is no expense entailed by an organization in the informal as well as formal speeches of employees, oral communication is the most economical medium for conveying the organization's messages.

Speech conveys information directly and rapidly to individuals and groups. It also provides for two-way communication as speakers not only convey information, but they also receive information from the people they address.

Oral communication has a strong impact created by the personality of the speaker as well as by the force of his delivery. Impersonal media of communication such as bulletin boards, magazines, films, and annual reports are important in public communication but they cannot supplant oral communication in public relations.

Speech in Public Relations

Speech is used in communicating with all publics. It informs employees about company policies and operations; trains them to be public relations spokesmen for the company; develops supervisors into more effective communicators with workers. In community relations, speech informs opinion leaders and community neighbors about a company's contributions to community welfare. In stockholder relations, management speaks to stockholders about earnings, operations, and corporate progress. Speeches are used to inform consumers about company policies and practices. In educational relations, oral communication informs students and teachers about a company or industry. Dealers and distributors hear from marketing executives about company policies and marketing programs. In government relations, executives testify before legislative committees and discuss pending legislation with local, state, and national government officials.

FIG. 24–1.   E. C. Klotzberger, General Manager, Fisher Body division, General Motors Corp., addressing 800 leaders of business and education and 40 young men who won scholarships in the annual Fisher Body model car competition.

TYPES OF ORAL COMMUNICATION USED IN PUBLIC RELATIONS

Several types of oral communications are used in public relations, depending upon the public to be informed, the objective of the presentation, and information to be communicated. Oral communications may be classified as: lectures, persuasive speeches, round-table conferences, panel discussions, question and answer discussions, oral testimony, informal conversation, demonstrations, and dramatizations.

Lectures

Lectures by skillful speakers are the quickest and most effective way of conveying information to small groups of employees, stockholders, suppliers, dealers, and neighbors. When a lecture is delivered over a public address system or radio or television broadcast, it may be heard by a large audience. Lectures are most useful in communicating factual information, making announcements, and for instruction.

Persuasive Speeches

Persuasive speeches appealing to the self-interest and emotions of the listeners are used by management in inducing employees, shareholders, and dealers to accept the policies, program, and proposals of management.

Round-Table Conferences

Round-table conferences are used in communicating with employees, stockholders, suppliers, community leaders, educators, and dealers to inform, correct misunderstandings, and exchange ideas about the company, its aims, and policies. Conferences provide a two-way flow of communication between management and its publics. They give the public an opportunity to express its views, discuss grievances, and secure answers to questions. They provide a valuable exchange of ideas and experience, leading to co-operative action. When the participants are prepared in advance and skillfully led, a round-table discussion is one of the most effective methods of communicating with small groups.

Panel Discussions

Panel discussions are used to present the views of specialists on a particular subject of interest to the audience. In the educational relations program of a corporation, for example, a panel to inform a group of teachers about the functions of a corporation should include representatives of management. Each executive discusses his functions, and together they would give the assembled teachers a better understanding of the operation of the business. Panels are useful in discussing controversial subjects involving management, employees, and stockholders and in presenting the views of several persons to groups of community neighbors, educators, suppliers, distributors, and dealers.

Question and Answer Discussions

A question and answer discussion, in which the audience asks questions of one or more speakers, is an effective method of communication when the audience is familiar with the subject under discussion. The opportunity to ask questions serves to correct misunderstandings and provides the questioners with supplementary information and new viewpoints. Question periods are used in stockholder meetings following a presentation by corporation officers of significant facts regarding finances and business operations, and outlook. The questions may be presented in advance in writing by shareholders and answered by officers of the corporation. Following a lecture by an executive to employees on a new employee benefit plan, a question and answer discussion provides a two-way exchange of ideas.

Oral Testimony

Oral testimony is frequently given by executives of companies and associations before local, state, and federal government legislative committees, boards, and agencies. Oral testimony is not only a medium of communication with representatives of government but through published testimony in the press it also informs the general public.

Informal Conversation

The informal conversation of management executives including foremen and supervisors with individual employees as well as dealers, suppliers, and neighbors is the most effective communication. "The impact of word-of-mouth public relations is greater than the combined effect of all other efforts," says the director of public relations of a large corporation. Some companies have corporate information programs to enable employees to informally discuss the company with their friends and neighbors.

Demonstrations

Product demonstrations are used to show the public advantages and features of the products of a corporation. They are combined with lectures and discussions to secure attention, arouse interest, and convince the audience of the merits of the product.

Dramatizations

Dramatizations or short plays are staged to inform and entertain employees, stockholders, consumers, dealers, and other groups. A play may be used to show employees the right and wrong ways to discuss company policies and operations with friends and neighbors.

ORGANIZATION FOR ORAL COMMUNICATION—SPEAKERS' BUREAU

Responsibility for developing an oral communications program should be assumed by the public relations department at headquarters. Execution of the program should be by the public relations managers of local plants, where speakers' bureaus should be established as a feature of the plant community relations program.

The headquarters public relations department may conduct a nation-wide public speaking program in addition to assisting local plants in establishing speakers' bureaus.

The principal function of a speakers' bureau is to recruit and train employee volunteer speakers and to secure speaking engagements for them. A speakers' bureau also carries on speech research and collects and prepares source material for speeches by executives and employee volunteers. It aids the management of subsidiary companies and local plants in organizing and conducting speaking programs in plant communities.

General Electric Company's product departments have established speakers' bureaus in local plants to provide speakers for community groups. The volunteer speakers of the speakers' bureau of Esso Research and Engineering Company, Linden, New Jersey, made 58 talks to 3,810 members of community groups within a 50-mile radius in a recent year.

The Wabash Railroad Company, St. Louis, Missouri, has a speakers' bureau with volunteer speakers recruited from its general officers and local traffic and operating officials. The purpose of this bureau is to keep on-line communities appraised of the national railroad situation and the progress and development of the company.

Members of the Ford Motor Company's community relations committees in 35 cities throughout the country accept speaking engagements for business, educational, and church groups to discuss company operations.

Speakers' bureaus have been established by national associations and unions as an important feature of their public relations programs. The National Association of Manufacturers' speakers' bureaus prepares speech material and schedules three professional speakers who travel continuously throughout the country addressing clubs and organizations. N.A.M. speakers address more than 500 meetings annually, with a total audience in excess of 145,000. The American Federation of Labor and Congress of Industrial Organizations' speakers' bureau is staffed by 26 speakers who address social, fraternal, religious, and other groups on the accomplishments of the trade-union movement.

Functions of a Speakers' Bureau

The basic functions of a speakers' bureau include recruiting speakers, training speakers, preparing speeches, securing engagements for speakers, handling bookings, providing visual aids for speakers, and following-up speeches.

Recruiting Speakers. The first step in organizing a speakers' bureau is to recruit personnel, both men and women executives, supervisors, and employees of the company or institution who are available and qualified to speak authoritatively on company policies and activities, technical subjects, and other public interest topics.

Some large corporations and associations employ professional speakers to speak before groups of educators, businessmen, students, women, and bankers. Professional speakers have the confidence, poise, good speaking voice, and forceful delivery often lacking in volunteers. However, the majority of speakers in public relations programs are non-professional volunteers.

In recruiting speakers, a survey should be made of the speaking talent in the organization and each person evaluated according to his subject knowledge, public speaking experience, and personal characteristics.

Speakers are usually not compensated for speaking, and speeches are usually made on the speaker's own time, although expenses of speakers may be paid by the company. Recognition is given to employees for their services as speakers. A roster of speakers may be started with a small group of experienced, effective speakers and enlarged gradually. The number of engagements a speaker should be expected to fill should be limited in order not to destroy interest in a speaking program.

Speakers may be recruited by consultation with division heads, by announcements in the employee publication, on bulletin boards, or by personal contact by the public relations staff.

A folder should be maintained for each speaker to include biographical data, glossy photographs, and reports on audience response to speeches made by the speaker.

Training Speakers. Although some volunteers are skillful speakers, many have limited public speaking experience and require speech training to insure that they make a good public impression. Speakers may be enrolled at company expense in a speech course at a night school. Teachers of public speaking are employed by some companies to train employees in speech. Membership in toastmaster clubs gives persons interested in public speaking an opportunity to improve their speaking ability.

Speech Preparation. The effectiveness of a public speaking program depends not only on good speakers but also on the speakers having something worthwhile and interesting to say. A speakers' bureau should collect and organize speech material for use by speakers. A list of speech topics approved by management should be selected, with background information on each topic. A speech material file, including copies of speeches given by organization personnel, is maintained by speakers' bureaus.

The Ford Motor Company's public relations department distributes copies of speeches, made by executives, to volunteer speakers. Subject areas include: citizenship, sales, education, industrial relations, management, economics, and highway safety.

Public relations staff writers prepare speeches for speakers who use these prepared speeches verbatim. Some speakers use them as a basis for their addresses, adapting the prepared speech to their own vocabulary and method or presentation. Others prefer to write their own speeches, using prepared material and supplementing it with subject matter of current interest or material related to local conditions.

Speech Clearance. It is the policy in many organizations to require speeches prepared by speakers to be submitted to the public relations department for approval before they are delivered. This is particularly essential in defense industries dealing with classified information or in military organizations.

The United States Air Force requires speakers to submit all speeches, speech outlines, or items of information to be used in speeches to an information services officer for review for accuracy, propriety, and conformance with policy and security.

The speakers' bureau of Esso Research and Engineering Company requires that all speeches be cleared by public relations, legal, and other divisions concerned.

Speech Subjects. Public relations speeches are made on a wide variety of subjects. Subjects are determined by the interests of the audience, the time available, the nature of the occasion, the public relations objectives of the organization, and the knowledge and experience of the speaker. The following speech subjects presented by speakers in the Esso Research and Engineering Company's speaking program illustrate the subjects discussed by corporation speakers: "What Makes Your Car Go?" "These Peaceful Atoms," "World of Wax," "The Origin of Oil," and "Opportunities in Petroleum Science."

Speakers associated with the Atomic Power Division of Westinghouse Electric Corporation have addressed groups in the Pittsburgh area on "The Atom and You," "Atoms and Women," and "The Atom Power Group."

Speakers' Guide. Suggestions for speakers may be combined into a speakers' kit or guide prepared by the public relations department. The kit suggests subjects for speeches, tells how to prepare a speech, and includes copies of speeches, speech outlines, and background material.

The public relations department, Wabash Railroad, has prepared for

Promotion of Speaking Engagements

Following the recruiting of speakers, selection of subjects, development of visual aids, and training of speakers, the Bureau initiated a publicity program to obtain engagements for speakers. The first announcement of the Speakers' Bureau was made in the company's monthly magazine, *Employees Bulletin,* with a full-page feature story illustrating speakers and listing their subjects.

A news release offering to supply speakers to local clubs and organizations was distributed by the Bureau to all newspapers, radio and television stations in plant communities. A news release announcing each speech and facts about the speaker is sent in advance to all news media in the community where the speech is to be delivered. A follow-up news release summarizing the speech is sent to local news media after the speech.

The Bureau is advertised in commercial radio programs sponsored by the company on local stations to obtain engagements for speakers from community organizations.

A 12-page brochure describing the operations of the Bureau is mailed to program chairmen of fraternal organizations, civic, service, school, and church groups and women's clubs within a 50-mile radius of Weirton. This brochure contains a picture of each speaker, a short résumé of his speech and a form for arranging an engagement. One page is devoted to "A Word of Appreciation" to the newspapers, radio and television stations in the district which have publicized the Bureau.

Area Served by Speakers' Bureau

A policy of restricting speaking engagements to a 30-mile radius of the main plant in Weirton was adopted when the Bureau was established because it was deemed desirable to first concentrate on the immediate plant communities which included Weirton and Wheeling, West Virginia and Steubenville, Ohio, with a combined population of more than 250,000. However, as the demand for speakers increased from outside the immediate area, the radius served was extended to 50 miles which includes Pittsburgh, Pennsylvania. Bureau speakers have gone to more distant points for state-wide meetings.

Number of Engagements

There is no limit to the number of engagements which a speaker for the Bureau may accept. The number of speeches made by individuals varies widely from five or six a year to as many as five a month. Some speakers speak on several subjects and some speeches are more popular than others.

A total of 800 speeches to audiences of more than 70,000 persons at the rate of 25 speeches a month were made by speakers for the Bureau in seven years.

Management of the Bureau

The Speakers' Bureau is managed by the assistant director of the Publications and Publicity Department with the assistance of a secretary. He acknowledges and processes requests for speakers, contacts and schedules speakers, arranges for substitute speakers in the event a speaker is unable to keep an engagement, prepares news coverage and a monthly report to management summarizing the activities of the Bureau.

Cost of the Bureau

The cost of organizing the Bureau in 1955 was about $4,000, including the services of the professional speech trainer, the brochure, and visual aids. Two subsequent expansions have cost an additional $5,300. (Operation of the Bureau takes only a portion of the time of the assistant director of the Publications and Publicity Department and his secretary.) In addition mileage payments are made to speakers for the use of their automobiles to and from speaking engagements.

Effectiveness of the Bureau

The Weirton Steel Company Speakers' Bureau, in the opinion of the management, has been an exceptionally good investment in community relations. It has contributed to a better understanding of the steel industry and the company. Speakers have established numerous personal relationships with people in the area, which is essential to good community-company relations. The Bureau is one of the best known and widely used services of the Publications and Publicity Department. Employees have shown their interest in promoting good relations for the company by volunteering to tell the company's story in plant communities. The Bureau is a very inexpensive public relations activity.

Numerous letters have been received from officials and members of civic and fraternal organizations, service, church, school, and women's groups which have heard Weirton speakers, expressing their appreciation and complimenting the ability of the speakers. Such expressions as "We were amazed at the wide scope of activities of your company," "Listening to your talk has given us a much better understanding of the steel industry," and "You are to be congratulated for this outstanding community relations program," testify to the favorable public reception of the company's public speaking program. Editorial comments on the speeches have been favorable and much publicity has been given the Bureau in the local press.

QUESTIONS

1. What is your opinion of the value of the Speakers' Bureau of Weirton Steel Company?
2. What changes should be made to improve the effectiveness of the Weirton Speakers' Bureau program?
3. Is the Weirton method of recruiting and training speakers, as described in the program, sound?
4. Is the Bureau's method of promoting speaking engagements satisfactory? If not, what other promotion should be used?
5. Is the company's method of appraising the effectiveness of this speaking program satisfactory? If not, what other methods should be used?
6. Are the visual aids to speakers used in this speaking program desirable? What other visual aids should be used?

Problem 24–1

ORAL COMMUNICATIONS

Middle Atlantic Telephone Company

The Middle Atlantic Telephone Company was established, in 1890, in a large Eastern city to provide telephone service to more than one million subscribers in two Middle Atlantic States. The annual revenue of the company is about $100 million. Shareholders number 50,000 individuals and organizations; 10,000 men and women are employed by the company in its exchanges, offices, and operating departments.

The public relations department of the company is headed by a vice-president and director of public relations who is aided by an assistant vice-president in charge of administration. The department is organized in three divisions: field services, creative services, and information services. The field services division contacts and counsels local managers in employee and community relations, cultural and youth activities. The creative services division is staffed by writers, photographers, and artists who edit the employee monthly magazine, *Telephone Topics,* and prepare the annual and interim financial reports, and publications describing the company's operations. The information services division serves the press, radio, and television editors with press releases, answers inquiries of the press and public, and maintains the department library.

The public relations department is advised by a professional public relations counseling firm, Wickstrom and Company, which makes annual opinion surveys, recommends specific courses of public relations action, and proposes plans involving a statement of objectives, policies, what to do and when, where, and what media of communications to use.

The company carries on extensive employee and community public relations programs through its field services division. Good employee relations are achieved by company-sponsored employee profit sharing, group life insurance and pension plans, and employee recreational activities. There is a 100-acre sports park and summer resort in the Appalachian Mountains at which employees may spend their vacations with their families and enjoy golf, tennis, fishing, swimming with low-cost accommodations. Periodic employee opinion surveys are conducted by the public relations counsel to determine employee attitudes toward the company.

In communicating with employees, the company employs in addition to the employee magazine, *Telephone Topics,* a number of other media. Bulletin boards located in all offices, exchanges, and operating departments are supervised by the field services division with the assistance of an employee in each location responsible for posting notices of interest to employees and maintenance of the boards.

Management letters are mailed quarterly to all employees at their homes, over the signature of the president, giving information on important company developments such as plant expansion, rate increases, labor negotiations, and fringe benefits.

Annual and interim financial reports prepared by the creative services division describing the company's financial status and development are mailed to each employee, who is invited to ask questions about company finances on an enclosed reply card addressed to the treasurer of the company.

A series of newspaper advertisements featuring long service employees is published in the principal daily newspapers of the major cities in which the company operates. These advertisements promote good employee relations by giving recognition to men and women associated with the company 25 years or more who are members of the employee Quarter Century Club. They are prepared and placed by the company's advertising agency in community newspapers.

Employee handbooks and manuals are prepared by the creative services division in co-operation with the industrial relations and personnel departments. They serve to inform new employees about company organization, policies, procedures, benefits, and regulations and to remind all employees of the advantages of working for the company.

Open houses at the company's exchanges and other facilities are held once a year for employees and their families to give workers an opportunity to show their families their part in the company's service and give supervisors an opportunity to meet personally the families of employees. This special event designated as "Family Nights" is arranged by the field services division of the public relations department with assistance of the operating staff at each location.

The community relations of the company is the responsibility of the field services division which, with the cooperation of the creative services division, publishes a monthly *Community News Letter*. This periodical is mailed to opinion leaders including professional people, doctors, lawyers, teachers, and ministers to inform them about the company's activities in the communities which it serves.

The major community relations activity of the company is assisting youth groups including Junior Achievement, Boy Scouts, Girl Scouts by contributing guidance and funds for scholarships, athletic events, contests, educational trips, hobby clubs, and teenage canteens. Employees of the company are recognized by management for participating in community youth organizations.

The cultural welfare of the communities served by the company is promoted by an annual art competition and exhibit of the work of local artists in the principal art galleries of the communities involved. Substantial cash prizes are awarded by the company for the best paintings exhibited. Substantial local publicity in newspapers, radio, and television is given the company in connection with this event.

The company contributes to the educational development of the communities it serves by sponsoring merit scholarships for outstanding high school boys and girls to enable them to attend the college of their choice. The scholarships are awarded by a committee of educators after careful consideration of the scholastic records of the applicants. Considerable publicity is given to the awards by the press.

Financial assistance is given by the company to community health projects by matching the contributions of employees up to a specified limit toward the construction of hospital facilities. The time of company personnel and company funds are contributed to heart, tuberculosis, diabetes, and crippled children fund drives.

Open houses at the company's exchanges and facilities are held annually for neighbors in the communities served by the company. Tours of facilities are conducted by trained guides; exhibits of telephone equipment, the company's safety program, and employee relations are arranged and guests are served refreshments and given a souvenir booklet describing the company's operations. Persons who attend these events are questioned to secure their reactions and evaluate the good will created by the occasion.

Press relations of the company are the responsibility of the information services division which prepares and distributes news publicity to newspapers and radio and television stations about company activities of genuine news value and public interest, answers inquiries from representatives of the press, and maintains good working relations with the press.

Press conferences are called by the information services division for the purpose of informing the press of important company news. The president of the company makes announcements and answers questions of the press. Photographs and background information are supplied the press.

Feature stories, photographs, and articles for daily and Sunday newspapers in the area served by the company are prepared by the information services division.

The principal feature of the company's press relations is an annual "Press Day" held at the company's headquarters to which leading business and consumer newspaper and magazine editors and writers are invited to see and hear about new developments in telephone communication. Luncheon is served and guests are conducted on a tour of company facilities.

Inquiries from the public, teachers, and students are answered by the information services division with booklets descriptive of the services of the company. These booklets are produced by the creative services division which has also prepared a Teachers' Kit containing a bibliography, course outlines, test questions, posters, and booklets on telephone communication for use by teachers in intermediate grades, secondary schools, and colleges.

The president of the company approved of the extensive public relations program but believed that more oral communications should be used to supplement the printed communications with the employee, community, and general publics. Spoken communications are most effective and economical and have a strong impact on public opinion. Impersonal communications by the employee periodical bulletin boards, newspaper advertising, and publicity are important but none of them can take the place of person-to-person communication in the public relations program.

The public relations director was asked to propose oral communication media for transmitting the company's messages to employees, communities, the press, and general public.

QUESTIONS

1. Describe in detail specific oral communication methods which should be used in transmitting information about the company to the employees.

2. Describe in detail oral communication methods which should be used in transmitting information about the company to the communities in the area of the company's operations.

3. Describe in detail specific oral communications methods which should be used in relations with the press, radio, and television.

4. Describe in detail the oral communications methods which should be used in communicating with: (*a*) stockholders, (*b*) suppliers, (*c*) educators, and (*d*) government officials.

BIBLIOGRAPHY

BIBLIOGRAPHY

ABELSON, H. I. *Persuasion; How Opinions and Attitudes Are Changed.* New York: Springer Publishing Co., 1959.

ALBIG, WILLIAM. *Modern Public Opinion.* New York: McGraw-Hill Book Co., Inc., 1956.

ASPLEY, J. C. *Public Relations Handbook.* 3rd ed. Chicago: Dartnell Corp., 1962.

ASSOCIATION OF NATIONAL ADVERTISERS, INC. *The Dollars and Sense of Business Films.* New York, 1954.

BARNOUW, ERIK. *Mass Communication: Television, Radio, Film, Press.* New York: Rinehart & Co., Inc., 1956.

BAUS, HERBERT M. *Publicity in Action.* New York: Harper & Bros., 1954.

BENTLEY, GARTH. *Editing the Company Publication.* New York: Harper & Bros., 1953.

BERNAYS, EDWARD L. *Public Relations.* Norman: University of Oklahoma, 1952.

———. *Your Future in Public Relations.* New York: Richards Rosen Press, 1961.

BIDDLE, WILLIAM W. *The Cultivation of Community Leaders.* New York: Harper & Bros., 1953.

BIKLEN, PAUL F., and BRETH, ROBERT D. *Successful Employee Publications.* New York: McGraw-Hill Book Co., Inc., 1945.

BLACK, GEORGE. *Planned Industrial Publicity.* Chicago: Putnam Co., 1952.

BLANKENSHIP, ALBERT B. *Consumer and Opinion Research.* New York: Harper & Bros., 1943.

BRISTOL, LEE J., JR. (ed.). *Developing the Corporate Image.* New York: Scribners, 1960.

BROWNELL, CLIFFORD, *et al. Public Relations in Education.* New York: McGraw-Hill Book Co., Inc., 1955.

BRYAN, JAMES E. *Public Relations in Medical Practice.* Baltimore: Williams and Wilkins Co., 1955.

BURNETTE, VERNE. *You and Your Public.* New York: Harper & Bros., 1943.

———. *Solving Public Relations Problems.* New York: B. C. Forbes & Sons, 1952.

CENTER, ALLEN H. *Public Relations Ideas in Action.* New York: McGraw-Hill Book Co., Inc., 1956.

CHILDS, HARWOOD L. *An Introduction to Public Opinion.* New York: John Wiley & Sons, 1940.

CUTLIP, SCOTT M., and CENTER, ALLEN H. *Effective Public Relations.* 2nd ed. Englewood Cliffs, N.J.: Prentice-Hall, Inc., 1958.

CUTLIP, SCOTT M. *A Public Relations Bibliography.* Madison: University of Wisconsin Press, 1958.

DAVIS, KEITH. *Human Relations at Work.* New York: McGraw-Hill Book Co., Inc., 1962.

DEAN, HOWARD H. *Effective Communication.* New York: Prentice-Hall, Inc., 1953.

DOOB, LEONARD W. *Public Opinion and Propaganda.* New York: Henry Holt & Co., 1948.

DORIS, LILLIAN. *Modern Corporate Reports.* New York: Prentice-Hall, Inc., 1948.

FINANCIAL PUBLIC RELATIONS ASSOCIATION. *F.P.R. 1958 Yearbook.* Chicago, 1958.

FINE, BENJAMIN. *College Publicity in the United States.* Rev. ed. New York: Harper & Bros., 1951.

FINLAY, W. A. (ed.). *Human Behavior in Industry.* New York: McGraw-Hill Book Co., Inc., 1954.

FITZGERALD, STEPHEN E. *Communicating Ideas to the Public.* New York: Funk & Wagnalls Co., 1950.

FLESCH, RUDOLF. *The Art of Plain Talk.* New York: Harper & Bros., 1946.

GALLUP, GEORGE. *A Guide to Public Opinion Polls.* Rev. ed. Princeton, N.J.: Princeton University Press, 1948.

GRISWOLD, GLENN, and GRISWOLD, DENNY. *Your Public Relations.* New York: Funk & Wagnalls Co., 1948.

HARLAN, GENE, and SCOTT, ALAN. *Contemporary Public Relations.* New York: Prentice-Hall, Inc., 1955.

HARLOW, REX F., and BLACK, MARVIN M. *Practical Public Relations.* Rev. ed. New York: Harper & Bros., 1952.

HARLOW, REX F. *Public Relations and the Social Sciences.* New York: Harper & Bros., 1957.

HARRAL, STEWART. *Tested Public Relations for Schools.* Norman: University of Oklahoma Press, 1952.

HARTER, D. LINCOLN, and SULLIVAN, JOHN. *Propaganda Handbook.* Philadelphia: Twentieth Century Publishing Co., 1953.

HARTLEY, E. L. and RUTH E. *Fundamentals of Social Psychology.* New York: Knopf, 1952.

HENKIN, SHEPARD. *Opportunities in Public Relations.* New York: Grosset & Dunlap, 1951.

HETTINGER, HERMAN S. *Financial Public Relations for the Business Corporation.* New York: Harper & Bros., 1954.

HILL, JOHN W. *The Role of Public Relations in Industry.* New York: Hill & Knowlton, 1953.

————. *Corporate Public Relations.* New York: Harper & Bros., 1958.

HODAPP, WILLIAM. *The Television Manual.* New York: Farrar, Straus and Young, Inc., 1953.

HODGES, WAYNE. *Company and Community.* New York: Harper & Bros., 1958.

HOVLAND, C. I., JANIS, I. L., and KELLEY, H. *Communications and Persuasion.* New Haven: Yale University Press, 1953.

INSTITUTE OF PUBLIC RELATIONS. *Guide to the Practice of Public Relations.* London: Newman Neame, Ltd., 1958.

IRION, FREDERICK C. *Public Opinion and Propaganda.* New York: Thomas Y. Crowell Co., 1950.

KATONA, GEORGE. *The Powerful Consumer.* New York: McGraw-Hill Book Co., Inc., 1960.

KATZ, E. and LAZARSFELD, P. *Personal Influence.* Glencoe, Ill.: Free Press, 1955.

KELLEY, STANLEY, JR. *Professional Public Relations and Political Power.* Baltimore: Johns Hopkins Press, 1956.

KEY, V. O. *Politics, Parties and Pressure Groups.* 4th ed. New York: Thomas Y. Crowell Co., 1958.

KILLIAN, L. M. and TURNER, R. H. *Collective Behavior.* Englewood Cliffs, N.J.: Prentice-Hall, Inc., 1957.

KINDRED, LESLIE W. *School Public Relations.* Englewood Cliffs, N.J.: Prentice-Hall, Inc., 1957.

KLAPPER, JOS. T. *The Effects of Mass Communications.* Glencoe, Ill.: Free Press, 1960.

LEE, ALFRED M. *How to Understand Propaganda.* New York: Rinehart, Holt & Winston, 1952.

LESLY, PHILIP (ed.). *Public Relations Handbook.* 2nd. ed. New York: Prentice-Hall, Inc., 1962.

LEWIS, H. T., and ENGLAND, W. B. *Procurement: Principles and Cases.* 3rd. ed. Homewood, Ill.: Richard D. Irwin, Inc., 1957.

LINDQUIST, ROBERT. *The Bank and Its Publics.* New York: Harper & Bros., 1956.

LIPPMANN, WALTER. *The Public Philosophy.* Boston: Little, Brown & Co., 1955.

LUNDBORG, LOUIS B. *Public Relations in the Local Community.* New York: Harper & Bros., 1950.

MACDOUGALL, CURTIS. *Understanding Public Opinion.* New York: Macmillan Co., 1952.

MAHONEY, TOM and HESSION, RITA. *Public Relations for Retailers.* New York: Macmillan Co., 1949.

MARSTON, JOHN. *The Nature of Public Relations.* New York: McGraw-Hill Book Co., 1963.

MCCARTY, JOHN T. *Community Relations for Business.* Washington, D.C.: Bureau of National Affairs, 1956.

MCCLOSKEY, G. E. *Education and Public Understanding.* New York: Harper & Bros., 1959.

NATIONAL INDUSTRIAL CONFERENCE BOARD, INC. *Communicating with Employees.* Studies in Personnel Policies, No. 129. New York, 1952.

NEILANDER, WILLIAM A. and MILLER, RAYMOND W. *Public Relations.* New York: Ronald Press Co., 1951.

NEWCOMB, ROBERT and SALMONS, MARG. *Employee Communications in Action.* New York: Harper & Bros., 1961.

OGLE, MARBURY C., JR. *Public Opinion and Political Dynamics.* Boston: Houghton Mifflin Co., 1950.

PARADIS, ADRIAN. *For Immediate Release: Careers in Public Relations.* New York: David McKay, 1955.

PARTEN, MILDRED B. *Surveys, Polls and Samples.* New York: Harper & Bros., 1950.

PERSONS, C. E. *Public Relations for Colleges and Universities.* Oakland, Calif.: Stanford University Press, 1946.

PETERS, R. W. *Communication within Industry.* New York: Harper & Bros., 1950.

PHILLIPS, D. C. *Oral Communication in Business.* New York: McGraw-Hill Book Co., 1955.

PINKHAM, RICHARD P. *Public Relations for Bar Associations.* Chicago: American Bar Association, 1954.

PLACKARD, DWIGHT H., and BLACKMON, CLIFTON. *Blueprint for Public Relations.* New York: McGraw-Hill Book Co., Inc., 1947.

POWELL, NORMAN JOHN. *Anatomy of Public Opinion.* New York: Prentice-Hall, Inc., 1951.

P. R. Reporter. Meriden, New Hampshire: P. R. Publishing Co.

Public Relations Journal. New York: Public Relations Society of America.

Public Relations News. New York.

PUBLIC RELATIONS SOCIETY OF AMERICA. *Public Relations Register.* New York, 1963.

RAMSBERGER, JACK. *How to Make Publicity Work.* New York: Reynal and Hitchcock, 1948.

RAMSBERGER, JACK, and SOUTHERLAND, R. H. *How to Think about Public Relations.* Montclair, N.J.: Economics Press, 1959.

REDFIELD, CHARLES E. *Communication in Management.* Chicago: University of Chicago Press, 1953.

REUTER, HENRY F. *Shareholder Relations: Corporate Annual Report Requirements.* Pittsburgh: Reuter and Bragdon, Inc., 1951.

RILEY, J. W., JR. (ed.). *The Corporation and Its Publics.* New York: John Wiley & Sons, 1963.

ROSS, IRWIN. *The Image Merchants.* New York: Doubleday & Co., 1959.

ROSS, M. G. *Community Organization, Theory and Principles.* New York: Harper & Bros., 1955.

RUBIN, BERNARD. *Public Relations in the Empire State.* New Brunswick, N.J., Rutgers University Press, 1958.

SAMSTAG, N. *Persuasion for Profit.* Norman: University of Oklahoma Press, 1957.

SANDERS, IRWIN T. *The Community: An Introduction to a Social System.* New York: Ronald Press Co., 1958.

SCHOENFELD, CLARENCE A. *The University and Its Publics.* New York: Harper & Bros., 1955.

SCHRAMM, WILBUR. *The Process and Effects of Mass Communication.* Urbana: University of Illinois Press, 1954.

SHAPIRO, LEO J. *Company Giving.* Chicago: Dwight Bohmbach & Co., 1960.

SILLS, THEODORE R. and LESLY, PHILIP. *Public Relations: Principles and Procedures.* Homewood, Ill.: Richard D. Irwin, Inc., 1945.

SIMON, H. A. *Administrative Behavior.* New York: Macmillan Co., 1947.

SMITH, CHARLES W., JR. *Public Opinion in a Democracy.* New York: Prentice-Hall, Inc., 1942.

SMITH, GEORGE H. *Motivation Research in Advertising and Marketing.* New York: McGraw-Hill Book Co., Inc., 1955.

STEINBERG, CHAS. S. *The Mass Communicators, Public Relations, Public Opinion and Mass Media.* New York: Harper & Bros., 1958.

STEPHENSON, HOWARD (ed.). *Handbook of Public Relations.* New York: McGraw-Hill Book Co., 1962.

STEPHENSON, HOWARD and PRATZNER, WESLEY F. *Publicity for Prestige and Profit.* New York: McGraw-Hill Book Co., Inc., 1954.

WHYTE, W. H., JR. and editors of *Fortune. Is Anybody Listening?* New York: Simon and Schuster, 1952.

WRIGHT, J. HANDLEY and CHRISTIAN, BYRON H. *Public Relations in Management.* New York: McGraw-Hill Book Co., Inc., 1949.

INDEX

INDEX

This book has been set on the Linotype in 10 and 12 point Garamond #3, leaded 1 point. Section and chapter numbers are in 10 and 30 point Spartan Medium; section and chapter titles are in 18 point Spartan Medium. The size of the type page is 27 by 46½ picas.

DATE DUE

GAYLORD			PRINTED IN U.S.A.